Introducing Employment Relations

D1493069

Introducing Employment Relations

A critical approach

THIRD EDITION

Steve Williams

OXFORD
UNIVERSITY PRESS

OXFORD
UNIVERSITY PRESS

Great Clarendon Street, Oxford, OX2 6DP,
United Kingdom

Oxford University Press is a department of the University of Oxford.
It furthers the University's objective of excellence in research, scholarship,
and education by publishing worldwide. Oxford is a registered trade mark of
Oxford University Press in the UK and in certain other countries

First edition 2005
Second edition 2010
Impression: 1

Published in the United States of America by Oxford University Press
198 Madison Avenue, New York, NY 10016, United States of America

British Library Cataloguing in Publication Data
Data available

Library of Congress Control Number: 2013949166

ISBN 978-0-19-964549-7

Printed in Great Britain by
Ashford Colour Press Ltd, Gosport, Hampshire

Contents

Acknowledgements

My principal thanks go to Derek Adam-Smith for his contribution to the first two editions of this book, without which I wouldn't have got this far. This new edition has benefited from discussions with my colleagues at the University of Portsmouth, particularly Peter Scott and Iona Byford. I am grateful to them. Undergraduate and postgraduate students at Portsmouth have often been a fount of ideas: especially Emma Thompson, Andy Robinson, Samm Coley, Natalie Wright, and Amy Street. Thanks also to Rebecca Harris for her help with some of the figures. And of course Anna deserves much gratitude for supporting me while I was writing the book.

The following people and organizations kindly gave permission to use their material: the Ethical Trading Initiative, to reproduce clauses from its Base Code; Sarah Pass, for her article on high-commitment management; Martin Upchurch, for material from his analysis of a survey of employment relations academics; Sam Bairstow, for material from her doctoral study of gay and lesbian members in trade unions; the European Trade Union Confederation, for content from its Athens Manifesto; and the Trades Union Congress, for material from its 2012 Equality Audit. I continued to benefit from the outstanding support of Oxford University Press while working on the latest edition of this book, particularly from Lucy Hyde and Kirsten Shankland. My thanks go to them. I would also like to thank the reviewers who provided very useful feedback on both the initial proposal and draft chapters.

I also acknowledge the kind permission of the following publishers for permission to use their copyright material:

Cambridge University Press for Table 7.1

John Wiley for Tables 6.1, 6.2, and 9.1.

Steve Williams, June 2013

Guide to key learning features

There are a number of key features included throughout the chapters of *Introducing Employment Relations* that are designed to help you develop and check your learning.

 Chapter objectives

The main objectives of this chapter are

- examine the characteristics of work
  economies, and to develop an under
  relations;

Chapter objectives

Every chapter opens with a bullet point list designed to signpost the key information and outline what you can expect to learn.

 Introductory case study:

The relevance of employment relations can b
coffee and sandwich chain Pret a Manger. Fo
British high streets. It operates over 300 shop
some £377 million. The company prides itsel

Case studies

The book is filled with case studies that link theory to real-world organizations and help you to understand employment relations in action.

 Insight into practice 1.1:

The way in which employers try to manipulat
claims that postal workers are being expected
the allocated time. The postal operator Royal
it is looking at making efficiency savings. On

Insight into practice boxes

This feature explores how organizations are affected by employment relations in a range of real-life situations.

Employment relations reflectio
employment relations

During the 2000s there was a growth of intere
Traditionally, matters like trade unions and co
attention to gender relations—defined as rela

Employment relations reflection boxes

These boxes give you a chance to pause and consider different viewpoints on a particular issue, as well as help you develop your critical thinking skills.

 International perspective

State repression of trade unions and workers
relations in many countries. The Internationa
survey of violations of trade union rights arou
of trade unions to organize workers in some

International perspective boxes

There are plenty of international examples to ensure you have a broad understanding of employment relations in a global context.

Historical perspective 1.7: Indu

During the 1960s and 1970s, there was a wav
(Poole 1986). Threats of plant closures and jo
a number of 'work-ins' in which workers and
plants themselves. The most famous instance

Historical perspective boxes

To understand where we are now, you need to know where we have come from. These boxes offer historical context to current employment relations issues.

LEGISLATION AND POLICY 2.2: The

The coalition government's Work Programm
2011, at a cost of up to £5 billion, its schem
experience opportunities, to improve their jo
had helped just 3.6 per cent of the long-ter

Legislation and policy boxes

The key legislative issues that build the framework of contemporary employment relations are explained and analysed in this feature.

Contesting employment rel
Kettle Chips

Until 2010 Kettle Chips was owned by th
Diamond Foods, it makes upmarket snac
and General Workers' Union (TGWU)—n

Contesting employment relations boxes

This feature takes a closer look at real-life examples of when the employment relationship is contested, including the causes and outcomes for employees and organizations.

Section summary and furthe

- The employment relationship should
  or effort bargain. This refers to the o
  employment relationships between a
  productive effort, and an employee, v
  wages and better working condition

Section summaries and further reading

The section summaries allow you to check your progress at the end of every section. This will also help you to organize and prioritize your revision.

1.5 Conclusion: the value o

The main purpose of this chapter has be
relationships, to consider employment r
actors, processes, and outcomes of em

Conclusions

Each chapter ends with clear conclusions that draw together your learning and summarise the important issues.

? Assignment and discussion

1. What are the main features of the en
2. With regard to the objectives of emp
   and 'voice'.
3. What is meant by the concept of m

End of chapter assignment and discussion questions

Check your progress at the end of every chapter with a range of questions that will allow you to practice for your exams, as well as develop your skills of reasoning and argument.

Key terms and concepts

Agenda for Change: a national pay and grading scheme that covers employees in the National Health Service.

Annualized hours: arrangements that specify the

Equality bar
designed to
intervention

Equal oppor

Key terms and concepts

This comprehensive glossary offers a list of key technical terms and concepts.

How to use the Online Resource Centre

There are a wide range of accompanying online resources available for students and registered lecturers. Visit the Online Resource Centre at www.oxfordtextbooks.co.uk/orc/williams3e/ to access all of the supporting content.

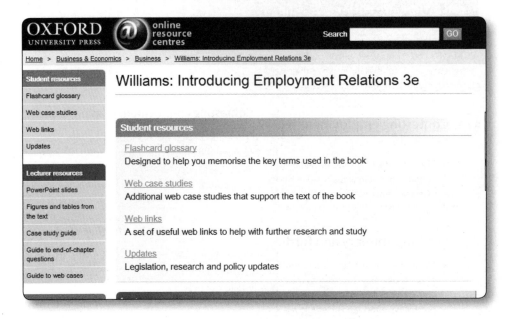

For students

There is a wealth of data on occupational and labour mar[ket]
the Office for National Statistics:
www.statistics.gov.uk/hub/labour-market/index.html

The Work Foundation undertakes research and produce[s]
work and employment in the UK:
www.workfoundation.com

Annotated web links

If you are unsure where you can find reliable and up-to-date sources of information online, or where exactly to locate content from professional associations, then these chapter-by-chapter web links will take the guesswork out of internet searches.

Williams: Introducing Employment Relations 3rd ed

Instructions: Click on the card to flip it, use the buttons to view the previous/next cards, and th[e] additional functionality.

Glossary

Test your knowledge and prepare for exams with our flashcard glossary of key terms.

> **Web case: banning strikes and industrial action**
>
> In the UK, only members of the armed services, the
>
> officers are prohibited by law from taking industrial a
>
> Conservatives speculated about the need to tighten

Web case studies

A set of additional case studies are hosted online, with questions for you to consider and discuss in class.

> **Research update: employment relations in a rece**
>
> Economic developments have a major influence on
>
> demonstrate in chapter two of the book. In 2008 the
>
> recession, part of a global economic slowdown caus

Updates

This resource is designed to help keep you informed of developments in the field.

For registered lecturers

> **The 'Wage-Work' Bargain**
>
> - The concept of the contract of employm
> - Power imbalance in the relationship
> - Employers 'buy' labour capacity

PowerPoint slides

Chapter-by-chapter slides are provided for use in your lecture presentations. The slides are adaptable and can be customized to match your own presentation style.

> **End of chapter case study questions: chapter**
>
> 1. What factors have contributed to the employm
>
> Among the factors that have led to the difficulti
>
> authoritarian way in which employment relation

A guide to case studies

This resource offers some suggestions and points on what students may include in their answers to the end of chapter case study questions.

> **Assignment and discussion questions**
>
> 1. Why and how do managers seek to retain their p
>
> Managers seek to retain their prerogative in emp
>
> because of their expertise and status they have t

A guide to end of chapter questions

A bank of suggested answers to the end of chapter questions for use in seminars.

> **Web case study questions**
>
> Chapter one: Why was the closure of the Vestas
> generate so many protests?
>
> The closure of the Vestas plant which made wind
>
> controversial for a number of reasons. For one th

A guide to web cases

Suggested answers to the web cases hosted on the student site can be used to prompt discussion in seminars.

Figures and tables from the text

The figures and tables from the book can be downloaded and used with course materials or assignments.

List of tables

List of figures

List of boxes

International perspective

Historical perspective

Legislation and policy

Contesting employment relations

List of abbreviations

ACAS	Advisory, Conciliation and Arbitration Service
ASBO	Anti-Social Behaviour Order
ATL	Association of Teachers and Lecturers
AWB	Agricultural Wages Board
BA	British Airways
BIS	(Department of) Business, Innovation and Skills
BMA	British Medical Association
BME	Black and minority ethnic
BUIRA	British Universities Industrial Relations Association
CAC	Central Arbitration Committee
CBI	Confederation of British Industry
CEEP	European Centre of Enterprises with Public Participation and of Enterprises of General Economic Interest
CEF	College Employers' Forum
CIPD	Chartered Institute of Personnel and Development
CSA	Child Support Agency
CSO	Civil society organization
CWU	Communication Workers Union
DDA	Disability Discrimination Act
ECA	Electrical Contractors' Association
ECHR	European Court of Human Rights
ECJ	European Court of Justice
EEC	European Economic Community
EES	European Employment Strategy
EHRC	Equality and Human Rights Commission
EIF	European Industry Federation
EO	Equal opportunity
EOC	Equal Opportunities Commission
EPOS	Electronic point of sale
EPZ	Export processing zone
ERA	Employment Relations Act (1999)
ET	Employment tribunal
ETI	Ethical Trading Initiative
ETUC	European Trade Union Confederation
ETUI	European Trade Union Institute

EU	European Union
EWC	European works council
FBI	Federal Bureau of Investigation
FBU	Fire Brigades Union
FDI	Foreign direct investment
FLA	Fair Labor Association
GLA	Gangmasters Licensing Authority
GMB	General, Municipal and Boilermakers' Union
GSP	Generalized System of Preferences
GUF	Global Union Federation
HCA	Healthcare assistant
HMRC	Her Majesty's Revenue and Customs
HPWS	High performance work system
HR	Human resources
HRM	Human resource management
ICE	Information and Consultation of Employees (Regulations)
ICO	Information Commissioner's Office
ICT	Information and communications technology
IDS	Incomes Data Services
IFA	International Framework Agreement
ILO	International Labour Organization
IMF	International Monetary Fund
IPA	Involvement and Participation Association
ITF	International Transport Workers Federation
ITUC	International Trade Union Confederation
JIB	Joint Industry Board
JIC	Joint Industry Council
LGB	Lesbian, gay, and bisexual
LGBT	Lesbian, gay, bisexual, and transexual
LIFO	Last in, first out
LPC	Low Pay Commission
MD	Managing diversity
MFGB	Miners' Federation of Great Britain
MNC	Multinational company
NASUWT	National Association of Schoolmasters Union of Women Teachers
NCB	National Coal Board
NEF	New Economics Foundation
NGO	Non-governmental organization

NHS	National Health Service
NMW	National Minimum Wage
NUM	National Union of Mineworkers
NUT	National Union of Teachers
OBR	Office for Budgetary Responsibility
OECD	Organization for Economic Cooperation and Development
OMC	Open method of coordination
ONS	Office for National Statistics
PAMSU	Pret a Manger Staff Union
PAT	Police Arbitration Tribunal
PCS	Public and Commercial Services Union
PCSO	Police community support officer
PNB	Police Negotiating Board
PRB	Pay review body
PRP	Performance-related pay
QMV	Qualified Majority Voting
RCN	Royal College of Nursing
RMT	Rail Maritime and Transport Union
SEA	Single European Act
SIPTU	Services, Industrial, Professional, and Technical Union
SNB	Special negotiating body
TGWU	Transport and General Workers' Union
TUC	Trades Union Congress
UCATT	Union of Construction Allied Trades and Technicians
UCU	University and College Union
UDM	Union of Democratic Mineworkers
UEAPME	European Association of Craft, Small and Medium-Sized Enterprises
ULR	Union Learning Representative
UN	United Nations
UNICE	Union of Industrial and Employers' Confederation of Europe
USDAW	Union of Shop Distributive and Allied Workers
VoC	Varieties of Capitalism
VPS	Variable payment system
WERS	Workplace Employment Relations Survey/Study
WTD	Working Time Directive
WTO	World Trade Organization
WTR	Working Time Regulations

Preface: about this book

The fundamental concern of employment relations as a field of study is with investigating the nature of the relationship that exists between employers and their employees or workers—or the employment relationship as it is generally known. Given that work and employment is such an important aspect of people's lives in advanced industrialized societies like the UK, the need to understand work and employment relationships is evidently highly important.

Traditionally, studies of employment relations were often dominated by a concern with understanding the role of trade unions, membership bodies comprised of workers, and how their activities helped to regulate work and employment relationships. In other words, the emphasis was on how people's terms and conditions of employment—wages, hours, holidays, benefits, etc.—were influenced by the actions of trade unions who bargained collectively with employers on behalf of the workforce as a whole. Such joint regulation, as it is known, remains an important element of contemporary employment relations.

Yet, as will become evident, simply focusing on how work and employment relationships are regulated is an inadequate foundation for understanding employment relations. We also need to consider the experiences of workers themselves, and how, often collectively in trade unions, they challenge and contest aspects of their employment relationships. Moreover, the decline of the trade unions means that we also have to fashion a broader, less restrictive approach to understanding contemporary employment relations, one that builds on the traditional features of employment relations as a field of study, but which also takes into account the circumstances of the twenty-first-century environment in which it operates.

This book is distinguished by four main characteristics. First, it adopts an explicitly critical approach to employment relations. What is meant by this? Rather than understanding employment relations just as concerning the regulation of employment relationships, the subject is conceptualized as the study of the way in which employment relationships are regulated, experienced, and contested. Clearly, we need to understand the ways in which the rules that govern the employment relationship are constituted; but how do workers experience the employment relationship, and how far, and in what ways, do they challenge, or contest, their employment situations? This is what distinguishes the approach taken in this book from those on human resource management (HRM), which, by tending to adopt an explicitly managerial focus, largely neglect the implications of management decisions for employees, and their responses.

Second, the book treats employment relations in a more thematic way than is often the case in conventional accounts. These tend to be influenced by an assumption that trade unions and collective bargaining constitute its principal subject matter. Though still important, the diminishing significance of joint regulation means that such an approach is no longer tenable (Ackers and Wilkinson 2003). Rather than devote chapters to trade union organization and collective bargaining in their own right, instead the focus is on the broader themes of employee representation (see Chapter 6), and developments in pay determination and working time (see Chapters 7 and 8). This more thematic approach better captures the broader conceptualization of employment relations advanced in this book.

Third, an important aim of this book is to establish the contemporary relevance of employment relations. The broader, critical approach, one that focuses on the ways work and employment relationships are regulated, experienced, and contested, means that a range of current employment relations issues can be considered. Perhaps the key purpose of this book is to demonstrate the continued importance of employment relations, based on the assumption that, as a field of study, its boundaries are wide-ranging and cannot be restricted just to the study of trade unions and collective bargaining. This has been particularly evident during the harsh economic climate produced by the 2008 financial crisis and subsequent economic recession. The impact of the post-2008 economic slump and the government austerity programmes on work and employment relations is a theme that pervades much of this book. Along with job cuts, efforts by employers to secure cheaper, more flexible working arrangements—through pay freezes, reduced hours, falsely claiming employees are working on a self-employed basis, and so on—have produced a major crisis in many people's standard of living (see Chapter 2). Unsurprisingly, then, campaigns for 'fair pay' and a 'living wage'— sufficient to keep workers and their families out of poverty—have become more prominent (see Chapter 7).

This is not to suggest that trade unions and collective bargaining are unimportant. On the contrary, they are important features of contemporary employment relations, as is evident throughout the book. But employment relations cannot be restricted just to the study of joint regulation; it encompasses a much broader range of structures, processes, and activities, including living wage campaigns. Much of the book, but Chapters 2, 3, and 4 in particular, are informed by the need to consider employment relations in a broader context. What happens at work is influenced by economic, political, and social changes. Thus there is the need to recognize that factors constituted mainly outside the workplace, such as gender, shape employment relations patterns and activities (see Chapter 4). The contemporary focus is further informed by the inclusion of material taken from a wide range of recent and up-to-date research findings.

Fourth, while for reasons of space we concentrate largely on developments in Britain, it is important to recognize that employment relations is a topic which is of international significance. European Union (EU) policies influence employment relations in important ways (see Chapter 3). Examples taken from the experience of other countries are provided at various points in the book, including references to developments in leading emerging economies, such as the 'BRIC' countries (Brazil, Russia, India, and China), where appropriate. Moreover, in Chapter 2 the implications of economic globalization for employment relations, and the policies and practices of multinational companies, are considered.

Before setting out the main features of this book, it is necessary to consider why it goes under the title of 'introducing employment relations' rather than 'introducing industrial relations'. As other writers have noted (e.g. Blyton and Turnbull 2004), the term 'industrial relations', although still widely used, is often associated with developments in traditional industries, like manufacturing, and with an emphasis on trade unions and joint regulation; 'employment relations', however, is more appropriate to understanding greater diversity in work and employment patterns. For this reason, it is better suited to the approach adopted here even though 'industrial' and 'employment' relations can be, and often are, used interchangeably.

The book is organized in five main sections. In Part One, comprising Chapter 1, an introduction to employment relations as a field of study is provided, presenting the main actors, processes, outcomes, and contexts of employment relations. In Part Two, the thematic assessment of issues, debates, and developments in employment relations commences with a focus on the important influence of contextual developments. Chapter 2, for example, considers the impact of the post-2008 economic downturn on work and employment relations. It also focuses on the implications of economic globalization, assesses the approaches taken by multinational companies, and evaluates the relevant trade union responses. Chapter 3 is about the political dimension of employment relations. It covers relevant public policy developments, including the nature of the coalition government's policy agenda, and also assesses the implications of European integration for employment relations. In Chapter 4, the concern is with the implications of social divisions for employment relations. Inequality and disadvantage are durable features of jobs and the labour market, and the chapter considers the effectiveness of interventions designed to tackle them.

The thematic approach is continued in Part Three of the book, which is devoted to four major topics in contemporary employment relations. Chapter 5 considers the management of employment relations, including the nature and impact of sophisticated HRM approaches to managing people at work. In Chapter 6 the focus is on how workers' interests are represented in employment relations. While traditionally trade unions were the main vehicle representing the interests of workers, their decline has stimulated interest in non-union representation arrangements. Nevertheless, unions have made efforts to enhance their representational capacities, through engaging with employers in a more cooperative, partnership-based manner, or using a more assertive approach to organizing and mobilizing workers. Chapter 7 is concerned with developments in pay determination. Due to the decline of collective pay-setting mechanisms by means of trade unions there is now greater interest in the managerial role in determining pay. Moreover, the regulation of low pay is a topical matter, as is evident from the interest in 'living wages'. Issues relating to working time have become important features of employment relations. Chapter 8 covers the key working time trends and patterns, examines how working time is used, and assesses the effectiveness of laws designed to regulate excessive working hours.

Part Four of the book is concerned with conflict in employment relations. One of the principal features of work and employment relationships is that, because of their different interests, there is always the potential for conflict to arise between an employer and an employee. Chapter 9 is concerned with investigating the various manifestations of labour conflict—which includes, but is not restricted to, strikes. Chapter 10 is devoted to the main processes designed to prevent conflict from occurring, or to resolve it when it does occur.

Part Five of the book consists of a brief concluding chapter in which the main themes of the book are drawn together to demonstrate the relevance of employment relations to contemporary societies.

Each chapter includes a number of supporting pedagogical features. Regular boxes devoted to employment relations reflections, insights into employment relations practice, international and historical perspectives, legislation and policy interventions, and exemplars of how work and employment relationships are contested, are used to illustrate the material in the main text. Each main section comes with a summary of the key points of the material covered in the preceding pages, and guidance on further reading suggestions, including appropriate website links. All the main chapters commence with a brief introductory case study, which is designed to demonstrate the relevance of the subject matter, and a longer case study at the end, with questions attached. There are also assignment and discussion questions to reinforce learning activity. The companion website contains further relevant features, such as additional case studies and research updates. Although this book makes reference to some initial data from the 2011 Workplace Employment Relations Study (WERS) (van Wanrooy et al. 2013), it was completed before the full findings became available. The companion website will provide any necessary updates.

Part 1

·····································

Introducing employment relations

·····································

The nature of employment relations

Chapter objectives

The main objectives of this chapter are to:

- examine the characteristics of work and employment relationships in market economies, and to develop an understanding of the nature of employment relations;
- consider the perspectives applied to employment relations as a field of study;
- provide a critically informed assessment of approaches to employment relations; and
- introduce the main employment relations actors, processes, outcomes, and contexts.

1.1 Introduction

Employment relations, which concerns how work and employment relationships are regulated, experienced, and contested, affects the majority of people who live in advanced, industrialized societies. In the UK, for example, some 30 million people are in employment of some kind; many of those who are not depend on the income generated from a parent's or partner's job for their subsistence. The purpose of this chapter is to consider the nature of employment relations, in three main sections. First, in Section 1.2 the focus is on the nature of the employment relationship in market economies. Second, in Section 1.3 the main perspectives that have been applied to employment relations as a field of study are assessed. Third, Section 1.4 introduces the main actors and processes in employment relations, highlights the principal outcomes of employment relations, and says something about the contexts in which employment relations functions. The concluding Section 1.5 then emphasizes the value of studying employment relations.

Introductory case study: The relevance of employment relations

The relevance of employment relations can be seen from events that took place during 2012 in the coffee and sandwich chain Pret a Manger. Founded in 1986, it is a well-established feature of many British high streets. It operates over 300 shops across the country, and in 2012 enjoyed record sales of some £377 million. The company prides itself on creating a happy and contented workforce. Staff are selected on the basis of their positive personality, and the company refers to creating a 'sense of fun'

(continued...)

at work and operating with a 'genuinely friendly' environment. For Pret, all this enhances the service offered to customers, giving the company a competitive advantage over its rivals. Yet wages are rather low. Workers—many of whom, especially in London, are immigrants—receive a starting rate of £6.25 per hour, just 6p more than the National Minimum Wage (2012–13 figures), although bonuses, linked to positive reports from mystery shoppers, can add an extra £1 an hour to their wages.

In 2012, a group of workers organized a new trade union to represent their interests—the Pret a Manger Staff Union (PAMSU). Among other things, the union campaigns against alleged incidents of bullying by Pret managers. Its main goal, however, is to raise workers' wages to the minimum level which it is possible for them to live on adequately—the recommended, but non-compulsory, 'living wage' (£8.45 in London, £7.45 elsewhere—2012–13 figures). PAMSU emphasizes its independence from the company.

> That means no managers, no politicians, and no bureaucrats. We don't rely on the law or the goodwill of the company when it comes to fighting for the interests of Pret workers. Instead, PAMSU believes all Pret workers—whether you're a barista, team leader, kitchen staff, or any other position—should come together to support each other. Only by standing together will we make sure we get the respect we deserve. It's only through solidarity that we'll make Pret a better place to work.

Pret, however, appears to have taken a rather hostile approach to the formation of a workers' union in the company. It dismissed a leading PAMSU activist, claiming that this was because of homophobic comments he was alleged to have made. The union, though, asserts that the sacking was motivated by a desire to suppress the nascent workers' organization and to reassert managerial control over staff.

Knowledge and understanding of employment relations are essential if we are to comprehend properly the background to, and implications of, developments like the campaign to organize a trade union and raise pay levels in Pret a Manger. We need to understand how the relationship between employers and workers operates, and the factors that influence it, including the broader economic, political, and social circumstances. It is important to understand and explain why the relevant employment relations actors, especially managers, workers, and trade unions, behave in the ways that they do. Understanding why workers take action to protest against, or change, the terms of their employment relationships, and the methods they use to do so, are also integral features of employment relations. Effective knowledge and understanding of contemporary employment relations makes important events like the campaign by Pret a Manger workers for better pay and union representation more readily comprehensible.

Sources: Myerscough (2013); PAMSU website, http://www.pamsu.org/

1.2 The employment relationship and employment relations

As a field of study, employment relations is concerned with understanding work and employment relationships, and has a particular focus on the relationship between employers and their employees (BUIRA 2009; Colling and Terry 2010). Although the main emphasis is on the employment relationship, not all workers are directly employed by employers; they may be formally self-employed or hired on a temporary basis through specialist agencies, while to all intents and purposes being employees. By conceiving of employment relations as covering work and employment relationships in a broad sense, then, it enables us to accommodate such changing patterns of work, while upholding a special concern with the employment relationship. This section is concerned with the nature of the employment relationship as a wage–work bargain; examining how employment relationships are regulated; and identifying the sources of the rules that govern work and employment relationships, and that take the form of terms and conditions of employment like pay, benefits, and working conditions.

1.2.1 **The employment relationship as a 'wage–work bargain'**

One way of understanding the employment relationship is to view it as a market exchange in which an employer hires a worker to undertake a particular job for an agreed price (e.g. wages, benefits). Work and employment relationships are thus an integral feature of capitalist market economies, which are characterized by the central importance of contracts and the capacity of the law to enforce contractual obligations and property rights (Sisson 2010). From a market-based perspective, work is a commodity like any other; and both a worker and his or her prospective employer are equally free to choose whether or not they want to enter into a contractual relationship (Budd 2011). The employment relationship is viewed as a contract, like any other, 'and the parties owe no responsibilities to one another beyond those expected of participants acting in good faith' (Sisson 2008: 11). The employment contract captures the reciprocity evident in the agreement by an employer to provide workers with wages in exchange for their willingness to engage in productive effort. Thus it is ostensibly characterized by the free and equal willingness of the parties to exchange resources.

But is there such a thing, in reality, as an employment contract? The advantage of using a market-based contractual framework to characterize the employment relationship is that it captures the way in which the employment relationship is an economic transaction, something that concerns the willingness of workers to offer their capacity to labour in exchange for the promise of wages (Kahn-Freund 1977). But there are three fundamental problems with viewing the employment relationship in purely market-based, contractual terms.

'First, the notion of a contract assumes that both parties to it come together in a free and equal way, without any obligation or pressure on them to participate. However, the individual worker is in a much weaker position than the prospective employer. It is rare for workers to be in a position where they have as much freedom to choose between alternative offers of employment as employers have in selecting employees. Moreover, the consequences of refusing an offer of employment are potentially much more serious for the worker, since jobs, and the wages they attract, are most people's primary source of income. Employers can simply offer the job to someone else (Fox 1974). In reality, therefore, work and employment relationships are generally characterized by a marked imbalance of power between a relatively powerful employer and a relatively powerless individual worker (Sisson 2008, 2010).

• Second, by accepting an offer of employment, workers come under the authority of an employer. A purely contractual approach, then, fails to capture the way in which work and employment relationships are infused by power, characterized by the capacity of an employer to command and the obligation on the worker to obey (Kahn-Freund 1977; Sisson 2010). Thus the 'brute facts of power' (Fox 1974: 183) mean that it is inappropriate to consider the employment relationship as a market-based contract, in the sense of a voluntary agreement between two equal parties (Wedderburn 1986). Indeed, a key advantage of the employment relationship for employers concerns the scope it gives them to direct the activities of employees, through what Sisson (2008: 25) calls 'residual control rights', something which is not possible where a worker is hired as a self-employed contractor to undertake a specific one-off task.

'The third reason why work and employment relationships cannot be understood in purely contractual terms is that labour is not a commodity in the conventional economic sense.

Employers do not buy employees in the way that a consumer purchases a tin of baked beans from a supermarket. Rather, they secure the capacity of employees to engage in productive work—their potential labour power. Having hired an employee, the employer must then convert latent labour power into productive effort—through systems of control and supervision, for example, or by eliciting the employee's motivation and commitment. Labour power, then, is an 'entirely fictitious commodity' (Polanyi 1957: 72); employers buy the capacity of workers to engage in productive effort. The distinctive characteristic of labour is that it is not an inanimate commodity, but is embodied in actual human beings (Edwards 2003; Sisson 2008; Kaufman 2010*a*).

A key implication of this is that the employment relationship is 'open-ended' or 'indeterminate' (Fox 1974; Marsden 1999; Sisson 2010). What this means is that when an employment contract is formed, it is impossible for the parties to specify all of the likely obligations. Neither the employer nor the employee can foresee all of the eventualities that may arise during the term of the contract. 'In a commercial contract, a product or service is supplied for a price. In the labour contract, the worker sells their ability to work, which is translated into actual labour during the course of the working day. Expectations about standards of performance have to be built up during the process of production' (Edwards 2003: 14).

The result is that the characteristics of the employment relationship are the outcome of both 'market' and 'managerial' relations (Flanders 1975; Sisson 2008). Market relations determine wages, or the price of a worker's employment, whereas managerial relations are concerned with establishing how much work is to be undertaken by the employee, of what kind, how quickly, and the sanctions for non-compliance (Edwards 2003; Colling and Terry 2010).

Rather than viewing the employment relationship as a contract, then, it is more accurate to consider it as an ongoing series of contracts, which are continually being re-negotiated between employers and their employees as changes in their circumstances alter the expectations of the parties, and thus their behaviour (Commons 1924; Colling and Terry 2010). Workplaces are best conceptualized as 'negotiated orders', marked by 'dialogue, day-to-day consensus building and "give-and-take"' between employers and employees (Sisson 2008: 34). The employment relationship is not a one-off transaction, as the market-based perspective would suggest. Rather it has to be viewed as a dynamic process: one in which an employer, due to an efficiency-driven concern to produce goods or deliver services more cheaply, seeks greater effort from employees, whose main interests (e.g. improvements in pay and working conditions) are often different.

For Budd (2004), the key managerial objective in employment relations—enhancing organizational efficiency—has to be reconciled with employees' demands for equity and voice. The equity objective refers to the desirability of ensuring that fair employment standards that reflect human dignity are in place, like an appropriate level of wages for example, or protection from being dismissed without adequate justification. The voice objective concerns the ability of employees to enjoy meaningful influence over decisions that affect them at work (Budd 2004: 7–8). While these three objectives can sometimes complement one another—workers who are treated fairly (equity) and have an opportunity to influence managerial decision-making (voice) may perform better (efficiency)—they often come into conflict. Managerial demands for greater work effort, for example, may lead to employment standards being undermined, or employees' views being disregarded, in pursuit of efficiency savings.

Insight into practice 1.1: The effort bargain in action

The way in which employers try to manipulate the effort bargain can be illustrated with reference to claims that postal workers are being expected to work faster to complete their delivery rounds within the allocated time. The postal operator Royal Mail faces greater competitive pressures; consequently, it is looking at making efficiency savings. One way of generating efficiencies is by working staff harder. In December 2008, the Communication Workers Union (CWU) claimed that the introduction of a new software system, known as Pegasus, which calculates the most efficient load that can be delivered in a round, was putting postal delivery workers under too much pressure. In particular, there was an assumption that delivery workers would maintain an average walking speed of four miles per hour while undertaking their rounds. The union claimed that such a speed was unachievable in practice, especially when you factor in the time postal workers spend waiting at doors to deliver packages that need signing for. Postal workers report that they frequently come under pressure to complete their rounds as quickly as possible. Bob Gibson, an official from the CWU, claimed that 'Royal Mail is using this system to meet financial savings without considering the physical realities of delivery needs. This is putting pressure on delivery workers and leading to bullying and harassment'. The Royal Mail denied it expected its delivery workers to walk so quickly, and stated that any bullying and harassment of staff would not be tolerated.

Sources: http://www.cwu.org http://news.bbc.co.uk/1/hi/uk/7777287.stm

The employment relationship is best conceptualized as a 'wage–work' or 'effort bargain' (Behrend 1957), marked by attempts by both the employer and the employee to influence and adjust its terms in ways that are beneficial to their own interest (see Insight into practice 1.1 for an illustrative example). As a result, there is always the opportunity for the interests of employers and employees to come into conflict (Baldamus 1961). Underlying the employment relationship is a constant potential struggle over its terms—over what Goodrich called 'the frontier of control' (Hyman 1975). Some perspectives characterize the employment relationship as a 'stark conflict of interests' (Hyman 1975: 27) between an employer who is concerned to extract the maximum effort from employees at minimum cost, and an employee whose concern is to secure better wages and limit the amount of work he or she is expected to undertake.

But it is overly simplistic to view the employment relationship just in terms of conflict between employers and employees; cooperation is also an essential feature (Edwards 1986, 2003). Employees share an interest with their employer in maintaining the competitiveness of their firm, for example; otherwise their jobs, and hence their livelihoods, are jeopardized (Kelly 1998). The employment relationship is, then, characterized both by cooperation and the potential for conflict (Sisson 2010). The power differential in favour of the employer renders it an essentially exploitative relationship; employers use their superior power to shift the terms of the wage–work bargain in a way that benefits their interest. Employees react to this, often by organizing themselves collectively in trade unions, to combat the imbalance of power. Although cooperation is an important characteristic of the employment relationship, there remains a basic antagonism between employers and employees that generates an inherent potential for conflict (Edwards 1986, 2003).

1.2.2 Regulating work and employment relationships

As has been established, the employment relationship is best viewed as a dynamic social and economic relationship, rather than a straightforward market-based transaction. But where do the rules that govern work and employment relationships come from, and how do they operate? How are matters such as pay, working hours, holiday entitlement, and the extent to which employees are able to influence decisions that affect them at work determined? The tensions and uncertainties evident in work and employment relationships mean that understanding how they are regulated, in the sense of devising and operating rules that govern them, is a central feature of employment relations as a field of study (BUIRA 2009; Colling and Terry 2010).

The systems-based approach to understanding employment relations, for example, is concerned with how the rules which govern employment relationships are established (Dunlop 1958). An employment relations system comprises four key elements (see Figure 1.1). First, there are three main groups of actors: managers, workers and trade unions, and governmental agencies. Second, these actors interact within specific contexts, for example the nature of the economic environment. Third, their interaction results in the production of a body of rules ('rule-making') which govern how employment relations operates (e.g. pay, working conditions). Negotiation between managers and unions is an example of a rule-making process. Fourth, an employment relations system is held together by an ideology: a 'set of ideas and beliefs commonly held by the actors that helps to bind or to integrate the system together as an entity' (Dunlop 1958: 16). An example of an ideology would be the preference for non-state intervention, or 'voluntarism' which long dominated employment relations in Britain (see Chapter 3).

The rules-based approach, focusing on the regulation of the employment relationship, had a major influence on the development of employment relations as a field of study. It became defined as 'the study of the rules governing employment, together with the ways in which the rules are made and changed, interpreted and administered. Put more briefly, it is the study of job regulation' (Clegg 1979: 1). If the regulation of the employment relationship is so important to developing an understanding of employment relations, how then are the rules generated?

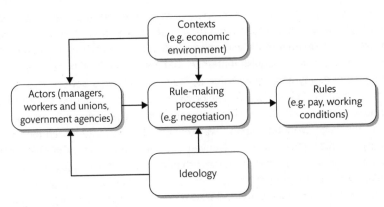

Figure 1.1 A simplified version of Dunlop's systems model

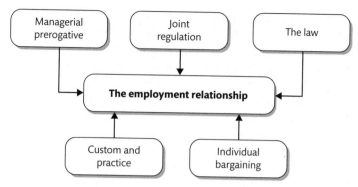

Figure 1.2 Sources of rules in employment relations

Five main sources of rules can be identified which govern work and employment relationships (see Figure 1.2), although it is important to recognize that the influence of each
will vary according to the context. First, managers attempt to determine the terms of the
employment relationship unilaterally, through the use of their prerogative. Exercising control over employees—the terms and conditions of their employment, and their behaviour—
is an essential feature of management activity. The concept of managerial prerogative, or
the 'right' to manage, is integral to understanding the management of employment relations. It should be understood primarily in ideological terms since it 'reflects an area of
decision-making over which management believes it has (and acts as if it does have) sole
and exclusive rights of determination and upon which it strenuously resists any interference' (Storey 1983: 102).

What factors influence this belief in the right of managers to exercise control over employment relations? Most obviously, managerial prerogative rests on the role of management as the legitimate agent of the employer—the organization and its shareholder
owners. This is supported by statutory obligations that compel managers to undertake their
function and operate in the interests of the shareholders. Managerial prerogative is also
founded on the belief that managers have the right to exercise control over employment
relations by virtue of their abilities, expertise, and leadership skills (Storey 1983: 103–4). The
right to manage, then, is important as an ideology, or set of ideas, to which many managers,
especially senior ones, subscribe. In practice, though, managerial prerogative is constrained
in two important ways.

First, it is necessarily influenced by the characteristics of the organizational environment,
such as the state of product and labour markets. Low unemployment levels may oblige managers to improve pay and conditions in order to attract and retain employees. Second, the
efforts of workers themselves who, to a varying degree, challenge and contest managerial
imperatives often limit the extent to which managers can exercise control in practice (Blyton,
Heery, and Turnbull 2011). Thus the nature of the employment relationship itself, as a wage-
work bargain, implies that managerial prerogative, though important as an ideology that informs managers' behaviour, is never absolute.

The second source of rules concerns the ability of some workers to influence aspects of
their own terms and conditions of employment by engaging in individual bargaining with
employers. Given the power differential that exists in the employment relationship, few have

the ability to exercise significant influence in this way, though individuals may obtain their employer's consent to relatively minor changes in work arrangements, such as starting and finishing times. Workers who possess particular skills for which there is high demand—in certain types of professional information technology work, for example—enjoy greater power to extract more favourable terms from employers. Perhaps the most obvious example of individual bargaining in practice concerns the activities of top professional sportspeople, footballers and the like, who, because of their exceptional individual talent, can negotiate with prospective employers (i.e. their clubs) from a genuine position of strength.

Third, more commonly (though less so than used to be the case), the rules that govern work and employment relationships are determined by collective bargaining between employers and trade unions, through 'joint regulation'. The unequal balance of power between the individual employee and the employer in the employment relationship impels employees to combine in, and organize, trade unions. One of the main purposes of these collective organizations of employees is to influence, principally through negotiations with employers, the terms of the wage–work bargain. Collective agreements are the outcome of the collective bargaining process. They may be procedural, setting out rules that govern the bargaining relationship between the employer and the union, or substantive: those that deliver concrete results to employees in the form of pay rises or changes to working hours, for example.

The fourth source of rules that govern work and employment relationships emanates from the state, legislation in particular. Whereas the emphasis in Britain used to be on the desirability of joint regulation as a source of rules in employment relations (Flanders 1974), in recent years legislation has come to exercise an ever greater influence, in order to challenge discrimination for example (see Chapter 4), or to alleviate low pay (see Chapter 7). Rules that govern work and employment relationships also reflect broader societal values, and changes in those values (Sisson 2010). A good example of this concerns the growing use of corporate codes of conduct to regulate international labour standards in a supposedly more ethical manner (see Chapter 2).

Fifth, rules are also generated informally through the day-to-day experiences of, and relationships between, managers and workers. Often referred to as 'custom and practice', informal rules are tacitly understood expectations of what is, and what is not, acceptable, and are important features of employment relations (Blyton, Heery, and Turnbull 2011). Numerous workplace studies demonstrate the way in which unwritten, informal, and tacit understandings influence the terms of the wage–work bargain (e.g. Brown 1973; Scott 1994)—see Contesting employment relations 1.2 for an illustration.

Contesting employment relations 1.2:   Custom and practice in action

In December 2004, a dispute arose between management and staff working in Post Office Counters, the retail arm of the Post Office, over Christmas opening hours. It was customary practice for staff to cease work at lunchtime on Christmas Eve, even though this had never been put in writing. Managers, however, wanted post offices to remain open until 5.30pm on 24 December, just like any other normal working day. They were concerned that the business would suffer if customers went elsewhere to do their last-minute Christmas shopping for stationery products and the like. This example demonstrates the importance of custom and practice rules in employment relations.

These sources of rules do not exist in isolation from each other. Plenty of research studies demonstrate, for example, that the presence of robust joint regulation enhances the effectiveness of legislation designed to protect workers. Workplace health and safety legislation, for example, tends to be more rigorously enforced where trade unions are present.

Although it highlights the important role that trade unions often have in influencing managerial decision-making through joint regulation, the rules-based approach to understanding employment relations has a number of related weaknesses (Hyman 1975). First, it tends to concentrate on the formal institutions of job regulation, trade unions, and collective bargaining in particular, perhaps to an unwarranted degree (Colling and Terry 2010). Second, following on from this, the rules-based approach implies an emphasis on stability and order in the employment relationship. Dunlop's model, in particular, has been criticized for being too static (Kaufman 2011). The processes by which workplace rules are challenged and changed, and the dynamic nature of the wage–work bargain, influenced as it often is by informal expectations and understandings based on custom and practice, can be neglected. Third, perhaps most importantly, the rules-based approach overlooks the way in which the employment relationship, understood as a wage–work bargain, is concerned with struggle as employees attempt to exercise control over their working lives. A proper understanding of employment relations, then, not only demands an analysis of how the employment relationship is regulated, but also how employees experience, challenge, and contest the rules.

 ### Section summary and further reading

- The employment relationship should be conceptualized not as a contract, but as a wage–work or effort bargain. This refers to the ongoing process of struggle over the terms of work and employment relationships between an employer, who wishes to convert latent labour power into productive effort, and an employee, who is concerned with increasing the return, in the form of wages and better working conditions, from his or her labour.

- Conceptualizing it as a bargain implies that the potential for conflict is an inevitable feature of the employment relationship. Not only is there is a basic antagonism between employer and employee, but work and employment relationships are also exploitative, characterized by an imbalance of power between a powerful employer and a relatively powerless individual employee.

- There are five sources of rules governing work and employment relationships: managerial regulation; joint regulation; individual bargaining; the law; and custom and practice expectations. While the regulation of employment relations is a key feature of employment relations as a field of study, we also need to understand how workers experience, challenge, and contest the rules.

Both Edwards (2003) and Colling and Terry (2010) are excellent guides to the nature of employment relations. The contributions made by Keith Sisson (2008; 2010: Chapter 3) are also highly recommended. Flanders (1975) examines the nature of 'market' and 'managerial' relations in the employment relationship.

1.3 Employment relations as a 'field of study'

Employment relations is not an academic discipline in its own right; it is better thought of as a 'field' or an 'area' of study (Edwards 2003; Heery et al. 2008; Sisson 2010). It is multidisciplinary in nature, drawing on concepts and debates from disciplines such as sociology, economics, political science, and law (Colling and Terry 2010; Sisson 2010).

The origins of employment relations as a field of study can be traced to the nineteenth century. This period saw the first major studies of the trade unions and collective bargaining, for example (Webb and Webb 1920a). It was also characterized by significant instances of worker unrest, the causes of which governments and official agencies were anxious to understand (Hyman 1989). A concern with investigating what became known as the 'labour problem' thus stimulated early studies of employment relations (Budd 2004; Heery et al. 2008; Kaufman 2012).

For much of the twentieth century, this was manifest in an emphasis on how the institutions of job regulation, the bargaining role of trade unions in particular, shaped work and employment relationships (Ackers and Wilkinson 2003; Frege 2008). Indeed, the development of employment relations as a field of study 'was part and parcel of a practical and intellectual response to the rise of trade unions and collective bargaining, as central institutions of twentieth century industrial society' (Ackers 2011: 45). Perspectives in this tradition were heavily influenced by the need for a proper historical understanding of the institutions they described. They were characterized by intricately detailed historical accounts of the development of trade unions, and collective bargaining arrangements in particular (see Flanders and Clegg 1964).

1.3.1 Unitary and pluralist perspectives on employment relations

One of the leading writers on employment relations during the 1960s and 1970s, along with Flanders and Clegg, was Alan Fox. In 1966, he established a distinction between unitary and pluralist 'frames of reference' in employment relations. These frames of reference are perspectives that can be applied to employment relations; they are not theories of employment relations (Blyton and Turnbull 2004). Fox articulated them as 'ideologies of management' (Fox 1966: 10), beliefs held by managers about how employment relations should operate. They can be likened to lenses, tools which people use to 'perceive and define social phenomena'— in this case the nature of the employment relationship—and which thus influence and shape their actions (Fox 1974: 271).

· The unitary perspective is characterized by an emphasis on cooperative relations at work. Since the relationship between employees and their employer is marked by a 'unity of interests' (Budd and Bhave 2008: 103), it rejects the assumption that a basic antagonism exists between them; conflict is largely caused by external agitators—trade unions—whose interference disrupts the harmonious state of relations that would otherwise exist. Holders of unitary beliefs rely on the 'liberal use of team or family metaphors' (Fox 1974: 249) when conceptualizing the nature of the employment relationship. Managers, in particular, often use the team analogy to describe relations in their organizations, based on the assumption that employers and their employees share the same goals—something that renders managerial prerogative legitimate, and trade union representation unnecessary. In his evidence to the 1994 House of Commons Employment Committee investigation into the future of trade unions, for example, the then chief executive of Zurich Insurance contended that it is 'the job of the company to create an environment in which a trade union becomes irrelevant . . . the very nature of the unions, sitting in there in a divisive capacity, stops the employees and managers of an organization getting together as one team' (House of Commons Employment Committee 1994: 342).

The unitary perspective on employment relations is often criticized for advancing an unrealistic view of workplace life, in particular for denying the basic antagonism that characterizes the employment relationship. Yet, as a perspective on the nature of employment relations, and, furthermore, one which is subscribed to by a large number of managers (Poole and Mansfield 1993), it must be taken seriously (Edwards 2003). For one thing, unitary thinking underpins much of the current emphasis on engaging and securing the organizational commitment of employees (Budd and Bhave 2008), as Chapter 5 demonstrates. Moreover, most managers, if asked their views about the nature of the employment relationship, would articulate a unitary perspective, stressing the importance of common goals, shared objectives, and the supposed absence of any conflict of interest between the employer and employee. These beliefs influence their behaviour, most notably the importance of upholding managerial prerogative, and of resisting what they see as trade union interference in the operation of their organizations (Cullinane and Dundon 2012). In a study of hotels, for example, Head and Lucas (2004) found that managers expressed hostility towards trade unions, rejected the notion that there was antagonism in the employment relationship, and emphasized the extent to which their organization was a 'happy team'.

By contrast, the pluralist frame of reference is a perspective which recognizes the existence of a basic antagonism in the employment relationship, and hence the inevitable potential for conflict. The concept of pluralism is derived from political theory, where it is used to capture the way in which states and governments have to mediate between a potentially highly diverse range of competing interest groups when formulating their policies. Having to accommodate the views of a diversity—or plurality—of interests means that political power is not exercised in a straightforwardly top-down manner, but is more diffuse, linked to the respective influence of different interest groups over policy outcomes.

With regard to employment relations, pluralism recognizes that employers and employees have different interests, which need to be reconciled if the organization is to function effectively. The principal concern of pluralists is with ensuring that any conflict that arises from differences of interest is managed appropriately, and contained in a way that prevents it from causing too much disruption. Thus there is an emphasis on developing procedures that are designed to resolve conflict, in particular establishing bargaining relationships with trade unions, given the array, or plurality, of interests that potentially exist within the organization.

Therefore, 'management has to face the fact that there are other sources of leadership, other focuses of loyalty, within the social system it governs, and that it is with these that management must share its decision-making' (Fox 1966: 8). In other words, managers cannot assume that the organization is characterized by shared interests and common goals; in particular, employees will have divergent interests, and may want to express them through their own independent institutions, trade unions. 'At the heart of the pluralist position is a conviction that the employment relationship embraces two equally legitimate sets of interests, those of employers and those of employees' (Heery et al. 2008: 14–15). Unions, then, are not external agitators to be resisted if harmonious relations are to be upheld, but are the legitimate representatives of employees' interests. They intervene to support the interests of workers in the employment relationship, whose position is generally subordinate to that of their employer. Moreover, from a pluralist perspective, government regulation in employment relations, in the form of laws that protect working people (e.g. minimum wages), is also justified on the grounds that, like trade union organization, it helps to rectify the inherent imbalance of power in favour of employers (Budd 2011).

The pluralist frame of reference was enormously influential in the development of employment relations as an academic field of study (Ackers and Wilkinson 2003; Frege 2008). The emphasis on employment relations as the 'study of the institutions of job regulation' (Flanders

1975) was informed by a belief in the legitimacy of trade unions, and accorded a special role to collective bargaining as the means by which they secured their goals, something that became the 'dominant paradigm' (Ackers and Wilkinson 2003: 7; Kaufman 2012).

During the 1960s and 1970s, the pluralist orthodoxy developed in the context of the emergence of employment relations as an important public policy issue (Hyman 1989; Ackers and Wilkinson 2003). Governments were concerned that the growth of workplace bargaining between union representatives and managers generated unnecessary levels of disruptive labour conflict and inflationary wage increases. From a pluralist perspective, the solution was not, as the holders of unitary views would argue, to resist the encroachment of the unions as a means of reasserting managerial authority; rather, stronger bargaining relationships between employers and unions should be encouraged, given the advantages of developing robust and effective procedures for containing, or institutionalizing, conflict through the joint regulation of the workplace. According to one leading pluralist, the 'paradox, whose truth managements have found it so difficult to accept, is that they can only regain control by sharing it' (Flanders 1975: 172). Until the 1980s, then, the pluralist perspective exercised an important influence over both public policy and even management attitudes towards employment relations, though not at the expense of the latter's fundamentally unitary beliefs.

1.3.2 Challenges to pluralist orthodoxy

The main challenge to the pluralist employment relations orthodoxy of the 1960s and 1970s initially came from the development of radical perspectives on employment relations. These share with pluralism a belief in the essentially antagonistic nature of the employment relationship. However, they do not accept its assumption that conflict can be resolved by the development of procedures, or even that it is desirable to attempt to do so. Radical approaches reject the assumption that conflict in employment relations can be accommodated in a straightforward fashion. Rather, the employment relationship is marked by a 'structured antagonism' arising out of the different interests of employers and employees. This means that not only is there always the potential for conflict to arise, but also that efforts to contain it will always be partial and incomplete (Edwards 1986). Moreover, radical approaches put a pronounced emphasis on the persistence of unequal power relations in the employment relationship, the reality of managerial control and domination over employees, and the role played by wider social forces in creating and maintaining inequalities and exploitative relations at work (Budd and Bhave 2008).

One of the most prominent perspectives coming under the radical label is that of Marxism. Kaufman (2011: 17) observes that the 'essence of the employer-employee relationship under capitalism, from a Marxist perspective, is domination, control and exploitation of labour in order to provide profit so firms can further accumulate capital'. The principal feature of Marxism, which distinguishes it from the radical approach in general, is the emphasis it places on how the exploitation of workers in the employment relationship generates class conflict between the working class, who produce goods and services, and the owners of capital—something that results in deepening class consciousness and the development of a socialist political project (see Gall 2003b).

What criticisms, then, do radical perspectives such as Marxism make of the pluralist perspective? First, they contend that pluralism fails to address the issue of power seriously

enough, assuming that, in an environment where bargaining relationships have been established, a balance of power exists between employers and unions (Fox 1974), although this has
been challenged by pluralist writers (Clegg 1975). Employers, by virtue of their ownership of,
and control over, the production of goods or delivery of services, enjoy far greater power than
even the most well-organized union (Fox 1974).

Second, radical writers argue that pluralism is an essentially conservative ideology, concerned with upholding the existing order in society rather than challenging it (Fox 1974;
Goldthorpe 1977). Thus, while pluralism ostensibly appears to advance the interests of employees, by recognizing the desirability of union organization and collective bargaining, in
fact the development of procedures ensures they are kept within narrow limits, and do not
challenge the economic power of employers. Joint regulation contains conflict, resolves it,
and thus ameliorates its potential for disruption in a way that helps the interests of capital
rather than those of labour.

Following on from this, the third main criticism of the pluralist approach is that by focusing
on procedural reform, it neglects the important substantive outcomes for employees (Hyman
1989). In other words, pluralism is more concerned with the system of joint regulation than
whether or not it produces anything worthwhile for employees. Some have suggested that the
radical approach places an unwarranted emphasis on conflict and disorder in employment
relations (Ackers and Wilkinson 2003). However, the main value of taking a radical, critical
perspective is that it draws our attention to the inadequacy of institutions of job regulation,
such as collective bargaining, when it comes to challenging prevailing systems of managerial
control and domination. It also highlights the large extent to which developments in employment relations reflect broader economic and social structures.

A number of important sociological studies of workplace employment relations were strongly
influenced by a radical perspective. Huw Beynon's study of Ford's Halewood car manufacturing
plant is a particularly notable example of the genre (Beynon 1973). Since the 1980s, though, the
influence of radical perspectives has waned (Ackers and Wilkinson 2005), largely because of
the marked decline in the level of trade union membership and organization, decreasing strike
levels, and the dwindling extent of collective bargaining activity. The main challenges to pluralist orthodoxy in employment relations increasingly come from elsewhere, from other critical
perspectives such as feminism (see Employment relations reflection 1.3), and in particular from
the resurgence of unitary thinking associated with the rise of new management techniques.

Employment relations reflection 1.3: The feminist critique of
employment relations

During the 2000s there was a growth of interest in feminist perspectives on employment relations.
Traditionally, matters like trade unions and collective bargaining were studied without paying much
attention to gender relations—defined as relations between men and women—and how they affect
employment relations (Wacjman 2000), though there were some notable exceptions (e.g. Pollert 1981).
The feminist critique of orthodox employment relations means that there is now a better appreciation of
the influence on employment relations of factors that are constituted outside of workplaces, particularly
gender for example (Greene 2003). The development of feminist perspectives has contributed to a
welcome broadening of the employment relations field (Heery et al. 2008); the challenges of reconciling
paid work with family responsibilities, like childcare for example, have received more attention as a result.

As shown in Chapter 5, there is growing interest in how organizations can develop so-phisticated human resource management (HRM) approaches to engage and enhance the commitment of their staff as a means of realizing improvements in business performance. Contemporary 'human resource management follows the unitarist belief that effective man-agement policies can align the interests of employees and employers and thereby remove conflicts of interest' (Budd 2004: 6). Growing interest in the 'neo-unitary' (Farnham and Pim-lott 1995) character of HRM demonstrates the extent to which perspectives drawn from the discipline of psychology, in particular those concerning human relations at work (Edwards 2003), such as the relationship between work, commitment, and performance, influence the study of employment relations.

The development of sophisticated HRM, and the associated ascendency of the unitary perspective, has challenged the position of employment relations as a field of study, given the extent to which, notwithstanding the increasing importance of radical perspectives, it was concerned with the joint regulation of the workplace. The study of employment relations was founded upon the importance of trade unionism and collective bargaining, and underpinned by a dominant pluralist perspective (Ackers and Wilkinson 2005; Heery et al. 2008).

By the 2000s, though, a field of study which 'focused on trade unions and collective bargain-ing had found it increasingly difficult to conceptualize a society in which both were increas-ingly marginal to the world of work' (Ackers and Wilkinson 2003: 12–13). While perspectives drawn from academic disciplines such as law (e.g. Davies and Freedland 2007), geography (e.g. Herod, Peck, and Wills 2003), and politics (e.g. Ludlum and Taylor 2003) have increasingly enhanced our understanding of employment relations, its importance as an academic field of study nevertheless dwindled during the 1980s and 1990s.

Yet employment relations is about more than just trade unions and collective bargaining. Key elements of what makes employment relations distinctive as a field of study—the focus on work and employment relationships and how they are regulated, experienced, and con-tested, and a concern with recognizing and promoting the interests of working people—mean that it remains a vital topic of contemporary enquiry (Ackers and Wilkinson 2005). Studying employment relations means that one has to recognize the importance of topics such as power and justice, and that employers and employees may have competing interests, things that are largely absent from HRM texts (BUIRA 2009). Moreover, issues relating to work and employment relations are integral to the way in which many emerging economies such as China have developed (e.g. Friedman and Lee 2010). Thus an understanding of employment relations is essential in order to comprehend, and critically evaluate, some of the key issues that affect business and management in twenty-first-century societies.

 ## Section summary and further reading

- The unitary perspective, which denies the basic antagonism in the employment relationship, can be criticized for being unrealistic, though its tenets influence the attitudes and behaviour of managers.

- Pluralism recognizes the potential for conflict, but tends to focus on how it can be contained by the development of procedures, particularly collective bargaining arrangements.

- Radical approaches, which developed out of a critique of pluralism, reject the assumption that conflict in employment relations can be accommodated in a straightforward fashion. Not only is the potential for conflict to arise ever-present, but also efforts to contain it will always be partial and incomplete.

● As a field of study, employment relations was traditionally concerned with understanding the rules that govern employment relationships, in particular joint regulation and collective bargaining between trade unions and employers. This is too narrow an approach; it has been rendered untenable, moreover, by declining unionization and falling levels of collective bargaining. However, key elements of what makes employment relations distinctive as a field of study, notably a concern with the interests of workers, make it a valuable topic of contemporary enquiry.

Budd and Bhave (2008) are good on 'frames of reference' in employment relations. See Heery et al. (2008) for an assessment of pluralist orthodoxy in employment relations and the principal challenges to it. Hyman (1975) is the standard Marxist introduction to employment relations. For the nature of employment relations as a field of study, see Ackers and Wilkinson (2003).

1.4 Employment relations: actors, processes, outcomes, and contexts

Having outlined the nature of the employment relationship and considered the main perspectives on employment relations as a field of study, the purpose of this section is to introduce the main actors, processes, and outcomes of employment relations, and illustrate the context which affects how it operates.

↑principle

1.4.1 Employment relations actors

Clearly there are two fundamental actors in employment relations—workers and employers—without whom work and employment relationships could not exist. For the most part, though, employers vest day-to-day control of employment relations matters in the hands of appointed managers. Moreover, employers may combine in associations to handle employment relations matters. While the experiences of workers are integral to the approach taken in this book to employment relations as a field of study, they frequently organize in trade unions—collective bodies of workers that act to support and protect their interests. We have already established that legislation plays an ever-increasing role in regulating employment relationships. Thus, as well as examining the role of employers, managers, employers' associations, and unions in employment relations, the nature of state intervention is also worthy of scrutiny. In this section, then, we offer a brief introduction to the roles of three main employment relations actors—employers and management, trade unions, and the state. However, researchers have begun to note the increasing array of other actors who play an important role in contemporary employment relations (see Employment relations reflection 1.4).

Employers and management

Except in very small firms, employing organizations entrust day-to-day control to salaried managers who are responsible, among other things, for managing employment relations. As has already been seen (see Section 1.2.2), a belief in managerial prerogative, or the 'right' to manage employment relationships unilaterally, without interference from third parties like trade unions, underpins managers' behaviour in employment relations. Yet managerial efforts to secure employee compliance will always be frustrated and thus incomplete. The

---

Employment relations reflection 1.4: New and emerging actors

Most studies of employment relations understandably focus on the activities of key actors like employers, workers, and trade unions. However, during the 2000s there has been a growing amount of scholarly interest in the role of other actors who are involved with employment relations matters in some way, like community groups and non-governmental organizations (NGOs). This is consistent with a shift towards the articulation of a broader understanding of employment relations in contemporary societies, one that expands its 'terrain to explore the links between employment and other spheres of social and economic life, and research new and previously neglected actors' (Heery and Frege 2006: 603). Williams, Abbott, and Heery (2011*a*), for example, focus their attention on the employment relations role and activities of 'civil society' organizations (CSOs), a label that encompasses living wage campaign groups, faith bodies, public interest legal organizations, charities, pressure groups, social movement organizations, and community groups. The campaigning organization, Stonewall, for example, lobbies on behalf of lesbian, gay, and bisexual people, and works with employers to improve the way they manage sexual orientation issues. Vulnerable workers, particularly those who are based in parts of the economy where trade unions are weak, often rely on agencies like the network of Citizens Advice Bureaux for help and support with employment-related matters (Abbott 2004). The increasing attention being given to these new and emerging employment relations actors illustrates how the boundaries of employment relations as a field of study are being widened.

---

nature of the employment relationship as a wage–work bargain invariably limits the scope of managerial prerogative, and also provides workers with opportunities to challenge managerial control. Therefore, in understanding how the employment relationship is managed, it is important not to oversimplify by concentrating solely on managerial attempts to secure control (Storey 1985; Hyman 1987). To realize the efficient production or delivery of goods and services, managers must secure a degree of legitimacy, or consent, among those they manage (Legge 2005).

Historically, employers sought to uphold managerial prerogative in the workplace by externalizing collective bargaining with trade unions through employers' associations. By bargaining with unions away from the workplace, on a multi-employer basis, employers aimed to 'neutralize' union power in the workplace. In matters that went unregulated by collective agreements, particularly those pertaining to the organization and pace of work, the assumption was that management prerogative would predominate (Sisson 1987). Although employers' associations sometimes engaged in crude anti-union activities, such as undermining strikes, their role in the joint regulation of employment relations, particularly through multi-employer collective bargaining and procedures for resolving disputes, became an important means of maintaining managerial control, and thus upholding employers' interests (McIvor 1996). Since the 1960s, however, the role of employers' associations has declined in significance, linked to the erosion of multi-employer bargaining. Increasing numbers of firms, especially larger ones, chose to develop organization-specific procedures for handling employment relations matters (Gospel 1992)–see Chapter 7.

One of the most notable features of contemporary employment relations concerns the growing extent to which employers have sought to regain control over their own arrangements, and manage employment relations directly. At first, this took the form of a pluralist concern with responding to, and managing the consequences of, trade unionism. Since the 1980s, though, the managerial employment relations agenda has taken on a more unitary ethos, linked to the decline of joint regulation. The rise of a sophisticated HRM approach to managing people at work, based on the use of techniques designed to raise organizational commitment and boost business performance, is emblematic of a more assertive managerial agenda in employment relations. Much more interest has been directed at the role of employers and management as a result (Kaufman 2011). One indication that employers are taking the management of employment relations more seriously concerns the growing proportion of workplaces with access to specialist employment relations managers, who have specific responsibility for managing human resources in organizations. Moreover, the influence in contemporary employment relations enjoyed by non-HR specialists in organizations, such as line managers, has increasingly been recognized (e.g. Purcell et al. 2003).

Trade unions

As has already been established, there is an imbalance of power in the employment relationship in favour of the employer. The main way in which workers attempt to challenge this power differential is to combine in collective organizations, trade unions, so that they can influence the terms of their employment relationships from a position of greater strength. One of the earliest and most well-known definitions of a trade union, dating from the end of the nineteenth century, refers to it as 'a continuous association of wage earners for the purpose of maintaining or improving the conditions of their working lives' (Webb and Webb 1920b: 1).

For our purposes, however, a trade union can be defined as a body comprised mainly of workers that, by means of collective organization and mobilization, represents and advances their interests both in the workplace and in society at large. It does so by providing workers with protection from the arbitrary exercise of managerial prerogative, bargaining with management over the terms and conditions of their employment, giving them influence over decisions that affect them at work, and by providing them with a means of bringing about political changes that are favourable to their interests. Trade unions are ostensibly democratic bodies: organizations which comprise, and work on behalf of, their members. Trade union members pay a subscription—usually between £10 and £25 per month—to benefit from the services of their union, including the right to influence its policies.

While one can trace their ancestry further back in time to the trade clubs and friendly societies of the eighteenth century, the trade unions originated during the period of sustained and rapid industrialization. The first stable and permanent national bodies date from around the middle of the nineteenth century and were mainly combinations of local organizations in industries such as engineering, construction, and printing (Hyman 2001b: 72). Early union organization developed as a means by which skilled workers could maintain control of their craft, and regulate the terms and conditions of their trades (Clegg, Fox, and Thompson 1964). A major function of the early trade unions was to provide their skilled craft-worker members with 'friendly benefits' such as unemployment and sick pay (Webb and Webb 1920b).

During the second half of the nineteenth century, trade unionism began to take root in industries such as coal mining, the railways, and steel making where craft practices, while evident, were much less deep-rooted (Hyman 2003), something that placed a greater onus on collective bargaining as a means of regulating pay and employment conditions. The main functions of the developing trade unions were thus to provide their members with benefits, and to regulate the terms and conditions of employment, first through craft control but, as time progressed, more commonly through collective bargaining, and also through political activity.

The main functions of the trade unions today continue to include regulating employment relationships through collective bargaining and political activity aimed at supporting the interests of working people; while most trade unions are independent of any political party, some major unions are affiliated to the Labour Party, and all of them view political campaigning as a legitimate method of achieving their objectives. The rise of the welfare state during the twentieth century meant that providing membership benefits became a less important union function. Nevertheless, trade unions now play an important role in supporting and protecting workers, for example by representing them in grievance and disciplinary cases.

See Table 1.1 for a list of the major trade unions in Britain (those with more than 100,000 members). The largest unions tend to be so-called 'general' unions, which recruit members from across a wide range of industry sectors and occupations. A good example is Unite, which was formed in 2007 following the merger of the Transport and General Workers Union (TGWU) and Amicus. The list of unions in Table 1.1 also includes some notable unions which organize largely on the basis of a single industry, like the Union of Shop, Distributive and Allied Workers (USDAW) in retail. Some unions operate on a narrower occupational basis, though because they tend to be rather small, they are largely absent from the list in the table. However, two organizations which do appear in the table—the Royal College of Nursing (RCN), a union of nurses, and the British Medical Association (BMA), which represents doctors—do possess a strong occupational identity.

Another feature of Table 1.1 worth noting concerns the relatively large number of major trade unions which operate in the public sector—education unions like the National Union of Teachers (NUT) and the University and College Union (UCU) for example. During the nineteenth and twentieth centuries, the development of trade unions was concentrated among primary and manufacturing industries. However, since the 1970s employment in these areas

Table 1.1 Major trade unions in the UK

Trade union	Membership
Unite	1,515,206
Unison	1,374,500
General Municipal and Boilermakers union (GMB)	602,212
Royal College of Nursing (RCN)	415,019
Union of Shop, Distributive and Allied Workers (USDAW)	398,859
National Union of Teachers (NUT)	375,042
National Association of Schoolmasters Union of Women Teachers (NASUWT)	326,810
Public and Commercial Services Union (PCS)	292,091
Communication Workers Union (CWU)	208,714
Association of Teachers and Lecturers (ATL)	202,509
British Medical Association (BMA)	144,428
University and College Union (UCU)	122,398
Prospect	121,173
Union of Construction Allied Trades and Technicians (UCATT)	110,539

Source: Certification Office (2012)

Insight into practice 1.5:   The role of the Trades Union Congress

Traditionally, the Trades Union Congress (TUC), which was founded in 1868, fulfils three broad roles in employment relations. First, it is involved in adjudicating disputes between unions concerning which of them should represent particular groups of workers, though this activity is now only of relatively minor importance (McIlroy and Daniels 2009). Second, it provides its union affiliates with services like education and training provision. Third, the TUC represents, and acts on behalf of, the trade union movement in general, in relations with government for example. In recent years the TUC's role has changed in two key respects. One of the changes concerns the development of a more explicit campaigning role on matters such as better rights for part-time workers, for example, and the need for vulnerable workers, like migrant workers, to have more protection. Linked to this, moreover, the TUC is trying to develop a role as the organization which speaks on behalf of working people as a whole, rather than just as the voice of the trade union interest (Heery 1998*b*, 1998*c*). However, union mergers and amalgamations threaten the TUC's role. The trend towards so-called 'super-unions' like Unite, for example, which was formed from the merger of the Transport and General Workers Union and Amicus, potentially erodes the authority of the TUC (McIlroy and Daniels 2009).

has fallen substantially. At the same time, workers in the public sector have become increasingly unionized. The growing proportion of trade union members who work in the public sector, many of whom are women employed in professional occupations like teaching, has had a marked effect on the character of trade unionism.

Finally, in this introduction to the role of the trade unions, it is important to mention the role and activities of the Trades Union Congress (TUC)—see Insight into practice 1.5. The TUC is a confederation of unions, and acts as the voice of the trade union movement in Britain. Very few major unions are not affiliated to the TUC; of those that appear in Table 1.1, only the RCN and BMA are outside it.

The state

Although management and unions are the principal parties in employment relations, it is also important to emphasize the strong, or 'pervasive' (Kelly 1998), influence of the state and its bodies. It is conventional to understand the effects of state activity on employment relations in four ways. First, employment in the state, or public, sector is a major element of contemporary employment relations, and at various points in this book we consider some of its distinctive features, such as pay determination for example (see Chapter 7). Second, states enact legislation in the area of employment relations, such as that designed to regulate trade union behaviour (see Chapter 3) or establish minimum wages (see Chapter 7). Third, states operate arrangements to help employers and unions resolve disputes, notably arbitration and conciliation machinery (see Chapter 10). Fourth, the economic and political policies pursued by the governments of national states also have important implications for employment relations.

Liberal-pluralist perspectives on the state focus on the way in which policy outcomes are the end result of a process of discussion, negotiation, and compromise between organized groups of citizens which is supported and overseen by governments (Pierson 1996). In employment relations, the state's role is generally seen to involve maintaining a balance between the competing interests of employers and workers, and accommodating the demands of both. Where an imbalance of power arises, particularly in favour of employers, the state acts to ameliorate it, for example by introducing legislation. However, there are two fundamental problems with liberal-pluralist perspectives. First, they fail to account for the marked tendency of state policy to favour the interests of employers. Second, they assume that state intervention produces an equivalence of power between capital and labour when in reality the odds remain stacked against the latter (Miliband 1973).

By contrast, the neo-liberal perspective views state intervention as a fundamental threat to liberties, particularly those of employers: it stifles market forces and is liable to undermine the free society. Whereas liberal-pluralist approaches consider state intervention in the area of employment relations as a largely progressive development, helping to ameliorate the imbalance of power between capital and labour, from a neo-liberal perspective, laws that make it easier for unions to operate endanger the liberties of individual workers and their employers to conduct their affairs in a manner of their own choosing. The main problem with this approach, however, is the assumption that workers and employers enjoy equal freedom to contract (or not to contract), when in reality, as has already been demonstrated, this is far from being the case.

For a critical and more sophisticated appreciation of the role of the state in employment relations Marxist perspectives have rather more to offer. Although Marx himself did not develop an explicit theory of the state under capitalism (Hyman 1975), two distinct approaches to understanding its role can be inferred from his work. In his early writings, the state is treated as an instrument of class rule by the dominant capitalist interest (see Jordan 1985; Pierson 1996). In this approach, the emphasis is on the coercive, repressive role of the state, and the way its offices and policies operate to suppress trade unions and the interests of working people (Kelly 1998)—see International perspective 1.6 for examples.

Yet state policy is not characterized just by the repression of the labour interest. Thus the second broad approach to understanding the role of the state under capitalism that can be inferred from Marx's writings holds that in order to maintain the long-term viability of capitalism, states need to win the consent of those they govern. This provides a stable and ordered

 International perspective 1.6: Union repression around the world

State repression of trade unions and workers' rights is a marked feature of contemporary employment relations in many countries. The International Trade Union Confederation (ITUC) publishes an annual survey of violations of trade union rights around the world. Whereas many countries restrict the ability of trade unions to organize workers in some way, or limit opportunities for collective bargaining, the ITUC's reports demonstrate the violence exhibited towards independent trade unionism in some places. In Zimbabwe, for example, the government has harassed and intimidated union activists. One leader of a teachers' union died a few weeks after having been arrested and tortured by Robert Mugabe's regime. By far the most dangerous place to be a trade unionist, however, is Colombia in South America. While the number of assassinations of union activists declined during the 2000s, there were still forty-nine such murders in 2010. The Colombian government claims that the violence is a consequence of years of civil war and the activities of numerous powerful armed groups of guerillas who control much of its territory. But there is evidence that the Colombian state encourages the killings.

Sources: ITUC (2008, 2012)

environment within which the capitalist order can flourish (Pierson 1996). From this perspective, then, policies and legislation ostensibly designed to favour the labour interest in fact benefit employers in the long term (Hyman 1975). By seemingly favouring the interests of labour, they give the capitalist system, and the exploitative nature of the employment relationship that underpins it, added legitimacy. Thus in order to maintain the long-term viability of capitalism, states adopt policies or enact legislation that runs counter to the short-term interests of employers (Dunleavy and O'Leary 1987).

All this points to a rather sophisticated understanding of the influence of the state on employment relations, suggesting that its approach is characterized by a mixture of coercion and consent (Kelly 1998). Government policy-makers and officials do not just respond to demands from employers; they also have to be responsive to the concerns of working people (Edwards 1986). That said, the state still operates within a capitalist order, something that shapes, but does not necessarily determine, the character of its policies.

1.4.2 Employment relations processes

As highlighted above (see Section 1.2.2), the regulation of employment relationships is of central importance to employment relations as a field of study. The traditionally dominant pluralist perspective on employment relations is marked by a concern with understanding joint regulatory processes, especially collective bargaining. In its narrow sense, collective bargaining is simply a means of determining pay and conditions of employment involving unions, who negotiate or bargain with employers. Beatrice and Sidney Webb, the first serious students of collective bargaining, suggested that it is largely an economic process, the collective equivalent of individual bargaining (Webb and Webb 1920a).

By acting collectively through trade unions, workers can secure more for themselves from the employment relationship than would be possible just from their own individual efforts. This is because it gives them more bargaining power, particularly where they are prepared to use forms of industrial action like strikes—temporary stoppages of work—as a lever to enforce their demands. Disputes which arise from conflicts of interest over the terms and conditions of employment relationships often cannot be settled internally by employers and employees, or unions, themselves. Therefore, to mitigate any disruptive effects, states generally operate third-party arrangements for resolving them. In the UK, for example, the Advisory, Conciliation, and Arbitration Service (ACAS) not only helps to settle collective disputes between unions and employers, but also intervenes in the case of individual disputes, after a worker has submitted a claim against their employer to an employment tribunal—see Chapter 10 for further details.

Collective bargaining is more than just a means of determining employment terms. It also fulfils a broader, political function. Flanders (1975) stressed that collective bargaining is a rule-making process. Not only does it set the terms and conditions on which labour is hired, but it also gives workers, through their unions, rights to challenge and influence managerial decisions over such things as the organization of work. Thus collective bargaining, as a process of 'job regulation', is an important means of giving workers voice over, and enabling them to participate in, matters that affect them in their working lives. This was a particularly strong theme of the 1960s Donovan Royal Commission which, heavily imbued with the dominant pluralist thinking of the time, stated that where it was properly undertaken 'collective bargaining is the

Historical perspective 1.7: Industrial democracy at work

During the 1960s and 1970s, there was a wave of interest in workers' control and industrial democracy (Poole 1986). Threats of plant closures and job cuts associated with industrial restructuring stimulated a number of 'work-ins' in which workers and their unions attempted to maintain the operation of plants themselves. The most famous instance occurred following the announcement of the closure of the Upper Clyde Shipbuilders yard near Glasgow. Workers and shop stewards occupied the yard for a period of time to prevent its closure (Foster and Woolfson 1986). There was also much interest in how workers' interests could be represented on company boards of directors (Brannen 1983). In the 1970s, a government committee of inquiry recommended that union representatives should have equal parity with shareholders on the boards of large companies, with an 'intermediary' group of ostensibly independent directors appointed by mutual consent maintaining a balance between the two sides. Employer opposition and the hostility of influential union leaders, who were concerned about the threat to the primacy of collective bargaining, ensured that the proposals came to nothing. However, there is now renewed interest in the benefits of greater industrial democracy. Some in the trade union movement argue that the UK would do well to follow the example of Germany, with its highly successful economy, where union representatives sit on the supervisory boards of major companies (TUC 2012a). A majority of UK employees support the principle of having workforce representation on company boards, and the TUC is reportedly taking a greater interest in the topic (Fair Work Commission 2013).

most effective means of giving workers the right to representation in decisions affecting their working lives, a right which is or should be the prerogative of every worker in a democratic society' (Royal Commission 1968: 54). Yet, as a form of worker participation, collective bargaining on its own only goes so far; in theory, more direct forms of worker control give workers greater influence over how their organizations are run by making them more democratic (see Historical perspective 1.7).

For the pluralists, collective bargaining not only gives workers a voice over matters that affect them at work, but is also an important means by which the inherent conflict in the employment relationship can be accommodated—or, as it is often put, institutionalized. In other words, the presence of collective bargaining enables managers to contain conflict, to keep it within acceptable limits, and is therefore an effective means of managing employment relations and extending managerial control (Flanders 1975). The principal radical critique of collective bargaining is that it contains workers' militancy within boundaries that are acceptable to employers. By institutionalizing conflict, it runs counter to the real interests of workers. Moreover, by becoming enmeshed in the process of bargaining with management, unions come to adopt a fundamentally conservative ethos, concerned with the procedural details of negotiations and agreements rather than with advancing the substantive interests of their members. Whereas workers want to improve their terms and conditions of employment, and to secure greater influence over workplace decisions, in the bargaining process union leaders may prefer to focus on establishing and maintaining stable relationships with employers, thus sustaining the institutional security of the union, rather than challenging them (Hyman 1989). In practice, however, one cannot readily distinguish between union leaders' concern with stable and secure bargaining relationships and the desire of their members for improved pay and conditions. Workers have a concern with the security and survival of their union because without it they have no means of winning better employment terms. Moreover, the position of union leaders becomes problematic if, in the bargaining process, they are not seen to be delivering benefits for their members (Smith 2001).

Workers also collectively influence their employment relationships and express their voice through the process of joint consultation. Whereas collective bargaining involves employers having to negotiate with a union over the terms and conditions of employment relationships—something that may require them to make concessions in order to secure an agreement—consultation is less threatening to managerial prerogative. For this reason, it is often preferred by managers, in as much as they can secure employees' views without being bound by them (Hall and Purcell 2012). With consultation, workers 'influence but in no way determine managerial policy and practice' (Poole 1986: 71). Consultation is often seen to be an appropriate process for handling matters where there is a supposed greater propensity for cooperation and a commonality of interests between management and workers, such as health, safety, and welfare issues, as opposed to the more explicitly conflictual collective bargaining relationship (Clegg 1979; Marchington 1989). However, it is often difficult to maintain a rigid distinction between consultation and collective bargaining, not least because union representatives often try to use consultation machinery as a bargaining forum.

There is a great diversity of consultation arrangements evident in practice (Marchington 1994; Hall and Purcell 2012). They are now used more expressly as managerial, rather than joint regulatory, processes (see Chapter 6 for further details). This is consistent with the broader decline of trade unions and collective bargaining, and the rise to prominence of a more unitary employment relations ethos. As a result, there is now a much greater concern with the role played by managerial processes in employment relations (Sisson 2010). These include HRM interventions such as performance management and absence management tools, which are used by employers to control the behaviour of employees in a more rigorous manner. Managerial processes for handling the grievances of employees and improving their behaviour and conduct—their 'discipline'—have become a more central feature of employment relations (see Chapter 10).

Perhaps the most notable example of this greater emphasis on the role played by managerial processes in regulating employment relationships concerns the question of worker voice. As we have seen, in a pluralist employment relations environment, workers have a say, and can gain some influence over decisions that affect them at work, through the process of collective bargaining by trade unions, supplemented by joint consultation. However, a prominent feature of the more unitary employment relations climate concerns the greater use of managerially-driven and controlled techniques for communicating with and involving employees. The term 'employee involvement' can be applied to managerial initiatives that are designed to further the flow of communication at work as a means of enhancing the organizational commitment of employees (Hyman and Mason 1995). This encompasses measures such as 'team briefings'—arrangements that enable managers to convey information about the organization and the workplace to employees on a regular basis (see Chapter 5).

Trade unions and collective bargaining remain important features of employment relations, particularly in public sector organizations and among many large private sector companies. However, as a field of study which is concerned with the regulation of employment relationships as well as how they are experienced and contested, employment relations is also concerned with developing a critical understanding of relevant managerial regulatory processes (Sisson 2010). Moreover, it encompasses the process of legal enactment, something which has become more important given the greatly increased extent to which employment relationships have come to be governed by statutory regulation (Colling and Terry 2010). Examples include laws prohibiting discrimination against certain defined categories of workers (see Chapter 4) and laws enacting minimum wage protection (see Chapter 7). Nor must we overlook the important extent to which informal expectations and custom and practice understandings play a prominent part in influencing the wage–work bargain (Colling and Terry 2010). As a field of study, then, employment relations is not just concerned with collective bargaining, important though that still is; it has a broader, more inclusive dimension, being concerned with all of the processes that are used to regulate work and employment relationships.

1.4.3 The outcomes of employment relations

Clearly, the production of rules that govern work and employment relationships is the most obvious outcome of employment relations. The traditional focus in employment relations concerned how collective bargaining, involving the joint regulation of work and employment relationships, produces rules in the form of negotiated collective agreements between employers and trade unions. There are two types of collective agreement. Procedural agreements set out the details of how collective bargaining operates, specifying the topics that come within the scope of bargaining activity for example. Substantive agreements concern the actual outcomes of the bargaining process: any changes to pay, hours, holidays, etc.—the substance of employment relationships—that result from a bargaining exercise.

Managerial regulation also generates procedural rules in the form of arrangements for handling performance and absence issues, dealing with grievance and disciplinary cases, and for informing and consulting with employees. Where unions are absent, managers not only enjoy more scope to determine rules governing these matters unilaterally, but can also exercise more control over the determination of pay and employment conditions. When it comes to substantive outcomes, managerial goals in employment relations tend to focus on matters such as work effort and productivity rates, and levels of attendance and organizational commitment. There has been growing interest in how employment relations can be managed to engage and win the organizational commitment of staff, with the goal of improving business performance (see Chapter 5). This development is associated with the neo-unitary challenge to pluralist orthodoxy mentioned above (see Section 1.3.2).

However, a key feature of employment relations as a field of study, and one that distinguishes it from HRM, is a concern with the outcomes for employees, not just with regard to tangible benefits like wages and benefits, but also more intangible effects such as job satisfaction, justice, and dignity at work (Ackers and Wilkinson 2005; Heery et al. 2008). Moreover, the dynamic nature of the employment relationship as a wage–work bargain means that there is always the potential for employees to challenge the rules under which they operate. When it comes to employment relations, then, efforts by workers to contest employment relations collectively, through strikes, protests, and other forms of industrial action, or on a more individual basis (e.g. grievances and legal cases against employers, or more informal means like withholding effort), should also be seen as outcomes.

Clearly, much of the interest in employment relations outcomes is concerned with workplace and organizational matters, such as pay, working conditions, and productivity. However, employment relations operates at multiple levels, influencing matters beyond the boundaries of the organization (BUIRA 2009; Sisson 2009). In much of the public sector, like local government for example, employers and unions conclude collective agreements over pay and some employment conditions at industry sector level. Moreover, even in the absence of multi-employer bargaining, there is evidence that firms in the same industry sector operate similar pay arrangements (Arrowsmith and Sisson 1999). Employment relations also produces outcomes which are of broader significance for economic and social life more generally, illustrating its multi-level nature. For example, there has always been a strong interest in the social and economic implications of collective bargaining arrangements on matters such as wage inequality and inflation (Heery et al. 2008). Keith Sisson (2009; 2010: Chapter 3), moreover, examines how the nature and structure of employment relationships influence a wide range of indicators, including business performance, economic growth, health, living standards, family lives, and personal development. This demonstrates the importance of employment relations as a field of study.

1.4.4 The contexts of employment relations

Employment relations operates in particular contexts, being affected by a wide range of economic, political, legal, and social influences. Here we provide an overview of the main contextual factors, supported by some illustrative examples.

First of all, employment relations is influenced by the nature of the economic environment. The implications of the post-2008 economic downturn for work and employment relations are considered in more detail in Chapter 2. However, the high level of unemployment has generated a greater level of job insecurity. Among other things, this has encouraged a sense of injustice among some workers about employers' use of cheap foreign labour, leading to disputes in parts of the country (Gall 2012b). Economic recession and high unemployment levels have also had a marked impact on wage levels as employers have either restricted pay rises or, in many cases, have instituted pay freezes. The consequence has been the most pronounced squeeze on people's living standards in over sixty years as rises in prices (as measured by inflation) have substantially outstripped income growth (Resolution Foundation 2012a).

Work and employment relations are also affected by changes in the labour market and the composition of employment, like the use of more flexible employment arrangements, such as part-time and temporary work, and the growing proportion of female employment (see Chapters 2 and 4). The harsh economic climate has had a powerful impact in this respect too, evident in the record proportion of people working on a part-time basis (nearly 20 per cent) because they cannot secure full-time hours. Chapter 2 also contains material relating to the profound impact of economic globalization on employment relations around the world.

Employment relations also operates within a political and legal context. The law is an important source of the rules that govern employment relationships; and, of course, the nature of the political system determines the kinds of laws that are enacted. During the 1980s and 1990s, for example, one of the key political aims of the Conservative governments under Margaret Thatcher and John Major was to weaken the role of the trade unions. This resulted in a number of pieces of legislation that heavily restricted how trade unions operate (see Chapter 3).

Political change, in the form of the Labour governments of Tony Blair and Gordon Brown between 1997 and 2010, produced a change in emphasis. While Labour did little to reverse the anti-union measures of their Conservative predecessors in government, it did not add to them. Labour was also more ready to enact legislation protecting the interests of workers, through interventions like the National Minimum Wage, and by signing up to European Union (EU) laws designed to favour workers' interests. Since 2010, though, the Conservative-Liberal Democrat coalition government has initiated a marked change in emphasis. Believing that people have too many rights at work, it has enacted a series of laws which ease the supposed burden of employment regulation on employers, including measures designed to restrict the capacity of aggrieved workers to claim legal redress (see Chapters 3 and 10).

Finally, employment relations operates within a social context; the underpinning values and beliefs that influence people's attitudes and behaviour affect employment relations in important ways. There is evidence that since the 1980s Britain has become a more tolerant society. For example, the annual British Social Attitudes Survey demonstrates that prejudice against homosexuals has declined markedly. People have also become less prejudiced against working women. Changes in social attitudes of this kind influence employment relations, for example by encouraging greater awareness and acceptance of equality and diversity measures. However, while the level of racial prejudice fell substantially during the 1990s, it appeared to edge up again during the 2000s, perhaps because of the negative way in which the media report immigration issues. Nearly one in five employees (18 per cent) believes that workers of Asian origin experience prejudicial treatment in their own workplace (Creegan and Robinson 2008).

Section summary and further reading

- The main employment relations actors are employers and managers, workers and trade unions, and the state. However, the role of 'new actors' like community-based organizations and other civil society organizations is receiving greater scrutiny.

- The key employment relations processes include collective bargaining and consultation arrangements. Managerial processes used to regulate employment relationships, such as communication techniques, are also important—nor should the importance of informal expectations and understandings in employment relations be overlooked.

- In terms of outcomes, traditionally the emphasis was on how collective bargaining and other processes generated procedural and substantive rules that govern employment relationships. Employment relations is not just concerned with improvements in organizational efficiency; it is also marked by a focus on the implications for workers, notably the extent to which they experience fair and equitable treatment at work and the degree to which they can influence decision-making in organizations. As a multi-level field of study, it is also responsible for a range of broader social and economic outcomes.

- Employment relations operates in a number of contexts: economic, industrial, political, and social changes all influence how employment relations functions.

See Heery et al. (2008) for further insights about the main employment relations actors, processes, and outcomes. Sisson (2009; 2010: Chapter 3) is very good on examining the broader social and economic outcomes of how work and employment relationships are organized.

1.5 Conclusion: the value of employment relations

The main purpose of this chapter has been to introduce the nature of work and employment relationships, to consider employment relations as a field of study, and to introduce the main actors, processes, and outcomes of employment relations, set against the key contexts in which employment relations operates. The subject matter of employment relations is sometimes thought to be restricted to the trade unions and collective bargaining; because of their diminished significance, it is therefore no longer very important as a field of study (Emmott 2005). However, while unions and collective bargaining still play a major role, employment relations is about much more than just these things (Sisson 2009, 2010). It views work and employment relationships as more than just market transactions, expressing a concern with how they are regulated—in the form of rules that govern work and employment relationships, and that comprise terms and conditions of employment. Given that the 'employment relationship is something that the great majority of us are involved in for much of our lives' (Sisson 2008: 6), this is clearly something which is highly relevant. Moreover, it is not enough just to take into account the regulation of work and employment relationships; how workers experience these relationships, and the circumstances under which they come to contest them, and mobilize against their employers, are also important matters. From this perspective, the continued value and relevance of employment relations as a field of study is evident from the Pret a Manger case discussed in the introductory case study for this chapter.

The subject matter of employment relations is thus concerned with the 'totality' of work and employment relationships (Kaufman 2010a: 102). In addition to a concern with the role of employers, unions, and collective bargaining, the study of employment relations incorporates the activities of a wide range of new and emerging actors such as civil society organizations, recognizes the manifold processes involved in the regulation of employment relationships, and pays heed to a broad range of outcomes at multiple levels. As a consequence, employment relations as a field of study is 'uniquely placed' to develop a more effective understanding of how business and management operates (Colling and Terry 2010: 4), not least because it recognizes the importance of the broader economic, social, and political dimensions which affect, and in turn are influenced by, work and employment in organizations. As a field of study which is concerned with managing people at work effectively, HRM is 'narrow and impoverished' by comparison (Colling and Terry 2010: 4). It is generally too managerialist, concerned with how managers can manipulate the attitudes, behaviour, and performance of employees in pursuit of organizational goals (BUIRA 2009). Employment relations, though, is characterized by an important critical dimension. It exposes managerial objectives and activities to rigorous scrutiny, not taking them at face value; recognizes that workers also have independent interests which they pursue; and attests to the tensions, uncertainties, and potential for conflict that underpin work and employment relationships (see Employment relations reflection 1.8).

See Figure 1.3 for a diagram illustrating how employment relations can best be conceptualized. At the heart of employment relations is the relationship between an employer and a worker ('work' and 'employment relationships'). Key employment relations actors (e.g. managers, unions, government agencies) are involved in regulating employment relationships (e.g. joint regulation or legal regulation). The regulation of work and employment

Employment relations reflection 1.8: The value of employment relations

In 2009, Martin Upchurch undertook a survey of academics about the teaching of employment relations in British universities (Upchurch 2009). He asked respondents why they thought the teaching of employment relations was still important. Among the comments he received in response were:

Business still operates within the bounds of rules, regulations and limited resources. [Employment relations] offers a conceptual way to explain the politics and relations of power in the world of work . . . [and] also draws the attention of students as it brings a more critical perspective to their understanding of management and work.

[The study of employment relations] is a valuable way of exposing students to new ways of thinking and challenging their pre-conceptions . . . By studying the inherent tensions in the employment relationship (through the use of hugely relevant current affairs examples) students can start to develop the all important skills of critical thought.

[Employment relations] recognises the issues of power and conflict in the workplace and how these dynamics are managed . . . We help students to challenge their misconceptions over how the employment relationship is really managed and we help produce future managers with a greater insight into the ways of the workplace.

[Employment relations is] probably one of the few subjects on a business degree that really requires any wider political engagement from students . . . and particularly also the recognition that there are alternative perspectives to viewing the world than 'managerialist' ones.

[Employment relations is] a vital part of the employment landscape and in the context of a globalising world is a very important subject of relevance to working people everywhere.

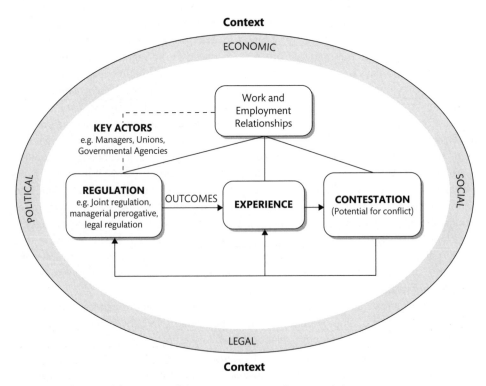

Figure 1.3 A framework for conceptualizing contemporary employment relations

relationships in this way produces certain outcomes—not just narrow workplace rules, but also in the form of broader, sometimes less tangible effects, like the implications for efficiency, equity, and voice (see Budd 2004). This latter point means that we have to be concerned with the way in which employees experience employment relations, and also with how the nature of this experience often puts them at odds with their employers. Thus work and employment relationships are marked by an inherent potential for conflict, the implication being that we need to understand the circumstances under which the terms of that relationship become contested, and also the form which that contestation takes. Finally, it has been established that <u>employment relations is influenced by aspects of the political, economic, legal, and social contexts in which it operates.</u>

Given that employment affects the majority of people in advanced industrialized societies like the UK, it should be evident that a good level of knowledge and understanding of employment relations is essential if one is going to appreciate properly the nature of contemporary business and management, and its relationship with society. While employment relations, conceived narrowly as the study of trade unions and collective bargaining, may have become marginalized, the broader perspective which we adopt here views it as a field of study that continues to be highly relevant. It concerns work and employment relationships, and all of the various features of, and influences over, these relationships—something that is of interest at an individual, organizational, and societal level.

 ## Assignment and discussion questions

1. What are the main features of the employment relationship as a 'wage–work bargain'?

2. With regard to the objectives of employment relations, explain what is meant by 'efficiency', 'equity', and 'voice'.

3. What is meant by the concept of managerial prerogative in employment relations? What are the main constraints on the exercise of managerial prerogative?

4. Which of the three perspectives—unitary, pluralist, or radical—most closely fits your own view of the world of work? Why?

5. Why is 'power' such an important concept in understanding employment relations?

 Visit the Online Resource Centre that accompanies this book to develop your understanding of this chapter, and keep up to date with the latest developments in this area. **www.oxfordtextbooks.co.uk/orc/williams3e/**

 ## Chapter case study: Employment relations in Amazon

Online retailer Amazon has become one of the most well-known firms in the world. First entering the UK market as a bookseller in 1998, the US company subsequently greatly expanded the range of products it sells, which now includes household goods, music downloads, and electronics. In September 2012, Amazon announced plans to create 2,000 new jobs at its depots across the UK, to add to the 5,000 permanent staff it already employed. Along with other leading multinationals, such as Google, Vodafone, and Starbucks, Amazon has been condemned for the way it structures its tax affairs. In 2011, for example, despite UK sales of some £3.35 billion, Amazon paid no corporation tax on any of the profits arising from that revenue. Some years earlier it had transferred the ownership of its UK business to a subsidiary based in Luxembourg, an arrangement that helps it to avoid paying tax in the UK.

But tax is not the only aspect of Amazon's business which has come in for criticism. The company's approach to work and employment relations matters has also sometimes been raised as a cause for concern. In early 2013, for example, an investigation by a German television station revealed that foreign temporary workers employed at one of Amazon's warehouses in Germany to cope with the pre-Christmas rush had experienced a brutal campaign of bullying and intimidation by military-style security guards wearing black boots and uniforms, employed by a contractor. Amazon subsequently announced that it would end its relationship with the security firm in question.

In the UK, trade unions claim that many of Amazon's workers have low pay and poor conditions, with wages often at, or just above, the statutory National Minimum Wage. Work in its warehouses is often highly insecure, with many staff taken on through temporary employment agencies rather than hired by the firm directly, meaning that they can be disposed of more readily when they are not needed. Workers have complained about the intense pressure involved in processing orders, with their movements constantly tracked throughout the warehouse to make sure they are keeping up to speed. In February 2013, the GMB union organized protests outside nine of Amazon's warehouses, including Doncaster, Swansea, and Milton Keynes. It says its aim was to draw attention to the low pay offered by Amazon, and to get the company to agree to pay its entire staff a 'living wage'—enough for workers to actually live on. One GMB official called for companies like Amazon to be given a 'corporate' Anti-social Behaviour Order (ASBO). This was justified on the grounds of its 'refusal to pay proper taxes or to treat its workers properly . . . Profitable companies like Amazon, dodging fair taxes while failing to pay their staff a living wage and treat them properly, deserve a corporate ASBO'.

Like many US companies, Amazon opposes trade union representation for its staff. When it was becoming established in the UK, it was able to prevent a union presence by using a combination of targeted rewards, the establishment of a staff consultative forum, and threats against employees with strong union sympathies. In 2012, the assistant secretary of the Scottish Trades Union Congress claimed that Amazon was a 'predatory, anti-union' employer, which offered jobs with weak employment standards. He criticized the company as:

> aggressively anti-union; workers in Scotland who dare even to ask about representation are bullied and harassed. While Amazon relies on effective enforcement of contracts to run its business and derive its significant profits, it does not afford its employees the security provided by decent employment contracts. Hours are often on the whim of the employer with shifts terminated half-way through if business tails off.

Amazon itself, however, rejects the claims that it is a bad employer, saying that it provides its staff with 'a safe and positive working environment, which includes on-the-job training and opportunities for career progression'. The company also says that its permanent workforce enjoys benefits such as healthcare and pension plans.

Sources: Kelly and Badigannavar 2004; Boyd 2012; BBC News Online 2013a; O' Connor 2013; Paterson 2013

Questions

To what extent do you agree with trade unionists who claim that companies like Amazon are bad employers? What, if anything, should be done to improve employment standards in such companies?

Part 2

Employment relations in context

2

Employment relations in the contemporary economy

◉ Chapter objectives

The main objectives of this chapter are to:

- examine the implications of changes in the economy for work and employment relations;
- consider the effects of the post-2008 economic slump on employment relations;
- explore how economic globalization and the activities of multinational companies have affected employment relations; and
- assess the main approaches to regulating labour standards on an international basis.

2.1 Introduction

This chapter examines the implications for work and employment relations of developments in the contemporary economy. Changes in the economic context, by altering the power held by the parties, exercise a profound influence on the character and conduct of work and employment relations, particularly as organizations come under pressure to reduce labour costs and increase the output of their staff, in order to maintain their competitiveness. In Section 2.2 the focus is on the influence of relevant economic, labour market, and employment developments on work and employment relations. There is a view that employment relations in the twenty-first century is marked by a shift towards greater cooperation between employers and workers, reflecting the development of a 'new' knowledge-based economy. However, some of the problems with this approach are highlighted by the impact of the post-2008 slump and the harsh economic climate it has generated. In Section 2.3 attention switches to the implications of economic globalization for work and employment relations. The focus here is on the nature of globalization, and how it has affected employment relations. This encompasses a concern with the role of multinational companies, and in particular how their activities have helped to undermine workers' rights and employment conditions around the world—something that has prompted growing interest in how labour standards can be regulated on an international basis.

Introductory case study: Agency workers and employment flexibility

One of the main themes of this chapter concerns demands from employers for cheaper and more flexible labour. Hiring workers through temporary employment agencies allows employers to adjust workforce numbers in response to variations in demand. Faced with rapidly declining car sales as the result of the economic recession, in February 2009 BMW ended weekend working at its Cowley plant near Oxford, which makes the Mini. Some 850 agency workers were sacked with just one hour's notice. Because they were not employed directly by BMW, the agency staff enjoyed few employment rights, and were not entitled to any redundancy pay. They were simply paid one week's wages to cover the notice period. Yet many members of the supposedly 'temporary' workforce had worked in the plant for some years. One agency worker said he had been treated like a 'second class' employee: 'I've worked here for three and a half years and now I'm being sacked for no reason. I've been used.' Angry workers reportedly booed and threw fruit at BMW managers on hearing that they were to lose their jobs. Union leaders, who were also targeted for criticism by some workers, expressed their disgust at the way the agency workers had been treated. Tony Woodley, joint leader of the Unite union, wrote to BMW accusing the company of treating workers with 'utter contempt'. He claimed that no one would 'treat a dog this way, never mind a loyal and committed workforce'. While the European Union has introduced legislation to give agency workers more rights (see Chapter 3), it did not come into force until 2011 and would not have given the workers affected by BMW's shift closure much additional protection anyway. This case shows that the benefits of employment flexibility, which in this case amounted to the freedom enjoyed by BMW to dismiss workers as easily as possible, are often one-sided in favour of employers.

Sources: BBC News Online 2009c; BBC News Online 2009d; Macalister and Pidd 2009

2.2 Work and employment relations: from the 'new economy' to recession

One of the most important influences on work and employment relations concerns developments in the economy, especially those relating to the changes in the composition of employment and the labour market. There are long-term changes evident, notably the process of de-industrialization and the shift in employment from manufacturing to services. The latter half of the twentieth century saw the decline of staple industries such as coal mining, iron and steel making, and shipbuilding, and also the erosion of the country's manufacturing capacity. There has been a pronounced shift in employment in favour of the service sector—banking, finance, retailing, leisure and hospitality, for example, and also the public services. See Table 2.1 for details of how the proportions of manufacturing and services jobs in the economy have changed since the 1980s. Whereas by 2012 just 8 per cent of the workforce worked in manufacturing (some 2.5 million people), over 80 per cent were based in the service sector. This change in the composition of employment has had some notable consequences for employment relations. For example, trade unions and collective bargaining have less of a presence in private services; therefore the decline of manufacturing employment has been one factor behind their decline (see Chapters 6 and 7).

Any analysis of the economic context, however, also has to encompass developments in the shorter term, most evidently the impact of the financial and economic crisis. Between

Table 2.1 The proportion of UK jobs in manufacturing and service industries, selected years 1979–2012

Year	Proportion of jobs in manufacturing (%)	Proportion of jobs in services (%)
1979	26.0	61.4
1984	20.5	67.5
1989	18.4	70.0
1994	15.8	74.2
1999	15.0	76.0
2004	11.6	80.0
2008	9.9	80.1
2012*	8.1	83.2

*Third quarter

Source: Office for National Statistics, http://www.statistics.gov.uk

2008 and 2013, many advanced economies experienced a pronounced economic downturn, which was instigated by the collapse in 2007 of the sub-prime mortgage market in the United States, followed by the failure of a number of major banks and investment firms (Mason 2009; Stiglitz 2010; Krugman 2012). The subsequent recession was the 'longest and deepest since the 1930s' (Lansley 2012: 5). While there was a return to growth in 2010, this was not sustained, and the economy fell back into recession for a period in 2011–12. The persistence of the economic downturn has been striking, with little apparent sign of any return to economic growth during the latter part of 2012 and into early 2013.

Economic recessions have pronounced adverse consequences for jobs. That of the early 1980s, for example, which hit the strongly unionized manufacturing sector particularly hard, generated a high level of unemployment. Between 1979 and 1984, the number of recorded unemployed rose from under 1.5 million (5.4 per cent of the workforce) to over 3 million (11.8 per cent). During the late 1990s and early 2000s, though, unemployment fell markedly, to less than 5 per cent of the workforce in 2004 (see Table 2.2). However, the 2008–9 recession prompted a sharp rise in unemployment; by the beginning of 2009 the number of unemployed had risen above the 2 million mark for the first time in twelve years. Between 2008 and 2012, unemployment grew by nearly 800,000, to 2.5 million—from 5.7 per cent to 8.0 per cent of the workforce—before stabilizing (see Table 2.2). Young workers have been particularly

Table 2.2 UK unemployment, selected years 1979–2012

Year	Total unemployed	Unemployment rate (%)
1979	1,432,000	5.4
1984	3,241,000	11.8
1989	2,082,000	7.2
1994	2,675,000	9.5
1999	1,728,000	6.0
2004	1,465,000	4.8
2008	1,777,000	5.7
2012	2,555,000	8.0

Source: Office for National Statistics, http://www.statistics.gov.uk

badly hit (Lansley 2012). Unemployment among 18–24 year olds increased by 53 per cent between 2008 and 2012; by the end of 2012 around a fifth of workers in this age group (over 800,000 young people) were unemployed. The coalition government's deficit-reduction pro-gramme, which includes austerity measures designed to produce over £80 billion worth of cuts to public expenditure (Lee 2011), means that job losses have been particularly evident in the public sector (Lansley 2012), with some 900,000 posts expected to be cut between 2010 and 2017.

Notwithstanding the intensity of the recession, and both the subsequent economic slump and the coalition's austerity measures, the level of unemployment did not reach as high a level as in previous recessions (Lansley 2012). Moreover, the number of people in employment actually grew during 2012, a period when there was no economic growth. As will be shown In Section 2.2.2, the paradox of seemingly rising employment levels during an economic down-turn can be explained by the flexibility employers benefit from when it comes to operating work and employment relations arrangements. There is very high demand for jobs when vacancies do arise. For example, in March 2013 a new Tesco Express store opened on East-ney Road in Portsmouth, near to where the author lives. It received 782 applications for the thirteen jobs on offer—around sixty for each new position. Moreover, many workers without jobs are part of the 'hidden' unemployed. For example, around 40 per cent of the 2.5 million people receiving incapacity benefits could be in a position to re-enter the workforce, but they are often based in areas of the country, like parts of the North of England and South Wales, where there are few jobs available (Lansley 2011).

During the 1990s and early 2000s there were claims that profound changes in work and employment relations were occurring, part of a shift to a so-called 'new economy' marked by a greater degree of cooperation between workers and employers. Three developments appeared to stand out. First, the employment relationship itself seemed to be diminishing in importance, given the increasing number of people who apparently work without one, in particular as supposedly autonomous and independent self-employed, freelance contrac-tors. Second, a dramatic shift towards more flexible forms of employment was held to be occurring, exemplifying a greater mutuality of interest at work. This is because employers are able to manage labour more efficiently, and workers can exercise more choice over their working arrangements. Third, changes in employment, most notably in the occupational structure, seemed to be transforming the nature of work itself, leading to a 'knowledge econ-omy' characterized by an increase in the proportion of people engaged in 'knowledge work'. These developments supposedly portend a shift away from emphasizing the inherent conflict of interest that exists between workers and employers to a more unitary concern with shared interests and consensus. However, the economic downturn and its effects highlight just how tenuous this 'new economy' thesis really is when it comes to interpreting changes in work and employment relations.

2.2.1 Self-employment: a harbinger of the 'new economy'?

One of the most prominent features of debates about the development of the 'new econ-omy' concerns the supposedly greater significance of work undertaken by self-employed, freelance contractors who are not subject to the disciplines of an employment relationship.

Table 2.3 Self-employment in the UK, 1984–2012

	No. of self-employed (000s)	Self-employed as a proportion of all those in employment (%)
1984	2,695	11.1
1988	3,216	12.3
1992	3,447	13.5
1996	3,506	13.5
2000	3,256	11.8
2004	3,618	12.7
2008	3,826	13.0
2012	4,194	14.2

Source: Office for National Statistics, http://www.statistics.gov.uk

People are thought to welcome the opportunity of working as 'free agents' (Barley and Kunda 2004)—as self-employed temporary contractors who sell their expertise to a range of organizations, thus being liberated from the constraints associated with being in a relationship with, and thus under the control of, a single employer. The decision to become self-employed is viewed by some as a positive choice by workers (Hakim 1988). It is held to signal a desire to escape the shackles of the employment relationship and to secure the independence that comes with working for oneself (Handy 1994; Leadbeater 1999).

As can be seen from Table 2.3, between the mid-1980s and mid-1990s the number of self-employed people in the UK grew by nearly a million. Self-employment was supported by successive Conservative governments, who viewed its growth, and also that of small businesses in general, as the mark of a dynamic and competitive economy in which enterprise thrived (Goss 1991). Self-employment is a particular feature of some industries, such as the media and IT sectors (Platman 2004; Tremblay and Genin 2010). There is evidence that people often do make a deliberate choice to become self-employed; the freedom and flexibility self-employment offers is viewed as highly desirable (Kirkpatrick and Hoque 2006), including the supposed ability to turn down offers of work. In the media industry, for example, many freelance workers welcome the autonomy they gain from being self-employed (Platman 2004). However, the degree of control and autonomy enjoyed by self-employed contractors varies according to such factors as their market situation. For example, self-employed translators with a wide client base have a rather high degree of autonomy, since they are not dependent on a small number of companies for work. Freelance editors and proofreaders, though, generally work for just one or two publishing clients and are dependent on them for commissions (Stanworth and Stanworth 1995; Fraser and Gold 2001).

It is important not to exaggerate the benefits of self-employment, since it can be associated with inferior employment conditions, like the absence of paid holidays, and may also be a source of considerable insecurity (Kirkpatrick and Hoque 2006). Many people who work from home assembling consumer products on an ostensibly self-employed basis, often low-paid women workers, undertake routine manual labour with minimal discretion (Felstead and Jewson 2000). Moreover, the extent to which the choice of self-employment is stimulated by a desire for independence, autonomy, and control on the part of the workers concerned should not be overstated. The decision to become self-employed is often more a function of the absence of alternative employment opportunities, particularly during periods of high unemployment, or the increased preference of some employers to replace directly employed staff with freelance contractors in some areas (MacDonald and Coffield 1991; Rees and Fielder 1992).

Despite the claimed benefits of self-employment and of freelance working arrangements, the number of self-employed scarcely grew between the early 1990s and late 2000s, fluctuating at a level close to the 3.5 million mark (see Table 2.3). The table also shows that the proportion of self-employed actually fell during the late 1990s, to under 12 per cent of the workforce, before gradually rising again in the 2000s, to 13 per cent in 2008. This constancy is hardly a sign of the growth of a 'new economy' (Nolan and Slater 2003). There was little appetite on the part of most workers to go freelance and become self-employed contractors (McGovern et al. 2007), particularly during a period of economic growth when jobs were relatively abundant. However, Table 2.3 indicates that between 2008 and 2012 there was an increase in the number of self-employed, to more than 4 million, with the proportion of the workforce in self-employment increasing to over 14 per cent. Much of the growth in self-employment occurred in 2011 and 2012 (ONS 2013).

This spurt in the number of people becoming self-employed by no means heralds a shift to a new economy in the manner anticipated by those who view freelance contracting as a positive choice by workers keen to secure greater control and autonomy over their working lives. Rather, as in the 1980s, it was more a function of the weak state of the labour market and the absence of alternative employment opportunities caused by the economic slump (CIPD 2012b). It is this rise in the incidence of self-employment which explains why the overall level of employment grew by a relatively small amount between 2008 and 2012, while the actual number of new employees actually fell. Some two-fifths of new 'jobs' created between the start of 2010 and the end of 2012 were on a self-employed basis, as people without jobs went freelance, tried to start their own businesses, or were pressed into 'false' self-employment (TUC 2013).

The concept of 'false' self-employment refers to the way in which much work that is supposedly arranged on a self-employed basis is simply disguised employment—albeit at a lower cost to the employer. False self-employment is a long-standing feature of work and employment relations, often evident in franchising arrangements—such as in the milk distribution sector (O'Connell Davidson 1994). Pushing workers into 'false' self-employment enables firms to realize cost savings, because they no longer have to provide many employment rights or pay welfare contributions. Yet this often leaves workers manifestly more exposed and vulnerable. They are obliged to bear more of the risks and costs of employment, given the unwillingness of companies to enter into a long-term and direct relationship with them. As supposedly self-employed contractors, workers do not benefit from the full range of employment rights, including access to holiday pay, sick pay, redundancy pay, and the right to be paid the National Minimum Wage. Moreover, although workers are often dependent on client companies for work, these companies have no reciprocal obligations to them beyond the terms of the immediate contract.

Insight into practice 2.1: The growth of 'bogus' self-employment

The economic downturn seems to have generated a growing amount of bogus self-employment, as some employers looked to take advantage of the weak labour market, and the relative paucity of jobs available, to hire workers on a cheaper and more flexible basis. Since they are not formally designated as 'employees', workers classified as self-employed miss out on a range of employment benefits, including rights to paid holiday, sickness pay, and redundancy pay. False or bogus self-employment is a long-standing feature of some parts of the economy, including construction and hairdressing, where workers are frequently expected to hire what are supposedly their own chairs on the premises of salons. Private cab firms, such as Addison Lee which operates in London, often hire drivers on a self-employed basis, saving money by not having to pay National Insurance contributions (Booth 2012). However, there are reports that the practice has spread, with some migrant workers in the food-processing sector being classified as working for themselves, when in reality they are doing a job of work for an employer just like any other employee (Leighton and Wynn 2011). The journalist John Harris has written about what he calls the 'fraudulent' way in which some employers have set about converting normal jobs into supposedly self-employed positions. He cites one online advertisement for a job which states: 'We are looking for a number of door supervisors, security guards and CCTV operatives . . . You will be employed on a self-employed basis' (Harris 2012). In 2010 the *Daily Mirror* newspaper launched its 'Gizza Proper Job' campaign, which drew attention to the scandal of bogus self-employment arrangements. The courier company Hermes Parcelnet, for example, operates with some 7,500 supposedly self-employed drivers, who can sometimes earn as little as £3 per hour, and are entitled to no compensation when they lose their jobs. Unlike genuinely self-employed workers, they seem to have little control over their working arrangements—for example, they cannot take a holiday when they choose (Sommerlad 2010, 2013).

The harsh economic climate prompted a growing incidence of 'false' or 'bogus' self-employment, as unscrupulous employers looked to push more of the costs of employment onto workers (TUC 2010)—see Insight into practice 2.1. While genuine self-employment is commonplace across the economy, particularly in sectors like media, publishing, and IT, it is often a function of organizations' decisions to divest themselves of responsibility for operating services on an in-house basis rather than a reflection of an increased entrepreneurial desire on the part of workers to become self-employed. Many workers are pushed into self-employment because of a lack of alternative jobs, something that was particularly noticeable during the post-2008 economic slump. Furthermore, the rising incidence of 'false' or 'bogus' self-employment indicates the way that some employers have responded to the recessionary climate by taking steps to operate with cheaper and more flexible sources of labour as a means of reducing costs.

2.2.2 Flexibility in work and employment relations

A second dimension of change relates to the use of more flexible forms of work and employment often associated with so-called 'non-standard' labour, such as part-time and temporary working arrangements. Their use is associated with the growing proportion of employment in service sector jobs, such as in retail, financial services, and hospitality (Felstead and Jewson 1999). By using part-time and temporary staff, rather than full-time and permanent employees, employers are able to align production or service delivery with anticipated demand and thus manage labour more efficiently. This is sometimes viewed as exemplifying a more

purposive, strategic approach to the management of labour. Moreover, one of the most powerful arguments in favour of flexible employment arrangements is that, in addition to being
convenient for employers, they allow people to exercise greater choice over their working
lives. People may opt for a temporary job if it provides a potential route into permanent
employment (Robinson 1999). However, a more critical, alternative interpretation views flexibility as less about operating innovative employment arrangements that satisfy the interests
of both workers and employers, and more about the search for stronger managerial prerogative, weakened trade unions, and a cheaper and more pliable workforce, who are expected to
work more intensively (e.g. Beynon et al. 2002). This is something that has been particularly
evident in the harsh climate of the post-2008 economic downturn.

When it comes to temporary work arrangements, one way in which employers can try to
gain flexibility is by using directly employed staff, but hired on fixed-term contracts. This allows managers to take on new staff to fill a vacancy, or to meet an anticipated short-term rise
in demand, without committing them to a long-term relationship. The use of fixed-term contracts is particularly common in the public services, especially health and education, where
funding uncertainties and budgetary constraints often conspire to make it difficult for employers to offer staff a permanent contract (Beynon et al. 2002). However, the use of this type
of flexibility is rather modest, and there is no evidence of any notable increase in temporary
employment arrangements. While the share of temporary employment rose during the early
1990s, to 7.1 per cent of the workforce in 1994, it fell back to just 5.5 per cent by 2008, before
gradually increasing again up to 2012 in the context of the economic downturn (see Table 2.4).
In 2004 just over one-fifth (22 per cent) of workplaces contained some employees on fixed-
term and temporary contracts; seven years later, in 2011, the proportion was largely the same
(23 per cent) (van Wanrooy et al. 2013).

What accounts for the lack of any notable increase in the use of directly-employed
temporary staff? One reason is that European Union (EU) legislation, which obliges employers
to treat temporary staff no less favourably than their permanent equivalents when it comes
to matters like pay, means that some of the cost benefits associated with using this form of
flexible employment have diminished (see Chapter 3). A further explanation is that because
of the economic climate many employers, particularly those in the public sector, have opted
to save money by not filling vacant positions; as employees' fixed-term contracts expire, they
are less likely to be replaced than was previously the case.

Table 2.4 The proportion of temporary and part-time workers in the UK,
selected years 1984–2012

Year	Temporary workers (%)	Part-time workers (%)
1984	5.5	21.0
1989	5.5	22.3
1994	7.1	24.5
1999	7.1	25.1
2004	6.1	25.9
2008	5.5	25.3
2012	6.4	27.3

Source: Office for National Statistics, http://www.statistics.gov.uk

A further manifestation of flexibility in work and employment relations concerns the use by employers of temporary labour hired through external employment agencies. Agency temps are a common feature of some parts of the economy—in the construction industry, for example (Purcell, Purcell, and Tailby 2004; Forde, MacKenzie, and Robinson 2008), and in other sectors where migrant workers comprise a large proportion of the workforce, such as hotels, food processing, cleaning, and social care (James and Lloyd 2008; Knox 2010; McKay and Markova 2010). There are estimated to be between 1.1 million and 1.5 million agency workers in the UK (BERR 2008). The agency employs the workers, or hires them as ostensibly self-employed contractors, thus sparing the organization from the costs, such as holiday pay, and duties that come with being an employer.

Using temporary agency labour benefits employers in a number of ways, most notably in relation to cost savings and greater flexibility. Such workers often have lower pay, worse employment conditions, and fewer employment rights than their directly employed counterparts. Moreover, hiring agency labour can be a relatively efficient way of accommodating short-term fluctuations in demand, or even, in some cases, of filling vacancies (McKay and Markova 2010). In theory, workers can choose whether or not they want to take on an assignment, thus enabling them to work in a flexible manner of their own choice. In reality, however, the mutuality embodied in this vision of the temporary assignment is rarely evident. In his study of temporary agency working in Leeds and Telford, Forde (2001) discovered that agencies reward people who they perceive to be good performers with regular assignments. Workers who refuse assignments, however, are less likely to be offered future ones.

The introductory case study shows how one company, in this case BMW, responded to economic difficulties by dismissing its agency workforce. They were, in the words of one of those who were sacked, treated as 'second-class' workers. Studies of temporary agency workers highlight the irregularity of their earnings and, for those who are designated as self-employed, the absence of paid holidays and other benefits. Many undertake temporary assignments only because they have been unable to secure a permanent position (e.g. Grimshaw, Earnshaw, and Hebson 2003). Some agency workers do choose such arrangements because of the flexibility they provide. Yet a much higher proportion—some 60 per cent—undertake temporary assignments not through choice, but because they cannot find permanent employment (BERR 2008).

There are numerous well-documented reports regarding the highly exploitative treatment experienced by agency workers, especially migrant workers (e.g. TUC 2007; Wilkinson 2012). They demonstrate the important extent to which employment flexibility is often synonymous with low pay, poor working conditions, extreme work pressures, and a high level of job insecurity (James and Lloyd 2008; McKay and Markova 2010). Competitive pressures in the food industry, and the demand for ever cheaper foodstuffs, work their way downwards through the supply chain to affect the workers responsible for picking, processing, and packaging the produce. The seasonal nature of the food business, as well as the short-term fluctuations in demand from the big supermarket chains, mean that it is advantageous for producers to make use of a source of labour that can be switched on and off as desired. The agriculture and food-processing industries make extensive use of migrant labour, often provided by local employment agencies known as 'gangmasters'. The firms that produce and process the food that goes on the supermarket shelves are thus relieved of the obligation to employ staff themselves, relying instead on using agency staff, sometimes on an hourly basis, in order to respond to fluctuations in demand from their supermarket customers. Migrant workers are often hired on so-called 'zero hours' contracts (see Chapter 8), meaning that while they are expected to be available for work when needed, they have no guarantee of receiving regular work themselves. For them, employment flexibility equates with irregular earnings and manifold insecurity (Shelley 2007).

Despite the apparent benefits of using temporary agency labour for employers, as with the case of directly employed temporary staff there is little sign of any notable increase in this type of flexibility in work and employment relations. In 2004, agency workers were present in 12 per cent of workplaces; seven years later, in 2011, they were present in 10 per cent of workplaces (van Wanrooy et al. 2013). EU legislation designed to give agency workers greater protection is unlikely to have acted as a constraint on the use of temporary labour. A more important factor, it would seem, concerns the way in which many employers responded to the economic downturn by reducing their use of agency staff, as in the case of BMW. Nearly a third (31 per cent) of workplaces in the public sector, for example, reduced the number of such workers between 2004 and 2011 (van Wanrooy et al. 2013).

Another way in which employers can gain flexibility in employment relations concerns changes to working time arrangements—something considered more fully in Chapter 8. Table 2.4 indicates the growth in the proportion of part-time workers (those working in jobs for fewer than 30 hours per week) in the economy during the 1980s and 1990s. In 1984 just over a fifth (21 per cent) of workers were employed on a part-time basis; by 1999 this had risen to a quarter (25.1 per cent). However, there was no further growth over the subsequent decade. Yet this was followed by a notable surge in part-time employment between 2008 and 2012. The number of people in part-time employment rose by around 621,000, to over 27 per cent of the workforce; over the same period there was a corresponding decline in full-time employment.

As was mentioned earlier, the provision of more flexible working time arrangements is often viewed as an unambiguously positive development inasmuch as it benefits employers, who are able to organize work schedules in a way that matches variations in demand for their products and services, and workers, who choose part-time working in order to reconcile employment with their family responsibilities. However, the emphasis on 'choice' pays insufficient heed to constraints such as childcare responsibilities (Felstead and Jewson 1999). There is plenty of evidence that women workers in particular are being trapped in low-paid part-time jobs, which generally offer few opportunities for advancement compared to full-time ones (Bradley et al. 2000).

The way many employers responded to the post-2008 economic downturn highlights the frequent absence of choice when it comes to flexible working time arrangements. Much of the growth in part-time employment during this period was involuntary, in the sense that workers went into part-time jobs only because full-time positions were unavailable. Nearly a fifth of part-time workers would prefer a full-time job (Cam 2012; Lansley 2012). But one of the key ways in which employers have responded to the downturn has been to cut costs through reducing working hours. In response to the recession, nearly a fifth (18 per cent) of workplaces curtailed opportunities for paid overtime, and a slightly smaller proportion (15 per cent) instituted cuts to the basic working hours of staff (van Wanrooy et al. 2013). One of the curious features of the post-2008 slump has been the relatively low peak in the level of unemployment, as mentioned in Section 2.2—bearing in mind, of course, that the headline number of unemployed does not capture the full scale of joblessness in the economy. One of the reasons for the relatively low unemployment figure is the marked rise in the level of 'underemployment', encompassing involuntary part-time workers and others who simply want to work for more hours in their job. The Trades Union Congress (TUC 2012b) has calculated that the number of underemployed people in the economy rose from 2.3 million in 2008 to 3.3 million in 2012—some 11 per cent of the workforce. By no means, then, can it be concluded that the rising level of part-time employment is the product of a shared belief among workers and employers in the virtue of flexibility.

This is even more apparent when another of the key ways in which employers responded to the economic downturn is considered, namely their pursuit of greater flexibility over pay and employment conditions. Wage cuts and freezes were evident in a substantial minority (42 per cent) of all workplaces, and a majority (63 per cent) of those in the public sector (van Wanrooy et al. 2013). In some cases, such as in the motor industry, measures were agreed with recognized trade unions as the price to be paid for maintaining the viability of the business and protecting jobs. Elsewhere, however, decisions to cut wages were highly contentious affairs, particularly in local government where some councils chose to institute pay cuts in order to save money. In 2011, for example, Shropshire Council dismissed its workforce of 6,500, before re-hiring them on new contracts, mostly at a lower pay rate. Evidently, the efficiency savings offered by such flexibility over pay and conditions enabled many employers to withstand the effects of the recession and protect jobs, one of the reasons why the overall level of unemployment did not rise as high as had been anticipated (CIPD 2013).

However, the cost to workers of such a sustained squeeze on wages, in terms of declining income and the threat to living standards, has been profound (Lansley 2010, 2011). Between 2009 and 2012, average pay fell by 3 per cent in real terms (after controlling for inflation), exacerbating a trend that had become evident even before the start of the recession (Lansley 2012). Given the large extent to which increases in prices exceed any rises in income, the consequence has been the most pronounced squeeze on people's living standards in over sixty years (Resolution Foundation 2012a). In 2013, the average worker in the UK earned no more than they had a decade earlier; one of the effects of such a pronounced squeeze on wages is that it is not anticipated that low- and middle-income families will see a return to their pre-recession income level until possibly 2023 (Resolution Foundation 2013).

LEGISLATION AND POLICY 2.2: The coalition's Work Programme

The coalition government's Work Programme seems to have been a costly failure. Introduced in June 2011, at a cost of up to £5 billion, its schemes are designed to provide unemployed people with work experience opportunities, to improve their job prospects. After just over a year in existence, however, it had helped just 3.6 per cent of the long-term unemployed who took part into jobs (Malik 2013). The Work Programme generated a considerable amount of controversy after it emerged that some unemployed people had been pushed into taking unpaid work, including cleaning homes and offices, with the threat of having their benefits withdrawn if they declined to participate (Malik, Ball, and Davies 2012). Some jobseekers on a Work Programme scheme were used as unpaid stewards during the Queen's Diamond Jubilee celebrations, and were obliged to sleep outside the night before under one of London's bridges over the River Thames (Malik 2012). Evidently, some employers have taken advantage of the Work

(continued...)

Programme to replace proper workers, who have to be paid at least the National Minimum Wage, with unemployed people on unpaid work experience schemes.

In February 2013 Cait Reilly, an unemployed geology graduate, won her court case against the government after she claimed that requiring her to undertake unpaid work for retail firm Poundland, or else lose her Jobseekers' Allowance, was unlawful. The Court of Appeal ruled that people like Reilly had been given insufficient information about their rights and the likely sanctions if they failed to participate in Work Programme schemes. According to Reilly, who had to give up her voluntary work for a local museum, the two weeks she spent at Poundland

> were a complete waste of my time, as the experience did not help me get a job . . . I was not given any training and I was left with no time to do my voluntary work or search for other jobs. The only beneficiary was Poundland, a multimillion-pound company. Later I found out that I should never have been told the placement was compulsory. I don't think I am above working in shops like Poundland. I now work part-time in a supermarket. It is just that I expect to get paid for working.
>
> (BBC News Online 2013*b*)

The government had to enact hasty retrospective legislation to avoid potentially costly claims for compensation from others who had been pushed into unpaid Work Programme schemes. Some major retailers, including Waterstones, Sainsbury's, and TK Maxx stopped their involvement in the Work Programme because of controversies like this, and also the campaigning efforts of unions and activists.

Perhaps the most contentious way in which employers try to secure greater flexibility over work and employment relationships is by taking measures to avoid paying workers for the jobs that they do altogether. The coalition government's Work Programme has attracted a great deal of controversy, not least because of the way in which some of its schemes have been used by employers as a source of cheap labour (see Legislation and policy 2.2). In some areas of work, particularly in the media industry, it has become increasingly commonplace to find menial, entry-level tasks being undertaken by a cadre of young and unpaid 'volunteer' staff—often known as 'interns'—who agree to work for no wages or just for expenses in exchange for training, work experience, and the opportunity to develop contacts, perhaps with the chance of securing a glamorous, well-paid job on a newspaper or in television as a result. Internships and unpaid work experience placements can be viewed as beneficial for workers, given the opportunity they provide to gain a foothold in otherwise hard to access careers.

However, there are growing concerns that interns are being used by employers as a source of cheap, or even free, labour (Perlin 2011; Bach 2012). While much of their work involves running errands or procuring refreshments, it can also encompass tasks that workers would normally expect to be paid for, such as handling reception duties. There have even been reports that some graduates have been charged fees to undertake work experience opportunities in the media industry. As Chapter 4 shows, the growing use of unpaid internships and work placements in some industries is a major career obstacle for people from low-income families, who cannot afford to work for free. There is also a concern that some unscrupulous employers are using them to avoid having to pay staff the National Minimum Wage (see Chapter 7).

The material covered in this section demonstrates the important extent to which employers try to secure flexibility and enhance their competiveness through efforts to operate with cheaper, more adaptable workforces. The post-2008 economic downturn, the coalition government's austerity programme, and the weak state of the labour market have given employers greater power to impose flexibility, manifest in cuts to wages for example. Flexibility in work and employment relations is not necessarily marked by a mutuality of interest between workers and employers. Moreover, unscrupulous employers have taken advantage of the weakened state of the economy and labour market to undermine employment standards, particularly in areas of the economy which are characterized by high levels of young workers and migrant workers. This approach to flexibility also helps to explain why, despite the intensity of the economic recession and the lack of economic growth, unemployment did not rise as high as had been expected and the level of private sector employment actually grew. Although these are desirable outcomes, they nonetheless came at the expense of a more insecure and cowed workforce, whose wages and living standards are in decline.

2.2.3 Occupational change: the rise of the knowledge worker?

A further feature of debates about the changing nature of work in the 'new economy' concerns the implications of occupational change for work and employment relations, in particular the supposed rise in the number of knowledge-based jobs undertaken by managers and professionals. The assumption is that the growth of knowledge work in the economy encourages a more cooperative employment relations environment. This is an area of long-standing interest. During the 1960s, for example, the concept of 'post-industrialism' was developed by the American writer Daniel Bell as a means of analysing how technological change generated an increase in professional, managerial, and technical occupations, in which jobs were more highly skilled and inherently more satisfying for those who undertook them, relative to declining manual labour (Kumar 1986). While evidence of such a change was decidedly lacking, the broad idea that technological change and innovation increasingly generate jobs that demand higher levels of knowledge on the part of those who undertake them has proven to be remarkably durable (e.g. Castells 2001). During the 2000s, for example, the UK Labour government emphasized the importance of the emerging knowledge economy as a source of future growth and prosperity (Warhurst 2008).

One way we can assess the nature of changes in jobs is by classifying them into particular occupational categories. See Table 2.5 for details of occupational change between 1984 and 2012. The data presented here would seem to indicate a pronounced shift towards a more knowledge-based economy, as signified by a growing proportion of managerial and

Table 2.5 Occupational change in the UK, 1984–2012 (% all in employment)

	Managers and senior officials	Professional occupations	Associate professional and technical occupations	Administrative and secretarial	Skilled trades	Personal services	Sales and customer service	Process, plant, and machine operatives	Elementary occupations
1984	12.1	8.4	10.1	15.0	16.4	4.1	6.1	11.8	16.1
2004	15.3	11.8	14.3	12.6	11.4	7.5	8.0	7.9	11.3
2012*	16.3	13.6	15.4	10.5	9.9	8.8	7.3	6.2	11.4

*July–October

Sources: Anderson (2009); Office for National Statistics, http://www.statistics.gov.uk

professional positions in the economy, which are generally associated with high-skill, non-routine, well-paid jobs. Between 1984 and 2012, the proportion of managerial and professional jobs in the economy rose from 12.1 per cent to 16.3 per cent, and from 8.4 per cent to 13.6 per cent, respectively. Over nearly three decades, the share of professional and managerial positions has risen from around a fifth of the workforce to approaching a third. At the same time, the proportion of jobs in 'elementary occupations', such as unskilled labouring work, has declined. Such occupational changes are thought to have major implications for work and employment relations. In particular, it is sometimes assumed that the rise of the information-based, knowledge economy, in which jobs will increasingly be of a managerial, professional, and technical kind, reduces the need for traditional management approaches, and erodes the potential for conflict in the employment relationship. Not only is extensive management control redundant in the new knowledge economy, but also greater cooperation between employers and their employees is inevitable given the harmony of interests that arises between them. Thus 'the new economy is identified with a fresh pattern of work relations free from long-standing hierarchical and conflictual employment relations' (Nolan and Slater 2003: 77).

However, there are three major problems with this way of thinking about the nature of occupational change and its implications for work and employment relations. First, the 'knowledge work' concept is a very crude and unsatisfactory tool for analysing the nature of occupational change (Thompson and Warhurst 1998). Much so-called 'knowledge work' consists of rather basic, routine, and mundane data-processing activities that are founded on the manual labour of workers, rather than what they contain in their heads (Poynter 2000). All jobs require workers to use knowledge, but the concept of 'knowledge work' implies the use of complex analytical and decision-making skills and a substantial amount of discretion and autonomy. Too often, though, 'simply using or applying knowledge in a job is enough for some to be regarded as a knowledge worker' (Warhurst and Thompson 2006: 792). Call centre workers and software developers both use sophisticated information and communications technologies as an integral feature of their jobs. Their work and employment relations arrangements, however, differ markedly. Software developers enjoy a far greater degree of discretion at work, and control over their own employment arrangements, than call centre workers (Baldry et al. 2007).

Even jobs in many so-called 'professional' occupations are marked by routine customer service work or information-processing activities, 'with low levels of discretion and analytical skill' (Fleming, Harley, and Sewell 2004: 735). In some cases, work restructuring and the reorganization of work processes mean that ostensibly 'knowledge workers' see their levels of discretion and autonomy being diminished. This was evident in the UK's HM Revenue and Customs (HMRC), where such changes meant that workers found themselves 'subject to systems of labour subordination and management control that would not have looked out of place in the mass production sites of the early twentieth century' (Carter et al. 2011: 94). When we examine the nature of occupations more closely, then, and in particular the content of the jobs that comprise them, we are presented with a rather different picture than that which has been advanced by advocates of the knowledge economy thesis. Far from necessarily promoting greater knowledge work, the introduction of new technology often reduces autonomy and intensifies workloads.

The second problem with the view that the development of a 'knowledge economy', marked by a growing proportion of managerial and professional jobs, has created a more cooperative and consensual climate of employment relations is that it neglects the important extent to which any kind of wage labour is marked by the potential to produce conflict, irrespective of the employment situation of the workers concerned. As private firms face ever greater competitive pressures, and with public sector organizations increasingly being constrained by austerity-driven budget cuts, efforts by employers to secure more work from their employees for less reward remain an enduring feature of work and employment relations. The behaviour of managers towards workers is often strongly influenced by pressure to comply with exacting short-term financial targets in a way that is inimical to the development of long-term, stable, and secure employment relationships (Beynon et al. 2002; Thompson 2011). Even genuinely 'knowledge' workers, such as staff employed in the Irish subsidiary of the US multinational studied by Cushen and Thompson (2012), can be highly discontented in their jobs if they feel that the wage–work bargain is being manipulated too much in favour of their employer. There is nothing intrinsic to 'knowledge work' that makes the workers involved more cooperative. Many schoolteachers, for example, have undertaken strikes and industrial action in protest over changes to their terms and conditions.

The third problem with the proposition that there is a growing knowledge economy which has encouraged a more cooperative employment relations climate concerns the assumption that the labour market is increasingly being dominated by a rapidly growing proportion of people working in professional, managerial, and technical occupations. For one thing, much of the expansion of professional occupations has occurred as a result of restructuring in the public sector, changes to the delivery of education and health services for example, not as part of a supposed shift to a knowledge economy. Assertions about the greater predominance of highly skilled, professional jobs in the economy should therefore be treated with a considerable degree of caution (Nolan and Wood 2003). Moreover, in reality the nature of occupational change is rather complex, involving the expansion of jobs both at the top end of the labour market and those at the bottom, where low-skilled routine work, which contains little discretion or autonomy, is commonplace (Warhurst 2008). Thus 'while management, professional and technical jobs are expanding, so too are routine services jobs, particularly in personal services and retail and hospitality' (Warhurst and Thompson 2006: 793). We need to be careful not to exaggerate the shift to a knowledge economy; there are still a good many routine and low-skilled jobs in the labour market, where conditions are poor and pay is low, and which offer limited employment rights (Lansley 2011).

The most important trend concerns the polarization of the occupational structure, with a growth in the proportion of both relatively highly skilled, well-paid, non-routine jobs at the top and low-skilled, poorly paid, routine jobs at the bottom (Lansley 2011; Holmes and Mayhew 2012). The occupational structure is said increasingly to resemble an 'hourglass' structure; as the proportion of 'good' jobs higher up the occupational structure and 'bad' jobs at the bottom both increase, there is a diminution in the number of middle-ranked jobs such as those involving semi-skilled manufacturing work or linked to clerical and administrative positions (Holmes and Mayhew 2012). While such intermediate jobs remain widespread in the economy (Anderson 2009), technological change and greater international competition associated with globalization (see Section 2.3) means that they are increasingly being squeezed. A 2012 report from the Resolution Foundation highlights the growing trend of the decline of middle-ranked jobs, with growth coming at the top and bottom of the occupational structure (Resolution Foundation 2012b).

Clearly the increasing number of 'bad' jobs in the economy, those that are routine, low-paid, and low-skilled in nature, highlights a major problem with the assumption that a knowledge economy marked by more consensual employment relations arrangements has come to predominate. The pursuit of flexibility by employers mentioned in Section 2.2.2 means that the jobs of many workers have become more insecure, vulnerable, and precarious (Kalleberg 2009; Pollert and Charlwood 2009). Migrant workers are often concentrated in jobs such as those arranged through agencies, which are of a precarious and vulnerable nature (McKay and Markova 2010; McDowell, Batvitzky, and Dyer 2012). Some commentators think that precarious work has become the 'dominant feature of social relations between employers and workers in the contemporary world' (Kalleberg 2009: 17), with adverse consequences for the economic well-being both of individual workers and the communities they inhabit. Guy Standing (2011) has written about the growing prominence of what he terms the 'precariat'—a category of workers, often young workers, whose jobs are marked by low pay, limited career opportunities, poor conditions, weakly enforced employment rights, and a high degree of insecurity and vulnerability.

Some contributions to the debate about the rise of 'precarious employment' are insufficiently rigorous, lack a broader perspective on the background to, and nature of, the 'precarious' concept, and present a rather exaggerated view on change in work and employment. Critics like Doogan (2009), for example, question just how much more insecure and precarious jobs in general have actually become. Nevertheless, what does seem evident is that assertions about the rise of a 'new economy', characterized by a greater degree of 'knowledge work' undertaken by highly skilled professionals and marked by a low propensity for conflict, are highly misleading (Nolan and Wood 2003). This is manifest in the growing number of people who work in jobs marked by low pay, poor conditions, limited employment rights, and a lack of security—matters that create the potential for all sorts of issues, problems, and grievances to arise. This situation has been magnified by the post-2008 economic slump. The International Labour Organization (ILO 2012) notes the increasing number of workers in the advanced economies who have taken part-time or temporary positions because of the lack of full-time, permanent jobs. Clearly the economic downturn has been responsible for some growth in the incidence of precarious employment. Based on this evidence, then, the prospects for cooperation and consensus in work and employment relations would appear very limited indeed. The potential for conflict in work and employment relationships is evidently growing rather than diminishing—not least because of the impact of the harsh economic climate and the extent to which it has exposed working people to greater pressures and rendered them more vulnerable.

Section summary and further reading

- There has been no fundamental transformation of employment relations consistent with the notion of a 'new economy'. The number of people who are self-employed is a rather small proportion of the total workforce. Much self-employment, moreover, is 'false' or 'bogus', disguising what is really an employment relationship—something which became more commonplace as a consequence of the economic downturn.

- Although many workers choose to make use of flexible employment arrangements in the form of part-time or temporary jobs, often their choices are constrained by a lack of appropriate alternatives, especially among women who have childcare responsibilities. Flexibility in work and employment relations is not necessarily marked by a mutuality of interest between workers and employers. Moreover, some unscrupulous employers have taken advantage of the weakened state of the economy and labour market in the recession to undermine employment standards.

- There are a number of problems with the view that the growth of a 'knowledge economy', marked by a growing proportion of managerial and professional jobs, has created a more cooperative and consensual climate of employment relations. They include the difficulties inherent in defining 'knowledge work' and the fact that occupational change involves the expansion of jobs at the top end of the labour market but also those at the bottom, where precarious low-skilled, poorly paid, routine work undertaken by vulnerable workers is commonplace.

Lansley (2012) provides a good analysis of the effects of the economic downturn on work and employment relations. See McKay and Markova (2010) and Wilkinson (2012) for details of the exploitative treatment often experienced by migrant agency workers. The Resolution Foundation is a good source of data on living standards (http://www.resolutionfoundation.org/). See Warhurst (2008) for a critical assessment of the 'knowledge economy'. Pollert and Charlwood (2009) and Standing (2011) focus on vulnerable and precarious work.

2.3 Employment relations in a global economy

The growing degree of global economic integration, or economic 'globalization' as it is often called, exercises a major influence over work and employment relations. What, then, do we mean by the currently fashionable concept of globalization? Although economic activity has long spread across national borders, it is suggested that there has been a major increase in the extent of economic interconnectedness on a worldwide scale, facilitated by innovations in information technology and communication networks (Held and McGrew 2007). This section commences by examining the broad implications of globalization for employment relations. This is followed by an examination of the major role played by multinational companies (MNCs) in the globalization process, and how their activities have contributed to a 'race to the bottom' in labour standards. As a result, efforts to regulate labour standards on an international basis have become a more prominent feature of employment relations.

2.3.1 Globalization and employment relations

The process of globalization is evident in five main respects: the increasing interconnectedness of financial markets on a worldwide basis; growing levels of international trade in goods and services; greater amounts of foreign direct investment (FDI) in the global economy; the enhanced importance and power of MNCs, often as sources of FDI themselves, particularly manifest in their use of cross-border supply chains and production networks; and higher levels of cross-border migration by workers—see Employment relations reflection 2.3 (Williams et al. 2013). Globalization is often perceived to be a neo-liberal project—one fostered by, and operated for the benefit of, multinationals and corporate elites (Frenkel 2006; Nichols and Sugur 2004). Central to neo-liberal ideology is the primacy accorded to free markets. Regulation of work and employment relationships by states and trade unions is viewed as highly undesirable: by constraining the freedom of individuals and companies to contract freely with one another, it impedes business competitiveness. Seen as a neo-liberal project, then, globalization involves efforts to liberalize trade and open up markets around the world (Kalleberg 2009).

> ### Employment relations reflection 2.3: Globalization and migration
>
> Migration, the movement of people across regions, national borders, or even continents, is a phenomenon of long-standing historical significance. Globalization has facilitated an increase in the extent to which people are willing and able to migrate. The impact of migration on 'receiving' countries is a source of particular political controversy. Most rich countries operate tight, and often increasingly strict, controls over immigrant labour, mostly to the detriment of migrant workers who are rendered more vulnerable (Anderson 2010). Yet they frequently fill jobs that indigenous workers are unwilling to take. They have an extensive presence in the agriculture and food-processing industries, for example, where they constitute a cheap source of labour for employers, enabling the major supermarket chains to keep prices low while at the same time improving their profitability. The existence of these migrant workers is rarely acknowledged except when a tragedy occurs, such as the deaths of twenty Chinese cocklepickers at Morecambe Bay in 2004. Following this, as a result of trade union campaigning efforts, legislation designed to regulate the affairs of unscrupulous gangmasters was enacted, including the establishment of a Gangmasters Licensing Authority (GLA). Although the GLA has taken action to clamp down on rogue gangmasters, accounts of life as a migrant worker demonstrate that low pay, insecurity, unpaid wages, and poor health and safety standards continue to be prevalent (e.g. Pai 2008).

What are the implications for work and employment relations? In order to compete more effectively in a more globalized environment, the neo-liberal agenda determines that countries should seek to deregulate their labour markets and promote greater employment flexibility (although, as Stiglitz (2002: 84) points out, by 'flexibility' globalization enthusiasts generally mean 'lower wages and less job protection'). One of the most profound effects of neo-liberal globalization is the impact of deregulatory policies on work and employment relations. To remain competitive, and thus make their countries attractive for investors, governments repress independent trade unions and weaken systems of employment regulation, such as legislation on pay and working conditions, or fail to enforce it effectively (Williams et al. 2013). Globalization is associated with greater job insecurity and the rise of more precarious work and employment relationships, particularly among young workers, migrant workers, and black and minority ethnic workers (Webster, Lambert, and Bezuidenhout 2008; Standing 2011).

It also poses some major challenges to union movements around the world. In particular, the increased power enjoyed by multinationals, arising from their greater capacity for mobility, has eroded the capacity of unions to effect the joint regulation of employment relations (Anner et al. 2006). Since unions are primarily national actors, whose power and capacity to influence employment relations stems from their ability to organize and mobilize workers in a specific country, and whose operations are to a large extent concerned with national-level employment regulation, the internationalization of economic activity has undoubtedly weakened them (Lillie and Martinez Lucio 2004).

Workers and trade unions in Europe and the United States often oppose globalization because of the perceived adverse consequences for jobs and labour standards in their countries. For example, some 600 manufacturing workers lost their jobs when Dyson moved production of its vacuum cleaners from Wiltshire in England to Malaysia in 2002. And in 2007, the clothing company Burberry closed its plant in Treorchy, South Wales, which made polo shirts, with the loss of some 300 jobs. It claimed that the factory had become commercially unviable, and that it was more cost-effective to switch production to sites in Asia and Southern and Eastern Europe where wages and employment costs were lower (Jenkins and Turnbull 2011).

Some, however, are sceptical of claims that globalization has been directly responsible for job losses in industrialized countries. In the US, for example, job losses in manufacturing have been caused more by domestic policy decisions than by greater exposure to international competition (Doogan 2009). However, as discussed in Section 2.3.2, firms do use threats of possibly relocating production to cheaper sites elsewhere to gain leverage over workers, getting them to moderate their wage demands and make other concessions.

It is sometimes believed that globalization has also engendered a process of 'convergence' of employment relations systems around the world. The concept of 'convergence' was originally used to refer to the way in which the process of industrialism, with its associated technical and institutional arrangements (such as collective bargaining, for example) generated greater uniformity in employment relations systems across nation-states (Kerr et al. 1962). However, globalization has stimulated renewed interest in the topic of convergence. It is held to be responsible for producing growing uniformity around a new employment relations 'paradigm' based on deregulated labour markets, employment flexibility, weak or decentralized collective bargaining arrangements, and increasingly powerless trade unions (Eaton 2000). Since these policies are viewed as essential to attracting multinational investment and competing effectively in the global economy, it is thought that countries have little option other than to implement them. Moreover, competitive pressures mean that firms are expected to operate a common set of 'best practice' arrangements, so-called because they are seen as the most economically efficient for managing work and employment relations, irrespective of the national context (Rubery and Grimshaw 2003; Frenkel 2006). Convergence pressures, then, would seem to make national differences in work and employment relations less important in a more globalized economy (Wailes, Bamber, and Lansbury 2011).

Yet, convergence pressures notwithstanding, national systems of work and employment relations seem to be highly resilient, suggesting that national-level diversity ('divergence') continues to prevail. Despite experiencing similar global economic pressures, national governments retain considerable discretion over the policies they choose in response (Wailes, Bamber, and Lansbury 2011). The concept of globalization is often used rhetorically by national governments as a means of persuading working people that, given the enhanced mobility of employers and the supposed pressures of global competition, deregulated labour markets and weakened trade unions are essential attributes of a competitive economy (Hirst, Thompson, and Bromley 2009).

The nature of cross-national diversity has been explored in a number of ways. Perhaps the most prominent approach is Hall and Soskice's 'varieties of capitalism' (VoC) model, which distinguishes between 'liberal market economies', including Britain and the United States, and 'coordinated market economies', such as Germany. The former are characterized by the predominance of a neo-liberal policy agenda such that the 'result should be some weakening of organized labour and a substantial amount of deregulation, much as conventional views predict' (Hall and Soskice 2001: 57). However, among the 'coordinated market economies', deregulatory pressures are more likely to be constrained, or at least moderated, by the presence of robust national-level employment relations systems. Here, trade unions and centralized systems of collective bargaining are less brittle in the face of pressures for enhanced flexibility.

The VoC framework has been criticized for not being sufficiently sensitive to the sheer range of policy approaches evident around the world, a trait it shares with other methods of conceptualizing cross-national diversity, and for being too static (Crouch 2005). It pays little heed to the efforts of working people and trade unions to challenge national systems and bring about change in work and employment relations arrangements (Hamann and Kelly 2008). That said, though, it does imply that globalization does not generate a straightforward process of convergence. Indeed, research suggests that there is a complex relationship between the convergence pressures associated with globalization and divergence imperatives based on national differences. The 'converging divergences' approach, for example, recognizes that there is evidence of convergence across countries, seen in trade union decline among other things. However, convergence is more prevalent in sectors of the economy which are more open to international competition, and marked by the presence of multinationals (Katz and Darbishire 2000). Moreover, while there have been quite strong moves to enact deregulatory, neo-liberal measures in coordinated market economies like Germany and Sweden, they have been moderated by the presence of robust institutional structures and political climates which remain broadly supportive of trade unions and collective bargaining. Convergence pressures, then, are by no means incompatible with the persistence of national diversity (Marginson and Sisson 2004).

2.3.2 Globalization, multinational companies, and the 'race to the bottom' in labour standards

Multinational companies have long been a feature of the international business environment. Since the 1980s, though, the scale and scope of their activities have grown markedly, and as a result they have contributed substantially to the process of economic globalization (Edwards and Ferner 2002). Investment flows from multinationals, rather than through patterns of trade between different countries, increasingly dominate international economic activity (Hirst, Thompson, and Bromley 2009). The activities of multinational companies (MNCs) are one of the clearest manifestations of economic globalization in action (Jones 2005). They 'span every sector of the global economy—from raw materials, to finance, to manufacturing—integrating and reordering economic activity within and across the world's major economic regions' (Held and McGrew 2007: 111). Companies including Coca-Cola, Microsoft, and IBM have been able to develop a massive worldwide presence, not only benefiting from the growing interconnectedness of the global economy, but also, through their activities, helping to stimulate it still further.

While it is easy to cite examples of prominent multinationals, and industries in which they predominate, how can they be conceptualized? The term MNC is used to refer to companies that invest in, and are thus directly responsible for, foreign subsidiaries beyond the boundaries of their national territorial base. By the late 2000s, there were some 82,000 multinationals in existence, responsible for hundreds of thousands of affiliates around the world (UNCTAD 2009). The UK economy, in particular, is dominated by the activities of multinationals since it is a notably open and attractive venue for investment by overseas companies (Marginson and Meardi 2010). Perhaps the most notable feature of globalization in practice concerns the cross-border arrangements MNCs operate for designing, sourcing, manufacturing, distributing, and retailing goods in a way that maximizes efficiency, particularly in sectors such as electronics, clothing, and footwear (Dicken 2007). They often do not own or even directly control the sites where goods are made; instead, factories are owned and managed through a complex network of contractor and sub-contractor firms in a way designed to minimize costs (Hale and Wills 2005). The manufacture of popular consumer electronics devices, like Apple iPods, iPhones, and iPads, is outsourced to a wide range of factories in the emerging economies of Asia. See International perspective 2.4 for an example of how service sector work has been affected by globalization and the growing integration of India into the global economy.

International perspective 2.4: Globalization and the growth of the Indian call centre industry

One of the most prominent—and controversial—aspects of the way globalization affects work and employment relations concerns the extent to which companies are able to switch their operations to developing and emerging economies, at the cost of jobs in Europe and the United States. India has become an attractive location for firms looking to relocate—or 'offshore'—some of their customer-facing and back office facilities, encompassing activities such as customer relations, telemarketing, payment processing, insurance claims, and credit card and loan applications. By the end of the 2000s, the Indian call centre sector comprised over 500 firms, directly employing half a million workers. There is a large pool of young, well-educated and English-speaking workers which firms can draw on to staff their operations (Poster 2007), at wage rates of between 10 and 15 per cent of those offered in the UK.

Companies tend to relocate operations that are high in volume and low in sophistication, resulting in very short job-cycle times for the Indian call centre operators. A study of Indian call centres found that they are geared towards undertaking 'standardized, low-value processes', resembling a 'mass production work model' (Taylor and Bain 2005: 269). Work in the call centres is highly regimented. Strict performance targets, extensive monitoring arrangements, and a systematic and punitive approach to enforcing workplace discipline contribute to creation of a 'stringent' work system (Noronha and D'Cruz 2009), all of which contribute to high levels of turnover of staff. A further source of pressure for Indian call centre workers is the requirement that they conceal their location, and even their identities as Indians, by speaking with 'neutral' accents and taking on anglicized pseudonyms, to meet the expectations of Western customers (Poster 2007).

Where multinationals operate in a highly integrated fashion, responsible for standardized products and services on a global basis, the easier it is for them to undertake detailed scrutiny of, and thus be able to compare, the respective performance of each of their subsidiaries (Marginson and Sisson 1994). Firms in this position enjoy the ability to make 'coercive comparisons' between different plants, whether operating in the same or in different countries (Mueller and Purcell 1992). The concept of 'coercive comparisons' is used to refer to the way multinationals use intricate financial, productivity, and output data to make detailed comparisons of the performance of their respective plants. These can then be used to exert pressure on workers and unions in plants that are found to be under-performing to increase their work effort or accept more flexible working arrangements as a means of catching up, with threats to relocate production acting to enforce compliance (Rubery and Grimshaw 2003; Marginson and Meardi 2009). Coercive comparisons seem to be extensively used in East European car factories owned by major US and German multinationals (Meardi et al. 2009).

Multinationals often attempt to replicate employment relations techniques that prevail at home in their foreign subsidiaries, making as little attempt as possible to adjust them to the nature of environment they inhabit. The way that American multinationals operate in the UK, for example, is marked by efforts to develop distinctive and innovative approaches to managing employment relations (Ferner 2003). However, the characteristics of the host country environment often exercise a profound influence over the way employment relations is managed in multinational subsidiaries (Edwards 2011). For example, in their study of an American multinational company, ITCO, Almond et al. (2005) discovered that it was able to implement its preferred non-union system of employment relations relatively easily in the UK and Ireland. Elsewhere in Europe, however, the presence of stronger national-level employment regulations meant that it was obliged to establish relationships with trade unions.

It should not be assumed that MNCs are supremely rational entities that are always capable of acting in a calculated and predictable manner. Just like any other organization, an MNC is characterized by the presence of power relations, something that may constrain its ability to secure the compliance of its foreign subsidiaries (Ferner and Edwards 1995; Ferner, Edwards, and Tempel 2012). Managers of subsidiaries often draw on aspects of work and employment relations in the country where they are based in order to challenge, or seek to change, policies emanating from corporate headquarters in the MNC's home country that are not viewed as appropriate (Edwards, Colling, and Ferner 2007; Ferner 2010). Therefore it is important to recognize that work and employment relations in MNC subsidiaries are not only influenced by a potentially complex mix of national and transnational factors, but they are also the product of relationships between different groups of managers, and between managers and workers, in specific workplaces (Elger and Smith 2005; Gamble 2011).

The growing power of multinational firms in a more globalized world has raised concerns about their ability to avoid, or subvert, national-level employment relations arrangements that obstruct their interests. In the fast-food industry, for example, companies like McDonald's often enjoy a level of power sufficient to enable them to avoid employment regulations, especially those governing collective bargaining and employee rights to information and consultation, that do not suit them (Royle and Towers 2002). Countries frequently offer MNCs incentives, including the relaxation of employment regulations, as a means of attracting investment, or of preventing it from going elsewhere. Multinationals can shrewdly use the threat of withdrawal, of disinvestment, to secure government favour or to control their employees' behaviour.

This highlights the potential for MNCs to engage in 'regime competition' (Streeck 1997), a term which refers to how multinationals base decisions about investment, or disinvestment, on the relative attractiveness of a country's employment 'regime'—that is, its set of employment laws and regulations. To attract investment in a globalized economy, then, governments come under pressure to relax the supposed regulatory burden for fear that if they do not do so, MNCs will transfer their activities to countries that will. This provokes competition between countries to attract multinational investment, based on which of them can offer the most desirable regulatory environment. During the 2000s, for example, major auto firms such as Toyota and Hyundai engaged in such a process when selecting locations for new manufacturing plants in Central and Eastern Europe (Meardi 2012).

In many emerging economies, like the Philippines, governments have established dedicated locations, sometimes known as 'export processing zones' (EPZs), in which planning, tax, and labour regulations are relaxed as incentives to attract foreign investment there (McKay

2006). China has instituted a number of 'Special Economic Zones' in the south of the country, in places like Shenzhen for example, where factories making products for international markets are concentrated (Cantin 2008). There are now some 3,500 EPZs in existence, operating in around 130 countries (Barrientos et al. 2011).

The Canadian writer Naomi Klein investigated EPZs in the Philippines, where workers making goods for the export market endure low pay and poor working conditions. She visited the Cavite free-trade zone, which covers nearly 700 acres to the south of the capital Manila. Here, Klein discovered over 200 factories employing some 50,000 workers engaged in producing goods for IBM, Nike, and Gap, among others. She found that the 'management is military-style, the supervisors often abusive, the wages below subsistence and the work low-skill and tedious' (Klein 2000: 205). In one case, a factory making computer screens for IBM, overtime working was rewarded with a doughnut and a pen. Abuses of labour rights were commonplace. Any 'workers who do attempt to organize unions in their factories are viewed as troublemakers, and often face threats and intimidation' (Klein 2000: 213). Perhaps most telling, however, was the prevailing climate of insecurity that characterized the zone. The government, factory owners, and workers were all aware of the inherently precarious nature of the jobs that multinational investment delivered and realized how easily they could be transferred elsewhere if the multinationals found alternative, cheaper sources of production.

By helping to undermine employment laws and regulations in this way, multinationals are responsible for producing a 'race to the bottom' in labour standards around the world, as countries compete with one another to offer lower labour costs and weaker employment protections, in the contest to attract MNC investment (Tsogas 2001). Violations of labour standards in the supply chains of multinationals, including very low wages, excessive hours of work, poor health and safety standards, child labour, harsh discipline, manifold employment discrimination, and trade union repression, have been extensively documented (e.g. Mosley 2011). Firms such as Monsoon, Primark, and Wal-Mart are among the many retailers who have faced allegations about unsafe and highly exploitative working conditions in some of their supplier factories in countries such as Bangladesh and China. The dreadful consequences of the drive for cheap labour and the neglect of basic employment standards were highlighted by the April 2013 collapse of the eight-storey Rana Plaza building, in the outskirts of the Bangladeshi capital Dhaka. It resulted in the deaths of over a thousand workers who were employed by a number of garment factories supplying Western multinationals.

One global brand that has attracted the most controversy about working conditions in the factories that make its products is Apple. During 2010, a series of suicides among Chinese workers employed in factories owned by the Taiwanese company Foxconn, which makes iPads and iPhones, drew attention to the highly alienating nature of work in such environments. Investigative reports document the extensive labour rights violations throughout Apple's network of supplier factories in China, including illegally high working hours, the use of child labour, unsafe and dangerous working conditions, extreme work pressures, and low pay (China Labor Watch 2012; Duhigg and Barboza 2012; FLA 2012).

Care needs to be taken not to assume that multinationals are supremely powerful entities helping to drive, and being the prime beneficiaries of, globalization. To be sure, they often use their power as dominant actors in the global economy in ways that damage the interests of working people, being responsible for manifold incidents of labour repression and violations of workers' rights around the world on a large scale. However, their activity is often vulnerable to challenges from activist groups and trade unions which campaign on behalf of working people around the world to protect and improve labour standards on an international basis (Seidman 2007, 2011).

2.3.3 Regulating international labour standards

Efforts to regulate labour standards on an international basis have a long history, dating back to the early twentieth century (Brown 2001). Since the 1990s, however, the development of globalization has generated much interest in how the greater mobility of employers across national borders can be reconciled with the effective protection of employment rights and working conditions of workers around the world (Hepple 2005; Royle 2011). Much of this concern has been driven by trade unions, non-governmental organizations (NGOs), and labour rights activists, who have mounted high-profile campaigns against leading multinationals, such as Nike and Reebok, which reportedly sourced some of their products from factories which operate exploitative practices such as child labour (Seidman 2007; Tsogas 2009). Moreover, the issue of international labour standards has also become more imperative because of the failure of national governments to enforce their own labour laws (Kuruvilla and Verma 2006). This is evident in China, for example, which in theory has a tough system of labour protections, including the right of workers to be paid a minimum wage. However, regional and local administrations are often unwilling to enforce compliance with minimum wage and other labour laws because of a concern that doing so would drive away investment (Yu 2008).

Globalization enthusiasts criticize attempts to regulate labour standards globally, on the grounds that they hinder efforts by developing countries wishing to use one of their key competitive advantages, low labour costs, to attract investment and pursue economic growth. They contend that workers in poor countries benefit from the prosperity generated by free trade and MNC investment. Rather than viewing it as a threat to labour standards, globalization should be welcomed, and indeed accelerated, since a globalizing economy offers the best hope of more jobs and increased prosperity (Flanagan 2006). While the jobs created are poorly paid by the standards of developed countries, the opportunities globalization gives to people, especially women, who would otherwise be entrenched in poverty, means that it should be welcomed. Moreover, MNCs and their suppliers tend to offer higher wages and better working conditions than do indigenous firms. In this interpretation, then, the proposition that globalization results in a 'race to the bottom' in respect of labour standards is nonsensical; rather, the investment it generates creates jobs, economic opportunities, and the potential for prosperity in places where they would otherwise be absent. Setting minimum employment rights, which developing countries are less likely to be able to meet, hinders free trade and unfairly protects companies and workers in the developed world from the rigours of global competition, leading to fewer job opportunities and reduced prosperity in poorer countries (Bhagwati 2004; Wolf 2004; Flanagan 2006).

However, this view has been challenged by studies which demonstrate that the presence of rigorous labour standards may contribute to economic growth rather than hinder it. Their absence encourages countries to follow a 'low road' route to economic development, based on promoting export-led growth with competitive advantage gained through low pay and weak employment protections. But such an approach is inimical to the long-term prosperity of developing countries. Instead a more sustainable economic model is desirable, one that is contingent on wage levels that are sufficient to boost demand-led growth and strong labour laws that encourage effective independent trade unions who can use their bargaining endeavours to raise wages (Palley 2004). Improvements in labour standards can complement productivity. Effective health and safety provision, for example, reduces the likelihood of workplace injuries, reducing welfare and absence costs for firms and raising employee morale (ILO 2009).

Nevertheless, the case for international labour standards does not rest on economic grounds alone. Rather, they are often advanced as a means of stimulating social justice, including dignity at work, something that has informed the perspective of the ILO in particular *[International Labour Organization]* (Leisink 1999). There are some interventions, such as the abolition of child labour for example, which might be seen as basic—and thus universally applicable—human rights, regardless of context. There is an argument that while child labour may be undesirable, it is nonetheless an indispensable feature of economic and social development in some societies because the additional wages are a vital contribution to family incomes. However, it is doubtful that economic development is contingent on the practice of widespread child labour. Rather, its existence helps to keep wages low to the advantage of unscrupulous employers (Tsogas 2001).

The assumption that a system of international labour standards is inimical to globalization, free trade, and increased prosperity is far too simplistic. Indeed, properly organized it could be used not just to restrict the pressure towards a 'race to the bottom' in labour standards, but also to stimulate 'a race to the top' (Hepple 2005: 24), by promoting positive economic freedoms for workers (Warnecke and De Ruyter 2010). Moreover, in so far as it has the potential to raise living standards in poorer nations, and to give the internationalization of economic activity greater support and legitimacy in richer ones, an effective system of minimum international labour standards could help to produce a fairer and more socially just process of globalization (Elliott and Freeman 2003).

The main approaches to regulating international labour standards are specified in Table 2.6: multilateral action by more than one country; the inclusion of so-called 'social

Table 2.6 The main approaches to promoting international labour standards

Type of approach	Main features
Multilateral efforts through the ILO or other international agencies (e.g. UN, OECD)	A quasi-legal, non-company-specific approach to setting labour standards, based mainly on encouraging and supporting countries in their efforts to ratify and comply with ILO conventions or adopt certain guidelines
Social clauses in trade agreements	A non-company-specific approach which involves inserting binding clauses that deal with labour standards into unilateral, bilateral, or multilateral trade agreements between different countries
Corporate codes of conduct	Unilateral, company-specific, and non-legally binding arrangements established by multinational companies, designed to promote minimum labour standards in their supply chains
Multi-stakeholder codes of conduct	Non-company-specific and non-legally binding arrangements designed to promote minimum labour standards in multinational supply chains, which involve unions, labour activist organizations, and NGOs as well as firms themselves
International framework agreements	Negotiated, company-specific, non-binding arrangements concluded between global union federations and leading multinational companies

clauses' that deal with labour rights issues in trade agreements; the efforts of multinational companies to develop voluntary codes of conduct, either by themselves or on a multi-stakeholder basis; and efforts made by global union federations (GUFs) to conclude international framework agreements with multinational companies.

With regard to multilateral arrangements, both the United Nations, in its 1999 Global Compact, and the Organisation for Economic Co-operation and Development (OECD), in its 2000 Guidelines for Multinational Enterprises, have published non-binding recommendations for good practice in international labour standards. Since they are largely exhortative in character, though, such interventions are weak when it comes to securing substantive changes (Hepple 2005; Kuruvilla and Verma 2006).

However, the main body responsible for promoting labour standards on a multilateral basis is the International Labour Organization (ILO). Founded in 1919, the ILO holds that economic growth should be reconciled with the 'creation of decent work', so that the benefits of globalization can be more equitably shared and not be achieved at the expense of workers' freedom, welfare, or dignity (ILO 2009: 10). An agency of the United Nations, the ILO comprises representatives of governments, trade unions, and employers' organizations from among its 183 member states. The main instruments it uses to promote labour standards are conventions, which its member countries are invited to ratify. By 2012, 189 conventions had been agreed. Among other things, they provide for the eradication of child labour (Convention 138, 1973), and the right of workers to enjoy freedom of association by being able to organize in trade unions and bargain collectively with employers (Conventions 87, 1948, and 98, 1949). Once a country has ratified a convention, it is obliged to uphold its provisions. However, countries are not obliged to ratify any of the conventions, and many do not do so (Kuruvilla and Verma 2006). About one-third have not ratified the convention prohibiting child labour, for example.

LEGISLATION AND POLICY 2.5:   The ILO'S Declaration of Fundamental Principles and Rights at Work

The ILO's Declaration of Fundamental Principles and Rights at Work consists of eight 'core' conventions covering freedom of association and the right to collective bargaining, the elimination of forced or compulsory labour, the elimination of workplace discrimination, and the abolition of child labour. All member states are required to comply with the obligations imposed by these conventions even if they have not ratified them.

- Freedom of Association and Protection of the Right to Organize Convention (Convention 87), 1948;
- Right to Organize and Collective Bargaining Convention (98), 1949;
- Forced Labour Convention (29), 1930;
- Abolition of Forced Labour Convention (105), 1957;
- Equal Remuneration Convention (100), 1951;
- Discrimination (Employment and Occupation) Convention (111), 1958;
- Minimum Age Convention (138), 1973;
- Worst Forms of Child Labour Convention (182), 1999.

During the 2000s, ILO more actively propagated the need for effective international labour standards as a means of regulating employment relations at a global level (Elliott and Freeman 2003). In 1998, it published a Declaration of Fundamental Principles and Rights at Work, containing a number of 'core' conventions (see Legislation and policy 2.5). For the ILO, these core standards embody certain basic principles and rights that all countries should aspire to respecting (ILO 2009). Unlike conventions in general, which have to be ratified before they impose any duty to comply, there is an obligation on all ILO members to work towards upholding the core labour standards. Yet the ILO possesses no sanctions to enforce compliance with its conventions (O'Brien 2002) apart from expulsion, and that is only ever used in extreme circumstances as a last resort. The question of whether or not countries that violate agreed international labour standards should be penalized, perhaps through the imposition of trade sanctions, has influenced the policy debate in this area. The main problem with a more rigorous enforcement regime is that it would discourage countries from ratifying ILO conventions, or even cause them to quit the organization entirely (Hepple 2005).

Increasingly, the ILO has come to focus on promoting the use of core labour standards—by influencing the policies of multinationals (explained later in this section), or through technical assistance work—rather than on standard-setting through conventions (Alston 2004). There is some evidence that interventions by the ILO can help to improve labour standards. In the Middle East, for example, ILO technical assistance has helped to promote the independent representation of workers' interests even in countries where trade unions are banned (Kuruvilla and Verma 2006). However, critics assert that this shift in emphasis has diminished the effectiveness of the ILO when it comes to protecting and advancing the interests of workers around the world (Alston 2004; Standing 2008, 2010). The main problem with an approach which is concerned with encouraging the adoption of core labour standards is that the work of the ILO has become too focused on upholding certain broad principles rather than with enforcing substantive labour rights through standard-setting and conventions (Royle 2011).

During the 1990s and 2000s, there were calls from some quarters for a more rigorous multilateral regime, set against the pursuit of global free trade. Following years of negotiations, the World Trade Organization (WTO) was established in 1995 with the purpose of determining a global framework within which free trade could flourish. In some quarters—in the United States labour movement for example—the formation of the WTO was viewed as an opportunity to enact a multilateral set of labour standards linked to free trade (Tsogas 2000; van Roozendaal 2002). The idea is that an obligation to uphold certain minimum labour standards, in the form of a so-called 'social clause', would be a condition of entry into the global free trade system ushered in by the WTO. Countries that failed to comply with the social clause, or did not enforce it effectively, could thus face penalties in the form of trade sanctions (Hassel 2008).

Following sustained opposition from many developing countries, the WTO, in its 1996 Singapore Declaration, rejected the idea of a social clause. Opposition stemmed from the belief that linking a country's ability to trade internationally to the operation of a minimum set of labour standards would put many developing countries at a competitive disadvantage. There are also doubts about whether the WTO is an appropriate vehicle for promoting labour standards given that its meetings are attended by trade ministers, whose main concern is with promoting free trade, not employment rights and protections. For these reasons, there seems little prospect that the WTO system will ever encompass international labour standards; it sees them as a matter for the ILO (Hepple 2005; Royle 2011).

That said, though, labour standards have been linked to trade agreements concluded on a unilateral or bilateral basis, those reached between individual countries or groups of countries, and also at a regional level. Essentially, 'regional' arrangements to promote labour standards are linked to the development of free trade agreements between groups of countries, of which the EU's 'social dimension' (see Chapter 3) is a prominent example. The bilateral approach involves including social clauses concerned with labour standards in trade agreements between individual countries or groups of countries; those between the United States and Jordan, and the United States and Singapore are examples (Kuruvilla and Verma 2006). The unilateral approach is marked by efforts by countries or groups of countries 'to secure compliance with specified labour standards by imposing trade and financial sanctions against countries that do not observe them, or by granting them trade or other preferences for doing so' (Hepple 2005: 89). Both the European Union (EU) and the United States, for example, operate Generalized System of Preferences (GSP) regimes whereby developing countries are given favourable trading rights in exchange for agreeing to abide by minimum labour standards. The failure of the multilateral approach may have encouraged further activity of a bilateral and unilateral kind (Kuruvilla and Verma 2006). However, the GSP process is extremely susceptible to political interference, with foreign policy considerations often playing an influential part in the selection of countries for inclusion (Tsogas 2009). Thus it would be unwise to expect that bilateral and unilateral approaches to promoting international labour standards will do much to improve employment conditions worldwide.

A further approach to regulating labour standards concerns the voluntary efforts of multinationals themselves to establish, and get their suppliers to abide by, codes of conduct governing employment practices and working conditions. Such private regulation became

---

LEGISLATION AND POLICY 2.6:   The Ethical Trading Initiative's 'Base Code'

The ETI Base Code is an internationally recognized voluntary code of labour practice which is founded on the conventions of the ILO. It contains nine clauses:

- Employment is freely chosen (e.g. there is no forced labour).
- Freedom of association and the right to collective bargaining are respected.
- Working conditions are safe and hygienic.
- Child labour should not be used.
- Living wages are paid (enough to meet basic needs and to provide some discretionary income).
- Working hours are not excessive (working hours comply with national laws and benchmark industry standards, whichever affords greater protection).
- No discrimination is practised (on a number of grounds, including race, nationality, gender, and trade union membership).
- Regular employment is provided.
- No harsh or inhumane treatment is allowed (e.g. no physical abuse or sexual harassment).

Source: http://www.ethicaltrade.org/eti-base-code

increasingly commonplace in the 1990s and 2000s, particularly in the sportswear and fashion industries, as companies responded to trade union campaigns and consumer pressures for reform by signing up to codes designed to specify minimum labour standards in their supply chains (Hepple 2005; Royle 2011). A code of conduct is a 'formal statement specifying the ethical standards that a [multinational] company holds and applies to the factories of its suppliers or to its trade partners' (Pun 2005: 102). In 1992, Levi-Strauss and Nike were the first major US corporations to establish their own corporate codes covering labour issues in their respective supply chains. Apple's Supplier Code of Conduct, for example, specifies that its suppliers should treat workers in a fair and non-discriminatory manner, not use forced or child labour, and respect workers' rights to associate in trade unions—albeit subject to national laws.

Nike is also a member of the Fair Labor Association (FLA), a US body that also includes Puma and Reebok among its membership. The FLA is a multi-stakeholder organization, comprising companies, universities, and non-governmental organizations, which has its own code of conduct requiring that, among other things, member firms ensure that their suppliers comply with local labour laws and respect workers' rights to organize in trade unions and bargain collectively. In the UK, the Ethical Trading Initiative (ETI), which includes Tesco, Marks and Spencer, and W H Smith among its members, as well as the Trades Union Congress (TUC) and leading non-governmental organizations like Oxfam, fulfils a similar function. It operates a voluntary 'Base Code', under which companies agree to source their products from suppliers who, among other things, respect workers' rights to form trade unions and pay 'living wages', defined as 'enough to meet basic needs and to provide discretionary income' (see Legislation and policy 2.6 for further details).

A key reason for the development of voluntary codes is the importance attached by corporations to protecting their reputation and safeguarding the image of their brands, in response to pressure from campaigns by labour rights activists and growing consumer awareness of the poor working conditions and exploitation experienced by many developing country workers producing goods for major global brands (Frenkel 2001; Frenkel and Scott 2002). There is some evidence that the presence of a code, particularly where it is rigorously enforced, through some kind of independent verification arrangement for example, is associated with improvements in labour standards (e.g. Barrientos and Smith 2006).

Yet the extent to which codes of conduct, which of course have no legal force, can generate effective international labour standards is questionable. Many US retailers have instituted codes of conduct only because of consumer pressure, not from a genuine commitment to improving working conditions in the developing world (Compa 2001); they are sometimes established with the aim of improving a company's public relations image (O'Brien 2002). Workers and trade unions generally have little influence over the content of corporate codes which, given that they come under the control of managers, is often highly selective (Esbenshade 2004; Merk 2009). Perhaps understandably, unions often doubt the value of corporate codes, viewing them as a weak approach to promoting improvements in labour standards, particularly where there are no independent verification arrangements (Kuruvilla and Verma 2006).

Some multinationals have responded to the criticism that their codes of conduct are ineffective by instituting improvements in monitoring arrangements, including opening them up to external scrutiny (e.g. Frenkel and Kim 2004; Locke et al. 2007). However, auditing and monitoring arrangements are often highly flawed (Royle 2011). In particular, suppliers have become adept at misleading auditors, giving the false impression that the code is being properly enforced, when the reality is rather different. Workers and managers in supplier factories report that codes are frequently violated in practice (Pun 2005; Egels-Zendén 2007). In advance of inspection visits, workers are often coached by their employers to give positive answers to the auditors. Both workers and employers have a vested interest in asserting that the codes are being complied with; otherwise a multinational might change to another supplier, threatening the viability of the firm and putting jobs at risk. A Chinese worker was clearly aware of the danger:

> You know we are afraid of losing production orders. We also don't want to give wrong answers and get into trouble.
>
> (Pun 2005: 107)

A further problem with codes is that while they might promote improvements in labour standards, this often comes at a price. Take the case of a Chinese factory that makes sports shoes for Reebok, for example. The only way that the firm could afford to comply with the specifications of Reebok's code and still remain profitable was by intensifying work and implementing a payment scheme that disadvantaged the workforce (Yu 2008). Demands from multinationals for lower prices make it difficult for suppliers to keep to the provisions of codes, given the potential increase in labour costs associated with compliance (Bulut and Lane 2011; Robinson 2010). MNCs expect suppliers in developing countries to abide by the terms of their codes, but they rarely give them any money to do so.

Since they are private voluntary arrangements, there is a high level of variation in respect of both the content of codes (Hepple 2005), and also their effectiveness. The presence of an independent trade union, for example, can help to ensure that codes operate to the benefit of workers in a more sustained way (Frenkel and Kim 2004). It needs to be recognized that corporate codes of conduct, in particular, are essentially managerial interventions, designed with managerial aims in mind; they are not put in place to foster the better representation of workers' interests (Pun 2005). The most effective way of improving labour standards would be to involve workers themselves, particularly by allowing them to organize in independent trade unions. There is also little knowledge and awareness of codes among the workers they are intended to help (Kuruvilla and Verma 2006). All this suggests that we should be careful not to assume that the presence of codes of conduct necessarily benefits workers in developing countries.

Unions themselves have given more attention to regulating labour standards on an international basis, particularly through the development of international framework agreements (IFAs). This stems from a growing recognition that unions need to operate more effectively internationally in order to advance the interests of workers around the world in a more globalized economy (Frege 2006). In the past, national-level union movements in rich countries have been accused of acting in their own self-interest when campaigning for more rigorous labour standards around the world. By making it more difficult for developing nations to compete, this would help to protect the jobs and wage levels of their members from foreign competition (Rubery and Grimshaw 2003). Yet international solidarity action is also a prominent feature of union responses to globalization. Workers and unions from around the world often take action to demonstrate their support for, and sympathy with, workers in a different country who are engaged in a dispute over their terms and conditions of employment. For example, such activity has a particularly long history in the port transport industry (Lillie and

Martinez Lucio 2004; Turnbull 2006). In Turkey, workers employed by Novamed, a subsidiary of a German multinational, won their dispute over union recognition partly because of the strong support provided by workers and unions from other countries, particularly solidarity action pursued by foreign trade unions (Fougner and Kurtoğlu 2011).

The development of IFAs symbolizes efforts by union movements to fashion a strategic response to the challenges of globalization (Croucher and Cotton 2009). They are negotiated arrangements between GUFs and individual MNCs which establish a set of non-binding rules designed to govern employment relationships on an international basis, in particular by establishing a set of minimum employment standards which sometimes extend to the supply chains (Riisgaard 2005; Stevis and Boswell 2007; Papadakis 2011). IFAs are important because they represent a new and innovative approach by the international trade union movement to regulating employment relationships above and beyond national borders (Hammer 2005).

While the first IFA, covering the French multinational Danone, was instituted during the 1980s, it was only in the 2000s that their number really grew, such that by 2012 there were seventy-five of them in existence, mainly in European companies such as the French retailer Carrefour, the Swedish retailer H&M, and the German motor vehicle manufacturer Volkswagen (Croucher and Cotton 2009). There is some evidence that IFAs can help to promote stronger trade union activity. The agreement between the multinational hotel chain Accor and the IUF (International Union of Food, Agricultural, Hotel, Restaurant, Catering, Tobacco and Allied Workers' Associations), for example, has enhanced the effectiveness of union organizing efforts, thus helping to improve labour standards (Wills 2002). Set against this, however, where knowledge and awareness of the IFA is lacking, then its potential to deliver positive change is much reduced (Riisgaard 2005). A further problem concerns the tendency for IFAs to focus on getting employers to comply with national labour laws, which in some parts of the world are often weak or poorly enforced (Croucher and Cotton 2009; Niforou 2012). IFAs are still relatively few in number (Niforou 2012). Yet, while their direct impact on work and employment relations has so far been somewhat limited, they are still just about the only directly negotiated international agreements between unions and multinationals in existence. This in itself is a positive development, one which the international labour movement can build on (Stevis and Boswell 2007). Although globalization poses many problems and challenges for workers and unions, the emergence of a progressive international trade union agenda, based on a common need to regulate effectively labour standards around the world, has been an important union response (Munck 2011).

Section summary and further reading

- Globalization involves the erosion of economic barriers between countries—it has been accompanied by a neo-liberal ideology which holds that deregulated labour markets, and greater employer flexibility over jobs, wages, and working conditions, are essential conditions for improvements in competitiveness.

- Multinational companies have not only been an important catalyst of economic globalization but they are also among its principal beneficiaries. They may use their economic power to weaken national-level employment regulations as the price of investment, and have been responsible for a 'race to the bottom' in labour standards.

(continued...)

- There has been growing interest in the desirability of regulating labour standards on an international basis. Though open to criticism that they hinder economic growth in a way that unfairly protects jobs in developing countries, international labour standards can help to stimulate improved social and economic well-being.

- A number of approaches to regulating labour standards on an international basis are evident, including multilateral efforts by the ILO, voluntary codes of conduct often put in place by multinational themselves, and international framework agreements (IFAs) negotiated between global union federations (GUFs) and leading MNCs.

The most rigorous and informative books on globalization are Dicken (2007) and Held and McGrew (2007). For a sceptical perspective on the significance of the globalization phenomenon, see Hirst, Thompson, and Bromley (2009). See Williams et al. (2013) for more about the implications of globalization for work and employment relations, especially Chapters 1, 3, and 5. Wailes, Bamber, and Lansbury (2011) is a good overview. For further information about the influences on the management of employment relations in multinationals, see Edwards (2011). The International Labour Organization (ILO) is a key source of information on international labour standards (http://www.ilo.org). For further information about international labour standards, see the work of Bob Hepple (2005). The chapter-length overviews provided by Royle (2011) and Williams et al. (2013: Chapter 4) are also highly recommended. Croucher and Cotton (2009) offer an excellent assessment of issues relating to trade union internationalism.

2.4 Conclusion

Perhaps the most notable theme to have emerged from our assessment of the implications of economic change for work and employment relations is the extent to which the competitive pressures associated with a capitalist market economy have impelled employers to find ever more efficient ways of managing labour, resulting in downward pressure on labour conditions. This is evident, for example, in the preference of employers for flexible employment arrangements that make labour cheaper and more adaptable; see the introductory case study of BMW, for example. For workers, the outcomes of this intensification of market competition are manifest in threats to their pay and conditions and greater job insecurity as employers seek to shift the terms of the wage–work bargain in a direction more favourable to their own interests. On a global scale, the efforts of powerful multinational companies to undermine national systems of employment relations, and to shift production to locations where it is cheaper to employ staff, are major consequences of the process of economic globalization. Moreover, the erosion of labour standards in the developing world is further evidence of how the neo-liberal process of economic globalization, as an intensification of capitalist relations, often undermines workers' interests.

Economic change, then, far from inducing a more cooperative character to employment relations, has made the potential for conflict in the employment relationship more starkly apparent. For many workers in developing countries, who produce clothes, shoes, and other consumer items for Western markets, conditions are often extremely poor, and their jobs precarious. The potential for conflict of interest that lies at the heart of the employment relationship is perhaps most readily apparent in the export processing zones and their like, which are increasingly dotted around the developing world. Although the relentless process of capitalist restructuring and the associated intensification of competitive pressures described in this chapter would appear to be wholly advantageous to employers, one would be mistaken in assuming that they have made both national systems of employment relations and organized labour impotent. For one thing, we have established that, despite the convergence pressures associated with globalization, national-level diversity remains an important feature of contemporary employment relations. Furthermore, the conditions under which labour operates make the mobilization of workers, and their organization in trade unions, an increasingly viable prospect. As long as the exploitative capitalist employment relationship endures, workers will endeavour to combine and look to secure improvements by means of collective action.

 ## Assignment and discussion questions

1 To what extent is working as a self-employed freelancer of greater benefit to workers than being employed by an employer within a conventional employment relationship?

2 Critically assess the proposition that flexible employment arrangements are equally advantageous for employers and workers.

3 What are the main ways in which globalization has affected work and employment relations?

4 'Investment in developing countries by multinational companies leads to improvements in living standards by providing opportunities for paid employment that would otherwise not be available. Such investment should therefore be encouraged.' Discuss.

5 Critically assess the main strengths and weaknesses of voluntary codes of conduct as arrangements for delivering improvements in international labour standards.

 Visit the Online Resource Centre that accompanies this book to develop your understanding of this chapter, and keep up to date with the latest developments in this area.
www.oxfordtextbooks.co.uk/orc/williams3e/

 ## Chapter case study: The effectiveness of voluntary labour codes

Just how effective are voluntary codes of labour conduct when it comes to protecting working conditions, tackling labour rights abuses, and improving employment standards in the supply chains of leading companies? There are frequent allegations that practices in factories around the world which produce goods sold by major UK retailers violate elements of the Ethical Trading Initiative's (ETI) Base Code. In 2010, for example, there were claims that the self-styled 'ethical fashion chain' Monsoon—a founder member of the ETI—had sourced some of its products from suppliers in India that use child labour and pay illegally low wages. In responding to the allegations, Monsoon emphasized the efforts it makes to tackle violations of labour standards in its supply chain. Other leading UK retail chains like Primark, Asda, and Tesco, all of which are members of the ETI, have been accused of sourcing clothes from factories in Bangladesh with poor labour standards. A series of investigations by the charity War on Want has unearthed numerous examples of labour practices that do not comply with the ETI Base Code. In its report, *Fashion Victims* (War on Want 2006), it accuses UK retailers of selling garments which have been made in factories where workers experience gross exploitation, for instance:

● extremely low wages—as little as 5p per hour in some cases—which are by no means enough for the workers to live on;

● excessive working hours—in some cases more than 80 hours per week;

● complaints that workers who complain that they have been sexually harassed are then sacked; and

● poor health and safety standards, such as inaccessible fire exits.

In 2008, War on Want published a follow-up investigation which showed that few concrete improvements had occurred as a result of its earlier report. It claimed that workers 'in Bangladesh continue to receive wages that are well below the cost of living, despite the huge profits being made by Asda, Primark and Tesco. They still work gruelling hours in order to earn enough to survive and feed their families, and continue to suffer harassment and intimidation as they struggle to meet unrealistic production targets' (War on Want 2008: 2). War on Want has also investigated the experiences of garment and textile workers in India who make products for ETI members such as Marks and Spencer, Debenhams, and Next. It alleges that insufficient progress has been made when it comes to ensuring that workers receive a living wage, and that they are often prevented from joining unions (War on Want 2010).

War on Want claims that pressure from retailers to keep the costs of production low, and thus ensure that the prices of items in their shops, such as jeans, t-shirts, and dresses are cheap, means that factories have no alternative but to violate the terms of the ETI Base Code. It criticizes the efforts made by corporations to improve labour standards, claiming that they are strong on rhetoric but weak on substance.

> For too long the UK government has supported purely voluntary initiatives for improving the rights of overseas workers. But as this report shows, there have been few steps taken to improve workers' rights, pay or working conditions within these mechanisms. Retailers cannot continue to pay lip service to corporate social responsibility whilst engaging in buying practices that systematically undermine the principles of decent work.

> (War on Want 2008: 1)

Retailers have responded by denying that pressure to cut production costs results in exploitation, emphasizing that their suppliers must comply with the appropriate ethical standards, and stressing that any violations of labour standards would be investigated.

Question

Why is it that major retailers seem to find it so difficult to ensure that the factories they use to source their products comply with the provisions of the ETI Base Code?

3 The politics of employment relations

 Chapter objectives

The main objectives of this chapter are to:

- demonstrate the influence of the political context on employment relations;
- examine the main public policy developments in employment relations, including those under the 1997–2010 Labour governments and the coalition since 2010; and
- consider the implications of European Union policy and the broader process of European integration for employment relations.

3.1 Introduction

In this chapter, the second of those that seek to contextualize employment relations developments, the concern is with the political dimension. One of the most distinctive features of employment relations as a field of study is that it is highly politicized; in other words, employment relations arrangements, institutions, and processes are infused by, and cannot be understood without reference to, the political context. This chapter considers the implications of public policy developments and explores the implications for employment relations of European integration, including the influence of the European Union's (EU) 'social dimension'. Section 3.2 starts by providing some historical context, outlining the main developments in public policy prior to 1997, when Tony Blair's Labour government was elected to office. This provides the background for the material in Section 3.3, which covers the main employment relations policy developments under Labour between 1997 and 2010. Section 3.4 focuses on the changes enacted by the Conservative-Liberal Democrat coalition government which took office in May 2010, and assesses the extent to which its policies vary from those of its Labour predecessor. Finally, in Section 3.5 the emphasis is on the implications of European integration for employment relations, which encompasses the waning impact of EU social and employment legislation under the 'social dimension', set against the context of economic recession, the privileging of deficit reduction, and the propagation of extreme austerity measures.

> **Introductory case study:** The European Union's Agency Workers Directive
>
> In June 2008, European Union (EU) employment ministers agreed to enact legislation, in the form of a directive, which would give workers employed through temporary agencies an entitlement to the same basic pay and conditions as workers directly employed to do the same job. The agreement came six years after the legislation was first proposed. The lengthy delay was in large part due to the then
>
> *(continued...)*

Labour government's opposition to the proposed directive. It agreed with employers' bodies that such legislation would impede the UK's labour market flexibility and hinder competitiveness. Following pressure from the trade unions, which supported the legislation, the UK government convened talks between the Confederation of British Industry (CBI), on behalf of employers, and the Trades Union Congress (TUC). In May 2008 they agreed a compromise whereby agency workers would have to serve a qualifying period of twelve weeks before they were entitled to equivalent pay and conditions. With this deal in place, the UK government dropped its opposition to the Directive, facilitating the following month's agreement between EU employment ministers.

The Directive passed into UK law in January 2010 in the form of the Agency Workers Regulations 2010, and was due to take effect the following year. In August 2010, though, the Prime Minister in the new coalition government, the Conservative David Cameron, emphasized his opposition to the new legislation. He said that with regard to the rights of agency workers, 'I think we have to look at this very carefully. Sometimes you find if you pile on extra rights and obligations, you just end up with fewer people in jobs'. Nevertheless, in October 2010 the then Liberal Democrat employment relations minister Ed Davey confirmed that the government would not be reviewing the Agency Workers Regulations, and they eventually came into effect in October 2011.

The lengthy, tortuous progress of this piece of EU employment legislation is instructive for what it tells us about the politics of employment relations in a number of respects. First, it demonstrates the increasing influence of EU legislation on employment relations, particularly after Labour under Tony Blair signed up to the Social Chapter in 1997. Second, the case demonstrates that EU legislation designed to guarantee minimum employment standards conflicts with successive governments' desire to respect employers' demands for flexibility, rather than improve protections for workers. Third, following on from this, the case highlights the contrast that exists between the UK, with its emphasis on limiting legislative intervention in employment relations, and the more regulated approach favoured by other EU countries. Fourth, the case is also instructive for what it reveals about the coalition government's preferred approach to employment relations. The Conservatives, in particular, view employment regulation with a pronounced disdain, something which has had a marked influence on developments in employment relations policy since the coalition took office in May 2010.

3.2 Public policy and employment relations

In order to understand contemporary developments in employment relations policy properly, key elements of the historical background need to be covered. The starting point is to explain the concept of 'voluntarism' and the important influence it has historically exercised over employment relations policy. The growth of state intervention in employment relations during the middle part of the twentieth century is considered, before the main features of Conservative policy towards employment relations under the governments of Margaret Thatcher and John Major between 1979 and 1997 come under scrutiny.

3.2.1 Voluntarism and employment relations in Britain

An appreciation of the importance of voluntarism is crucial to understanding the nature of employment relations in Britain. In essence, it refers to the preference for the terms of the employment relationship to be determined voluntarily by employers and trade unions, with state interference only as a last resort (Dickens and Hall 2010). The roots of the voluntaristic tradition can be traced as far back as the seventeenth and eighteenth centuries. During this period, the development of capitalism was informed by the complementary ideologies of economic laissez-faire and market individualism in which the recognition of private property interests predominated (Hyman 1975; Fox 1985a). Nascent capitalist entrepreneurs were resistant to state intervention in their affairs and preferred, wherever possible, to handle their own affairs.

The dominance of market individualism and laissez-faire ideologies provided the foundation for the development of 'collective laissez-faire' as the dominant state approach to employment relations—a preference that employers should deal with employment relations matters, and with unions, themselves, without direct intervention by the state (Davies and Freedland 1993). Employers could deal with union activities in ways that did not threaten their interests too severely, thus obviating the need for more explicitly repressive measures. Trade unions also favoured voluntarism because it allowed them to bargain freely with employers without interference from a pro-employer judiciary (Flanders 1974). The absence of state intervention in relationships between workers, unions, and employers is generally thought to have had a pronounced and long-standing influence on employment relations during the twentieth century (Kahn-Freund 1964). While some legislation was considered desirable, in the area of health and safety for example, unlike many other countries the regulation of the employment relationship in Britain came to be determined largely by a combination of collective bargaining and managerial prerogative, without the development of a comprehensive system of statutory employment rights (Fox 1985a; Hyman 2001b).

Howell (2005), though, contends that the state exercised a more profound influence over the development of employment relations than has hitherto been acknowledged, not so much through legislation, but rather by establishing and maintaining the conditions under which collective bargaining thrived. Moreover, during periods of sustained industrial unrest governments often intervened quickly to repress trade union activity (Geary 1985). Judicial hostility to organized labour—laws were interpreted in ways that benefited employers, for example (Fox 1985a)—frequently undermined unions' legitimacy. This demonstrates that the state's role in employment relations is far removed from that of a neutral, disinterested observer. Rather, it is largely concerned with providing an environment which privileges the interests of employers, something that has, for the reasons outlined above, generally implied limited direct state intervention in employment relations, but does not rule out a more coercive approach if that is dictated by circumstances (Hyman 1975).

3.2.2 Growing state intervention and employment relations

During the mid-twentieth century there was a marked increase in the extent of state intervention in employment relations. For one thing, the 1960s and 1970s saw a growth in the statutory regulation of work and employment relationships in areas such as redundancy payments, the dismissal of employees, equal pay, and sex and race discrimination. Hitherto, the prevailing assumption was that, apart from some exceptions like health and safety at work, employment rights were more effectively promoted through collective bargaining. For a number of reasons, including economic efficiency, social change, and pressure from workers for improved rights, this period saw a substantial growth (which continues in the present period) in the 'juridification'—that is the regulation of social and economic activity by the law—of work and employment relationships (Davies and Freedland 1993).

Perhaps the most notable manifestation of greater state intervention in employment relations, however, related to government efforts to manage the economy. The policy priority of
full employment, achieved through stimulating demand, caused upward pressure on wages
with potentially inflationary consequences. Governments therefore intervened to try and win
trade union agreement to restrain their wage-bargaining behaviour through a series of largely
voluntary 'incomes policies' (Kessler 1994). Prompted by growing membership discontent,
over time the unions became increasingly hostile to incomes policies, which impeded the
ability of governments to incorporate and integrate the unions in processes of state economic
management (Hyman 1975).

Alongside the development of incomes policies, during the 1960s and 1970s the development and evolution of tripartite arrangements for economic and industrial policy formulation was further evidence not only of greater state involvement in economic planning and
management, but also of government efforts to incorporate business representatives, union
leaderships, and the TUC into state policy-making processes (Davies and Freedland 1993).
'Tripartism' refers to the participation of unions, employers, and government representatives in operating state institutions. It is important to acknowledge the repressive basis of
this attempt to incorporate the union interest. Incomes policies and tripartite arrangements
reflected government efforts to accommodate trade union power, and to try to shape and
control it, in order to sustain economic growth and the long-term viability of the capitalist
market economy (Hyman 1989).

Historical perspective 3.1:   The 'winter of discontent' 1978–9

Whenever there is an increase in the level of strike activity in Britain, politicians and media commentators
invariably speculate about the parallels with the industrial unrest of 1978–9, which became popularly
known as the 'winter of discontent', a Shakespearean phrase in origin. So what was the 'winter of
discontent'? The term is used to refer to the series of strikes which affected road haulage, transport, and
public services during the winter of 1978–9. The industrial unrest of this period is often presented as
the result of excessive union militancy, a sign that the trade unions had become too powerful. In reality,
however, it expressed the profound discontent experienced by many workers, particularly in the public
services, who were unhappy at the relative decline in their standard of living as a result of wage restraint
policies. Nevertheless, the strikes, and particularly the way they were presented by the largely anti-union
media, undermined the popularity and legitimacy of the Labour government led by James Callaghan,
helping to usher in a Conservative administration under the leadership of Margaret Thatcher in May 1979.

In the area of employment relations policy, the 1974–9 Labour government was dominated
by the experience of the so-called 'social contract'. In exchange for legislation designed to
promote genuine social reforms, the TUC accepted the need for voluntary wage restraint as a
means of reducing inflation and securing improvements in economic competitiveness (Davies
and Freedland 1993). Despite its ambitious intentions, in practice the social contract ended
up as little more than a conventional incomes policy, since after 1976 the government came
under increasing pressure, not least from the International Monetary Fund (IMF) which made
it a loan condition, to scale back its social policies in order to pursue austerity measures (Marsh
1992). Wage restraint policies provoked a wave of industrial action during 1978–9, a period
which became popularly known as the 'winter of discontent' (see Historical perspective 3.1).

Pressure from workers, who had become increasingly hostile to wage restraint because of the adverse consequences for their living standards, thus restricted the extent to which unions were able to cooperate with governments in managing the economy (Hyman 1989).

3.2.3 Public policy under the Conservatives: towards neo-liberalism?

There was a marked policy shift during the 1980s and 1990s under Conservative governments led by Margaret Thatcher and John Major. On entering office in 1979, the Conservative government's economic policy was dominated by a concern to reduce inflation through tight control of the money supply and an explicit abandonment of the objective of full employment. It placed a greater emphasis on the free play of market forces as a source of enhanced economic competitiveness, rejecting demand management as a tool of economic policy. Moreover, the Conservatives had little regard for tripartite methods of economic policy formulation, and over time abolished most of the state institutions that exemplified tripartism (Crouch 1995). Thus there was a 'distancing of unions from the corridors of power' (Davies and Freedland 1993: 427).

The trend towards increasing juridification of employment relations did, however, continue under the Conservatives, albeit with a markedly different emphasis as they oversaw a large-scale programme of employment relations reform, by means of six major Acts of Parliament between 1980 and 1993, largely designed to weaken the trade unions (Crouch 1996; Dickens and Hall 2010). Excessive union power was perceived to be a major constraint on economic competitiveness; thus the reform of employment relations was central to attempts to boost the economy.

What, then, were the Conservatives' principal aims in reforming the legislation governing unions and employment relations? First, they wished to reduce the power of trade unions in the economy (Davies and Freedland 1993). Legislation was passed that severely restricted the ability of unions to undertake lawful industrial action, in particular by mandating that unions must win the support of a majority of members in a properly constituted postal ballot—see Chapter 9 for further details. The operation of closed shop arrangements (see Chapter 5) was also outlawed.

Second, Conservative governments were eager to diminish the scope for legitimate political activity by trade unions, something that involved attempts to challenge the links between the unions and the Labour Party (Davies and Freedland 1993). Many unions, even those that are not affiliated to Labour, maintain political funds and use them for general campaigning purposes. The 1984 Trade Union Act obliged trade unions operating political funds to win the support of their members for such arrangements in a ballot at least once every ten years.

A third aim of the Conservatives' legislative programme was to promote greater internal democracy in trade unions, to restore membership control of union policies and leaderships, and thus, it was anticipated, instil greater moderation in union behaviour (Martin et al. 1995). For example, the Trade Union Act 1984 mandated that union general secretaries and executive bodies be subject to periodic election in a ballot. It was reinforced by the 1988 Employment Act, which made postal ballots mandatory in union elections.

The policy of 'giving unions back to their members' was based on an assumption that the moderate mass of trade union members was being coerced by militant union leaderships into taking unnecessary industrial action, and thus their voice needed to be heard, principally through a greater role for ballots (McIlroy 1991). However, the Conservatives' real aim seems to have been to use the rhetoric of individual member rights as a way of undermining collective union power, thus reducing the effectiveness of trade unionism (Martin et al. 1995). Legislative measures made it easier for individual members both to dissent from, and challenge, collective decision-making processes (McIlroy 1991). The scale of the Conservative governments' legislative reform of employment relations during the 1980s and 1990s is suggestive of a marked shift towards the repression of union activity by the state, something that also extended to the use of its powers to combat industrial disputes (see Historical perspective 3.2).

Historical perspective 3.2:   The defeat of the 1984–5 miners' strike

Conservative governments of the 1980s and 1990s did not rely solely on the reform of employment law to suppress trade unionism, as the experience of the 1984–5 miners' strike demonstrates. In March 1984, the leadership of the National Union of Mineworkers (NUM), under Arthur Scargill, called a national strike in order to defeat the National Coal Board's (NCB) plan, backed by the government, to close twenty pits with the loss of over 100,000 mining jobs. Miners in Yorkshire walked out and were followed by those in other regions, including Scotland and South Wales. The strike was to last for a year. Controversially, the NUM's leadership did not authorize a ballot, largely on the basis that the strike was underway anyway, and many miners in areas where the pits were not under immediate threat of closure, Nottinghamshire for example, only participated reluctantly.

Throughout the course of the dispute, the extensive powers of the state were deployed to ensure that the miners were defeated. In the years preceding the strike, the government had made arrangements for alternative energy supplies, and had built up coal stocks in preparation for a lengthy struggle. A special cabinet sub-committee was instituted, chaired by the prime minister, Margaret Thatcher, to oversee the state's response once the strike had started. Figures associated with the Conservative Party, like businessman David Hart for example, helped to arrange support for miners who wished to return to work, and assisted the formation of a breakaway union, the Union of Democratic Mineworkers (UDM) in Nottinghamshire. They also backed legal actions by NUM members against their union for breaching its own rules by not holding a ballot. Eventually, in October 1984 the union had its assets seized, or 'sequestrated', by the courts.

The resources of the Security Service, MI5, were used to undermine the strike's effectiveness; it had an agent placed within the NUM's leadership. Extensive military-style policing tactics, including the use of roadblocks on motorways, were deployed to prevent NUM pickets from travelling around the country blocking the supply of coal to electricity-generating plants and obstructing efforts to return to work. Nearly 9,000 miners were arrested in 1984 as a result. In March 1985, after holding out for a year, the NUM called off the strike and organized a return to work, having failed in its attempt to use industrial action to prevent the pit closure programme.

Sources: Beynon 1985; Milne 2004

---

0   How should the Conservatives' programme of legislative reform be interpreted? What accounts for such a 'sustained assault' (Howell 2005: 133) on trade unionism in Britain? One approach puts the onus on the ideological character of the Conservatives' programme (Wedderburn 1989). The important influence of the right-wing political scientist Friedrich Hayek is acknowledged. He viewed unions as coercive organizations that used their illegitimate collective power to put pressure on employers to concede improvements in pay and conditions that distorted the free operation of market forces, thus generating adverse economic outcomes such as higher inflation and greater unemployment. Thus the Conservative legislative programme was underpinned by a coherent set of values and principles associated with the 'new right'. The reform of employment relations was based on a neo-liberal policy perspective which holds that free markets, deregulation, and weak trade unions are essential for economic competitiveness (Davies and Freedland 2007).

An alternative approach emphasizes the pragmatic and opportunistic aspects of Conservative policy-making (Auerbach 1990). Rather than reflecting a coherent neo-liberal ideology, anti-union laws tended to be passed in response to particular events or were influenced by prevailing circumstances. For example, the measures designed to restrict 'unofficial' industrial action that were included in the 1990 Employment Act resulted from a series of industrial disputes in transport the previous year.

A reasonable conclusion is that the Conservatives' legislative programme was founded on a combination of neo-liberal ideology and political opportunism (Davies and Freedland 1993; Howell 2005). Some measures, though, such as the abolition of the closed shop, for example, do seem to have been driven more by ideology than others (Davies and Freedland 1993). Yet the opportunistic character of much of the Conservatives' later legislative interventions demonstrates that, while the policy regime had become much more repressive, union resistance compelled the state to respond to particular challenges to its authority as and when they arose (Davies and Freedland 1993).

What were the effects of the Conservatives' legislative programme? To what extent did their reforms weaken union power? We should not ignore the possibility that Conservative governments were only able to enact such restrictive policies because of the degree to which the unions had already been weakened by economic developments, such as job losses in manufacturing and increasing levels of unemployment (Dunn and Metcalf 1996). Nevertheless, the sheer scale of state repression of the unions during this period, of which the legislation was but one part, significantly undermined the economic power of trade unionism.

However, the Conservatives were rather less successful in realizing their aim of challenging the political basis of trade union activity, by mandating political fund ballots for example. Trade union members support and value the political campaigning activities of their unions. Not only have they strongly voted in favour of retaining political funds, but also in some cases have supported establishing new funds (Leopold 1997, 2006).

Efforts to reform the internal government of the trade unions by encouraging greater 'democracy' as a source of union moderation were similarly unsuccessful. Given the complexity of its demands, legislation stimulated greater centralization of authority in the unions, enhancing the authority of union leaders but reducing members' participation in union affairs (Undy et al. 1996). There is no evidence that the balloting provisions encouraged moderation—in fact rather the opposite. In general, the obligation that union leaders be elected by postal ballot at least once every five years seems to have favoured radical challenges to more moderate general secretaries. In thinking that more effective balloting arrangements would induce greater union moderation, Conservative politicians were, then, profoundly mistaken. If anything, union leaders tend to exert a moderating influence on a generally more combative membership.

Overall, then, the Conservatives' programme of employment relations reform contributed to the diminution of trade union power, largely because of the severe constraints legislation imposed on strikes and other forms of industrial action. However, the Conservative's other aims—the depoliticization of the unions and the encouragement of greater union democracy and moderation—do not appear to have been so successful. Moreover, as shown in Section 3.5, the Conservatives' deregulatory agenda came under challenge from the growing amount of European Union legislation (Dickens and Hall 2010).

Section summary and further reading

- For many years, the principle of voluntarism, or collective laissez-faire, in which the state abstained from directly intervening in relations between employers, employees, and trade unions, characterized the role of the state in Britain.

- During the 1960s and 1970s, there was a marked increase in the degree of state intervention in employment relations. The use of incomes policies, the development of tripartite arrangements, and the growing statutory regulation of the employment relationship all eroded, but did not significantly undermine, the voluntarist ethos.

- During the 1980s and 1990s, Conservative governments used the machinery of the state, most notably by enacting repressive legislation, to undermine the power and legitimacy of the trade unions. Although it was informed by a neo-liberal ideological agenda, the opportunistic basis of the Conservatives' legislative programme is also evident.

For voluntarism in Britain, see Flanders (1974) and Hyman (2001*b*). Davies and Freedland (1993) offer the best account of the growth of state intervention in employment relations during the 1960s and 1970s. For a critical overview of the Conservatives' anti-union legislation, see McIlroy (1991). There is an overview of the policy background in Dickens and Hall (2010: 298–301). Howell (2005) offers a vigorous approach to understanding the role of the state in employment relations.

3.3 Labour and employment relations in Britain, 1997–2010

How far, and in what ways, did employment relations policy change under Tony Blair and Gordon Brown's Labour governments between 1997 and 2010? Because of its historic close links with the trade unions, it might have been expected that Labour would have looked to reverse some of the Conservatives' policies. Indeed, at the beginning of the twentieth century, it was the leading trade unions of the time, along with a group of prominent socialists, who played a key role in establishing the Labour Party—in order to give working people a more effective political voice in Parliament. For much of the twentieth century, the unions exerted a powerful influence over the politics of the Labour Party, provided much needed financial and organizational support, sponsored Members of Parliament, and often gave the Labour leadership the necessary backing to defeat left-wing challenges to its policies (Minkin 1991; Thorpe 1999).

During the 1980s and 1990s, though, the Labour leadership distanced the party from the unions. The union link was perceived to be unpopular with the electorate since it gave the impression that the Labour Party was too beholden to one special interest group (Alderman and Carter 1994; Howell 2005). Under the leadership of Tony Blair, Labour reduced its dependency on the unions for financial support, and looked instead for donations from business and wealthy individuals (Leopold 1997; Osler 2002). Moreover, measures were taken to reduce the influence of the affiliated trade unions in the party's internal structures and decision-making processes—though the Labour leadership remained careful to avoid antagonizing the unions too much since they were still important as a source of funds and organizational support (McIlroy 1998).

3.3.1 Labour's employment relations policies

Having originally opposed the Conservatives' legislative changes, during the early 1990s the Labour Party revised its employment relations policies following a string of election defeats, and came to favour retaining most of the changes. This formed part of a broader shift in Labour policy towards the endorsement, and indeed the celebration, of a dynamic free market economy (Coates 2000). In particular, Labour elaborated a notably enthusiastic acceptance of the desirability of a deregulated labour market as a source of economic competitiveness (e.g. DTI 2006), signalling a marked convergence with the neo-liberal policies that had been followed by previous Conservative governments. Labour's retention of the bulk of the anti-union legislation it inherited from its Conservative predecessors 'marked a shift in the political consensus of the most significant kind' (Davies and Freedland 2007: 111).

Although the unions enjoyed greater involvement in policy deliberations, over the level of the National Minimum Wage for example, this did not constitute a major revival of tripartism by any means (Davies and Freedland 2007). Set against this, though, Labour extended the scope of the juridification of employment relations (see Dickens and Hall 2009, 2010), instigating a major expansion in the scope of employment rights—something that distinguished its approach from that of its Conservative predecessors. Labour's policy interventions in employment relations between 1997 and 2010 can be categorized under five main themes (see Legislation and policy 3.3 for an overview of the relevant legislation).

LEGISLATION AND POLICY 3.3: The main elements of Labour's legislative programme

- Minimum Wage Act (1998): established the National Minimum Wage, and also a procedure for determining its level and scope (see Chapter 7 for further details).

- Employment Relations Act (1999): provided for a new statutory procedure whereby employers would be obliged to recognize a trade union for collective bargaining purposes where there is support from a majority of the workforce (see Chapter 5).

- Employment Act (2002): extended rights to paid maternity leave; introduced two weeks' paid paternity leave; gave parents of young children the 'right' to request flexible working arrangements (see Chapter 4).

- Employment Relations Act (2004): effected revisions to the statutory recognition procedure introduced by the Employment Relations Act (1999).

- Work and Families Act (2006): extended the 'right' to request flexible working arrangements to workers who care for adults; provided for the extension of paid maternity leave to a year, with the opportunity for some of it to be shared with fathers (see Chapter 4).

- Employment Act (2008): provided for measures to improve the enforcement of the National Minimum Wage (see Chapter 7); established new arrangements to encourage internal resolution of individual employment disputes (see Chapter 10).

- First, Labour was keen to encourage greater partnership between employers and trade unions (Brown 2000, 2011), something that informed the development of proposals incorporated into the 1999 Employment Relations Act, and discussed in Chapter 5, obliging employers to recognize a union for collective bargaining where this is wanted by a majority of the workforce. Labour's agenda, however, was marked by an explicitly unitary perspective on social partnership, one that envisages employment relations as being about the development of a 'harmony of interests' (Howell 2004); a union presence is viewed as legitimate only in so far as it helps to enhance business competitiveness.

Thus Labour's vision of employment relations partnership was one in which trade unions exist only as weak and powerless employment relations actors, dependent on the goodwill of employers (Smith and Morton 2006).

- Second, Labour also articulated the need for greater 'fairness' in employment relations, particularly through the establishment of minimum employment standards that prevent workers from being overly exploited (Dickens and Hall 2009, 2010). One can point to important policy initiatives like the National Minimum Wage (NMW) as evidence of Labour's commitment to creating a more extensive system of individual employment rights (see Chapter 7). At the same time, though, in emphasizing the benefits of Britain's 'flexible' labour market, Labour was wary of the supposed threat to economic competitiveness of extending employment protection beyond a minimum floor of rights (DTI 2006).

- A third feature of Labour's employment relations programme was the increased emphasis accorded to developing 'family-friendly' policies, designed to improve the balance between home and paid work responsibilities (Nash 2006). It introduced a 'right' to request flexible working, for example (see Chapter 8), extended the period of paid maternity leave, and enacted legislation providing for paid paternity leave and unpaid parental leave (see Chapter 4). Yet the extent to which Labour was genuinely committed to securing change in this area, given its reluctance to legislate effectively against excessive working hours (see Chapter 8), is perhaps questionable.

- Fourth, Labour extended both the breadth and depth of equality and anti-discrimination legislation, a topic which is considered in more detail in Chapter 4. Yet while equality issues became over time an increasingly important priority for Labour, its reluctance to antagonize employers made it unwilling to enact measures, like the Agency Workers Directive for example, which would have helped to reduce employment discrimination and disadvantage (Bewley 2006).

- The fifth and final theme of the Labour government's approach to employment relations policy concerns its efforts to encourage people to move off welfare benefits and into paid employment, the so-called welfare to work agenda (Davies and Freedland 2007). Measures like the minimum wage helped to improve the attractiveness of work and encourage people to leave welfare as a result. The centrepiece of Labour's welfare to work policy were the various New Deal programmes, offering skills training and employment advice to people who experience labour market disadvantage, like young workers for example. Between 1998 and 2006 around a million young people passed through the New Deal programme, making a substantial impact on reducing poverty (Brinkley, Coats, and Overell 2007). However, critics argue that Labour put too much emphasis on forcing people into work, by threats to withdraw benefits, and gave insufficient attention to altering the perceptions of employers, who are often prejudiced against people with little, or uneven, work experience.

Some parts of Labour's employment relations programme were influenced by the need to comply with EU legislation. It is important to acknowledge the more supportive approach taken by Labour to the regulation of employment relations by the EU than was the case under its Conservative predecessor in government, the most evident feature of which was the government's signing of the 'Social Chapter' after entering office in 1997 (see Section 3.5).

The result was to increase markedly the scope of juridification in employment relations with EU-derived legislation on such matters as parental leave, equality and discrimination in employment, information and consultation rights for employees, and new rights for part-time and fixed-term contract workers (Dickens and Hall 2009, 2010).

Yet Labour often enacted—'transposed'—EU legislation reluctantly and, where possible, with opt-outs from key provisions, as with the Working Time Directive for example (see Chapter 8). The argument about the Agency Workers Directive, highlighted in the introduction to this chapter, demonstrates how the Labour government was concerned not to introduce employment legislation that would mitigate business flexibility. This 'minimalist' approach to transposing EU directives accords with the emphasis Labour placed on the appropriateness of a flexible, deregulated labour market, both as a means of sustaining economic competitiveness and maintaining the goodwill of employers (Howell 2005; Davies and Freedland 2007).

3.3.2 Interpreting Labour's approach to employment relations

How, then, can Labour's approach to employment relations between 1997 and 2010 be interpreted? Clearly, Labour's legislative programme marked a change in emphasis from the approach taken by the Conservatives (Dickens and Hall 2010). The introduction of the NMW, the encouragement of partnership in employment relations, and the greater engagement with the EU's social dimension would all have been inconceivable under the Thatcher and Major administrations of the 1980s and 1990s. The breadth and depth of individual rights at work were extended by Labour in ways that significantly benefited workers—the development of legislation dealing with equality and work–life balance issues, for example, and the protection to vulnerable workers offered by policies such as the minimum wage (Bewley 2006; Brinkley, Coats, and Overell 2007).

This provoked some harsh criticism from business organizations like the CBI, who contend that the increase in the amount of labour market regulation imposed too great a burden on businesses, thus damaging economic competiveness. Nevertheless, Labour retained just about all of the Conservatives' anti-union legislation; and the scope of the legal regulation of the trade unions means that their activities remained highly restricted (Smith and Morton 2006). Continuity with the approach taken by its Conservative predecessors in government was also evident with regard to the importance Labour attached to the desirability of maintaining a flexible, competitive market economy in which business can thrive, and thus generate jobs, unfettered by the activities of trade unions (DTI 2006). Although Labour instituted policies ostensibly designed to support trade unions and to protect workers, some critics claimed that they were so insubstantial as to be of little real effect in practice (Smith and Morton 2009). Under Labour, then, employment relations policy continued to be underpinned by a dominant neo-liberal ideology (Daniels and McIlroy 2009).

Yet, while accepting that neo-liberalism exercised an increasingly marked influence over Labour's approach to employment relations between 1997 and 2010, it is necessary to offer a more nuanced assessment of its policy interventions than simply ascribing them to neo-liberal ideology. Three points are relevant in this respect. First, bear in mind that Labour was keener to progress change in some areas than it was in others. For example, it seemed more at ease promoting work–life balance policies, given the greater scope for securing support from employers, than it was with extending trade union rights (Dickens and Hall 2010).

Second, it is evident that Labour's approach changed over time. In its first term of office between 1997 and 2001, for example, Labour favoured what Davies and Freedland (2007) call 'light regulation'. In other words, measures such as the minimum wage were introduced which, while offering important minimum employment standards, did not greatly undermine business flexibility. As the 2000s progressed, however, Labour's policy stance became rather more incoherent, marked by a concern with further light regulation on the one hand (e.g. work–life balance legislation), and an outright deregulatory approach on the other (e.g. a concern with reducing the number of claims to employment tribunals). Nevertheless, it was increasingly concerned with promoting greater awareness of, and also enforcing, already existing employment legislation (DTI 2006). The Employment Act 2008, for example, included measures designed to improve the enforcement of the minimum wage following concerns about low compliance in some sectors of the economy, to the detriment of migrant and other vulnerable workers (see Chapter 7).

Third, following on from all this, we should remember not to overstate the overall coherence of Labour's approach in government. It is partly to be understood as an 'amalgam of competing values' (Dickens and Hall 2009: 340). Yes, there was a strong degree of continuity with the approach taken by the Conservatives in the 1980s and 1990s; but there were also important differences. While neo-liberal ideology was undoubtedly an important influence on policy interventions, it sometimes conflicted with pressures coming from both inside and outside (e.g. trade unions, campaign groups) government for greater regulation of employment relations. A good example of this was the response to the tragic deaths of twenty-four Chinese cocklepickers who drowned while working in Morecambe Bay in 2004. Following pressure from unions, and also some of its own supporters in Parliament, the Labour government established the Gangmasters Licensing Authority (GLA), whose job is to regulate labour providers in employment sectors with large numbers of migrant workers (such as agriculture).

The example of the GLA points to another distinctive feature of Labour's approach—a predilection for establishing institutions as a means of dealing with controversial areas of employment relations policy, and of reconciling the different interests of employers' bodies and trade unions in a way that promotes partnership and cooperation. The Low Pay Commission, which was established in 1998 to make recommendations about the level of the minimum wage, is perhaps the most obvious example of this—see Chapter 7. When it comes to employment relations, some contend that the durability of such institutions may end up to be the most notable legacy of Labour's period in government (e.g. Brown 2011).

In exchange for their continued financial support, the unions were able to obtain some modest improvements in employment rights from the Labour government, such as an increase in the statutory minimum annual leave entitlement (see Chapter 8). However, the relationship between Labour and the trade unions became increasingly strained during the 2000s. The unions were frustrated by Labour's unwillingness to strengthen union rights, its policy of extending private sector involvement in the delivery of public services, and its support for the virtues of a deregulated labour market as a source of economic dynamism (Ludlum and Taylor 2003). While there was internal pressure in some affiliated trade unions to reduce the amount of money they give to Labour, only two unions broke with the party entirely—see Employment relations reflection 3.4.

How, then, can the Labour government's approach to employment relations be assessed? Perhaps the main outcome was that voluntarism, which had already been undermined by

Employment relations reflection 3.4: The relationship between trade unions and the Labour Party

During the 2000s there was a growing rift between the Labour Party and its affiliated trade unions as the latter became increasingly disenchanted with the Labour government's policy programme. Two unions—the National Union of Rail, Maritime and Transport workers (RMT) and the Fire Brigades Union (FBU)—disaffiliated from the Labour Party. Other trade union affiliates threatened to withdraw their financial support and made some symbolic cuts. Yet most union leaderships, including that of Unison, which represents workers in the public services, strenuously resisted efforts to break with the Labour Party, fearing that such an outcome would prejudice their political influence and thus lose the unions a voice in government (Leopold 2006). The link with the Labour Party is presented as an essential way in which workers, collectively through their unions, can influence government policy. That said, though, the benefits of the link for the unions appear to have diminished during the 2000s, as Labour's attachment to the virtues of neo-liberalism became more pronounced. The relationship between Labour and the unions prevailed, but it came under increasing strain. At the same time, though, Labour became increasingly reliant on its affiliated unions for financial support, particularly as donations from wealthy individuals have dried up amidst controversies over political funding (McIlroy 2009).

Fifteen major unions, including Unison, Unite, and the GMB general union remain affiliated to, and thus formally part of, the Labour Party. In the ten years between 2001 and 2011, 63 per cent of Labour's funds came from the unions; in 2011 alone it was 84 per cent (Unlock Democracy 2012). The election of Ed Miliband as Labour leader in September 2010, following its defeat at the polls earlier that year, focused attention on the role of the trade unions in the Labour Party. Miliband squeezed past his brother David largely because of the support he gained from union members (Dorey and Denham 2011). Nevertheless, the Labour leadership's determination to back a pay freeze in the public sector in order to cut public expenditure has angered some trade union leaders, who resent Miliband's efforts to distance the Labour Party from the unions, still the main source of its funds.

the policies of previous governments, such as the Conservative anti-union legislation of the 1980s and 1990s, largely departed the scene. Under Labour, there was a marked increase in the juridification of the employment relationship, the result of which is that employment protection 'relies increasingly on legal rights not collective organization' in trade unions (Dickens and Hall 2010: 317). That said, though, there was an emphasis placed on ensuring that employment regulation was progressed in a way that enhanced, or at least did not damage, the competitive advantages held to result from labour market flexibility (Howell 2005). Historically, before the Conservative changes of the 1980s and 1990s, the primary purpose of employment regulation was to correct the imbalance of power in the employment relationship between a relatively powerless individual worker and a relatively powerful employer. Inspired by a neo-liberal ideology which held that the labour market needed to be deregulated and the power of the unions tamed if economic prosperity was to be increased, the Conservatives pursued a distinctively anti-union agenda.

Under Labour, however, between 1997 and 2010 the neo-liberal approach was modified rather than discarded. Rather than a wholesale emphasis on deregulation, as under the Conservatives in the 1980s and 1990s, Labour articulated a distinctive approach to employment relations policy which held that the main purpose of regulation is to support and enhance economic competitiveness (Davies and Freedland 2007). In this way, then, aspirations towards fairness and better employment standards can be reconciled with, but are clearly subordinate to, the need to maintain labour market flexibility as a source of improved business performance. This explains the Labour government's opposition to EU measures like the Agency Workers Directive, designed to improve workers' rights (see the introductory case study). Labour market regulation was pursued only in so far as it did not challenge the prevailing neo-liberal assumption that deregulation is the most effective means of generating improvements in economic competitiveness.

 ## Section summary and further reading

- The Labour governments of Tony Blair and Gordon Brown between 1997 and 2010 instituted some important changes in employment relations policy, notably the development of new statutory protections in the area of individual employment rights.

- Labour did, however, retain the overwhelming bulk of the anti-union legislation it inherited from the Conservatives, and its employment relations policy interventions were designed not to upset employers. This reflected a largely uncritical acceptance of neo-liberal ideology: that economic competitiveness is contingent on deregulated and flexible labour markets, making substantial improvements to union and workers' rights through stronger employment regulation undesirable.

- Although Labour's neo-liberal policy agenda, with its emphasis on the importance of deregulated labour markets as a source of economic dynamism, caused relations with the trade unions to become increasingly strained, there was no wholesale abandonment of Labour by the unions.

For an insightful analysis of Labour's approach to employment relations, see the work of Dickens and Hall (2006, 2010). You may find the book *Towards a Flexible Labour Market?* by Davies and Freedland (2007) a little hard going, but it offers the most detailed account of Labour's policies. For a robust critique of Labour's neo-liberalism, see the work of Smith and Morton (2006, 2009).

3.4 The coalition government's policy approach in employment relations

The outcome of the inconclusive May 2010 general election was the formation of a coalition government between the Conservative Party and the Liberal Democrats, with David Cameron as prime minister. In this section the main features of the coalition's policy approach in employment relations are examined.

3.4.1 The Conservatives and Liberal Democrats in opposition

As was mentioned in Section 3.2.3, when they were in office during the 1980s and 1990s the Conservatives pursued a robust anti-union and deregulatory policy agenda which was informed by neo-liberal ideology. Under David Cameron, who became its leader in 2005, the Conservative Party initially tried to 'modernize' itself, in the sense of formulating policies that would appeal to a broader range of voters and thus win electoral support. This included an apparent abandonment of the neo-liberal emphasis on the importance of markets and deregulation that had previously dominated its approach. Yet there were some doubts raised about the significance of the Conservative Party's modernization efforts under David Cameron, including whether or not it had ever really repudiated neo-liberalism (Kenny 2009; Lee 2009). Moreover, the Conservatives responded to the development of the financial and economic crisis in 2007–8 with an increased emphasis on free market policy solutions. In the run-up to the 2010 general election, a clearer deregulatory agenda became apparent, manifest in Conservative Party concerns that the perceived burden of 'red tape' was inhibiting employers' flexibility. Its modernizing efforts, then, were increasingly eclipsed by the growing predominance of a more conventional deregulatory agenda in the area of employment relations policy (Williams and Scott 2010, 2011).

Moreover, the leadership of the Liberal Democrats—the Conservatives' coalition partners—also increasingly came to favour neo-liberal policies. In the past, the Liberal Democrat policy agenda was dominated by a social liberalism approach. This views state intervention, including employment regulation, as a necessary and desirable means of promoting liberal principles, such as greater social justice and reduced inequality. From the mid-2000s onwards, however, the influence of social liberalism diminished. The publication in 2004 of the 'Orange Book', with contributions from a number of leading Liberal Democrat politicians, helped to revive the classical tradition of market liberalism in the party (Marshall and Laws 2004). The emphasis it places on the virtues of the small state and the desirability of free markets increasingly came to dominate the leadership of the Liberal Democrats, particularly after Nick Clegg became party leader in 2007 (Gray 2010; Grayson 2010).

3.4.2 The coalition's neo-liberal policy activism

The formation of the coalition was justified for practical reasons—on the basis that a stable government was needed to tackle the budget deficit, ensure economic stability, and provide the conditions to secure renewed economic growth. But it was also based on a shared neo-liberal ideological belief in the virtues of free markets and deregulation. The budget deficit was to be tackled through a programme of austerity measures unprecedented in modern times, initially amounting to £81 billion of public expenditure savings over four years (although the original aim of eliminating the deficit by 2014–15 has subsequently had to be abandoned). The coalition's deficit reduction plan has profound implications for employment relations in the public sector. Alongside the expected loss of over 700,000 jobs (HM Treasury 2011), many public sector workers have also had their pay frozen and their pension entitlements eroded, prompting a wave of strikes and protests (see Chapter 9).

The coalition's activism, exemplified by the ambition of its deficit reduction programme, is based on a neo-liberal belief that a marked reduction in the size of the state is an essential precondition for economic growth (Lee 2011; Taylor-Gooby and Stoker 2011). The government is concerned not merely with reducing the size of the state, but with instigating reforms to public services and how they are delivered, extending and accelerating the previous Labour government's policy of using private sector providers (Bach and Kessler 2012). As an incentive for private firms to participate, the coalition abolished the policy instituted by Labour under which staff employed by private sector providers to deliver public services enjoyed the same basic pay and conditions as their public sector counterparts (Grimshaw and Rubery 2012). Moreover, to give employers more flexibility, and consistent with its broader drive to reduce public expenditure, the coalition has encouraged greater localization of public sector pay (see Chapter 7).

All this is consistent with a reassertion of neo-liberal values when it comes to formulating policies on work and employment relations. Yet perhaps the most notable manifestation of the marked extent to which a renewed emphasis on neo-liberalism has driven the policy agenda in employment relations since the coalition took office concerns the importance attached to employment deregulation. The June 2010 coalition agreement—the *Programme for Government* (HM Government 2010)—specified the government's intention to reduce the supposed regulatory burden on businesses and review existing employment laws, in a way that would give employers more flexibility while also 'protecting fairness' for employees.

The coalition's policy approach shares some elements of Labour's advocacy of light regulation, particularly over matters such as parental leave and flexible working issues, calculated to attract electoral support from women voters (HM Government 2011a)—see Chapter 4. But there is an element of hypocrisy evident. At the same time as the coalition is promoting greater access to flexible working, it is also planning to change the employment conditions of its own civil servants to reduce their access to flexible working hours arrangements.

LEGISLATION AND POLICY 3.5:   The coalition's *Employer's Charter*

In January 2011 the coalition government published its *Employer's Charter*, a document which was extended and reissued in March 2012 (BIS 2012c). While largely symbolic, since it does not specify any proposals for reform or legislative change, the Charter is a useful indication of where the government's concerns rest. Among other things, it specifies that an employer is entitled to dismiss an employee for poor performance. The publication of the Charter was justified by the coalition government on the grounds that businesses 'feel they have no rights—the pendulum has swung too far in favour of employees' (BIS 2011: 5). This assertion sits uneasily alongside the claim, propounded in the same document, that internationally the UK already has a very lightly regulated labour market.

Whether or not the Charter actually helps employers is open to question. Perhaps it is best viewed as an 'ideological dog whistle' (CIPD 2011a), designed to reassure employers' bodies that the government is sensitive to their calls for less regulation. Nevertheless it could help to aid the confidence of unscrupulous employers who could use it to undermine workers' rights (Ewing 2011).

Notwithstanding these rather limited efforts to promote light regulation, the main feature of the coalition's approach to employment relations has been the emphasis accorded to employment deregulation, something which intensified during 2011 and 2012 as the economy fell back into recession. Coalition policy is based on the unverified assertion that hitherto there has been too much of a concern with promoting employee rights, with the result that the employment relationship has become 'one-sided' in favour of employees. Rather than emphasize worker protections, then, government needs to take more action to ensure that the 'rights' of employers are accorded greater priority (see Legislation and policy 3.5). Of course the problem with this assumption is that the balance of power in the employment relationship is nearly always markedly one-sided in favour of employers, as Chapter 1 showed. The coalition also believes that the excessive level of employment regulation has made employers fearful of taking on new staff. Making it easier to fire workers, it is presumed, will encourage employers to hire them in the first place and thus help to promote growth (BIS 2012a)—an archetypal neo-liberal claim, despite the lack of supporting evidence for it. Indeed, the government's own research shows that employment regulation does not generally put employers off from hiring new staff (BIS 2012b).

Central to the coalition's approach is an assumption that, beyond operating a non-specified 'core of fundamental employment protections', government should abstain from intervening to regulate employment relationships. The coalition propounds a rather idealistic and abstentionist 'vision for the labour market in which both employers and workers are informed and empowered, able to negotiate their relationship within a framework of funda-mental protections, with minimal intervention by the Government' (BIS 2011: 6).

The coalition's deregulatory drive has been evident in a number of areas of work and em-ployment relations policy, including the weakening of equality legislation (see Chapter 4) and the use of government schemes like the Work Programme to promote cheap labour and undermine minimum wage legislation (see Chapter 7). The main focus of the coalition's de-regulatory drive, though, relates to the package of measures that have been instigated under its Employment Law Review which, having commenced in 2010, is intended as a five-year, rolling programme of reform to tackle the 'deluge' of regulation (see BIS 2011: 5). Much of this Review is concerned with changes to arrangements for resolving employment disputes, particularly the system of employment tribunals, which are examined in Chapter 10. One particularly controversial coalition measure involves asking workers to give up a range of employment rights and protections in exchange for receiving at least £2000 worth of shares in their employer's business. Despite attracting very little support, and with criticisms ex-pressed by employers (BIS 2012d), the coalition has nonetheless pushed ahead with its pro-posal to bribe people to sacrifice their rights at work.

One area where the coalition's deregulatory aspirations have been most evident is work-place health and safety arrangements. The Conservatives, in particular, have expressed con-cern that the perception of a 'compensation culture', caused by employers' fear of litigation, has been responsible for an excessive amount of health and safety regulation (Young 2010). However, a government-commissioned review found that there was actually little wrong with the existing system of health and safety regulation, other than it perhaps needed simplifying, and that most of the problems arose from a lack of understanding by employers of their ob-ligations (Löfstedt 2011). Nevertheless, in its response to the review, the government chose to emphasize the desirability of deregulation, exemplified by the aim to reduce the number of health and safety regulations by half within three years (DWP 2011). The review thus gave legitimacy to the coalition's highly ideological programme of reducing employment regula-tion, with the added effect of transferring responsibility for workplace injuries and ill-health from employers to individual workers (James, Tombs, and Whyte 2013).

3.4.3 Interpreting the coalition's employment relations agenda

In accounting for the vigour and activism exhibited by the coalition government in general, there appears to be an emergent consensus that it is rooted in an ideological preference for neo-liberal policy solutions (Lee 2011; Taylor-Gooby and Stoker 2011). With specific regard to employment relations, there has been a marked emphasis on employment deregulation, evident in efforts to weaken the institutional framework developed by Labour between 1997 and 2010 (Bach and Kessler 2012; Grimshaw and Rubery 2012). This is predicated on the belief that businesses, particularly small and medium-sized enterprises, are too constrained by employment regulation, and removing this is a key precondition for economic growth.

The coalition's deregulatory drive intensified during 2011 and 2012, increasingly being justi-fied on the grounds, consistent with neo-liberal ideology, that weakening employment regula-tion is an important precondition of economic growth. There is little sign of any real concern with 'protecting fairness' for employees. Many Conservative politicians are clearly heavily wedded to the idea that free markets and deregulation are essential for increased competitiveness (Kwarteng et al. 2012). When it comes to employment regulation, though, there is little evidence for the claim that economic growth has been hindered by workers having too many rights and protections. Much of the supposed evidence base used by the coalition government to justify its deregulatory policies consists of unverified claims from employers' bodies which are hostile to employment regulation in the first place. Moreover, the level of employment regulation in the UK is already very low by international standards, something even the government recognizes (BIS 2011; CIPD 2011a). Other countries have recovered from the economic crisis more quickly than the UK, despite having stronger employment laws.

It is not excessive employment regulation which has been the main impediment to economic growth; rather it is a lack of demand in the economy. Making working people more insecure by weakening employment rights and protections seems unlikely to act as an effective spur to economic growth. Far from unleashing a recovery from economic recession, austerity programmes and deregulatory policies have in fact prolonged it (ILO 2012). Instead, the adverse economic climate has been used to justify an ideological attack on workers' rights and protections. There is some evidence that leading Liberal Democrat ministers have been able to resist certain of the more extreme deregulatory measures proposed by their Conservative coalition partners. That said, though, they largely share a predilection for weaker employment rights. The coalition's approach to employment relations since 2010 is best interpreted as a form of 'reasserted neoliberalism' (Grimshaw and Rubery 2012: 109), something evident from its emphasis on reducing the role of the state and advancing a more deregulated labour market. This can be contrasted with Labour's approach between 1997 and 2010, when there was more of a concern with operating a framework of minimum employment standards and basic workplace rights.

 ### Section summary and further reading

- The formation of the coalition government between the Conservatives and Liberal Democrats in May 2010 was based on a shared neo-liberal ideological belief in the virtues of free markets, which has strongly influenced its approach to employment relations policy.

- The main feature of the approach taken by the coalition since 2010 concerns the strong emphasis placed on deregulating employment relations, which has increasingly been justified on the grounds of promoting economic growth. Critics maintain that the coalition has used the adverse economic climate as a pretext for an ideological attack on workers' rights and protections.

See the Department of Business, Innovation, and Skills (BIS 2011) document, *Flexible, Effective, Fair*, for the coalition government's approach to employment relations. For material on the Conservative Party's approach to employment relations under the leadership of David Cameron, and the implications of the coalition, see Williams and Scott (2010, 2011).

3.5 Employment relations and the politics of European integration

Fundamentally, the project of European integration is economic in nature. It is centred on advancing 'four freedoms'—the free movement of capital, goods, services, and workers—throughout the countries of the European Union (EU). Alongside this emphasis on market integration, though, the EU also possesses a 'social dimension', which encompasses employment relations matters. In this section we examine the progress of the EU's 'social dimension' since the Treaty of Rome established the original European Economic Community in 1957. It comprises four main elements: (1) legislation, largely in the form of directives which the governments of individual member states are required to implement in their own territories; (2) social programmes, including assistance and support to help unemployed people into work, for example (outside the scope of this book); (3) 'social dialogue', discussions between employers' bodies and trade union organizations; and (4) something called the 'open method of coordination' (OMC), which encompasses voluntary, non-binding measures to realize employment-related goals.

The social dimension originally developed to facilitate the 'upward' or 'positive' harmonization of employment rules and regulations throughout the EU. Instituting a cross-Europe floor of labour standards would protect the interests of workers and help to maintain the existence of a 'European Social Model'—comprising strong welfare states, robust employment regulations, healthy trade unions, and effective collective bargaining arrangements—moderating the impact of market forces on the lives of workers (Meardi 2012). However, not only has the social dimension always been rather weak when set against the primacy of economic integration, but during the 2000s its influence dwindled in significance markedly as a more explicit neo-liberal concern with flexibility, competitiveness, and deregulation came to dominate the EU policy agenda.

Before proceeding any further, there are two things that require acknowledging. First, the respective roles enjoyed by the different EU institutions need to be understood. See International perspective 3.6 for details of the relevant EU institutions. Second, you should be aware that the EU is based on a series of treaties which establish its powers, or 'competences', relative to those of its member states (Hepple 2005). One of the biggest sources of political conflict in the EU has been the resistance of the UK government to reforms that are perceived to weaken its national powers, and this includes powers to effect employment regulation.

 International perspective 3.6: The institutions of the European Union

There are four principal EU institutions. The European Commission, comprising representatives of each member state, is responsible for promoting and effecting legislation, and monitoring its progress. The European Court of Justice (ECJ) deliberates on matters of EU law and on issues that are of EU-wide significance. The European Parliament, made up of directly elected members from all EU countries, has traditionally lacked much influence though it can now obstruct and amend legislation in some areas. Most power, however, rests with the Council of Ministers. It represents the interests of member state governments, comprising ministers from member states, and is the principal decision-making body of the EU.

In respect of employment relations, though, the role of the 'social partners', bodies representing the interests of employers and unions at EU level, must also be acknowledged. There are three main employers' organizations. Founded in 1958, since 2007 the Union of Industrial and Employers' Confederations of Europe (UNICE) has been called Business Europe (http://www.businesseurope.eu/). It acts on behalf of private sector employers. The Confederation of British Industry (CBI) is one of its forty-one affiliates from thirty-five different countries. The European Association of Craft, Small and Medium-Sized Enterprises (UEAPME) represents the interests of small and medium-sized employers (http://www.ueapme.com/). The European Centre of Enterprises with Public Participation and of Enterprises of General Economic Interest (CEEP) acts on behalf of public sector employers in more than twenty countries (http://www.ceep.eu/).

The European Trade Union Confederation (ETUC) is the social partner that represents the interests of the trade unions (http://www.etuc.org/). Founded in 1973, it encompasses over eighty national union confederations, including the British TUC, from thirty-six different countries. The ETUC supports the activities of ten European industry federations (EIFs), bodies that represent the interests of trade unions in specific industrial sectors—the European Metalworkers' Federation in the engineering industry for example.

3.5.1 The 'social dimension' to European integration

The EU was instituted as the European Economic Community (EEC), or the 'Common Market' as it became popularly known, in 1957 when France, Italy, West Germany (as it then was), and the Benelux countries (Belgium, the Netherlands, and Luxembourg) acceded to the Treaty of Rome. Britain joined the EEC sixteen years later. As its name suggests, the EEC was designed as a vehicle for greater economic cooperation across Western Europe: a means of promoting market integration. Apart from provisions designed to improve cross-border labour mobility and pay equality between men and women (Gold 1993), the Treaty of Rome covered social and employment matters relatively briefly. It mentioned improving working conditions, but this was considered relevant only in so far as it enhanced the operation of the common market and supported economic integration (Teague 1999). The emphasis on economic cooperation meant that 'labour law and social protection were seen as almost exclusively national functions' (Hepple 2005: 199). In the early stages of the EEC's development, then, little attention was paid to the 'social dimension' of European integration, embracing employment-related matters as well as social protection and benefits (Bridgford and Stirling 1994; Hyman 2010).

By the 1970s, there was a greater concern to give the EEC a more active social and employment dimension, characterized by 'more ambitious efforts to adopt directives which would ensure upward harmonization of employment regulations' (Hyman 2010: 59). However, the Conservatives under Margaret Thatcher opposed extending the competence of the EEC in matters relating to employment relations on the basis that such interventions would damage economic competitiveness (Hepple 2005). Nevertheless, from the mid-1980s onwards the social dimension was revived, and indeed accelerated, under the auspices of the then president of the European Commission, the former French finance minister Jacques Delors (Hyman 2010).

The activities of the European Community were increasingly dominated by the prospect of the 1993 completion of the Single European Market. Thus a central motivating force underpinning the increased emphasis given to social and employment policy during this period was the need to secure support for, and the legitimacy of, further economic integration in Europe (Bridgford and Stirling 1994). Moreover, without the development of minimum labour standards, the ability of multinational corporations to redirect investment, and therefore jobs, to locations where labour costs are lower—'social dumping' as it became known—would otherwise go unchecked (Adnett and Hardy 2005). By the end of the 1980s there was a growing acknowledgement that a more robust social and employment policy agenda was beneficial to the development and success of economic integration, and was not something that should be marginalized (Davies and Freedland 1993).

The then Conservative government was profoundly opposed to the expansion, however limited, of the European Community's competence in the area of social and employment policy (Davies and Freedland 1993). As a result, the 1993 Treaty of European Union, agreed in 1991 in the Dutch town of Maastricht, in fact comprised two distinct documents. One included a new 'Social Chapter' that gave the EU more scope to legislate on a range of social and employment matters, including information and consultation rights for workers, and was signed by all the member states except Britain. The other, which Britain signed, left this chapter out.

The 1993 Maastricht Treaty also gave a major boost to another aspect of the developing social dimension—the process of 'social dialogue'. During the 1960s and 1970s, the European Commission supported various initiatives designed to facilitate discussion between trade union bodies and employers' organizations on matters of mutual interest, notwithstanding the suspicion of UNICE (Hall 1994; Waddington and Hoffman 2003). Under the presidency of Jacques Delors, though, the European Commission took action to promote social dialogue as an integral part of the social dimension. The 1987 Single European Act obliged the Commission to encourage the development of social dialogue between the social partners at European level (Carley 1993; Bridgford and Stirling 1994). It was anticipated that legislative proposals in the field of social and employment policy would stand more chance of success if they already had the support of the trade unions and employers' organizations (Teague 1989; Hall 1994).

The Maastricht Treaty further encouraged the pursuit of social dialogue. It provided for the conclusion of 'framework agreements' between the social partners. In areas where directives had been proposed, trade unions and employers' organizations at EU level were given an opportunity to reach an agreement themselves, which could then be taken forward and adopted as legislation. The Maastricht Treaty also provided for 'framework agreements' between the social partners that could be implemented voluntarily across the EU member states without the need for legislative action (Keller and Sörries 1999). See Insight into practice 3.7 for details of how social dialogue has progressed.

 Insight into practice 3.7: The outcomes of social dialogue

Social dialogue operates in three broad ways. First, at EU-level the social partners (employers' organizations and trade union bodies) can reach their own negotiated 'framework agreement' on a proposal, which is then taken forward and enacted as EU legislation in the form of an appropriate directive. Directives regulating parental leave and the rights of part-time and fixed-term contract workers were all put into effect following agreement between the social partners (Keller and Sörries 1999). However, UNICE (now Business Europe) only participated reluctantly. Since the 1990s this element of social dialogue has produced rather little at EU level. In specific industry sectors, however, some progress has been evident. In 2008, for example, the social partners in the maritime industry struck a framework agreement, which was then enacted as a directive, establishing minimum standards for seafarers in Europe.

Second, social dialogue at EU level can also lead to voluntary framework agreements between the social partners, which do not have legislative effect. During the 2000s, three such agreements were reached: on telework (2002), workplace stress (2004) (see Prosser 2011), and harassment and violence at work (2007). A major problem with the voluntary approach is the difficulty of guaranteeing compliance across EU member states (Keller 2003). Moreover, employers' bodies can be reluctant to engage in meaningful dialogue because they are wary of encouraging cross-border bargaining with unions.

Third, social dialogue also operates at industry level between sector-specific employers' organizations and union federations. The European Commission has invested a great deal of effort encouraging dialogue between the social partners at industry sector level. While there has been a modest increase in the coverage of sectoral social dialogue during the 2000s, measurable progress, in terms of actual outcomes, has been rather disappointing (Keller and Weber 2011).

Following its 1997 election victory, Labour brought Britain under the aegis of the Social Chapter, which was formally instituted by that year's Treaty of Amsterdam. As a result, EU directives relating to matters such as parental leave rights and information and consultation rights for workers had to be implemented. Sex discrimination in employment had come within the purview of the EU since the Social Action Programme of the 1970s. Importantly, however, the Treaty of Amsterdam also extended the scope of the EU's competence in employment-related matters to cover matters relating to other aspects of discrimination, on the grounds of race and ethnicity, sexual orientation, religion or belief, and age (Davies and Freedland 2007). This resulted in two new directives being agreed in 2000: a framework directive covering equal treatment in employment and occupations, and a directive dealing with racial discrimination. See Legislation and policy 3.8 for details of the major EU directives in the area of employment policy that have been enacted since 1993.

LEGISLATION AND POLICY 3.8: Major European Union directives in the area of employment relations since 1993

- The Directive on the Adaptation of Working Time (1993): provides for the regulation of working hours, rest breaks, and holiday periods (see Chapter 8).

- The European Works Council Directive (1994): provides for the establishment of transnational information and consultation arrangements in multinational companies operating in Europe. A revised directive was agreed in 2009 (see Chapter 6).

- The Posting of Workers Directive (1996): gives workers who are posted abroad to another EU member state for a limited period of time the right to the same core pay and conditions enjoyed by local workers (see Section 3.5.3).

- The Parental Leave Directive (1996): provides for minimum standards of parental leave provision within the EU; a revised directive was agreed in 2009 (see Chapter 4).

- The Directive on Equal Rights and Treatment for Part-Time Workers (1997): prohibits employers from giving part-time workers less favourable pay and conditions than equivalent full-time staff (see Chapter 4).

- The Fixed-Term Contract Workers Directive (1999): prohibits employers from giving workers on fixed-term contracts less favourable pay and conditions than equivalent permanent staff (see Chapter 4).

- The Race Directive (2000): establishes minimum standards of Europe-wide legal protection for individuals on the grounds of racial or ethnic origins (see Chapter 4).

- The Framework for Equal Treatment in Employment and Occupations Directive (2000): prohibits direct or indirect discrimination on grounds of religion or belief, disability, age, or sexual orientation (see Chapter 4).

- The National Information and Consultation of Employees Directive (2002): provides for information and consultation arrangements among firms employing fifty workers or more (see Chapter 6).

- The Agency Workers Directive: first proposed in 2002, and eventually agreed in 2008, this directive provides for agency-supplied temporary workers to get pay and conditions that are comparable with those enjoyed by permanent employees—subject to certain conditions (see the introductory case study).

How can the EU's social dimension be interpreted? Business groups are often highly critical of the additional regulation created by EU legislation, citing the increased costs and inflexibility it generates. The Working Time Directive, which limits working hours (see Chapter 8), is seen as particularly harmful. Consistent with the neo-liberal, deregulatory ethos which increasingly informed its approach to employment relations policy in general, the last Labour government took a notably employer-friendly approach to the implementation of EU labour law, evident in its long-standing opposition to the Agency Workers Directive. Unsurprisingly, given the primacy of its neo-liberal ideological belief in the virtues of deregulation, the coalition government is instinctively hostile to social and employment laws emanating from

Europe. Set against this, however, EU employment laws have generally been welcomed by the trade unions; they see the directives as a source of important new rights and protections for workers, and as an important counterweight to the more neo-liberal policy approach favoured by successive UK governments.

A more critical perspective suggests that the social dimension has not been a very effective means of enhancing workers' rights (Wedderburn 1995); EU legislation is often weaker than that which already exists in most member states. Moreover, key aspects of employment relations policy, such as collective bargaining and the right of workers to associate in trade unions for example, still largely come within the prerogative of individual member states. The limited progress of social and employment policy is, however, not particularly surprising given the large extent to which the EU is primarily a vehicle for the promotion of market integration (Martin and Ross 1999); its policies are favourable, in the main, to the large multinational corporations that have benefited from the removal of economic and other barriers within Europe (Hyman 2001a). The principal justification for the development of the social dimension rested on the extent to which it could support, and add legitimacy to, the process of economic union.

3.5.2 The demise of 'Social Europe'

During the 2000s the already relatively weak social dimension of European integration was marginalized still further, meaning that a genuinely 'social' Europe has become a distant prospect indeed. There has been some progress. Perhaps the main advance came in 2009, when the new Lisbon Treaty of European Union came into effect, which included a number of measures relating to social matters, most notably the inclusion of the Charter of Fundamental Rights of the European Union as an appendix (Pochet and Degryse 2010). First published in 2000, the Charter contains fifty-four articles arranged in seven chapters. One of the chapters deals with the theme of 'solidarity', encompassing rights to fair and just working conditions, collective bargaining, and to take strike action (see Legislation and policy 3.9).

LEGISLATION AND POLICY 3.9:   The Charter of Fundamental Rights of the European Union

Among other things, the chapter on 'solidarity' contains these four articles:

Article 27. Workers or their representatives must, at the appropriate levels, be guaranteed information and consultation in good time . . . under the conditions provided for by Community law and national laws and practices.

Article 28. Workers and employers, or their respective organization, have in accordance with Community law and national laws and practices the right to negotiate and conclude collective agreements at the appropriate levels and, in cases of conflicts of interest, to take collective action to defend their interests, including strike action.

Article 30. Every worker has the right to protection against unjustified dismissal, in accordance with Community law and national laws and practices.

Article 31. (1) Every worker has the right to working conditions which respect his or her health, safety, and dignity; (2) Every worker has the right to limitation of maximum working hours, to daily and weekly rest periods and to an annual period of paid leave.

Responding to the concerns of employers' bodies that the Charter could potentially greatly strengthen employment rights across a range of areas, the then Labour government won agreement over an opt-out protocol whereby nothing in the new Treaty could be used to challenge existing UK legislation, or introduce new rights into UK law. This opposition to the Charter was roundly condemned by the trade unions, who saw it as further evidence of the Labour government's neo-liberal employment relations values, notably the pursuit of flexible and deregulated labour markets. The controversy over the opt-out perhaps deflects attention from the real significance of the Charter: how it has increasingly been drawn on by the ECJ to inform its deliberations and judgments in employment-related cases (Syrpis 2008). It may therefore come to exercise an ever greater indirect influence over EU employment relations, regardless of the fact that it is technically not legally binding. For this reason alone, then, the status of the opt-out must be viewed as 'ambiguous' (Hyman 2010: 61).

The Charter of Fundamental Rights excepted, though, during the 2000s the overall level of EU interest in social and employment policy initiatives diminished markedly. New legislative initiatives were few and far between; where changes to employment law have arisen they are largely concerned with revising existing directives (e.g. Parental Leave Directive, European Works Council Directive) rather than instituting anything new (Hyman 2010; Pochet and Degryse 2010). Moreover, EU policy-makers have increasingly eschewed measures that enhance labour standards, instead putting a greater emphasis on policies designed to improve economic competitiveness through increased labour market flexibility and employment deregulation (Hyman 2010). This is evident when the nature of the European Employment Strategy (EES) and the neo-liberal character of the 'Lisbon agenda' is understood.

The EES emerged in the mid-1990s, and was formally established by the 1997 Treaty of Amsterdam (Hepple 2005; Davies and Freedland 2007). Its purpose is to tackle unemployment and social exclusion across EU member states through measures which promote not just more jobs, but also better quality jobs, and thus facilitate greater social protection. The scope of the EES includes guidelines which among other things encompass: measures to encourage job creation; efforts to improve the standard of vocational training; anti-poverty initiatives; and the promotion of gender equality. The development of the EES signalled a shift in the EU's priorities away from legislating to establish minimum labour standards, towards a greater emphasis on using labour market measures to improve economic competitiveness.

This emphasis on competitiveness was symbolized by the so-called 'Lisbon agenda' which dominated EU thinking during the 2000s. At the Lisbon summit of 2000, EU governments established the strategic aim that by 2010 Europe would 'become the most competitive and dynamic knowledge-based economy in the world, capable of sustainable economic growth with more and better jobs and greater social cohesion' (Adnett and Hardy 2005: 86–7). The Lisbon agenda portended a more neo-liberal emphasis on markets, competition, and flexibility, something which became more evident as the 2000s went on (Pochet and Degryse 2010; Hyman 2011).

In this context, the EES has been increasingly favoured over legislation as a mechanism for realizing the EU's employment policy objectives. Under the EES, the key mechanism for promoting change is not employment legislation in the form of directives, but rather something called the 'open method of coordination' (OMC). The OMC is an approach to realizing employment objectives, set out in the guidelines that determine the scope of the EES, which relies on targets and other non-legislative intervention, with the aim of coordinating measures across EU member states. Individual EU member states draw up 'national action plans' which indicate how they are realizing the objectives of the EES. The aim is that individual governments can share and learn from each other's experiences. Thus the 'OMC is designed to assist member states in developing their own policies, whilst encouraging some element of coordination through peer pressure' (Adnett and Hardy 2005: 203).

Like much social dialogue, the OMC is a way of realizing EU social and employment objectives through 'soft' regulation. There is no compulsion to ensure specific outcomes are achieved, or penalties for non-compliance. 'Hard' regulation involves using legislation to effect compliance with EU goals. Within the EU, there has been an increased preference for 'soft regulation' through social dialogue and the OMC, rather than 'hard regulation' in the form of directives (Hepple 2005; Hyman 2005).

The importance attached to the EES suggests that social protection, including measures to combat discrimination for example, remains a major EU priority. That said, though, its overall results have been disappointing (Bieling 2012; Meardi 2012). More importantly, the development of the EES represents a key shift in the EU away from using legislation to improve labour standards, towards an approach that attempts to integrate the pursuit of economic competitiveness with the need to provide jobs of meaningful quantity and quality (Hepple 2005). The EU uses a rather ugly word—'flexicurity'—to capture the reciprocity of efforts that promote business flexibility while at the same giving workers more protection and security. Yet the onus is generally on diluting labour standards and facilitating employment deregulation, at the expense of measures that help employees (Meardi 2012).

Although trade unions and sympathetic politicians successfully opposed some of the more extreme deregulatory proposals, the neo-liberal emphasis in EU policy-making became increasingly apparent as the 2000s progressed. Nowhere was this more evident than in the European Commission's Europe 2020 strategy. Launched in 2010, and replacing the Lisbon agenda set in train a decade earlier, the Europe 2020 initiative is a ten-year programme designed to help steer European countries out of economic recession:

> Europe 2020 is the European Union's ten-year growth strategy. It is about more than just overcoming the crisis which continues to afflict many of our economies. It is about addressing the shortcomings of our growth model and creating the conditions for a different type of growth that is smarter, more sustainable and more inclusive.
>
> (European Commission 2013)

Europe 2020 contains three 'mutually reinforcing priorities': to produce growth which is 'smart', based on knowledge and innovation; 'sustainable', in the sense of being environmentally sustainable and competitive; and 'inclusive', based on high employment and social cohesion. Progress on these priorities is encouraged with reference to key targets—e.g. for 75 per cent of EU citizens aged 20–64 to be employed by 2020—and seven 'flagship initiatives', including 'an agenda for skills and jobs' which focuses on 'modernizing' labour markets and 'empowering' people to develop their skills (European Commission 2010; Daly 2012). A particularly notable feature of the Europe 2020 strategy concerns the emphasis placed on 'economic governance' arrangements, including a more interventionist role for the EU in monitoring member states' economies, and a focus on consolidating public finances and reducing budget deficits (Hyman 2011).

A careful analysis of the Europe 2020 strategy reveals the large extent to which it both continues and intensifies the neo-liberal EU policy agenda evident during the 2000s. There is a strong emphasis given to the importance of completing the Single European Market, tackling barriers that hinder cross-border economic activity. Major imperatives are to promote greater labour market flexibility and pursue further deregulation, with little attention given to advocating interventionist social policies that would improve people's working lives (Bieling 2012). Growth and efficiency are prioritized, at the expense of social rights. The role of government is to help people cope with more insecure environments, for example by encouraging a greater focus on skills development, not to moderate the sources of insecurity (Daly 2012). For Hyman (2011: 15), then, the Europe 2020 strategy exemplifies the 'neoliberal character, once at least partially contained, of European integration'. It also 'demonstrates how, within current EU governance, social policy has been reduced to a subsidiary component of economic policy' (Hyman 2011: 19).

The Europe 2020 strategy highlights an important shift in the EU's approach to social and employment policy that has occurred since the early 2000s. Until then, there was a general concern to progress what Hepple (2005) terms 'positive harmonization'. The aim was to promote a Europe-wide minimum level of labour standards, reducing the scope for social dumping by employers. Positive harmonization embodied progress towards a European system of employment relations based on certain minimum standards.

During the 2000s, however, EU policy-makers made 'negative harmonization' more of a priority (Adnett and Hardy 2005; Hepple 2005). This encompasses policies to reduce the barriers to job creation, enacting measures that support business flexibility and improve competitiveness. From this perspective, labour standards hinder economic prosperity, and so should be weakened. Negative harmonization involves the freeing up of markets, including labour markets, on a Europe-wide basis, minimizing the effects of employment regulation to give employers more flexibility (Hyman 2011; Meardi 2012). See Table 3.1 for the main differences between positive and negative harmonization.

The EU's response to the eurozone crisis stemming from the global financial crash and subsequent economic downturn shows just how deeply committed EU policy-makers are to advancing neo-liberal policies and negative harmonization. As previously mentioned, the Europe 2020 strategy makes provision for new economic governance arrangements, which some see as adding further momentum to the neo-liberal imperative for reduced social protection, weakened employment rights, and efforts to secure wage moderation (Hyman 2011). During 2011, moreover, EU governments agreed a number of measures designed to increase

Table 3.1 Positive and negative harmonization of labour standards

Positive harmonization	Negative harmonization
Preference for legal measures to promote employment protection ('hard regulation')	Preference for non-legal measures to improve the quantity and quality of jobs ('soft regulation')
Minimum employment standards	Improving labour flexibility
Active role for the social partners in advancing employment regulation	Reduced role for social partners, limited to social dialogue
Reducing social dumping	Promoting competitiveness
'Social Europe'	'Market Europe'

EU control over the budgets of member states, further entrenching negative harmonization. The December 2011 'fiscal pact', for example, which was agreed by all EU member states except the UK, obliges governments to balance their budgets, effectively creating a permanent austerity regime across Europe (Hyman 2011; Barnard 2012).

Requests from member states for financial help have been agreed only on condition that their governments institute wide-ranging programmes of labour market reform. As Barnard (2012: 98) observes, people have already suffered greatly because of the economic crisis and its 'devastating effect on jobs'; yet it is the response of the EU, and its emphasis on the desirability of employment deregulation, which presents the 'more pernicious threat to workers'. While Spain, Portugal, and Ireland have all been encouraged to weaken employment rights and protections as a condition of receiving financial assistance, nowhere have the combined effects of austerity and deregulation been quite as devastating as in Greece. Obliged to enact extreme austerity measures, including massive spending cuts, wage reductions, and tax rises for low-income households, by the so-called 'Troika' of the EU, European Central Bank, and International Monetary Fund, by 2012 the Greek economy had fallen into a deep recession, with over 25 per cent of the workforce unemployed. The Troika also insisted that Greece impose a widespread programme of labour reforms designed to promote greater labour market flexibility, including tearing up national collective bargaining agreements with trade unions. The International Labour Organization has forthrightly condemned the emphasis on austerity and deregulatory policies, claiming that they have simply prolonged the economic crisis in countries like Greece (ILO 2012).

 Contesting employment relations 3.10: The ETUC's *Athens Manifesto*

At its May 2011 Congress held in Athens, Greece the European Trade Union Confederation (ETUC) agreed a programme of fair, equitable, and socially just measures to address the continuing economic crisis. The *Athens Manifesto* (ETUC 2011), as it is called, expressed strong concern about the adverse consequences for working people and their living standards of the austerity measures and deregulatory policies imposed on countries such as Greece, Portugal, and Ireland, which have worsened the economic crisis in these countries; it demanded an urgent change in approach. Current policies leading to increased unemployment, greater inequality, and reductions in living standards must be abandoned. Instead, the ETUC calls for the implementation of a 'European New Deal' for workers, and for an economic governance model that 'serves the interests of European people and not markets'. Among the specific demands are that:

- 'fundamental social rights should take precedence over economic freedoms';
- more and better quality jobs should be prioritized on the EU's policy agenda;
- a 'coordinated attack on youth unemployment' is needed;
- there should be an emphasis on improving the working conditions of all European workers; and
- it is necessary to protect and advance the rights of migrant workers.

The financial and economic crisis and the recession it generated have both extended and intensified the use of neo-liberal policy measures already apparent in the EU. It seems evident that not only can the EU no longer be relied on for measures that protect working people, but also that it has become the main protagonist of a race to the bottom in labour standards across Europe (Barnard 2012). Whether or not this continues depends on the extent to which trade unions and others can resist, and provide an alternative to, Europe-wide austerity programmes and deregulatory policies (see Contesting employment relations 3.10). But at present the ideal of a 'social Europe' seems far removed from the grim reality of economic recession, rising un-employment levels, cuts to wages and pensions, and weakened labour rights.

3.5.3 European Union enlargement and employment relations

EU enlargement and the pressures for negative harmonization which it has generated have also contributed to the demise of the social dimension of European integration. Since 1957, when the Treaty of Rome was agreed, the European Union has expanded from the six countries that originally comprised the EEC (West Germany, France, Italy, and the 'Benelux' countries—Belgium, the Netherlands, and Luxembourg) to twenty-eight by 2013. The UK, for example, joined in 1973. During the 1980s and 1990s there was further expansion, with the accession of countries such as Greece, Spain, Austria, and Sweden. In 2004, ten countries, including Poland, Hungary, and the Czech Republic, which until the 1990s had been part of the Soviet Bloc, joined the EU. Romania and Bulgaria acceded three years later, and Croatia became the twenty-eighth member state in 2013 (see Table 3.2). This process of enlargement has had major ramifications for employment relations, including the social dimension, which it has weakened in a number of ways.

One of the effects of enlargement has also been to weaken political support for a rigor-ous social dimension that encompasses legislative interventions designed to enhance labour standards in the EU as a whole. While it is important not to over-generalize, many of the new accession states tend to be sympathetic to neo-liberal, deregulatory policies in the area of employment relations. This is particularly the case with the Baltic states. In Latvia, for exam-ple, neo-liberal market reforms have caused the erosion of employment standards: salaries are low, unions are weak, jobs are often marked by excessive working hours, and there is little protection for workers (Woolfson 2007).

Perhaps the most obvious impact of EU enlargement has been the increase in labour mi-gration it has generated; people from the so-called A8 Eastern European countries have more scope to travel to Western Europe in search of work. One of the key principles of the EU is free movement of workers between countries—in other words, the removal of barriers that prevent citizens of one member state from working in another. However, in the run-up to the 2004 enlargement there was some concern that the large disparity in pay and conditions

Table 3.2 Accession dates of EU countries

Countries	Date
Belgium, France, Italy, Luxembourg, Netherlands, West Germany	1957
Denmark, Ireland, UK	1973
Greece	1981
Portugal, Spain	1986
Austria, Finland, Sweden	1994
Cyprus, Czech Republic, Estonia, Hungary, Latvia, Lithuania, Malta, Poland, Slovakia, Slovenia	2004
Bulgaria, Romania	2007
Croatia	2013

between Western and Eastern Europe would prove overly disruptive. It was recognized that instituting the free movement of labour in a newly enlarged EU would need careful handling.

Thus existing EU member states (EU15) were given the right to operate transitional arrangements until 2011, enabling them to restrict the influx of migrant workers from the newly joined countries. Most made use of such arrangements, although the UK, along with Ireland and Sweden, effectively relaxed all controls. Nationals from Bulgaria and Romania, two countries which became part of the EU in 2007, faced tighter restrictions until the end of 2013. Two of the countries most affected by the influx of East European migrants were Ireland and the UK. Not only are migrants attracted by the wages on offer, often substantially higher than those available in their home countries, but also the economic boom which lasted until 2007 meant that there was a high demand for labour in the expanding service and construction sectors, much of which was met by migrants from Eastern Europe. In 2007 alone, around 112,000 A8 citizens migrated to the UK. Although the economic recession reduced the level of immigration from the A8 countries, after 2010 it started to increase again; by 2011 some 669,000 A8 citizens were working in the UK, most of them Polish (Vargas-Silva 2012).

Labour migration from Eastern Europe to Western Europe has had major implications both for the migrants' home and host countries. Countries like Poland and the Baltic states (Latvia, Lithuania, and Estonia) have suffered labour shortages as a result of the outflow of workers to Western Europe. In his study of Latvia, for example, Woolfson (2007) points to the adverse social consequences produced by widespread emigration, including disruption to family life.

With regard to the effects of migration on host countries, the conventional view is that it benefits the economy. Business organizations like the Confederation of British Industry vociferously support the free movement of labour. They contend that labour migration improves the supply of labour, allowing businesses greater flexibility and adaptability, thus producing a more dynamic and competitive economy. Increased labour mobility from Eastern Europe is generally viewed as beneficial; it helps to fill the gaps created by skills shortages, for example (Donaghey and Teague 2006), thus contributing to economic growth.

Critics, however, argue that the main benefit for employers is the flexibility to offer lower wages and weaker employment protections. Because migrant workers are willing to work for lower wages and with less employment protection, the indigenous population comes under pressure to lower its expectations and work for less reward. This results in downward pressure on wages and a lowering of labour standards. There is also a widespread popular belief that migrant workers take jobs that would otherwise have gone to the indigenous population.

Yet independent studies of the impact of migration from the A8 countries on employment levels and wages conclude that there is no evidence of any substantial negative labour market effects, though the wages of some may have fallen slightly (Sumption and Somerville 2010). While some groups of workers may have been disadvantaged as a result of migration from the A8 countries, overall there is no support for the view that the influx of workers from Poland and elsewhere in Eastern Europe has reduced employment opportunities for indigenous workers or significantly eroded wage levels. Thus 'the view of the tabloid press that migrants "take our jobs" and "cut our pay" is misplaced' (Reed and Latorre 2009: 34).

Nevertheless, in countries like the UK and Ireland there has been much discussion about the potentially adverse economic and social consequences of increased migration levels. Migrant workers from A8 countries often work in low-paid, unskilled, and precarious jobs, in sectors such as food processing for example (Sumption and Somerville 2010). They are viewed by employers as 'good' workers, in the sense of being compliant with managerial directives, such as working more hours at short notice (Thompson, Newsome, and Commander 2013). In Ireland, the influx of migrant workers allowed employers to rely on a low-paid workforce who experience poor conditions and have little employment protection (Dundon, González-Pérez, and McDonough 2007). One of the main effects of labour migration from Eastern Europe, then, has been the erosion of existing employment conditions and protections (Woolfson 2007). Moreover, concerns about the adverse social consequences of increased migration from Eastern Europe, particularly the strain put on local public services, have also been widespread.

But there is no automatic link between migration and the dilution of labour standards. The onus is on governments to enforce existing employment protection, or to enhance it, so that migrant workers are not used by employers as a cheap and easily disposable workforce in a way that contributes to the deterioration of labour standards. The UK government came under increasing pressure from trade unions and campaign organizations to enforce existing employment regulation, like the National Minimum Wage, more rigorously. Generally, trade unions support the free movement of labour and welcome migrant workers, because of the improvements in economic competitiveness it generates. However, they highlight the importance of improving and rigorously enforcing existing employment laws so that migrant workers are not exploited by employers and used as a cheap source of disposable labour. Unions have tried to develop innovative new ways of organizing migrant workers, including engaging with broader campaigning networks and alliances, sometimes at an international level (Fitzgerald and Hardy 2010).

While much of the attention has been directed towards the impact of migration from Eastern Europe on employment relations, EU enlargement has also helped to facilitate the more extensive use of 'regime competition' and 'coercive comparisons' (see Chapter 2) linked to the expansion of the single market. The dismantling of economic barriers has enhanced the capacity of multinational companies to engage in social dumping; it has become easier for them to move production to Eastern European countries, where wages are lower and labour standards generally weaker. Relocation, or merely the threat of relocation, means that workers in Western Europe come under pressure to moderate their wage demands, for example, or to accept worse employment conditions (Anderson 2011; Meardi 2012).

EU enlargement, then, has brought into sharper focus the contrast between 'positive' and 'negative' harmonization as competing visions of how labour regulation across Europe should operate (Hepple 2005; Meardi 2012). On the one hand, positive harmonization portends an interventionist role for the EU in setting or encouraging minimum employment standards to ensure that workers throughout Europe are adequately protected. On the other hand, however, the emphasis of negative harmonization is on creating a level playing field of employment standards through deregulation, allowing employers greater scope to benefit from an integrated and open market.

For those, like the trade unions for example, who want to maintain and improve on existing employment standards, the increased mobility of businesses and workers in an enlarged EU poses a major challenge. This has been evident in some high-profile industrial disputes. In early 2009, for example, there were walk-outs in the UK in support of workers at the Lindsey oil refinery who were striking in protest at the use of cheaper foreign construction labour (Gall 2012b). For Barnard (2009: 277), the dispute symbolized how the principle of market integration came 'face to face with angry protestors fearful about their jobs at a time of deep recession'. The end-of-chapter case study features another major dispute that erupted over the use by an employer of cheap foreign labour to undermine employment standards.

European Court of Justice (ECJ) rulings also pose a major threat to the future of the social dimension in an enlarged EU. In the 2007 Laval and Viking cases, for example, the ECJ held that industrial action by trade unions which hindered the free movement rights of employers in a single market was unlawful, even if the action in question complied with the national law of the country where it occurred (e.g. Woolfson, Thörnqvist, and Sommers 2010). The following year, the ECJ ruled in the Rüffert and Luxembourg cases that only in certain narrowly defined circumstances could governments and other public authorities mandate labour standards which had the effect of preventing employers in other countries from offering services (Hyman 2010).

There are a number of implications of this 'Laval quartet' of decisions. Although the ECJ recognizes the rights of workers and trade unions to engage in collective bargaining and to undertake industrial action, the scope of these rights is highly circumscribed—and they are clearly subordinate to the rights of employers to benefit from social dumping (ETUC n.d.). In general the rulings make it very much harder for unions in Western Europe 'to protect, through collective bargaining, established worker rights from undercutting by Central Eastern European providers' (Meardi 2012: 14). They highlight the potential threat that EU enlargement, in combination with a neo-liberal emphasis on free markets, poses to employment standards across Europe.

The ECJ, in trying to strike a balance between the principle of upholding labour standards on the one hand, and the principle of supporting market integration on the other, has come down on the side of the latter (Hyman 2010; Lindstrom 2010). EU law, based on the primacy of advancing the single market, takes precedence over, and may even negate, national-level efforts to enhance labour standards, jeopardizing the ability of governments to regulate employment relations within their own territories (Dølvik and Visser 2009; Cremers 2010).

The ECJ's rulings also highlight the weakness of the Posting of Workers Directive (1996), which was designed to give workers who are posted abroad to another EU member state for a limited period of time the right to the same core pay and conditions enjoyed by local workers. This would help to combat social dumping, by preventing employers from bringing in workers from abroad to do jobs on lower rates of pay and with worse conditions than indigenous workers. Yet the ECJ's rulings appear to validate the use of social dumping as a legitimate tool of labour management. While the Posting of Workers Directive was designed to help strike a balance between the desirability of a free market in the EU and the need to protect labour standards, in practice it has done little to prevent social dumping, suggesting that more needs to be done to make it an effective employment relations policy instrument (Cremers, Erik Dølvik, and Bosch 2007; ETUC n.d.).

Overall, then, EU enlargement has accentuated the potential for social dumping by exacerbating a 'race to the bottom' in labour standards, further contributing to the demise of 'social' Europe (Donaghey and Teague 2006; Meardi 2012). EU legislation in the area of social and employment policy has done little to counter the increased scope of multinational companies to benefit from the removal of economic and political barriers, including the use of social dumping as a way of reducing costs. Despite much rhetoric about the EU's social dimension, the material covered here demonstrates the large extent to which it has been subordinate to powerful pressures of market integration.

There have been campaigns to mitigate the effects of the ECJ's rulings, and calls for a renewed focus on enhancing social and employment rights in the enlarged EU (Lindstrom 2010). The mobilizing efforts of the ETUC and other union bodies do much to ensure that workers' interests are heard at EU level. Moreover, the democratically elected European Parliament has increasingly acted as a bulwark against neo-liberal policies that would otherwise weaken the social dimension still further. The foundering EU social dimension is unlikely to be revived through judicial interventions. Rather, the actions of trade unions and EU citizens themselves offer the best chance of shifting the process of European integration in a more socially desirable direction.

 ## Section summary and further reading

- During the 1980s and 1990s, the development of the 'social dimension', encompassing legislation in areas such as working time, and information and consultation rights for workers, became an increasingly important aspect of the process of European integration. Nevertheless, it remained subordinate to the process of market integration and was progressed largely in so far as it legitimized greater economic union.

- The importance of the social dimension has diminished during the 2000s, linked to the growing neo-liberal emphasis on free markets inspired by the Lisbon agenda and evident in the Europe 2020 strategy. EU policy-makers prefer to use 'soft' regulation, in the form of non-binding targets and guidelines, over 'hard' regulation, in the form of legislation, to realize social and employment goals.

- By exacerbating a 'race to the bottom' in labour standards, EU enlargement has further contributed to the demise of 'social' Europe. Major ECJ rulings exemplify the threat that EU enlargement, in combination with a neo-liberal emphasis on free markets, poses to employment standards across Europe.

The best short overview of the employment relations implications of European integration is Hyman (2010). Both Adnett and Hardy (2005) and Hepple (2005: Chapters 8 and 9) are also highly recommended. The *European Journal of Industrial Relations* contains relevant academic papers. For information about EU social and employment policy go to: http://europa.eu/pol/socio/index_en.htm

Details of the European Commission's Europe 2020 strategy are available online: http://ec.europa.eu/europe2020/index_en.htm

3.6 Conclusion

This chapter has examined the highly politicized nature of work and employment relations. It has considered the influence of government policies, and the implications of greater European integration for employment relations. One thing that will be evident is the large extent to which both UK governments and the EU have been concerned with developing and enacting policies that provide businesses with a supportive environment in which they can pursue growth more readily. The Conservatives' legislative reforms of the 1980s and 1990s, for example, were impelled by a belief that excessive union power was an obstacle to economic competitiveness, and that greater labour market deregulation was a necessary, and indeed desirable, component of wealth creation. Between 1997 and 2010 Labour made some notable policy interventions ostensibly designed to favour workers and trade unions; yet in general they were enacted in ways that ensure they do not conflict with the primacy of a neo-liberal belief that deregulated labour markets and weak trade unions are necessary components of a competitive economy. Since 2010, moreover, the 'reasserted neoliberalism' (Grimshaw and Rubery 2012) of the Conservative-Liberal Democrat coalition government is evident from its wide-ranging programme of employment deregulation. Looking beyond the UK, the impetus of the EU's 'social dimension' has dwindled markedly, reflecting its subordination to the process of market integration, something that the process of EU enlargement has brought into particularly sharp focus.

 ### Assignment and discussion questions

1. What is voluntarism in employment relations? Why has its significance declined?

2. Assess the extent to which Labour's employment relations policies between 1997 and 2010 were marked by continuity with the approach taken by its Conservative predecessors in government.

3. What have been the main influences on the employment relations policies of the coalition government since 2010?

4. What is meant by the 'social dimension' of the EU? How successful has the EU been in achieving its social objectives?

5. What have been the main effects of EU enlargement on employment relations?

 Visit the Online Resource Centre that accompanies this book to develop your understanding of this chapter, and keep up to date with the latest developments in this area.
www.oxfordtextbooks.co.uk/orc/williams3e/

 ### Chapter case study: The Irish Ferries dispute

The Irish Ferries dispute illustrates how EU enlargement potentially erodes labour standards since it allows companies wanting to pursue cost savings more scope to substitute their existing workforce with lower-paid workers from Eastern Europe. In 2004 Irish Ferries came into conflict with the Irish trade union SIPTU after the company started replacing its existing Irish workforce with cheaper, non-Irish workers on some of its routes. However, matters were exacerbated the following year when the company announced it wanted over 500 'voluntary' redundancies from its unionized Irish staff, who would be replaced by non-union agency workers from Eastern Europe at much lower wages (Donaghey and Teague 2006: 658). While many staff accepted voluntary redundancy, a significant number did not and faced a huge pay cut when Irish Ferries instituted the lower rate of pay.

Following legal action in the Irish courts by SIPTU and an intervention from the Irish Labour Court, which issued a non-binding recommendation that the company carry on employing Irish staff until 2007, the company took a harder line. This included sending replacement Eastern European workers onto the *Isle of Inishmore* vessel, accompanied by security guards disguised as passengers. When crew members realized what was happening they seized control of the ship and instituted anti-piracy measures, some locking themselves in the boiler room. The dispute then escalated as port workers refused to handle any Irish Ferries vessels. Tens of thousands of workers also took to the streets in a number of Irish towns and cities to demonstrate their support for the beleaguered workforce as part of a 'national day of protest' (Woolfson 2007: 211).

In December 2005 a legally binding settlement allowed the company to continue with its plans to restructure its labour force, with a more generous redundancy package in place for existing staff who agreed to depart. Irish Ferries was also required to ensure that replacement workers were paid at least the Irish minimum wage, considerably more than the company had originally intended. A year after the dispute, just twelve members of the directly employed unionized workforce remained with the company out of the more than 500 who previously had jobs there.

Question

To what extent, and in what ways, is it possible for EU enlargement to be reconciled with a robust 'social dimension' which protects workers' rights?

4 Social divisions and employment relations

 Chapter objectives

The main objectives of this chapter are to:

● explain the nature of employment disadvantage based on social divisions, and to consider the implications for employment relations;

● assess public policy and legislative developments designed to challenge disadvantage in employment;

● consider the extent, nature, and implications of employer-led initiatives designed to reduce disadvantage, including equal opportunities policies, diversity management, and work–life balance initiatives; and

● examine the efforts made by trade unions to represent the interests of workers from disadvantaged social groups.

4.1 Introduction

Following on from Chapters 2 and 3, which focused on employment relations in the contemporary economy and the politics of employment relations respectively, this chapter, the third of those that aim to analyse employment relations developments in a broader context, focuses on the influence of social divisions. By this we mean aspects of disadvantage and inequality that are socially constituted, reflecting people's shared social characteristics, like gender for example. The aim of this chapter is to provide you with a good knowledge of the nature, and principal features, of inequality and disadvantage in employment relations, and to enable you to develop a critical understanding of the main ways they have been addressed. The starting point—in Section 4.2—is a brief assessment of the dimensions of inequality and disadvantage at work, including a discussion of divisions based on social class. Following on from this, in Section 4.3 the focus is on the evolving legal and policy framework governing equality and diversity issues, including family-friendly and work–life balance measures. Section 4.4 is concerned with understanding and interpreting employers' interventions, particularly equal opportunities and managing diversity policies, and also examines the role played by the trade unions in promoting equality and diversity.

> **Introductory case study:** Pregnancy discrimination at work
>
> Despite it being unlawful, studies show there is a high incidence of pregnancy-related discrimination (James 2011). Between 2003 and 2005 the Equal Opportunities Commission (EOC) mounted a major investigation of pregnancy-related discrimination at work, including research with employers and a survey of 1,000 women who had worked during a recent pregnancy (EOC 2005). The EOC found that
>
> *(continued...)*

nearly half (45 per cent) of the women they surveyed reported being discriminated against, which included being sacked in some cases. Other discriminatory practices included failing to get appropriate pay rises, and missing out on training opportunities. Young women, black and ethnic minority women, women who are relatively new to their jobs, and women on low incomes seem to be particularly prone to discriminatory treatment.

The issue of pregnancy-related discrimination highlights a number of important topics considered in this chapter. One of these is the effectiveness of the law as a means of challenging employment disadvantage. Since discrimination on the grounds of pregnancy is unlawful, and has been since the mid-1970s, why is the law not a more effective instrument? Without effective enforcement the law can be a weak mechanism for protecting workers. The organization Maternity Action campaigns against pregnancy discrimination and gives advice to women. It reckons that few women take action against discriminatory employers, either because they are unaware of their rights, are harassed if they do try and assert their rights, or lack the time, energy, and resources to make a claim (http://www.maternityaction.org.uk). A second topic concerns the role of managers in organizations. The EOC found that insufficient knowledge and understanding of maternity rights on the part of line managers, and a failure to manage pregnancy effectively, were among the main causes of pregnancy-related discrimination. Third, how does pregnancy-related discrimination affect an employer's business? Employers who manage pregnancy effectively are more likely to retain talented and more productive staff (EOC 2005). Employers who make a concerted effort to tackle discrimination and promote equality may find that there are business benefits.

4.2 Discrimination, disadvantage, and inequality in work and employment relations

Workers often experience discrimination, disadvantage, and inequality in employment relations on the grounds of their social characteristics. For many years, the principal focus of studies of workplace inequality concerned the so-called status divide between manual and non-manual workers. In this section, the extent to which class-based disadvantage still affects work and employment relations—often expressed in concerns about stalled social mobility—is examined. The focus of attention then switches to the importance of other manifestations of inequality and disadvantage in work and employment relations, based on shared social characteristics such as gender.

4.2.1 Social class, the status divide, and employment disadvantage

Traditionally, the most fundamental divisions in society are those that are seen to arise from social class. The concept of class refers to hierarchical divisions in society which reflect differences in people's access to material resources. Social inequality and disadvantage are the consequences of differences in people's life chances, including access to education and employment opportunities, which reflect their class position. Historically, class differences in society both reflected, and in turn exercised an important influence over, work and employment relationships. While the concept of social class has long been the subject of much debate and controversy, one thing that is clear is that someone's economic situation, in particular their occupation, is a major determinant of their class position. You need only think about how strongly the term 'working class' is associated with routine, manual labour in factory settings. Thus the concept of social class captures the way in which people shared a sense of collective identity based on their work situation.

Traditionally in employment relations, class divisions were manifest in the status divide that existed between manual, blue-collar workers and their non-manual, white-collar 'staff' counterparts for much of the twentieth century. In manufacturing industry, for example, manual workers enjoyed the least favourable terms and conditions of employment, including a longer working week, shorter holidays, and fewer fringe benefits (Wedderburn and Craig 1974). Non-manual work, largely undertaken in office environments, was associated with higher status, better terms and conditions of employment, and greater job security. White-collar employees were more likely to benefit from sick pay arrangements, and enjoy longer holidays, a shorter working week, greater opportunities for promotion, and more autonomy at work (Price 1989).

In the twenty-first century does the concept of social class, with all that it entails for employment relations, still have any relevance? Politicians often refer to the UK as a 'classless society', implying that the importance of social class as a source of disadvantage has diminished, and that it no longer acts as a barrier to individual self-advancement. It is often held that the salience of class has declined (e.g. Pakulski and Waters 1996), and that other sources of social identity, like gender or ethnicity, for example, have become more important sources of social inequality and disadvantage. Alternatively, inequality and disadvantage do not arise so much from differences in people's collective class position, but rather reflect variations in the talent and ability of individual workers, and thus their capacity to improve their livelihoods and advance their careers (see McGovern et al. 2007: 81–3).

The decline of the trade unions (see Chapter 6) is sometimes said to reflect the dwindling relevance of class, as the working class occupations on which many unions were founded have become less prevalent. The supposed closing of the status divide at work, manifest in the apparent trend towards the 'harmonization' of employment conditions (Russell 1992), is a further reflection of the supposedly declining salience of class in employment relations. Organizational restructuring, in particular the demand for greater workplace flexibility, is held to have undermined traditional occupational patterns, and thus eroded the established distinction between manual and non-manual employees (Bradley et al. 2000). In some areas, such as in local government, unions and employers have concluded 'single status' agreements in order to promote harmonization, though progress towards implementation has been protracted (Wright 2011).

While undoubtedly an important aspect of contemporary employment relations, harmonization has been of limited overall significance. Although occupational change has rendered the distinction between manual and non-manual employment less important than it once was, not least because of the growth of non-manual jobs in the economy, the status divide remains a durable feature of employment relations, and thus a source of workplace inequality. Access to a variety of benefits, including occupational pension schemes, paid holiday entitlement, and sick pay is strongly linked to one's position in the occupational—and by implication the class—hierarchy (McGovern et al. 2007).

The enduring status divide at work is by no means the only evidence of the persistence of class-based inequality. During the 2000s there was growing concern in government about the supposed decline in social mobility—in other words, that fewer people from low-income backgrounds were progressing up the occupational hierarchy and securing relatively well-paid managerial and professional jobs. Lack of social mobility is held to be responsible for the persistence of inequality, for example by limiting access to top jobs and reducing opportunities for people from low-income backgrounds to progress up the career ladder. Parental income would seem to have a marked influence over a child's life chances; little more than 10 per cent of children whose parents are on low incomes reach the top 25 per cent of the income scale (HM Government 2011b). Thus the 'life-chances of children in Britain today remain heavily dependent on the circumstances of their birth' (Independent Commission on Social Mobility 2009: 4).

Studies of professions, like law, demonstrate the large extent to which top positions are not only filled by people from privileged backgrounds, but also seem to be becoming less socially diverse in respect of class (Ashley 2010; Milburn 2012). Particular concern has been expressed about the growing expectation in some occupations, such as journalism and the media, that people should have to undertake a period of unpaid work experience or an internship before securing paid employment. This often disadvantages young people from low-income families, who cannot afford to work for free, and is therefore a barrier to improved social mobility (Milburn 2012). The level of intergenerational inequality is higher in the UK than other comparable countries (OECD 2010). Not only is such ongoing inequality objectionable on the grounds of social justice—shouldn't people from low-income backgrounds have similar opportunities to those with richer parents?—but it also inhibits economic efficiency by restricting the pool of talent open to business (Independent Commission on Social Mobility 2009). Like its Labour predecessor, the coalition government has expressed a strong desire to improve social mobility (HM Government 2011b), and in 2012 it established a new Social Mobility and Child Poverty Commission under the chairmanship of former Labour minister Alan Milburn.

Some sociologists have raised questions about the government's strategy for social mobility, particularly its emphasis on improving diversity at the top through the provision of better educational opportunities. Goldthorpe and Jackson (2007) assert that intergenerational social mobility, as expressed by social class rather than income, has largely been constant for some thirty years. This followed a marked increase in social mobility between the 1940s and 1970s, which was the product of a major expansion in the number of jobs in managerial and professional occupations during this period. In the absence of similar changes in the employment structure, which seem unlikely, any genuine upward social mobility would need to be complemented by a corresponding level of downward mobility (i.e. fewer children from relatively well-off families going into good jobs), something which few politicians will find acceptable. Providing better educational opportunities or operating schemes designed to encourage a more socially diverse workforce in top professions will do little to change this.

Clearly, society remains 'riven' by social divisions centred on class (Erickson et al. 2009: 202). Not only are they still evident in employment, but work itself is an important source of the social class divide given the large extent to which one's occupation influences one's overall life chances (e.g. health, access to education, etc.). Moreover, in the absence of any trend towards greater upward social mobility, the class position of one's parents, derived from their occupations, and the way in which this affects the life chances of their children, continue to exercise a profound influence over work and employment relations.

4.2.2 Disadvantage at work: towards a broader agenda

Though important, on its own the persistence of class inequality is insufficient to account for employment disadvantage in contemporary workplaces. Other sources of social identity, like gender, for example, are also responsible for creating divisions in work and employment relations. Indeed, social class often intersects with them to compound inequality and disadvantage (Moore 2011). Low-paid women workers, for example, may encounter disadvantage on the basis of their class position and their gender.

Historically, women were channelled by employers, often with the support of male-dominated trade unions, into poorly paid, low-skilled jobs that offered few opportunities for promotion (Bradley 1989), or were excluded from the workforce entirely. There is evidence of progress towards greater gender equality. Over half (51 per cent) of employees are now women (van Wanrooy et al. 2013). Growing numbers of women have secured entry to professional and managerial jobs, in areas such as education, health, and the law (Crompton and Sanderson 1990; Walby 1997; EHRC 2010). By the mid-2000s around a third of workplace managers were female (Kersley et al. 2006).

Yet the progress towards greater gender equality at work should not be overstated. For one thing, although it has been eroded, the segregation of jobs and occupations based on gender remains a marked feature of contemporary employment relations. Women continue to be grossly under-represented in executive and managerial roles at the top of organizations. Such 'vertical segregation' is best illustrated by the lack of female directors. In 2010, just 12.5 per cent of FTSE 100 company board directors were women, up from 9.4 per cent in 2004—a rate of increase that if continued at the same pace will bring about gender parity in about seventy years (Davies 2011). There are important structural constraints that inhibit women from advancing in organizations, in particular efforts by relatively powerful men attempting to exercise power over, and exclude, them (Bradley 1999). The term 'glass ceiling' has been popularized to refer to the invisible barrier that seems to hinder women from getting to the top of organizations.

Segregation is also manifest on a 'horizontal basis', evident in the over-representation of women in particular occupations, such as that of supermarket cashier for example, or nursing, and their under-representation in others (Bradley et al. 2000). Work and employment relations are characterized by a marked degree of gender-based occupational and workplace segregation (Bradley and Healy 2008). Although female participation in the labour force has grown, much women's employment is concentrated in poorly remunerated, part-time jobs in the service sector, where opportunities for career progression are very limited (Women and Work Commission 2006), and which are often depicted as being less important than full-time jobs.

The persistence of gender segregation at work is perhaps one of the main reasons why the gender pay gap has proved to be so resilient. This is the difference between the average earnings of men and those of women, and is a major aspect of gender-based disadvantage. Over the years this gap has narrowed; in 2012 women in full-time employment on average earned 9.6 per cent less per hour than male full-timers, down from nearly 40 per cent in the early 1970s. However, the gap is wider when all employees, not just those employed on a full-time basis, are taken into account. Once this is done, it stands at 19.7 per cent (ONS 2012a). The reason the gender pay gap is wider when comparing the average hourly earnings of all male and female employees, not just full-timers, is because a disproportionately high number of women are concentrated in occupations marked by a predominance of low-paid, part-time jobs.

Although so far this discussion has largely been concerned with inequality based on gender, this should not imply that other sources of disadvantage are somehow less important. In spite of changing social attitudes and growing tolerance about people's sexual orientation, reports of homophobic bullying and discrimination persist (e.g. Bairstow 2004; EHRC 2010; Colgan and Wright 2011). Prejudice and discrimination against people on grounds of their age appears to be widespread (Sweiry and Willitts 2012). When it comes to religion or belief, people belonging to some social groups are markedly disadvantaged. For example, just 25 per cent of Muslim women are in paid employment, compared to some 70 per cent of women in general; and a fifth of mainly Muslim women of Pakistani and Bangladeshi origin report having experienced negative attitudes to religious dress at work (EOC 2006; EHRC 2010). There is also a long history of discrimination against disabled people in employment, who are especially prone to unemployment or segregation in poorly paid, low-skilled jobs as a result (Barnes 1992). The experience of disabled workers in organizations is often marked by incidents of bullying, harassment, and other examples of discriminatory behaviour (Foster 2011). Disadvantage on grounds of 'race' and ethnicity is also a feature of employment; generally, black and minority ethnic workers are more likely to be unemployed, or work in low-paid jobs with few career prospects, than their white counterparts, and are markedly less evident in managerial roles (Bradley and Healy 2008). Migrant workers frequently encounter discrimination and disadvantage in employment, often being concentrated in jobs that are of a precarious nature (McDowell, Batvitzky, and Dyer 2012). Many lack knowledge or awareness of their rights at work, which makes them vulnerable, and are liable to be treated unjustly by employers (Clark 2011).

Different dimensions of social divisions often intersect with one another, creating the potential for multiple disadvantages. Although large numbers of women have entered managerial and professional occupations, many others lack access to such positions and work in low-paid jobs with few opportunities for career progression, not just on account of their gender, but also because of their class position. Women from ethnic minorities may experience inequality on the grounds of their gender and their ethnicity (e.g. Kamenou, Netto, and Fearfull 2012). It is often women of Pakistani and Bangladeshi origin who suffer from the most pronounced disadvantage (Bradley and Healy 2008).

 ## Section summary and further reading

- Inequality at work has long been manifested in the status divide, reflecting divisions based on social class, something that harmonization initiatives have done relatively little to eradicate. The lack of improvement in social mobility also sustains class-based disadvantage.

- Notwithstanding the importance of social class, a broader conceptualization of social divisions at work is desirable, one that considers the implications for work and employment relations of disadvantage arising from other shared social characteristics, such as age, sexual orientation, disability, race and ethnicity, and gender, which often intersect.

There are some good studies of developments in female employment; Bradley (1999) and Bradley et al. (2000: Chapter 4) are particularly recommended. See Erickson et al. (2009: Chapter 8) for an overview of the relevance of social class and other aspects of inequality.

4.3 Public policy, anti-discrimination legislation, and equality at work

This section is concerned with examining the implications of the principal legislative inter-ventions designed to challenge inequality and disadvantage at work, and the public policy assumptions that underpin them. Following an analysis of the way the legislation evolved between the 1970s and the 1990s, we consider the manifold changes enacted by Labour governments during the 2000s, including the extension of protection from discrimination and the provision of rights to 'family-friendly' working arrangements. The legal framework relating to equality at work is then interpreted and assessed, including a critique of the coali-tion government's approach to equality and anti-discrimination issues.

4.3.1 The development of equality and anti-discrimination legislation

The development of anti-discrimination and equality legislation has been a notable feature of employment relations since the 1970s. Initially, governments were concerned with discrimi-nation on grounds of sex and race, though by the 1990s the need to challenge discrimina-tory treatment with regard to people with disabilities was also recognized. See Legislation and policy 4.1 for details of the main pieces of anti-discrimination and equality legislation between the 1970s and 1990s.

> **LEGISLATION AND POLICY 4.1: The main equality and anti-discrimination legislation of the 1970s to 1990s**
>
> - *Equal Pay Act (1970)*: provided for equal pay between men and women when engaged in 'like work'.
> - *Sex Discrimination Act (1975)*: prohibited direct and indirect discrimination in employment in relation to sex.
> - *Race Relations Act (1976)*: prohibited direct and indirect discrimination in employment in relation to race and ethnicity.
> - *Equal Pay (Equal Pay for Work of Equal Value) Regulations (1983)*: provided for equal pay between men and women when engaged in work of equal value.
> - *Disability Discrimination Act (1995)*: obliged employers to make 'reasonable adjustments' to ensure that a disabled employee, or potential employee, was not substantially disadvantaged; small firms were exempted.

During the 1970s, legislation designed to promote equality at work helped to erode the voluntarist basis of employment relations in Britain. The 1970 Equal Pay Act, which came into effect fully in 1975, provided for equal pay between men and women when engaged in 'like work'. Also in 1975, the principle that pregnant women be entitled to a period of paid maternity absence was established, alongside protection against discrimination on the grounds of pregnancy.

The 1975 Sex Discrimination Act made direct and indirect discrimination against women in employment unlawful. Direct discrimination refers to circumstances where, for example,

Table 4.1 Discrimination—key concepts

Concept	Definition
Direct discrimination	Unfair discrimination that arises where someone is treated less favourably in employment on account of their sex, race, etc.
Indirect discrimination	Unfair discrimination that arises where a condition of employment is applied which results in a worker being treated less favourably on account of their sex, race, etc.
Positive action	Measures designed to correct the under-representation of certain groups of workers through interventions which help their employment prospects (e.g. training and development)
Positive discrimination	Measures designed to correct the under-representation of certain groups of workers by giving them preferential treatment (e.g. quotas)—unlawful in the UK

a man or woman is not considered for employment, or for promotion, or a pay rise, among other things, purely because of their sex. The concept of indirect discrimination, however, concerns the situation where a condition of employment is applied 'to both sexes of a kind such that the proportion of one sex who can comply with it is considerably smaller. An example might be when a police force specifies that all candidates for the post of police officer must be two metres tall' (Cockburn 1991: 28–9). Similarly, the 1976 Race Relations Act prohibited direct and indirect discrimination in employment on the grounds of race. See Table 4.1 for key concepts related to the area of discrimination.

Pressure from campaigning groups and trade union activists was an important impetus for the enactment of legislation covering equal pay and sex discrimination in particular (Cockburn 1991). Yet the development of anti-discrimination legislation was, and to a large extent continues to be, marked by a 'liberal' approach to securing greater equality (Dickens 2000a). This involves trying to ensure that people are accorded equal treatment regardless of their social characteristics (Jewson and Mason 1986). Progress towards equality is achieved by using formal procedures, covering recruitment, selection, and promotion decisions for example, that encourage managers to treat people as if they are the same, reducing the salience of social differences (Liff and Wacjman 1996).

With the 'radical' approach to securing greater equality, however, there is a greater emphasis on the importance of influencing outcomes directly, rather than on ensuring that processes are in place to treat people the same, regardless of their social characteristics. Radical measures encompass, for example, 'positive action' to deal with, say, the under-representation of particular categories of workers, such as women or black and minority ethnic workers. This might take the form of dedicated training interventions designed to increase their participation. While the law traditionally has not encouraged positive action, unlike 'positive discrimination' it is not unlawful. Positive discrimination involves giving members of disadvantaged social groups preferential treatment in the jobs market or in promotion decisions. For example, Norway has instituted a controversial system of gender quotas for company boards (see International perspective 4.2).

International perspective 4.2: Gender quotas on company boards

One form of positive discrimination which has attracted growing interest concerns efforts to tackle the under-representation of women on company boards through some kind of quota system. Women comprise only around one in seven board members of major companies in Europe. Some European countries have already enacted measures to tackle the under-representation of women on company boards. Norway was a particularly notable pioneer. In 2003 it enacted controversial legislation requiring company boards to have at least 40 per cent representation of each sex by 2008. It would appear that 'the law has successfully challenged the under-representation of women on public limited companies' boards of directors, and made the boards appear more democratic and equal. This indicates that the hard strategy of legislation was a successful tool for improving the gender balance' (Seierstad 2011: 290). Much of the benefit, though, seems to have been accrued by a relatively small number of female directors, who sit on more boards; there are also concerns that any improvements have largely been cosmetic, with few advantages accruing to women in general. That said, though, the change has 'weakened the idea that a career in business is for "men only"' (Teigen 2012: 88). The Norwegian model has attracted the interest of EU policy-makers. In 2012, the European Commission proposed introducing a new Gender Balance Directive, which would set an objective of at least 40 per cent of non-executive positions on the boards of major companies being held by women by 2020 (European Commission 2012). However, this has been opposed by some member states, including the UK.

Conservative governments of the 1980s and 1990s largely eschewed legislative interventions as a means of effecting change, in favour of voluntary employer- and market-led efforts (Dickens 1997; Webb 1997; Dex and Forth 2009). They promoted 'a privatized route to equality, with an emphasis on individual organizations deciding what is in their interests' (Dickens 1999: 11). The principal exception was the 1995 Disability Discrimination Act, which obliged large employers to make 'reasonable adjustments' to ensure that people with disabilities, encompassing both physical and mental impairments, were not substantially disadvantaged in employment, or experience less favourable treatment without adequate justification—the result of many years of campaigning by pressure groups and disability activists. Conservative efforts at avoiding further legal intervention in the area of equality were stymied by the obligations that went with membership of the European Economic Community (EEC) (Davies and Freedland 1993; Dickens 1997). In 1992, for instance, the EU's Pregnant Workers Directive gave all women the right to a minimum of fourteen weeks' maternity leave; previously not all female workers were eligible for such leave.

4.3.2 Developments under Labour and the coalition since 1997

The extension of anti-discrimination legislation and the support given to 'family-friendly' working were two key elements of Labour's employment relations policy programme between 1997 and 2010. See Legislation and policy 4.3 for details of the main legislative provisions. It is also important to recognize that other policies enacted by Labour also helped to alleviate employment disadvantage. The National Minimum Wage (NMW), for example, has particularly benefited low-paid women workers (see Chapter 7).

LEGISLATION AND POLICY 4.3:   Equality and anti-discrimination legislation under Labour 1997–2010

- *Maternity and Parental Leave Regulations 1999*: enacted in order to comply with the EU's 1996 Parental Leave Directive. Established the right of parents to take up to thirteen weeks of unpaid parental leave, offered parents the right to unpaid time off work to attend to family emergencies, and increased the minimum period of maternity leave to eighteen weeks.

- *Race Relations Amendment Act 2000*: obliged public sector employers to promote positive race relations.

- *Part-time Workers (Prevention of Less Favourable Treatment) Regulations 2000*: prohibited employers from treating part-time workers less favourably than a full-time equivalent. Enacted in order to comply with the EU's 1997 Directive on Equal Rights and Treatment for Part-Time Workers.

- *Fixed-term Employees Regulations 2002*: prohibited employers from treating employees on fixed-term contracts less favourably than an equivalent permanent employee. Enacted in order to comply with the EU's 1999 Fixed-Term Contracts Directive.

- *Employment Act 2002*: extended the minimum period of paid maternity leave to twenty-six weeks, introduced two weeks' paid paternity leave, and established a new right for parents to request flexible working arrangements.

- *Employment Equality (Sexual Orientation) Regulations 2003*: gave workers protection against discrimination on the grounds of sexual orientation. This legislation was enacted in order to comply with the EU's 2000 Equal Treatment Directive.

- *Employment Equality (Religion or Belief) Regulations 2003*: gave workers protection against discrimination on the grounds of religion or belief. This legislation was enacted in order to comply with the EU's 2000 Equal Treatment Directive.

- *Disability Discrimination Act 1995 (Amendment) Regulations 2003*: among other things, this did away with the exemption for small employers, placed an obligation on public sector employers to promote disability equality, and, in order to comply with the EU's 2000 Equal Treatment Directive, reduced the scope for employers to avoid making reasonable adjustments.

- *The Employment Equality (Age) Regulations 2006*: prohibited age discrimination in respect of employment and vocational training, and introduced a new 'default' retirement age of 65, which was later rescinded; enacted in order to comply with the EU's 2000 Equal Treatment Directive.

- *Work and Families Act 2006*: extended the right to request flexible working to carers of adults, provided for the extension of paid maternity leave to a minimum of thirty-nine weeks along with the expectation that it would subsequently be increased to a year, and provided for the introduction of additional paternity leave, some of which could be paid.

- *Equality Act 2006*: provided for the establishment of the Equality and Human Rights Commission; imposed a new duty on public bodies to promote gender equality.

- *Equality Act 2010*: consolidated all existing equality and anti-discrimination legislation in one piece of overarching legislation; provided for greater consistency of treatment across the various 'protected characteristics'; imposed a 'general equality duty' on public authorities; and provided for some degree of positive action in selection and promotion decisions.

The scope of anti-discrimination law was extensively widened under Labour (Dex and Forth 2009). In 2004, for example, disability discrimination legislation was extended to cover all employers. Most of the impetus for reform was stimulated by EU legislation (Dickens 2007), in particular a 2000 framework equality directive that prohibits discrimination in employment on the grounds of age, sexual orientation, and religion or belief. EU legislation also influenced the equality agenda in other respects. For example, directives establishing that part-time workers and employees on fixed-term contracts should not be less favourably treated than their full-time and permanent counterparts were enacted, and subsequently implemented in the early 2000s, because of a concern to promote gender equality. The over-representation of women in part-time and temporary jobs meant that where employers treated people under-taking them less favourably than others then this could amount to discriminatory treatment on the grounds of gender. However, workers who believe they are disadvantaged as a result of their part-time status must identify appropriate full-time workers as comparators. Extensive job segregation, though, means that part-time workers generally do not undertake the same jobs as full-timers. This makes such comparisons problematic, and as a result few part-time workers are in a position to benefit from the legislation (McColgan 2000; McKay 2001).

The strengthening of equality legislation was a further aspect of change in the public policy framework during the 2000s, unrelated to Britain's membership of the EU. For example, the then Labour government responded to the report of the Macpherson inquiry into the murder of the black teenager Stephen Lawrence by enacting a new Race Relations Act 2000 that, among other things, obliges public sector employers to actively promote race equal-ity (Fredman 2001). Subsequently, corresponding duties to promote disability equality and gender equality were also enacted, though they did not apply to private sector firms.

The introduction of these positive duties to promote equality, a form of positive action, was rather significant (Dex and Forth 2009). They represent a move, albeit limited, away from a liberal conception of achieving equality, based on treating everyone in the same way, to a situation where it is recognized that in order to alleviate inequality at work, employers need to do more to assist people from disadvantaged groups. These duties marked a shift in think-ing, away from an approach dominated by an emphasis on reducing discrimination, towards a view that promoting equality is more desirable, 'which does not depend on discrimination already having taken place . . .' (Conley 2011: 24). In the public sector, at least, Labour pursued a 'stronger and broader' approach to equality and diversity issues: broader, through efforts to 'integrate equality and diversity in the public service workforce with the delivery of public services sensitive to diverse communities', and stronger, as exemplified by the shift to a more radical orientation, marked by the use of positive action, monitoring arrangements, and tar-gets. The equality duties were the 'most obvious representation of a stronger *and* broader approach' to equality and diversity matters under Labour (Bach and Kessler 2012: 89).

Perhaps the most important piece of equality legislation enacted by Labour—the 2010 Equality Act—came right at the end of its period in office. Its main purpose was to modernize the legal framework relating to equality and diversity matters, making it more straightfor-ward and ensuring greater consistency of approach (Conley 2011). The Equality Act consoli-dated all of the existing equality and anti-discrimination laws so that they are incorporated into one, single piece of overarching legislation. It did not enlarge the coverage of existing anti-discrimination law—discrimination on the grounds of age, disability, gender reassign-ment, marriage and civil partnership, pregnancy and maternity, race, religion or belief, sex, and sexual orientation were already unlawful. However, these categories are now defined as 'protected characteristics'. In some areas, the Equality Act extended the obligation on employ-ers not to discriminate against workers with certain protected characteristics; it prohibited indirect discrimination on the grounds of disability, for example, and it made employers liable when their staff were harassed because of a protected characteristic by a third party such as a customer or a client, if they had not taken sufficient steps to prevent it. Moreover, the Equality Act placed a 'general equality duty' on public authorities to eliminate unlawful discrimination and promote equality and 'good relations' across all of the protected characteristics except for marriage and civil partnership. It also encourages positive action by permitting an employer to take a protected characteristic into account when choosing between otherwise similarly qualified candidates for a vacancy or a promotion. This is a relatively minor, but potentially highly symbolic, departure from the hitherto dominant liberal approach to promoting equality and diversity which aspires to treat people as if they are all the same (Conley 2011).

Successive governments have also taken action to promote more 'family-friendly' employment policies and a better 'work–life balance'. The idea is to give as many people as possible, but especially women and lone parents, the opportunity to reconcile their family responsibilities with undertaking paid employment, something that is viewed as advantageous to businesses because it helps them to attract and retain talented staff (McKay 2001).

The 'family-friendly' label is used to describe a wide variety of different practices that may help parents and carers reconcile their work with their domestic responsibilities, including, among other things, provisions for maternity, paternity, and parental leave (see Table 4.2), childcare facilities, job-sharing measures, and other forms of flexible working arrangements. The term 'work–life balance' has increasingly been preferred to 'family-friendly', not least because it implies a focus on workers in general, not just those with family responsibilities. The main problem with the work–life balance concept concerns the assumption that a distinction can easily be made between people's 'work' and their 'lives' (Scholarios and Marks 2004). In reality, of course, they overlap and interact with each other in subtle, complex, and dynamic ways (Warhurst, Eikhof, and Haunschild 2008). Moreover, as will become evident later, it seems that work pressures increasingly affect and constrain the way people undertake the rest of their lives.

The family-friendly policy agenda was initially stimulated by the need to comply with the EU's 1996 Parental Leave Directive. As a result, the then Labour government enacted legislation in 1999 which established a new entitlement for parents to take up to three months' unpaid parental leave up until a child's fifth birthday, and gave employees the right to take unpaid time off work in order to manage family crises, such as the sickness of a child. The revised 2010 Parental Leave Directive, which gives parents the right to at least eighteen weeks' unpaid leave, came into effect in April 2013. During the 2000s, Labour further extended rights to family-friendly working, moving beyond what was required by the obligation to comply with EU legislation. It introduced the right of fathers to take up to two weeks' paternity leave, and extended the minimum period of paid maternity leave to nine months, although the plan

Table 4.2 Parental leave—key concepts

Concept	Definition
Maternity leave	Leave taken by the mother before, during, and after the birth of a child
Paternity leave	Leave taken by the father during and after the birth or adoption of a child
Parental leave	Leave that can be taken by either parent in the first few years after the birth or adoption of a child

to increase this to a year was abandoned because of the recession. Labour also established a means by which fathers can take up to twenty-six weeks' Additional Paternity Leave, some of which could be paid, if the mother returns to work, which took effect in 2011. It also legislated to give parents and carers of adults the right to have their requests for flexible working arrangements (e.g. part-time working) taken seriously by employers—see Chapter 8.

The coalition government has expressed an intention to extend the ability to request flexible working to cover all employees, not just parents of children and carers of adults, in 2015, as part of its Modern Workplaces initiative. However, it reckons that the existing 'right' is too cumbersome and bureaucratic, and imposes too much of a burden on employers. Instead, the coalition plans to place a duty on employers to consider requests in a 'reasonable manner' and within a 'reasonable' amount of time; this will be accompanied by a new statutory code of practice to provide guidance over what constitutes 'reasonable' for the purposes of this provision (HM Government 2012a).

Some concerns have been evinced that family-friendly measures may accentuate, rather than diminish, gender disadvantage at work by reinforcing the presumption that it is largely the responsibility of mothers to adapt their employment arrangements, not fathers. Most requests for flexible working come from women, reflecting the gendered assumptions that govern the respective roles of mothers and fathers. Yet part-time working arrangements and other forms of flexible employment, which are dominated by women, often provide limited opportunities for career development or progression. Moreover, the relatively long period of maternity leave available, compared to the provision for paternity leave, allied with feeble parental leave arrangements, potentially reinforce gender disadvantage by sustaining the belief that it is the job of the mother, rather than the father, to take time away from work to look after children (EHRC 2009).

Thus too much family-friendly legislation reinforces the assumption that women's careers are of secondary importance relative to those of men. For Dickens (2007: 472), measures 'targeted at men may offer more in terms of gender equality'. While she acknowledges that some progress has been made to support fathers, the introduction of paternity leave for example, most family-friendly legislation 'appears still to embody gendered assumptions about the nature of the father's role'. The coalition government's Modern Workplaces initiative is designed to increase the involvement of fathers in child-raising activities. It proposes a new system of shared, flexible parental leave designed to take effect from April 2015. While the default of fifty-two weeks of maternity leave (thirty-nine weeks of paid maternity leave) will continue to apply, where both parents qualify a woman will be able to end her period of maternity leave early, with the remaining balance of unused maternity leave and maternity pay shared between the parents as flexible parental leave and pay (HM Government 2012b).

4.3.3 Evaluating the legal and policy framework

In assessing developments in the legal and policy framework governing discrimination and equality at work, it is important to recognize that there are a number of positive and progressive features of recent government interventions. The scope of anti-discrimination legislation has been considerably widened; it is no longer lawful for an employer to discriminate against a worker on the grounds of his or her sexual orientation, for example. The right to request flexible working, while modest in its purpose, seems to have stimulated the greater use of flexible working arrangements, to the benefit of workers with caring responsibilities—see Chapter 8. Moreover, the extension of anti-discrimination legislation has influenced employers' equal opportunities policies, as will be seen in Section 4.4. There is also a growing emphasis on promoting parental leave, designed to enable greater involvement of fathers in child-raising activities, rather than assuming this is a role for mothers.

Nevertheless, there are a number of major problems with the legal framework. First, efforts to tackle discrimination and promote equality at work have been tempered by a desire to avoid overly disturbing business interests (Dean and Liff 2010). The prevailing assumption behind the approach taken by policy-makers is that voluntary interventions by employers are a more effective way of improving equality outcomes than legislative measures, and that equality action has to be 'justified in terms of promoting efficiency and competitiveness' (Dickens 2007: 468), rather than for reasons of social justice (Dex and Forth 2009). Pursuing equality is desirable, but only in so far as it accords with the interests of employers—an 'inadequate basis for the pursuit of equality' (Dickens 2007: 474). For example, Labour resisted extending the equality duties to private sector employers, limiting their overall impact (Dean and Liff 2010). This desire not to antagonize employers was particularly evident when it came to implementing EU legislation, like the original Parental Leave Directive, where Labour was concerned not to go beyond the minimum requirements.

A second problem concerns the liberal, equal treatment approach that underpins most of the legislative framework, something which leaves the structural causes of inequality at work largely unchallenged. Disadvantage is presented as a problem for the individual worker, rather than as something that stems from how the organization operates (see Insight into practice 4.4). Although the 2000s saw the introduction of some limited duties to promote equality, for the most part any kind of positive action designed to achieve greater equality has been eschewed by policy-makers. The emphasis on establishing a level playing field, on which, in theory, people compete on the same terms, fails to appreciate the extent to which the rules of the game conform to the experiences of relatively privileged sections of the workforce, like men (Dickens 1992).

 Insight into practice 4.4: The individualized basis of responses to disability discrimination legislation

The Disability Discrimination Act (DDA) 1995 obliges employers to make 'reasonable adjustments' to accommodate disabled workers so that they are not put at a substantial disadvantage in employment, or when looking for employment. Based on interviews with disabled workers in the public sector, Foster (2007) demonstrates that the adjustment process is often damaging to the worker concerned, some of whom experience stress or ill-health as a result. Even when the process of adjustment produced a satisfactory outcome for the worker concerned, delays in implementation could cause difficulties. The most significant finding, however, concerns the informal, individualized basis of the adjustment process: much depended on the disabled employee's relationship with their line manager. The problem with such a highly individualized approach, though, is that it lacks transparency, contributing 'nothing to the development of broader policy-making and practice' (Foster 2007: 81). Moreover, a worker's disability comes to be perceived as a problem for the individual, to be resolved through negotiation with his or her line manager, rather than a structural issue for the organization as a whole.

A third problem with the legal framework relating to equality and discrimination at work concerns the rather weak arrangements for enforcing rights. Two types of enforcement mechanism exist: administrative measures and legal arrangements (Dickens 2007). With regard to the former, until 2007 separate bodies covered the areas of gender discrimination, race discrimination, and disability discrimination respectively. Although they were entitled to investigate employers suspected of operating discriminatory practices, these powers were only used sparingly, and they enjoyed little scope to enforce changes. In 2007, these bodies were merged into a new Equality and Human Rights Commission (EHRC). The rationale for creating an all-encompassing equality body was that with the introduction of new discrimination laws covering age, sexual orientation, and religion or belief, it made sense to establish a single agency, one which would be a more effective guardian of equality, than lots of smaller, issue-specific bodies (Dean and Liff 2010). In theory, a single equality body should be able to articulate a more integrated and systematic approach to tackling discrimination and promoting equality. However, its progress has been disappointing, not least because of the damage inflicted on it since 2010 by the coalition government (as explained later in this section).

The second type of enforcement mechanism concerns attempts by workers who have experienced unlawful discrimination to gain legal redress by submitting a claim to an employment tribunal (ET), which can award financial compensation to successful claimants. The weaknesses of ETs as vehicles for enforcing the legal rights of employees are considered in more detail in Chapter 10. Here, though, the focus is on their limitations as arrangements for challenging unlawful discriminatory practices. One problem is that the onus is on an individual worker to take the appropriate action, when they might either lack knowledge about how to make a discrimination claim, or may be anxious about the consequences of submitting one (Dickens 2007).

One way of resolving this would be to allow individual claimants to come together as a group to submit so-called 'class actions', since discrimination rarely affects just one individual worker, but is generally a collective experience (Bradley and Healy 2008). Because such 'class actions' are prohibited in the UK, ETs often have to handle multiple individual claims together—see the end-of-chapter case for an example. And after submitting a claim, having to go through a tribunal hearing can be an unpleasant experience for the workers involved (Aston, Hill, and Tackey 2006). Even in the small minority of cases where a discrimination claim is upheld, the remedy is usually in the form of financial compensation, generally less than £10,000. Moreover, employers are under no obligation to eradicate the discriminatory practice that prompted the claim in the first place (Dickens 1997). The impact of a provision in the 2010 Equality Act for employment tribunals to recommend changes relating to the workforce in general, following a successful discrimination claim, remains to be seen.

During the 2000s, Labour largely favoured employer-led efforts when it came to promoting equality at work, with legislative action treated as an undesirable last resort when voluntary efforts failed (Roper, Cunningham, and James 2003). Little was done to oblige employers to eradicate discriminatory practices at work. The system remained geared towards the readiness of individual workers who experience disadvantage to submit claims to employment tribunals, with little hope of adequate redress even if they win their case. The idea was that equality action is best fostered by a relatively light touch legislative regime within which employers are encouraged, because it is in their own interests, to take voluntary initiatives to promote equality (Dickens 2007).

One might have expected the Conservative-Liberal Democrat coalition, which took office in 2010, to have been sympathetic to advancing equality and diversity in the workplace. Before the 2010 general election, for example, under David Cameron's leadership the Conservative Party placed a great deal of emphasis on the importance of promoting greater gender equality and improving people's work–life balance, part of a policy agenda calculated to appeal particularly to women voters (Williams and Scott 2010). However, perhaps the most overwhelming feature of the coalition government's approach is its marked lack of concern for equality matters. Even the much vaunted Modern Workplaces agenda, with its proposed new system of shared parental leave and the extended right to request flexible working, is not due to take effect until 2015 at the earliest because of concerns about the supposed potential regulatory burden on employers. The revised EU Parental Leave Directive was implemented in 2013, a year later than it should have been.

In many respects, the coalition's policies seem destined to compromise equality. Its broader deregulatory agenda (see Chapter 3), which encompasses measures designed to restrict access to employment tribunals (see Chapter 10), possesses major adverse consequences for equality, not least because of the difficulties workers who experience discrimination will face when trying to win redress. The EHRC is ill-placed to help. The coalition has instigated drastic cuts to the organization's budget, which has lost many experienced campaigning staff as a result. The EHRC's capacity to promote equality and combat discrimination, particularly in the area of race, has been severely compromised, in some people's view deliberately so because otherwise it might have mobilized opinion against coalition policies (Conley 2012; Holloway 2012).

Perhaps the most notable example of the coalition's lack of support for equality matters concerns the abandonment of key measures contained in the 2010 Equality Act, but which had yet to pass into law when it took office, and the repeal of some that had. Plans to implement compulsory equal pay audits for companies deemed to have made insufficient progress in tackling gender pay differentials and a proposed new duty on public bodies to tackle inequalities based on social class—the first instance of the law being proposed to tackle class-based disadvantage—were discarded (Conley 2011). At the time of writing, the coalition has not been able to achieve its objective of repealing the 'general equality duty' as part of its commitment to reducing employment regulation; however, the provision making employers liable for harassment of their staff by third parties is due to be abandoned. Moreover, its overall policy agenda, which is dominated by the pursuit of austerity, has severely compromised equality, particularly in respect of gender. The impact of cuts to jobs, wages, and pensions in the public sector is felt disproportionately highly by women; they are also more likely to be disadvantaged by the withdrawal of public services, and often have to bear the burden of tasks left undone by the retreat of state provision (Fawcett Society 2012). For these reasons, then, the 2010 election of the coalition government would appear to mark something of a turning point in respect of equality and anti-discrimination legislation. Progress that was made during the 2000s under Labour came to a pronounced halt, with the 2010 Equality Act marking the zenith of governmental efforts to tackle inequality and disadvantage using the law. It is not just that the coalition has not really been terribly interested in promoting greater equality, but taken together its policies have had the effect of markedly increasing inequality.

Section summary and further reading

- Legislation prohibiting discrimination in work and employment on the grounds of sex and race developed during the 1970s. It was informed by a liberal conception of equality which holds that disadvantage is best alleviated by establishing measures which ensure that people are treated the same, irrespective of their gender or ethnicity. Conservative governments of the 1980s were ill-disposed towards further legislation. However, the need to implement EU directives and, in the case of disability discrimination, campaigns by activists, meant that some legislative intervention occurred.

- During the 2000s, Labour governments made some notable changes to the legal framework, including extending the scope of anti-discrimination legislation, for example, and establishing a range of policies designed to promote more family-friendly working arrangements.

- The policy and legal framework relating to equality and discrimination matters has a number of major weaknesses, including a reluctance to challenge the interests of employers, the predominance of a liberal, equal treatment ethos which fails to address the structural causes of employment disadvantage, and the presence of a weak enforcement regime which puts too much responsibility for tackling discrimination onto individual workers and not enough of an onus on employers.

For further information about the legislative and policy framework governing equality, see Kirton and Greene (2010: Chapter 6) and Dean and Liff (2010: 429–33). The work of Linda Dickens on equality and anti-discrimination legislation is highly recommended (e.g. Dickens 2007). See Jewson and Mason (1986) for further details of the liberal and radical approaches to equality. See the Equality and Human Rights Commission's website for details of its work (http://www.equalityhumanrights.com).

4.4 Equality and diversity at work

In this section the concern is with organizational initiatives designed to challenge inequality and disadvantage at work. Equal opportunities (EO) policies are the main tool used by employers to promote equality in the workplace. There has been an increasing amount of interest in the concept of managing diversity (MD) as a means of challenging disadvantage at work. Many organizations have also established policies dealing with work–life balance and family-friendly working issues. However, trade unions play a key part in promoting effective action in this area.

4.4.1 Understanding equal opportunities policies

During the 1980s and 1990s, many large employers in the public and private sectors increasingly committed themselves to the pursuit of equal opportunities, in particular by styling themselves as 'equal opportunity employers' and enacting formal EO policies (Dex and Forth 2009). This trend continued during the 2000s. In 2004, 67 per cent of workplaces with five or more employees were covered by a formal policy; by 2011, this had risen to 76 per cent (van Wanrooy et al. 2013). Much of the increase reflects the growing prevalence of EO policies in smaller, private sector workplaces (Walsh 2007; Dex and Forth 2009; van Wanrooy et al. 2013). Whereas in the past EO policies were generally restricted to the areas of sex and race, there is evidence that, under the influence of legislation, their scope is widening to cover disability, and also age, religion, and sexual orientation (Walsh 2007).

Under the influence of the legislative framework, organizational EO policies are typically marked by a 'liberal' orientation when it comes to tackling inequality at work (Jewson and Mason 1986; Bach and Kessler 2012). There is, therefore, an overwhelming emphasis on the development of a 'level playing field' (Webb 1997), so that workers are treated in the same way. As applied to the recruitment and selection of staff, for instance, the emphasis is on ensuring that procedures exist which enable employers to choose staff on the basis of their suitability for the job, irrespective of their social characteristics (Kirton and Greene 2010).

Why, though, have EO policies become so commonplace among organizations? Compliance with the law is the most significant influence on organizational practice; EO policies are designed to ensure that the organization is less liable to actions on grounds of sex, race, and, more recently, disability, religious belief, age, and sexual orientation. Bradley and Healy (2008: 81) acknowledge that concerns about the weakness of the legislation protecting workers from discrimination are well justified. Nevertheless, they maintain that legislative provisions 'may act as an incentive for good practice' in organizations. Employers have been encouraged to develop EO policies in order to avoid discrimination cases that could potentially damage their reputation. The pursuit of EO in organizations has also been informed by a belief that inequality and unfair discrimination at work are inherently undesirable and, in the interests of social justice, should be eradicated (Davies and Thomas 2000). However, the social justice rationale for equality action has been eclipsed by the one that stresses the advantages to businesses of reducing inequality and disadvantage in the employment relationship (Dickens 1997; Glover and Kirton 2006; Kirton and Greene 2010).

There is no one business 'case' for equality action. Rather, it is proposed that the promotion of equality will, to varying degrees, generate certain business advantages (Dickens 1994; Liff 2003). These include being able to draw on a wider pool of talent when recruiting employees, retain important staff, benefit from the contribution of groups whose skills and potential contribution might otherwise have been neglected, match the characteristics of customers, and sustain a positive corporate reputation (Dickens 2000a; Liff 2003). Since the desirability of equality action is bound up with its potential contribution to improving organizational performance, business arguments may be more effective in generating positive reform, in particular by securing the commitment of managers, than a social justice rationale (Dickens 1994; Liff 2003).

The growing adoption of organizational EO policies would seem to reflect 'a progressive increase in employers' commitment over time' (Dex and Forth 2009: 253). They have made a positive difference to the position of some groups of workers, particularly relatively well-off women who are better able to gain access to managerial and professional jobs (Webb 1997). This is evident in the case of the airline company studied by Rutherford (1999). Over a long period of time it had developed a range of sophisticated EO practices, job-sharing arrangements for example, designed to increase the number of women in management roles. Yet the proportion of women in senior management roles remained stubbornly low—largely, it seems, because of an assumption that such jobs required excessive working hours, something that was difficult to reconcile with women's family responsibilities.

4.4.2 Equal opportunities policies: a critical assessment

There are four main problems with EO policies as tools for challenging discrimination and disadvantage at work. The first is that they are often merely rhetorical statements of intent that help to conceal the presence of discriminatory workplace practices (Kirton and Greene 2010). In other words, the presence of a formal policy need not have much of an effect at all on employment relations processes and arrangements. Just because there is an equal opportunities policy in place should not be taken as a sign that unfair discrimination is absent (Aitkenhead and Liff 1991; Bradley and Healy 2008). The experiences of the black trade union activists studied by Healy, Bradley, and Mukherjee (2004) were marked by incidents of racial discrimination, even in companies that were noted for their supposedly eager pursuit of equal opportunities. See Insight into practice 4.5 for evidence of the persistence of racist and sexist attitudes and behaviours in organizations.

 Insight into practice 4.5: Racial disadvantage at work—the experiences of black and minority ethnic women trade unionists

Despite the growing use of equal opportunities policies, Bradley and Healy's (2008) study of the experiences of black and minority ethnic (BME) women trade union activists demonstrates that discrimination on grounds of race and ethnicity remains a prevalent feature of organizational life. Four aspects of discriminatory practice seem particularly noteworthy. First, the organizations in which the women worked were highly segregated on the grounds of both gender and race. Black women managers were rare. Second, racism was reportedly commonplace, albeit in a less explicit fashion than in the past. Bradley and Healy (2008: 146) point to the persistence of what they call 'everyday racism', meaning the 'remarks, actions and behaviours which, in a small way but persistently, emphasise difference from the majority'. Examples include the use of phrases such as 'you people' or 'you lot' when referring to BME staff. Third, racial stereotyping seemed to be a common feature of organizational life. The women were often made to feel as if they were inferior on the grounds that they were black. According to one woman, 'managers make us feel like as if we don't have brains, even if you do cleaning they say you are not doing it properly . . . This is the way they treat us . . .' (Bradley and Healy 2008: 148–9). Fourth, sometimes managers were accused of failing to take complaints of racial harassment seriously. The experiences of these women indicate that we should take care not to assume that the expansion of equal opportunities policies in organizations has necessarily eradicated racist and sexist attitudes and behaviours.

In practice, EO policies are often just 'empty shells'. This means that in many workplaces covered by a formal EO policy there are either few practices to support it, or if there are they are restricted to certain groups of workers, such as the ability to undertake job-sharing for example (Hoque and Noon 2004). Rigorous arrangements for evaluating the operation of EO policies tend to be rather rare (Dex and Forth 2009). For example, fewer than a quarter (23 per cent) of workplaces are covered by formal arrangements for monitoring recruitment and selection (van Wanrooy et al. 2013). Overall, then, while formal EO policies have become more prevalent in organizations, inadequate arrangements for monitoring and evaluating how they operate limit the extent to which they can be used as effective tools for mitigating discrimination and disadvantage.

A second problem with organizational EO policies is that their focus is often rather narrow, concerned with assisting women managers to break the 'glass ceiling' and secure more senior positions, for example. This was apparent in the case of the airline discussed in Section 4.4.1 (Rutherford 1999). However, employers are often uninterested in developing interventions that would benefit the many more female workers who are employed in jobs characterized by low pay and poor working conditions, and whose prospects are obstructed more by the presence of a 'sticky floor' rather than a glass ceiling (Cockburn 1991; Dickens 1997). For example the National Health Service (NHS) has pursued a gender equality agenda that prioritizes increasing the proportion of women in professional and managerial jobs. Such an approach, however, has 'little relevance to women in clerical and administrative grades, much less ancillary workers such as cleaners, catering staff and health-care assistants' (Richards 2001: 27).

The third obstacle to the progress of employer-led equality initiatives concerns the attitudes and behaviour of line managers, who are generally responsible for implementing them in practice. But many such managers continue to make decisions based on prejudiced or stereotypical assumptions (Kirton and Greene 2010). Equality initiatives are often treated as unimportant, or even resisted, by managers who see them as an infringement on their prerogative, especially during periods of organizational change. This was apparent in a civil service agency that, among other things, gave line managers more discretion over equal opportunities. Although a minority of managers did take the opportunity to progress these issues, most had only a 'hazy perception of the role they were expected to play in maintaining and developing' equal opportunities (Cunningham, Lord, and Delaney 1999: 70), and some expressed downright hostility.

Linked to this, the fourth weakness of EO policies as devices designed to reduce unfair discrimination at work is that they generally fail to challenge those features of the cultures and structures of organizations that privilege men. This was evident in the case of a high street bank. The company had a long-standing formal commitment to equal opportunities. In practice, however, major barriers to women's progress existed. Managers were expected to undertake excessive working hours—something of a problem for women with family responsibilities. Moreover, it was assumed that once they had children, women would lack the appropriate level of organizational commitment necessary for promotion. If a woman expressed an interest in flexible working, so as to combine work and family responsibilities more easily, this was taken as a sign that she was not interested in pursuing a career. Thus management in the organization, especially senior roles, was dominated by men. 'Formal equality statements expressed concern about this situation but there were far more powerful informal practices which reinforced it' (Liff and Ward 2001: 30).

It is important not to underplay the significance of EO initiatives. In some areas they have fostered a 'climate of equality', enabling women to challenge long-established structures of job segregation (Bradley 1999). By itself, though, employer-led equality action is a rather weak means of challenging such discrimination in employment (Dickens 2000a). A major source of this weakness is that it is underpinned by an assumption that equality is best promoted on the basis that it delivers important business benefits. Yet there are a number of problems with this approach. For one thing, employers may focus their efforts on improvements in areas where it is easier to secure change, or where the business benefits are more easily identifiable (Dickens 1999). This explains the popularity of initiatives designed to erode the glass ceiling and increase the proportion of female managers in senior positions. Challenging long-established patterns of job segregation and low pay, which operate to the disadvantage of women workers in particular, is a much more complicated and difficult area and will not be in the interests of employers who secure important cost advantages by maintaining a pool of cheap, low-paid female labour (Dickens 1994). In such cases 'a business case can be articulated against [equal opportunities] action' (Dickens 1999: 10).

A further problem is that the supposed business benefits of equality action may be difficult to identify at an organizational level (Colling and Dickens 1998). They are also likely to be of a relatively long-term character, something that is problematic given the pressure on organizations to deliver short-term performance gains (Kirton and Greene 2010). Equality initiatives, then, are more likely to be perceived by employers as business costs, rather than as investments that can help to enhance organizational performance, and are liable to be withdrawn if no advantage is apparent (Dickens 2000a). As a result, employer-led efforts to challenge inequality at work are bound to be 'partial' and 'selective' (Dickens 1997), varying between organizations and over time according to managerial preferences, and not those of disadvantaged employees (Kirton and Greene 2010).

4.4.3 **Towards managing diversity?**

In contrast to the emphasis on equal treatment and fair procedures that characterizes the liberal model of equal opportunities approaches, interventions designed to produce equal outcomes are at the heart of the radical model. 'It seeks to intervene directly in workplace practices in order to achieve a fair distribution of rewards among employees, as measured by some criterion of moral value and worth' (Jewson and Mason 1986: 315). The radical model recognizes that structural factors particular to certain socially disadvantaged groups inhibit their participation in employment, for example women's greater share of domestic responsibilities (Webb and Liff 1988). Thus equality 'of access is an illusion while the white, male, full-time worker with few domestic responsibilities is seen as the norm' (Kirton and Greene 2010: 123). Positive discrimination, then, such as setting employment quotas for example, may be necessary if equality at work is to be achieved.

The main problem with the radical approach is that it invites the complaint that certain groups of workers are the unworthy beneficiaries of 'special treatment', which may erode support for equality initiatives. Nor does it 'promise any improvement *in the nature of the organisation itself'* (Cockburn 1989: 217, original italics). Instead, Cockburn (1989) proposes that it is more useful to distinguish between 'short' and 'long' equality agendas. Whereas the short agenda is concerned with rather superficial managerial interventions designed to improve equality of opportunity, at its longest the equal opportunities agenda should be a transformative programme, dedicated to challenging the power of privileged groups of white, male employees. It recognizes that 'disadvantage can be perpetuated through an organization's structure, culture and practices, rather than just through the biased decision-making of managers' (Liff 2003: 440), and that it is these that should be reformed.

One of the claims made for the managing diversity (MD) approach is that it holds out the promise of transformative organizational change as a means of eroding disadvantage in employment (Blakemore and Drake 1996). It offers the prospect of 'a more radical challenge to the problem of disadvantage and discrimination by requiring organizations to adapt to individuals and groups rather than vice versa' (Dean and Liff 2010: 428). The MD approach has become increasingly influential, particularly in the United States, as a means of challenging discrimination and disadvantage in the employment relationship (Glover and Kirton 2006; Greene and Kirton 2009; Oswick and Noon 2012). What, then, are the main assumptions that underpin, and the principal characteristics of, the MD model?

Table 4.3 The key characteristics of equal opportunities and diversity management approaches

Equal opportunities	Diversity management
A 'liberal' approach (sameness)	Recognizing and celebrating difference
Emphasis on the 'level playing field'	Attractive to managers
Equal treatment (group-based)	A more individualistic approach
The use of formal procedures (e.g. selection)	Emphasis on culture change

Whereas the liberal equal opportunities approach emphasizes the importance of equal treatment and sameness as the best way of reducing disadvantage, the MD model contends that disadvantage is more effectively tackled by acknowledging and lauding differences between employees (Kandola and Fullerton 1994; Greene and Kirton 2009; Healy, Kirton, and Noon 2010). 'In contrast to equal opportunities approaches, which aim for workplaces where an individual's sex and race is of no greater significance than the colour of the eyes in determining the treatment they receive, the core idea behind managing diversity seems to encourage organizations to recognize difference' (Liff 1997: 13). See Table 4.3 for the key characteristics of the EO and MD approaches.

In the MD approach, the emphasis on individual differences stands in marked contrast to the primacy of tackling group-based disadvantage that is central to liberal EO programmes (Liff 1997). Thus there 'is a move away from the idea that different groups should be assimilated to meet an organizational norm' (Kirton and Greene 2010: 127)—one which is often, of course, based on the experiences of those who are relatively privileged in the labour market, such as white males (Liff and Wacjman 1996).

A further aspect of the MD approach which distinguishes it from an equal opportunities approach is that it is supposedly more attractive to managers (Liff 1997; Noon 2007). The emphasis on managing individual employees, and of realizing their potential in a way that benefits the business, is something that line managers, who might otherwise be sceptical of the value of equal opportunity initiatives, can more easily appreciate (Greene and Kirton 2009). In contrast to the EO approach, which is often perceived as an external imposition, particularly through government regulation, MD is said to be more easily aligned with, and supportive of, the needs of the business (Ross and Schneider 1992; Glover and Kirton 2006; Healy, Kirton, and Noon 2010; Oswick and Noon 2012). For example, the use of employee networks, or 'affinity groups' as they are sometimes called, is a feature of diversity management in the United States, and now appears to have spread to the UK (see Insight into practice 4.6).

The most profound claim for the MD approach, though, is that if organizations are to acknowledge and manage individual differences effectively, and thus realize the full potential of their employees, they should review the way they operate. Underpinning the MD approach, therefore, is the assumption that an organization must 'recognize that *it* has to change to adapt to employee differences rather than simply expecting employees to fit in with its pre-existing practices' (Liff 1999: 68).

There is some evidence that where organizations take diversity seriously, and alter their practices accordingly, it can benefit employees. This is apparent from a study of the experiences of lesbian, gay, and bisexual (LGB) workers in sixteen 'good practice' case study

Insight into practice 4.6: Affinity groups as a diversity management tool

The development of employee networks, or affinity groups as they are sometimes called, is an increasingly important feature of organizational efforts to manage diversity effectively. They are managerially sponsored groups of employees based around some aspect of social identity, like sexual orientation for example, which operate within a specific organization. The development of such employee networks has been particularly evident in the City of London. Between 2005 and 2007 Merrill Lynch established five employee networks, including a Women's Leadership Council, a black professional network, a lesbian, gay, bisexual, and transgender (LGBT) group, and a parents and carers network with some 800 members. Deloitte & Touche has instituted, among other things, a disability group called Workability and a Globe (gay, lesbian, or bisexual employees) network (Smethurst 2007). These groups and networks are not just part of a broader attempt to recognize diversity, but are also viewed as a means of enhancing business performance, by helping firms to attract and retain talented staff for example, and also because they help to make people feel more comfortable at work. Some argue that because they operate under the aegis of employers these networks rarely enjoy the power to challenge undesirable discriminatory practices in organizations (e.g. Healy and Oikelome 2007). However, in places they seem to have become an increasingly prominent diversity management tool, helping to shape and influence the organizational diversity agenda. Colgan and McKearney's (2012: 373) study of LGBT networks suggests that they provide workers with a 'mechanism for visibility, community, and voice'.

organizations which had committed themselves to operating in ways that supported and enhanced diversity, for example by developing LGB networks. Even though LGB staff were aware that the employers had not done all they could to recognize and promote the benefits of diversity, they recognized that their experience of employment had been enhanced by the adoption of an MD approach (Colgan et al. 2007).

Managing diversity, then, appears to hold out the potential for a transformation in employer attitudes towards equality, consistent with the 'long' approach discussed earlier in this section. In many cases, the diversity agenda has given equality practitioners in organizations more influence and authority, particularly because of the greater scope it gives them to integrate their goals with the overall needs of the business (Kirton and Greene 2009). Generally, however, the MD approach promises significantly more than it actually delivers. There are three major problems. First, in practice it is often difficult to distinguish between an EO and an MD approach. Line managers prefer to deal with individual differences in a standardized way, more akin to a conventional equal opportunities mode of action (Greene and Kirton 2009: 163). MD may involve little more than a simple re-labelling of conventional equal opportunities initiatives (Kirton and Greene 2010), perhaps to make them more palatable to managers.

Second, the MD approach has been criticized for offering a 'sanitized' and 'unthreatening' perspective on workplace differences (Webb 1997: 163). It is a model that is designed to be comfortable for managers, not to challenge their assumptions or prejudices (Noon 2007). Workers themselves rarely have any input into how diversity management operates, with the result that the policies and practices associated with it often lack credibility (Greene and Kirton 2009). The emphasis on individuals, moreover, means that pressure to change potentially discriminatory organizational practices is often absent; they do not have the collective power to effect reforms enjoyed by socially disadvantaged groups (Webb 1997). As a result, understandings of 'differences', and of whether and how they should be valued, generally come within the prerogative of managers, who may support diversity only as long as it delivers explicit organizational benefits, or does not cost them anything (Webb 1997; Glover and Kirton 2006).

Third, although in theory the MD approach holds out the promise of transformative organizational change in order to enable individual differences to be recognized and valued, in practice it generally leaves established beliefs and practices unchanged (Dickens 2000a). Its focus on individual difference fails to recognize that disadvantage is a collective, social phenomenon which is group-based, and thus is rarely used to challenge those long-standing features of organizations that systematically privilege, say, men (Liff 1997; Dean and Liff 2010). Often diversity 'may have more to do with corporate image-building than with the kind of interventions designed to facilitate more egalitarian work organization and increased inclusion of women' (Webb 1997: 166).

Ashley's (2010) study of diversity initiatives among City of London law firms exemplifies the limits of the MD approach. Efforts to diversify the class base of the legal profession, by acknowledging and rewarding individual difference based on social class—for example, opening up positions to more working class candidates—were largely unsuccessful. Although good for the corporate reputation, they did very little to challenge the perception among senior lawyers that a more diverse class base would damage the image of their profession— an attitude which is 'deeply entrenched' in institutional structures and practices. Indeed, the presence of diversity initiatives notwithstanding, the expectation that 'non-traditional candidates should assimilate to existing organizational norms . . . remains unchanged' (Ashley 2010: 723). Effective action to promote diversity is contingent on using a more conventional EO agenda, based on tackling group-based disadvantage, rather than through a focus on lauding individual difference (Ashley 2010).

Like conventional equal opportunities approaches, to which they often bear a marked resemblance, MD policies are, given their status as employer-led methods of generating change, somewhat weak interventions for challenging inequality and disadvantage in employment (Greene and Kirton 2009). As Noon (2007) observes, the rationale for the MD approach is based on similar business case arguments to those that inform the development of equal opportunities initiatives more generally, and suffers from the same kind of problems. These include a tendency to focus solely on short-term performance improvements, which might not immediately be apparent, and a realization that there are often considerable benefits for employers of not taking action to deal with workplace disadvantage. Greene and Kirton's (2011) research in a government department demonstrates that the diversity management approach is more robust and durable when it is grounded in more than just narrow business case arguments. Despite a major restructuring exercise and associated job losses, diversity management in this public sector organization was sustained through the involvement of trade unions and employee representatives, and by the requirement to comply with its statutory obligation to promote equality.

4.4.4 Managing work–life balance in organizations

As was seen in Section 4.3.2, growing concerns about the need for more family-friendly working arrangements and better work–life balance have been a major influence over employment relations policy, evidenced by the establishment of the 'right' for some employees to request flexible working patterns, the extension of paid maternity leave, and the institution of new rights to paid paternity leave and unpaid parental leave. During the 2000s, Labour placed a particular emphasis on using legislation as a means of prompting voluntary action on the part of employers, not least because of the supposed business benefits, like improved staff morale, reduced absenteeism, and easier recruitment (HM Treasury and DTI 2003). Policy interventions by the coalition government have also been predicated on business case arguments. Its Modern Workplaces policy agenda, for example, makes reference to the positive outcomes for companies such as Lloyds Banking Group and Centrica of operating extensive work–life balance arrangements.

There is some evidence that employers accept the business rationale for family-friendly and work–life balance policies. In the hospitality industry, recruitment and retention difficulties encouraged some major employers to invest in flexible working time arrangements in order to hold on to women staff with young children (Doherty 2004). The presence of work–life balance arrangements is associated with lower turnover of staff and reduced levels of employee absence (Beauregard and Henry 2009). Overall, however, there are rather mixed findings when it comes to the relationship between flexible working time arrangements and performance outcomes, suggesting that there is no 'unequivocal' business case for work–life balance in organizations (de Menezes and Kelliher 2011).

During the first half of the 2000s, there was an increase in the provision of flexible working and other family-friendly working arrangements by employers (Hayward, Fong, and Thornton 2007). This occurred not so much because of the supposed business benefits, but in response to the expectations of workers. The availability of flexible working and other family-friendly practices tends to be much more commonplace in organizations with some characteristics than it is in others. In particular, they are concentrated among public sector employers, and in workplaces in the retail and hotel and catering sectors, generally where there are relatively high proportions of female and part-time workers (Walsh 2010).

For a number of reasons, it is doubtful that voluntary action by employers alone will lead to the widespread adoption of robust family-friendly and work–life balance policies in a way that promotes greater equality at work. For one thing, despite all the rhetoric about supposed business benefits, work–life balance arrangements are rarely a priority for employers (Hyman and Summers 2004: 421). There does not appear to have been any increase in employer provision during the latter half of the 2000s (van Wanrooy et al. 2013). Indeed, among workplace managers the view that it is the responsibility of individual workers, rather than employers, to take care of work–life balance issues has become more widespread. In 2004, 66 per cent of managers agreed or strongly agreed with the view that it was up to individual employees to balance their work and family responsibilities; by 2011 the figure had risen to 76 per cent (van Wanrooy et al. 2013).

Family-friendly and work–life balance policies are often presented by employers, and perceived by employees, as perks: additional benefits that may be, and indeed are, withdrawn, or at least not accorded as much importance, in periods of economic difficulty (Lewis 1997; Doherty 2004; Hyman and Summers 2004). If seen as perks, moreover, policies directed at workers with family responsibilities can be a cause of disaffection among staff who do not enjoy access to them (e.g. Greene and Kirton 2009), in what has been termed a 'family-friendly backlash' (Walsh 2010).

Even when family-friendly working arrangements are operated, it cannot be assumed that they will promote equality between men and women at work. Indeed, they may reinforce disadvantage. Women who undertake flexible working, especially part-time employment, may be perceived by male managers as lacking the commitment to the job and the organization necessary for promotion. This was particularly evident in the firm of chartered accountants studied by Lewis (1997). She found that organizational commitment was largely equated with time spent at work. Female employees who were unable to match the number of hours at work put in by their male counterparts, or who were on reduced hours, were seen as less promotable.

Unsurprisingly, then, there has been some reluctance on the part of employees to make use of family-friendly and work–life balance practices, resulting in a 'take-up gap' (Kodz, Harper, and Dench 2002). People sometimes shun them, reluctant to damage their careers by risking the appearance of being less committed to the organization. However, there is some evidence that the take-up gap narrowed as demand from employees for more flexible working arrangements grew (Holt and Grainger 2005; Hayward, Fong, and Thornton 2007). Nevertheless, the take-up of unpaid parental leave continues to be very low indeed; little more than one in ten employees who are parents of young children make use of it (Tipping et al. 2012), evidently because they cannot afford to.

Perhaps the biggest obstacle to take-up of family-friendly and work–life balance practices is that they often come under the control of line managers who can be reluctant to allow employees to make use of them (Hyman and Summers 2004), in spite of what the organizational policy might say. This gap between the espoused policy of an organization and what managers actually allow to happen in practice has been identified as a considerable impediment to the take-up of family-friendly working arrangements (Visser and Williams 2006). See Insight into practice 4.7 for details of the experiences of professional women. In some parts of the economy, such as in call centres and the retail sector, there is often a conflict between the flexibility needed by managers, in particular the expectation that staff will work additional hours at short notice to cope with an unanticipated rise in calls, and the demand from workers for predictable working time arrangements so that they can plan their family responsibilities effectively (Hyman and Marks 2008; O'Brien-Smith and Rigby 2010).

 Insight into practice 4.7:   Family-friendly working—the experiences of professional women

Catherine Gatrell interviewed twenty working mothers, including teachers, architects, and lawyers, for her book *Hard Labour: The Sociology of Parenthood*. Nearly all of them were either treated badly by their employer or experienced discrimination as a result of their pregnancy. On returning to work following maternity leave, moreover, these women often found that their managers were unsupportive, making it difficult for them to balance their careers with their child-rearing responsibilities, even in organizations that claimed to support equal opportunities and family-friendly working arrangements. Managers turned down requests for reduced hours, for example. There was also some evidence that mothers who switched to part-time employment experienced detriment because they did not conform to male-dominated career paths that put a premium on full-time employment. As a result, Gatrell (2005: 194) observes that 'organizations which claim to have put "family-friendly" policies in place may be paying lip-service to the idea, and might have no real intention of implementing or promoting the policies'—making sure that managers follow them, for example. While the business case for operating family-friendly working arrangements was recognized in some organizations, particularly those headed by working mothers themselves, for the most part it was not widely accepted.

Increasing work demands are a further significant constraint on the effectiveness of policies designed to enable people to strike a better balance between the requirements of their job and their family lives (Hyman et al. 2003; O'Brien-Smith and Rigby 2010). In the local authority studied by Tailby et al. (2005), extensive work pressures had contributed to a growing 'work–life imbalance' as the increasingly demanding nature of people's jobs adversely affected their lives outside work. Indeed, around a third (31 per cent) of full-time employees in general claim that work interferes with their life outside work (van Wanrooy et al. 2013). The provision of work–life balance arrangements does not necessarily help to reduce the potential conflict between people's paid work and the rest of their lives (Beauregard and Henry 2009), perhaps because their presence is often coupled with greater work pressures. Kelliher and Anderson (2010) found that the use of flexible working time arrangements is associated with higher levels of job satisfaction; ironically, however, it is also linked to greater job demands. 'In this case a policy ostensibly about assisting employees to gain a more satisfactory work–life balance, also produced outcomes that could have negative implications for work–life balance and employee wellbeing in the longer term' (Kelliher and Anderson 2010: 99).

4.4.5 Trade unions, collective bargaining, and the pursuit of workplace equality

Clearly managerial interventions are of limited effectiveness in challenging discrimination and disadvantage in employment. In this section the contribution of trade unions and collective bargaining is examined. The emphasis is largely on gender equality, which is where most union activity has been concentrated. Such efforts present major challenges for the unions, which have traditionally been reluctant to eschew the belief that workers in the same industry, occupation, or organization might have different interests based on aspects of their social identity, like gender or ethnicity (Kirton and Greene 2010: 180).

Historically, trade union practices and collective bargaining activity have often operated to the detriment of women and black and minority ethnic workers. With regard to gender, for example, unions often colluded with employers to exclude women from skilled, and therefore more highly paid, jobs, helping to reinforce patterns of occupational segregation and a sexual division of labour that privileged the work of men over that of women (Bradley 1989). Union collective bargaining priorities, moreover, reflected dominant male assumptions concerning the inferior value of women's labour (Charles 1986). It is important to recognize, therefore, that historically the trade unions were largely uninterested in promoting gender equality at work. Indeed, their activities helped to support 'those very mechanisms in the organization of work which makes patterns of gender segregation so difficult to break down' (Rees 1992: 85). Unions tended to operate in ways that privileged the interests of men, and developed an overly masculine culture in which women, and their interests, were marginalized (Cunnison and Stageman 1993).

Since the 1980s, though, the unions have, albeit rather slowly and unevenly, sought to represent the interests of an increasingly diverse workforce more effectively, those of women in particular. They have done so for three related reasons. First, economic change has eroded the traditional heartlands of trade unionism in male-dominated manufacturing industry. Employment growth has been concentrated largely in the service sector, which is characterized by high levels of female employment. Second, with the decline of male-dominated manual industries, trade unionism is increasingly concentrated in areas such as health and education, disproportionately populated by female employees. During the 2000s, the proportion of women employees who are trade union members overtook that of male employees; in 2011 nearly 29 per cent of women were trade unionists compared to just 23 per cent of men (Brownlie 2012). Third, influenced by feminism, women themselves have challenged the male-dominated structures and decision-making processes of trade unions (Cunnison and Stageman 1993; Colgan and Ledwith 2002). For these reasons, then, unions have made equality and diversity issues more of a priority (Kirton and Greene 2010; Moore 2011). This extends beyond gender equality: for example, the trade union movement has made greater efforts to challenge discrimination and disadvantage in employment on the grounds of race and ethnicity (Sullivan 2011). That said, though, unions have emphasized the pursuit of women's equality far more than that of other groups, such as gay and lesbian workers (Kirton and Greene 2010).

One of the key levers used by unions is to ensure that equality issues are covered in collective bargaining with employers. The concept of equality bargaining refers to initiatives undertaken by trade unions that are designed to reduce the employment disadvantage of particular groups, such as women workers for example, through interventions directed at employers (Colling and Dickens 1989, 2001). In the past, union bargaining priorities and activities discriminated against women at work by systematically undervaluing the contribution of their labour. Moreover, unions often supported pay structures that disadvantaged women—for example, those that accord high value to length of service.

However, while collective bargaining has done much to sustain workplace inequality, it also has the potential to erode it (Cockburn 1991). Unions may be more capable of securing equality action on the basis of social justice, rather than for narrow, insecure, and partial business reasons (Colling and Dickens 1998). Through trade union action, collective bargaining may give women workers greater influence over their pay and employment conditions. It 'provides a way of giving women a voice; an ability to define their needs and concerns and to set their own priorities for action' (Dickens 2000b: 197).

There is a good deal of evidence that a union presence has a positive influence on the organizational equality agenda, not least by putting pressure on employers to improve their practices (Heery 2006). Unions have increasingly been active in promoting and articulating equality issues as priorities for collective bargaining, including demands for pay equality between men and women, and greater access to family-friendly working arrangements (Bewley and Fernie 2003). The shop workers' union USDAW, for example, has used legislative changes and drawn on business case arguments in bargaining for improvements in work–life balance provision among major retail firms (O'Brien-Smith and Rigby 2010; Rigby and O'Brien-Smith 2010). There are also a growing number of trade union equality representatives, whose activities seem to have contributed to the improved treatment of equality and diversity matters in those employing organizations where they are based. Their presence enables unions to represent the interests of a diverse workforce more effectively (Moore 2011; Bacon and Hoque 2012). Equality practices are more evident, and equality outcomes are generally better, in unionized workplaces compared to non-unionized workplaces (Dex and Forth 2009; Dean and Liff 2010; Kirton and Greene 2010). See Insight into practice 4.8 for an assessment of union effectiveness in negotiating equality issues.

Insight into practice 4.8: Auditing union progress in the area of equality bargaining

In 2012, the Trades Union Congress (TUC 2012c) published an equality audit which gives an indication of the areas where trade unions made progress in negotiating with employers over equality issues:

- 69 per cent of unions reported some negotiating successes in the area of flexible working and work–life balance arrangements;
- 58 per cent reported having negotiated improvements in conditions for parents and carers;
- 53 per cent reported some negotiating success in the area of equal pay between men and women;
- 44 per cent reported negotiating improved rights for lesbian, gay, bisexual, and transgender workers; and
- 50 per cent reported successes negotiating improvements on age-related issues.

However, union negotiators found it difficult to advance equality issues during the economic recession; the 'tougher climate' means that 'most unions feel it has been harder to get employers to address equality issues'. There is often more of a concern with preserving existing measures in the face of cutbacks. Nevertheless, the 'report suggests unions and their negotiators have not abandoned the push for equality' (TUC 2012c: 6).

One of the areas where trade union action has been most prominent is that of equal pay. Groups of largely female workers, such as speech therapists for example, have benefited from pay rises generated by successful union equal value campaigns (Bradley 1999). Trade unions have sometimes been able to use legislative measures, and the threat of potential discrimination claims on a mass scale, to secure employer action (Colling and Dickens 1998). They have been the subject of legal action themselves, by women workers encouraged by an aggressive breed of 'no-win, no fee' lawyers who contend that union efforts to resolve equal pay claims through collective agreements with employers have been negligent (Dean and Liff 2010; Kirton and Greene 2010)—see the end-of-chapter case study for further details.

The extent to which unions have been successful in promoting effective equality action is related to the degree of internal pressure for change (Heery 2006). Some unions have taken steps to alter their representative structures, and the way their decision-making processes operate, to accommodate the interests of a diverse membership. Efforts by unions to reform their decision-making structures and representative arrangements in order to promote greater internal equality and diversity have been a major trend (see Kirton and Greene 2010: 189–92).

In assessing the extent and nature of these changes, it is useful to employ, in modified form, the distinction between liberal and radical approaches discussed in Section 4.3.1. The liberal approach is concerned with reducing the barriers that prevent people from disadvantaged groups participating in unions or benefiting from their services; by seeking to remove discriminatory practices it seeks to establish a 'level playing field' (Kirton and Greene 2002). Certain measures, including the appointment of equality or women's officers and ensuring that union meetings are made more accessible by offering childcare facilities, for example, have been taken in order to help promote equality of access (Colgan and Ledwith 2002). See Insight into practice 4.9 for details of how the unions have sought to represent the interests of their lesbian and gay members.

Insight into practice 4.9:   Representing the interests of lesbian and gay members in British trade unions

Sam Bairstow studied the way in which trade unions in Britain represent the interests of their lesbian and gay members (Bairstow 2004). She found evidence of the existence of a dual approach in union practice. Some unions were characterized by bottom-up, activist-led efforts to secure change. This made for a more participatory, informal, and inclusive approach to the advancement of lesbian and gay interests. In others, though, the development of internal structures for lesbian and gay representation was a more top-down, leadership-driven affair. In these cases, links between lesbian and gay representative structures and mainstream union decision-making bodies seem to be more effectively realized. The problem here, however, lies in ensuring that centralized and bureaucratic union initiatives are sensitive to the particular needs of gay and lesbian members. Unions are also using their educational facilities and other programmes to build awareness of the issues facing lesbian and gay members, and to secure effective representation of their interests. There is little evidence of concerted resistance to these developments on the part of more conservative union members and officials. Most members, for instance, do not appear to be interested. Nevertheless, Bairstow (2004) does suggest that unions are sometimes uncomfortable with, or uncertain about, dealing with issues relating to sexual orientation.

Most trade unions have typically adopted a liberal approach to the way they promote internal equality, particularly with regard to gender. The main weakness of this approach, however, is its failure to challenge male-dominated union power structures that often operate in ways that disadvantage women (Kirton 1999; Bradley and Healy 2008). Liberal measures are viewed by some as an ineffective means of securing the effective participation of under-represented groups, such as black and women members, in trade unions, and that more radical interventions may be necessary (Healy and Kirton 2000). The radical approach implies that positive action is required in order to enable union members from disadvantaged social groups to participate in trade unions and thus have their interests represented more effectively (Kirton and Greene 2002; Dean and Liff 2010). See Figure 4.1 for an illustration of how unions use liberal and radical interventions.

There are two principal measures that come under the 'radical' label. The first concerns the provision of special, or 'reserved', places for representatives from particular social groups, mainly women workers, on union decision-making bodies. This has become a more common feature of trade union practice, though it is still limited to a minority of unions, such as the public services union Unison (McBride 2001). However, trade unionists, including many women, often dislike the potential divisiveness generated by having reserved seats (Bradley 1999). Women who take them up are often made to feel inferior; they can be treated as second-class union representatives whose contributions should be limited to issues that specifically concern women members, and thus can be easily marginalized (Kirton and Healy 1999; Colgan and Ledwith 2002). Perhaps the most fundamental criticism of reserved seats, though, is that although their presence advances the representation of individual women within trade unions, they are less effective in promoting the interests of women as a disadvantaged social group. In other words, tinkering with policy-making structures in a way that enables more women to participate as individuals does little to challenge the embedded,

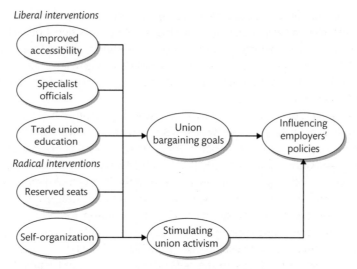

Liberal interventions

Radical interventions

Figure 4.1 Liberal and radical interventions used by trade unions to promote equality

and collectively generated, male-dominated norms and assumptions that determine union action (McBride 2000, 2001).

The second 'radical' measure used by some unions to promote internal equality and diversity concerns the establishment of internal structures that enable members from disadvantaged groups to organize and represent themselves through what is known as 'self-organization' (Virdee and Grint 1994). This refers to arrangements that provide a separate space for collective organization and action by union members and activists, on the basis of their shared social characteristics. To secure more effective representation, self-organization offers a means by which members from disadvantaged social groups can work together, separate from established union decision-making structures, to pursue their collective interests. Of all unions, Unison has the most sophisticated set of arrangements; black, disabled, lesbian and gay, and women members all have the opportunity to self-organize (Terry 1996; McBride 2000).

Whereas reserved seats focus on improving representative democracy in unions, self-organization is designed to enhance the participation of members from disadvantaged groups. It enables them to work together, constructing 'a sense of identity, political consciousness, confidence and solidarity and to develop and practice activist skills' (Colgan and Ledwith 2002: 178). Self-organization, therefore, explicitly challenges the notion that workers are a homogeneous group with a single set of common interests that can be articulated and represented by a trade union in an unproblematic manner. It recognizes that, by virtue of belonging to particular social groups, workers may have diverse interests, and that traditional assumptions about participation in trade unions, which assumed a commonality of interest, are therefore inappropriate. One particularly prominent instance of self-organization was promoted by the GMB union, which established a dedicated branch for Polish migrant workers (Fitzgerald and Hardy 2010).

Studies of self-organization in practice show that, while rare, it nonetheless gives members and activists a forum that they can use to develop participation, and to bring issues that specifically concern them onto the union agenda (Colgan and Ledwith 2000; Parker 2002). Women-only groups in trade unions help to provide female trade union officers with an effective base of support (Kirton and Healy 2013). Moreover, black members' networks are not only an effective way of stimulating involvement and participation, but also serve to encourage greater discussion of race equality issues in a trade union context (Bradley, Healy, and Mukherjee 2002). Self-organization arrangements may also serve to generate union activism, giving members a sense that they are able to effect changes that benefit their working lives (Colgan 1999; Bradley and Healy 2008).

The positive effects of self-organization may, however, sometimes be limited in practice. For one thing, it relies on the willingness of members to participate in union affairs, something that cannot be assumed. Moreover, apart from in Unison, separate organizing is generally limited to women (Kirton and Greene 2002). Where the links with established policy-making bodies are tenuous, self-organization can also lead to the interests of disadvantaged social groups being marginalized. Autonomy, then, may foster exclusion (Colgan and Ledwith 2002), particularly if powerful union interests feel challenged. In Unison, for example, the policy issues discussed in the women's self-organized groups rarely made it onto the agenda of the powerful mainstream decision-making bodies (McBride 2000, 2001).

Although the relationship between the self-organized groups and established decision-making structures may improve over time (Colgan 1999), self-organization may reinforce rather than ameliorate the under-representation of disadvantaged groups in trade unions. That said, however, there is no doubting that the self-organizing approach has fostered greater trade union involvement among workers who belong to groups that often experience exclusion, like black and minority ethnic women for example. Their enthusiasm for the self-organization approach indicates that despite the problems we have identified, it can be a valuable means of revitalizing union organization and of enabling trade unions to represent diversity in a more effective manner (Bradley and Healy 2008).

 ## Section summary and further reading

- There has been an increase in the extent and coverage of equal opportunities policies among public and private sector organizations. EO policies are characterized by a liberal approach to challenging disadvantage in employment, in which the importance of using formal procedures to ensure equality of treatment is emphasized.

- The managing diversity approach is concerned with how organizations can manage and take advantage of individual differences. In practice there is often some overlap with traditional equal opportunities approaches. Moreover, the MD model does not do much to challenge those aspects of organizational structure and culture that continue to privilege white males.

- During the 2000s, the proportion of workplaces claiming to operate work–life balance and family-friendly practices increased markedly, linked to the espoused business benefits that come from using them. However, there is some evidence that the reach of family-friendly working remains limited. The extent to which workers have benefited by achieving a better work–life balance is questionable, not least because of the reluctance of managers to apply organizational policies appropriately along with increased job demands.

- Trade unions play an important part in advancing greater equality at work. Through their bargaining and other efforts unions are able to promote a higher incidence of equality practices and better equality outcomes, based on a social justice rationale. They have also taken steps to improve the representation of members from disadvantaged social groups, though such initiatives have largely been of a liberal nature.

For an overview of the issues pertaining to managing equal opportunities and diversity in organizations, see Kirton and Greene (2010) and Dean and Liff (2010). Bradley and Healy's (2008) interviews with black and minority ethnic women trade unionists highlight some negative features of organizational practice. For an in-depth analysis of MD in practice, see Kirton and Greene (2009). Hyman and Summers (2004) and Walsh (2010) provide good insights concerning the management of work–life balance issues. For an overview of trade unions and equality, see Kirton and Greene (2010: Chapter 7) and Dean and Liff (2010: 433–6).

4.5 Conclusion

Inequality and disadvantage, linked to social divisions, are important features of work and employment relations. Like Chapters 2 and 3, the material in this chapter demonstrates that relationships between employers and employees at work cannot simply be understood in the context of the workplace, but are informed by wider economic, political, and social influences that transcend particular employment situations. For example, although the practice of trade unionism is clearly founded on collective values and the need for unity to combat hostile employers, historically it was also often concerned with excluding groups of workers, such as women for example, in order to advantage a privileged male minority. Nevertheless, unions have come under pressure to operate more inclusively, not least because their traditional constituencies, male-dominated industries based on manual labour, have dwindled in significance. They have taken up the interests of women workers and other socially disadvantaged groups more readily, and have altered their structures to enable them to be more effectively represented.

Union activity in these areas, while not without its difficulties, is an important catalyst for greater equality in work and employment relations. Employer-led efforts, based on a rather narrow and insecure conception of the business advantages of equality action, can be of limited effectiveness. Equal opportunities policies, which emphasize the need to treat everybody the same regardless of their social characteristics, are strong on rhetoric, but often short on action. The managing diversity model, despite its ostensibly more transformative approach, does little to challenge socially generated disadvantage and inequality at work, and in practice is often little different from the more conventional equal opportunities agenda. A trade union presence, though, can exert pressure on employers to deliver a more effective set of equality policies, such as better work–life balance arrangements.

Nevertheless, the 'initiative in addressing equality issues now rests substantially with employers, prompted and shaped to some extent by the law' (Dean and Liff 2010: 436). Equality and diversity action in organizations increasingly occurs within, and is informed by, a legal framework which is the product of growing state intervention in this area of work and employment relations (Dex and Forth 2009). While anti-discrimination and equality laws have been in place since the 1970s, in general they lack effectiveness; the liberal, equal treatment values that underpin the legislation discourage positive action, and employers are rarely obliged to undertake initiatives that promote equality, even if they are found to be operating discriminatory practices. During the 2000s, Labour extended the scope of anti-discrimination legislation and encouraged organizations to adopt family-friendly policies and work–life balance arrangements for their staff, although it was extremely reluctant to compel businesses to improve their practices. However, notwithstanding its concern with promoting improved work–life balance and greater social mobility, many of the measures instituted since 2010 by the coalition government have adverse consequences for equality and diversity in work and employment relations.

 ## Assignment and discussion questions

1. Why have governments prioritized improvements in social mobility? In your view, how could improved social mobility best be achieved?

2. Critically assess the main strengths and weaknesses of the legal framework relating to discrimination and equality at work.

3. To what extent do organizations' equal opportunities policies help to combat disadvantage and inequality in work and employment relations?

4. Why might employers be more sympathetic to the managing diversity agenda than to the liberal equal opportunities approach?

5. Critically assess the main ways in which the trade unions have responded to the particular problems of disadvantaged groups in work and employment relations.

 Visit the Online Resource Centre that accompanies this book to develop your understanding of this chapter, and keep up to date with the latest developments in this area.
www.oxfordtextbooks.co.uk/orc/williams3e/

 ## Chapter case study: Equal pay in local government—unions v lawyers

Since the early 2000s many current and former female employees in local government and the health service have instigated legal action against public sector employers on the grounds of equal pay. In April 2010 some 5,000 mainly female Birmingham City Council staff won an employment tribunal claim over equal pay. Workers in female-dominated jobs, such as cleaners, cooks, and care assistants, had been excluded from bonus payments given to workers in jobs like refuse collection which are filled largely by men. Some took legal action in pursuit of compensation for the lost earnings that resulted. The Council appealed the case up to the Supreme Court, but in October 2012 it upheld the claims of 174 of the women concerned, ruling that they were entitled to pursue compensation. The cost to Birmingham City Council of settling all of the claims could eventually amount to some £750m.

In local government, the 1997 single status agreement was designed to harmonize pay and conditions and secure equality, putting an end to pay structures which historically had discriminated against women. However, the process of implementation was rather slow. Cash-strapped councils often found it difficult to fund the changes to pay and conditions required by the agreement. A further difficulty concerned the need to tackle long-standing pay anomalies between different groups of workers. For example, those employed in jobs mainly filled by men (e.g. refuse collection) often enjoyed access to trade union-negotiated bonus payments, whereas those in female-dominated occupations (e.g. school catering staff) did not. Given the potentially high cost to employers of compensating staff for lost earnings as a result of discriminatory pay and grading schemes, agreements negotiated with the trade unions over the implementation of the single status agreement generally did not incorporate compensation for any discrimination arising out of the previous arrangements. However, seeing an opportunity, some law firms, Newcastle-based Stefan Cross Solicitors being the most prominent, encouraged women workers to instigate legal action against local authorities and other public sector employers for compensation arising out of the lost earnings on a no win, no fee basis. This meant that while claimants did not have to pay the costs of any legal fees up front, a sizeable portion of any compensation arising from a successful claim would be due to their lawyers.

Lawyers like Stefan Cross contend that unions who negotiate settlements with employers which, while improving the pay of women workers, do not fully compensate them for any lost earnings arising out of the operation of discriminatory pay systems in the past, are not effectively representing their members' interests. His law firm represented a group of Middlesbrough workers which successfully litigated against the GMB trade union on the grounds that it had made it insufficiently clear to its members that a deal negotiated with the employer, which it advised them to accept, was overly favourable to workers in male-dominated jobs and offered less than might have been achieved through litigation. Unions like the GMB are alleged to have been too concerned with protecting the interests of male members of the union, and insufficiently vigorous in securing gender equality.

However, the unions resent accusations that they have been deficient at representing their members. They argue that whereas the only concern of lawyers is with maximizing the financial compensation due to their individual clients, unions have broader concerns, such as the implications of any settlement for public sector employers. The activities of no win, no fee lawyers undermine union efforts to secure a fair deal for all workers through collective bargaining, and may jeopardize public services and jobs as employers struggle to find the money to fund compensation payments. Unions resent the activities of lawyers like Stefan Cross, who in 2010 reportedly boasted about changing his car from a Porsche to a Ferrari, claiming that they have become wealthy as a result of taking a sizeable cut of the financial compensation due to low-paid public sector workers. Trade unions represent their members for free. These equal pay claims highlight one of the difficulties arising out of the increasing influence of the law over work and employment relations, namely the encouragement given to workers, aided and abetted by rapacious lawyers, to pursue individual redress through litigation without necessarily any concern for the consequences. While not opposed to the use of litigation as a last resort—indeed the Unison trade union supported workers in Birmingham—unions consider collective bargaining to be a fairer and more sustainable means of promoting gender pay equality in public sector organizations.

Question

What are the main strengths and weaknesses of litigation, compared with collective bargaining, as a means of delivering greater gender pay equality in public sector organizations?

Part 3

Key issues in contemporary employment relations

5 Managing employment relations

◎ Chapter objectives

The main objectives of this chapter are to:

- examine how the management role in employment relations developed in a context of growing unionization;
- examine how employers have challenged the role and influence of trade unions;
- consider the implications of the statutory procedure for union recognition;
- explore the extent to which the rise of sophisticated human resource management has transformed the management of employment relations; and
- consider the inherent tensions evident in the management of employment relations.

5.1 Introduction

This chapter is concerned with developments in the management of employment relations. Union decline means that there is now a much more sustained 'focus on management as the prime mover in industrial relations, both in terms of organizational practice and in the amount of academic research' (Marchington and Harrison 1991: 286). Rather than having to react to and accommodate trade unionism, managers would appear to enjoy an environment in which they are much better able to innovate in respect of employment relations. This chapter starts by tracing the historical development of employment relations management, and the important concern with managing with trade unions that dominated the managerial agenda before the 1980s. Section 5.3 focuses on the nature, scope, and dimensions of the managerial challenge to trade unionism that has dominated employment relations since the 1980s, before considering the implications of legislation which compels employers to recognize a union where this is desired by a majority of the workforce. Union decline was, in part, influenced by the development of new techniques for managing employment relations associated with the development of human resource management (HRM). Section 5.4 examines the main features of a sophisticated HRM approach to managing employment relations, and interprets its significance. This is followed, in Section 5.5, by an assessment of the main challenges and tensions inherent in managing work and employment relationships.

Introductory case study: Engaging employees at McDonalds

One of the main themes of this chapter concerns the extent to which the management of employment relations has changed, away from a focus on working with trade unions and managing the implications of unionization, towards a more contemporary focus on improving business performance by engaging employees and securing their commitment to the organization without the need for trade unions. The fast-food chain McDonalds is well known for its non-union status; it is often portrayed as a low-wage employer, whose employment practices are based on securing employee compliance with organizational standards through rigorous control systems, resulting in low discretion. However, David Fairhurst, a senior McDonalds executive in the UK, asserts that this stereotype is no longer appropriate. Rather, the need to improve customer service, and thus deliver better performance, has made jobs in the fast-food company more rewarding, increasing the commitment of employees. Since 2005, he claims, 'we have focused our efforts on engaging our people to deliver an outstanding experience for our customers by creating an outstanding employment experience for them' (Fairhurst 2008: 326). Critics of McDonalds, however, point out that many jobs in the fast-food company still attract low rates of pay, at or just above the minimum wage, casting doubt on its claim that employees are valued assets. In this chapter we question how far a concern with engaging employees and securing their organizational commitment, linked to the development of sophisticated human resource management (HRM), has come to dominate approaches to managing employment relations.

5.2 Managing with trade unions

As Chapter 1 showed, a belief in managerial prerogative, or the right to manage, underpins management behaviour in employment relations. Historically, although managements vigorously attempted to exclude trade unions from their workplaces, in practice the strength of union organization in many areas of the economy obliged them to try to sustain their prerogative by accommodating workers' demands. During the twentieth century, employers often recognized unions for collective bargaining so as to mitigate disruption, and foster order and stability (Hyman 1975). This was, however, in large part a reaction to the pressure coming from workers themselves to organize unions (Clegg, Fox, and Thompson 1964). Attempts to exclude unions caused too much disruption, given the collective power that workers were able to wield. Thus employers took a pragmatic approach, recognizing unions, but doing so in a way that disturbed managerial prerogatives as little as possible (Gospel 1992).

During the 1960s and 1970s, in a context of growing union power, companies that had hitherto not recognized a union found it advantageous to do so in order to quell workplace militancy. For example, management in the biscuit works studied by Scott (1994) were aware of a growing union presence in the factory and chose to accommodate it by means of a centralized negotiating relationship with full-time union officers, from which workplace union activists were distanced. The company embraced collective bargaining with a recognized union, but did so in a way that upheld managerial rights and secured workplace order. Although, for pragmatic reasons, employers may have chosen to recognize unions, by no means does this mean that they accepted their legitimacy, and indeed they made every effort to restrict union influence over employment relations in the workplace. For much of the twentieth century, many employers chose to try to exclude unions from their workplaces by dealing with them through employers' associations (see Chapter 1). However, the growth of workplace bargaining prompted employers to look for more sophisticated ways of managing employment relations in unionized environments.

5.2.1 Managerial innovation in employment relations: the pluralist agenda

Attempts to bargain with unions by means of employers' associations contributed to the widespread neglect of employment relations management in many firms, or what Hyman (2003) refers to as the 'tradition of unscientific management'. The historical weakness of the personnel management function in Britain has long been acknowledged (e.g. Flanders 1975). Writers point to the history of unsophisticated managerial control systems, the lack of complex managerial hierarchies in firms, and the slow, and indeed relatively late, diffusion of scientific management techniques (Tolliday and Zeitlin 1991; Gospel 1992). Employers exhibited a preference for ad hoc, informal, and unsophisticated ways of managing their workforces, such as a reliance on simple payment by results techniques.

What factors contributed to managerial neglect of employment relations matters? Clearly the externalization of relations with trade unions was one influence. Three other elements were also important: first, the process of industrialization in Britain, which started earlier than in other competitor economies, delayed the emergence of the modern corporate firm; second, diverse and fluctuating product markets and an ample labour supply were obstacles to modernization; and third, in some industries a pre-industrial craft ethos prevailed, in which workers enjoyed a degree of control over the content of their jobs (Gospel 1992).

Employers therefore found it increasingly hard to maintain managerial prerogatives in the workplace. During the 1940s and 1950s, there was a marked growth in the incidence of workplace bargaining in Britain, particularly in the engineering sector (Gospel 1992). Not only did this reflect the increasing difficulty employers had in upholding managerial rights in the workplace, but the weakness of agreements reached by means of multi-employer bargaining and a tight labour market created by full employment—which enhanced workers' bargaining power—were also contributory factors (Terry 1983). The reluctance of senior managers to take control over their own employment relations during this period in a resolute and strategic way and to come to terms with, and accommodate the growth of, workplace unionism, rather than see it as a threat to be nullified, was seen by the pluralists as a major error, contributing to industrial disputes and workplace disorder (Flanders 1964, 1975).

They were encouraged to secure greater control over employment relations in the workplace by recognizing, formally, the legitimacy of shop-floor unionism rather than by trying to extinguish it, something that would only cause greater disruption. Such a prescription characterized the findings and recommendations of the 1965–8 Royal Commission on Trade Unions and Employers' Associations, established under the chairmanship of Lord Donovan. It was set up to examine the system of employment relations and to make proposals for its reform, given the detrimental effect aspects of it were held to have on economic performance, in particular 'wage drift'—inflationary increases in earnings caused by workplace bargaining—and the associated high level of labour conflict. Influenced by prominent pluralist writers such as Allan Flanders, Donovan identified managerial weakness as a prime source of Britain's employment relations problems and strongly recommended that, in order to rectify them, managers should secure greater control over workplace employment relations (Royal Commission 1968).

During the 1960s and 1970s, in a context of growing union militancy, managers adopted a notably more interventionist approach in respect of workplace employment relations anyway, in order to contain and accommodate trade union power and thus exercise greater control. Employers were increasingly the 'main instigators in reshaping the system of industrial relations in Britain' (Gospel 1992: 140). Perhaps the most significant managerial intervention during this period was the rise of 'productivity bargaining', heralded as a major managerial initiative in the reform of employment relations. The theory and practice of productivity bargaining were popularized by Allan Flanders's celebrated study of the negotiation of a path-breaking collective agreement, known as the 'Blue Book', at Esso's Fawley oil refinery near Southampton during the early 1960s (Flanders 1964).

What were the features of the Blue Book deal struck between management and unions at Fawley? Its major targets were the perceived 'under-utilization' of labour and excessive overtime working. The high level of overtime allowed workers to supplement low basic wages with premium payments for doing the extra work. This not only contributed to wage drift, since earnings became increasingly distant from formally negotiated pay rates, but it also encouraged workplace bargaining over overtime rates and allocation. Furthermore, the prospect of supplementing earnings through opportunities for overtime was detrimental to productivity since it gave workers an incentive to reduce their effort during their normal working time in the hope that this would make overtime necessary. The productivity agreement struck at Fawley, then, saw management 'buy out' overtime and other inefficient practices in return for higher basic earnings and a fixed working week. It was envisaged that this approach would encourage order and stability as well as generating productivity improvements (Flanders 1964).

Over and above the features of the agreement itself, the deal struck at Fawley was held to be significant in two important respects. First, it was an example of managerial innovation in employment relations, standing out from the hitherto ad hoc, unsophisticated, and reactive approach to employment relations exhibited in most British firms (Flanders 1964). Second, the agreement appeared to possess a 'higher order function', being the 'very embodiment of pluralist industrial relations' (Ahlstrand 1990: 61, 60). It represented an attempt by management to secure control of the workplace through cooperative means, by explicitly recognizing the legitimacy of the unions as the representatives of the workforce, rather than trying to marginalize or exclude them (Flanders 1964).

The Fawley experiment, then, appeared not only to be beneficial for the employer, in that it led to improved economic performance, but it also seemed to secure, and legitimize, the interests of employees through the establishment of a cooperative relationship with the unions. Ensuing productivity gains, though, were limited and largely the result of staffing cuts rather than the more efficient utilization of labour, and overtime working remained commonplace. Managers, moreover, never eschewed their unitary beliefs; indeed, they used productivity agreements to undermine union power in the workplace, part of a long-term strategy to manage without unions altogether (Ahlstrand 1990).

During the late 1960s and early 1970s, there was a marked increase in the popularity of productivity agreements, though they varied considerably in their scope, detail, and outcomes. Perhaps their most important function, however, was to signal the growth of a more resolute and sophisticated approach to the management of employment relations in British firms (Clegg 1979), contributing to the declining incidence of multi-employer bargaining through employers' associations. Moreover, workplace trade unionism, particularly the role of shop stewards (see Chapter 6), became increasingly formalized as managers encouraged, or 'sponsored', them in an attempt to accommodate union power (Terry 1983). In the Cadbury's confectionery plant at Bourneville, for example, managers acceded to the operation of a closed shop arrangement (see Historical perspective 5.1) as part of an attempt to contain and accommodate the growing influence of the shop stewards, and to direct it in a 'responsible and realistic' direction (Smith, Child, and Rowlinson 1990: 195).

Historical perspective 5.1:   Managing with the closed shop

Union membership agreements, or 'closed shops' as they are more popularly known, were a major feature of British employment relations for many years. Under closed shop arrangements, union membership was a condition of employment. The 'pre-entry' closed shop restricted particular jobs to members of a specific union. The more commonplace 'post-entry' closed shop made union membership mandatory when a worker commenced employment. While union pressure was an important factor stimulating the growth of closed shop arrangements (McCarthy 1964), they became increasingly widespread in British industry during the 1970s, largely due to management acquiescence (Dunn and Gennard 1984; Marchington and Parker 1990; Gospel 1992). This was part of the broader concern of managers to accommodate and contain workplace trade unionism, to push it in a moderate and cooperative direction.

By 1980, some 5 million workers may have been covered by closed shop arrangements, mostly of the post-entry type (Millward et al. 1992). Margaret Thatcher's Conservative governments, however, made reform of the closed shop a key feature of their legislative assault on the trade unions until, with the enactment of the 1990 Employment Act, the operation of a closed shop was effectively made unlawful altogether. Perhaps a more influential factor contributing to the decline of the closed shop—by 1990 only about half a million workers were still covered by such an arrangement (Millward et al. 1992)—was the decline of employment in those industries, such as printing for example, where it was prominent.

From this overview of how employment relations was managed before the 1980s, it should be clear that while employers accepted trade unionism, this reflected a pragmatic response to circumstances, notably union power, rather than a genuine belief in the virtues of a pluralist approach. If managers had to deal with trade unions, they tried to do so in such a way that it contained workplace militancy. Managers may have been obliged to respond constructively to the implications of growing union power, but their fundamentally unitary values generally remained constant.

Section summary and further reading

- Employers have long played a leading role in employment relations by initiating union recognition, albeit under pressure from workers for union representation. In forming employers' associations and instituting multi-employer bargaining arrangements, employers sought to maintain managerial prerogative in the workplace by externalizing their relationship with trade unions.

- Among other things, this process of externalization contributed to a tradition of 'unscientific management', and the weakness of managerial structures and systems in respect of employment relations. The growth of workplace bargaining and its effects encouraged firms to develop a more

(continued...)

sophisticated approach to managing employment relations in the workplace, accommodating trade union power rather than attempting to repulse it.

- The reform of employment relations in the 1960s and 1970s, the conclusion of productivity agreements for example, while predominantly management-led, was encouraged by the need to accommodate growing union power. There was no general shift in managerial philosophy away from unitary values, rather a pragmatic acceptance of pluralist approaches as the most effective means of ensuring stability in employment relations.

Gospel (1992) is the most authoritative study of the historical development of the management of employment relations. McIvor (1996) assesses the growth and development of employers' associations. Allan Flanders's classic 1964 account of the Fawley experiment, *The Fawley Productivity Agreements* (Flanders 1964), is seminal. It should be read in conjunction with Ahlstrand (1990).

5.3 Challenging unions

Since the 1980s, the changes in the economic and political environment discussed in Chapters 2 and 3 have made it easier for employers to challenge the influence of trade unions, compounding the fundamentally unitary preferences of managers and the frequently held view that a union presence is undesirable because it would restrict managerial prerogative, raise labour costs, and hinder organizational flexibility (Poole and Mansfield 1993; Cullinane and Dundon 2012). Managers no longer find it necessary reach pragmatic accommodations with the unions in order to contain their power. Even where they had hitherto encouraged a union presence, such as in the Cadbury's Bourneville plant for example, managers attempted to undermine, and even extinguish, a formal union presence (Smith, Child, and Rowlinson 1990). In this part of the chapter, the concern is with the ways in which employers have sought to challenge trade unionism, and with the implications of the statutory union recognition procedure introduced in 2000.

5.3.1 Union exclusion

Perhaps the most obvious measure of union exclusion in Britain is the substantial fall in the incidence of union recognition which occurred between the 1980s and 2000s, particularly in the private sector (Blanchflower and Bryson 2009; Simms and Charlwood 2010). As can be seen from Tables 5.1 and 5.2, union recognition levels in the public sector have generally held

Table 5.1 Percentage of workplaces with a recognized union, 1980–98

	All workplaces	Private manufacturing	Private services	Public sector
1980	64	65	41	94
1984	66	56	44	99
1990	53	44	36	87
1998	41	29	23	87

Workplaces with twenty-five or more employees

Sources: Millward, Bryson, and Forth (2000: 96), Kersley et al. (2006: 120)

Table 5.2 Percentage of workplaces with a recognized union, 2004–11

	All workplaces	Private manufacturing	Private services	Public sector
2004	24	13	14	89
2011	21	11	11	19

Workplaces with five or more employees

Source: van Wanrooy et al. (2013: 14)

up rather well; the most significant falls have occurred in the private sector, where by 2011 unions were recognized for collective bargaining purposes in only around a tenth of workplaces with more than five employees (van Wanrooy et al. 2013).

The main reason for the decline in the level of union recognition is that private sector employers have been increasingly 'turning their back on trade unions' (Blanchflower and Bryson 2009: 56). For most of the twentieth century, an employer's decision to recognize a union, or not to recognize one, was a voluntary matter—influenced, of course, by the organizing efforts of workers and unions. In general, employers were never legally obliged to deal with a union. In theory, they could withdraw recognition from, or 'derecognize', trade unions as they saw fit. This was certainly one reason for the decline in the level of union recognition between the 1980s and the 2000s. One of the best-known examples concerns the newspaper industry and the withdrawal of union recognition by Rupert Murdoch's News International, owner of *The Times*, *The Sunday Times*, and *The Sun* titles, prompting a bitter industrial dispute in 1986–7 (Littleton 1992).

During the 1990s, the trend of union derecognition accelerated, and was even extended to the Fawley oil refinery, which thirty years previously had been celebrated as the epitome of pluralist employment relations (Smith and Morton 1994; Claydon 1996). A further notable example of union derecognition occurred in 2005 when, following its purchase by two private equity funds, the vehicle rescue firm the AA derecognized the GMB union (Clark 2010). Yet complete derecognition is a relatively rare occurrence; where it does happen it is largely an opportunistic response by managers to declining union membership and organization. In 2012, for example, Virgin Media cited the purported lack of support for trade union representation among its employees to justify derecognition, on rather dubious grounds, prompting union claims that the company was 'stealing' union recognition.

Union derecognition by itself insufficiently accounts for the overall decline in union recognition in Britain between the 1980s and 2000s. We also need to acknowledge the growing importance of non-recognition of unions by employers in new workplaces (Machin 2000; Blanchflower and Bryson 2009). Newly established workplaces operating in growing sectors of the economy, such as high-tech industries, are unlikely to recognize unions in the first place.

While not as prominent as the headline fall in union recognition, even where unions do retain a formal workplace presence employers have become keener to challenge their role. In some circumstances this involves nakedly aggressive attempts to suppress trade unions, by victimizing union representatives for example (Gall 2010c). Employers have also tried to restrict the influence of unions over the regulation of employment relationships by reducing the scope of union recognition, limiting the number of matters which it covers (Blanchflower and Bryson 2009). New methods of direct communications between management and employees, such as team briefings for example, which are designed to encourage greater organizational loyalty and commitment and to foster among the workforce a sense of identification with their employer, have also been used to exclude trade unions and reduce their influence (see Section 5.4.2). Moreover, as Chapter 6 shows, so-called 'partnership agreements' between employers and unions exemplify the way in which employers may, for pragmatic reasons, uphold union recognition, but seek to shape the relationship in a manner that better suits their interests.

5.3.2 Statutory union recognition in Britain

Except for the 1970s, when statutory procedures existed for a time (see Beaumont 1981), until 2000 employers were never under a legal obligation to recognize a union. The third statutory recognition procedure was enacted by the 1999 Employment Relations Act, and came into effect in June 2000. It was the outcome of the 1997 Labour government's commitment to introducing a measure that would oblige employers to recognize a union where the majority of the workforce wanted it (DTI 1998). The Trades Union Congress (TUC) anticipated that the new statutory recognition procedure could produce as many as a million new trade union members. For further details of how the procedure operates see Figure 5.1 and Legislation and policy 5.2.

LEGISLATION AND POLICY 5.2: **The statutory union recognition procedure in Britain**

Under the procedure, if a union has a recognition claim for a particular group of workers dismissed by the employer it can make an application to a state body, the Central Arbitration Committee (CAC), which decides if the claim is a valid one for the purposes of the statutory procedure. It does not apply where fewer than twenty-one workers are employed. CAC must also determine whether there is sufficient support for unionization among the workforce: at least 10 per cent must be union members, with the likelihood that a majority of the workforce would vote in favour of union recognition in a ballot. If these tests are met, and no other union is recognized for the group of workers in question, then CAC can mandate union recognition if 50 per cent or more of the relevant workers are members of the union, or it can order a ballot of the workforce. To secure recognition, a union must win approval from a simple majority of those voting, as long as this constitutes a threshold of 40 per cent of the relevant workforce. For example, in a workforce of 100 people if 39 people vote in favour of union recognition, and none vote against, then recognition would not be awarded because the 40 per cent threshold would not have been met. See Figure 5.1 for a diagrammatic representation. A code of practice (DTI 2005) governs matters like union access to the workforce in the run-up to a recognition ballot. The Employment Relations Act (2004) made some changes to how the statutory union recognition procedure operates. In particular, employers and unions are prohibited from engaging in 'unfair practices', namely the use of incentives, threats, or some other kind of 'undue influence' to sway workers' votes.

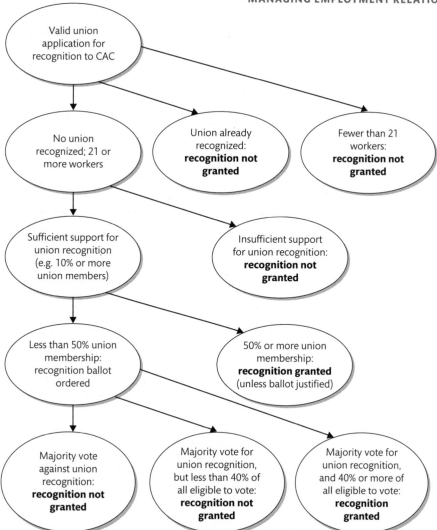

Figure 5.1 A simplified model of the statutory union recognition procedure

The introduction of the new statutory recognition procedure would, at first glance, appear to be a distinctly union-friendly act; the principle underlying the policy is that union recognition should be granted where the majority of the workforce votes in favour of it. However, the procedure was enacted in a way that was largely favourable to employers (Wood and Goddard 1999; Gall 2012a). For example, it does not apply where there are fewer than twenty-one employees. Even if an employer is obliged to recognize a union by means of the statutory route, the scope of bargaining is limited to pay, hours, and holidays. Moreover, there are no guaranteed outcomes since the right to recognition is limited to simply the 'right to invoke a procedure' (Brown et al. 2001: 183; Gall 2012a). Some have criticized the limited scope of the statutory recognition procedure, particularly its rather narrow conception of what constitutes legitimate union representation, based on demonstrating majority support in a workplace ballot (e.g. Bogg 2012).

As mentioned in Legislation and policy 5.2, the principle of majority support for union recognition is qualified by the need for a union to win the support of at least 40 per cent of the relevant workforce, including non-voters. The government's aim was that the existence of the statutory procedure would encourage employers and unions to reach their own voluntary recognition agreement (Oxenbridge et al. 2003; Gall 2010b; Brodtkorb 2012). The statutory procedure should prevail only if they were unable to reach a deal themselves. Gall (2012a: 412) characterizes this approach as 'legally induced voluntarism' in the sense that the 'explicit intention of its creators was to use the law to thereby allow unions to *try* to effect change in behaviour of employers in the voluntary arena'.

What, then, have been the effects of the statutory union recognition procedure since it came into existence in 2000? The first thing to appreciate is that the upsurge of new union recognition agreements dates from the mid-1990s, before the statutory procedure took effect (see Table 5.3). Knowing that legislation could soon compel them to recognize a union, some employers struck voluntary deals with trade unions beforehand. Table 5.3 shows the number of new recognition deals identified between 1995 and 2010. It indicates that the incidence of new agreements peaked in the early 2000s, soon after the statutory procedure was introduced (Gall 2012a).

The overwhelming majority of new recognition agreements since 2000 have been voluntary arrangements. By April 2013, the statutory recognition procedure had directly resulted in just 249 new agreements, 115 of them without a ballot, from a total of 839 applications by unions. Among the companies to have signed recognition deals with trade unions as a direct result of the procedure are: Kwik Fit, the car repairer; Global Casinos; Xansa, the business services firm; and Honda, the car manufacturer. Yet in the period 2000–10 there were nearly

Table 5.3 New cases of union recognition, 1995–2010

Year	Number of new recognition deals
1995	88
1996	86
1997	109
1998	131
1999	366
2000	554
2001	702
2002	394
2003	265
2004	241
2005	158
2006	152
2007	149
2008	141
2009	73
2010	59
Total	3,668

Source: Gall (2012a)

3,000 new recognition agreements reported overall, covering more than three-quarters of a million workers (Gall 2012a). Clearly, the main effect of the statutory procedure has been to stimulate voluntary union recognition by employers (Wood, Moore, and Ewing 2003), as its designers intended. The preference for voluntary agreements demonstrates that in some cases unions have been successful in putting pressure on employers to concede recognition without needing to invoke the statutory procedure, though its existence is clearly an influence.

As can be seen from Table 5.3, since 2001 the number of new recognition agreements has declined, a trend which accelerated as the 2000s progressed. The number of applications for recognition submitted to CAC also fell; for example, just twenty-eight were made in 2010–11. Unions initially focused on firms which they knew would be relatively easy targets for recognition claims, those with strong union support among the workforce. As the years went on, though, these firms were picked off, meaning that the unions have increasingly had to operate on 'harder terrain' (Gall 2007). They have found it difficult to make contact with workers in non-union workplaces in the private services sector, where employers are often hostile to unionization (Gall 2010b). Moreover, the economic recession also seems to have contributed to the diminishing trend of new recognition agreements; cost pressures make employers more reluctant to contemplate recognizing a union (Brodtkorb 2012). Recognition successes for unions have largely come about in sectors of the economy where they are already strong, particularly manufacturing industry (Blanden, Machin, and Van Reenan 2006). There is little sign that unions have been able to expand their influence by securing recognition agreements in key parts of the 'new economy', like the telecommunications and retail sectors (Gall 2007).

5.3.3 Employers' responses to union recognition claims

The large extent to which some employers will go to resist unionization has impeded attempts by unions to secure recognition agreements (Heery and Simms 2011). Growing employer opposition to union recognition seems to have contributed to the declining number of new recognition agreements (Gall 2007, 2012a). See Contesting employment relations 5.3 for the determination of Kettle Chips to avoid union recognition.

 Contesting employment relations 5.3: Resisting union recognition at Kettle Chips

Until 2010 Kettle Chips was owned by the private equity firm Lion Capital. Now part of the US-based Diamond Foods, it makes upmarket snacks and crisps at its factory in Norwich. In 2007 the Transport and General Workers' Union (TGWU)—now part of the Unite trade union—submitted a claim under the statutory union recognition procedure. Following an acrimonious battle between the union and employer, in October 2007 the workforce voted 206: 93 against union recognition. The firm claimed that its staff were relatively well paid and enjoyed good benefits, including twenty-five days' holiday and comprehensive sick pay. Controversially, though, Kettle Chips hired the subsidiary of a prominent US union-busting firm, the Burke Group, to dissuade workers in the factory from voting for union recognition. Unite also claimed that managers had put undue influence on workers not to support unionization; one of its officials asserted that Kettle Chips had conducted a 'long and poisonous campaign' against the union. Nevertheless, because of a lack of evidence, CAC did not uphold Unite's complaint that Kettle Chips had engaged in 'unfair' practices through its anti-union threats and insinuations.

While it is difficult to detect a common, dominant pattern (Heery and Simms 2010), there are three broad ways in which employers can try and resist union recognition claims. First, some have followed an aggressive strategy of 'union suppression', involving the use of anti-union consultants, the victimization of union activists, and other intimidatory tactics designed to forestall a union presence (e.g. Moore 2011). Heery and Simms (2010: 9) discovered 'plentiful examples of unlawful and unethical action by employers, a proportion of whom were ruthless in trying to squash attempts at unionisation'. There are cases where employers have attempted to influence the outcome of a recognition ballot by threatening to close or relocate the workplace if the vote was to go in favour of the union, claiming that union recognition would threaten the viability of the workplace, and thus put people's jobs in jeopardy (Gall 2003a). The satellite broadcaster, BSkyB, for example, allegedly hinted that if its call centre workforce supported union recognition this could undermine their competitiveness, particularly when set against the low costs of operating in India. Unsurprisingly, most workers voted against. Although it is unlawful to dismiss workers for activities relating to union recognition, some employers have tried to resist unionization by firing union activists, illustrating their preparedness to 'invest whatever is necessary to defeat unions' (Moore 2004: 16). Employers in the United States often pursue a markedly aggressive anti-union policy in order to protect managerial prerogatives (see International perspective 5.4).

 International perspective 5.4: Anti-unionism in the United States

Visceral hostility towards trade unionism and collective bargaining has been a long-standing feature of employment relations in the United States. Attempts by unions to gain recognition for collective bargaining purposes have generally been met by robust employer opposition, something that seems to have increased since the 1970s (L. Richards 2008). Companies wanting to remain union-free frequently employ specialist anti-union consultants to advise on ways of resisting unionization efforts (Logan 2006). In *Fast Food Nation*, Eric Schlosser details some of the methods used by McDonalds to remain free of the unions. It uses, for example, managerial 'flying squads' comprising experienced senior managers, who descend on a restaurant to encourage the workforce to desist from unionization, by means of threats if other approaches fail to do the trick, as soon as a hint of union activity emerges (Schlosser 2002). In his book on work and employment relations in the US, *The Big Squeeze*, Steven Greenhouse recounts similar stories of workers across a range of firms being fired, in violation of federal law, for supporting unionization efforts. For example, following years of struggle to resist union recognition, numerous legal challenges, and the use of specialist anti-union consultants, the EnerSys company eventually frustrated the stated wish of the majority of the workforce in its South Carolina battery factory for union recognition by closing it down (Greenhouse 2008).

Second, more commonly employers make use of a 'substitutionist' approach to forestall unionization: providing employees with alternative, in-house methods of representation such as a company council, or by using rewards, like pay rises, to demonstrate that union recognition is unnecessary (Gall and McKay 2001). Companies like The Body Shop and Pizza Express have developed sophisticated employee involvement and communications arrangements in an attempt to demonstrate to their staff that union representation is unnecessary. While this may be a more sophisticated way of resisting recognition than the union suppression approach, it should not in any way be portrayed as the 'benign face of anti-unionism';

rather, substitution is 'simply one tactic among others that employers use to remain union free' (Heery and Simms 2010: 10). The third way in which employers try to resist unionization is by refusing to engage meaningfully with the union even after recognition has been granted. This was the case in a marketing company's call centre. In the two years following the recognition agreement, the employer refused to bargain seriously with the trade union. As a result the workforce began to question the effectiveness of union representation, and support for it dwindled (Kelly and Badigannavar 2004).

Any overall assessment of the effectiveness of the statutory recognition procedure and its contribution to extending unionization must acknowledge the large amount of employer resistance it has generated. Given such opposition to trade unionism, and the way in which the relevant legislation was designed not to antagonize employers, the direct impact of the statutory union recognition procedure on its own has been relatively limited. Nevertheless, indirectly it seems to have stimulated a substantial upsurge in voluntary recognition activity during the 2000s (Gall 2012a). As a result, some consider the procedure to have been a modest success, a 'work in progress' which can be built on to encourage a stronger union presence in the economy (Brodtkorb 2012: 86). Others, though, offer a more pessimistic prognosis, seeing the declining number of new recognition agreements in general, and CAC applications in particular, as evidence of the much diminished relevance of the statutory recognition procedure. As one commentator puts it, the 'statutory recognition procedure is dying—not with a bang, but with a whimper' (Bogg 2012: 410) as the number of new agreements falls away, with little prospect of any turnaround in the near future (Gall 2012a).

A major challenge for the unions, and one that militates against any easy turnaround in their fortunes, concerns the growing proportion of non-union workplaces in the economy, linked to changes in the composition of employment. New recognition agreements notwithstanding, the overall level of union recognition continued to decline during the 2000s (Blanchflower and Bryson 2009). By 2011, unions were recognized in little more than one in ten private sector workplaces (van Wanrooy et al. 2013). The number of new recognition deals has been outweighed by the growing number of new firms and workplaces that do not recognize a trade union in the first place. By itself, the statutory recognition procedure holds out little prospect of reversing the process of union exclusion, given the opposition of employers and the weaknesses in the procedure itself (Gall 2012a).

Section summary and further reading

- The process of union exclusion is best illustrated by the decline in the level of union recognition by employers. Although some employers have derecognized trade unions, the fall in the prevalence of union recognition mainly reflects the growth of non-union workplaces, with newly established sites operating in growing sectors of the economy being unlikely to recognize unions in the first place.

- A statutory union recognition procedure was introduced in 2000. An employer is obliged to recognize a union for collective bargaining purposes where the majority of the workforce wants it. The procedure, however, was implemented so as not to antagonize employers, and its direct impact has therefore been limited.

- There was a marked increase in union recognition activity during the early 2000s, most of it on a voluntary basis, as anticipated by the designers of the statutory procedure. As the decade progressed, however, there was a notable fall in the number of new recognition agreements,

(continued...)

with employer resistance being a major impediment. Moreover, the growing proportion of new non-union workplaces means that the overall level of union recognition in the private sector has continued to decline.

For data on union recognition trends, see Blanchflower and Bryson (2009). The best overview of union derecognition in the 1980s and 1990s is Claydon (1996). For the implications of the statutory union recognition procedure see Gall (2007) or Gall (2012a). Go to the CAC website—http://www.cac.gov.uk—for its annual report (e.g. CAC 2012), and also for details of specific cases under the statutory procedure. Moore (2004) is a study of employers' resistance to recognition claims; there are also good insights in Heery and Simms (2010).

5.4 Sophisticated human resource management and employment relations

Given the diminution of union recognition between the 1980s and 2000s, to what extent have managements been able to develop new, more sophisticated techniques for managing employment relations? The terms 'personnel management' and 'personnel manager' have come to be replaced by 'human resource management' (HRM) and 'human resource manager' in organizational vocabularies. There is an assumption that the rise of a sophisticated HRM approach is associated with a change in the focus of managing employment relations, away from a concern with securing employee compliance with organizational rules and accommodating the potential for conflict in the employment relationship, towards a much greater emphasis on securing employees' engagement, cooperation, and commitment to the organization. This section considers the nature of sophisticated HRM as a managerial approach, accounts for its growing importance, and critically assesses whether or not it has transformed the management of employment relations by raising organizational commitment and delivering better business performance.

5.4.1 Sophisticated HRM and the management of employment relations

An initial obstacle to be overcome when discussing the concept of HRM concerns its tendency to be used in different ways. On the one hand, 'HRM' is sometimes used as an umbrella label for managing people in organizations, being interchangeable with the term 'personnel management'. On the other hand, a second way of interpreting HRM, and the one preferred here, is to view it as a particular approach to managing the workforce, based on engaging and involving employees, winning their commitment to the organization, and thus driving improvements in business performance. The term 'sophisticated HRM' is used here to refer to this second, narrower conceptualization, distinguishing it from the broader approach.

Whereas in the past the job of managing employment relations was dominated by the issues that arose from having to deal with unions, the focus now is said to be on using effective people management skills to build relationships with and engage employees. Thus the principal concern of those responsible for managing employment relations in organizations is with developing and sustaining a climate in which employees feel valued, and are thus inspired to work more effectively and perform better, to the advantage of the employing organization (Emmott 2005).

There are a number of features of sophisticated HRM that supposedly make it distinctive. It puts a greater emphasis on the fit between employment policies and the overall business objectives of the organization. The management of employees is undertaken not for its own sake, but is carried out in a way that enables it to contribute to overall business goals. Linked to this there is a concern with managing people in a way that helps to enhance business performance, through interventions designed to involve employees and to increase their organizational commitment and engagement. In contrast to the traditional personnel management approach, which tended to rely on bureaucratic methods such as the provision of regular pay increments to enforce control in the workplace, under a sophisticated HRM regime the emphasis is placed more on techniques for managing organizational culture (Legge 2005). Employers are now engaging with hearts and minds and, some would say, souls as a means of harnessing employee commitment and gaining competitive advantage' (Bolton 2004: 47). This is done through the manipulation of symbols, values, and beliefs in the workplace, sometimes including efforts to encourage employees to identify with their employer's brand, and behave accordingly (Cushen and Thompson 2012).

Perhaps most importantly, a sophisticated HRM approach to managing employment relations is also associated with a preference for weak or non-existent trade unions. Sophisticated HRM is marked by a unitary ethos; it threatens unions by seeking to bind individual employees to the organization, and reduce the potential for conflict of interest. The onus is on the cooperative and harmonious nature of relations between managers and workers. Any conflict is either frictional, down to short-term, easily resolved problems, like personality differences for example, or is the product of external agitators, such as trade union activists. Sophisticated HRM, then, is not presented as an anti-union approach to managing employment relations, in the sense of seeking to drive unions out or actively resisting them. Rather, it is thought of as a 'substitute' for trade union organization. Unions are therefore simply unnecessary, and indeed their presence would disrupt the cooperative and harmonious relationship between managers and workers that has been so carefully fostered (McLoughlin and Gourlay 1994).

The management style of the multinational courier company studied by Dundon and (Rollinson 2004) would seem to embody such an approach. Characterized by an emphasis on developing a strong organizational culture, it was supported by the use of a range of sophisticated HRM interventions, including an extensive system of direct communication methods. The company's approach to managing its staff was perceived to be a crucial component of its business strategy—for example, by helping to enhance customer service. DeliveryCo did not recognize a trade union. But the company claimed that this was not because it was against unions; rather its 'pro-individual' stance, which meant that employees were treated well, made a union presence irrelevant. This seems to have been acknowledged by some of its staff. According to one of DeliveryCo's call centre agents: 'I don't think we need a union, you can always go to somebody. If you are not happy with your manager's decision then you can go to the big boss, and they don't mind you doing that' (Dundon and Rollinson 2004: 145).

Yet the sophisticated HRM approach is marked by an important ambiguity. On the one hand, it is often portrayed as a way of managing employees centred on involving and developing them. This 'soft' approach to sophisticated HRM treats employees as individuals; they are 'valued assets, a source of competitive advantage through their commitment, adaptability and quality' (Legge 2005: 105). Thus the emphasis is placed on supporting employee well-being, for example through sophisticated stress-management interventions and work–life balance policies (Bolton and Houlihan 2007). The result is a more engaged workforce, whose high morale and organizational commitment drives improvements in business performance.

On the other hand, with the 'hard' approach to HRM, employees are treated as a resource, a factor of production, to be used, and discarded if necessary, in a way that supports organizational objectives. Performance improvements come not from a more committed and engaged workforce, but from managers exercising greater control over, and intensifying, people's work activities. Whereas 'soft' HRM is driven by the aim of winning employee cooperation, 'hard' HRM is marked by a more coercive logic, akin to a compliance-based approach to managing the workforce. The growing use of arrangements to monitor and manage the performance of staff testifies to the control-based dimension of HRM. In call centres, for example, workers are often subjected to a highly regimented pattern of work, including having to meet very detailed targets governing call handling (e.g. number of calls per hour), with extensive monitoring of their activities by supervisors (Baldry et al. 2007).

While the 'soft' HRM model implies that business objectives can be more effectively realized if an emphasis is placed upon developing employees and fostering their commitment, in practice organizations often view their employees as costs, which have to be minimized. The language of 'soft' HRM is important since it helps to obscure the commodity status of employees. Often, 'even if the rhetoric of HRM is "soft", the reality is almost always "hard", with the interests of the organization prevailing over those of the individual' (Gratton et al. 1999: 57). Not only is the presence of 'soft' HRM somewhat rare, but it is also difficult to distinguish between 'soft' and 'hard' approaches in practice (Legge 2005). Sophisticated HRM practices sit easily alongside, and may even help to uphold, more traditional coercive management approaches (Bacon 1999). The promotion of workplace fun in some call centres, for example, is in part designed to obviate efforts by workers to contest aspects of their otherwise mundane and intensive jobs (Baldry et al. 2007).

Claims that the sophisticated HRM approach makes unions redundant, and that it is not anti-union, often fail to stand up to closer scrutiny. It has a political agenda, marked by the desirability of weakening the power of the unions and enhancing managerial prerogatives in the workplace. Its unitary ethos reflects the dominant political climate, one in which the trade unions, given the decline in their power and the hostile public policy environment, have largely been on the retreat (Legge 2005). Employers' claims to be 'non-union' rather than 'anti-union' should be treated with caution. Sophisticated HRM often operates as a benign façade obscuring the more authoritarian reality. In the steel company 'Ministeel', for example, the elaboration of HRM techniques was part of a policy designed to exclude the union from the workplace, and there were complaints from trade unionists of intimidation (Bacon 1999). The reluctance of employees to embrace trade unionism in such circumstances is often not a reflection of progressive management policies, but more the result of an inability to see what value union membership could offer them or, in some cases, an aversion to trade unions (McLoughlin and Gourlay 1994; Dundon and Rollinson 2004).

The supposed rise of a sophisticated HRM approach should not divert attention from the way in which organizations commonly make use of more efficiency-driven approaches to managing employment relations, often involving tighter control over performance standards—see Insight into practice 5.5 for the example of Ryanair. This is particularly evident in efforts by employers to take the matter of employee absence from work more seriously

Insight into practice 5.5:   Managing employment relations in Ryanair

The successful airline Ryanair takes an approach to managing employment relations that is consistent with, and indeed exemplifies, the low-cost model on which it has based its business growth. It demonstrates not only that the sophisticated HRM approach is by no means universal, but also that there are alternative methods of managing human resources which may be as effective, if not more so, in business terms. Cabin crew staff are employed on short-term contracts through agencies not the airline itself, with pay and other benefits, like holiday entitlement for example, that are low by industry standards. Workers enjoy few opportunities to be involved in, or to influence, decision-making processes. Rather, the degree of involvement is minimal. The airline takes a 'low-road' approach to managing employment relations based on its low-cost, efficiency-driven business model (O'Sullivan and Gunnigle 2009). Ryanair has become well known for its prominent anti-trade union stance. In situations where its workers have asked for union representation, the company has vigorously opposed it.

(Taylor et al. 2010). The economic recession seems to have encouraged the development of a more assertive approach to managing employment relations, arising from the need to remain competitive in challenging market conditions. Roche and Teague's (2012) extensive study of Irish firms, for example, shows that while efforts had been made to motivate and secure increased organizational commitment from staff, the priority attached to 'getting the business back in shape' meant that a much more robust approach was being taken with regard to matters of employee discipline and performance.

Based on such evidence, then, it would be unwise to claim that the development of sophisticated HRM has transformed employment relations. As shown in Section 5.5, competitive pressures and the need to enhance short-term financial performance preclude many organizations from investing in the kind of sophisticated, progressive management techniques necessary to foster greater organizational involvement and commitment. This is not to say that there has been no change in the way employment relations is managed, however. Perhaps the most notable development concerns the greater degree of control enjoyed by managers over elements of the employment relationship as a result of the decline of the trade unions and joint regulation (Brown and Marsden 2011); approaches to managing employment relations are often still dominated by the desirability of preserving managerial prerogative (Cullinane and Dundon 2012).

5.4.2 Managing employee voice and engagement

The question of employee voice is central to debates around sophisticated HRM and the desirability of managing employment relations in a way that stimulates greater organizational commitment and engagement from employees (Marchington 2008; Budd, Gollan, and Wilkinson 2010). Voice mechanisms are designed to provide employees with a say over workplace and organizational decisions (Dundon and Rollinson 2004; Wilkinson and Fay 2011). Voice was traditionally associated with trade union representation; it was expressed through the medium of collective bargaining, based on a pluralist understanding that employees and employers have different interests which need to be reconciled. Much of the growing interest in managing employee voice, however, reflects the more dominant unitary paradigm under which it operates as a central feature of efforts by employers to effect high-commitment management and raise levels of employee engagement (Wilkinson and Dundon 2010). In this context, then, voice can be seen to involve the 'transmission of ideas to managers in order to improve organizational performance' (Dundon et al. 2005: 312), in the absence of, or as a substitute for, trade unions.

There are three main types of arrangement for articulating employee voice present in organizations, two of which—direct communications and direct participation—are considered here; the third—indirect voice mechanisms, using some kind of representative structure, such as a consultation forum—features in the section on non-union employee representation in Chapter 6. Taking direct communication arrangements to start with, it is very evident that between the 1980s and 2000s there was a substantial increase in the use of employee voice techniques by employers, notably arrangements for communicating information between managers and staff (Kersley et al. 2006; McGovern et al. 2007; Willman, Gomez, and Bryson 2009). The 'cascading' of information downwards through the management hierarchy has become a commonplace feature of workplace life. Moreover, regular workforce meetings, newsletters, and team briefings have become increasingly popular methods for communicating information to employees.

There has also been a less pronounced increase in the incidence of arrangements that enable staff to communicate their views 'upwards' to managers. Such upward forms of communication encompass surveys of staff attitudes, the use of electronic mail to convey views and information to managers, and suggestion schemes, which enable employees to propose ways of improving organizational practice. While such practices seem to be linked to a more positive workplace climate, increasing employees' job satisfaction and trust in management (Willman, Gomez, and Bryson 2009), there is not much evidence that it improves their organizational commitment or work performance (Marchington 2001). In the past, opportunities for employees to communicate their ideas, concerns, and suggestions upwards to managers were rather limited (Scott 1994; Gratton et al. 1999); the flow of information was generally one-way, from managers to workers, with the latter accorded few opportunities to express their voice. Managers still often favour direct communications over other voice arrangements, though. They can be used simply to convey information to employees and to influence their behaviour, rather than as a mechanism for allowing employees to exercise genuine voice (Danford et al. 2005).

The second type of voice arrangement considered here concerns mechanisms that enable employees to participate directly in matters relating to the organization of their work and job tasks—in problem-solving or work improvement groups for example, or through teamworking arrangements (Gallie et al. 1998). It is often thought that giving employees greater influence and voice over the organization of work and changes in work processes is essential if companies are to secure the levels of commitment necessary for the production of high-quality goods and services, and thus thrive in increasingly competitive global markets (Boxall and Purcell 2011). Moreover, direct participation arrangements are among the major best practice HRM practices thought to deliver improvements in business performance (Marchington and Wilkinson 2005). Work improvement groups, for example, have been portrayed as a form of 'intelligent' workplace flexibility; participating employees 'must draw on their job experience and use it creatively to identify and solve problems' (White et al. 2004: 46).

Teamworking arrangements can also be viewed a manifestation of 'intelligent flexibility' (White et al. 2004). They potentially enable workers collectively to organize and manage part of the process of production or service delivery without the need for direct supervision by management. In so far as it holds out the promise of a significant increase in the degree to which employees are able to exercise an influence over the organization of their work, self-managed teams are often portrayed as the 'ultimate in direct participation' (Marchington and Wilkinson 2005: 406). However, managers sometimes use teamworking initiatives as a means of extending their control over labour. In his study of a plant manufacturing car components, Danford (1998) shows that the company introduced teamworking in order to undermine workers' influence over the production process. The new arrangements enabled management to institute flexibility on its terms rather than those of the workers, exercise greater control over the way in which work tasks were undertaken, and raise effort levels.

On the positive side, it is evident that during the 1990s there was a substantial increase in the prevalence of 'intelligent flexibility', evidenced by the growing incidence of problem-solving groups and teamworking arrangements for example (White et al. 2004). On a more pessimistic note, though, this growth appears to have stalled during the 2000s; for example, there has been little change in the prevalence of problem-solving groups (van Wanrooy et al. 2013). The use of 'intelligent flexibility' is still only evident in a minority of workplaces, contributing to a widespread perception among workers that they should have more influence over issues that affect them at work (McGovern et al. 2007).

Employee voice is often thought to be a key dimension of efforts to promote greater employee engagement, a topic which has attracted a growing amount of attention since the publication of the government-supported MacLeod Report in 2009 (MacLeod and Clarke 2009). As the introductory case study showed, even the fast-food chain McDonalds claims to be concerned with engaging its staff so that they can deliver improved customer service (Fairhurst 2008). What, then, is meant by 'employee engagement'? According to one interpretation, it can be defined as: 'being positively present during the performance of work by willingly contributing intellectual effort, experiencing positive emotions and meaningful connections to others' (CIPD 2010: 5). Workers can be engaged: intellectually, by thinking hard about their jobs and how they can be done better; affectively, by feeling positively about doing a good job; and socially, by actively taking opportunities to discuss work-related improvements with others at work (CIPD 2010).

For MacLeod and Clarke (2009), the key drivers of greater employee engagement are: the commitment and vision of senior organizational leaders; consistency of approach to managing people by front-line managers; provision of effective employee voice arrangements; and an integrity of approach, such that organizational leaders and managers subscribe to its values and principles, setting an appropriate example to others through their behaviours. In theory, greater engagement benefits both employers—through enhanced business performance and innovation—and employees—by creating a more positive and stimulating working environment (MacLeod and Clarke 2009). It is claimed that greater levels of employee engagement are the product of: the provision of meaningful work; the commitment of senior management in the organization; the support of front-line managers; and the presence of opportunities for workers to express voice over workplace and organizational decisions (CIPD 2010).

All this sounds highly unobjectionable; who could be against having a more engaged workforce? The problem is that studies consistently show that most employees are in fact not engaged at work—fewer than 40 per cent according to one study (CIPD 2012a). The main obstacle appears to be the presence of a pervasive 'climate of low trust' (Sanders 2012: 1), based largely on the widespread belief evident among employees that senior organizational managers are too distant, lack interest in staff issues, and are not sufficiently concerned with giving them effective voice (CIPD 2012a; Purcell 2012; Sanders 2012). For Coats (2010: 42), the low level of employee engagement is an indictment of the inadequacy and ineffectiveness of attempts by employers to develop sophisticated management techniques and voice arrangements, something he describes as a 'failure of enlightened HRM'. In late 2012, a government-backed initiative to revive the engagement agenda and tackle the problem of the 'engagement deficit' was launched with a great deal of publicity—the Engage for Success campaign. But it is doubtful that it will have much of an impact; for one thing, the recessionary economic situation means that engagement does not seem to be much of a priority for employers (Purcell 2012). Moreover, low levels of job discretion and the lack of genuine opportunities to exercise voice experienced by many employees also militate against progress towards better engagement. Perhaps most importantly, though, the nature of the financial and economic climate in general means that employers increasingly have to treat employees as costs to be minimized, rather than as assets to be valued, and are thus simply unable to deliver the kind of environment in which higher levels of engagement are possible (Thompson 2011).

5.4.3 Managing employment relations and performance

As mentioned in Section 5.4.1, one of the most distinctive aspects of a sophisticated HRM approach is the emphasis on managing employees in a way that enhances business performance. This contrasts with the traditional pluralist approach in which the priority was to manage with, and accommodate the effects of, trade unionism and collective bargaining. During the 1990s and 2000s there was a surge of interest in how the presence of so-called 'high commitment', 'high involvement', or 'high performance' practices can impact positively on organizational performance (Godard 2004; Purcell and Kinnie 2007; Proctor 2008).

Why has there been such a growth of interest in the relationship between HRM and organizational performance? The quest for business credibility on the part of human resource practitioners is an important influence since historically this function was largely seen as a cost and not as a source of added business value. If the presence of sophisticated HRM practices can be demonstrated to have a positive impact on the financial bottom line of organizations, then not only could this help to justify the existence of a specialist personnel or human resource function, but it would also enhance its credibility and status (Purcell and Kinnie 2007).

What kinds of management interventions are encompassed by the high commitment approach? Writers like Pfeffer (1998) have produced a list of practices which are assumed to be universally applicable when it comes to generating performance improvements. Yet one of the problems in demonstrating a link between commitment-based HRM and business performance is that there is no consensus about the practices that should be included under the 'high commitment' label (Purcell and Kinnie 2007). Different studies rarely rely on the same set of practices when assessing the impact of the high commitment management approach. Some consider the impact of a broad range of traditional personnel practices, including formal selection procedures, grievance procedures, and regular appraisals, on performance.

More justifiably, others work to a tighter, more restrictive definition of high commitment practices, focusing on those interventions that are specifically designed to motivate, involve, and reward employees in a way that increases their engagement with the business. This narrower interpretation suggests there are four main features of the high commitment approach in practice (White et al. 2004; Kersley et al. 2006):

- The presence of formal teamworking arrangements, particularly those which allow team members some responsibility for deciding how work should be done and who should do it.

- The existence of a functionally flexible workforce, who are well trained and have the necessary skills to be able to undertake a variety of jobs in their workplace.

- The use of employee involvement practices. Where staff are able to exercise some influence over managerial decision-making, by participating in problem-solving groups for example, this can be taken as evidence of a high commitment approach.

- The use of sophisticated reward mechanisms which offer incentives to workers for demonstrating commitment and performing well.

High commitment practices are claimed to improve business performance by producing a better quality workforce who are more committed to, and engaged with, business goals because they enjoy more fulfilling working lives. To the extent that they develop a greater sense of identification with the organization and are more involved in decisions that affect them in the workplace, employees will, it is assumed, perform better and be more productive (Wood and de Menezes 1998). The high commitment management approach increases 'discretionary work effort' (Huselid 1995); people who are managed well at work and feel engaged will contribute more (see Figure 5.2).

The positive impact of so-called high commitment or high performance management practices is, it is argued, more pronounced when they are used not in an idiosyncratic, ad hoc way, but in a mutually supportive fashion, or in 'bundles' (Huselid 1995; MacDuffie 1995). Teamworking arrangements, for example, should produce better results where they are operated in combination with appropriate recruitment and selection and reward practices. There has been growing interest in how high commitment management practices can be used in a systemic fashion, as part of a mutually supportive and interlocking set of arrangements that can be used to enhance organizational performance. The high performance work system (HPWS) model is relevant here. It holds that firms which operate an integrated and mutually supportive

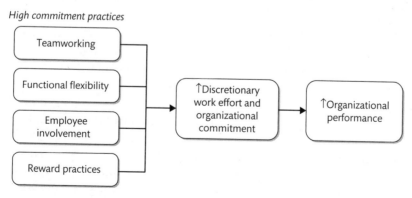

Figure 5.2 The high commitment model

set of sophisticated HRM practices—that allow workers to participate in workplace decisions, enhance their skills, and reward them for contributing extra effort—will benefit from having a more committed and empowered workforce, with positive outcomes for business performance (Applebaum et al. 2000; Boxall and Macky 2009). Although the HPWS model derives from the United States, there is some evidence that it is increasingly capturing the attention of firms around the world, especially in Asia (Kim and Bae 2005; Som 2008; Zhang and Li 2009). However, work and employment relations in emerging economies like China, the Philippines, and Turkey are often marked by highly authoritarian management regimes, based on compliance with organizational standards rather than commitment-based HRM, which give workers few opportunities for participation (Nichols and Sugur 2004; Cooke 2005; McKay 2006).

There is some evidence of an association between the use of high commitment practices and workplace financial performance in private sector companies (e.g. Huselid 1995). Survey data suggest that while there is a link between the use of high commitment practices and greater productivity, this relationship does not extend to a positive effect on financial performance (Wood and Bryson 2009). A major study of a number of large public and private sector organizations, including the Nationwide Building Society and Jaguar Cars, demonstrates that there is a connection between the use of sophisticated HRM practices, organizational commitment, and business performance. However, the behaviour of line managers seems to be of crucial importance; a large part of the success of the high commitment approach depends on how effectively the practices are operated in particular workplaces (Purcell et al. 2003).

How valid are the suppositions that, first, the use of high commitment management practices has become more commonplace and, second, that their presence generates improved business performance? There are a number of difficulties in assuming that the high commitment paradigm has come to dominate the way employment relations is managed (Legge 2005). Six major problems can be identified.

- To begin with, the prevalence of high commitment practices remains rather low; relatively few workplaces make use of a substantial number of them as a coherent package. The high commitment approach to managing people at work is present in only a minority of workplaces, and does not appear to be becoming more widespread (Kersley et al. 2006; Wood and Bryson 2009). In the US many employers prefer to operate a more conventional 'command and control' approach to managing employment relations, based on extensive rules and little employee involvement (Kaufman 2010b).

- A second problem concerns the proposition that there is a link between high commitment HRM and business performance. Research studies in this area tend to exaggerate the extent of any association. Closer analysis of the relevant data reveals that the relationship between high commitment practices and business performance is often less clear-cut (Godard 2004; Wall and Wood 2005).

- There is no consensus on what practices should comprise the high commitment management approach (Purcell and Kinnie 2007). This means that we have to exercise a great deal of care when considering the relationship between sophisticated HRM and business performance. There is also some evidence that traditional personnel management techniques, which recognize and reward employees' contributions for example, may have a more profound effect on performance (see Insight into practice 5.6). The high commitment approach promises a lot, but in reality may deliver rather less than simply conventional good personnel management practice (Godard 2004).

Insight into practice 5.6: High commitment working—the view from below

Undertaken over a period of four years, Sarah Pass's (2005) study of four manufacturing departments in a major healthcare company demonstrates some of the problems with the assumption that high commitment management practices cause performance improvements. As well as the interviews she undertook with workers, one of the strengths of her investigation is that she actually worked in a production capacity in the firm herself, and so is particularly well placed to comment on its activities. Pass discovered that performance improvements came from the exercise of close managerial control over the workforce and heavy work pressures, not the kind of sophisticated HRM interventions that are supposed to engender greater organizational commitment. Increases in performance were also seen to result from the use of traditional personnel management practices which offered recognition and respect, and thus generated good relationships. When workers felt their contribution was recognized, were treated by managers with respect, and were able to form robust and supportive relationships, they responded more positively to managerial interventions.

- One of the key assumptions underpinning the high commitment approach, that improvements in business performance result from better quality of working life for employees because it raises their productivity, is questionable. Improvements in performance are often the result of heavier workloads, and come with few of the benefits for workers that are supposed to be associated with new ways of working (Kaufman 2010b). In the case of an aircraft manufacturer which had adopted key elements of the high commitment model, for example, performance improvements were the result of increased work pressures, not a more committed workforce (Danford et al. 2004).

- In the high commitment approach there is often a tendency to treat human resource practices as formal managerial interventions, readily identifiable and thus, when presented as variables, making the effects of their presence supposedly easy to measure. But the management of the employment relationship is a process; it possesses a dynamic, and should not be reduced to a set of formal practices. How these function in workplaces, where, for example, managers and workers contest their operation or interpret them in different ways from those intended, is a much more complex and less easily measurable matter. Studies of the relationship between high commitment management practices and business performance increasingly recognize the important role played by front-line managers in influencing the extent to which practices are actually put into effect (Purcell and Hutchinson 2007), as well as the responses of employees. When considering the effects of high commitment practices, a distinction should be made between 'intended' practices (those that the organization aims to enact), 'actual' practices (those that line managers actually do enact), and 'perceived' practices (those that are experienced by the workforce) (Purcell and Kinnie 2007; Purcell et al. 2009).

- Finally, the research methodology that underpins studies of the relationship between sophisticated HRM and performance raises doubts about the appropriateness of the high commitment paradigm and its contribution. One leading commentator accuses much of the extant research of being 'riddled with error both with respect to data on HRM and on outcomes' (Guest 2011: 10). We have already seen that there is no consensus on what practices constitute a high commitment approach, but the specification and measurement of business performance are also often somewhat rudimentary too (Purcell and Kinnie 2007). Research studies rely for their data on responses from managers who, unsurprisingly, offer a biased and partial perspective, and may know little of how the practices they identify are interpreted in the workplace (Legge 2001). While there may be an association between sophisticated HRM and business performance, it is not necessarily a causal one. Firms that are performing well may be in a better position to afford to implement expensive HRM interventions, suggesting that it may be difficult to disentangle cause and effect when it comes to measuring the impact of sophisticated HRM (Wall and Wood 2005). Taken together, these methodological criticisms mean that we have relatively little knowledge of 'which practices or combinations of HR practices have the most impact, nor when, why or for whom they matter' (Guest 2011: 10–11).

It is increasingly being recognized that in order to understand the relationship between sophisticated HRM and performance properly, the impact of management practices on workers, and how workers respond to them, needs to be considered (Purcell and Kinnie 2007; Purcell et al. 2009; Guest 2011). Too much of the interest in high commitment HRM has been concerned with managerial objectives in the employment relationship and how they can be realized, whereas the implications for workers tend to be rather neglected (Kaufman 2010b). Studies that draw on the experiences of workers tend to reveal that performance improvements are driven by more intensive managerial control and greater work pressures, rather than the presence of a more committed workforce.

However, it is not just workers' experiences that we need to consider, but also their interests. If we view the employment relationship as a wage–work bargain, marked by the potential for a conflict of interests, then it helps us to understand why the high commitment management approach—indeed any managerial interventions—will ultimately prove unsatisfying to managers. This is because workers have different interests to those of their employers, and will thus experience, and react to, management practices in ways that do not conform to managerial expectations. Teamworking arrangements, for example, may upset existing social relationships in an organization and thus damage morale, commitment, and ultimately performance (Jenkins and Delbridge 2007). Writers on human resource management often criticize the assumption of those like Pfeffer (1998) who propagate a set of universal best practice techniques for managing people at work in a way that enhances business performance, preferring to take a contingency perspective instead. This asserts that firms would do better to operate practices that best fit in with their overall business strategy instead (Boxall and Purcell 2011). An employment relations perspective, though, highlights another, perhaps more important, dimension of the 'best fit' concept—that in order to improve the effectiveness of their practices, managers must make an effort to ensure that they conform with the expectations of employees.

The importance of this is evident from Cushen and Thompson's (2012) study of Avatar, the Irish-based subsidiary of a US multinational company, which employed highly skilled workers in a knowledge-intensive environment. The firm operated an extensive range of best practice management techniques designed to promote the organizational commitment and engagement of staff, and was high-performing. You might think, then, that the use of high commitment practices was linked to the financial success of the firm, by increasing discretionary work effort in the manner assumed by the proponents of sophisticated

HRM. This assumption would be wrong though. The workforce regarded efforts by the company to promote commitment and engagement with something close to contempt, viewing them as patronizing and insulting. They were particularly aware of the marked contradiction between the positive messages espoused by managers about how wonderful everything was, and that they should take pride from identifying with the company's values, and the reality of the strict controls over pay and growing job insecurity that were engendered by the need to conform with tight financial constraints. The workforce was high-performing, not because they were committed to the organization and its values, but out of an intrinsic interest in their knowledge-intensive and challenging jobs, over which they could exercise control.

How, then, should sophisticated HRM and the high commitment approach, and their impact on employment relations, be interpreted? While their prevalence is lower than some had anticipated, they have nonetheless exercised an important influence on management thinking when it comes to work and employment relationships (Wood and Bryson 2009). It is clear that some changes have occurred, the growth of direct communications arrangements for example, which are now present in a substantial number of workplaces; however, this hardly amounts to a transformation of the way employment relations is managed. Changes occurred in part because the decline of trade unionism opened up opportunities for innovation, but more commonly have been elaborated because of a desire to challenge union influence. Not only does the take-up of sophisticated HRM and the high commitment approach seem to have slowed during the 2000s, but it has also been somewhat uneven, with more evidence for the use of some practices, for example teamworking, than others (Wood and Bryson 2009).

Even in situations where managers have been able to develop and sustain a sophisticated HRM approach, this does not necessarily mean that they are going to be effective in influencing and shaping employees' attitudes and behaviour. In the case of the multinational courier company mentioned in Section 5.4.1, despite the use of a high commitment approach, many staff remained unhappy about the lack of influence they had over decisions that affected them at work (Dundon and Rollinson 2004). The different interests of employees mean that the effectiveness of managerial interventions of any kind is always going to be partial and incomplete.

 ## Section summary and further reading

- Whereas traditional approaches to managing employment relations were dominated by a concern to manage the consequences of trade unionism, it is claimed that contemporary organizations are taking a more sophisticated HRM approach to managing employees. Rather than accommodating the potential for conflict, the prime focus of managerial endeavour in employment relations is concerned with building employee engagement, winning organizational commitment, and improving business performance.

- Yet the extent of change has been somewhat limited, and falls well short of being a genuine transformation. While elements of a 'soft' approach to HRM are increasingly evident, the management of employment relations is dominated by a concern to control employees and enhance managerial prerogative, rather than use innovative new practices to encourage their voice, commitment, and engagement.

(continued...)

● There is much interest in how the presence of sophisticated HRM, and so-called high commitment or high performance practices in particular, contributes to improvements in business performance. However, there are some major problems with the high commitment approach, not least a tendency to overlook the experiences and attitudes of employees.

Legge (2005) remains the best critical assessment of the HRM phenomenon. For the management of employment relations in non-union firms, see Dundon and Rollinson (2004). Marchington (2008) offers a good overview of employee voice. See Proctor (2008) for high performance management, and Purcell and Kinnie (2007) for some of the problems inherent in drawing an association between HRM and business performance. Thompson (2011) offers a rigorous critique of the sophisticated HRM approach and its limits, while the case study of Avatar illuminates some key themes (Cushen and Thompson 2012). For details of the Engage for Success campaign go to its website: http://www.engageforsuccess.org/

5.5 Conceptualizing the management of employment relations

The growing influence of management as an employment relations actor has generated an increasing amount of interest in how its role should be conceptualized. Care needs to be taken, however, not to exaggerate the degree of consistency evident in managerial approaches. Two features of how work and employment relationships are managed hinder the capacity of managers to develop consistent approaches to the management of labour: the nature of the employment relationship as a wage–work bargain and the tensions arising from the dual function of labour in a market economy.

5.5.1 Managing the wage–work bargain

Given that the employment relationship is to be conceptualized as a wage–work bargain (see Chapter 1), managers need to exercise control over employees while at the same time gaining their cooperation. Understandably, the ways in which managements exert control over their employees have been a long-standing feature of workplace studies. For example, a distinction has been made between two types of managerial control strategy: 'direct control', in which managers closely regulate and supervise the activities of workers; and 'responsible autonomy', where control is exercised by deliberately ceding to workers some degree of discretion over how they carry out their work tasks (Friedman 1977).

In order to sustain management prerogative, organizations have been compelled to design ever more sophisticated techniques; the growth of formal personnel policies and procedures can be seen as an attempt to secure 'bureaucratic control' (Edwards 1979). The rise of sophisticated HRM, given the extent to which it is concerned with securing organizational culture change, is, in some interpretations, a more robust and, in so far as it is concerned with manipulating the meaning employees attach to their work, a more insidious way of securing managerial control (Willmott 1993).

In service industries, where the relationship between the employee and the customer is a key source of competitive advantage, managers have been obliged to develop novel techniques in an attempt to exercise control (see Insight into practice 5.7). This may, for example, involve using customers themselves (Korczynski 2002). Some companies use fake, or 'mock',

Insight into practice 5.7: Tipping as a source of management control?

In some parts of the economy, restaurants for example, customer tips, as part of the 'total reward system' for front-line customer service staff, are viewed as an important component of workers' remuneration since they offset low rates of basic pay (Mars and Mitchell 1976). The practice of tipping, moreover, particularly where it has been 'institutionalized'—that is, become a standard and accepted feature of workplace life—can serve to enhance managerial control of customer service workers, such as waiting staff for example. In a study of the Central Restaurant Group, Ogbonna and Harris (2002: 730–1) noted that the use of tipping was an 'integral part of reward', and had 'a long history in the organization', a reflection of its founder's belief that 'the best way to generate enthusiasm, loyalty and the required customer service behaviour from front-line staff was in encouraging them to keep their own tips'. Three main reasons underpinned the institutionalization of tipping in Central Restaurant Group. First, as a motivational tool it helped to improve employees' performance. Second, it allowed the company to pay a low basic wage, helping to keep labour costs down. Third, it enabled management to maintain control, albeit indirectly, over employee behaviour during the customer service encounter.

The institutionalization of tipping in Central Restaurant Group served to reinforce managerial control over employee behaviour in three ways. First, competition for tips encouraged self-interest among the workforce and thus impeded the development of a collective ethos which might challenge managerial standards. Second, by keeping basic pay low managers fostered among the waiting staff a sense of dependency on the tips. Third, the company used a number of means, including communications processes, to promote its approach to tipping.

Since tips comprised a substantial proportion of their earnings, workers were understandably supportive of the Central Restaurant Group's approach. Nevertheless, there was some dissatisfaction among workers over the behaviours it was felt necessary to produce in order to receive tips. Managers sometimes encouraged flirting, a form of potentially exploitative sexual labour, as a means of keeping customers happy. Ogbonna and Harris (2002: 742) suggest that such activity is a 'degrading and debasing' feature of front-line customer service work, and that workers may feel obliged to 'prostitute' themselves in exchange for the possibility of additional tipped income. They conclude, however, that despite the high level of management manipulation inherent in the institutionalization of tipping and its potentially exploitative implications, workers nonetheless used the system for their own ends. They were not the passive dupes of managers, but rational and calculative actors aware of what they needed to do to maximize their earnings.

customers. Their job is to establish that employees are fulfilling their role in the prescribed manner while pretending to be consumers (Fuller and Smith 1991). In some sectors, most famously the airline industry but also in call centres, companies have attempted to control the operation of the service encounter through the manipulation of workers' feelings or emotions (Hochschild 1983; Taylor 1998). Delta Airlines, for example, used wide-ranging and sophisticated training methods to ensure that its cabin crew acted appropriately, in particular by smiling, in all of their interactions with customers. Thus, 'the emotional style of offering the service is part of the service itself' (Hochschild 1983: 5).

The importance of control notwithstanding, managers also need to secure the cooperation and consent of their staff. Thus 'management strategy is always a blend of consent and co-ercion, though the nature of that blend varies between companies and between the various levels within each company hierarchy' (Fox 1985b: 66). Consent was traditionally secured by means of ad hoc accommodations with trade unions (Hyman 2003). Yet, even in non-union environments, managers must operate in such a way as to gain the cooperation of, and thus secure legitimacy among, those they manage (Dundon and Rollinson 2004).

It is sometimes assumed that small firms offer environments where employers enjoy untrammelled prerogative. It is certainly rare to find a union presence, and small firm employers often express a marked hostility towards trade unions, regarding them as a potential obstacle to their ability to run the business as they like (Rainnie 1989). One of the owner-managers interviewed in a study of manufacturing businesses in the East Midlands told the researcher: 'I'll never be told what to do by a bloody trade unionist; this is my business' (Marlow 2002: 33). The absence of unions from small firms should not lead us to assume that there is a harmonious employment relations climate within them, the accepted wisdom for many years (Rainnie 1989). Yet we would be well advised not to replace one over-simplistic view, that employment relations in small firms are inherently harmonious, with another, that management autocracy is unconstrained and that pay and conditions are inevitably poor. Typologies have been constructed which capture the diversity of employment relations arrangements in small firms, based on the influence of product and labour market factors (e.g. Rainnie 1989; Goss 1991). For example, in sectors of the economy like the clothing trade the emphasis is on treating workers as a cost, to be hired and fired according to the vagaries of the market, with little need for stability, and with vulnerable, often female workers from ethnic minorities being employed, who are highly dependent on the employer for paid work (Goss 1991: 84).

Yet there has been an increasing concern to recognize the importance of factors other than markets in influencing management approaches to employment relations in small firms. It is not just market forces that are important, but also how they shape the activities and behaviour of employers and workers (Ram and Edwards 2003). This demands a more sensitive and dynamic interpretation of employment relations in small firms. There are three related dimensions of this. First of all, the importance of managerial choices needs to be acknowledged; the management of employment relations in small firms, just like elsewhere, is not determined solely by markets, but also to a degree reflects the choices made by managers themselves, albeit within specific contexts (Ram and Edwards 2010).

The second dimension concerns the need to recognize the 'embeddedness' of small firms in wider familial, ethnic, and community networks, as well as their market presence (Ram and Edwards 2003, 2010; Edwards et al. 2006). For example, many Asian-owned firms in the clothing and restaurant sectors operate with low pay and highly exploitative working conditions; yet the presence of common ethnic bonds means that generally workers are more tolerant of their circumstances (Jones and Ram 2010). There is plenty of evidence indicating that in general workers in small firms express relatively high levels of satisfaction. Yet this 'does not mean that there is a wholly shared view of the firm or that workers naively accept managerial authority. It means that they work closely with these managers and can deal with issues in an immediate and informal way. This removes some of the distance and anonymity of large firms, and enables workers to appreciate the efforts made by managers' (Ram and Edwards 2010: 247). Importantly, there seems to be nothing inherent about the greater level of job satisfaction evident among workers in small firms; rather, it constitutes a tactical, 'pragmatic' response to their specific situations. Even relatively well-paid workers in small professional service firms would contemplate changing jobs if it meant gaining higher pay and better benefits by going elsewhere (Tsai, Sengupta, and Edwards 2007: 1802).

Third, a dynamic approach also captures the 'complex, contested and conflictual nature of employment relations in small firms' (Ram and Edwards 2010: 238). Although 'bound by market constraints', employment relationships in small firms are nonetheless 'socially negotiated' (Marlow 2002: 39), and thus constitute a wage–work bargain, just like elsewhere. For example, in their examination of WaterCo, a company that supplies water facilities to offices and other locations, Dundon and Rollinson (2004: 91) found that even in the absence of a trade union, 'workers were not passive recipients of the conditions they experienced. Rather, they exerted influence in return and, in so doing, partially shaped how management regulated the employment relationship'. Employment relations in small firms is often marked by a high degree of informality, with a lack of formal arrangements and procedures for dealing with human resource matters. But even this informality is based 'mainly on unwritten customs and the tacit understandings that arise out of the interactions of the parties at work' (Ram et al. 2001: 846), rather than the unconstrained use of managerial prerogative by employers in the absence of joint regulation or statutory provisions.

Even in small low-wage firms, where it would be anticipated that workers would be extremely vulnerable to the vagaries of the market, they do exercise some influence over the nature of their employment relationships, not least because employers often need to elicit their cooperation (Edwards and Ram 2006). This is evident from a study of employment relations in small Asian-owned firms in the West Midlands clothing industry. Monder Ram's (1994) *Managing to Survive* focuses on the dynamic nature of the employment relationship, conceptualizing it as a 'negotiated order'. Ram (1994) discovered that to portray employment relations in these firms as autocratic was far too simplistic an approach. Rather, managerial authority was bounded by the need to construct and reconstruct bargains with workers over the pace of work tasks, and the wages payable for undertaking them. Space for 'informal accommodations' was created by the workers' intricate knowledge of the production process, given the imperative for a steady flow of output. Thus 'workers were not passive in the face of authoritarian managements; they would endeavour to alter the terms of the effort bargain if they felt that they were not "fairly" rewarded' (Ram 1994: 122). Familial, ethnic, and community ties, no matter how much they cause workers to identify with their employers, do not necessarily eradicate the potential for conflict in the small firm employment relationship, and the importance of 'negotiated consent' as the basis for managing employment relations, even in parts of the informal economy where the flouting of labour law is manifest (Ram, Edwards, and Jones 2007; Jones and Ram 2010).

This material on small firms provides some key insights into the nature of managing employment relations, particularly the onus on employers to win the consent and cooperation of their employees as well as exercising control over them. While the extent of managerial prerogative is pronounced, employers' behaviour is affected not just by market forces, but also by the influence of the social contexts in which their firms operate, and the need to reach accommodations with workers themselves. The absence of unions does not imply a harmonious employment relations environment; nor does it necessarily mean that an autocratic managerial approach prevails. Rather, managing the employment relationship, as a wage–work bargain, in these circumstances involves a complex and dynamic process of tacit and informal negotiation with workers who have interests of their own.

5.5.2 Managing employment relations in a financialized market economy

A second factor that hinders managerial consistency concerns the tension that is created by the dual function of labour in a capitalist market economy. The experience of Esso's oil refinery at Fawley, mentioned in Section 5.2.1, illustrates the tension that can exist between an imperative to cut labour costs as a means of enhancing productivity, something that involves workforce reductions, and the need to secure greater employee commitment as a means of generating flexibility (Ahlstrand 1990). Thus the management of labour in a capitalist economy is beset by contradiction (Legge 2005). Managements have to reconcile two seemingly conflicting interests, 'to cut costs to the bone and yet at the same time promote the security, autonomy and teamwork, which are the conditions for innovation into new markets, products and services' (Sisson and Storey 2000: 29).

Financial imperatives, and the constant need to keep labour costs under control, are a major obstacle to the development of a sophisticated HRM approach in firms operating in Britain. The case of HP, a firm which espoused a sophisticated HRM approach, is instructive. Intense competitive pressures compelled the firm to reduce its workforce, resulting in increased pressure and lower morale among those who remained. Inevitably, such feelings influenced the perceptions and behaviour of employees, thus ensuring that HRM techniques were rendered less effective as a result (Truss 2001). The dominance of short-term pressures on companies to improve their financial performance is particularly acute in Anglo-Saxon economies such as Britain, where firm performance is judged according to strict financial criteria. In manufacturing environments, for example, the predominance of finance-based forms of control has encouraged a particular form of labour flexibility, one founded on the intensive use of relatively unskilled workers, rather than contingent on the use of a better developed, more committed workforce (Ackroyd and Proctor 1998).

During the 2000s, financial imperatives have come to exercise an ever greater influence on the management of employment relations, especially in the context of the recessionary economic climate. They are a particular impediment to the effective delivery of a commitment-based, sophisticated HRM approach to managing employment relations. The concept of 'financialization' is relevant here. It captures the growing dominance of international finance, in particular how economic life in general has come to be permeated by the operation of financial markets (Lapavitsas 2011). Firms have increasingly been required to engage in continual change and restructuring initiatives, including merger and acquisition activity, and bear down on costs, in order to retain the confidence of financial markets. Among the main consequences are job cuts and increased workloads for remaining staff, as firms look to make themselves more competitive. 'The general trend has been associated with downsizing and delayering as firms seek ways of cutting costs to improve financial performance. Taking labour out and extracting greater labour effort remains a focal point of restructuring activities' (Thompson 2011: 362). This is particularly evident when it comes to the private equity model of ownership; see Employment relations reflection 5.8 for details of how it affects employment relations.

Short-term market pressures for greater profitability and returns to shareholders militate against efforts to build consistent, long-term approaches to managing employment relations in a way that builds trust, and thus delivers better commitment and engagement (Sisson and Purcell 2010). The result is a kind of 'disconnected capitalism' (Thompson 2003), marked by the inability of employers to develop long-term, trust-based relationships with

Employment relations reflection 5.8: Private equity and employment relations

The trend towards greater 'financialization' is particularly manifest in the rise of the private equity model of business ownership (Clark 2009). During the 2000s, the growth of private equity funds attracted a considerable amount of attention. Private equity funds borrow large sums of money from institutional investors, in combination with small amounts of their own, to buy out under-performing companies, taking their shares off the stock market. The idea is that through rigorous control over costs, and away from the public eye, the fortunes of the company are improved. This helps to service the repayments on the debt incurred and leads to handsome rewards for the members of the private equity fund. Among the companies taken over by private equity funds during the 2000s were Alliance Boots, Birds Eye, and the car park firm NCP. Over 3 million workers in the UK (10 per cent of the workforce) are employed in companies under the control of private equity.

The impact of private equity ownership on employment relations has prompted a lively debate. Some argue that its effects have been positive. While private equity takeover sometimes results in job losses, in general it helps to stabilize and even raise employment levels. This is because previously under-performing companies are made more secure, thus supporting jobs. The emphasis on improving financial performance may even generate greater interest in using high commitment management practices and more extensive use of arrangements for consulting with employees. Moreover, for the most part private equity ownership seems to have no effect on managerial approaches to joint regulation and union recognition (Bacon et al. 2010; Bacon and Wright 2008).

However, critics contend that pressure to reduce costs has adverse consequences for staff employed in firms taken over by private equity. Not only do private equity funds look for efficiency savings through job cuts, but they also try to lower costs by eroding terms and conditions of employment and making remaining employees work harder. Legislation that exists to protect employees' pay and conditions when their business is sold does not apply to private equity takeovers (Clark 2008). In some cases, new private equity owners have terminated union recognition agreements. In 2004, for example, the private equity funds CVC Capital Partners and Permira took joint control of the car rescue firm the AA in a deal worth £1.75 billion. A year later the AA derecognized the GMB union, replacing it with a body which purported to act as an independent trade union, when in reality it was a management-controlled staff association. Clark (2010) focuses on how the AA's private equity owners—following the merger with Saga in 2007 it is now owned by the Charterhouse private equity fund—sought to extract greater value from its workforce by cutting jobs, eroding working conditions, and disposing of union recognition.

their employees given the presence of ever more intensive demands on firms to focus on short-term improvements in financial performance (Thompson 2011).

All this highlights the relevance of what Thompson (2011) calls a 'political economy' perspective, one that highlights the influence of the structural constraints imposed by markets on firms, and how they shape the management of employment relations within them. The case of Avatar, the Irish-based subsidiary of a major US multinational mentioned in Section 5.4.3, illustrates this well. The firm put a strong emphasis on using an extensive range of best practice approaches to managing employment relations, designed to elicit greater employee commitment. However, Avatar's obligations to the financial markets, particularly its pledge to increase returns to shareholders, meant that it was obsessed by cutting costs, including through voluntary redundancies and outsourcing business activities. As a result, not only was it unable to deliver on its commitment-based promises, but also its employees were enraged by the hypocrisy evident in its stance, given their high levels of insecurity (Cushen and Thompson 2012).

The management of employment relations in market economies is marked by two contradictory tendencies: first, the need to exercise control over employees, as well as to secure their consent and cooperation; and second, the desirability of treating employees as resources to be developed and the obligation to consider them as commodities to be discarded if necessary. They pose immense challenges to organizations which are keen to manage employment relations in a long-term, purposive, or 'strategic' way. For Hyman (1987: 30), 'there is no "one best way" of managing these contradictions, only different routes to partial failure'. In other words, management can never enjoy complete control over employment relations, and the results of their interventions may differ substantially from the intended outcomes.

 ### Section summary and further reading

- It is important to recognize the obstacles to developing a consistent and long-term pattern of managerial action in employment relations. Evidence from small firms demonstrates that managing the employment relationship, as a wage–work bargain, involves a complex and dynamic process of tacit and informal negotiation with workers who have interests of their own.

- The nature of employment relations makes it difficult for managers to pursue effective long-term and strategic approaches. On the one hand, managers view their employees as valued assets whose cooperation and consent is deemed essential to achieving organizational objectives. On the other hand, managers also have to exercise control over the workforce, exploiting and discarding them as necessary.

Sisson and Purcell (2010) is the most useful recent overview of the main issues and challenges relating to the management of employment relations. For employment relations in small firms, see the chapter by Ram and Edwards (2010). The article, 'The trouble with HRM', by Thompson (2011) espouses the value of a 'political economy' approach to managing employment relations. For a classic thought-provoking and sophisticated conceptualization of the management of employment relations, see Hyman (1987).

5.6 Conclusion

What, then, are the salient aspects of the way contemporary employment relations is managed? Clearly, pressures to sustain and expand the scope of managerial prerogative and accommodate the influence of trade unions are long-standing features of the management of employment relations. Employers have taken advantage of a more favourable economic and political climate to challenge the influence of trade unions. Among newly established workplaces, union recognition is rare; where unions do retain a formal presence, managers have attempted to erode their influence through the use of sophisticated HRM techniques. The way in which some employers have responded to the introduction of the statutory union recognition procedure demonstrates that anti-union values remain commonplace.

The development of sophisticated HRM and the use of high commitment management practices supposedly portend a transformation in the management of employment relations. Whereas in the past the managerial agenda was dominated by the need to accommodate the trade unions, the key emphasis now, it is claimed, is concerned with engaging employees and building their organizational commitment as a key source of improved business performance. As indicated in the introductory case study, McDonalds claims that employee engagement is a main priority. However, the extent to which the fundamental basis of managing employment relations has changed is questionable. There is little sign that the high commitment approach has become widespread. Moreover, the activities of those non-union firms that espouse a sophisticated HRM approach demonstrate that their main concern is with preventing a union presence from becoming established—something that makes the distinction between 'non-unionism' and 'anti-unionism' approaches difficult to uphold in practice (Blyton and Turnbull 2004).

Although attempts to expand the scope of managerial prerogative are a defining feature of the way in which employment relations is managed, the very nature of the employment relationship, as a 'negotiated order', means that it is inevitably limited in practice. In order to realize the efficient production of goods and services, managers must not only seek to exercise control over their employees, but are also compelled to win their consent and cooperation. Even in small non-union workplaces, where 'passive acquiescence' is all that might be expected from employees (Goss 1991), employers are obliged to secure a degree of legitimacy from them in order to operate efficiently. Thus the scope of managerial prerogative is inherently limited by the nature of the employment relationship as a wage–work bargain.

The need to exercise control over employees as well as gain their cooperation is an important contradictory feature of the management of employment relations. As such, it militates against consistency in managerial interventions, making the elaboration of a purposive, or strategic, approach difficult to pursue in practice. This is reinforced by a further contradictory feature of the way the employment relationship is managed in capitalist market economies: that which exists between the desirability of treating employees as resources, whose skill, commitment, and dedication contribute to raising organizational performance, and the need to consider them as commodities, to be discarded should competitive pressures dictate it. These contradictions render consistency in managerial approaches, such as the pursuit of sophisticated HRM, difficult to achieve in practice. An espoused policy goal of high commitment may be undermined by the effects of more intense competitive pressures, leading to job cuts, insecurity, and a lowering of employee morale. Despite a more favourable political climate and the dramatic decline of trade unionism, it is clear that there has been no real transformation in the way in which employment relations is managed.

Assignment and discussion questions

1. Why and how do managers seek to retain their prerogative in employment relations?

2. Critically assess the effectiveness of the statutory union recognition procedure as a mechanism for enhancing recognition levels.

3. In theory, why might a sophisticated HRM approach to managing employment relations based on the operation of 'high commitment practices' lead to improved business performance? What are the main obstacles in practice?

4. What arguments have been put forward to support the view that employers cannot take a longer-term, strategic approach to the management of employment relations? Explain whether you agree or disagree with these arguments.

5. How does a 'political economy' approach help with understanding the way employment relations is managed?

 Visit the Online Resource Centre that accompanies this book to develop your understanding of this chapter, and keep up to date with the latest developments in this area.
www.oxfordtextbooks.co.uk/orc/williams3e/

Chapter case study: Blacklisting trade unionists in the construction industry

Employers are sometimes prepared to take extreme measures to undermine the legitimate role and activities of trade unions. Blacklisting, for example, has a long history. It involves operating covert lists of the names, personal details, and employment history of trade unionists, which are shared among employers in order to deny them employment. The GMB union calls blacklisting 'illegal corporate bullying', claiming that it is a deep-rooted feature of the construction sector. During the twentieth century a business association called the Economic League maintained a list of trade union activists and others thought to be undesirable subversives, which it made available to sympathetic employers. However, blacklisting hit the news during 2009 following a raid by the Information Commissioner's Office (ICO) on the premises of The Consulting Association, a firm run by Ian Kerr apparently on behalf of the major construction company Sir Robert McAlpine (BBC Panorama 2013). It operated a database which contained the names and details of over 3,000 workers. Major construction companies, such as Balfour Beatty, Carillion, and Wimpey paid The Consulting Association an annual fee, and an additional amount each time they wanted the name of an individual worker to be checked against The Consulting Association's records. Its database contained details of individuals' personal lives (including car registration numbers) and unfavourable comments on their supposed conduct. Workers were labelled as 'militants', 'bad news', or 'extreme troublemakers'. Kerr was convicted and fined £5,000 for data protection offences. But the case drew attention to the scandalous treatment experienced by some workers, who had been sacked or denied employment because of legitimate trade union activities or for raising health and safety concerns. Professor Keith Ewing, a prominent human rights expert, calls blacklisting 'a nasty, secretive and unaccountable practice that causes untold misery for individuals who are entrapped unwittingly by its covert nature, incapable of challenging what is being said and used against them, and unable to understand why their lives are being blighted by the failure to secure work' (Ewing 2009: 2).

The case of electrician Steve Acheson is instructive. Following the death at work of a colleague, Acheson became determined to ensure that construction firms complied with health and safety legislation. As a consequence, his name and details, such as his address and mobile telephone number, found their way onto The Consulting Association's database and his work activities were monitored. Being the unwitting victim of blacklisting, Acheson found it difficult to hold down a job, and was dismissed a number of times during the first half of the 2000s, winning unfair dismissal cases as a result. But, having been made aware that he has been blacklisted himself, Acheson is determined to campaign against the practice, and has protested outside the premises of a former employer. He said: 'I've not been out of work because I'm a bad electrician—but because I cared about health and safety and was an active union member' (Ewing 2011).

Successive governments have failed to tackle the problem of blacklisting effectively. Only in 2010, in the aftermath of The Consulting Association scandal, did Labour take action. It put into effect powers to prohibit the operation of blacklists and to make it unlawful for employers to deny a worker employment, or to dismiss or demote them, because of a blacklist entry. However, there is concern that the legislation is inadequate. Blacklisting has not been made a criminal offence. Moreover, workers do not have a specific right not to be blacklisted (Ewing 2010). None of the companies that used The Consulting Association's services have faced any sanctions. Trade unions are concerned that blacklisting still continues surreptitiously, and that the penalties are insufficient. There are indications that blacklisting still occurs on major construction projects, such as London's Crossrail project (Ewing 2011; Milne 2012; BBC Panorama 2013).

Questions

Why is blacklisting a particularly prominent feature of the construction industry? What insights does the blacklisting scandal provide about the employment relations approach taken by major construction companies?

6 Representation at work

 Chapter objectives

The main objectives of this chapter are to:

- examine the ways in which trade unions represent the interests of workers;
- consider the effectiveness of non-union arrangements for the representation of workers' interests;
- assess the implications for employers and trade unions of 'partnership agreements'; and
- evaluate the extent to which organizing unionism can enhance workers' interests.

6.1 Introduction

In this chapter, the concern is with how the interests of workers are represented, something that has traditionally been done through the 'single channel' of trade unionism. Therefore Section 6.2 begins by considering how unions represent workers' interests. However, declining unionization levels have reduced the extent to which workers enjoy effective representation of their interests. To understand developments in the representation of workers, there is a need to consider both how unions have sought to respond to the decline in membership, and alternative forms of worker representation. In Section 6.3 the focus is on non-union forms of employee representation, including an assessment of the implications of European Union (EU) legislation concerning information and consultation rights for workers. As will become evident, though, non-union arrangements are rather ineffective when it comes to representing the interests of workers. Thus the onus is on how trade unions can be revitalized, improving their representational capacities. One approach, examined in Section 6.4, advocates that unions can best demonstrate their relevance, and improve their prospects, by engaging with employers in a cooperative fashion, as is manifest in the rising number of 'partnership agreements' concluded during the 2000s. The alternative 'organizing unionism' approach, however, holds that union renewal is more likely to arise from an emphasis on mobilizing new members, in opposition to employers. This is the focus of Section 6.5.

 Introductory case study: Organizing workers in a sandwich factory

This chapter considers the main approaches unions have developed to expand their representational capacities—by instituting more cooperative partnership working with employers, for example, or by organizing new members. Holgate (2005) studied a union organizing drive in a factory that makes sandwiches for high street retail outlets. The low-paid workforce comprised a large number of black and minority ethnic staff, many of them migrants, who were treated in ways that suggest the presence of

(continued...)

racial discrimination. Although the organizing campaign led to an increase in union membership in the factory, from forty to 150, it was not enough to secure recognition from the employer. The effectiveness of the initiative was undermined by language difficulties and the presence of ethnic divisions within the workforce. Union officials also played down the relevance of racism, declining to use it as an organizing tool. As a result, 'the opportunity to organize around issues that the workers felt to be most important to them was lost, and the failure to acknowledge the racialized nature of the employment practices at the factory did nothing to build trust and respect in the union' (Holgate 2005: 475). This case highlights some of the challenges unions face when trying to expand their reach, by organizing workers in growing sectors of the economy where there is a highly diverse workforce.

6.2 Trade unions, worker representation, and the 'representation gap'

The main functions of the trade unions were covered in Chapter 1. This section examines the principal ways in which trade unions represent the interests of workers, set against an outline of how the unions developed, before focusing on the decline in union membership that commenced in the 1980s, and assessing the factors that contributed to it.

6.2.1 Trade unions and the representation of workers' interests

There are four main ways in which trade unions represent the interests of workers. First, unions insure workers against difficulties and problems that arise during the course of their working lives. The provision of friendly benefits was a major function of the early unions of skilled workers (Webb and Webb 1920a). During the twentieth century, the importance of friendly benefits as a union function declined markedly, not just because collective bargaining became the principal way in which unions sought to regulate the employment relationship, but also because the state's role in providing welfare benefits, like unemployment assistance for example, expanded considerably. Nevertheless, one of the defining features of union organization is that it reflects the wishes of workers collectively to insure, or protect, themselves against problems at work. Nevertheless, while union membership may be predicated on workers' demands for insurance against individual problems at work, it is something that is achievable only through robust collective organization (Williams 1997).

The second way in which unions represent the interests of workers is by bargaining on their behalf with managers over pay and other terms and conditions of employment. Importantly, collective bargaining is not just an economic process, concerned with setting the terms on which workers are hired, but it is also a political activity since it enables workers, through their union representatives, to influence, and thus regulate jointly with managers, workplace decision-making (Flanders 1975). Contemporary trends in collective bargaining activity are discussed in Chapter 7.

The third way in which unions represent the interests of workers concerns the activities of stewards, unpaid union representatives based in the workplace. These lay representatives are generally the first point of contact for union members, and act to advocate their interests to managers, supporting and standing up for them in the workplace (Coates and Topham 1980), sometimes as a safeguard against hard-line employers. Workplace union representatives have long played a key role in representing the collective interests of workers (Terry 2010). However, one problem is that stewards and lay representatives are essentially concerned with representing the (sometimes narrow and sectional) interests of their own members, which hinders union efforts to expand their membership base. Moreover, the way stewards represent their members' interests is often shaped by their assumptions about the kinds of issues that are legitimate for union action. Munro's (1999) study of shop steward organization among ancillary staff in the health service demonstrates the influence of a relatively narrow 'trade union agenda' dominated by the concerns of male workers. This affects stewards' behaviour in that they may ignore issues of particular importance to women workers, such as childcare provision.

Fourth, unions do not just represent the interests of their members in the workplace, but also in the broader political arena. Indeed, by seeking to advance the interests of workers in general, and not just those of their members, unions act as a 'sword of justice' (Flanders 1975)—campaigning for effective laws governing employment rights, for example. In Chapter 3, the influence of unions in the Labour Party was highlighted. The introduction of the National Minimum Wage in 1999 (see Chapter 7), the culmination of a successful campaign run within the party by some trade unions to secure a manifesto commitment to introduce it, demonstrates how unions can use political channels to advance workers' interests. Unions have increasingly looked to alternative, broader ways of representing workers' interests politically, other than through the Labour Party. For example, in the 2000s the union movement has campaigned to improve the rights and employment conditions of mostly non-unionized 'vulnerable' workers, such as migrants (TUC 2008).

6.2.2 Declining unionization and the 'representation gap'

One of the most prominent features of employment relations during the twentieth century was the growth of trade union membership, as workers organized collectively to ensure that their interests were represented effectively. Table 6.1 shows that overall trade union membership numbers and union density (the proportion of employees who are union members) rose in two distinct phases. First, the period between 1880 and 1920 saw a major expansion of trade unionism. The development of 'general' unions, in industries such as the docks, transport, and gas for example, in two waves (first during the 1880s, and second during the 1910s) demonstrates how, under the influence of prominent leaders, many of whom were imbued with a socialist outlook, increasing numbers of semi-skilled and un-skilled workers became organized (see Hyman 2001b). Unlike their skilled craft counterparts, most of the workers who unionized in this period looked to secure improvements in their pay and conditions through widespread collective organization and a readiness to use strikes and engage in political activity. By 1910, trade union membership had reached over 2.5 million, albeit concentrated in certain areas such as coal mining—the Miners' Federation of Great Britain (MFGB) was the largest union in the country—engineering, railways, and cotton production.

Although trade union membership had already started to edge upwards during the late 1930s, after falling back to under 5 million during the economic depression, the second main period of growth occurred between the 1940s and 1970s. Economic recovery after

Table 6.1 Trade union membership, 1892–1979

Year	Union membership	Union density (%)
1892	1,576,000	10.6
1900	2,022,000	12.7
1910	2,565,000	14.6
1917	5,499,000	30.2
1920	8,348,000	45.2
1926	5,219,000	28.3
1933	4,392,000	22.6
1938	6,053,000	30.5
1945	7,875,000	38.6
1950	9,829,000	44.1
1955	9,741,000	44.5
1960	9,835,000	44.2
1965	10,325,000	44.2
1970	11,187,000	48.5
1975	12,026,000	51.0
1979	13,447,000	55.4

Source: Bain and Price (1983)

the Second World War was predicated on the growth of manufacturing industry, the mass production of electrical goods and other standardized products such as motor vehicles. Full employment encouraged greater shop-floor bargaining activity, creating the conditions that enabled trade unionism to flourish at workplace level (Terry 1983). Moreover, the rather monotonous nature of the assembly-line work in large-scale factory environments, allied with the more vigorous exercise of managerial prerogative, generated increasingly adversarial and 'low-trust' relations between managers and workers (Fox 1974). Although the shop steward position originated in the first two decades of the twentieth century (Hinton 1973), the growth of workplace bargaining saw a massive rise in their numbers, particularly in engineering and parts of manufacturing industry, thus generating a 'shift in authority' in the trade unions away from the salaried cadre of full-time professional officials (Royal Commission 1968; Terry 1983). Shop steward organization spread to the public sector, and their numbers reached 335,000 by the early 1980s (Charlwood and Forth 2009). Legislation of the 1970s, which obliges employers to give shop stewards of recognized unions reasonable paid time off work to undertake union activities, reflected the prevailing pluralist policy assumption that by accepting and integrating workplace unionism, rather than challenging it, managers could effectively contain labour conflict.

By the 1970s, perhaps the most striking feature of employment relations in the UK was the strength of trade unionism. Trade union membership peaked at over 13 million in the late 1970s, with some 55 per cent of employees being unionized (see Table 6.1). Much of the rapid acceleration in union membership during the 1960s and 1970s reflected the increased unionization of 'white-collar' workers in office-based occupations in sectors such as central and local government administration. By 'the end of the 1970s nearly 40 per cent of all trade unionists were in white-collar jobs' (Price 1983: 155).

However, while trade unionism has traditionally constituted the 'single channel' by which workers have had their interests represented in the UK (Terry 2010), declining levels of unionization mean that many people no longer enjoy effective representation at work. Although the fall in the number of union members has attracted most attention, it has to be seen in the context of the broader diminution of joint regulation as a means of regulating employment relationships. Chapter 5 considered the falling incidence of union recognition since the 1980s. The decline in the level of collective bargaining coverage is discussed in Chapter 7. Union workplace organization has also been rendered less effective by the increased preference of managers for bypassing shop stewards, and communicating with workers directly (e.g. Marchington and Parker 1990). In 1980, lay trade union representatives were present in 53 per cent of workplaces, whereas in 2004 they were present in just 38 per cent of workplaces (Kersley et al. 2006); over the same period the number of union representatives fell by two-thirds (Charlwood and Forth 2009). Since 2004, however, this decline appears to have stabilized (van Wanrooy et al. 2013), and new union representative roles have developed during the 2000s (see Employment relations reflection 6.1).

Nevertheless, membership decline is perhaps the starkest indication of the collapse of the union movement's fortunes. Table 6.2 shows that in 1980 there were over 12 million union members in Britain, some 54 per cent of the workforce. During the 1980s union membership fell by a third. Membership decline continued during the 1990s, albeit at a more gradual pace; by 2000 fewer than three in ten employees (29.8 per cent) were union members. Union membership continued to fall during the twenty-first century. Table 6.2 shows that by 2011 there were around 6.4 million union members in the UK. In the three decades between 1980 and 2010 the overall level of trade union membership fell by around 6 million; by 2011, only around a quarter of employees were union members.

Employment relations reflection 6.1: Union learning representatives and union equality representatives

Employers who recognize a trade union are obliged to give union representatives—such as shop stewards—a reasonable amount of time away from their work to undertake their union duties. A recognized union is also entitled to appoint safety representatives whose activities include investigating health and safety issues and making representations to managers. The 2002 Employment Act provided for the establishment of union learning representatives (ULRs), allowing them time off work to undertake their role. ULRs work to promote learning, training, and development activities, by raising awareness of the opportunities that are available to workers for example, or by encouraging employers to improve their provision. According to the Trades Union Congress (TUC), by 2010 it had trained some 23,000 ULRs (Moore 2011). They make an effective contribution to widening participation in learning activities at work. Not all employers, however, support the objective of enhancing opportunities for workplace learning. Some have failed to engage constructively with ULRs, and managers are markedly less convinced that they have a positive impact on training than ULRs themselves (Wallis, Stuart, and Greenwood 2005; Cassell and Lee 2009; Hoque and Bacon 2011). Although some have criticized the ULR initiative, claiming that it is designed to weaken unions by encouraging them to take too cooperative a stance towards employers, Moore (2011) suggests that ULRs are helping to revitalize unions by mobilizing members and generating activism. The union learning representative model has been taken forward as a useful way of achieving progress in other areas of employment relations, such as the development of union equality representatives (see Chapter 4).

Table 6.2 Trade union membership and density (employees), 1980–2011

	Union membership*	Density (%)§
1980	12,239,000	54.5
1985	10,282,000	49.0
1990	8,835,000	38.1
1995	7,125,000	32.4
2000	7,120,000	29.8
2005	7,056,000	28.6
2011	6,389,000	26.0

*Great Britain (1980–90), UK (1995–2011); § proportion of employees

Sources: Waddington (2003); Brownlie (2012)

What explains such a dramatic reversal of fortunes for the unions? Trade union decline can be attributed to the interaction of a complex range of relevant factors (Simms and Charlwood 2010). Economic changes, for instance, have had some influence. For one thing, workers do not have the same incentive as they once did to organize in unions. While it still exists, the extent of the union wage premium (the extra amount typically earned by unionized workers through collective bargaining compared to non-unionized workers) has considerably narrowed (Metcalf 2005; Blanchflower and Bryson 2009). Moreover, as was mentioned in Chapter 2, economic globalization enables companies to become more internationally mobile, something which has reduced the bargaining power of workers and unions (Anner et al. 2006). Periods of economic recession have also had an adverse effect on union membership levels. During the recession of the early 1980s, for example, factory closures and job losses were concentrated in what were then strongly unionized parts of the economy such as manufacturing.

Union membership decline continued, however, albeit at a slower rate, even during periods of economic growth when employment levels rose (Fernie 2005), such as during the mid-1990s and in the first half of the 2000s. This suggests that declining unionization is influenced by long-term changes in the economy, particularly changes in the composition of employment. The compositional approach asserts that, since the 1980s, employment has been contracting in areas where unions are strong and increasing in areas where they are weak. Thus the number of full-time, male-dominated jobs in large manufacturing enterprises, where unionization tends to be commonplace, has dwindled considerably. Most employment growth has been in the private services sector, where jobs are often held by women on a part-time basis, and where unions are relatively weak. Much of the decline in the level of unionization can therefore be attributed to the failure of unions to organize in new workplaces, and thus gain recognition from employers in expanding areas of the economy (Machin 2000).

Some argue that changes in the structure of employment have eroded the kind of collective experiences and values that used to bind working people together, and which underpinned unionization (Simms and Charlwood 2010). In the past, workers in large-scale manufacturing enterprises, for example, developed a sense of collective endeavour, based on a strong sense of shared interests. Workers today, however, tend to be located in relatively small office environments or industrial units, often isolated from others engaged in similar jobs. They are no longer so exposed to unions, and as a consequence are less likely to see their relevance.

However, compositional change seems to have only been responsible for around a third of the fall in union membership (Blanchflower and Bryson 2009).

Economic restructuring and changes in the composition of employment have had adverse consequences for trade union membership levels across many advanced economies. However, the decline has been more marked in the UK than it has elsewhere (Simms and Charlwood 2010), suggesting that there are other factors which have had an effect. For Blanchflower and Bryson 2009: 56), union membership decline has largely been caused by 'employers turning their back on trade unions', manifest in a greater unwillingness to contemplate union recognition, and efforts to weaken their influence by using techniques associated with a sophisticated human resource management approach) (see Chapter 5). Moreover, efforts by employers to avoid unions have been aided by important developments in the political and legal spheres. As Chapter 3 shows, during the 1980s and 1990s Conservative governments led by Margaret Thatcher and John Major passed laws which strictly regulated the behaviour of the unions (Simms and Charlwood 2010), just about all of which were retained by Labour. Employers have thus been able to challenge and restrict the influence of unions with a greater degree of confidence.

In terms of an overall assessment, it would seem that the dramatic fall in union membership during the first half of the 1980s was the product of compositional change and the massive job losses linked to the recession of that period. By the 1990s, the effects of the Conservatives' legislative changes were beginning to take effect, fostering a climate in which the exercise of managerial prerogative was strengthened and union confidence undermined. Moreover, the decline in the wage premium associated with union membership meant that workers had less of an incentive to join unions, while ongoing compositional change continued to erode membership levels. During the late 1990s and early 2000s, the decline in the overall level of trade union membership largely stabilized. Labour provided the unions with a less hostile public policy climate than its Conservative predecessors, even if, as was shown in Chapter 3, it was far from being pro-union, and encouraged employers and unions to work more in partnership (see Section 6.4.2). The unions also started to devote more resources to recruiting and organizing new members (see Section 6.4.3). However, such efforts seemingly did little to counteract the effect of ongoing compositional changes which have continued to nibble away at union density in the private sector.

Nevertheless, employment growth during the 2000s in the public services, a sector where the level of unionization is robust, helped stabilize the overall level of union membership. Bear in mind that union density varies markedly by sector and industry—see Table 6.3. In the public sector 56.5 per cent of employees are trade unionists, compared to just 14.1 per cent of employees in the private sector. Over a half (51.5 per cent) of employees in education are trade union members, compared to fewer than one in twenty-five (3.6 per cent) employees in hotels and restaurants. Austerity measures instigated by the Conservative-Liberal Democrat coalition government resulted in the loss of some 370,000 public sector jobs by the end of 2012, many of which would have been filled by trade union members. Along with the major economic downturn and the rising level of unemployment up to 2012, this seems to have had an adverse impact on unionization levels, manifest in a notable acceleration in the decline of union density between 2009 and 2011.

Yet by no means have all unions equally experienced membership decline. Some trade unions, particularly those representing professional employees mainly in the public sector,

Table 6.3 Union density by sector and industry, UK 2011 (selected industries)

	Union density (%)*
All	26.0
Private sector	14.1
Public sector	56.5
Public administration and defence	53.4
Education	51.5
Electricity and gas	41.5
Health and social work	41.4
Transport and storage	38.9
Manufacturing	18.7
Financial services	16.7
Construction	14.8
Wholesale, retail, and motor trade	11.9
Hotels and restaurants	3.6

*proportion of employees

Source: Brownlie (2012)

such as teachers and nurses, have increased their membership (Simms and Charlwood 2010). Unions which are prepared to challenge employers by threatening and engaging in strikes and other forms of industrial action, like the Rail, Maritime, and Transport (RMT) union, also benefited from membership growth during the 2000s. Nevertheless, the overall diminution of trade union membership, allied with declining levels of union recognition (see Chapter 5), has given rise to a 'representation gap', in the sense that growing numbers of workers have little or no opportunity to have their interests represented at work (Towers 1997; Heery 2009a). Some might say that unions are not really needed any more given the growth in statutory employment rights, such as the National Minimum Wage, enacted by Labour between 1997 and 2010. Yet the legal framework of employment rights and protections is a far from effective substitute for trade union representation—not least because when they have problems aggrieved workers are expected actively to pursue redress themselves, when they may not have the knowledge or resources to do so (see Chapter 10). Without a union presence, statutory employment rights and protections are much more difficult to enforce (Terry 2010).

Section summary and further reading

- Trade unions represent the interests of workers by providing them with protection, or insurance, against problems that affect them at work, bargaining collectively with employers on their behalf, acting as a workplace advocate, and in the broader, political arena.

- For much of the twentieth century union membership increased; it became a particularly prominent feature of some industrial sectors, like manufacturing for example. By the 1960s and 1970s union membership among white-collar workers had become commonplace.

- There has been marked fall in the overall level of trade union membership since the 1980s. This has been caused by a combination of factors, including changes in the composition of employment, employer policies of union exclusion, and the hostile anti-union policy climate propagated by Conservative governments during the 1980s and 1990s.

While the fall in overall union membership is perhaps the starkest dimension of union decline, it is just one aspect of the broader diminution of union power, something that also includes falling levels of union recognition and dwindling numbers of workplace union representatives. The result has been a growing 'representation gap', with workers increasingly unable to have their interests effectively represented at work.

For an overview of union membership trends and the factors that influence them, see Simms and Charlwood (2010). The Department for Business, Innovation, and Skills (BIS) produces an annual analysis of trade union membership data (e.g. Brownlie 2012).

6.3 Non-union forms of employee representation

The decline in the 'single channel' of union representation has prompted an increased amount of interest in alternative methods of promoting worker voice—non-union systems of employee representation, like information and consultation arrangements for example. Would works councils, as found in many European countries, be an effective alternative? The German 'dual system' of employee representation (see International perspective 6.2), based on the formal separation of collective bargaining from participation rights, has received a considerable amount of attention (e.g. Towers 1997). This section is devoted to assessing the phenomenon of non-union systems of employee representation, explaining why it has become such an important employment relations topic.

International perspective 6.2: The system of works councils in Germany

Collective bargaining in Germany is largely conducted at multi-employer level between trade unions and employers' associations. Works councils (which can be established in all private sector companies with five or more employees and which enjoy specific rights to information, consultation, and co-determination), however, are technically independent from the unions. Co-determination, which in effect allows the works council the right to reject management proposals, applies to 'social' issues, including payment methods, overtime arrangements, and the allocation of working hours. Works councils have information and consultation rights over matters pertaining to, among other things, the working environment, job design, and new technology, as well as information rights on financial issues. Nevertheless, their formal separation notwithstanding, the respective roles of unions and works councils generally overlap to a large degree (Gumbrell-McCormick and Hyman 2010). Works councillors are elected by the entire workforce, have a term of office of four years, and are obliged by law to cooperate with management 'in a spirit of mutual trust' for the benefit of employees and the establishment. While the powers of works councils should not be overstated, their presence places considerable limits on the ability of managers unilaterally to reform working conditions (Hyman 1996: 71). However, the legacy of unification in 1990, competitive pressures, and increasing demands from employers for greater flexibility, particularly over the determination of pay and conditions, may have weakened the system of works councils in Germany (Gumbrell-McCormick and Hyman 2010).

6.3.1 The development of non-union forms of employee representation

There is nothing new about non-union systems of employee representation; indeed, information-sharing and consultation arrangements can exist in unionized and non-unionized firms alike. Historically, though, consultation was viewed by trade unions as inferior to, and less desirable than, collective bargaining as a method of articulating workers' interests (Marchington 1994; Hall and Purcell 2012)—see Chapter 1. This is because with consultation managers retain the right to make the final decision, whereas bargaining means managers may have to compromise and moderate their objectives to produce a negotiated, and thus jointly agreed, settlement to a problem or dispute.

The decline of union representation has prompted a growing level of interest in the role of non-union systems of employee representation as a means of promoting greater worker voice (Gollan 2007, 2010; Kaufman and Taras 2010; Gollan and Lewin 2013). Generally, non-union employee representation arrangements are established by employers with the purpose of enabling managers to inform and consult with staff indirectly, often by means of elected or appointed employee representatives. They can be described as: 'employer-sponsored bodies of formally organized employee voice' (Donaghey et al. 2012: 164). Companies like Pizza Express, B&Q, and Standard Life, which do not recognize unions and view maintaining their non-union status as desirable, have developed in-house arrangements for informing and consulting staff in the form of 'employee forums' or 'company councils'.

What has prompted employers to consider non-union systems of employee representation, in the form of arrangements that enable managers to inform and consult with employee representatives for example? Three main factors are evident. First, most commonly managerial interest in non-union systems of employee representation stems from the concern to avoid, or discontinue, union recognition. In other words, they are designed to act as a substitute for union representation, helping to preclude an 'active union presence' (Gollan 2007: 104). Some of the enthusiasm for non-union systems of employee representation is linked to the introduction of the statutory union recognition procedure discussed in Chapter 5, and is best understood as an attempt to avoid unionization (e.g. Heery and Simms 2010).

Second, there is also some evidence that non-union systems of employee representation are increasingly being used as an integral part of a 'sophisticated HRM' approach which is designed to enhance business performance by giving workers more opportunity to express their voice at work. This is often a key feature of high-performance work systems (Kaufman and Taras 2010)—see Chapter 5. Employee voice is conceptualized in a unitary manner (Terry 2010), with non-union systems of employee representation being designed to facilitate improved communications with staff, as a way of facilitating organizational change or to improve levels of engagement (Gollan 2007; Hall and Purcell 2012). While union avoidance is the most important reason for establishing non-union employee representation arrangements, the way they come to be used by managers as tools for promoting cooperative relations and a harmony of interests in the workplace should not be overlooked (Butler 2009; Donaghey et al. 2012). However, the outcome of employee representation arrangements that are driven primarily by a desire to improve organizational performance is a highly restricted form of employee voice, one over which management enjoys significant control (Hall and Terry 2004).

The third main reason for the growing interest in non-union systems of employee representation relates to the introduction of European Union (EU) legislation concerning information and consultation rights for workers in areas such as redundancy and health and safety (Terry 2010; Hall and Purcell 2012). In public policy terms these developments are rather significant. For one thing, under certain circumstances employers become obliged to establish formal information and consultation arrangements, involving elected employee representatives, a marked shift in emphasis away from the previously voluntarist approach (Hall and

Edwards 1999). Moreover, EU legislation has eroded the hitherto dominant single-channel system of employee representation. Perhaps its main effect, though, has been to articulate an increasingly pronounced framework of legal rights underpinning employee representation (Terry 2010). This is particularly evident when we consider two later pieces of EU legislation, brought in under the 'Social Chapter', which are specifically concerned with information and consultation arrangements: the Information and Consultation Directive (see Section 6.3.3) and the European Works Council Directive (Section 6.3.4) respectively.

Employment relations reflection 6.3: Representing workers' interests beyond the workplace

Much of the interest in non-union forms of employee representation has justifiably been concerned with workplace-based arrangements, like systems for informing and consulting with staff for example. However, bodies which operate outside the workplace, in society at large, may also act in ways that help to protect and support the interests of workers. Civil society organizations (CSOs) include charities, pressure groups, and other non-governmental organizations. Some provide workers with advice, support, and legal representation. The gay rights organization Stonewall, for example, sometimes sponsors legal cases by workers who have been discriminated against on the grounds of their sexuality. CSOs lobby governments for legislative and policy changes that benefit workers, including better family-friendly working rights. They often work with employers to improve conditions for workers who frequently suffer from employment disadvantage, such as migrant workers. CSOs also sometimes campaign alongside trade unions to improve the pay and employment conditions of specific groups of workers, such as homeworkers (Williams, Abbott, and Heery 2011b).

Changes in the law, and the encouragement given to non-union arrangements, mean that the pattern of employee representation has become increasingly complex and fragmented (Gospel and Willman 2003). See Employment relations reflection 6.3 for details of how the activities of civil society organizations provide workers with voice. While the single channel of union representation remains important in some areas—in the public sector, for example, and among large private employers—its significance has markedly waned. Moreover, there is growing interest in the use of 'hybrid' employee representation arrangements (Charlwood and Terry 2007; Terry 2010). This is where some employees in the same firm have access to union representation, and others non-union arrangements, or no representation at all. Essex County Council, for instance, operates an employee forum alongside trade union recognition for collective bargaining (IDS 2011a). Cullinane et al.'s (2012) case study of a British multinational and its Irish subsidiary provides a good example of 'double-breasted' employee representation in practice. The company pursued a determinedly non-union approach in its Irish operations, despite operating with union recognition in its home country base. The erosion of the single channel of representation even in unionized firms, and the rise of a hybrid approach, signal the 'gradual displacement of union by non-union forms as employers seek to persuade employees that they can enjoy the benefits of representation without the costs of union membership' (Charlwood and Terry 2007: 336).

Notwithstanding the supposed benefits of non-union systems of employee representation for employers, such arrangements are relatively rare. Indeed, the prevalence of representative forms of voice, both union and non-union, has declined, particularly in small firms (Charlwood and Forth 2009; Willman, Gomez, and Bryson 2009; van Wanrooy et al. 2013).

The most notable consequence of the diminishing significance of the 'single channel' of employee representation through collective bargaining by trade unions is that many employees go without any kind of representation at all. Only around a half of all employees work in workplaces where representation, either through a union or some kind of non-union system such as a company council, is available (Charlwood and Terry 2007: 323).

6.3.2 **Non-union systems of employee representation in practice**

Studies of non-union systems of employee representation demonstrate how diverse they are in practice (Kaufman and Taras 2010). In some cases, like that of Delta Airlines for example, they are used as part of a long-term sophisticated HRM strategy which is designed to encourage employee participation (Kaufman 2013). Nevertheless generally non-union systems of employee representation are inadequate substitutes for trade unions when it comes to articulating the interests of employees. This is primarily because they operate as managerial tools, lack the power to challenge organizational decisions, and are therefore not seen as representing the interests of employees effectively. Being too closely controlled by managers, non-union systems of employee representation thus lack legitimacy.

Non-union systems of employee representation, precisely because they are management tools, rarely have sufficient power to influence managerial decision-making, and are thus viewed by employees as ineffective arrangements for protecting and supporting their interests at work (e.g. Terry 1999; Lloyd 2001). They are used as negotiating forums very infrequently; workers may get some additional voice, but without the 'muscle' to enforce it (Kaufman and Taras 2010: 268). In a study of non-union employee representation at the Eurotunnel call centre, Gollan (2003) discovered that managers largely saw the company council as a vehicle for communicating information to staff rather than giving them voice. Most employees surveyed 'stated that the company council was not effective in representing general employee interests' (Gollan 2003: 537).

Kaufman and Taras (2010) maintain that non-union systems of employee representation can produce some positive benefits for employees, because it is in the employer's interest for them to do so. Their very existence means that workers will expect to be able to express their voice or have their interests represented; if this not does happen, they will lack legitimacy and fall into disrepute as a result, with adverse consequences for morale and the increased prospect of unionization. However, it is difficult to sustain non-union systems of employee representation; keeping them 'energized and productive over the longer term is a major management challenge' (Kaufman and Taras 2010: 269). They often do not live up to employee expectations (Donaghey et al. 2012).

Some of the challenges inherent in operating non-union systems of employee representation are evident from Butler's (2009) case study research in a bank and a company making refrigeration products. In the latter, financial difficulties, and the priority placed by the firm on the need for speedy decision-making, meant that consultation became less important, and the non-union employee representation system was marginalized as a result. The initially 'proactive approach to consultation was frustrated by financial imperatives and ultimately both sets of workers viewed consultation as a marginal, remote and peripheral exercise' (Butler 2009: 210). The highly competitive environment in which the bank operated meant that it had to take decisions, for instance over branch closures, quickly. Employees were critical of the quality of the consultation process and felt that the non-union system of employee representation operating in the company lacked sufficient influence over managerial decision-making processes.

For these reasons, then, non-union employee representation systems are generally seen by workers as ineffective substitutes for a union presence, often because they become restricted to straightforward information-sharing (Gollan 2007; Donaghey et al. 2012). In both Eurotunnel and South West Water, for example, attempts to replace unionized systems of employee representation with non-union arrangements proved to be unsuccessful, as unions regained recognition rights (Bonner and Gollan 2005; Gollan 2007). Although they can sometimes produce initial benefits for employees, the effectiveness of non-union systems of employee representation often diminishes over time because of an unsupportive climate, the absence of employee influence, and their lack of independence from management (Donaghey et al. 2012).

6.3.3 The Information and Consultation of Employees Regulations

One key piece of EU legislation dealing with information and consultation matters is the Information and Consultation Directive, which was agreed in 2002 and implemented in the UK by means of the Information and Consultation of Employees (ICE) Regulations 2004. This legislation is highly significant, in theory at least; for the first time all employees in the UK are covered by a comprehensive statutory framework governing rights to information and consultation (Hall et al. 2013). The purpose of the Directive was to ensure that employers have arrangements in place for informing and consulting with their staff. The legislation establishes the circumstances under which employers may be obliged to inform and consult with employee representatives over certain matters, including likely employment changes for example, and to ensure that staff are kept informed about matters like business performance. Consultation is defined as 'the exchange of views and the establishment of dialogue' (Hall and Purcell (2012: 55–63).

Lobbying from employers meant that one of the Labour government's main objectives when designing the ICE Regulations was to ensure that firms were given a considerable amount of flexibility over their information and consultation arrangements (Hall 2006; Hall and Purcell 2012). As a result, the 'way the regulations are drawn up in the UK gives considerable freedom to choose the form and frequency of consultation' (Purcell and Hall 2012: 7). An additional feature of the government's approach to implementing the Information and Consultation Directive was to stress the positive contribution that employee involvement can make to business performance (Gollan and Wilkinson 2007). In other words, arrangements for informing and consulting staff should be viewed primarily as managerial tools, designed to help employers realize their business goals, not to enhance the representation of workers' interests in the employment relationship (Hall and Purcell 2012).

The implementation of the ICE Regulations was staged. Initially in April 2005 they applied to employers with 150 or more employees; coverage was extended to all employers with fifty or more employees in 2008. Their main features include the following:

- There is no automatic obligation on employers to establish arrangements for informing and consulting with employees or their representatives; at least 10 per cent of the workforce must submit a written request, either to the employer or to a state body—the Central Arbitration Committee (CAC).

- In the event of a valid request, arrangements must be put in place to enable appropriate employee representatives to be elected or appointed.

- The employer and employee representatives then have six months to reach a negotiated agreement governing the operation of information and consultation arrangements.

- In some circumstances an employer is entitled to claim that employees are already covered by appropriate information and consultation arrangements. So-called 'pre-existing arrangements' must satisfy certain conditions (e.g. they have to be in writing and cover all employees).

- Where there is a pre-existing arrangement in place, then any request to change it must be supported by a majority of employees in a ballot, and by at least 40 per cent of all those eligible to vote (including abstainers).

- Where a valid request is made, but is ignored by an employer, or where negotiations do not produce an agreement within the six-month time period, then a default statutory model procedure for information and consultation, as prescribed by the Regulations, applies.

The UK government's 'minimalist' (Hall and Purcell 2012: 82) approach to implementing the legislation in a way that prioritizes business flexibility means that it is unlikely to enhance the representation of workers' interests through stronger provisions for information and consultation. For one thing, there is no automatic 'right' of employees to be informed and consulted; employers need not do anything unless the 10 per cent 'trigger' is pulled—a very unlikely prospect in most cases (Hall and Purcell 2012)—and there is no formal role envisaged for trade unions (Terry 2010; Hall and Purcell 2012). Moreover, the ICE Regulations also permit employers to obtain their employees' agreement to 'direct' forms of information and consultation—that is, directly between managers and staff, without the need for employees to have representatives to act on their behalf. This is consistent with the government's view that informing and consulting with employees should primarily be seen as a means of involving staff, improving their commitment to organizational goals, and thus enhancing business performance, and not as a means of enabling them to have their interests more effectively represented. With the exception of the default model, there is nothing in the Regulations governing the structure and content of information and consultation, whether they are pre-existing arrangements or those negotiated under the Regulations (Hall and Purcell 2012). The ICE Regulations, therefore, 'give substantial latitude to employers, either to do nothing, or to design a consultative arrangement in whatever way they want' (Purcell and Hall 2012: 13).

For these reasons, they are unlikely to have much of an impact on information and consultation arrangements. This has been borne out by research into the impact of the legislation. Where firms do operate information and consultation arrangements, it is generally for internal managerial reasons, such as avoiding trade unions (Hall et al. 2013). There are signs of 'considerable voluntary activity in terms of reviewing, modifying, and introducing information and consultation arrangements but this has largely been employer-led', not a direct result of the legislation (Hall and Purcell 2012: 112). This is consistent with a 'risk assessment' rather than 'compliance' approach (Hall 2006). In other words, employers have been concerned with reviewing, altering, and strengthening their existing information and consultation practices in the light of the new legislation, rather than with having to take action to ensure that their arrangements comply with it. This has been the case with the retail chain B&Q, which revised its 'Grassroots' system of employee consultation partly as a consequence of the ICE Regulations (Hall 2005). While some employers have taken purposive action to improve their information and consultation arrangements, including allowing employees and their representatives to exercise an influence over the results, this has been driven by 'internal organizational dynamics' and not the legislation, the effect of which has been 'largely peripheral' (Hall et al. 2013).

The trade unions reacted to the ICE Regulations cautiously. On the one hand, the legislation provides unionized employers with an opportunity to challenge existing union-based representation arrangements centred on collective bargaining (Hall 2006). On the other hand, it gives unions an opportunity to secure a foothold in non-union firms by organizing a request for information and consultation arrangements, for example, or by using information and consultation machinery as a platform for union representatives. Research on the impact of the ICE Regulations shows that trade unions have generally been reluctant to use the legislation as a mechanism for developing and expanding a union presence (Hall et al. 2013). There is little to suggest, then, that the ICE Regulations will do much to advance the representation of workers' interests in employment relations; information and consultation arrangements are generally tightly controlled by employers. On paper, employees would seem to have much stronger rights to be informed and consulted by their employers than in the past; however, in reality, these supposed rights are highly circumscribed, given the extensive control over information and consultation arrangements enjoyed by employers and managers, and their 'continued managerial indifference to employee representation and... preference for unilateral managerial action', the lack of legal enforcement arrangements, and the continued weakness of trade unions (Terry 2010: 294).

6.3.4 **European works councils**

European works councils (EWCs) are transnational arrangements for informing and consulting with employee representatives on a Europe-wide basis. In 1994 the EU agreed legislation—the European Works Council Directive—which provides for the establishment of transnational information and consultation machinery in 'community-scale undertakings'— multinational companies that employ at least 1,000 employees in the European Economic Area (EU member states plus Iceland, Norway, and Liechtenstein), including at least 150 in each of two or more of these countries. The purpose of the EWC Directive was to promote more effective information and consultation arrangements in multinational firms operating in Europe (Waddington 2011a).

The completion of the Single European Market, and the process of internationalization it encouraged, meant that there was greater pressure to institute arrangements that would allow employees to influence corporate decisions increasingly being made at a European level (Hall and Marginson 2005). The aim of the EWC Directive was to ensure that worker representatives are informed and consulted about matters with a transnational bearing including, among other things, the economic and financial situation of the firm, likely employment trends, the implications of investment decisions, and substantial changes to working methods and production processes.

Strong importance was attached to allowing firms to operate arrangements that suited their particular circumstances (Hall and Purcell 2012). Thus Article 13 of the EWC Directive gave multinational companies operating in Europe scope to develop their own machinery for informing and consulting with worker representatives. Until 1996, they were able to establish arrangements which could be 'tailored to the circumstances of the enterprise' (Carley and Hall 2000: 105). Over 400 'Article 13' agreements, as they became known, were eventually concluded, in firms such as Deutsche Bank and Unilever. Because the EWC Directive was enacted under the 'Social Chapter' (see Chapter 3), the UK did not come under its aegis until 2000, after the Labour government under Tony Blair reversed the 'opt-out' secured by John Major, his Conservative predecessor as prime minister. Nevertheless, a number of UK firms which had a substantial presence in other European countries, and were thus obliged to set up transnational information and consultation machinery for staff there (United Biscuits, for example), extended the coverage of their EWCs to the UK voluntarily.

After 1996, firms could no longer take advantage of 'Article 13' agreements; that route was closed. Instead, the mechanism for establishing EWCs is specified in Article 6 of the Directive, and involves the establishment of something called a 'special negotiating body' (SNB). Firms that meet the definition of 'community-scale undertaking' are obliged to institute an SNB on receiving a written request from 100 or more employees, or their representatives, in at least two EU member states; or they can set one up voluntarily themselves. The purpose of the SNB is to determine the constitution and procedure of the EWC, including its coverage (what areas of the firm and which employees will it cover?), its scope (what issues will it handle?), its composition (e.g. the balance between managerial and employee representatives, and the process for choosing employee representatives), and how it is intended to operate (e.g. the timing and format of EWC meetings), subject to certain minimum specifications set out in the Directive. If the SNB process fails to reach agreement on how the EWC should operate, or where an employer ignores a valid request to establish an SNB, the EWC Directive lays down a default model, in the form of a set of 'subsidiary requirements' which have to be applied, such as a minimum of one meeting each year. While there are no reported cases of the EWC's subsidiary requirements being put into effect, the content of so-called Article 6 agreements often resembles them in important respects (Hall and Marginson 2005: 206), suggesting that SNBs use them as a model when negotiating their own firm-specific arrangements. See Insight into practice 6.4 for the details of an EWC agreement.

 Insight into practice 6.4: The EWC agreement at Diageo

Diageo is a UK-based multinational drinks company whose brands include Baileys, Guinness, and Johnnie Walker. In 1998 it negotiated an EWC agreement with employee representatives, establishing the Diageo Europe Forum. It was revised in 2002, following further negotiations between the company and employee representatives. The Forum, which meets once a year, comprises two senior management representatives and thirty-five employee representatives, drawn from across the company's European operations, though nearly half come from the UK (with ten representatives) and Ireland (seven). Half of the UK's representatives are trade union representatives, mainly from Diageo's Scottish operations, and half are non-union representatives, mainly from London. The Forum is designed to act as a vehicle by which Diageo can inform and consult with employee representatives on matters relating to, among other things, business performance, company strategy, the employment situation, organizational change, and the introduction of new working methods and production processes. While the approach to consultation is restricted to that laid down by the original EWC Directive, namely the 'exchange of views and establishment of dialogue', the Diageo agreement also specifies that the views of employee representatives must be heard, and that managers should respond to them in a timely fashion.

Sources: EIRO (2002); European Works Council database, http://www.ewcdb.eu/show_body.php?body_ID=918

Consultation was limited by the Directive to 'the exchange of views and establishment of dialogue' between management and employee representatives (Carley and Hall 2000: 105), and few companies went beyond this when instituting Article 13 EWCs (Marginson et al. 1998: 25). Panasonic, for example, emphasized that the scope of its EWC was strictly limited to 'consultation' as defined in the Directive (Kalman 1999). Trade union bodies criticized this element of the EWC Directive, contending that consultation obligations should be strengthened, something that has informed their approach to the revision of the EWC Directive—described later in the section. In particular, they argued that there should be a greater onus on firms to respond to proposals put forward by employee representatives in EWC meetings.

At the beginning of 2013, the European Trade Union Institute's (ETUI) EWC database recorded 1,020 active councils, across 945 multinational companies (MNCs) (some firms are covered by more than one body). About 38 per cent of eligible multinationals have an EWC in place (remember that there is no obligation on companies to establish an EWC without a valid request being made that triggers the SNB process). However, the growth in the number of new EWCs has slowed, as smaller MNCs seem less inclined to accommodate requests (Jagodzinski 2011).

Studies of EWCs show that they are marked by a high degree of variation. While most comprise both management and workers' representatives, some consist solely of workers' representatives. A typology of EWCs has been developed by Lecher et al. (2001) based on how active they are, as cited in Hall and Marginson (2005: 216):

- 'Symbolic EWCs': marked by a low level of information provision, with no formal consultation apparent.

- 'Service EWCs': marked by exchanges of information, without any sign that the EWC is developing its own distinct agenda.

- 'Project-oriented EWCs': marked by the tendency of workers' representatives to develop their own approaches relatively free from managerial control.

- 'Participatory EWCs': marked by extensive and highly formalized consultation, and sometimes even negotiation, between workers' representatives and management.

There are a number of competing influences on the way EWCs operate in practice. As shown later in this section, a firm's product market strategy can exercise an important effect. EWCs tend to be more active in companies which have highly integrated, internationalized operations, relative to those whose product lines are more diverse and nationally oriented. The influence of the multinational's home country is also important; EWCs in UK-based companies, for example, tend to be less active than those whose headquarters are in France or Germany (Hall and Marginson 2005).

There are three major reasons why EWCs, as provided for by the original EWC Directive, have been inadequate arrangements for improving the representation of workers' interests at a transnational level. First, they lack the power to influence managerial decisions effectively. This was evident in the case of the Swedish multinational companies studied by Huzzard and Docherty (2005), for example. Waddington (2006) surveyed EWC worker representatives in the engineering sector. In general, they did not consider that their respective EWCs had much of an influence over managerial decisions.

Second, linked to this, the absence of a formal role for trade union representatives can contribute to the ineffectiveness of EWCs. One of the main weaknesses of the original EWC Directive was that it did not provide for a formal trade union presence. Not only did this lead to a perception that EWCs were insufficiently powerful relative to management (Waddington 2006), but it may also have helped to legitimize union-avoidance tactics. Panasonic, for example, needed to establish arrangements to select employee representatives to its EWC from its non-unionized sales company. Instead of extending union recognition, it chose to establish a new non-union consultative committee from which the EWC delegates could be nominated (Kalman 1999).

Third, studies of how EWCs operate indicate that in general they are seen by employers as a means of helping them realize their business objectives, rather than as arrangements that help to ensure that, through a process of genuine consultation with their representatives, workers have their interests protected. EWCs tend to be used by senior managers as vehicles for communicating with staff, helping to disseminate information and legitimize managerial decision-making (Redfern 2007; Waddington 2011a). The security firm G4S, for example, claims its EWC is a 'really useful communications channel', although employee representatives have noticed a greater willingness by management to listen to their views (IDS 2011a). The EWC representatives surveyed by Waddington (2011b) rated the quality of consultation by managers as poor, with the councils used largely as vehicles for information-sharing. Interviews with worker representatives in a UK-based manufacturing company pointed to 'a concerted effort on the part of central management to use the EWC as a means by which to communicate the need for restructuring, to build company culture and to co-ordinate a Europe-wide strategic HRM policy' (Timming 2007: 255).

Article 13 agreements, in particular, tend to be used as managerially-led devices to stimulate improved business performance through better communication with employees. In the case of the fast-food chain McDonald's, for example, the EWC was used by the company as 'just another institution to be captured for management; another method of "getting the message across" ' (Royle 2000: 193). In such cases, EWCs are primarily used as one of a range of techniques designed to improve the management of human resources in multinationals, rather than as arrangements for strengthening worker representation at a transnational level. There are further factors, moreover, that limit the representational capacity of EWCs. Generally, there are few formalized arrangements that enable EWC representatives to forge effective relationships with national-level systems of information and consultation (Waddington 2006). The activity of worker representatives is often overly influenced by a national frame of reference, reflecting conditions in their home countries, rather than a genuinely transnational mode of understanding—though this may be changing as representatives develop a more 'European' outlook (Waddington 2006).

It would be wrong, though, to imply that EWCs have made no contribution to enhancing the representation of workers' interests at transnational level. Although the original EWC Directive did not provide the unions with a formal role, the presence of union representatives on many EWCs gives these bodies some degree of independence from managerial control (Waddington 2011a). Moreover, in some cases union representatives have used EWCs as mechanisms for building networks of international cooperation and information-sharing (Huzzard and Docherty 2005; Waddington 2011a). Yet some notable difficulties exist in practice. This was clear in the case of an unnamed multinational manufacturing and merchanting company. Genuine consultation was rare; managers came to EWC meetings to report on decisions that had already been made. Delegates had no opportunity to challenge managerial decision-making or to influence decisions. A frustrated British representative claimed: 'We should be able to challenge things. What happens now is we are just told things. The unions put forward an alternative plan and the company ignores it. That surely isn't right?' (quoted in Wills 2000: 94).

It is important to recognize that the effectiveness of EWCs varies according to the presence of specific factors, particularly the extent to which production and other operations are integrated transnationally (Hall and Marginson 2005). In his study of six UK-based multinationals, for example, Redfern (2007) found that EWCs were more active, in terms of networking and information-sharing between representatives, in unionized companies with a single product line and a Europe-wide management structure. In the highly internationalized and integrated vehicle manufacturing sector, the trade unions have used EWCs as the building blocks of a stronger, more transnational union movement (Greer and Hauptmeier 2008). The quality of information-sharing and consultation is better where senior union representatives are involved with the EWC (Waddington 2011a).

Undoubtedly, EWCs 'have become an established feature of the international employment relations landscape' (Hall and Purcell 2012: 53). However, the extent to which they are able to operate in ways that advance the interests of workers at transnational level largely depends on the capacity of trade unions to cooperate across national borders and use them as vehicles for enhancing international labour solidarity. The revised ('recast') EWC Directive, which took effect in 2011, may help in this respect. Among other things, it provides for a greater trade union role and establishes stronger, clearer, and more detailed obligations on multinationals when it comes to the process of information-sharing and consultation (Waddington 2011a: Chapter 7). Employee representatives have greater scope to express their views, and have them taken into account by the employer, before organizational decisions are made, rather than just over how they are implemented (Jagodzinski 2011: 210–12; Hall and Purcell 2012: 63–4).

Section summary and further reading

- The decline in the 'single channel' of union representation has prompted an increased amount of interest in alternative methods of promoting worker voice—non-union systems of employee representation, like information and consultation arrangements for example.

- There is a business case for systems of non-union employee representation, based on promoting employee voice; however, union avoidance is a more important reason for the development of information and consultation arrangements. They are typically established in order to enhance managerial prerogative and act as a substitute for trade unionism, not to give workers adequate independent representation of their interests.

- The Information and Consultation of Employees (ICE) Regulations implement an EU directive which is designed to ensure that staff have access to information and consultation arrangements. However, the government transposed the directive in a way that minimizes its impact, not least the requirement that at least 10 per cent of employees make a written request for information and consultation arrangements before an employer is required to do anything.

- While there are signs that in some cases EWCs have developed their own distinctive agenda, and can operate in ways that support the transnational representation of workers' interests, overall the experience of EWCs in this respect has generally been rather disappointing. Indeed, they are often used more as additional channels which multinational companies can use to communicate with staff.

Terry (2010) offers a critical overview of employee representation developments. Hall and Purcell (2012) provide an extensive study of consultation in employment relations. The most extensive study of non-union systems of employee representation is Gollan (2007). The chapter by Kaufman and Taras (2010) is also recommended. Jeremy Waddington has written a comprehensive account of EWCs, focusing on the experiences of representatives (Waddington 2011a). You can access the ETUI's EWC database at: http://www.ewcdb.eu/index.php

6.4 Cooperative trade unionism and partnership agreements

The weaknesses of non-union arrangements mean that more attention should be given to how trade unions can be revitalized if workers are to have their interests represented effectively. One key way that trade unions have tried to demonstrate their relevance is by promoting cooperative relations with employers, on the basis that a union presence can help to enhance business performance and enable the successful management of change in a way that protects jobs. A good example of this occurred in May 2012 with the decision by the US multinational car firm General Motors to invest in the production of the new Astra model at its Vauxhall subsidiary's Ellesmere Port plant on Merseyside, starting in 2015. This new investment is expected to preserve over 2,000 existing jobs, and to create some 700 new jobs. A key part of the package was the Unite union's agreement to a four-year pay and conditions deal, which included a move to a round-the-clock production schedule and an increase in the number of shifts at the plant from two to three, something that was backed by the overwhelming majority of the current workforce.

There is nothing new about cooperative employment relations arrangements. During the 1980s, for example, there was much interest in so-called 'new style' collective agreements, which were actively promoted by some moderate trade unions. Under these agreements, employers guaranteed recognition to a single union in exchange for accepting greater flexibility and a commitment to act responsibly, eschewing strikes and industrial action (Bassett 1987; Garrahan and Stewart 1992). Since the late 1990s, though, there has been a renewed interest in cooperative relationships between employers and unions, manifest in the form of 'partnership agreements', which have become a major feature of employment relations (Stuart and Martinez Lucio 2005; Bacon and Samuel 2009).

6.4.1 Partnership—principles and practice

Under partnership, the emphasis is on promoting cooperative relations between managers and unions, to the supposed benefit of all parties, including the employer, the workforce, and the union (Simms and Charlwood 2010; Terry 2010). The assumption is that union revitalization is best achieved through 'mutual cooperation', something which 'is likely to result in more harmonious industrial relations, including higher levels of trust, and in the financial success of the enterprise, thereby ensuring job security and better pay for workers, and increased membership and influence for unions' (Badigannavar and Kelly 2011: 6). A total of 248 new partnership agreements were recorded over the ten-year period from 1998 to 2007, with 10 per cent of employees working in organizations covered by them (Bacon and Samuel 2009). Among the well-known companies which have signed partnership agreements with trade unions are Barclays Bank, Legal and General, and Tesco. Most agreements, though, seem to be situated in the public sector, for instance in health organizations (Bacon and Samuel 2009).

One of the problems in assessing partnership agreements concerns the rather ambiguous concept of partnership itself, which is open to differing interpretations (Stuart and Martinez Lucio 2005). Nevertheless, partnership agreements can be defined as: 'formal collective agreements to enhance cooperation between employers and independent trade unions or staff associations', based on a 'mutual recognition of competing and shared interests' (Bacon and Samuel 2009: 232). They are generally rooted in a series of core principles: sets of 'shared values and beliefs that establish the behaviours, attitudes, and expectations required for co-operative industrial relations' (Samuel and Bacon 2010: 432).

The core partnership principles articulated during the 1990s by the Trades Union Congress (TUC) and the Involvement and Participation Association (IPA) have commanded a great deal of attention, even though they do not seem to have had much of an influence over actual partnership agreements in practice (Samuel and Bacon 2010). Among the TUC's six principles of partnership are: the importance of 'a commitment to the success of the organization', the desirability of recognizing and respecting the 'legitimate roles of the employer and the trade union', and the employer's 'commitment to employment security' (TUC 1997). The latter is a central aim of partnership as far as the unions are concerned, often in exchange for agreement to greater flexibility over working practices. However, guarantees of employment do not generally feature in partnership agreements, and any commitments to promote employment security tend to be expressed in a vague and aspirational way, without containing much substance. As a consequence, partnership agreements tend to 'display only modest aims' (Samuel and Bacon 2010: 439).

In addition to the broad principles of partnership agreements we also need to be concerned with their specific provisions. The content of partnership agreements tends to be dominated by matters relating to employee voice, especially arrangements providing for consultation and representative participation, enabling unions in particular to exercise greater influence over organizational decision-making (Johnstone, Ackers, and Wilkinson 2009; Johnstone, Wilkinson, and Ackers 2010). Yet, reflecting their modest aims, partnership agreements generally lack much substance. They tend to be marked by a concern with process issues—arrangements for operating voice through recognized unions, for example—rather than specific goals (Samuel and Bacon 2010).

6.4.2 **Why partnership?**

Why has partnership become a prominent feature of employment relations? Partnership agreements have generally been initiated by employers (Oxenbridge and Brown 2005). They are attractive to firms which are operating in increasingly competitive market conditions since they offer the prospect of both a harmonious employment relations environment and a more flexible, committed workforce, matters that are seen as crucial to improvements in business performance (Badigannavar and Kelly 2011). Managers in the banking sector, for example, viewed partnership as a key means of breaking away from traditionally adversarial relationships with trade unions and disruptive strikes (Johnstone, Wilkinson, and Ackers 2010; Geary and Trif 2011). In the public sector, where most partnership agreements reside, partnership has contributed to the reform of public services by securing union cooperation with reform initiatives (Bacon and Samuel 2009; Bach and Kessler 2012).

Partnership agreements also assist managerial efforts to secure, and gain support for, organizational change (Oxenbridge and Brown 2005; Johnstone, Ackers, and Wilkinson 2009). In his study of a financial services firm, for example, Samuel (2007) observed that the main managerial motive for developing a partnership approach was the belief that securing support from the unions would help the company adapt more effectively to changing market conditions. Partnership working is also seen to benefit employers by generating higher levels of employee trust, involvement, and security (Butler, Tregaskis, and Glover 2013). There is a presumption that if organizations want greater effort and commitment from their staff, then, in the interests of 'mutuality', they should give them opportunities to express their views (Guest and Peccei 2001).

For the unions, partnership is viewed as attractive because it enables them to maintain an organizational presence, and may even give them more influence over decisions (Guest and Peccei 2001). Yet the partnership agenda is to a large extent a reflection of trade union weakness. In the case of Tesco, for example, the union was concerned that the company was contemplating derecognition. In an otherwise hostile environment, partnership appears to guarantee the unions a presence, a degree of institutional security, and some (however limited) influence over organizational decision-making (Wills 2004: 335).

The rise of partnership during the late 1990s and 2000s was also aided by the presence of a supportive political context. Partnership agreements were given considerable encouragement by the Labour administrations of 1997–2010, based on the belief that cooperative relationships at work are a central feature of a 'modernized' system of employment relations (Johnstone, Ackers, and Wilkinson 2009; Bacon and Samuel 2009; Stuart and Martinez Lucio 2005). For example, Labour made money available in a special fund to support partnership working. Yet it tended to conceive of partnership in an explicitly unitary fashion (Ackers and Payne 1998). If there is to be a role for the unions, it is a very restricted one, limited to working with businesses in a cooperative way in order to improve competitiveness.

6.4.3 **Partnership—an assessment**

When it comes to evaluating the impact of partnership agreements, there are three broad perspectives: the 'mutual gains', 'constrained mutuality', and 'pessimistic' viewpoints (Geary and Trif 2011). The concept of the 'mutual gains enterprise' captures the ways in which employers can benefit from instituting cooperative management–union relationships, in particular by easing the introduction of new working practices and helping to boost business performance (Kochan and Osterman 1994). Advocates of partnership working contend that it not only benefits employers, but also that workers enjoy greater job security, are better informed about decisions, and retain union representation. From this viewpoint, partnership agreements 'establish the basis for a progressive workplace consensus' (Samuel and Bacon 2010: 432) and render union representation more effective.

There is some evidence to support the 'mutual gains' perspective on partnership, with benefits accruing to the employer, the workforce, and the recognized trade union (e.g. Danford, Richardson, and Upchurch 2002; Kochan et al. 2009). In NatBank, for example, partnership meant that the union enjoyed a stronger influence over decision-making, employees felt more informed and involved when it came to decisions that affected them, and managers profited from having better quality information and feedback (Johnstone, Wilkinson, and Ackers 2010). There is evidence that partnership working can strengthen trade unionism (Haynes and Allen 2001). In the financial services firm Legal and General, for example, the partnership agreement meant that while the union lost influence over pay determination, it gained more involvement over a wider range of issues, such as staff training and development.

The union gained members, and also benefited from the development of a stronger cadre of activists, as a result of partnership (Samuel 2005).

The second perspective on the outcomes of partnership holds that it is characterized by 'constrained mutuality'. Workers and unions generally benefit from partnership agreements, but employer interests dominate to such an extent that it is inappropriate to see them as involving mutual gains (e.g. Guest et al. 2008). Within trade unions, support for partnership is often strongest among union leaderships and full-time officers, who may sign agreements over the heads of shop stewards and lay representatives (e.g. Marks et al. 1998). While these deals give unions 'institutional security', that is they help to secure a formal presence for the union at an organizational level, they nonetheless shift the balance of power firmly in favour of management. In the case of Barclays, for example, although the recognized union secured greater access to, and influence over, organizational decision-making, this generated its own tensions. From the point of view of its members and activists, senior union representatives were too closely identified with managerial decisions. Therefore the union did not seem to be fighting on behalf of its members' interests as strongly as it ought to have done; it appeared to have developed a relationship with the bank that was too cosy and cooperative (Wills 2004). Therefore one of the main dangers of partnership for the trade unions concerns the distance that is potentially opened up between those union representatives who are party to managerial decision-making, and use their position to influence it, and the members, who may become disillusioned about the extent to which, as they view it, the union is really representing their interests in opposition to management (see Oxenbridge and Brown 2004).

The third—'pessimistic'—perspective on the outcomes of partnership agreements offers a much more negative appraisal of the prospects of partnership to enhance the representational capacities of the trade unions. It sees partnership as having been advanced primarily as part of an employers' agenda to circumscribe the influence of recognized trade unions and enhance managerial prerogative, with few, if any, genuine benefits accruing to workers. Partnership, then, is inimical to robust trade unionism and the effective representation of workers' interests. Partnership agreements are used as instruments for reinforcing managerial prerogative, with the aim of weakening trade union influence (e.g. Evans, Harvey, and Turnbull 2012). For example, Danford et al.'s (2005) study of two aerospace firms suggests that the 'business case' for partnership rests not so much on the desirability of achieving mutual gains, but rather on the belief that partnership working could enhance managerial prerogative by weakening trade union power.

The pessimistic viewpoint recognizes that management almost always drives partnership, often with the threat of union derecognition, or of major workforce reductions, hanging in the background if the unions do not concur (Kelly 2005a). This was the case at both United Distillers and Allied Domecq, where partnership was initiated by the respective companies 'as part of a restructuring and closure package' (Marks et al. 1998: 217). Partnership agreements, because they have been jointly concluded, even if it is by senior officials on the union side, have a level of legitimacy that makes them difficult to counter, even when they have detrimental results for the employees and undermine workplace unionism. When shop stewards in a supermarket chain tried to represent workers' grievances, they were rebuffed, told by managers that their actions ran counter to the provisions of the partnership agreement. Trade unionism, 'in the short term, is acceptable as long as it does not interfere with managerial prerogatives on the shop floor' (Taylor and Ramsay 1998: 137). At United Distillers, a shop steward explained how partnership had strengthened management power:

> The people who work with us day in day out in the office or on the lines haven't changed, and these people are still going to manage us in the way that they always have, except now they have got an agreement which the union signed up to and they will beat us with it.
>
> (quoted in Marks et al. 1998: 221)

From a pessimistic perspective, workers enjoy few, if any, benefits from partnership (see Insight into practice 6.5); it is designed to serve managerial interests. There is little evidence that partnership arrangements provide workers with genuine employment security (Oxenbridge and Brown 2002; Evans, Harvey, and Turnbull 2012). Indeed, organizations with partnership agreements have a higher rate of job losses than those without them in place (Kelly 2005a). The few studies which compare workers in partnership organizations with those in similar

 Insight into practice 6.5: Partnership at Borg Warner

Studies of partnership agreements that consider how far they benefit employees are rare. Suff and Williams (2004), though, asked employees at Borg Warner in South Wales, a manufacturer of specialist components and systems for vehicles that has developed a celebrated partnership approach with the Amicus trade union, about whether or not they had benefited from it. The partnership agreement, known as the 'Margam Way', after the location of the plant, comprises a ten-point plan that, among other things, emphasizes the importance of transparency and good communications. Managers and union representatives cited the positive impact of partnership, in particular the way in which the development of cooperative relations enabled the business to grow.

What were employees' views, though? How did they experience partnership in practice? Most of those surveyed (57 per cent) thought it had improved their working lives, and had enabled the union to participate more effectively in organizational decision-making. Thus there was general backing for the partnership approach. Nevertheless, despite the emphasis on communications many staff felt that they had limited influence over decisions that affected them at work. While partnership had increased their job security, in general people considered themselves to be insecure, a reflection of the competitive market environment and the history of job losses in the plant. Job satisfaction was high, but generally employees did not see this as a product of the partnership agreement. Although partnership had to some extent helped to improve the reputation of Borg Warner as a 'good' employer, employees nevertheless exhibited a low level of trust in management.

In this case, a partnership agreement did produce some benefits for employees, and the plant had remained open, ensuring that some jobs were secured. However, it did not prevent extensive job losses from occurring during the 2000s, which generated an increased sense of insecurity among the workforce (Evans, Harvey, and Turnbull 2012). Moreover, the level of cooperation between management and employees was strictly bounded, and fell well short of that proposed by the 'mutual gains' model. The partnership agreement was dominated by management. Ensuring the competitiveness of the plant was used as a device for securing cooperation from shop stewards, resulting in reduced support for the union from a workforce who considered it to be ineffective at representing their interests (Evans, Harvey, and Turnbull 2012).

non-partnership organizations indicate that for the most part it is those working in the non-partnership organization who have the more positive experiences (e.g. Badigannavar and Kelly 2004).

Efforts to capture the complexity of partnership in practice focus on how partnership agreements sometimes exhibit elements of all three perspectives. The bank studied by Geary and Trif (2011), for example, was characterized by 'mutual gains', yet managers benefited more than employees ('constrained mutuality'), while the development of a more intensive work regime marked by more rigorous arrangements for exercising managerial control is consistent with the 'pessimistic' outlook on partnership. Crucial, it seems, was the quality of employees' relationships with line managers, suggesting that a contingent perspective on partnership may be appropriate. Others maintain that partnership needs to be understood as a complex and evolutionary process, a work in progress if you like, meaning that its effectiveness cannot just be reduced to a concern with the specific features of partnership agreements and their outcomes (Johnstone, Ackers, and Wilkinson 2009).

Nevertheless, the overall assessment must be a negative one. Since they are arrangements that are designed to alter existing management–union relations, partnership agreements do little for the millions of workers without access to union representation (Badigannavar and Kelly 2004). Generally, the partnership agenda is firmly under the control of managements, and has for the most part been elaborated under conditions of union weakness (Kelly 2005a). Even though partnership agreements may acknowledge that legitimate differences of interest exist between an employer and union, 'that is about all they do say, and the language is otherwise overwhelmingly unitarist in flavour' (Terry 2004: 212). While it is important to recognize that it may at least help to secure a trade union presence, partnership is a largely managerial initiative, one that reflects the general weakness of the union movement (Terry 2004), and does little to close the representation gap in workplaces.

By the late 2000s, the Labour government's enthusiasm for partnership seemed to have dissipated (Guest et al. 2008). The Conservative-Liberal Democrat coalition, which took office in May 2010, has evinced little interest in advocating partnership in employment relations, being more concerned with promoting greater deregulation (see Chapter 3). As the limits of the partnership approach become increasingly evident, it is notable that support for it has dwindled among a new generation of trade union leaders who are more sceptical about the benefits of an approach to revitalizing unions that depends on cooperating with employers. That said, however, partnership has been surprisingly durable (Bacon and Samuel 2009), and partnership agreements continue to be a prominent feature of employment relations.

The economic recession, though, has posed some major challenges for employers operating partnership agreements, particularly that of maintaining high-trust relations under highly adverse economic conditions (Butler, Glover, and Tregaskis 2011). Although cooperative relations with unions may have helped some major firms to endure the recession more easily, by enabling agreements on short-time working arrangements and other cost-cutting measures, such actions are undertaken largely on the employer's terms. In relation to the case of Vauxhall, mentioned in Section 6.4, without the union's cooperation, and its agreement to the introduction of a more flexible package of pay and conditions, General Motors could very easily have taken its investment elsewhere.

Section summary and further reading

- The development of partnership has been a notable feature of employment relations during the 1990s and 2000s. In general, partnership agreements offer workers the promise of greater employment security and new forms of employee involvement and representation, in exchange for union agreement to greater job flexibility and a more cooperative stance.

- Encouraged by the government, which saw partnership as a means of modernizing employment relations, employers have been the main protagonists of partnership working. The concept of mutual gains which underlies partnership implies that employers, unions, and workers all benefit from partnership working. In practice, however, partnership agreements largely serve the interests of employers, and are used as instruments that enhance managerial prerogative.

- While partnership agreements may help to secure the position of a recognized union, allowing them some limited influence over organizational decision-making, this comes at the expense of workplace trade unionism, which is weakened by the shift in the balance of power in favour of management. Nevertheless, the inherent ambiguity of the partnership concept may in certain circumstances be used by unions to secure greater influence.

For overviews of the partnership phenomenon see Terry (2010: 291–3) and Simms and Charlwood (2010: 138–9). The chapter by Stuart and Martinez Lucio (2005) is also particularly useful. Peter Samuel and Nicolas Bacon have studied the adoption and content of partnership agreements (Bacon and Samuel 2009; Samuel and Bacon 2010). See Johnstone, Wilkinson, and Ackers (2010) for a case study of partnership in a bank; compare their analysis with the more critical perspective offered by Evans, Harvey, and Turnbull (2012).

6.5 Organizing unionism

In 1899, the Workers' Union's first full-time district organizer, Will Buchan, initiated a recruitment drive at Sir Thomas Lipton's City Road warehouses in London. The 1,300 workers were badly paid, and experienced poor working conditions. As Hyman (1971: 19) reports: 'Girls worked a 10-hour day with only one half-hour break, carrying heavy loads in unhealthy conditions; often they fainted, and the time lost was deducted from their wages'. Perhaps unsurprisingly, Buchan's attempts to organize these workers met with considerable success at first, and a new branch of the Workers' Union was established. As the union became more powerful, however, Lipton took measures to undermine its position, and dismissed many of the leading union activists among the workforce. By early 1900, union organization in the warehouses had collapsed (Hyman 1971). The Workers' Union was to go on to become one of the most important general unions in Britain during the first two decades of the twentieth century, eventually to become a part of the Transport and General Workers' Union (TGWU), which is now Unite. Nevertheless, its failure to secure a presence because of intense employer hostility at Lipton's warehouses in 1899 demonstrates that the process of organizing workers into unions can be a daunting task.

6.5.1 'Servicing unionism' and 'organizing unionism'

As this case shows, there is a long history of efforts to organize workers into unions in the UK (Simms, Holgate, and Heery 2013). However, by the late twentieth century, union organizing activity had dwindled markedly (Beaumont and Harris 1990). One of the few unions to experience membership growth during the 1980s was the shop-workers' union, USDAW. While this was partly a reflection of increasing retail employment, the union's own recruitment efforts were also important. USDAW officials were mandated to spend a certain proportion of their time on recruitment activity (Upchurch and Donnelly 1992). Generally, though, unions focused their energies on providing representational services to existing members, like collective bargaining. Such a 'servicing' approach to trade unionism, which focuses on supporting the current membership, is to be contrasted with an organizing approach, which is concerned with pursuing membership growth by organizing workers in new areas. Traditionally, most union officials' expertise lay in supporting and providing services to existing members, not in going out and finding new ones. This is something that has long inhibited recruitment and organizing activity by unions (Kelly and Heery 1994).

Consistent with an emphasis on a servicing approach, one of the key ways in which the union movement has responded to declining membership has been through merger activity. The largest trade union in Britain—Unite—was formed following the 2007 amalgamation of Amicus and the Transport and General Workers' Union, both of which had a long history of being involved in merger activity themselves. Trade union mergers have been a commonplace response to membership decline (Simms and Charlwood 2010). Rationalization in this way is attractive because it raises the prospect of delivering union services, especially collective bargaining, more efficiently, although mergers rarely deliver the anticipated efficiency gains (Undy 2008). However, such 'market-share' unionism, whereby unions seek to gain members through mergers and amalgamations, only increases individual unions' share of the existing 'market' for members, without doing very much to extend it (Willman 1989). Since the 1990s, however, there has also been an increased emphasis on how unions themselves can rebuild their strength and expand their membership through intensive and focused activity to expand their territories, by organizing new workers.

6.5.2 The 'organizing model'

The 'organizing unionism' approach, based on mobilizing workers collectively and challenging the interests of employers, serves as a model for union renewal (Byford 2011; Heery and Simms 2011; Simms and Charlwood 2010). The increased focus on organizing activity has been called 'probably the most significant development in British trade unionism of recent years' (Simms, Holgate, and Heery 2013: 1). The statutory union recognition procedure (see Chapter 5) has been an important catalyst for organizing; it encourages unions to build up membership in firms in order to be well positioned to submit a claim for recognition (Heery and Simms 2011; Simms, Holgate, and Heery 2013). Some writers (e.g. Kelly 2005a) argue that such an approach is more likely than partnership working to revitalize the trade unions. This suggests that an adversarial approach, based around contesting the way in which employers manage employment relationships, is a more effective method of strengthening trade unionism than a cooperative, partnership-based orientation (Badigannavar and Kelly 2011).

The 'organizing model' of trade unionism is marked by four key characteristics. First, 'organizing' is distinguished from straightforward 'recruitment' of new members because of its emphasis on 'union building': changing the culture of unions by fostering greater participation and activism among union members (Bronfenbrenner and Juravich 1998; Simms, Holgate, and Heery 2013). Thus, the 'term organizing is most commonly used to describe an approach to union building that relies on unions facilitating local leadership at workplace level so that workers are empowered to act for themselves' (Simms and Holgate 2010a: 358). As such, organizing unionism is marked by an ongoing process of developing and strengthening workplace organization, consistent with a bottom-up approach to trade union renewal (Fairbrother 1996; Heery et al. 2000c).

Second, organizing unionism is characterized by an emphasis on the unionization of groups of workers that the unions have largely neglected in the past, and who frequently suffer from labour market disadvantage (Simms, Holgate, and Heery 2013). For example, the TUC has emphasized improvements to the representation of part-time and young workers (Heery 1998b; TUC 1997)—see Employment relations reflection 6.6 for prospects for unionization among young workers. In the United States, though, the organization of immigrant workers, particularly those from Latin America, is seen as crucial to the revival of the trade unions, notwithstanding the poor historical record of American unions in this area (Milkman 2000). There is also an associated concern with broadening the reach of trade unionism, manifest in efforts to extend union representation into non-union parts of the economy (Simms and Holgate 2010a).

Employment relations reflection 6.6: Prospects for unionization among young workers

More vigorous efforts by unions to organize young workers could help to revitalize trade unionism. Unionization rates among young workers are low. Just 3 per cent of 16 to 19 year old employees, and 11 per cent of 20 to 24 year olds, are union members, compared with 26 per cent of all employees (Brownlie 2012). Research shows that such low union density does not reflect a more hostile attitude to trade unions on the part of young workers. In fact, they tend to be rather well-disposed towards unions, but they often work in parts of the economy where union organization is either weak or absent entirely, like hotels and restaurants (e.g. Waddington and Kerr 2002; Freeman and Diamond 2003; Byford 2009). Tailby and Pollert (2011) conducted a survey of around 500 young workers aged between 16 and 29. Despite workers having manifold problems and grievances, such as experiencing bullying or not receiving holiday pay to which they were entitled, their efforts to resolve issues at work on an individual basis were largely unsuccessful. Asked why they had not joined a union, the most common responses from workers were that there was no union present in their workplace, or that they had not been asked. There was 'almost no evidence of hostility to unions' (Tailby and Pollert 2011: 515). While the youngest group of workers—16 to 21 year olds—tended to be 'uninformed' and 'have no opinions' about unions, those aged between 22 and 29 were knowledgeable about unions, and expressed a 'relatively pro-union' stance (Tailby and Pollert 2011: 518).

Third, perhaps the most distinctive feature of organizing unionism is the use of a specialized cadre of skilled, professional organizers, whose role is to build union organization (Simms, Holgate, and Heery 2013). After looking at initiatives in Australia and the United States, in the late 1990s the TUC established a dedicated 'Organizing Academy', whose purpose was to develop a 'cadre of specialist organizers' (Simms and Holgate 2010a). Union-sponsored trainees undertook a year-long training programme, combining classroom-based learning and real-life organizing activity with their union sponsors (Heery et al. 2000b; Simms and Holgate 2010b). The intention was that, on completing their training, participants should be well placed to become dedicated union organizers who are able to use their skills to expand union organization in Britain.

The fourth characteristic of organizing unionism concerns the use of innovative organizing tactics. These include 'mapping' the workforce in particular establishments, identifying those workers who are more susceptible to trade unionism, person-to-person recruitment techniques, and the choice of particular 'levers' or grievances that union organizers can use to build support (Heery et al. 2000*a*; Heery and Simms 2011; Simms, Heery, and Holgate 2013). In the United States, there has sometimes been a moral dimension to organizing initiatives as unions campaign on the basis of giving workers 'justice' or 'dignity'. An emphasis on the importance of collective mobilization, as a means of challenging employers' interests, is generally a prominent feature of organizing campaigns. Research shows that union organizers use a 'set of arguments that stressed the value of collectivism and which were oppositional in their stance to the employer' (Heery and Simms 2011: 33).

Notwithstanding these features, there is some doubt about the extent to which a distinctive 'organizing model' operates in practice (e.g. Gall and Fiorito 2011). Some leading unions, the GMB general union for example, have not been involved in the Organizing Academy, sometimes preferring to establish their own initiatives (Heery and Simms 2008; Daniels 2009). Simms and Holgate (2010*b*: 165) emphasize that 'different unions have developed different organizing approaches that reflect different objectives and contexts'. Unite, for example, has focused on expanding into new, non-union areas of the economy. The GMB has not used a specialist cadre of specialist organizers, instead encouraging its generalist officials to engage in organizing activity alongside their servicing tasks. USDAW has not been very interested in promoting a culture of activism; rather, organizing work is focused on sustaining union density. Different unions use the organizing approach for different purposes (Simms and Holgate 2010*b*). This is evident when we look at the experiences of two unions that have successfully increased membership—the Public and Commercial Services (PCS) union and the Rail, Maritime, and Transport (RMT) union. Their approach to union organizing emphasizes 'collective workplace mobilization through industrial action' (Gall and Fiorito 2011: 238). Greater union effectiveness comes from a preparedness to threaten and engage in strikes and industrial action, based on the mobilization efforts of lay union activists against employers (Simms and Holgate 2010*b*). In the case of the RMT, for example, collective mobilization and strikes have manifestly helped to strengthen union organization in the London Underground (Darlington 2012).

6.5.3 Evaluating organizing unionism

The organizing unionism approach is now sufficiently well established for us to be able to consider its effectiveness. There is some evidence that unions have used it effectively to secure recognition from employers. The Communication Workers Union (CWU), for example, was recognized by 'Typetalk', a not-for-profit call centre service operated as a joint venture between a charity and the telecommunications firm BT, following an intense organizing campaign. The language used to frame the campaign was carefully fashioned. A contrast was drawn between the progressive policies the organization pursued with regard to its client base and its opposition to unionization. Union organizers developed a 'language of "dignity", "fairness" and "respect", stressing union membership as a human right and emphasising that the rights of employees were as equally important as the rights of clients' (Simms 2007: 125). They identified a series of specific grievances, health and safety problems for example, which they could use to mobilize support from the workforce for union recognition. The recognition campaign also involved the establishment of an organizing committee, comprising union activists, who took the leading role in recruiting new members and raising awareness of the union's activities. A key objective was to 'encourage activists to be independent of officials and to address their own problems' (Simms 2007: 127). As a result, the organizing campaign was rather successful, in the sense of securing the objective of union recognition, despite managerial opposition to unionization. That said, however, the emphasis in the Typetalk campaign of organizing in the workplace means that union activists there are not effectively integrated within the structures of the wider union (Simms 2007).

Elsewhere, though, the effectiveness of organizing unionism has often been hindered by a number of major constraints (see Heery and Simms 2008). The most important external obstacle has been employer opposition to union organizing initiatives (Heery and Simms 2011). Gall's (2005) study of organizing campaigns indicates that opposition from employers is commonplace. Employer hostility to unionization in the charity Scope, for example, was a major reason why the organizing campaign there did not result in union recognition (Simms 2007).

Opposition from employers is not the only obstacle impeding the effectiveness of the organizing model, by any means. There are also some notable internal constraints within unions themselves. One is that organizing unionism demands considerable investment on the part of the unions involved (Simms 2003), something which is generally lacking as resources are limited (Heery and Simms 2011). Moreover, internal union opposition to the development of an organizing approach is also relatively widespread (Heery and Simms 2008). Servicing existing members is often viewed as more of a priority than organizing activity, the effectiveness of which is constrained as a result (Simms and Holgate 2010a; Byford 2011). Where organizing activity does take place, there is a tendency for unions to concentrate on consolidating their existing membership bases in sectors like manufacturing, rather than attempt to take the resource-intensive step of seeking to organize workers in areas of the economy where their presence is weak (Daniels 2009; Heery and Simms 2011). A good example of such 'infill' activity (Simms, Holgate, and Heery 2013) concerns the efforts of a union in the higher education sector to organize contract research workers in universities (Badigannavar and Kelly 2005).

Where the organizing approach is pursued, unions tend to make use of selected elements of it in their campaigns, those that are most appropriate to their particular circumstances, rather than adopt the model in its entirety. Nevertheless, the use of innovative organizing techniques appears to have been effective (Heery and Simms 2011). Person-to-person recruitment has been the most popular method, while workforce mapping appears to be relatively rare. Some use of a moral discourse of 'dignity' and 'justice' has been reported. A union organizing drive among restaurants in London's Covent Garden district was accompanied by pressure to establish a 'Respect at Work Zone'. Nevertheless, British unions have blanched at the overly evangelistic tone of some American organizing campaigns (Heery et al. 2000b, 2000c).

Two other difficulties with the organizing unionism approach have also been identified. First, the underlying assumption that workers are relatively easily organized, especially where they have demonstrable grievances, is often mistaken (Heery and Simms 2008). As Badigannavar and Kelly (2005) show in their study of contract university researchers, a number of factors, including the extent to which workers blame their employers for their grievances, and the degree to which they expect a union to remedy them, help to explain why some organizing campaigns succeed whereas others fail. Organizing campaigns may also stall because the workers concerned do not identify with the union. There are 'instances of women, members of ethnic minorities and younger workers proving difficult to recruit because unions were not perceived as "their" institutions' (Heery and Simms 2008: 35). Organizing campaigns sometimes fail because unions are insufficiently attuned to, and respectful of, workplace diversity—as was evident in the case of the sandwich factory in the introductory case study (Holgate 2005).

A second difficulty with the organizing unionism approach is the contradiction that exists between, on the one hand, the need for union officials to exercise some degree of control and, on the other hand, the emphasis on encouraging workers themselves to organize and pursue unionization. Although without some degree of coordination from above it is difficult to see how unions can mobilize effectively to improve people's working lives, initiatives designed by union leaderships to boost workplace unionism may be of limited effectiveness since they are perceived to be bureaucratic interventions and thus lack support on the ground (Carter 2000). Perhaps the best way of characterizing organizing campaigns is to see them as involving a degree of 'managed activism' (Heery et al. 2000c). To be effective they require coordination from above and management by union officials; but they also depend on the participation and activism of the workers concerned for their success (e.g. Simms 2007). What, then, are the implications of organizing unionism for the representation of workers' interests? The approach has an ostensibly inclusive character, given that a leading objective is to expand union organization into areas where it has hitherto been weak, and thus offer representation to workers who would previously have lacked it. However, most British unions have been reluctant to adopt organizing unionism wholeheartedly and have preferred to concentrate on building membership in areas of existing strength (Heery et al. 2003; Daniels 2009). Consequently, it has not resulted in an influx of new trade union members. Greater emphasis on organizing has 'at best stabilized union membership rather than generated renewal' (Heery and Simms 2011: 43). Perhaps the most notable effect of the unions' concern with organizing, then, has been to reinforce their 'institutional security', in much the same way as the partnership approach. This is not, of course, something that should be derided. Robust trade unionism is vital to the effective representation of workers' interests, and those who accept that there is an inherent imbalance of power in the employment relationship should welcome anything that secures a union presence. The challenge for the unions is how they can expand their representative capacity to cover the millions of workers without the means of independent and effective representation at work. While 'organizing has risen up the list of many unions' agendas over the last decade... it is no panacea. In and of itself, it cannot reverse the severe decline [in union membership] that has occurred over the last three decades' (Daniels 2009: 275).

Section summary and further reading

- While the recruitment of new members has always been an essential feature of union activity, during the 2000s there has been a marked revival of interest among unions in organizing workers, associated with the concept of 'organizing unionism'.

- The organizing unionism model is held to differ from traditional union recruitment effort in a number of key respects. First, it is concerned with 'union building', that is the ongoing development of workplace organization, and not just recruitment on its own. Second, it is designed to attract into union activity workers who have previously been marginalized by the union movement. Third, it involves specially trained union organizers. Fourth, it uses novel organizing techniques such as 'workplace mapping'.

- The diffusion of organizing unionism in Britain has so far been somewhat limited. Most unions remain conservative in their recruitment priorities. Moreover, attempts to initiate novel organizing campaigns have come up against both external constraints, like employer opposition, and internal obstacles, such as a lack of resources.

The most substantial overview of the organizing approach is the book *Union Voices* (Simms, Holgate, and Heery 2013). Daniels (2009) and Simms and Charlwood (2010: 139–40) are good briefer assessments of the organizing phenomenon. Heery and Simms (2011) rigorously evaluate organizing efforts; in an earlier article they assess the constraints on union organizing (Heery and Simms 2008).

6.6 Conclusion

For many years trade unions have been responsible for representing workers' interests. By virtue of their collective organization, unions can provide individuals with protection, or insurance, against problems at work. They also bargain with management on behalf of their members, seeking to alter the terms of the wage–work bargain in favour of their members. Unions operate in the workplace itself, where the lay union representative, or shop steward, not only negotiates with management, but also advises, supports, and represents his or her members. Finally, unions represent the interests of workers in the wider political arena, for example by influencing the legislative process. Nevertheless, the complex nature of workers' interests poses considerable challenges for unions as they attempt to carry out their representative functions. Workers generally want protection for themselves as individuals, but this requires collective action to be effective. Unions must therefore demonstrate their relevance to individuals, while at the same time operating as a collective agency on behalf of what may be a considerably diverse membership. Thus effective trade unionism depends on the extent to which the unions are able to translate diverse, individual interests into collective action (Hyman 1994).

Moreover, unions frequently face difficulties when seeking to construct a broader representative agenda. Campaigning on political and social issues can lead to discontent among members who, understandably, would prefer their union to concentrate its resources on representing their 'sectional' interests in the workplace rather than waste money, as they see it, on irrelevant causes. Thus unions are caught between narrow and broad understandings of interest representation (Hyman 1994). Perhaps the most important implication of this overview of employee representation in the workplace is that it is not representation mechanisms, by themselves, that give workers influence over the decisions which affect their working lives, but those that are effective (Kelly 1998). Non-union systems of employee representation are generally used as management tools to improve communications, or to avoid a union presence. They lack the power and legitimacy of agencies that are independent of the employer, like trade unions, and thus do not help to offer workers adequate representation of their interests. Although a trade union presence is a necessary condition of effective representation, it is not a guarantee. Unions often have to engage with employers in a cooperative fashion, if only to secure a presence, while at the same time acting to challenge their interests. The concept of 'partnership' has become popular among union leaderships specifically because, in a hostile environment, cooperation with employers is seen as the most effective way of guaranteeing 'institutional security'. But is this in the interests of their members? Clearly a union presence, however constrained, is important. Without it, workers would have little protection against threats to their pay and employment conditions. However, partnership agreements may not only damage workplace union organization, but also do not seem to provide workers with any real job security.

Finally, workers' interests are not constant, but are fluid, and subject to ongoing adjustments as the characteristics of their environments change. The process of interest representation does not simply mean that trade unions act on behalf of, or 'for', their members. Unions themselves play an active part themselves in shaping, influencing, and controlling the interests of workers and thus exercising power 'over' them (Hyman 1975). In one sense, organizing unionism may be viewed as a kind of 'managed activism' (Heery et al. 2000c), something that enhances the power of union leaderships. Unions are to a large extent, however, agencies that embody the collective power of their members. Not only does this limit the authority of union leaderships, since policies depend for their effectiveness on mobilization from below, but it also highlights the tension that exists in all unions between the desirability of coordination from above by union leaderships and the pressure for democratic control from below.

 ## Assignment and discussion questions

1. Critically assess the proposition that 'workers no longer need to be represented at work by a trade union or other body since, in the twenty-first century, management fully take account of the needs and views of workers when making decisions that affect them'.

2. What factors were responsible for the decline in union membership between the 1980s and 2000s?

3. What are the main strengths and weaknesses of non-union arrangements for promoting employee representation at work?

4. Why have some unions promoted partnership? What do workers and unions gain from partnership agreements? What are the main drawbacks of partnership agreements when it comes to advancing the representation of workers' interests?

5. You have been asked to advise a trade union on how it might go about recruiting younger workers into membership. In small groups, or by talking to friends, identify what younger people want from employment, and explain what unions could do to meet these needs.

 Visit the Online Resource Centre that accompanies this book to develop your understanding of this chapter, and keep up to date with the latest developments in this area.
www.oxfordtextbooks.co.uk/orc/williams3e/

 ## Chapter case study: Community unionism

There has been an increasing recognition among some unions that in order to organize workers who suffer from labour market disadvantage more effectively, and to improve their livelihoods, the focus of union activity needs to extend beyond the workplace to encompass the wider communities in which workers are based (see McBride and Greenwood 2009). There are three main types of community unionism. First, some unions have themselves tried to develop a more community-based orientation. The Community union was formed in 2004 from a merger of two unions representing steel workers, and footwear and textile workers. Both predecessor unions had deep roots in specific industrial communities but, because of economic change, membership levels were dwindling. The focus on community was designed to stem this decline. In addition to the conventional functions that we would expect from a trade union—bargaining with employers, and providing members with employment advice, support, and representation—Community also emphasizes the importance of taking a broader, community-based approach to promoting the interests of its members, one which is not just restricted to the workplace. It provides members with lifelong learning opportunities, for example, and fights for 'justice and social rights of working people and within the communities where they live' (http://www.community-tu.org). Trade unions have long been an integral part of many industrial communities, in coal mining areas for example. Yet the example of Community demonstrates that unions are exploring new ways of representing the interests of their members.

The second type of community unionism has become increasingly commonplace in the United States. It takes the form of organizations that support and campaign on behalf of workers who experience labour market disadvantage. Perhaps the best known examples of this type of community unionism are the immigrant worker centres, organizations that work to improve the prospects of poorly paid, vulnerable, and disadvantaged workers (Fine 2006). The third type of community unionism involves joint initiatives between traditional labour unions and community-based organizations, such as faith groups. The idea is that broad-based coalitions can raise awareness of labour market disadvantage and campaign for effective ways of reducing it. The London Citizens group and its London living wage campaign has been one of the most effective of its type in the UK (Holgate 2009). Engaging with community organizations in this way can enhance the mobilizing capacity of unions, giving them more power to achieve their objectives (Tattersall 2009).

The development of community unionism raises the prospect of a profound revitalization of the trade union movement. A community focus enables unions to engage with, and potentially represent, a more diverse workforce, helping to combat labour market disadvantage. Union activity in communities operates beyond the confines of the workplace, meaning that it is less dependent on the attitudes of employers. There are some problems however. The strength of the unions traditionally rests on their workplace organization. Existing union members may be unhappy with, and challenge, efforts to develop a community orientation. Added to which, the interests of communities, and particularly community bodies, and unions may come into conflict. There has been some trade union opposition to working with faith bodies, because they are sometimes perceived as being prejudiced against gay people (Holgate 2009).

Question

What are the main strengths and weaknesses of 'community unionism' as a means of revitalizing the trade unions?

7 Pay determination and employment relations

◎ Chapter objectives

The main objectives of this chapter are to:

- provide an overview of the development and contraction of collective bargaining;
- explore the reasons for the resilience of collective bargaining as an influence on the terms of the wage–work bargain in the public sector;
- assess the ways in which employers have used their greater freedom to manage arrangements for pay determination;
- examine the main issues and implications relating to the National Minimum Wage; and
- investigate the purpose, characteristics, and outcomes of 'living wage' campaigns.

7.1 Introduction

Pay is at the heart of employment relations as a field of study: the 'receipt of a wage in return for an employee's labour under guidance of an employer's authority is the conventional definition of an employment relationship' (Grimshaw and Rubery 2010: 350). The purpose of this chapter is to look more closely at key developments in pay determination. In Section 7.2 the initial focus is on the joint regulation of pay through collective bargaining with trade unions. It covers the evolution, development, and decline of collective bargaining as a means of setting pay, set against an appreciation of the important degree to which collective bargaining has proved to be resilient in the public sector. Section 7.3 is concerned with a key implication of the diminution of collective bargaining, which is the increased level of unilateral managerial control over pay determination, particularly in private firms. The last major part of the chapter (Section 7.4) is devoted mainly to the statutory regulation of pay, with a particular emphasis on the background to, and the operation and consequences of, the National Minimum Wage, which has been in existence since 1999. By the end of this chapter, therefore, you should have gained some important insights into the main pay-setting trends in employment relations, and the key issues and implications that arise from them.

Introductory case study: The 'fair tips' campaign

For low-paid workers in the service sector, the protection provided by the National Minimum Wage (NMW), which since 1999 has set a legal minimum floor for wages, is a very important feature of their jobs. Most employers in low-paying sectors of the economy have complied with the NMW relatively easily. However, some restaurant chains, like Café Rouge and Strada for example, initially took advantage of a loophole in the minimum wage legislation which allowed them to pay their waiting staff an hourly rate of pay that was less than the NMW, and use revenue taken from service charges to top up wages to the legal minimum. Only tips left for waiting staff directly on the table could not be counted towards the NMW.

In May 2008, the trade union Unite launched a 'fair tips' campaign to draw attention to this loophole in the NMW legislation whereby money taken from customers in the form of service charges, supposedly to reward good service, was actually being used to supplement staff wages so that they reached the legal minimum. Leading newspapers like the *Daily Mirror* and *The Independent* supported the campaign to stop revenue from tips being used to make up the minimum wage. Unite published a 'Fair Tips Charter', inviting employers to commit to 'pay all employees at least the minimum wage with 100% of tips added on top as a bonus with no hidden charges'. Some restaurant chains, like Pizza Hut and TGI Fridays signed up to the Charter. As a result of the campaign, and lobbying by trade unions, in July 2008 the government announced that it would close the legal loophole which allowed employers to use tips and service charges to count towards the NMW. According to Unite's then joint general secretary Derek Simpson, this meant that 'unscrupulous employers will no longer be able to use the tips left for staff to subsidise low wages. Workers in restaurants, hotels and bars across the country have waited a long time for what they deserve'.

Sources: BBC News Online (2009*b*), Sommerlad (2009)

7.2 Collective bargaining and pay determination

Historically, most employees had their pay set through collective bargaining between employers, or employers' associations, and trade unions. One of the most notable recent developments in employment relations has been the diminished importance of collective bargaining as a pay-setting tool, particularly in the private sector. Nevertheless, collective bargaining, including multi-employer arrangements, has proven to be more resilient in public sector organizations, albeit mitigated by pressures for greater flexibility and occupational restructuring. While the importance of collective bargaining as a means of determining pay has declined, it continues to influence earnings for millions of workers throughout the economy.

7.2.1 The evolution and development of collective bargaining

At the beginning of the 1980s collective bargaining was the predominant method of pay determination in Britain (Marginson 2012), with over 70 per cent of employees covered by collective agreements (Daniel and Millward 1983). It found favour among employers, as well as among union leaders, because it enabled conflict to become 'institutionalized', accommodated and contained within the bargaining relationship. The alternative was continuing instability and disorder as unions struggled to secure a presence. Thus the decision to recognize and bargain with unions reflected an acceptance on the part of employers that a union presence was inevitable—as the 'lesser of two evils' (Blyton and Turnbull 2004: 228). For much of the twentieth century, formally at least, collective bargaining commonly operated on a multi-employer, industry-wide basis. Moreover, national bargaining arrangements also became established across the public sector (Carter and Fairbrother 1999).

The main advantage of multi-employer arrangements for employers was that they could be used to exclude union influence from the workplace. However, the inadequacies of industry-level collective agreements enabled more localized bargaining to flourish in the private sector (Royal Commission 1968; Hyman 1975). During the 1950s and 1960s, in a climate of full employment, shop stewards in the engineering industry were able to negotiate with managers over bonuses, overtime arrangements, and incentive payments, and reach local settlements that were outside of, and in addition to, the industry agreements (Sisson and Brown 1983; Brown 2010).

The influence of multi-employer bargaining was inevitably eroded, and concerns about the consequences arose. The increasing gap between the rates agreed by means of industry-level bargaining and the actual earnings of workers, augmented by locally negotiated supplements—or 'wage drift' as it became known (Royal Commission 1968; Brown 1973)—was perceived to have inflationary consequences. Added to this, informal workplace bargaining tended to 'sap management control over work' (Brown, Marginson, and Walsh 2003: 200), and generated a multitude of small-scale, often short industrial disputes which, taken together, were deemed by policy-makers to be detrimental to economic performance.

Although dominated by the experience of the engineering sector, the Donovan Royal Commission (1965–8) found that much of the blame for these problems could be laid at the door of management who, it was asserted, should take a greater degree of responsibility for shaping their own employment relations arrangements (Royal Commission 1968). While the extent of Donovan's influence is questionable—single-employer bargaining was rising in popularity anyway as employers sought to develop organization-specific arrangements—the 1970s saw a diminution in the incidence of multi-employer bargaining (Brown 1981, 2010; Brown, Bryson, and Forth 2009).

7.2.2 The contraction of collective bargaining

However, since the 1980s there has been a marked diminution in the role played by collective bargaining in employment relations (Brown, Bryson, and Forth 2009; Marginson 2012). This contraction of collective bargaining has been expressed in three main ways: the substantial decline in the coverage of collective bargaining; the decentralization of bargaining where it does exist, manifest in the almost complete disappearance of multi-employer bargaining from the private sector; and the narrowing of the scope of collective bargaining.

First, with regard to the diminution of collective bargaining coverage, whereas in 1984 collective bargaining covered some two-thirds of workplaces with 25 or more employees, by 2004 this had fallen to just a third. Moreover, over the same twenty-year period the proportion of employees covered by collective bargaining declined from 70 per cent to 39 per cent—see Table 7.1 for further details. While much of the decline occurred during the 1980s and 1990s, the contraction of collective bargaining coverage continued during the 2000s (Brown and Nash 2008; Brown 2010). By 2011, collective bargaining was present in just 13 per cent of all workplaces with five or more employees, and just 6 per cent of private sector

Table 7.1 The contraction of collective bargaining coverage, 1984–2004

	1984	1990	1998	2004
Workplaces with any collective bargaining (%)				
All workplaces	66	52	40	32
Private sector	47	38	24	16
Public sector	99	86	84	82
Employees in workplaces with any collective bargaining (%)				
All workplaces	70	54	42	39
Private sector	52	41	32	25
Public sector	95	78	67	79

Workplaces with 25 or more employees

Source: Brown, Bryson, and Forth (2009)

workplaces (van Wanrooy et al. 2013). Only one in six (16 per cent) employees in the private sector is covered by collective bargaining—see Table 7.2. This table shows that the proportion of all employees covered by collective bargaining also declined between 2004 and 2011, from 29 per cent to 23 per cent, largely because of an apparently substantial fall in collective bargaining coverage in the public sector. Nevertheless, there remains a marked differentiation between collective bargaining coverage in the public sector, where it is still commonplace, and the private sector, where it has become much rarer. Collective bargaining and pay determination arrangements in public sector organizations are examined in Section 7.2.3.

There is a pronounced association between workplace size and collective bargaining coverage. Collective bargaining is rarer in smaller workplaces than in larger workplaces. Table 7.3 shows that whereas just 17 per cent of employees in workplaces with fewer than fifty employees are covered by collective bargaining, this proportion rises to 44 per cent of employees in larger workplaces, those with fifty or more employees. Collective bargaining

Table 7.2 Changes in collective bargaining coverage, 2004–11

	2004	2011
Workplaces with any collective bargaining (%)		
All workplaces	16	13
Private sector	8	6
Public sector	70	58
Employees in workplaces with any collective bargaining (%)		
All workplaces	29	23
Private sector	17	16
Public sector	69	44

Workplaces with 5 or more employees

Source: van Wanrooy et al. (2013)

Table 7.3 Collective bargaining coverage by workplace size and industry sector, 2011

	Employees' pay covered by collective bargaining (%)
All	31.2
Workplaces with fewer than 50 employees	17.3
Workplaces with 50 or more employees	44.1
Public administration and defence	71.1
Education	59.0
Electricity and gas	50.9
Transport and storage	47.2
Health and social work	43.8
Financial services	25.0
Manufacturing	23.2
Construction	18.0
Wholesale, retail, and motor trade	16.0
Hotels and restaurants	4.6

Selected industries

Source: Brownlie (2012)

coverage also varies extensively by industry sector. The most obvious variation is that which exists between the private and public sectors, as mentioned already. However, there are further variations in collective bargaining coverage which are worth noting. In some industries the presence of collective bargaining is rare indeed. Fewer than 5 per cent of hotel and restaurant employees, for example, are covered by collective bargaining, compared to around a half of workers in the electricity and gas and transport and storage sectors. These variations show that, while its coverage has clearly diminished substantially, collective bargaining continues to be present in many parts of the economy. In some parts of the private sector, such as in electricity, railways, and chemicals, collective bargaining has maintained an important influence, whereas in others, such as construction and food manufacturing, it has declined markedly (Brown 2010: 259).

What, then, accounts for the large-scale 'retreat' (Brown, Bryson, and Forth 2009: 31) of collective bargaining in the private sector? There are a number of factors which could plausibly explain the decline of collective bargaining, including the presence of a hostile legal and public policy environment during the 1980s and 1990s. Conservative governments of that period discouraged collective bargaining, a reflection of their espoused belief in individualism. It was portrayed as an archaic process that, by restricting managerial flexibility, undermined business performance. There may also have been a compositional effect. The changing composition of the workforce, in particular the increasing proportion of employees working in the private services sector, where collective bargaining had never been widespread anyway outside a few sectors such as food retailing, may have contributed to the diminution of collective bargaining. It is much rarer in newer workplaces, those established since the 1980s, than it is in older workplaces.

However, Brown, Bryson, and Forth (2009: 22) contend that the influence of such public policy and compositional effects on the 'collapse' of collectivism when it comes to determining employees' pay and conditions has been limited. Collective bargaining coverage continued to decline even during the 2000s under Labour governments that offered it an ostensibly more favourable climate (Brown 2010). Moreover, just 10 per cent of the decline in collective bargaining coverage in the private sector is estimated to be attributable to compositional change. Instead, collective bargaining has diminished largely because of the rise of more competitive market conditions, including greater international competition, which have encouraged employers to pursue greater control and flexibility over pay determination (Brown 2010). Whereas for much of the twentieth century relatively slack product markets gave employers a certain degree of latitude when it came to pay, making them receptive to demands from trade unions for collective bargaining arrangements, since the 1980s increasingly tough market conditions and greater competition has forced 'employers to tighten their control over employment, of which reducing the leeway for unions and reducing their influence over the conduct of work is a part' (Brown, Bryson, and Forth 2009: 22).

While robustly expressed, this explanation for the decline of collective bargaining based on the primacy of product markets, and intensified competition within them, is by no means entirely convincing. What about the role of actors like employers and unions, the choices they make, and the nature of the political-legal environment that shapes these choices (Marginson 2012)? These questions help to direct our attention to the diminution of union power in the private sector. Not only have unions been increasingly unable to secure bargaining arrangements in new workplaces, but employers have also attempted, often successfully, to exclude them from existing ones, in an effort to forge more direct relations with their staff. It should not be forgotten that collective bargaining has always been something that managers were willing to accept, often reluctantly, as a way of avoiding disruption. Thus the decline in collective bargaining coverage reflects the determination of managers to extend their prerogative to the area of pay determination, something that was enabled by, and further contributed to, the frailty of the trade union movement.

The second major collective bargaining trend since the 1980s concerns the decentralization of pay bargaining activity. During the 1980s and 1990s, multi-employer bargaining in the private sector almost disappeared, except for a few industries like electrical contracting (Gospel and Druker 1998). In 2004, just 4 per cent of private sector employees had their pay set in this way (Brown and Nash 2008). Where collective bargaining prevails in the private sector, it is now almost always undertaken at single-employer level (Brown, Bryson, and Forth 2009). Although the importance of multi-employer bargaining had been dwindling well before the 1980s, that decade saw the termination of national agreements across a range of sectors, including retail banking, engineering, and food retailing (Brown and Walsh 1991; Brown, Marginson, and Walsh 1995). This trend continued into the next decade in such a way that multi-employer bargaining 'which had greatly diminished in importance in the 1980s, became even more of a rarity in the 1990s' (Cully et al. 1999: 228). The principal reason for the decline of multi-employer bargaining concerned the ambition of firms to align pay more closely with business performance, and to exert greater control over pay outcomes in a more competitive environment. Without control over their own bargaining arrangements, firms found it difficult to secure increasingly necessary flexibility over pay (Brown and Walsh 1991; Brown, Marginson, and Walsh 2003).

The third key collective bargaining trend concerns its narrowing scope. Collective bargaining has become less about hard negotiation, and more likely to take the form of managers sharing information with union representatives, or consulting with them, rather than actually negotiating. Particularly in the private sector, collective bargaining is marked by 'a lack of confrontation and by a more consultative style over a relatively wide range of issues' (Brown and Nash 2008: 102). While the role of collective bargaining is most evident when it comes to pay-setting, it is also important to remember that the scope of bargaining can cover a potentially wide range of other employment issues, like holiday entitlement, for example, or grievance and disciplinary procedures. In the private sector, the scope of collective bargaining has narrowed markedly—the range of issues on which employers are willing to negotiate with trade unions fell substantially during the 2000s (van Wanrooy et al. 2013). Not only has the coverage of collective bargaining declined, but where it remains its scope has often been narrowed as the range of issues subject to joint regulation has diminished (Brown and Nash 2008). Evidently, it is not just the coverage of collective bargaining that has declined, 'but also its influence where it is still to be found' (Brown 2010: 262).

7.2.3 Collective bargaining in public sector organizations

While the extent of unilateral regulation of pay by managements has undoubtedly risen, by no means does this imply that collective bargaining has become extinct. We have already seen that there is a widespread variation in the incidence of collective bargaining arrangements throughout the economy. In the public sector, collective bargaining, often of the multi-employer type, continues to exert a powerful influence over the determination of pay. In 2011, collective bargaining covered 58 per cent of public sector workplaces—see Table 7.2. However, this table also shows a marked decline in the coverage of collective bargaining in the public sector during the 2000s. Whereas 69 per cent of employees in public sector workplaces were covered by collective bargaining in 2004, by 2011 this had fallen to 44 per cent. This decline seems to be partly related to the greater role played by pay review bodies (PRBs) in determining pay and conditions in the public sector, especially in health (van Wanrooy et al. 2013)—though some see the PRB process as a form of collective bargaining, rather than as supplanting it (see later in this section).

 Insight into practice 7.1: The erosion of national bargaining in the further education sector

Apart from the Civil Service, where the more direct role of government as employer appears to have been critical, the only other part of the public sector where national bargaining has been significantly eroded is the further education sector in England and Wales. Until 1993, further education colleges came under the control of their respective local authorities, which were the employers of college staff. Pay rates were negotiated nationally between representatives of the local authorities and the appropriate trade unions. Conditions of service were also determined by multi-employer bargaining at national level. The national 'Silver Book' agreement—as it was called because of the colour of its cover—among other things set upper limits on the number of teaching hours that lecturers could work on a weekly and annual basis.

In 1993, the colleges were taken out of local authority control and, in a process called 'incorporation', became employers of college staff in their own right. Although the arrangements would change, there

(continued...)

was no expectation that national bargaining would cease. It was anticipated that the newly established College Employers' Forum (CEF), an employers' association which took on the job of representing the colleges' employment relations interests, would continue to negotiate agreements with the unions which would then apply throughout the sector. The CEF's leadership, however, developed an ambitious reform agenda. Since college budgets were to be squeezed, it proposed replacing the Silver Book with a 'flexible' contract that placed no specific limitations on college lecturers' workload. This provoked a lengthy and bitter industrial dispute as the main lecturers' union tried to resist the imposition of new contracts. While some colleges were able to impose the CEF's contract, many introduced, either unilaterally or after negotiations with local union representatives, a version of their own which included some workload limits. By the end of the 1990s, then, a large variety of different contractual arrangements existed in the sector.

Pay remained formally subject to national bargaining, although the inability or reluctance of many colleges to implement annual recommended awards in full—or at all in some cases—because of purported financial difficulties led to an increasingly disparate set of pay rates across the sector as well as a number of industrial disputes. During the 2000s, attempts have been made by the employers and the unions to reinforce the authority of national agreements linked to the availability of more funds for the sector. It has proved difficult, though, to reinstate their influence given the diversity of employment arrangements present in the college sector.

Source: Williams (2004)

During the 1980s and 1990s, Conservative governments encouraged the reform of pay determination arrangements in the public sector, in particular by promoting the desirability of greater local managerial flexibility. Decentralized bargaining was seen as complementing the devolution of operational decision-making to local managers, hence making employment relations more 'responsive to the needs of managerial efficiency and labour market conditions, and more sensitive to employee performance' (Winchester and Bach 1999: 45). During this period, however, national bargaining in the public sector proved to be rather resilient (Corby 2000). The main exception was the Civil Service, where responsibility for pay determination was devolved to individual executive agencies, such as the Benefits Agency. Change in the Civil Service was more profound largely because of the government's direct influence over employment relations arrangements—although even here decentralization was moderated by the desirability of exercising close control over pay settlements (Bach 2010; Bach and Kessler 2012). Elsewhere, except for further education colleges, where there were a specific set of factors that led to the erosion of national bargaining (see Insight into practice 7.1), the extent of decentralization was limited. In the health service, for example, efforts to promote local pay deals were undermined by a combination of management ambivalence and union opposition (Thornley 1998; Carr 1999; Bach and Kessler 2012).

During the 2000s, Labour governments focused their efforts on 'modernizing' pay arrangements in the public sector. In this context, 'modernization' involved tackling problems of gender inequality, putting more of an emphasis on linking pay with performance, and enabling greater local managerial flexibility over employee reward—all to be achieved through partnership working with relevant public sector trade unions (Bach and Kessler 2012). This was manifest in the development of national frameworks applying to broad pay and conditions matters; but they contained space to give managers sufficient flexibility at local level when implementing them. The best known example came in the health service. The ambitious 2004

'Agenda for Change' agreement established a highly centralized national pay and grading system, designed to be operationalized by managers in individual health service trusts (Bach 2010). These efforts to build in space for local flexibility notwithstanding, overall the Labour government's efforts during the 2000s to 'develop more integrated and coherent systems of pay determination' represented a shift towards greater centralized control over pay determination arrangements (Bach, Givan, and Forth 2009: 323).

Nevertheless, there is one further aspect of the modernization agenda in public sector employment relations which has encouraged localization, namely the growing use of 'assistant' roles, such as teaching assistants in schools, healthcare assistants (HCAs), and police community support officers (PCSOs) (Bach 2011). Faced with pressures to improve service delivery, make cost savings, and improve efficiency, public sector managers have attempted to secure greater local flexibility by altering the composition of their workforce. One popular way of re-profiling the workforce has been to use greater proportions of auxiliary staff, whose pay and conditions, unlike those of established occupations, are generally not subject to determination at national level. Although HCAs now come under the national Agenda for Change pay and grading system, workforce re-profiling initiatives have been a commonplace way of promoting employment flexibility and realizing efficiency savings. Increasing numbers of teaching assistants and police community support officers testify to the attractiveness of this approach for employers (Bach, Kessler, and Heron 2006; Loveday, Williams, and Scott 2008).

Perhaps the foremost reason for the durability of centralized, national-level arrangements for determining public sector pay concerns the role of the system of pay review bodies (PRBs). These are formally independent institutions, whose members are appointed by the government, which, after evaluating appropriate data and submissions from interested parties such as trade unions, make non-binding recommendations to the government on pay increases and any other relevant matters within their remit. PRBs were originally created for specific groups of public sector employees, such as doctors and dentists and senior civil servants, and also members of the armed forces. However, their remit subsequently widened to encompass nursing staff and 'professions allied to medicine', including midwives and health visitors, and schoolteachers, in 1983 and 1991 respectively. In 2001, prison officers were also given a pay review body. Linked to the Agenda for Change agreement, during the 2000s the scope of the pay review body for nursing staff and professions allied to medicine was widened to encompass all NHS staff, with the exception of doctors and senior managers, and renamed the NHS Pay Review Body. The pay of over 2 million public sector workers is set by PRB recommendation (see Table 7.4).

Governments came to prefer PRBs over traditional collective bargaining arrangements because they helped to mitigate labour conflict in key public sector occupations. The PRB process, with its ostensibly rational, ordered, and consensual approach to determining pay outcomes, seemed less likely to cause disputes than traditional collective bargaining, with its more adversarial dynamic, and also help to reduce the power of the public sector unions. For example, PRBs were introduced for nurses and schoolteachers in the aftermath of large-scale industrial disputes. For governments, the two main attractions of PRBs are: first, that they offer a 'more stable and less conflictual system of pay determination than existed previously' (White 2000: 94); and second, that they give the impression that the government is an indifferent bystander, allowing it to avoid being drawn into potentially messy employment relations issues while still being able to exercise a strong influence (Bach, Givan, and Forth 2009;

Table 7.4 The system of pay review bodies

	Year established	Coverage
Senior Salaries Review Body	1971	Judges, senior civil servants, senior officers of the armed forces
Armed Forces Pay Review Body	1971	Members of the navy, military, and air force
Review Body on Doctors' and Dentists' Remuneration	1971	Doctors and dentists with any part in the National Health Service
National Health Service Pay Review Body	1983	Originally covered nurses and 'professions allied to medicine' (e.g. radiographers); in 2003 its remit was extended to all health professions, and extended again in 2007 to cover all non-clinical support staff
School Teachers' Review Body	1991	Schoolteachers
Prison Service Pay Review Body	2001	Prison officers, prison governors, and operational staff

Source: Office for Manpower Economics, http://www.ome.uk.com

Bach and Kessler 2012). Moreover, compared to 'traditional forms of national pay bargaining, the review body process has encouraged a more systematic analysis of a wider range of issues relating to affordability, recruitment and retention, morale, workload and job roles' (Bach 2010: 162).

During the 1990s and 2000s the presence of PRBs in certain parts of the public sector undoubtedly hindered the development of local bargaining arrangements since recommendations generally apply nationally, restricting the ability of managers to secure local pay flexibility. But how should the PRB process itself be understood? In some interpretations, it is treated as a form of pay determination that is distinct from collective bargaining (e.g. Kersley et al. 2006). More plausibly, PRB arrangements should be viewed as a 'particular type of collective bargaining' (Brown and Nash 2008: 95), perhaps akin to bargaining at 'arms' length' (Winchester and Bach 1995). Rather than being a 'substitute' for the collective bargaining process, pay review bodies, as a kind of third-party intervention, are in fact 'part of it' (Burchill 2000: 155). In other words, the review bodies mediate between the claims of the unions, representing the collective interests of their members, and the counter-claims of the employer representatives (Burchill 2000). Just because the parties do not meet with each other directly over a single negotiating table does not invalidate the status of the PRB process as a distinctive form of bargaining.

On this basis, then, studies which purport to show a dramatic decline in collective bargaining coverage in the public sector during the 2000s (e.g. van Wanrooy et al. 2013) should be treated with a certain degree of caution. Much of this supposed decline may simply reflect the expansion of the PRB system in the health sector. Since 2007, however, more vigorous government efforts to influence the PRB process, either through the guidance it gives review bodies or its decision about whether or not to implement their recommendations, means that it has become less easy to view it as a specific type of collective bargaining. Labour increasingly used PRBs explicitly as tools to moderate public sector pay rises (Bach 2010). For this reason, they seemed to have lost some of their effectiveness as tools for preventing disputes. In 2008, for example, the National Union of Teachers held a national one-day strike in England and Wales in pursuit of a 4 per cent pay claim, following a recommendation by their review body of a three-year pay deal, with a rise of just 2.45 per cent in the first year. The PRB process was also used by Labour as a means of delivering aspects of its modernization agenda, namely a push for greater local managerial control over pay and conditions. In schools, for example, the PRB 'delegated increasing levels of responsibility to head teachers to reduce the workload of teachers, to assess and award merit payments, and enhanced flexibility to decide on the grade of staff within national structures' (Bach, Givan, and Forth 2009: 322). Clearly, the PRB process gives governments a greater degree of control over public sector pay arrangements— one reason why it is seen as suitable for the police (see Contesting employment relations 7.2).

 Contesting employment relations 7.2: Reforming pay and conditions in the police

Police pay and conditions have prompted a growing degree of discontent. Matters relating to pay are determined by negotiation by means of a Police Negotiating Board (PNB), which comprises representatives of the police staff associations (police officers are not allowed to join unions) and employers, and makes recommendations to the government, in the form of the home secretary. Where negotiation fails to produce an agreement over a particular matter, it can be referred to an independent Police Arbitration Tribunal (PAT), although the government has the final say. In 2007–8, the then Labour government accepted the PAT's recommendation to award the police a pay rise of 2.5 per cent; but because this increase was not backdated, it amounted to only a 1.9 per cent annual overall rise. Police officers were incensed by this decision. Forbidden by law from undertaking industrial action, many thousands of police officers instead protested by marching through London. The association for rank and file police officers, the Police Federation, organized a ballot which showed that an overwhelming majority of its members wanted to see the law that prevents them from engaging in strikes and other forms of industrial action overturned. It also fought, and lost, a legal battle to overrule the home secretary's decision.

Since 2010, relations between the coalition government and the police have become increasingly strained, partly because of budget cuts of around 20 per cent. But the most controversial feature of the coalition's approach concerns the commissioning of a major two-part review of police pay and conditions under Tom Winsor, which reported in 2011 (part one) and 2012 (part two). Among the Winsor Review's recommendations were that the system of annual pay progression should be replaced by arrangements that put greater emphasis on individual skills and contribution. The Review wants the starting salary for police constables to be cut by some £4,000 to around £19,000 per annum, a recommendation which has been accepted by the government. It also calls for the PNB system to be replaced by an independent pay review body. All this created further calls from rank and file police officers for the right to take industrial action. In early 2013, the Police Federation initiated another ballot of its members on the issue; although there was a majority vote in favour of taking industrial action, it was not large enough to force a change in policy.

Since 2010, pressure for the 'erosion of national pay and conditions' across the public sector has increased (Bach 2012: 411). The Conservative-Liberal Democrat coalition government is instinctively hostile to national collective bargaining arrangements. Soon after taking office it abolished a national negotiating body covering school support staff which had only just been established under Labour. Much of the impetus for reform has been driven by right-wing lobbyists and pressure groups calling for greater localization of public sector pay determination (e.g. Wolf 2010; Holmes and Oakley 2012). They argue that local pay would enable public sector employers like local authorities and health service trusts to operate flexible pay and conditions arrangements, thus improving productivity. Public sector pay levels, being nationally determined, are deemed to be insensitive to local labour market conditions, making it difficult for private sector employers in relatively low-wage areas of the country to compete for workers; high public sector pay, it is claimed, is responsible for 'crowding out' private sector employment. In 2011, the coalition announced that it wanted to press ahead with the localization of public sector pay. PRBs were given a remit to examine how pay arrangements which are 'more market facing in local areas' could be introduced.

Not only have government efforts to decentralize pay determination in the public sector met with a great deal of opposition from the trade unions, but there is also much evidence that the assumptions upon which the localization agenda is based do not stand up to careful scrutiny. The Trades Union Congress (TUC) commissioned research which indicated that local pay in the public sector would not boost private sector employment. Reductions in public sector wage levels could also cost local economies up to £10 billion, because of the consequent fall in demand for goods and services. Moreover, it is unfair to expect workers doing the same jobs to get different pay, simply because of where they happen to live (TUC 2012*d*). The most rigorous challenge to the pay localization agenda has come from the pay experts Incomes Data Services (IDS). IDS research concludes that the idea that 'public sector pay levels crowd out private sector jobs and investment is highly flawed' (IDS 2012: 57). This is mainly because comparisons of pay levels which show that on average public sector pay is higher than in the private sector do not take into account marked differences in occupational structures between the sectors. They are not comparing 'like with like' (IDS 2012: 57). The public sector contains a larger proportion of people in professional and associate professional jobs, such as teachers and healthcare workers.

By 2013, much of the impetus for local pay determination in the public sector seemed to have dissipated. Union opposition and the generally unsupportive stance of most public sector employers have blunted the government's enthusiasm; even the PRB reviews broadly came down in favour of retaining national arrangements for determining pay and conditions, although individual schools are to be given greater flexibility over pay-setting arrangements within a national framework. Nevertheless, some health trusts in the south-west of England announced their intention to opt out of national pay and conditions agreements, allowing them greater scope to realize efficiency savings through reductions in pay, holiday entitlement, and sick leave. Pressures for greater decentralization also exist elsewhere in the system. Austerity measures, for example, have resulted in some cash-strapped local authorities opting to implement pay cuts, eroding the efficacy of national agreements.

Moreover, the greater opening up of public services to private sector providers increasingly undermines national pay and conditions of service agreements. In education, for example, the operators of new types of school, such as academies and 'free schools', are, in principle, able to set their own terms and conditions of employment for schoolteachers. 'Alongside ongoing opportunities for schools to convert into academies, the growth of free schools and all hospitals becoming foundation trusts, this is establishing a public service landscape in which many organizations have scope to opt out of national pay and conditions' (Bach 2012: 411). While national, multi-employer arrangements for determining public sector pay and conditions have proved to be remarkably resilient, increasing private sector involvement in the delivery of public services may erode it in future.

Section summary and further reading

- For much of the twentieth century, collective bargaining, often in the form of multi-employer arrangements, was the principal pay-setting method in employment relations.

- Multi-employer bargaining in the private sector has become rare indeed. In order to secure greater flexibility over their own employment relations, employers increasingly prefer to bargain with trade unions themselves. Moreover, there has been a general contraction of collective bargaining coverage in the private sector linked to changes in competitive conditions and the decline of union power relative to employers.

- In the public sector, collective bargaining, often manifest in multi-employer arrangements, has been somewhat resilient. The operation of pay review bodies for key groups of workers, a form of 'arms' length bargaining', has contributed to the durability of national arrangements for determining pay. However, pressures for greater local managerial flexibility may be encouraged by both austerity measures and the growing opening up of public services to private sector providers.

Collective bargaining trends are amply covered by Brown, Bryson, and Forth (2009) and Brown (2010). See Bach and Kessler (2012) and Bach (2010) for an overview of developments in public sector pay determination. White (2000) analyses the role of pay review bodies. More information about the operation of pay review bodies can be found at the website of the Office for Manpower Economics: http://www.ome.uk.com

7.3 Unilateral managerial regulation of pay

What, then, are the implications of the contraction of collective bargaining? How do employees have their pay determined, if not through the process of collective bargaining? In the private sector the most notable development concerns the large extent to which pay is now regulated unilaterally by management (Brown and Nash 2008; Druker and White 2009; Grimshaw and Rubery 2010). As Grimshaw and Rubery (2010: 353) make clear, the 'reality for the vast majority of private sector employees in the UK is that management sets their pay, not trade unions'. The purpose of this section is to examine the nature and extent of managerial innovation in pay-setting arrangements. How well have employers used the greater freedom they would seem to enjoy when it comes to managing pay issues? And what are the implications of systems for determining pay based on some kind of assessment of an employee's performance?

7.3.1 Managerial innovation in pay-setting arrangements: variable pay systems

There has been growing interest in how pay can be used as part of a sophisticated human resource management (HRM) approach (see Chapter 5) to managing employees. The term 'reward', rather than pay, is often used to refer to broader and more innovative methods of remunerating employees that assist the achievement of organizational goals. The decline of collective bargaining, with its common rate for the job, supposedly gives managers greater scope to implement more variable arrangements for determining pay, enhancing their flexibility when it comes to rewarding individual staff (Kersley et al. 2006; Druker and White 2009). Rather than basing pay on relatively unsophisticated criteria, such as the number of hours employees spend at work each week, for example, their grade, or their length of service, reward schemes may offer employees greater flexibility over their methods of remuneration, or align wages with performance, at the level of the worker, the work-group, or the organization. This is seen to embody a more strategic approach to the management of pay issues. For Druker and White (2009: 11), the management of reward 'is one of the key levers to be deployed in pursuit of effective HRM. If pay is to "deliver the goods" in terms of HR strategy, then it must be structured, it is argued, in order to meet HR objectives'.

Central to the idea that the management of reward issues should not only be aligned with, and supportive of, broader HRM objectives, but also integrated with the overall strategic goals of the organization, is the concept of 'new pay'. The 'new pay' approach is also marked by a greater emphasis on aligning reward levels with the contribution and achievements of workers as individuals, rather than as part of a collective (Corby, Palmer, and Lindop 2009). One of the main advantages of the greater flexibility offered by the 'new pay' approach for managers concerns the way in which pay outcomes are more closely linked to individual or organizational performance, passing on more of the risks of a lack of business success to the workforce (Arrowsmith and Marginson 2010).

Arrangements for determining pay whereby pay levels may vary according to, or be contingent on, levels of output, performance, or profitability are a key source of managerial flexibility. So-called 'variable' or 'contingent' pay systems became a more commonplace feature of employment relations during the 1980s and 1990s (Pendleton, Whitfield, and Bryson 2009; Brown and Marsden 2011). However, there is nothing new about variable pay systems (VPS). Incentive-based payment systems, which link an element of workers' pay to a measure of their output, have a long history in work and employment relations. Managers are often attracted to such schemes because they offer a relatively straightforward way of motivating and securing more effort from workers without the need for close supervision (Brown and Walsh 1994; Grimshaw and Rubery 2010). In practice, though, such arrangements rarely operate as effectively as managers anticipate. Workers, for example, may restrict their output, in order to maximize the earnings of them all as a group, and not go flat out in pursuit of a higher individual wage. Moreover, the effect of incentive payments on motivation is rarely unambiguous (Brown, Marginson, and Walsh 2003); the demotivation resulting from a failure to be awarded an expected wage bonus, for example, can outweigh any motivational advantages.

Such incentive payment schemes, where pay or bonuses are linked to output in some way—'payment by results'—are one type of VPS. The 'new pay' agenda, though, is more commonly linked with two other types of VPS: organizational-level arrangements that link reward to the success of the organization in some way, perhaps profitability for example, or through opportunities to purchase company shares; and performance-related pay (PRP) arrangements, whereby some or all of an employee's pay is linked to a managerial assessment of their performance, either as part of a team, or more commonly on an individual basis (Arrowsmith and Marginson 2011). There are two main reasons why they are attractive to employers. First, they are consistent with a 'new pay' approach in which there is an emphasis on managing reward in a way that supports overall business objectives, and puts more of an onus on securing greater organizational flexibility and improvements in business performance. The use of VPSs 'signifies a HR management strategy that responds to the more rapidly changing business environment, and often the decentralization of business and HR responsibilities to local managers' (Arrowsmith et al. 2010: 273). Second, they are consistent with efforts to promote

Table 7.5 Use of variable payment schemes, 2004–11, percentage of workplaces

	2004	2011
Any payment by results	31	28
Any system of pay based on an assessment of merit/performance	15	20
Any payment by results or based on merit/performance	40	40
Any profit-related pay	30	29
Any share schemes	17	9
At least one variable payment scheme	54	54

Source: van Wanrooy et al. (2013: 25)

a more individualized approach to managing employment relations, and would appear to make collective bargaining through trade unions, with its emphasis on standardized pay rates, unnecessary (Marginson 2009; Grimshaw and Rubery 2010).

Given the lack of progress made towards sophisticated HRM in general (see Chapter 5), perhaps it should come as no surprise that management-inspired innovations in respect of pay arrangements have been somewhat limited. The presence of VPSs is far from widespread (Corby, Palmer, and Lindop 2009), though there are signs that they have become present in a broader range of workplaces (Pendleton, Whitfield, and Bryson 2009). While there was a marked increase in the proportion of workplaces using them in the 1980s and 1990s, this growth did not continue during the 2000s (Brown and Marsden 2011; van Wanrooy et al. 2013). Table 7.5 shows that between 2004 and 2011 there was little change in the proportion of workplaces operating particular VPSs.

Managers are often reluctant to change systems for determining pay. They prefer to tread carefully, restricting their efforts to instituting incremental, minor adjustments (Kessler 2000). Overall, managers have 'not taken advantage of the demise of collective bargaining to implement new integrated systems of individualised employee relations and pay determination' (Charlwood 2007: 43). Generally, the decline of collective pay-setting arrangements has produced 'procedural individualization' rather than 'substantive individualization' when it comes to determining pay. In other words, while the decline of collective bargaining means that procedures for determining pay have become increasingly de-collectivized, in the sense that the influence of trade unions has diminished, managers still prefer to operate standardized arrangements for rewarding staff (Charlwood 2007).

Why has change been so limited when it comes to the reform of pay systems? One reason is that managers are often reluctant to bear the risks of innovation. Attempts to reform pay arrangements can disrupt employment relations, by undermining established norms of fairness and the legitimacy they offer. Managers are wary about making changes to existing payment systems. The 'tried and tested nature of arrangements, it seems, invests them with a high degree of legitimacy in the eyes of managers and employees' (Arrowsmith and Sisson 1999: 66). A second reason concerns pressures for equity, which arise from the need to operate arrangements for determining pay that comply with statutory requirements, particularly when it comes to equal pay matters, for example. There are other external pressures limiting the capacity of managers to innovate in respect of pay, and reducing the significance of VPSs. Decisions over pay settlements are influenced by the need to offer rises that are in line both with inflation, and with what other comparable groups of workers have been awarded (Druker and White 2009).

7.3.2 **The implications of performance-related pay**

Perhaps the most notable type of VPS involves attempts to link some element of an employee's reward to an assessment of their merit or performance by their manager. Through a focus on the rationale for performance-related pay (PRP) and how it operates, we are better placed to understand some of the difficulties and challenges that apply when trying to innovate in respect of pay-setting arrangements. The term PRP is conventionally associated with arrangements for determining pay that link an element of a worker's wages to some assessment of their worth, or merit. Under PRP, or individual PRP as it is sometimes called, an element of an employee's remuneration is based, over a given period of time, on an often subjective assessment of the quantity and quality of his or her work, normally by an immediate manager, set against a series of targets. Its use in white-collar jobs in particular represents a shift away from pay based on job grade or length of service 'towards relating pay more directly to individual characteristics' (Kessler and Purcell 1995: 350), particularly in some parts of the public sector, where PRP schemes have been introduced in occupations such as schoolteaching (Perkins and White 2010; Bach and Kessler 2012); however, they are more commonly found in the private sector (van Wanrooy et al. 2013).

What is the purpose of PRP? Kessler and Purcell (1995) suggest that three sets of managerial goals provide the rationale for PRP arrangements. First, managers use it as a way of stimulating pay flexibility. PRP ostensibly gives them greater latitude to restructure pay systems so that they support organizational objectives, though this is rarely done in a strategic way. The second set of goals relates to the desirability of enhancing employee motivation, commitment, and loyalty. If pay is made more contingent on their performance, then it is presumed that employees will identify with, and become more attached to, managerially determined organizational goals.

In his study of PRP in four local authorities, Heery (1998*a*) identified a contradictory rationale underpinning the decision to adopt PRP. On the one hand, managers sought to use it to gain greater employee compliance; PRP could help to reduce shirking and augment management control. On the other hand, the implementation of PRP was also seen as a way of generating culture change, towards a climate in which an ethos of flexibility and commitment predominated. Perhaps this should not be surprising given that the management of the employment relationship is driven by the need to secure employee compliance, as well as elicit their commitment, as we saw in Chapter 5.

The third set of managerial goals concern the use of PRP as a way of challenging collective bargaining arrangements and marginalizing the influence of trade unions. PRP is often seen as inimical to collective bargaining for a number of reasons, not least because it is often marked by an emphasis on rewarding individuals, and also because it threatens the role of unions as the bargaining agents of the workforce, perhaps as a prelude to, or a consequence of, derecognition (Gunnigle, Turner, and D'Art 1998; Heery 2009*b*).

Yet the existence of PRP is not incompatible with a trade union presence and collective bargaining (Grimshaw and Rubery 2010). While a desire to reduce the influence of trade unions and collective bargaining is a major rationale for the adoption of PRP schemes, a union presence can help to regulate how they are implemented, and shape the details (Heery 1997). Trade unions can work to improve how they function, perhaps by limiting the amount of an employee's reward that is contingent on performance or by insisting on constraints when it comes to the scope for managerial discretion (Heery 2009b). In the banking sector, for example, unions have been rather successful in ensuring that PRP is subject to joint regulation through collective bargaining, rather than just being subject to unilateral control by management (Arrowsmith and Marginson 2011). There is evidence that 'unions have proven able to redraw the lines of collective negotiation around the size of the available pay pot and its distribution. Combined with their ability to secure greater transparency and consistency in the functioning of schemes, unions in banking have obtained a degree of standardisation of outcomes' (Marginson 2009: 115).

Moreover, the effectiveness of PRP, as with any other kind of managerial intervention in employment relations, to a large degree rests upon how far it is viewed as legitimate by the workforce, particularly the extent to which it corresponds with their sense of fairness (Arrowsmith et al. 2010). When operating PRP schemes, managers have to take into account the expectations and reactions of employees. In his study of local government, Heery (1998a: 85) considers that 'PRP has been the subject of a tacit exchange between managers and employees, in which managers have refrained from an exacting application of formal procedures for fear of alienating employees'. This helps to explain, for example, the reluctance of managers to give employees low performance ratings. The experience of PRP schemes suggests that the need to win the consent of employees places important constraints upon managerial discretion over how pay is determined. Like any management initiative in employment relations, then, the implementation of PRP is conditioned by the need to elicit employees' cooperation as well as their compliance.

To what extent, though, is PRP effective, in managerial terms, as a way of increasing employees' motivation, and thus their levels of performance? Key features of PRP schemes, such as the manipulation of performance targets, the subjective evaluation of performance by managers, and the fact that the performance element to pay is generally a very small proportion of overall earnings, conspire to reduce their effectiveness (Kessler 2000). Given its potential to produce variations in earnings between employees, individual PRP can lead to increased jealousies and erode staff morale. See Insight into practice 7.3 for the case of schoolteachers.

 Insight into practice 7.3: Performance-related pay for schoolteachers

The most ambitious system of PRP in the whole of the public sector to be introduced during the 2000s was brought in for schoolteachers in England and Wales. The Labour government claimed that enhancing the pay of effective classroom teachers would lead to improved pupil performance, and thus generate improvements in educational standards. Once teachers have reached the top of the main pay scale, they can apply to cross a 'performance threshold' which involves having their performance assessed against certain criteria, including pupil attainment for example, by their headteacher. If successful, they can move to an upper pay scale, receiving an immediate £2,000 pay rise (Bach and Kessler 2012: 62). Teachers overwhelmingly opposed the PRP scheme; most felt that it would not

(continued...)

lead to improvements in teaching and better pupil performance (Farrell and Morris 2004). Moreover, expectations that PRP would raise the performance of teachers, and thus improve pupil performance, do not seem to have been realized (Farrell and Morris 2009). Four main factors account for the failure of the PRP scheme to have had the desired effects. First, individual PRP is considered to be inappropriate in school environments. Improvements in pupils' performance are generally seen by teachers as the result of their collective effort, and are sometimes attributable to factors beyond their control, such as parental support. Second, teachers consider PRP to be unsuited to the complicated task of improving children's education. Third, teachers dislike the potential for favouritism in the way that the PRP scheme operates, particularly the subjective judgement of headteachers as to whether staff meet the threshold or not. Fourth, teachers sometimes view PRP as a divisive mechanism, with negative consequences for their morale (Farrell and Morris 2004).

The overwhelming majority of teachers applying have been successful. This suggests that the new pay arrangements were not so much related to rewarding high performance, but more a general pay increase for teachers as a whole that, for political reasons, such as the reluctance of the government to be seen as giving away something for nothing, had to be disguised (Bach and Kessler 2012). Despite their hostility to PRP, teachers complied with the new arrangements on the basis that, since the additional pay was available, they might as well take it (Farrell and Morris 2004). However, a further effect of the PRP scheme has been to increase record keeping requirements and other forms of bureaucracy. Perhaps most significant long-term consequence of the introduction of PRP in schools is its contribution to the erosion of teachers' professional autonomy, and increasing managerial control (Farrell and Morris 2004). In early 2013, the coalition government announced plans to introduce a more extensive system of PRP in schools. Rather than being automatic, annual pay progression up the main scale is to be based on an assessment of teachers' performance.

There is plentiful evidence that in practice PRP schemes may have a greater demotivating effect, rather than increasing workers' motivation (Marsden 2009), as can be seen from the experiences of two government agencies, the Inland Revenue and the Employment Service (Marsden and French 1998). Although most employees supported the principle of PRP, in general they were highly critical of the way the respective schemes operated in practice. In the Employment Service, for example, the individual performance targets were a source of discontent since it was difficult for employees, given that they had insufficient control over their workloads, to attain them. It was widely felt, moreover, that managers manipulated the performance review process to give higher ratings to favoured employees. In both organizations, PRP appears to have led to a significant decline in morale, caused jealousies, and reduced the level of cooperation between managers and employees.

While the principle of PRP is generally seen as fair, in practice it is often implemented in a way that disrupts established pay arrangements and, in doing so, upsets existing norms of fairness and the sense of legitimacy that they create, something which forms the basis of workplace order. Any alterations to pay-setting arrangements, particularly those that link an element of pay to performance in some way, unless handled very carefully and with due sensitivity, seem likely to have a demotivating effect (Brown and Nolan 1988; Brown, Marginson, and Walsh 2003). That said, however, PRP schemes in the public sector, while not motivating employees into supplying greater work effort, do seem to be associated with improvements in organizational performance. How is this apparent paradox to be explained? The contribution of Marsden (2009) is important here. He explains that PRP arrangements, as part of broader systems of performance management in organizations, enable workers and managers to clarify objectives and work priorities, and provide workers with a means of influencing, and indeed negotiating over, the process of goal-setting. Therefore the effectiveness of PRP schemes, and indeed VPSs in general, seems to depend 'less on their effect on motivation than on their direct association with a radical change in performance norms and renegotiation of job design and work rules' (Grimshaw and Rubery 2010: 361). This is consistent with viewing the workplace as a 'negotiated order' (see Chapter 1), marked by an ongoing process of negotiation and re-negotiation over the terms of the wage–work bargain (Sisson 2010).

 ### Section summary and further reading

- The contraction of collective bargaining coverage in general in the private sector means that the majority of employees in Britain have their pay determined unilaterally by management.
- The growth in the use of 'variable' or 'contingent' pay schemes seen in the 1980s and 1990s did not continue into the 2000s, and employers often prefer to operate standardized arrangements for determining pay even in the absence of trade unions and collective bargaining.
- Managers find arrangements that associate pay with performance attractive, since they offer more flexibility and help to secure the commitment of employees to business goals. While sometimes designed to undermine collectivism, PRP is not inimical to joint regulation and trade unionism. Nevertheless, despite the apparently greater freedom they enjoy to reform pay systems and influence pay settlements, managers have been reluctant to upset existing, 'tried and tested' arrangements.

There is some good material on managerial approaches to pay determination in Grimshaw and Rubery (2010). Charlwood (2007) demonstrates the continuing relevance of standardized pay-setting processes. Druker and White (2009), Heery (2009b), and Marginson (2009) are useful when it comes to understanding trends and developments in pay determination.

7.4 Regulating low pay

One of the main implications of the diminution of collective bargaining as a pay-setting mechanism and the consequent increase in unilateral managerial regulation has been growing pay inequality. The gap between high earners and those lower down the wage hierarchy grew markedly during the 1980s and 1990s, alongside the declining reach of joint regulation. As a consequence, the question of how best to protect low-paid workers became a more topical issue. The main purpose of this section is to examine the regulation of low pay, looking at the rationale for, and impact of, statutory regulation in the form of the National Minimum Wage (NMW), which was introduced in 1999. As will become evident, although the NMW is generally reckoned to be an example of a highly successful government policy intervention, it has done rather little to reduce the problem of low pay in the economy. As a result, among campaigners on behalf of the low-paid there is growing interest in other ways of tackling poverty pay, such as the living wage approach.

7.4.1 Regulating low pay through minimum wages

The first major task concerns specifying what is meant by low pay. It is generally conceived of in relative terms, not as an absolute measure (e.g. Rubery and Edwards 2003). In other words, determining the level of pay beneath which workers are classified as low-paid should be done in relation to the general level of earnings characteristic of a particular society, something which varies across regions and countries, and which changes over time. In this respect, the Organisation for Economic Co-operation and Development (OECD) defines low pay as that which falls below a level of two-thirds of overall median earnings. In 2011 some 4 million workers in the UK, two-thirds of them women, earned less than two-thirds median hourly pay—below £7.49 per hour, or a salary of £13,600 based on a thirty-five-hour week (Pennycook and Whittaker 2012).

Women are more likely than men to be engaged in low-paid work, and low pay is also a more commonplace feature of jobs held by young workers (Pennycook and Whittaker 2012). It is concentrated in particular occupations (e.g. cleaners, sales assistants, catering workers, bar staff) and in certain sectors of the economy—especially hospitality, social care, retail, clothing and textile manufacturing, and hairdressing. Low pay is a prominent feature of hotels and restaurants; two-fifths (41 per cent) of workplaces in this sector had at least a quarter of the workforce earning the adult minimum wage or less. Yet it is much less evident in other sectors, such as transport and communications (van Wanrooy et al. 2013).

Broadly speaking, there are two main ways in which low pay is regulated in modern economies: either by collective agreements, or by means of a statutory minimum wage (Rubery and Grimshaw 2003). In the case of the first of these arrangements, a floor of wages is sometimes set by collective bargaining on an industry-by-industry basis, such as in Germany for example, with governments sometimes having the power to extend the settlement to all employers in the sector, even those that are not directly party to the agreement. Centralized systems of collective bargaining can often be quite effective ways of regulating low pay, and of impeding the growth of wage inequality, especially for full-time employees. This is because they act to compress wage differentials in the sectors where they have coverage (Hayter and Weinberg 2011).

 International perspective 7.4:   Minimum wage issues around the world

Minimum wages are often a topic of political interest and controversy around the world. Germany is one of the few advanced economies not to have a statutory minimum wage; instead, multi-employer collective bargaining sets a floor of wages on an industry sector basis. However, this approach means that workers in sectors where collective bargaining coverage is weak—often women, the low-skilled, and migrants—are disadvantaged. There is growing pressure in Germany for the introduction of an economy-wide minimum wage to help the low-paid. The United States operates a federal minimum wage—currently $7.25 (£4.86) per hour—which sets a pay floor across the country, although some individual states also have their own higher rates. In early 2013, the newly re-elected President Obama proposed raising the federal minimum wage to $9.00 (£6.03) per hour, much to the consternation of political opponents and business leaders, who contend—erroneously given the findings of most research—that this would damage economic competitiveness and lead to job losses. But even with this rise, the minimum wage would still be lower than it is in many other advanced economies, including the UK. In Greece, though, economic recession and pressure to pursue austerity policies mean that movement has been in the other direction. Under pressure from the European Union and the International Monetary Fund to reform its labour market and increase its economic competitiveness, in 2012 the Greek government slashed the value of the country's minimum wage by nearly a quarter (22 per cent). This is just one of the measures in Greece which has provoked furious opposition, including major strikes and demonstrations, against the austerity regime.

The second type of arrangement, a statutory minimum wage, exists in countries such as France, Spain, Portugal, and, since 1999, in the UK too. Even in Germany there has been much debate about the merits of operating a minimum wage system (see International perspective 7.4). While the NMW is the first national, cross-sectoral arrangement for regulating low pay by law in the UK, it is by no means the first attempt by government to regulate low pay (Sargeant 2010). Fair Wages Resolutions, for example, which originated in 1891, obliged employers to respect minimum standards when working on government contracts, largely to prevent unfair competition arising from the undercutting of wages (Bercusson 1978; Coats 2007). In the early 1980s, the then Conservative government repealed them. In 1993, the Conservatives also abolished all bar one of the remaining wages councils, which, for a large part of the twentieth century, had fixed wage rates, and sometimes employment conditions, in a range of low-paying sectors. They were seen as outdated and anachronistic institutions which inhibited labour market flexibility, were ineffective at tackling poverty, and, given the claim that they priced workers out of jobs, impediments to employment growth (Dickens et al. 1993; Rubery and Edwards 2003).

However, the abolition of the wages councils was responsible for increased wage inequality (Butcher 2012), without any positive impact on employment. According to Coats (2007: 17), 'an important 'effect of wages councils abolition was significantly to increase the number of low paid workers in the UK'. The one body that survived—the Agricultural Wages Board (AWB)—is scheduled for abolition by the coalition government, which contends that it is no longer needed given the existence of the NMW, as part of the Enterprise and Regulatory Reform Act 2013. Trade unions representing workers in agriculture strongly opposed getting rid of the AWB, pointing out that its role involves more than just setting basic wages, also covering matters like sick pay, overtime rates, and accommodation arrangements. Abolishing it would exacerbate the problem of rural poverty. However, the government's decision received plenty of support from landowners and business interests who would benefit from having a cheaper agricultural workforce.

What reasons lay behind the establishment of the NMW in 1999? Two factors were particularly important. First, one of the motivating influences behind the introduction of the NMW was the growing concern about rising wage inequality and its adverse social and economic consequences. There is a powerful body of evidence which demonstrates that the size of the gap between high and low earners matters in some very important ways. In their book *The Spirit Level*, for example, Wilkinson and Pickett (2009) show that countries with relatively high levels of inequality (e.g. US, UK) suffer from greater social problems, higher crime rates, and poorer health outcomes, than those which are more equal. Obesity, for example, is more prevalent in the UK than it is in countries with less inequality, like Sweden.

There was a marked growth in wage inequality during the 1980s, which continued into the 1990s, albeit at a slower rate (Machin 2011). The gap between high earners and low earners widened considerably, 'reaching the highest levels experienced in the twentieth century' (Machin 1999: 185). Rising inequality was fuelled by the trend for pay rises of high and relatively high earners to far outstrip increases for people on more modest earnings. In part it was also driven by technological change and the employment consequences of economic globalization, which reduced demand for semi- and low-skilled workers (Resolution Foundation 2012b). However, the then Conservative government's deregulatory policies, manifest in the abolition of the wages councils, the diminution of trade union power, the fall in collective bargaining coverage, and greater unilateral regulation of pay by management all helped to generate increased inequality during the 1980s and 1990s (Brown, Marginson, and Walsh 2003; Coats 2007). With the exception of Ireland, where wage inequality also rose, in the rest of the EU it largely remained stable or even diminished in this period (Machin 1999).

But a second factor was also important in the establishment of the NMW; this concerns the 'political momentum' for minimum wage regulation given by Tony Blair's Labour government, elected in 1997 (Butcher 2012: R26). Labour's eventual commitment to establishing an NMW was the outcome of protracted debates and struggle within the party as supporters of the policy, particularly in some trade unions, tried to overcome the traditional ambivalence towards statutory wage-fixing that had characterized attitudes in much of the labour movement (Coats 2007; Arrowsmith 2009). Following its victory at the 1997 general election, the Labour government set up a Low Pay Commission (LPC), comprising employer and union representatives, as well as academic experts. The LPC's initial role was to make recommendations to government over such matters as the coverage of the minimum wage (i.e. to whom would it apply?), the elements of pay that could be counted towards the minimum wage (e.g. what should happen to tips?—see the introductory case study), and the minimum wage rates themselves. After the NMW came into effect, the LPC remained in existence with its role largely devoted to investigating the effects of the minimum wage, and making recommendations to the government over changes to the minimum wage rates (or 'upratings') and other relevant matters in a series of annual reports (e.g. LPC 2013).

Since their introduction in 1999, the NMW rates have been uprated several times, as can be seen from Table 7.6. A lower 'development' rate applied to workers aged between 18 and 21 (20 since 2010). It was introduced largely because of a concern that if young workers were

Table 7.6 National Minimum Wage rates, 1999–2013

	Workers aged 22 and over*	Uprating	Workers aged 18–21*	Workers aged 16–17	Apprentices
April 1999	£3.60		£3.00		
June 2000	£3.60		£3.20		
October 2000	£3.70	2.8%	£3.20		
October 2001	£4.10	10.8%	£3.50		
October 2002	£4.20	2.4%	£3.60		
October 2003	£4.50	7.1%	£3.80		
October 2004	£4.85	7.8%	£4.10	£3.00	
October 2005	£5.05	4.1%	£4.25	£3.00	
October 2006	£5.35	5.9%	£4.45	£3.30	
October 2007	£5.52	3.2%	£4.60	£3.40	
October 2008	£5.73	3.8%	£4.77	£3.53	
October 2009	£5.80	1.2%	£4.83	£3.57	
October 2010	£5.93	2.2%	£4.92	£3.64	£2.50
October 2011	£6.08	2.5%	£4.98	£3.68	£2.60
October 2012	£6.19	1.8%	£4.98	£3.68	£2.65
October 2013	£6.31	1.9%	£5.03	£3.72	£2.65

*The main NMW rate extended to 21 year olds in 2010

to be covered by the main NMW rate it would make them too expensive for employers to hire, thus significantly damaging their labour market prospects (Metcalf 1999; Coats 2007; Sargeant 2010). Initially, the use of the lower rate for young workers was far from common-place; employers were reluctant to use it (e.g. Heyes and Gray 2001; Langlois and Lucas 2005). There are difficulties recruiting, motivating, and retaining younger workers at rates of pay that are below the main 'adult' NMW level; many managers view it as unfair to discriminate against them on the grounds of age (Williams, Adam-Smith, and Norris 2004), even though it is lawful, being exempt from age discrimination legislation (Sargeant 2010). Some employers, like Tesco, have turned away from pay structures related to age, although they are still com-mon in sectors like fast-food restaurants and pubs which employ lots of young people (IDS 2011b). As the main NMW rate increased, some employers reintroduced age-based differen-tials as a way of managing the extra costs of compliance; and there is evidence that the young workers' rate is becoming more widely used (LPC 2012).

Originally, the NMW did not cover workers aged below 18. The LPC and the government did not want to discourage teenagers from leaving full-time education (Sargeant 2010). How-ever, in October 2004 the government introduced a new, lower rate of £3.00 per hour that applied to 16 and 17 year olds. This was done because of concerns raised by trade unions that some young workers were being exploited by unscrupulous employers who were paying them very low rates of pay, less than £2.00 an hour in some cases (LPC 2004). In 2010 the full 'adult' rate was extended to cover workers aged 21 and over; the same year saw the introduc-tion of an 'apprentice' rate, payable to apprentices aged below 19 or, if older, who are in the first year of their training (LPC 2010; Butcher 2012).

The operation of the LPC, in particular the high level of consensus that informs its recom-mendations, has been praised. It has also been lauded for retaining its independence from the government, its pragmatism, and the importance it attaches to basing its recommenda-tions on rigorous evidence and analysis (Brown 2009; Butcher 2012). By bringing employer and union representatives together to discuss and reach agreement on matters relating to the NMW, the way the LPC operates has been heralded as an example of 'social partner-ship' that could be used to improve other aspects of employment relations (Brown 2009; Butcher 2012). Yet, while no one could doubt the effective role played by the LPC in helping to make the NMW such a durable feature of the employment relations environment, it has been overly cautious, particularly when it comes to its recommended minimum wage rates—too willing to be oversensitive to claims from employers about the undesirable consequences of raising them too far (Grimshaw and Rubery 2010), especially during the post-2008 economic downturn (LPC 2013).

One of the LPC's most important concerns has been to avoid any adverse economic con-sequences of implementing NMW rates that are too high, or that increase too quickly (Brown 2009). The fear is that employers in low-paying sectors of the economy could react to any increase in labour costs by reducing jobs. Therefore, a key challenge for the LPC is striking a balance between 'a desire to have a high minimum, to benefit low-paid workers, against the concern that job losses might arise if that minimum were to be set too high' (Manning 2012: 3). One former member of the LPC has defended the deliberately cautious stance ini-tially followed by the LPC, which favoured introducing an NMW at a relatively low level, just in case there were any adverse effects on the economy, and building from there through regular upratings. He maintains that once 'it was clear that there were no negative effects on employment... the LPC had scope for somewhat greater ambition in testing the boundaries' (Coats 2007: 49).

During the first half of the 2000s, the value of the main NMW rate grew quite substantially, exceeding both inflation and rises in average earnings. Table 7.6 shows that in some years—notably in 2001, 2003, and 2004—there was a pronounced annual uprating: nearly 11 per cent in the first of those years, and over 7 per cent in the others. Although the NMW rate was initially set at a low level, reflecting the cautious approach taken by the LPC, it was subsequently raised by a relatively large amount until 2006 (Stewart 2011; Butcher 2012). Whereas in 1999 the main NMW rate amounted to a rather meagre 46 per cent of median adult hourly earnings, by 2006 it had reached 51 per cent (Butcher 2012).

Since then, though, the LPC has reverted to a more conservative approach, with the annual average uprating amounting to just 2.5 per cent. Some attribute this to pressure from employers (Grimshaw and Rubery 2010); but the recession also seems to have prompted a greater degree of caution from the LPC, which does not want to undermine any economic recovery by raising the minimum wage rates too far (LPC 2012, 2013), a position which the government has evidently encouraged (BIS 2013). Indeed, in 2012 there was no annual increase in the NMW rates for young workers, in recognition of their fragile employment situation (LPC 2012). Supporters of the LPC's approach recognize that it has become more cautious since 2007, but nonetheless stress that over the entire period since 1999 the value of the NMW has grown relative to average earnings (Butcher 2012). In 2012 it stood at 52 per cent of median adult hourly earnings (LPC 2012). Yet this has not been sufficient to offset the initially low level at which the NMW was set (Stewart 2011). Moreover, its value in real terms—relative to rises in prices—declined between 2010 and 2012, meaning that it was effectively at the lowest level for ten years (Pennycook and Whittaker 2012; Resolution Foundation 2012c).

7.4.2 The impact of the National Minimum Wage

In considering the impact of the NMW we first need to ascertain who has benefited from it. Around 5 per cent of the workforce—some 1.2 million workers—gained directly from the 1999 introduction of the NMW (Metcalf 2008; Butcher 2012). Later upratings affected between 4 and 5 per cent of the workforce; in 2011, for example, 4.4 per cent of all jobs in the economy were affected by that year's increase in the adult NMW rate (LPC 2012). Yet because the incidence of low pay is concentrated among certain sectors and occupations, increases in the NMW have had much more of an effect in some types of jobs than in others. Most of the beneficiaries, some two-thirds, are women workers, especially those employed in part-time jobs. Workers in low-paying sectors of the economy—notably hairdressing, hospitality, retail, and social care—and those employed by small businesses have benefited disproportionately from the presence of the NMW.

The NMW has been widely praised as an example of a highly effective government policy intervention, not just in employment relations, but also more broadly. In a 2010 poll of political experts it was voted the most successful UK government policy since 1980, beating the Northern Ireland Peace Process into second place (Butcher 2012; Manning 2012). Initially, though, it by no means commanded universal support. During the 1990s, the Conservative Party and many business organizations opposed the minimum wage policy, claiming that it would push up inflation and have a massively adverse impact on employment; some speculated that introducing an NMW would put up to 2 million jobs at risk (Manning 2011, 2012; Stewart 2011). The simple economic reasoning behind these claims is that any rise in the price of labour, wages that is, without a corresponding increase in productivity, will reduce employers' demand for it. Alternatively, firms will pass on the higher costs of adapting to the NMW to customers in the form of higher prices. Such problems would be exacerbated if, as critics of the minimum wage expected, other groups of workers were to secure corresponding increases in their wages in order to preserve their relative position in the pay hierarchy or, in other words, restore their existing pay 'differentials'. Some US labour economists emphasize that minimum wages are associated with reductions in employment levels (e.g. Neumark and Wascher 2008).

Yet, contrary to these expectations, the introduction of the NMW appears to have had little adverse effect on the British economy; it arrived with a 'whimper rather than a bang' (Dickens and Manning 2003: 202). The low level at which the NMW was initially set meant that most firms, even in low-paying sectors of the economy, were not affected directly by its introduction; and many of those that were found the necessary increases in wage rates easily affordable. Overall, neither the introduction of the NMW, nor its subsequent uprat- ings, seems to have had a detrimental impact on employment levels (Manning 2012; Metcalf 2008; Stewart 2011). Indeed employment in low-paying sectors of the economy, where the NMW will have had a more powerful effect, has grown more quickly than throughout the economy in general, even during the recession (Butcher 2012). The Conservatives dropped their opposition in the early 2000s, and the coalition government has affirmed its support for the NMW, recognizing the protection it gives low-paid workers and the incentive to work it provides. However, while all the major political parties support the principle of having a mini- mum wage (Butcher 2012), this does not necessarily include a commitment to maintaining its value. As already mentioned, since 2010, when the coalition took office, this has declined.

What explains the absence of a negative impact on employment levels? Some economists specify that minimum wages can have a positive effect because they provide people outside the labour market with an incentive to take up a job (Manning 2012). No doubt the prevailing economic context also helped. Until 2008 the UK economy grew, meaning that any increased costs to employers arising from the NMW were easily absorbed, and indeed were relatively minor compared to the revenue arising from expanding product markets (Brown 2009). Metcalf (2008) posits five plausible reasons why the NMW has had no discernable adverse employment effects:

- Employers have coped with the increased costs of the NMW by raising productivity, rather than reducing employment.
- Some of the increase in costs has been passed on to consumers in the form of higher prices.
- Firms have coped by taking a smaller share of profits.
- Employers have reduced hours of work rather than cut jobs.
- Employers have a degree of market power and thus some flexibility when determining wages; this means that they did not necessarily react to the NMW by cutting jobs.

This last point is important for understanding why the NMW has not created a 'labour market shock' and reduced employment levels, in the manner expected by some (e.g. Brown and

Crossman 2000). The NMW has been relatively easily absorbed by firms in low-paying sectors of the economy, who have a variety of options open to them when it comes to offsetting the resultant higher wage costs: increasing productivity; reducing working hours; adjusting bonus payments and shift premiums; taking less profits; or increasing prices (LPC 2011; Butcher 2012). Far from being a shock to firms in low-paying sectors of the economy, the minimum wage is simply a further influence among the many that shape employment relationships within them (Adam-Smith, Norris, and Williams 2003). It is unlikely that a consistent pattern of responses to the NMW will be identified, particularly with it being set at such a low level. Rather, affected firms will react in idiosyncratic and diverse ways, influenced by the characteristics of their product and labour market environments (Arrowsmith 2009). Indeed, many employers have adapted to the increased costs of the NMW rises simply by 'muddling through' (Metcalf 2008).

Of course, another way in which employers in low-paying sectors of the economy can avoid the consequences of the NMW legislation is by failing to comply with it. While the extent of non-compliance is difficult to measure, overall it seems to be quite rare (Manning 2012). Nevertheless, concerns have been expressed that the level of non-compliance in the informal economy, particularly among migrant workers, may be an issue (Croucher and White 2007; LPC 2010). In 2010, for example, the Channel Four *Dispatches* programme revealed that some clothing and textiles factories in the UK, which made goods for leading high street chains like New Look, were paying workers as little as £2.50 per hour (Channel Four 2010). There is a growing awareness that the practice of employers providing opportunities for unpaid work experience should be more closely scrutinized (see Employment relations reflection 7.5). Generally, though, it is the technical aspects of the NMW regulations that cause the biggest problems, including calculating the hourly wage rate in jobs where the pay is linked to production in some way, rather than time spent actually working, suggesting that some non-compliance is inadvertent (Patel 2011).

Employment relations reflection 7.5: Unpaid work experience—opportunity or exploitation?

Chapter 2 highlighted the use of unpaid internships by employers as a means of gaining cheaper labour. Some trade unions claim that employers use unpaid work experience as a way of reducing costs, and of avoiding having to pay the minimum wage, with little benefit for the workers involved. The media and broadcasting union BECTU claims that any training element is largely absent, and that the use of volunteer labour in this way 'amounts to the exploitation of young people desperate to gain a foothold in the film/TV sector' (TUC 2008: 121). The Low Pay Commission is very concerned that some employers classify unpaid positions as 'internships' to avoid complying with the NMW, when in fact the people filling them are undertaking real jobs, and that this practice is becoming more widespread (LPC 2012, 2013). The government has published guidance which specifies that unless they are a genuine volunteer, or a student undertaking a placement of less than a year's duration, then workers directly engaged in work activities—having a role that extends beyond simply observing others—are entitled to receive at least the NMW (Gateways to the Professions Collaborative Forum 2011). However, the government's own policies seem to have played a part in undermining the NMW's effectiveness. One of the reasons why its Work Programme (see Chapter 2), which aims to get the unemployed back into employment, has been so controversial is because jobseekers are often compelled to take up unpaid work placements which some employers use instead of proper paid positions.

However, there is growing evidence that some unscrupulous employers have been try-ing to escape their obligation to pay workers the minimum wage. The LPC claims that non-compliance is a particular problem in some areas, such as in the hotel cleaning and social care sectors (LPC 2013). In October 2011, the BBC's *Panorama* programme (2011) highlighted the methods used by some employers to avoid having to comply with the NMW. In the social care sector, for example, workers are often only paid for the time they actually spend attend-ing to users, not the time spent travelling between different clients. Moreover, reductions in the time supposed to be devoted to particular clients mean that workers, if they are to carry out their duties properly, can only do so on an effectively unpaid basis (Ramesh 2013). At least 150,000 direct social care workers (9 per cent of this workforce) do not receive the NMW as a result of such tactics (Hussein 2011). Employers that do not comply with the NMW are generally aware that they are breaking the law, but believe they are not going to be caught. They assume that their workers are happy to have a job, no matter how badly paid, and are therefore unlikely to make a complaint (Ipsos Mori/Community Links 2012).

There are two methods of enforcing the NMW. First, workers themselves are entitled to pursue their right to be paid the minimum wage by litigating against employers. There are around 500–600 complaints about non-payment of the NMW made to employment tribu-nals each year. However, there are a number of problems with this method of enforcement. For one thing, workers may lack the appropriate knowledge of their rights under the NMW legislation, and so may not be aware that they have a justified complaint (TUC 2008). More-over, even if they do have adequate knowledge, workers can be reluctant to complain about underpayment of the minimum wage—with good reason, since there is some evidence that employers victimize workers who make their voices heard. Thus workers may be discouraged from making a complaint against their employer because of a fear that it would jeopardize their jobs (Croucher and White 2007).

The second method of ensuring compliance with the NMW concerns proactive enforce-ment by HM Revenue and Customs (HMRC). In the eighteen-month period up to October 2012 it identified £6.2 million of pay arrears which were owed to some 36,000 workers (BIS/HMRC 2013). However, the HMRC's enforcement arrangements have been criticized for being inadequate (Croucher and White 2007). On average, an employer can expect a visit from an enforcement officer once every 320 years; perhaps the really remarkable thing is 'that so many employers *do* comply with the NMW' (Metcalf 2008: 499). Prompted by pressure from trade unions, campaigners for the low-paid, and also the views of the LPC itself, during the latter half of the 2000s the government took steps to improve the enforcement of the NMW legislation. This included increased resources and better targeted enforcement activity by HMRC officers, focusing on industries like clothing and textiles where there were known problems of non-compliance (LPC 2010; Patel 2011; BIS/HRMC 2013). Moreover, Labour's 2008 Employment Act established a new penalty regime under which an employer can be fined up to £5,000 for a failure to pay the NMW, as well as improving the arrangements whereby workers could claim any wage arrears.

However, the LPC has expressed a worry that coalition budget cuts could damage enforce-ment efforts, particularly by compromising attempts to publicize the NMW effectively (LPC 2011). It has also been concerned that HMRC is insufficiently committed to instituting pro-ceedings against employers found to have broken the law (LPC 2012); during the NMW's first ten years in existence there were only seven successful prosecutions for non-payment, and none since the coalition took office. The LPC also thinks that more needs to be done to raise awareness of employers who have broken the law by not paying staff the minimum wage, by naming them in public (LPC 2013).

7.4.3 From the minimum wage to the living wage

The NMW seems to have had some effect in moderating wage inequality, in particular by helping to increase the income of the poorest working households (see Coats 2007: 57; Metcalf 2008). During the 2000s, rises in the level of the minimum wage helped to narrow the ratio between the average earnings of the lowest-paid and median pay—so-called 'lower-tail inequality' (Manning 2012). That said, however, 'upper-tail inequality'—the gap between the median and top earners—has continued to grow (Machin 2011; Manning 2011). The incomes of a very small minority of people at the very top of the earnings hierarchy have risen sharply relative to other groups (Resolution Foundation 2013), 'racing away' from those of people further down the hierarchy (Brewer et al. 2008). This has been fostered by the diminution of collective bargaining, increased unilateral managerial regulation of pay issues, and the preference of governments for a light regulatory environment. As a result, the UK has become 'more unequal than at any time since modern records began' (Turnbull and Wass 2011: 274). Very high earners, those at the very peak of the income distribution scale, like boardroom directors for example, have been able to secure ever higher levels of remuneration relative to others; this has prompted a debate about the desirability of regulating top people's pay (see Employment relations reflection 7.6).

Employment relations reflection 7.6: Directors' pay and the growth of pay inequality

One of the contributory factors to the growth of pay inequality in Britain has been the ever-increasing level of remuneration enjoyed by the directors of public limited companies, relative to average wages. In 1979, for example, the most highly paid executive in BP earned sixteen and a half times the salary of the average employee in the company; by 2011, this had grown to sixty-three times the average employee's salary (High Pay Commission 2011). Top pay often bears little relationship to how well the company has performed. According to the government, between 2002 and 2012, 'directors' pay in the UK's largest listed companies has quadrupled with no clear link to company performance. Top pay appears to go up when performance is good, but there is comparatively less elasticity downwards when performance is average or poor. As a result, average levels of executive pay have ratcheted upwards' (BIS 2012e: 9). Business groups, such as the Institute of Directors, claim that companies are operating in a global market for talent, and thus need to offer high basic salaries, and also the prospect of share options and generous bonuses, in order to attract key executives. Nevertheless, since the size of a director's remuneration package signals their importance relative to others, status, rather than the market, would appear to be the foremost influence on boardroom pay.

One feature of executive pay that has caused widespread concern is that directors frequently receive large pay-offs on leaving their companies, regardless of their performance (High Pay Commission 2011). During the 2000s, for example, the top executives of British banks benefited from massive bonuses, despite presiding over a banking system which almost collapsed in 2008, and was only kept afloat with the infusion of billions of pounds of taxpayers' money. In early 2009 there was a public outcry when the pension arrangements of Sir Fred Goodwin, the former chief executive of banking group RBS, came to

(continued...)

light. Despite presiding over what were perhaps the largest corporate losses in UK history—RBS lost £24 billion in 2008—Goodwin managed to secure a lifetime annual pension payment of nearly £700,000 at the age of 50. Many experts believe that the City of London's profligate bonus culture, by encouraging executives to behave imprudently, was a significant cause of the banking system's failure, and thus a major contribution to the economic recession which it spawned. Excessive remuneration, moreover, contributes to a range of social and economic problems, not least growing wage inequality (Machin 2011). Some argue, therefore, that more effective regulation of executive pay would be in the wider public interest, particularly by tackling the bonus culture at the top of companies (High Pay Commission 2011).

Successive governments have been reluctant to legislate to regulate boardroom pay, believing that responsibility for directors' remuneration should rest in the hands of a company's shareholders. During the 1990s, both Conservative and Labour administrations encouraged self-regulation, in particular the adoption of the Cadbury, Greenbury, and Hampel codes of practice, which, among other things, recommended the establishment of dedicated remuneration committees made up of non-executive directors, and greater transparency and disclosure of directors' pay arrangements. The presumption was that it was for the shareholders of companies to challenge excessive and unjustified pay awards. Nevertheless, during the early 2000s Labour introduced legislation which gave shareholders the opportunity to vote on directors' remuneration arrangements at company annual general meetings. Such votes, though, are merely voluntary, and companies can ignore them if they wish. However, widely reported corporate excesses have prompted further regulatory intervention from the coalition government. It has proposed a series of measures in response to growing disquiet, including a proposal that shareholders should have an annual binding vote on a company's remuneration arrangements (BIS 2012e). Yet the government nonetheless evinces a firm belief in the fundamental principle that executive pay should primarily be a matter for a company's shareholders. Given that in 2012 Aviva was only the fourth company to lose a vote on its remuneration arrangements in a decade, it does not seem very likely that further increasing the influence of shareholders will do much to check excessive rises in top pay.

Although the NMW has made a positive contribution to reducing wage inequality at the bottom end of the income distribution scale, it has been rather less effective when it comes to tackling the problem of low pay in general. There is a tendency for it to be used 'not as a floor to pay rates but as the going rate for many occupations' in low-paying sectors of the economy (Grimshaw and Rubery 2010: 357). While the NMW has been highly beneficial in protecting workers who are in extremely badly paid jobs, there are still at least 4 million people who, despite receiving at least the minimum wage, are classified as being 'low-paid'. Indeed the UK 'has the second highest level of low pay among advanced economies, behind the US' (Resolution Foundation 2012c: 48). The system of in-work benefits reduces the onus on employers to raise wage levels. Moreover, workers in low-paying sectors of the economy are generally excluded from the influence of collective bargaining arrangements, something which helps poverty wages to endure (Grimshaw and Rubery 2010). As a result, around one-fifth of the workforce—people working in bars, restaurants, hotels, care homes, and shops for example—do not earn enough to be able to support an adequate standard of living (KPMG 2012).

While the concept of the 'living wage' is not new (Bennett and Lister 2010), during the 2000s the focus of many campaigners against low pay shifted away from minimum wage provision towards greater advocacy of a 'living wage', particularly in the United States (Luce 2004). In 2001, the London Living Wage campaign was launched; it has subsequently grown substantially under the auspices of networks of community organizations like Citizens UK, with grassroots fair pay and living wage campaigns spreading around the country. The living wage is based on the notion that workers should be entitled to a minimum level of pay sufficient to enable them to maintain an adequate standard of living for themselves and their families, based on the cost of food, housing, and other essentials, keeping them out of poverty (Bennett and Lister 2010; Manning 2012). There are separate living wage rates for London (where living costs are higher) and the rest of the UK, calculated by the Greater London Authority's Living Wage Unit and Loughborough University's Centre for Research in Social Policy respectively. In 2012–13, the living wage rates were £8.55 in London and £7.45 elsewhere, amounts substantially in excess of the statutory NMW.

Sometimes working in collaboration with trade unions, during the 2000s living wage campaigners made strenuous efforts to get employers to agree that workers are paid a living wage, including those employed indirectly by contractors in cleaning, catering, and security roles. Protests and demonstrations were organized to raise awareness of low pay in leading companies like Barclays and KPMG, leveraging change by exposing them to negative publicity and the threat of reputational damage. 'The various living wage campaigns have been the most successful examples of grassroots community organizing in recent years' (Manning 2012: 21).

In 2011, Citizens UK established a Living Wage Foundation (http://www.livingwage.org.uk), whose role is primarily concerned with encouraging and supporting the voluntary efforts of employers to ensure that workers receive a living wage. The case for paying a living wage is increasingly grounded in 'appeals to ethical business best practice and anecdotal evidence of the potential benefits to business of paying low-paid workers a higher wage' (Pennycook 2012: 5). The Living Wage Foundation claims that there are advantages for employers in adopting a living wage, including reduced absenteeism and better work quality, which more than offset the financial costs of paying higher wages. The cosmetics chain Lush, for example, has introduced the living wage for its workforce in London, and plans to extend it further. The company claims it has benefited from having more loyal and less tired workers, because they do not have to take additional jobs to supplement their incomes (BBC News Online 2012a).

The concept of a living wage seems to have a lot going for it; it is attractive to members of the public, and also for employers wanting to demonstrate their ethical credentials (Bennett and Lister 2010). Many local authorities, including those in York, Cardiff, and Newcastle, have raised pay levels of their staff to observe the living wage. Leading politicians from all the major political parties have given it their public backing. Yet living wage campaigners have struggled to make progress for contract cleaners and other workers in government departments in the face of employer opposition to pay increases.

However, there are a number of problems with the living wage approach, which cast some doubt on its efficacy as a means of tackling the issue of low pay. Since the needs of households and families vary so widely, it is not possible to specify a rate of pay which encompasses them all (Coats 2007). There are a range of factors other than pay which influence household living standards, such as how many earners there are in the household (Manning 2012). A further problem relates to the rather low number of workers that have benefited from the living wage movement; between 2005 and 2011 only around 10,000 workers received a pay rise as a result of organizations agreeing to become living wage employers (Pennycook 2012). The roster of living wage employers is dominated by large public sector organizations, many of whose workers have their pay influenced by collective bargaining, and private companies such as financial and legal firms who have relatively few low-paid workers among their direct and contractor staff. For them, the costs of agreeing to pay a living wage are minor, but the reputational gains of being viewed as a living wage employer are potentially very large indeed. Yet for firms that employ large numbers of low-paid workers, such as major retailers, any supposed business benefits could well be outweighed by the adverse impact of the increase in labour costs that would arise from paying a living wage (Pennycook 2012). Nevertheless, working people and their representatives often use the living wage issue to mobilize against and challenge the interests of employers—see Chapter 9. Protests outside the premises of companies charged with being low-paying employers, such as Next and Amazon, have helped to generate increasing momentum behind living wage campaigns.

 ## Section summary and further reading

- While many countries operate statutory minimum wages, the first National Minimum Wage (NMW) in the UK was introduced by Labour in 1999. The establishment of the NMW was in large part a response to concerns about rising wage inequality, and its adverse social and economic effects; it was designed to reduce the scale of in-work poverty by setting a legal floor for wages.

- The Low Pay Commission (LPC) is charged with overseeing the operation of the NMW, including making recommendations on minimum wage rates to the government. It has taken a rather cautious approach, concerned that if the NMW was introduced at too high a level, or was increased too precipitously, it would jeopardize jobs in low-paying sectors of the economy.

- There have been no adverse effects of the NMW on employment. It has been accommodated by firms in low-paying sectors of the economy with relative ease. Nevertheless, there are growing concerns about non-compliance in some parts of the economy, and that unscrupulous employers can exploit loopholes to avoid paying the NMW.

- The NMW has been praised as a highly successful government policy intervention. It has played some part in reducing inequality at the lower end of the earnings scale. However, the NMW does not appear to have been a very effective tool when it comes to reducing the extent of low-paid work in the economy. There is growing interest in the extent to which this is likely to be addressed through voluntary efforts by employers to commit to paying staff a living wage.

See Turnbull and Wass (2011) for earnings inequality. Grimshaw and Rubery (2010) provide a good overview of matters relating to low pay and the NMW. The Resolution Foundation publishes research and analysis about low pay and related topics (http://www.resolutionfoundation.org/). There is an extensive overview of how the NMW developed in Butcher (2012). Croucher and White (2007) deal with compliance and enforcement issues. The Low Pay Commission produces regular reports, available online, which contain masses of detail about the operation of the NMW (http://www.lowpay.gov.uk). For more information about the living wage approach, see Pennycook (2012) and Manning (2012).

7.5 Conclusion

One of the most important changes in work and employment relations concerns the declining importance of collective bargaining as a means of determining pay, particularly in the private sector. Nevertheless, collective bargaining remains commonplace in the public sector, especially if the pay review body system is considered as a form of 'arms' length' bargaining. What have been the main implications of the contraction of collective bargaining coverage? This chapter considered three particularly noteworthy developments. First, the increased extent of unilateral regulation of pay issues by management was identified. However, managers do not appear to have used their apparent new-found freedom to innovate very much in pay arrangements. Rather, they prefer to rely on established, tried and tested, and standardized approaches to pay determination. In attempting to pursue changes in employment relations, managers are constrained by the need to secure their legitimacy among the workforce. This is very important since it demonstrates that, even though the power of the trade unions has declined substantially, the wage–work bargain remains relevant as a way of conceptualizing the employment relationship, and that there are notable limits to the exercise of managerial prerogative. Second, although other factors have played a part, the decline of collective bargaining as a means of determining pay has contributed to the growth of pay inequality. Moreover, as was mentioned in Chapter 1, collective bargaining is not just a pay-setting mechanism; its presence also allows workers a say, or voice, over decisions that affect them at work. The diminution of trade union power has enabled employers to secure changes to the wage–work bargain in ways that are advantageous to them, something that has helped to promote inequality. Third, the implementation of the NMW has been a significant development, given that it creates a statutory floor for wages. Such regulation of work and employment relationships through the law, however, is a weak substitute for collective bargaining. The NMW was initially set at a deliberately low, or cautious, level that was designed to alleviate the most extreme cases of low pay in a way that would not be disruptive to employers. While it has played a part in reducing wage inequality in the lower half of the income scale, it has done little to diminish the incidence of low pay, which is still extensive in some parts of the economy. Thus statutory regulation of the employment relationship is, by itself, not an adequate replacement for joint regulation as a means of securing improved pay and conditions for workers. Living wage campaigns, inasmuch as they involve workers' mobilizing collectively in pursuit of higher pay, may prove to be a more effective method of tackling the problem of low pay.

 ## Assignment and discussion questions

1. Identify the main reasons for the decline in collective bargaining coverage since the 1980s.

2. What are the main issues and challenges of operating performance-related pay schemes for employers?

3. What are the main trends when it comes to wage inequality? What are the main factors that have contributed to high levels of wage inequality in the UK?

4. In your view, are the current NMW rates set too high, too low, or about right? Or would you get rid of the NMW entirely? Justify your answer.

5. What are 'living wage' campaigns? To what extent do you support the idea of a 'living wage', and why?

 Visit the Online Resource Centre that accompanies this book to develop your understanding of this chapter, and keep up to date with the latest developments in this area.
www.oxfordtextbooks.co.uk/orc/williams3e/

 ## Chapter case study: Campaigning for fair pay in supermarkets

Campaigns for fairer pay for workers employed in supermarkets have become increasingly vocal and well organized. The Fair Pay Network is an alliance of unions and civil society organizations, including Oxfam, the Child Poverty Action Group, the Migrant Rights Network, and the Fawcett

Society. It campaigns against low pay, and the poverty that often results for people who are in work. In 2012 it published a report on low pay in four major national supermarket chains—Asda, Morrisons, Sainsbury's, and Tesco—called *Face the Difference*, based on interviews with 100 employees. These firms employ around 900,000 staff, have been expanding rapidly, and are highly profitable. Their respective chief executives enjoy pay and benefits packages of between £3 million and £6 million each year. Yet many of the workers employed by these supermarket chains are paid wages so low that it keeps them in poverty.

The firms are not doing anything which is unlawful; they pay all their staff hourly rates of pay which comply with the NMW. However, the Fair Pay Network believes that the major supermarket chains could easily afford to give all of their workers a higher rate of pay which is sufficient to keep them out of poverty. The report shows that many low-paid supermarket workers face major financial problems, including increasing levels of unsecured personal debt, and that most (52 per cent) had cut their spending on food items over the twelve months prior to the research. The Fair Pay Network states that 'it cannot be acceptable to employers, employees, government or public that the gigantic employer block formed by Tesco, ASDA, Sainsbury's and Morrisons, enjoying quite colossal profits and vast executive pay packages at the top, will not commit to paying all of its employees a wage rate that keeps them out of poverty' (Fair Pay Network 2012: 8). Among other things, the Fair Pay Network recommends that the major supermarket chains should commit to paying all their workers at least a living wage (in 2012–13 this was £8.45 per hour in London, £7.45 elsewhere), and to ensuring that low-paid staff have sufficient opportunities for career progression. The report also calls on the trade unions to make more vigorous efforts to organize supermarket workers and boost union membership, so that they have more protection.

Other campaigns have focused on changing the employment practices of major supermarket chains. Sainsbury's, for example, has been specifically targeted by the 'Pay Up' campaign, which highlights the extensive profits made by the supermarket chain and the massive increases in remuneration enjoyed by its directors. Yet between 2004 and 2012 its lowest-paid workers actually saw their pay cut in real terms (after inflation), and many rely on credit cards or payday loans to get through the month. In May 2012, supporters of the Pay Up campaign, some of whom are linked to the activist organization UK Uncut, held a protest outside the London headquarters of Sainsbury's. A Pay Up spokesperson claimed that the supermarket chain 'has seen rising profits and booming CEO pay, but real-terms pay cuts for workers on basic rates. We want the workforce to take home a greater slice of the Sainsbury's pie. Workers at Sainsbury's have been demanding a living wage for over a year, and Pay Up is echoing that demand'. For its part, Sainsbury's claims to treat its staff fairly, and that the most recent pay review had resulted in a 2.7 per cent increase in basic hourly rates of pay, well above the retail industry average. Its arch-rival, Tesco, has not escaped the attention of low pay activist campaigns. In February 2012 one of its Express stores in Central London was forced to close for an hour because of a protest over claims that the supermarket chain had offered unpaid 'work experience' positions as part of the coalition government's controversial Work Programme to get unemployed people back into employment.

These campaigns and protests demonstrate very clearly that employment relations is not just about the regulation of employment relationships, but also concerns the experiences and differential interests of workers and how the dominant interests of employers are often challenged as a result. The protests and mobilization efforts evident in these cases show how new networks of activists and campaigning coalitions are finding innovative ways of putting traditional employment relations concerns—pay and employment conditions—on to the agenda of policy-makers, unions, and employers.

Sources Fair Pay Network (2012); Taylor (2012); Pay Up website, http://www.payup.org.uk/.

Questions

What is the purpose of campaigns for fairer pay in supermarkets? To what extent do you think they are necessary?

8 Working time and employment relations

◎ Chapter objectives

The main objectives of this chapter are to:

- demonstrate the importance of working time as an employment relations issue;
- identify and account for the main working time trends;
- examine how working time is used by employers, and the reasons for, and consequences of, high levels of work intensity; and
- explain how working time matters are subject to legal regulation, in particular the scope of the Working Time Regulations.

8.1 Introduction

Working time—its length, its pattern, and its use—is a central concern of employment relations. As was discussed in the introductory chapter of this book, the principal feature of the employment relationship is the exchange of wages for latent labour power—an employee's capacity to work. When a job is started it is not the worker's labour that an employer is buying, but, in effect, his or her time. It is then the task of the employer to ensure that this time is used productively (Arrowsmith and Sisson 2000). Moreover, working time has long been an issue on which trade unions have campaigned, for a shorter working week in particular. In order to understand contemporary employment relations properly, then, it is essential to consider trends in working time, how it is used, and also how it is regulated.

For a number of reasons the topic of working time has attracted a greater amount of attention in recent years. Concerns have arisen about the harmful effects of excessive working hours, linked to the rise of what has popularly become known as the 'long hours culture'. Working time is now affected by a greater degree of legal regulation; in particular, the European Union's (EU) Working Time Directive has attracted rather a lot of controversy. Employers are interested in how working time can be arranged in ways that improve organizational efficiency and generate performance improvements. Moreover, policy-makers have taken measures to encourage more flexible working time arrangements, not least because of the potential they have to improve gender equality (Grimshaw and Rubery 2010; Eurofound 2012). The chapter commences in Section 8.2 with an overview of the importance of working time as an employment relations issue and how it can be understood, before some key working time trends, including the prevalence of flexible working time arrangements, are outlined and discussed in Section 8.3. The focus of Section 8.4 is on how working time is used, with a particular emphasis on explaining prevailing high levels of work intensity. As just mentioned, the EU Working Time

Directive, and the Working Time Regulations (WTR) in the UK, mean that some working time matters have become more regulated by law. We look at this legislation, explain why it has been controversial, and consider its implications in Section 8.5.

 Introductory case study: Overtime bans on the railways

Working time, and how it is organized, managed, and remunerated, is an integral feature of employment relations. Some industries rely heavily on the use of overtime arrangements—getting workers to undertake more work over and above their normal working hours, often in return for a premium payment. But an over-reliance on paid overtime working can, when handled badly, create difficulties, particularly in those parts of the economy where unions are well organized and thus try to exercise a degree of control over working time arrangements. This is evident on the railways, where unions have used restrictions on overtime as a bargaining lever in disputes with employers. In December 2005, Central Trains, one of the UK's passenger rail operators, cancelled all of its services on the Sunday before Christmas because too few train drivers had reported for work. Sunday working was undertaken on the basis of voluntary overtime, in return for a premium payment. Most of the time this meant that Central Trains had sufficient drivers to maintain its Sunday timetable. In this instance, though, the failure of enough drivers to report for work was intensely damaging for the business. Since then, train companies have experienced similar problems on a regular basis. In November 2009, for example, First Capital Connect was forced to cancel hundreds of Sunday services after its drivers declined to undertake voluntary overtime; and in March 2011 train drivers employed by the London Midland company instituted a ban on Sunday overtime working following the employer's decision to withdraw the premium double time payment which it attracted, causing considerable disruption.

8.2 Working time and employment relations

As mentioned in Section 8.1, the question of working time is integral to the wage–work bargain that characterizes the employment relationship. 'Under the traditional or standard employment relationship it is labour time that is sold, primarily in continuous daily blocks under open-ended contracts, and it is up to the employer to extract the anticipated labour power through the management of work organization and employee effort and performance' (Grimshaw and Rubery 2010: 362). Managing working time effectively is a crucial way in which employers can secure improvements in productive efficiency. Like any other aspect of the employment relationship, though, attempts by employers to control working time have always been challenged by workers. One way in which they can contest working time is by absenting themselves (Ackroyd and Thompson 1999)—see Chapter 9. But there are also other ways in which workers have manipulated working time to suit their interests.

In particular, in workplaces based around production lines workers have opportunities to exert control over their working time, by working 'back up the line' for example. This refers to the process, commonplace in vehicle manufacturing at one time (e.g. Turner, Clack, and Roberts 1967), by which an increase in the pace of work enables workers to generate short, informal rest breaks as the production line catches up. This is particularly effective in situations where workers are able to manipulate job timings set through work study techniques. If workers can slow a job down and make it look difficult when it is being measured, this is likely to result in a 'loose' rate, making it easier to accumulate informal rest periods if they revert to their normal, faster pace or, alternatively, allowing them to work in a more leisurely way, at the pace set for the work study engineers, without any loss of pay (Roy 1952). While it may have become harder for workers to manipulate working time to their advantage, attempts to do so remain an important feature of the employment relationship.

Working time has long been a key source of contestation between unions and employers, and campaigns to reduce its length were 'fundamental to the organization of the working class and the development of labour solidarity' (Arrowsmith 2002: 114). This can be seen in the long-running attempts by workers, collectively through trade unions, to shorten the length of both the working day and the working week. Although nineteenth-century campaigns by prominent liberal philanthropists helped to secure reduced working hours for women and child workers, it is important to recognize that legislation was largely the outcome of working-class pressure for reform (Arrowsmith 2002).

The reduction of working time has been a central aim of organized labour ever since, and working time issues, such as the length of the working week, have long been important matters for collective bargaining between employers and trade unions (Grimshaw and Rubery 2010; Eurofound 2012). During the 1980s and 1990s, for example, engineering unions in Germany and Britain successfully used industrial action to reduce the length of the working week, to thirty-five hours in the case of the former. However, this often came at a price as employers conceded fewer hours in return for greater flexibility over the utilization of working time (McKinlay and McNulty 1992; Hyman 2001b). Nevertheless, trade unions have an important role in successfully campaigning for, and wresting from employers, reductions in working time, and also paid holiday entitlement (Green 1997). In recent years, the Trades Union Congress (TUC) has made the excessive working hours experienced by some groups of workers a campaign priority (Blyton 2011).

Perhaps the most notable recent example of how working time issues are often central to the collective bargaining agenda between employers and unions relates to the introduction of short-time working arrangements as an attempt to mitigate the effects of the economic recession. Such agreements, which were particularly evident in Germany and Italy, involve unions consenting to reduced working hours on a temporary basis in order to reduce costs and thus preserve jobs (Eurofound 2010). In the UK, some of the major car producers instituted short-time working; for example, in 2009 Toyota and the Unite trade union negotiated an agreement that would temporarily reduce employees' hours and pay by 10 per cent as a way of avoiding redundancies.

However, the decline of the trade unions and the diminishing scope and importance of collective bargaining mean that in general joint regulation plays a less powerful part than it once did, with employers enjoying greater freedom to manage working time issues unilaterally (Grimshaw and Rubery 2010; Blyton 2011). That is not to say, however, that working time matters go uncontested, as is evident from the case of the railways discussed in the introductory case study. The increased degree of managerial regulation over working time produces its own problems, tensions, and conflicts, since workers often challenge and contest efforts by employers to exercise control over this area of employment relations. Workers can use and adapt working time for their own purposes, in ways that do not necessarily conform with managerial expectations. In call centres, for example, where the pressure of customer service roles is often fairly intense, there is evidence that front-line managers may take a more lenient approach to employee absences from work in situations where the staff have developed a strong collective identity, which expresses itself in an ability to influence custom and practice expectations of how working time should be used (Deery, Iverson, and Walsh 2010). The whole question of working time, then, demonstrates very clearly the nature of the employment relationship as a 'contested terrain', and the potential for conflict that exists between employers and employees as a result, in spite of the greater degree—formally at least—of unilateral managerial control—or perhaps even because of it (Grimshaw and Rubery 2010; Blyton 2011).

 Section summary and further reading

- Working time is a key feature of employment relations, being central to the wage–work bargain that underpins the employment relationship.

- Working time has long been a prime source of contestation between employers and unions; working time issues are often a key feature of the collective bargaining agenda.

- Although the decline of the unions means that organizations enjoy greater scope to exercise managerial control over working time issues, it is nonetheless an area of employment relations which is marked by a pronounced potential for conflict between employers and employees.

The best overviews of working time and employment relations are provided by Blyton (2011) and Grimshaw and Rubery (2010). For a historical perspective on the role of working time in employment relations, see Arrowsmith (2002).

8.3 Working time: patterns and trends

Having considered the importance of working time in employment relations, and the way trade union efforts have been directed at reducing it, what, then, have been the main trends when it comes to working hours? Two main issues are considered in this section. First, the pattern of overall working hours is assessed, with particular attention paid to accounting for the rise and diminution of the so-called 'long hours culture'. Second, the trend of more flexible patterns of working time is discussed and interpreted.

8.3.1 Overall working hours

Historically, the overall trend, at least until the 1990s, was towards the reduction in the average number of weekly working hours for full-time employees. During the 1990s, however, this trend came to an end, resulting in British full-time employees achieving the dubious distinction of having the longest average working week in the EU. This raised significant concerns about the rise of what has come to be known as the 'long hours culture' (Arrowsmith 2002; Grimshaw and Rubery 2010).

There are a number of reasons why the average weekly working hours of full-time employees rose during the 1980s and early 1990s. For one thing, greater competitive pressures encouraged many businesses to find ways of increasing output while freezing, or even reducing, staff numbers. Thus employees, particularly those in white-collar jobs like professionals and managers, were obliged to work more hours, usually unpaid, to make up the slack (Beynon

International perspective 8.1: The 35-hour working week in France

The regulation and control of working time has long been a central concern of trade unions in France, and a prime source of contestation in employment relations. For much of the twentieth century, reductions in working hours, either through legislation or employer concessions, were the outcome of intense periods of mobilization and struggle by organized labour (Jefferys 2000). Following the 1981 election of François Mitterrand as president of France, and the establishment of a coalition government of socialists and communists, a 1982 law fixed the maximum working week, before overtime payments apply, at thirty-nine hours, with the progressive reduction to thirty-five hours as a longer-term aim, and increased the minimum period of paid annual leave to five weeks.

Realization of the thirty-five-hour limit had to await the 1997 election of a socialist government under the premiership of Lionel Jospin. The first 'Aubry' law of 1998, named after its ministerial sponsor, offered incentives for employers who negotiated thirty-five-hour agreements that created jobs. The second 'Aubry' law of 2000 made the maximum thirty-five-hour week mandatory for all those working in firms with more than twenty employees. The ostensible aim of the legislation was to create job opportunities, and thus reduce the level of unemployment. But the legislation was also driven by another imperative, 'that of a continuing process of state modernization of industrial relations in which working time was held out as bait' (Jefferys 2003: 142). The aim, then, was to encourage firms to negotiate workplace agreements with local union representatives over the more flexible use of working time. This would, it was hoped, not only stimulate workplace bargaining, and thus challenge the authority of the unions and their national power bases, but also enhance productivity through the more intensive use of working time.

Understandably, therefore, many manual workers, who bore the brunt of such flexibility initiatives, were rather restrained in their support of the thirty-five-hour week. However, the main challenge came from the right-wing presidency of Nicolas Sarkozy, who was elected in 2007 on a platform which included a pledge to loosen the thirty-five-hour limit before workers become entitled to premium overtime payments. Reforms introduced in 2008 allow employers to reach agreements with unions and employees which provide for greater flexibility over working hours. The Sarkozy administration also reduced taxes and charges on overtime working in an attempt to dilute the effectiveness of the thirty-five-hour limit. However, this policy was reversed by François Hollande's socialist government, which came into power in May 2012, with the result that the thirty-five-hour working week seems likely to continue to be an important feature of French employment relations.

et al. 2002). Moreover, unlike other EU countries, where specific statutory limits on working time are commonplace (see International perspective 8.1 for the example of France), before the advent of the Working Time Regulations in 1998 (see Section 8.5.2) in the UK working time matters were generally left outside the scope of legal regulation (Grimshaw and Rubery 2010). An additional factor was the decline in the power of the trade unions who, through their collective bargaining endeavours, had hitherto been a major influence on the shortening of the working week.

Since the late 1990s, though, the problem of so-called 'long hours' working appears to have diminished in significance, as measured by the proportion of employees working more than forty-five hours a week. Tables 8.1 and 8.2 show that while this figure rose in the first half of the 1990s, it subsequently declined. In 1996, 23.5 per cent of employees usually worked for more than forty-five hours a week; by 2008 this had declined to 18.8 per cent, and by early 2013 to 18 per cent. Between 1992 and 2011 the average number of hours worked each week by all those in employment fell by nearly 5 per cent (ONS 2011).

Table 8.1 Usual weekly hours of work in main job by percentage share of employees, 1992–2008

	1992	1996	2000	2004	2008
Fewer than 6 hours	1.6	1.8	1.4	1.2	1.1
6–15 hours	8.4	8.3	7.7	7.4	6.5
16–30 hours	13.6	15.2	16.1	17.6	18.0
31–45 hours	55.3	51.3	52.3	54.3	55.5
Over 45 hours	21.1	23.5	22.5	19.6	18.8

Source: Office for National Statistics, http://www.ons.gov.uk

Table 8.2 Usual weekly hours of work in main job by percentage share of employees, 2013*

	All employees (%)	Men (%)	Women (%)
Fewer than 6 hours	1.2	0.8	1.6
6–15 hours	6.6	3.3	10.0
16–30 hours	19.8	8.4	31.4
31–45 hours	54.3	61.3	47.4
Over 45 hours	18.0	26.3	9.6

* January to March

Source: Office for National Statistics, http://www.ons.gov.uk

The decline in the proportion of employees working 'long hours', and a fall in the average number of hours usually worked each week, are trends which are evident across Europe (Messenger 2011; Eurofound 2012). While the number of weekly working hours for full-time employees in the UK is relatively high by European standards (Grimshaw and Rubery 2010), contrary to popular perception it is no longer the highest in the EU (see Table 8.3).

Indeed, taken as a whole, the average length of the working week in the UK is unremarkable compared to other EU countries. The relatively high number of part-time jobs means that

Table 8.3 Average number of weekly hours usually worked by full-time employees, selected EU countries, April–June 2011

Country	Hours worked (full-time employees)
Austria	43.7
Greece	43.7
UK	42.7
Germany	42.0
Spain	41.6
EU average	41.6
France	41.1
Italy	40.5
Ireland	39.7
Denmark	39.1

Source: ONS (2011)

Table 8.4 Average number of weekly hours usually worked by all in employment, selected EU countries, April–June 2011

Country	Hours worked (all in employment)
Greece	42.2
Czech Republic	41.2
Spain	38.4
France	38.0
Italy	37.6
EU average	37.4
UK	36.3
Germany	35.6
Ireland	35.0
Netherlands	30.5

Source: ONS (2011)

there is a wide spread of working hours in the economy; some work for many hours in an average week, whereas others may only work for a relatively small number of hours (Grimshaw and Rubery 2010). Table 8.4 shows that when the working hours of all those in employment are taken into account—people in part-time as well as full-time jobs—the average number of hours usually worked each week in the UK is below the average for the EU as a whole. The Netherlands is the EU country with the highest proportion of part-time employees, accounting for its position at the foot of Table 8.4.

High levels of weekly working hours tend to be concentrated among certain types of workers, namely full-time male managers and professionals, and male workers in specific sectors of the economy (Kersley et al. 2006; Walsh 2010; Blyton 2011). This reflects the large amount of overtime working that has long characterized employment relations in Britain—work that is undertaken in excess of the 'normal' working day or week. But we need to bear in mind that for workers in general there are two distinct motivations for undertaking overtime. Manual workers, particularly in transport, manufacturing, and process industries, often depend on overtime arrangements, with any additional hours they do being paid at a higher, premium

 Contesting employment relations 8.2: The TUC's Work Your Proper Hours Day campaign

The Trades Union Congress (TUC) campaigns against excessive working hours, claiming that they undermine people's work–life balance and damage their health. It reckons that over 5 million workers in the UK undertake some unpaid overtime work each year, amounting to some £29 billion worth of 'free work' for employers. In order to raise awareness of excessive working hours and their adverse consequences, every year the TUC announces a 'Work Your Proper Hours Day'. In 2013, it was 1 March, chosen because it was the day of the year that the average worker undertaking unpaid overtime stops working for free, and actually starts earning for him or herself. The TUC says that on this day at least workers should make sure they take a proper lunch break, and leave work on time. http://www.worksmart.org.uk/workyourproperhoursday/

rate, to supplement regular wages which might be quite low, and thus maintain their liveli-hoods. Among the occupations with the highest average working weeks are the drivers of cranes and heavy goods vehicles (ONS 2011).

For managers and professionals, though, overtime working is largely unpaid, and arises because the demands of their jobs mean that their work duties cannot be completed within normal working hours. Managers undertake an average of 7.6 hours, and professionals an average of 6.8 hours, of unpaid overtime working each week (ONS 2011). The TUC estimates that over 5 million people perform some unpaid overtime, worth some £29 billion to the economy (TUC 2011). It also runs a campaign designed to challenge the culture of unpaid overtime which exists in many organizations (see Contesting employment relations 8.2). Managerial and professional staff often have little choice other than to undertake unpaid overtime, because without it they are unable to perform their jobs to their employer's satis-faction, or demonstrate the requisite commitment to their position, jeopardizing their em-ployment prospects (Blyton 2011).

There is a view that we need not be concerned about the number of working hours peo-ple undertake, even if they appear to be excessive. This is because they are a function of the choices workers make about how to balance their paid work and non-paid work responsi-bilities. People who work for lots of hours seem to have greater job satisfaction; they may put in more working hours because they find their jobs interesting and gratifying (Green and Whitfield 2009; Walsh 2010), or because the prospect of additional overtime payments is seen as desirable.

Yet an over-reliance on paid overtime working can cause employers problems. It is a po-tentially very inefficient way of organizing working time. Workers may work more slowly during their normal contractual working hours in order to ensure that overtime—paid at a premium rate—is needed to complete their tasks. The preponderance of overtime working has long been criticized. Flanders (1975) viewed the existence of 'systematic overtime' as a sign of managerial irresponsibility; it was an inefficient, albeit relatively easy, way of secur-ing increases in output without hiring new staff or, more importantly, investing in capital machinery, and thus stifled innovation. Workers welcomed the opportunity to undertake overtime since it enabled them to supplement their low basic wages. In the 1950s and 1960s, then, overtime working became 'institutionalized', particularly among male manual workers (Arrowsmith 2002). This refers to the way in which overtime came 'to be accepted as a habit—as a way of life in industry—for which all kinds of justifications are then invented'. It gained 'a self-perpetuating character' (Flanders 1975: 56).

Excessive hours of work have further adverse consequences, which extend beyond the confines of the workplace. In addition to being an inefficient way of managing working time in organizations, and a potentially important constraint on productivity, too many hours at work can impair workers' health and well-being and also, by creating a 'time squeeze', have a detrimental impact on their lives outside work (Walsh 2010). More hours spent at work mean that the time workers can spend with friends and family members is diminished, a major cata-lyst for work–life imbalance (see Chapter 4).

Indeed, it would seem that greater demand from workers for working time arrangements that enable them to balance the competing demands of their working and non-working lives means that the question of long-hours working, while it has by no means gone away, has become less imperative—as evidenced by the falling share of employees who usually work for more than forty-five hours per week. There are other reasons why the extent of long hours working has diminished. Structural changes in the economy have played a part; in particular, the growth in the proportion of employment which is located in services—retail, care, hotels and restaurants, etc. Most jobs in these sectors are organized on a part-time basis, depressing the overall working hours figure (ONS 2011). Moreover, the recession of the late 2000s, in particular the distinctive way in which it has affected the labour market through the marked shift in favour of part-time employment (see Chapter 2), may also have contributed to the trend of declining working hours. Beyond this, though, perhaps we are simply seeing a reversion to the broad historical trend of falling working hours, linked to greater levels of affluence, which was evident through most of the twentieth century, with the increases of the 1980s and 1990s being a deviation from the norm (Green 2011). Some people argue, however, that working hours remain far too long and that drastic measures are needed to alleviate the problems this causes (see Employment relations reflection 8.3).

Employment relations reflection 8.3:   The '21 hours' campaign

In February 2010, the New Economics Foundation (NEF) think tank published its *21 Hours* report (NEF 2010). The principal aim of this initiative is to encourage a shift towards a reduction in the length of the normal working week to around twenty-one hours. NEF claims that such a drastic reduction in many people's working hours would help to tackle the problem of overwork, reduce unemployment, improve people's well-being, reduce over-consumption, and promote greater equality, by distributing paid work more evenly across the working population. Such a change should be gradual, NEF contends, enabling workers and employers to adapt effectively, and in particular making sure that annual wage increments offset any pay reductions that result from working fewer hours. One of the report's co-authors, Anna Coote, said:

> Spending less time in paid work could help us to break this pattern. We'd have more time to be better parents, better citizens, better carers and better neighbours. We could even become better employees— less stressed, more in control, happier in our jobs and more productive. It is time to break the power of the old industrial clock, take back our lives and work for a sustainable future.
>
> (BBC News Online 2010)

8.3.2 'Flexible' patterns of working time

As well as the excessive working hours characteristic of some occupations and sectors, the other main feature of working time concerns the increasing prevalence of flexible patterns of working time, defined as working time arrangements that depart from the conventional 'standard' full-time working week of, say, seven or eight hours per day from Monday to Friday. The significance of this temporal flexibility is particularly evident when it comes to the notable growth in the proportion of the workforce working on a part-time basis—see Tables 8.1 and 8.2. In 1992, 23.6 per cent of employees worked for up to, and including, thirty hours per week; this figure rose to 25.6 per cent in 2008, and to 27.6 per cent in 2013. Table 8.2 also shows that there is a marked gender influence on working hours. Some 43 per cent of female employees work on a part-time basis (up to and including 30 hours per week), whereas just 13 per cent of male employees do so.

Although most employees continue to work a standard working week, it is by no means as commonplace as it once was, as working time arrangements become more variable and irregular (Grimshaw and Rubery 2010; Walsh 2010; Eurofound 2012). More than one in ten female employees usually work fewer than fifteen hours a week; and employers in some parts of the economy, like the retail and social care sectors, make use of highly changeable patterns of working time, which can change from week to week, or even from day to day. This means that the concept of 'standard' working time needs to be used with some care given the extent to which many people's 'normal' working hours now depart from the conventional model, including in evenings and weekends (Blyton 2011). Working hours have also become increasingly polarized. Some managers and professionals regularly work in excess of fifty hours a week, whereas over half of employees usually work for fewer than thirty-one hours each week.

There are three main reasons why flexible working time arrangements have become more common. The first concerns changes in the economic context. Shifts in the composition of employment, particularly the growing proportion of the workforce based in the service sector—e.g. shops, hotels, restaurants—where part-time working is more commonplace, have had a notable effect (ONS 2011). In manufacturing, for example, just one in twenty workers is employed on a part-time basis, compared to more than a half (53 per cent) of workers in hotels and restaurants (Kersley et al. 2006).

The second reason for the growing prevalence of flexible working patterns is because it suits employers, by enabling them to manage labour in a more efficient manner. Using part-time work schedules helps employers to operate services outside of the conventional 'standard' working day, including in the evenings and at weekends, without having to pay out for premium overtime payments (Grimshaw and Rubery 2010). It also enables them to respond more easily to variations in demand, particularly in customer service industries.

Third, the increased female participation in the workforce, and the rising number of dual-earner households (where both partners are in employment), have also stimulated demand for more flexible patterns of working time. Flexible working time arrangements are often seen as desirable because they enable workers—especially female workers—to combine paid employment with unpaid household labour more readily. Warren, Pascall, and Fox's (2010) study of low-waged women in heterosexual couples illustrates just how important flexible work schedules are when it comes to accommodating childcare and fitting it around paid work. Given that their partners largely undertook full-time jobs, the bulk of the responsibility for childcare rested on the shoulders of these women, meaning that part-time working arrangements, often in the evenings and weekends when their partners were at home and could look after the children, were the only viable option for them, even though many would have liked to increase their hours.

Employers have responded to the greater demand from workers for flexible working time arrangements. In addition to part-time work, the availability of other forms of working time flexibility (such as compressed working weeks, where a standard number of working hours is worked over fewer than five full days, or flexi-time arrangements, which give workers some element of discretion over starting and finishing times) have become more commonplace—see Table 8.5 for a list of specific practices. The most commonly used forms of flexible working arrangements are: flexi-time, working from home, and part-time working (Tipping et al. 2012). Governments have encouraged employers to increase the availability of flexible working time arrangements, including establishing a legal right for working parents and carers

Table 8.5 Glossary of major flexible working time practices

Practice	Definition
Part-time working	Work that is undertaken on a less than full-time basis; any job which requires fewer than 30 hours each week is generally considered to be of part-time status.
Flexi-time	A form of working time arrangement that gives staff some discretion over their working hours, in particular their starting and finishing times.
Compressed working week	A way of organizing working time such that a standard number of working hours is worked over fewer than five full days; sometimes organized on the basis of a fortnight (e.g. nine days).
Annual hours	A type of working time arrangement in which people's hours are calculated on the basis of a year, rather than say a week. This gives organizations more flexibility to adjust the working hours of their staff to cope with seasonal fluctuations in demand without the use of expensive overtime.
Term-time working	An arrangement that enables staff with school-age children to work only during periods when the children are attending school.
Job-sharing/splitting	This involves an arrangement whereby a job is shared, or particular functions associated with a job are split, between two or more workers.
Voluntary reductions in working time (V-time)	This term is used to refer to instances where workers and their managers agree to cut back on the number of hours worked.

of adults to request them, based on the belief that they generate important business benefits, including lower absenteeism and better recruitment and retention (see Legislation and policy 8.4). Nevertheless, flexible working time arrangements are generally more common in public sector organizations, and in companies which have a high proportion of female staff (Dex and Forth 2009; Walsh 2010).

LEGISLATION AND POLICY 8.4:   The right to request flexible working

In 2003, parents of young or disabled children gained the right to have a request for flexible working arrangements, such as moving from full-time to part-time employment, taken seriously. Employers are entitled to refuse such a request on business grounds—if it would result in a substantial increase in costs, for example. Since it is not a right to flexible working, merely a right to have any request to work flexibly taken seriously by an employer, the government was criticized for not doing enough to encourage flexible working (Anderson 2003). Nevertheless, during the second half of the 2000s the scope of the right to request flexible working was extended to carers of adults and also to all parents of children aged below 17. The coalition government has expressed its intention to extend this right to all workers, albeit in a way that gives organizations more scope to refuse requests (HM Government 2011a). There is some evidence that the right to request flexible working has been responsible for encouraging more widespread availability of flexible working arrangements (Walsh 2010). Studies of its impact indicate that most requests from workers are either fully or partly agreed by employers (e.g. Holt and Grainger 2005). However, care is needed not to exaggerate the impact of the right to request flexible working, given the importance of pressure for change from workers themselves. While perhaps playing a part in securing wider consensus about the desirability of flexible working, the legislation seems to have 'been swimming with the tide of opinion, rather than initiating change' (Green 2011: 118).

Although there would appear to be a consensus that, since they benefit both workers and employers, the greater prevalence of flexible working time arrangements is something to be welcomed, there are a number of major problems which should not be overlooked. For one thing, as seen in Chapter 4, just because flexible working time arrangements are available in theory does not necessarily mean that workers can make use of them in practice. A second problem with flexible working time arrangements concerns the adverse consequences for gender equality that arise from their use. Part-time jobs predominate in low-paid and low-skilled sectors of the economy, with the result that those who undertake them, the large majority of whom are women, often experience considerable employment disadvantage (Grimshaw and Rubery 2010; Warren, Pascall, and Fox 2010). The question of social class is also relevant here. It is far easier for workers in relatively well-paid managerial and professional jobs to contemplate being able to reduce their hours, and thus take a cut in pay as a result, than it is for their less well-remunerated counterparts further down the organizational hierarchy. They are also more likely to be able to exercise a degree of control over their own working time arrangements, such as starting and finishing times. Thus 'the location of individuals within particular employment hierarchies exerts a critical influence over access to working time discretion and flexibility' (Blyton 2011: 314).

A third problem with flexible working time arrangements concerns their 'dual logic': to what extent are they capable of meeting both the needs of employers and those of employees (Messenger 2011)? There is often a mismatch between organizational demands for flexibility—based on an efficiency rationale—and workers' demands for flexibility—which are predicated on the desirability of combining paid employment with family life. Part-time jobs are 'often organized and designed to maximize employer flexibility, to meet fluctuations in customer demand or to provide cover for sickness and holidays. There is thus a strong potential for conflict between the flexibility requirements of employers and those of employees' (Grimshaw and Rubery 2010: 370). In call centres, for example, conflict arises because the flexibility demanded by managers, in particular the expectation that staff will work additional hours at short notice to cope with an unanticipated rise in calls, clashes with demands from workers for predictable working time arrangements, so that they can plan their family responsibilities effectively (Hyman and Marks 2008). Moreover, one of the key labour market consequences of the recession concerns the rapid growth of involuntary part-time employment, part of a broader trend of greater 'underemployment' in the economy (see Chapter 2). For many workers the problem is not one of a 'long hours culture', but of having insufficient hours to maintain their standard of living.

This is related to a fourth problem with flexible working time arrangements, which concerns the increasing variability of working hours in some parts of the economy, such as retail and social care, as employers try to manage labour as efficiently as possible by constantly tweaking staff numbers to match varying patterns of demand (Grimshaw and Rubery 2010; Blyton 2011). The difficulty for workers is that their working hours become increasingly unpredictable, making it difficult for them to plan activities—including childcare provision—around the demands of their paid jobs. Blyton and Jenkins (2012b) talked to workers in South Wales who had been made redundant when the Burberry clothing factory closed in 2007 about the characteristics of their new jobs. Many 'were subject to working time patterns that not only varied from week to week but were also highly unpredictable, in terms of both timing and duration', creating serious difficulties (Blyton and Jenkins 2012b: 35).

For example, a worker who had found a job as a hotel receptionist observed that the worst thing about the position was the timing and unpredictability of the shifts, which varied from week to week:

> You can't plan anything. I've just had to cancel a dentist's appointment because they've called me in for a shift and I can't make another appointment because I won't know what I'm working next week.
>
> (Blyton and Jenkins 2012*b*: 36)

Nowhere are such difficulties more evident than when it comes to the increasing number of workers who are employed on 'zero-hours' contracts by companies such as the retailer Poundland and security firm G4S (Inman 2013). Under these arrangements, an employer is not obliged to provide work to an employee; nor is there any obligation on the employee to accept work from their employer. Thus the number of hours to be worked, and when they are to be worked, are not specified in the employment contract. Employees are only paid for the hours that they work. Advocates of zero-hours contracts claim that not only do they give employers flexibility to adjust working time in response to patterns of demand in a very cost-effective way, but that they are also good for workers, who benefit from the flexibility to work when it is suitable for them to do so, enabling them to accommodate family responsibilities more easily.

 Insight into practice 8.5:   Zero-hours contracts in a recession

The incidence of zero-hours contracts grew markedly during the late 2000s. In 2011, nearly a quarter (23 per cent) of workplaces with more than 100 employees used such contracts, up from just 11 per cent in 2004 (van Wanrooy et al. 2013: 10). In August 2012, the BBC's *Newsnight* programme featured a report about the increasing prevalence of zero-hours contracts. Employers benefit from the flexibility they offer. People only need to be paid when there is specific work for them to do. But this creates huge problems for employees—and they are employees—who have little guarantee of a regular income, despite being required to be available for work by their employer, meaning that they cannot take up alternative employment. Anna (not her real name), for example, gets a text message at 11.30am each day telling her whether or not she is required for a shift of picking and packing work at a local factory, starting two hours later. An employee of fast-food chain McDonald's observed that his zero-hours contract had lasted for five years, and that in the outlet where he worked only managers enjoyed regular, guaranteed work. His total working hours, and their timing, differed from week to week. 'They're not fair; they're not right—they're exploitative', he said. 'The free labour market's for companies, not for us. I'm not free.' However, McDonald's defended its employment arrangements, saying that many of its workers were looking for shift patterns that gave them flexibility to fit work around study, childcare, and other commitments. http://www.bbc.co.uk/news/uk-19263787

But the flexibility offered by zero-hours contracts is very one-sided. They provide 'temporal flexibility for employers to a far greater extent than for employees—increasing employers' ability to adjust working time patterns but at a cost of greater irregularity and unpredictability for employees' (Blyton 2011: 300). There is evidence that the use of zero-hours contracts by employers has grown in the recession as employers take advantage of a wide pool of unemployed and underemployed workers to reduce their labour costs (see Insight into practice 8.5). Concerned about their potential to cause exploitation, by not providing workers with any guaranteed earnings, some unions have campaigned against zero-hours contracts, and have called for them to be banned.

Finally, all this talk of temporal flexibility should not conceal the relative lack of managerial innovation when it comes to reforming working time arrangements, as is evident from rather limited use of 'annualized hours' schemes. While they vary in their detail, the main feature of annualized hours arrangements is the specification of a certain number of hours to be worked by an employee in any given year, in exchange for a guaranteed wage. Among the companies that have instituted annualized hours schemes for some of their staff are RAC Motoring Services and Siemens (Arrowsmith 2007). The main benefit of annualized hours for employers is that it enables them to manage peaks and slumps in demand for a product over a year without having to resort to the use of expensive overtime when it is high, or having workers sitting around idle when it is low.

Given that, for the employer, the aims of introducing annualized hours are to secure greater flexibility and eliminate overtime, employees are understandably often wary about it, even though their overall working time may fall and basic earnings rise (Arrowsmith 2007). Managers may pledge that the average guaranteed wage will leave most employees better off, but the loss of overtime may have a significant negative impact on the income of some (see Heyes 1997); and a greater likelihood of 'unsocial hours' working under an annualized hours arrangement may prove to be difficult for people, usually women, who have childcare responsibilities (Rubery and Grimshaw 2003).

Since annualized hours offer employers some major benefits, including reduced overtime payments, enhanced flexibility, and greater control over how working time is used, why is it not more commonplace? In 2011, fewer than one in ten (8 per cent) of workplaces used annual hours contracts, although this was higher than in 2004 (van Wanrooy et al. 2013). Arrowsmith (2007) posits two reasons why annualized hours arrangements have not become more widely used. First, employers are satisfied with the flexibility offered by other types of working time arrangement, part-time working in areas like retail for example, or shift-working in manufacturing industry. Moreover, there remains a strong preference for using overtime as a source of working time flexibility, in order to respond to fluctuations in demand for products and services, despite its expense and inefficiency.

Second, instituting annualized working arrangements demands a high degree of strategic management commitment, not least because of the need to overcome potential resistance from employees—something that is often absent. It is no coincidence that most annualized hours schemes operate in workplaces where there is a formal union presence, enabling the employer to negotiate their introduction in a way that helps to satisfy the interests of the workforce (Arrowsmith 2007). The rarity of annualized hours schemes suggests that many employers are either incapable or unwilling to bear the risks of innovating when it comes to managing working time arrangements. The preponderance of overtime working indicates a preference on the part of employers for relatively straightforward methods of securing working time flexibility. Despite its association with weak and ineffective management (Flanders 1975), the institutionalization of overtime working continues to be a commonplace feature of contemporary employment relations.

Section summary and further reading

- Overall working hours have resumed their historical downward trajectory after an increase during the 1990s prompting concern about the effects of a 'long hours culture', evident particularly among managers, professionals, and certain groups of manual workers.

- The other main working time trend concerns the growth of working time flexibility, manifest in the increasing proportion of part-time jobs in the economy. While in theory both employers and employees can benefit from temporal flexibility, in practice flexible working time arrangements can exacerbate labour market disadvantage, strengthen exploitation, and generate conflict.

- The greater use of flexible working time arrangements notwithstanding, managerial innovation in this area has been limited. Employers tend to prefer relatively straightforward measures for securing working time flexibility, particularly by means of paid and unpaid overtime.

Good overviews of working time trends are provided by Grimshaw and Rubery (2010) and Blyton (2011). Messenger (2011) and Eurofound (2012) offer a broader European perspective. For annualized hours, see Arrowsmith (2007).

8.4 Work pressures and work intensification

Having discussed working time trends, developments in one further feature of the wage–work bargain need to be assessed. This concerns how working time is actually utilized by employers. What do workers do when they are at work, and how intensively, or with how much effort, do they perform their jobs? This is an important area of analysis since the concept of 'effort' is critical to employment relations. Employers, when they hire workers, as we know, buy their potential labour power, or their capacity to engage in productive effort. How this latent effort is then used is subject to an ongoing process of negotiation and re-negotiation between managers and workers. Thus the questions of how working time is used, and also why heightened work pressures seem so prevalent in modern workplaces, are worthy of scrutiny.

8.4.1 Work intensification trends

Problems of measurement render judgements of work effort difficult to calculate with any degree of certainty (Nichols 1986; Green 2001). While one can attempt to measure the speed at which a job is undertaken, its physical and mental intensity is personal to the individual performing it, and is thus an inherently subjective phenomenon (McGovern et al. 2007). Work effort, then, is an ambiguous concept (Green 2006). Nevertheless, studies of work effort demonstrate that during the 1980s and 1990s work in the UK became more intensive, stabilized at a relatively high level during the early 2000s, before increasing in intensity again between 2006 and 2012 (Green 2006; Felstead et al. 2013). Greater work pressures are also evident in other industrialized countries (Green, Huxley, and Whitfield 2010).

In the 1980s, both survey and case study evidence highlighted the importance of work intensification linked to demands from employers for improved flexibility in the utilization of labour (Elger 1990). For much of the ensuing decade there was a 'palpable increase in work intensity, with workers being required to work harder during the hours they were at work'

(Green, Huxley, and Whitfield 2010: 383), something which is evident from a number of relevant research studies (e.g. Gallie et al. 1998). In 1992, for example, 31 per cent of employees strongly agreed that their jobs required them to work very hard; this had risen to 40 per cent of employees by 2000 (McGovern et al. 2007). In a study of twenty workplaces for the Joseph Rowntree Foundation, researchers asked employees whether the speed of their work, and the effort they expended in undertaking it, had increased or decreased. Sixty-four per cent of employees reported an increase in the speed of their work, and 61 per cent claimed an increase in effort (Burchell et al. 1999; Burchell 2002).

While the intensity of work may have stopped rising during the early 2000s, it nonetheless evened out at a high level indeed (Green and Whitfield 2009; Green 2011). Perhaps it is the case that physically and mentally workers simply are incapable of working any harder, with the trend of work intensification having reached its natural limits (Green 2011). However, the economic slump seems to have sparked a further increase in levels of work intensity; those 'in jobs are working harder, faster and to tighter deadlines than they did in the past' (Felstead et al. 2013: 6). A third of employees (34 per cent) claim that their job requires them to work very hard, and one in seven (14 per cent) never seem to have enough time to get their work done (van Wanrooy et al. 2013: 40).

8.4.2 **The causes of work intensification**

But what has caused greater work pressures? Perhaps jobs have become more intrinsically satisfying, with workers more willing to exert additional effort as a result? Work intensification is linked to increasing skill levels (Gallie et al. 1998). Some employees now enjoy greater responsibility and discretion in their jobs, making them harder, yes, but also more challenging (see Beynon et al. 2002: 280-1). The importance of such 'supply-side' factors—that greater work pressures are the result of workers supplying more effort—should not be entirely discounted. However, work intensification seems to have mainly been demand-driven (Gallie 2005), with three interrelated sources of added work pressure being particularly evident (see Table 8.6).

First, increasing competitive pressures have led employers to pursue greater flexibility, and ruthlessly manage costs in such a way that the same number of employees, or fewer, is obliged to produce ever greater quantities of work (Burchell 2002). For example, in their study of seven private and public sector case study organizations, Beynon et al. (2002) noted the large extent to which demands for enhanced organizational competitiveness and efficiency savings drove managers to intensify the labour of their staff. For the private sector companies, the obligation to satisfy the expectations of financial institutions, and thus enhance shareholder

Table 8.6 The potential sources of work intensification

Supply-side factors	Demand-side factors
Greater job satisfaction	Greater competitive pressures
More highly skilled jobs	More sophisticated information and communications technologies (ICT)
Greater discretion and responsibility	Rigorous performance management arrangements

value, resulted in pressure to prune staff numbers as a means of taking out costs. Competitive pressures mean that managers are often impelled to try and increase the work effort of their staff as a means of realizing short-term improvements in organizational performance. Job cuts can result in the workload having to be shared out between the remaining employees. When, for example, managers in a further education college were made redundant, lecturers were obliged to take on their public relations and marketing duties (Hudson 2002).

Developments in the food processing sector illustrate particularly well how increased levels of work intensity arise from competitive pressures. Supermarkets constantly badger their suppliers for cheaper products, and also often demand faster, more flexible delivery arrangements, in order to reduce their own costs. Supply chain pressures result in factories trying to pass cost savings down the line, with the burden falling on their production workers, in order to maintain their own competiveness. One way of achieving this is to increase the speed of production lines, meaning that staff are obliged to work at a quicker pace (James and Lloyd 2008). Investments in new automated technological processes that speed up production also have a marked effect. In a fruit and vegetable processing factory studied by Newsome, Thompson, and Commander (2009: 153), the implications of automation for work intensity were particularly evident. The 'speed of the lines is often so intense that it causes motion sickness. One line operator reported that she took travel sickness tablets to try to deal with the effects of motion sickness from working for long periods on the line'.

In front-line service work, moreover, where people have responsibility for dealing with customers, managers may use this relationship as a means of extracting greater work effort from staff. The telecommunications company studied by Beynon et al. (2002), for example, had given greater priority to service quality considerations, and expected its workers to be more sensitive to customer needs—an added source of pressure. The way in which customer expectations contribute to raised work intensity is particularly evident in some sectors. In hotels, for example, working around guests and responding to their needs are added sources of pressure for housekeeping and room cleaning staff (Sherman 2011). In the airline industry, competitive pressures have encouraged operators to adopt an approach to managing staff so dominated by the imperative to reduce costs that it intensified workers' labour, damaged their health, and potentially undermined safety standards. On short-haul routes brief turnaround times between incoming and outgoing flights, often less than thirty minutes, create added strains for cabin crew. Pressure to sell products to passengers also contributes to their workload. A worker observed that:

> we spend eight out of ten services running around like headless chickens. During turnaround we are treading on cleaners and caterers while getting the aircraft ready for the next sector. Our endeavour to satisfy the passengers means that we compromise safety.
>
> (quoted in Boyd 2001: 447)

A second source of added work pressure emanates from the greater capacity for managers to exercise control over employees, linked to the decline in workplace power of the trade unions (Green 2011). This is manifest in the use of increasingly robust performance management systems (McGovern et al. 2007). In a study of two financial services companies and two public sector organizations, Poynter (2000) demonstrates how managers use sophisticated performance management techniques to increase the work effort of their staff, and to enhance their own control. In financial services, for example, the use of performance targets is an effective means of generating faster work rates, not least because in some areas employees faced the threat of disciplinary action should their output be deemed unacceptable (Baldry, Bain, and Taylor 1998).

Third, greater scope for managerial control of this kind is enhanced by the use to which new forms of information and communications technology (ICT) are put, in particular by enabling managers to monitor and adjust work flows more effectively (Green 2011). What Green (2006) calls 'effort-biased technological change' has been a major source of increased work pressure. In other words, ICT helps managers to secure extra effort from their subordinates, because their activities are more easily monitored and recorded. Evidently, innovations 'like the mobile phone and the laptop computer—devices that enable work to be carried out at what, previously, had been idle times—are only the most tangible signs' of how technology can be used to increase work effort (Green 2006: 174). More importantly, the profusion of ICT-based monitoring systems, and the way they are used to inform performance management arrangements, allows managers to secure greater employee compliance with organizational norms, standards, values, and targets.

The effectiveness of performance management systems is often based on the use of information and communication technology to monitor workers—so-called ICT-based monitoring techniques. Electronic Point of Sale (EPOS) arrangements can be used to monitor the performance of checkout staff in retail stores, for example. In call centres and other office-based environments, ICT monitoring systems can be used to record the number and length of telephone calls, and even the keystrokes on a computer. Over a half of employees (52 per cent) in one survey reported that their work activities were recorded in some way by a computer system; nearly a quarter (23 per cent) indicated that information gathered in this way was used to monitor their performance (McGovern et al. 2007: 170). Call centres are environments where the use of ICT enables managers to control the pace of work and monitor staff with particular ease, a source of work intensification. According to one worker:

> The major pressure is ... the calls ... and that is understandable because we work in a call-centre environment, and you also get the pressure ... because you haven't got time to literally stand up and do what you need to do or take two minutes. You feel as though you're under pressure by taking the calls because it [the indicator] could be flashing 'there's eight minutes of calls waiting' which is quite regular in the evening.

(quoted in Beynon et al. 2002: 289)

Clearly, the most obvious way in which technological change leads to increased work pressures is by enabling managers to monitor work flows and workers' activities more closely. Private care firms use sophisticated monitoring devices to track how long their staff spend visiting home-based clients (Ramesh 2013). But email and other forms of electronic communication also mean that in some cases employers can contact employees, and expect them to undertake work duties outside of normal working hours, even when they are at home (Walsh 2010).

However, we should be careful not to exaggerate the capacity of managers to secure control over, and extract more effort from, their staff. Workers are capable of challenging the encroachment of managerial control initiatives in rather imaginative ways. Moreover, there is evidence that employers have had to pay a price for increases in work effort, in particular, the use of financial incentives, in the form of increased wages, to encourage higher effort.

'Additional earnings provide employees with the motive to increase effort, and employers have developed methods of monitoring and control to ensure that effort is increased' (McGovern et al. 2007: 186).

 Contesting employment relations 8.6: The National Gallery dispute

In 2011 a dispute broke out at the National Gallery in London over its decision to increase the number of rooms gallery assistants are required to guard from one to at least two. It argued that the change would enhance security, pointing out that the new arrangement was standard practice in other museums and art galleries. However, the gallery assistants were outraged by the change, claiming that it was prompted by the need for substantial reductions in staffing costs. What they called 'doubling-up' would—in their view—in fact compromise security, since it would be less easy to ensure that works of art were protected effectively, and reduce the amount of help they would be able to provide to visitors. As a result, during 2012 the PCS union organized a series of relatively short walk-outs by gallery assistants in protest against the change, resulting in the temporary closure of many of the National Gallery's rooms.

While the weakness of the trade unions means that workers are less well defended from work intensification, increases in work effort are nonetheless accompanied by higher earnings, suggesting that managers cannot simply impose higher workloads, but rather have to bargain over them with employees. Moreover, as the case of the dispute at the National Gallery shows, under some circumstances workers challenge attempts by managers to increase their workloads (see Contesting employment relations 8.6).

8.4.3 The effects of work intensification

What, though, are the effects of work intensification? For organizations, it seems that the conditions for increases in the levels of trust and cooperation necessary to stimulate long-term, real improvements in economic performance are unlikely to exist. Employers often prefer to 'sweat' their staff, generating short-term improvements in output by intensifying workloads or using overtime. One of the main effects is the exhaustion of the workers concerned. This is particularly evident among hotel cleaning and room staff who work to stringent quotas specifying the number of rooms that need to be serviced per shift. The resulting 'imperative of speed' creates an 'atmosphere of stress' as the staff labour to complete their duties as quickly as possible (Sherman 2011: 24). In order to realize efficiency savings, and thus improve their competitiveness, hotels operate onerous work schedules, and put a lot of pressure on their housekeeping staff to increase their efforts. In September 2012, for example, BBC Newsnight reported that contract cleaners at the prestigious London Hilton Waldorf hotel had their quota raised from two to three rooms per hour, with disciplinary action threatened if they did not comply. In the study of hotel cleaners by Guégnard and Mériot (2009: 106) a worker commented:

We have to rush, and they tell us to work faster. The hotel should hire more staff. In eight hours, I am supposed to achieve my work, but whereas one hour is supposed to be enough to clean two rooms, each room generally takes at least 40 minutes.

The work is not easy; the physical effort required by their jobs, and the pace at which they have to be performed, ends up exhausting the workers concerned, as this comment indicates:

> After a single working day, I am already broken. I even got problems with my muscles that I have never had before. And that tires me even more. I would like to take another job. If only I could stop!

(Guégnard and Mériot 2009: 107)

While pressure is an aspect of all work, and can have an important part in stimulating and maintaining motivation, excessive workloads not only undermine performance at work, but can also make people ill. Perhaps the most notable outcome of increased work pressures, then, concerns the adverse effects they have on workers' physical and psychological well-being. Excessive work pressures account for some 25 per cent of work-related mental health problems experienced by workers. Stress, which can be defined as 'the adverse reaction a person has to excessive pressure or other types of demand placed on them' (HSE 2008: 1), can have serious adverse consequences for workers' mental and physical well-being, including an increased risk of heart disease and depression. It is unsurprising that high levels of work-related stress persist given the pressures under which many people work (Green and Whitfield 2009; Green 2011). This is evident in the food industry, for example, where the burden of constant demands from supermarkets for lower costs and greater flexibility is passed by factory managers on to the production workers in the form of increases in the pace of work, to the marked detriment of their well-being (James and Lloyd 2008).

The evidence of a 'widespread intensification of work effort and its detrimental impact on well-being is unambiguous' (Green 2006: 174). The following quotations, the first from a call centre operator, and the second from a further education lecturer, illustrate the psychological and physical damage to individuals of excessive work pressures.

> I know a lot of people are off with stress. Because you get customers on the telephone and I have seen women sit there and cry because of the calls they are getting . . . In this job women get sworn at and cry.

(quoted in Beynon et al. 2002: 281)

> So many people are going home with work to do that they haven't really got time to do. I find myself going home feeling physically exhausted, although I've hardly done anything physical.

(quoted in Nolan 2002: 122)

The experience of the Child Support Agency (CSA), the organization responsible for assessing and collecting child maintenance payments from non-resident parents, demonstrates how excessive workloads can damage employee well-being. Delays in processing claims became a matter of particular concern, and the CSA was widely castigated for its ineffectiveness. However, restructuring initiatives designed to resolve these problems were undertaken with little regard for their effects on staff, and seemed to make matters worse. Pressures of work, those associated with performance targets in particular, adversely affected the workforce in terms of generating excessive stress, something which compromised operational efficiency. Staff morale was extremely low. There was a high incidence of long-term sickness absence, largely due to stress-related complaints. According to one member of staff, 'every single day someone in their office would be crying through stress and frustration' (Atkinson and McKay 2005: 75).

Section summary and further reading

- Although there are difficulties associated with measuring how much effort people expend in their jobs, there is nonetheless overwhelming evidence that employment relations in the 1980s and 1990s was marked by work intensification, after which effort levels stabilized at a high level during the 2000s.

- While an increase in their job responsibilities may in part have led some people to work harder, the principal causes of increased work pressures are the growing competitive pressures on organizations that have compelled them to increase staff workloads, and extensive use of new systems for managing performance, linked to developments in information technology.

- It is unlikely that the increases in work effort seen in the UK will generate long-term improvements in economic performance. Moreover, there is evidence of adverse consequences for workers' health and well-being.

For data on work effort, and explanations of why it has increased, see Green (2006: Chapters 3 and 4) and McGovern et al. (2007: Chapters 5 and 6). Green (2011) offers the most up-to-date review of trends in work intensification. For case studies, see Beynon et al. (2002) and James and Lloyd (2008).

8.5 The legal regulation of working time

As was mentioned in Sections 8.2 and 8.3, unlike elsewhere in Europe, traditionally the law played little role in regulating working time in the UK, with the exception of historical legislation restricting the working hours of women and children. In unionized sectors of the economy matters such as the length of the standard working week were regulated through collective bargaining; however, the diminishing reach of joint regulation since the 1980s has reduced the effectiveness of this approach (Grimshaw and Rubery 2010). Since the 1990s, though, EU legislation, particularly the 1993 Working Time Directive (WTD), and the Working Time Regulations (WTR) 1998 which enact it in the UK, has come to play a prominent part in efforts to regulate working hours and associated matters.

8.5.1 The impact of excessive working hours

There is now a large body of evidence demonstrating a link between excessive hours of work and adverse health outcomes. The adverse effects of night work and other unsocial hours of work on employees' physiological and psychological well-being have long been recognized, as has excessive working hours (e.g. Bara and Arber 2009). Virtanen et al. (2010), for example, demonstrate that people who regularly undertake ten- or eleven-hour working days are more liable to developing heart disease. The TUC (2009) highlights the range of conditions, including increased risk of heart disease, mental ill-health, diabetes, and bowel problems, which are associated with people who habitually work for more than forty-eight hours a week.

During the 1980s, there was growing concern in the European Commission that the regulation of working time needed to be addressed across the EU as a health and safety measure (Bridgford and Stirling 1994). The principal outcome of this interest was agreement to enact a Directive on the Adaptation of Working Time (the 'Working Time Directive') in 1993. However, John Major's Conservative government tried to prevent its application, arguing that because the Directive was a 'social' measure it could only be enacted through the so-called

'Social Chapter', from which the UK, because of its Maastricht 'opt-out', was at the time exempt (see Chapter 3). Yet the European Court of Justice (ECJ) ruled that the Directive was, as the European Commission maintained, a 'health and safety' measure and thus fell outside the 'Social Chapter' and, having thus been enacted, had to be extended to the UK.

8.5.2 **The 1998 Working Time Regulations**

Nevertheless, Tony Blair's Labour government, which took office in 1997, was able to win some significant concessions when the WTR were eventually enacted in 1998, notably the so-called 'right' of workers to choose whether or not they want to work for more than forty-eight hours a week, a source of much controversy as we see in Section 8.5.3.

The WTR provide for:

- a limit of forty-eight hours that a worker is required to work (including overtime), normally averaged out over a seventeen-week reference period;
- workers to have at least eleven consecutive hours of rest in any twenty-four-hour period;
- workers to have a rest period of at least twenty-four consecutive hours in any seven-day period, or forty-eight hours in a fourteen-day period;
- workers to have at least a twenty-minute unpaid rest break if the working day is longer than six hours;
- night workers, who are defined as workers who normally work at least three hours between 11pm and 6am, to be limited to an average of eight hours of work in any twenty-four-hour period; and
- a minimum of four weeks' paid annual leave.

There are additional restrictions that apply to workers aged below 18: for example, they are limited to an eight-hour working day and a forty-hour working week.

Some groups of workers—junior doctors and workers in transport, for example—were originally excluded from the scope of the forty-eight-hour maximum working week, as were senior managers, and others whose working time is said to be 'unmeasured'. Employers can reach a collective agreement with a recognized trade union, or by means of a 'workforce agreement' with elected employee representatives in the absence of a recognized union, to benefit from certain flexibilities; for example, the seventeen-week reference period over which the forty-eight-hour maximum limit is calculated can be extended to up to a year. The most controversial aspect of the WTR, and something that the British government fought hard to include, and even harder to retain, is the provision that workers can, by virtue of an 'individual agreement' with their employer, exceed the forty-eight-hour average weekly limit.

Employers frequently use such individual agreements automatically, routinely asking new employees to sign opt-out clauses when they commence employment (Neathy and Arrowsmith 2001; Barnard, Deakin, and Hobbs 2003; Crail 2007). Nearly a third of all workplaces (32 per cent) contain at least one employee who has signed an opt-out clause; and all employees have opted out in 15 per cent of workplaces (van Wanrooy et al. 2013). Many workers, it is argued, have very little real 'choice' about whether or not their working week is limited to an average of forty-eight hours. The TUC (2009) claims that in many cases employers put pressure on employees to 'agree' to opt out.

Yet both workers and their employers have a vested interest in ensuring that the opt-out remains, and that excessive working hours continue (Barnard, Deakin, and Hobbs 2003). Workers either need the additional income provided by paid overtime or, where it is unpaid, do the extra work in order to ensure that they keep their jobs, or are well regarded for promotion purposes. Employers, as we have seen, are reliant on overtime working as a key means of securing workplace flexibility. The widespread use of opt-outs is suggestive of a certain amount of 'pragmatic collusion' between workers and their employers (Goss and Adam-Smith 2001). In the food processing sector, for example, where extensive use is made of overtime to respond to fluctuating patterns of demand, there is evidence that workers willingly agree to sign opt-outs because of the extra income that working more hours brings (James and Lloyd 2008).

During the 2000s, the legal regulation of working time developed and evolved in three broad ways. The first thing to be aware of is that working time legislation has been extended to cover groups of workers who were excluded from the WTR. For example, the EU's Horizontal Amending Directive (2000)—what a charming name!—extended the scope of the WTD to cover, among others, non-mobile workers in the road transport industry and rail workers. The EU's Road Transport Directive (2002) took effect in 2005; it restricts drivers' weekly hours to forty-eight, averaged over a four-month reference period, with an absolute upper limit of sixty hours in any one week. Perhaps the most controversial development, however, was the decision to bring junior doctors within the scope of the WTR, with their weekly hours capped at forty-eight since 2009 (see the end-of-chapter case study for more details).

Second, during the 2000s the then Labour government altered the regulations governing paid holiday entitlement in two important respects. When the WTR were enacted the entitlement to four weeks' paid annual leave was subject to a thirteen-week qualifying period, and did not include bank holidays. Some employers included the eight bank holidays as part of the four-week entitlement, meaning that a full-time worker could be left with just 12 days of paid leave. However, following legal action from the trade unions, in 2001 the European Court of Justice (ECJ) ruled that the qualifying period did not comply with the Working Time Directive, and was thus unlawful. Workers are entitled to start accruing annual leave entitlement from the time they start a job. Unions also secured a further alteration—the exclusion of bank holidays from the four-week entitlement to paid annual leave. As a result, paid holiday entitlement increased to 4.8 weeks (twenty-four days for people working a five-day week) in 2007, and to 5.6 weeks (twenty-eight days) in 2009.

Third, there have also been some important case law developments, with the provisions of the WTR being subject to close scrutiny by the ECJ. Perhaps the most important topic concerns what is actually meant by 'working time', particularly for people in professional and managerial jobs who might be dealing with work-related emails while at home or on their way to and from work, outside of usual office hours (Brinkley 2012). New communication technologies mean that some workers are 'always on' (Grimshaw and Rubery 2010: 368), available for, and actually undertaking, work-related activities during ostensible periods of leisure. Management consultants, for example, find that working and non-working time becomes blurred because of the pressure they are under to satisfy their clients (Donnelly 2011).

An issue which has caused particular difficulty concerns how periods when workers are not actually engaged in work duties, but are 'on call'—that is, available on the employer's premises to work if required—should be treated for the purpose of the Working Time Directive. ECJ judgments have specified that the period of time when workers are 'on call' should be counted as working time, even if the workers concerned use it to rest or sleep. This has caused considerable difficulties for employers across Europe who operate such 'on call' arrangements, particularly in the health sector where around-the-clock availability of medical staff is often essential.

Although you would be forgiven for thinking otherwise, given the fuss made by businesses, the actual impact of the WTR has been rather modest. Perhaps most notably, they appear to have had little effect on working time patterns. As we have already observed, during the 2000s, average weekly hours of work for full-time employees have fallen. Yet there are a number of reasons why this decline is unlikely to be linked to the WTR. For one thing, it commenced in the mid-1990s, before the legislation came into effect (Green 2011). Moreover, the existence of the individual opt-out has means that the effect of the forty-eight-hour maximum working week provision has been diluted (Green 2011; Green and Whitfield 2009).

This raises the important question of whether or not workers should be entitled to opt out of legal coverage designed to protect their health and safety at work. Even Walsh (2010: 493), who suggests that there is a link between the WTR and the trend of declining working hours, acknowledges that 'a significant proportion of British employees still work more than forty-eight hours a week, especially male employees, and long hours working remains widespread among managers'.

The existence of the opt-out has other potential consequences. In theory, by restricting the use of overtime as a means of securing working time flexibility, the WTR could have prompted employers to develop other, more efficient ways of organizing working time, perhaps by investing in production methods or reorganizing work. However, the ease with which employers can secure opt-outs means that they have less of an incentive to undertake such changes (White et al. 2004). This has potentially adverse consequences for productivity, since the quality of work performed by people working excessive hours often declines, as they tire, leading to reduced output per hour (TUC 2009).

There are other, more plausible explanations for the decline in working hours since the mid-1990s. One is that it marks a return to the long-term trend of falling working hours, evident for much of the twentieth century, which is a function of greater prosperity and more desire for leisure time (Green 2011). Similarly, the decline in working hours reflects the greater extent to which workers have been demanding, and employers instituting, more family-friendly working arrangements, and the growth of a broader concern with securing a better work–life balance. Economic factors also seem to have played a part too, with the impact of the economic recession evident in fewer working hours being required by employers, and a notable rise in part-time working arrangements, since the late 2000s.

Yet the forty-eight-hour week aside, the force of working time regulation is evident in other respects, particularly the provision of statutory paid holiday entitlement. The enactment of the WTR meant that, for the first time ever in the UK, workers were given a legal entitlement to paid annual leave, a provision that benefited perhaps as much as 10 per cent of the workforce (Green 2003; Green and Whitfield 2009). However, there is some evidence that unscrupulous employers fail to give their staff the holiday leave to which they are legally entitled (Citizens Advice 2011).

8.5.3 The Working Time Directive: current debates and future prospects

As mentioned already, the 'individual agreement' provision, which allows workers to opt out from the forty-eight-hour upper limit placed on the average working week, is perhaps the most controversial feature of the WTD. In 2003, the European Commission launched a review of the individual agreement provision. Between 2004 and 2008, various attempts to reach a compromise were blocked, as EU member states failed to agree on an approach that satisfied all their interests.

The UK government and CBI lobbied vociferously for the retention of the opt-out on the grounds that, without it, employers would enjoy less flexibility over working time arrangements, and thus be rendered less competitive. The TUC, though, wanted to see the opt-out scrapped. It contended that even without the opt-out the WTD gives employers plenty of flexibility; the seventeen-week reference period for calculating working time (which can be increased to fifty-two weeks if there is union agreement) enables them to cope with variations in demand.

> If a business genuinely cannot survive without its staff working excessive hours on a permanent basis, then management need to think again about how work is organised. However, in most cases managers would find that they could manage these working time limits quite easily if they had to. All too often the problem is that they do not want to bother to manage this issue.
>
> (TUC 2009)

In 2008, the EU's Council of Ministers finally reached an agreement under which the individual opt-out would remain, albeit subject to certain conditions: that workers should not be asked to sign an opt-out agreement during the first month of their employment; that workers who do not sign, or repudiate, an opt-out agreement should not be victimized; and that a new, absolute upper limit of sixty hours in any one week should be instituted. The Council of Ministers also secured a deal on the matter of on-call time. However, this settlement was rejected by the European Parliament, which voted overwhelmingly for the opt-out to be scrapped entirely. Further efforts to reach another, more acceptable, compromise failed, meaning that the existing state of affairs continued (i.e. with the opt-out supposedly protected).

This was not the end of the matter, however. In March 2010 the European Commission began a consultation process with the social partners (trade union and employer bodies) over a proposed review of the WTD. In framing the review, the Commission highlighted some major working time trends, notably the decline in working hours in general and greater variability in working hours, and how these 'fundamental changes' meant that a full and comprehensive review of the Directive was merited. Specifically, the Commission wants the review to cover the opt-out provision, the question of on-call time, and whether or not more flexibility could be instituted (e.g. extending the seventeen-week reference period) (EIRO 2010). While the social partners have agreed to negotiate the content of a revised WTD, it is difficult to see how a deal can be reached. On the one hand, the main employers' body at EU level, BusinessEurope, wants to see workers continue to have access to opt-outs, that when workers are on call this should not be treated as working time, and that business flexibility should be prioritized. On the other hand, the European Trade Union Confederation (ETUC) has called for the opt-out to be scrapped, for existing ECJ rulings on on-call time to be respected by any new legislation, and to maintain the existing arrangements when it comes to reference periods (EIRO 2012).

The question of the WTD has intruded onto the domestic political arena. Prior to 2010, the Labour government fought to maintain the individual opt-out because it was viewed as so crucial to employers' flexibility. Rhetorically, at least, the coalition is even more hostile to the Directive. The May 2010 coalition agreement includes an aspiration to 'work to limit the application of the WTD in the UK', though little tangible progress has been made when it comes to actually challenging or repudiating it, other than commissioning a review of the legislation as it applies to junior doctors. Yet there can be little doubt about the Conservative Party's antipathy towards the WTD, notwithstanding the evidence that its practical effects have been rather limited. Hostility to the legislation is emblematic, not just of Conservative opposition to employment regulation, but also of many in the party's deep hostility to the EU (Gall 2011c).

Many see the WTD as a key example where powers over social and employment legislation can be repatriated from the EU. Even prominent Liberal Democrat members of the government, like deputy prime minister Nick Clegg and business secretary Vince Cable, who are ostensibly more supportive of the EU and less hostile to protective employment legislation, have suggested that working time matters should not be a matter for EU regulation. Perhaps the most telling indication of the eagerness of the government to rid the UK of European working time legislation was evident in late 2011 when the government raised the prospect of making reform of the WTD a condition of agreeing to future EU treaty revisions.

 ## Section summary and further reading

- Due to concerns about the adverse consequences of excessive working hours for workers' health, in 1993 the EU enacted the Working Time Directive (WTD), which among other things provides for a maximum average working week of forty-eight hours, minimum rest periods and rest breaks, and a minimum of four weeks' paid leave. It was put into effect in the UK by the 1998 Working Time Regulations (WTR).

- One of the most controversial features of the WTR concerns the provision for opting out of the forty-eight-hour week, meaning that the legislation has done little to tackle the phenomenon of excessive working hours.

- The future of the WTD is somewhat uncertain, with the European Commission engaged in a review of the legislation.

Studies of the impact of the WTR include Goss and Adam-Smith (2001) and Barnard, Deakin, and Hobbs (2003). For an overall evaluation, see Green (2011).

8.6 Conclusion

This chapter has demonstrated the importance of working time as an employment relations issue: its length, the way in which it is organized, how it is used, and how it is regulated. For much of the twentieth century the duration of working time was commonly regulated jointly through collective bargaining between employers and trade unions. The diminution of joint regulation, however, has given managers more scope to exercise unilateral control over working time, something that is particularly manifest in the greater incidence of flexible working hours, rising work pressures, and expectations that work duties should be undertaken outside of 'normal' working hours. Working time patterns are marked by an increasing amount of variation and unpredictability, as employers endeavour to manage labour as efficiently as possible by constantly adjusting staff numbers to match changes in demand for services. While it is important not to overlook the extent to which flexible working hours can be operated in ways that benefit workers, overall working time trends would appear to have had some major adverse consequences for them, particularly the harm to their well-being caused by excessive working hours and high work pressures.

That said, though, some aspects of working time—including the maximum length of the working week, paid holiday entitlement, rest breaks, and rest periods—have come within the scope of legal regulation, mainly as a result of the EU's 1993 Working Time Directive (put into effect in the UK by the 1998 Working Time Regulations). However, given the scope for opt-outs enjoyed by employers, the WTR have evidently done little to challenge excessive working hours in Britain. This further demonstrates how statutory regulation of the employment relationship is, by itself, not an adequate replacement for joint regulation as a means of securing improvements in working conditions. Nevertheless, the law has had a more positive effect when it comes to guaranteeing most workers a minimum amount of paid holidays each year. Whether or not working time regulation can have a more profound impact on working hours depends on the extent to which trade unions in Europe can mobilize effectively to secure changes in the WTD which support workers' interests.

 ### Assignment and discussion questions

1. Account for the main working time trends since the 1990s.

2. What are main advantages and disadvantages for workers and employers of overtime working arrangements?

3. To what extent do you agree with the view that flexible working hours arrangements are overwhelmingly beneficial for workers?

4. Assess the main causes of work intensification.

5. Critically assess the arguments for and against using the law to regulate working time arrangements.

 Visit the Online Resource Centre that accompanies this book to develop your understanding of this chapter, and keep up to date with the latest developments in this area.
www.oxfordtextbooks.co.uk/orc/williams3e/

 ### Chapter case study: Junior doctors and the Working Time Directive

The application of the Working Time Directive (WTD) in the health sector has provoked a considerable degree of controversy. During the 1990s, junior doctors engaged in postgraduate training in clinical environments regularly worked for more than 100 hours each week. Amidst concerns about the need for patient safety and ensuring effective training, the implementation of the WTD was staged for junior doctors, with the forty-eight-hour limit finally coming into force in August 2009. This provoked a lot of opposition from some quarters, particularly doctors' organizations like the Royal Colleges, who claimed that the maximum working week would mean that there was insufficient time to provide training, and would hamper the response to medical emergencies. The president of the Royal College of Surgeons warned that the WTD would lead to a dramatic reduction in the level of contact between doctors and patients, with potentially damaging consequences for patient care. In September 2012, the Royal College of Physicians published a report—*Hospitals on the Edge*—which asserts that the forty-eight-hour working limit has adversely affected continuity of patient care, increased the hours of senior doctors (consultants), and reduced the effectiveness of the training offered to junior doctors by consultants (RCP 2012).

Conservative MP Charlotte Leslie has campaigned to exempt junior doctors from the forty-eight-hour maximum working week. She claims that doctors in acute medical and surgical units find it necessary to work for more than forty-eight hours. Moreover, the working time limit adversely affects the standard of patient care by eroding continuity of care, reducing the amount of training given to junior doctors and limiting the availability of appropriate clinical expertise. In an April 2012 Westminster Hall debate, Leslie claimed that, while she was not advocating a return to the days when junior doctors worked an excessive number of hours, the WTD was 'compromising' care, 'devastating the NHS', and 'eroding that professional ethos which upholds the NHS and beginning to replace it by a clock on, clock off culture'. As a result, the safety of patients is 'being seriously jeopardized on a day-to-day basis'. The coalition government has promised to review the application of the WTD, and wants to see more flexibility over how the maximum working week operates in areas like the health sector.

However, others argue that the application of the WTD to junior doctors has been put into practice relatively smoothly, with few of the negative outcomes claimed by the Royal Colleges and Conservative politicians. The NHS Employers organization, for example, emphasizes the effective way in which hospitals and other organizations have adapted to the maximum working week, for example through revised shift patterns and the use of more sophisticated flexible working time arrangements. The independent Temple review of the implications of the WTD for junior doctors' training found that, with the exception of out-of-hours services, high-quality training could be delivered in forty-eight hours a week, as long as there was proper supervision. There is also evidence that reducing junior doctors' hours so that they are compliant with the WTD enhances patient safety by reducing the number of errors made. Following a House of Lords debate on the issue, in October 2012 the chair of the British Medical Association's Junior Doctors Committee, Ben Molyneux, recognized that while there was a range of opinion on the matter, the maximum working week was beneficial overall. He said:

> Tired doctors make mistakes, and we must think of the welfare of doctors and the resultant impact fatigue can have on patient care ... There is a mounting body of evidence to support the move to reduced working hours in terms of patient safety. While flexibility may be appropriate, scrapping the [WTD] is not.

Sources: BBC News Online 2009*e*, 2011*b*; BBC Democracy Live 2012; RCP (2012); http://www.bma.org.uk

Questions

To what extent is it desirable to regulate the working hours of junior doctors by law? How can working time legislation be implemented in ways that do not jeopardize patient safety?

Part 4

Conflict and employment relations

9 Labour conflict and employment relations

◉ Chapter objectives

The main objectives of this chapter are to:

- demonstrate the relevance of labour conflict in contemporary employment relations;
- examine the nature and purpose of strikes, and their significance as a form of labour conflict;
- account for recent strike trends, and discuss their implications for employment relations;
- examine the contribution made by mobilization theory to understanding the circumstances under which labour conflict arises; and
- assess the nature and significance of forms of labour conflict other than strikes.

9.1 Introduction

Chapter 1 observed that the employment relationship, given that it is a wage–work or effort bargain, is characterized by a basic antagonism; thus there is always the potential for conflict to arise in the relationship between employers and employees (Edwards 1986). Labour conflict, however, is often overlooked, particularly in texts on human resource management. This is justified with reference to a diminution of strike activity and other forms of industrial action (e.g. 'overtime bans'), particularly in the private sector. Yet all around the world there is evidence that strikes and labour conflict remain an important feature of work and employment relations. Even the well-known retail chain Walmart, which has successfully managed to avoid recognizing unions in its US stores, was affected by strikes, protests, and walk-outs by many of its workers during 2012. Labour conflict is commonplace in some parts of the world, most notably in China where strikes and protests by workers demanding higher wages and better working conditions have become endemic (Seymour 2013). Moreover, economic recession has been responsible for a marked increase in the incidence of strikes and labour conflict internationally (ILO 2011). In many European countries, for example, there have been mass strikes by workers in protest against government austerity measures which involve job losses, cuts to wages and pensions, and weakened employment protection.

In this chapter the resurgence of strikes and labour conflict in the context of ongoing economic recession is highlighted. There is also an examination of the main influences on strike levels and the key features of the legal framework governing industrial action by trade unions. It is important to bear in mind that conflict in employment relations is about much more than strikes, manifesting itself in a variety of forms. The concept of 'labour conflict' is used to refer to a variety of behaviours undertaken by workers and their allies, both inside and outside the workplace, which reflect the basic antagonism underlying the employment relationship. Mobilization theory helps us to understand the circumstances under which workers' grievances translate into instances of actual labour conflict, and that this conflict when it does arise can take a variety of forms, and is not just restricted to strikes.

 Introductory case study: The 2012 pensions strikes at Unilever

In January 2012, employees of Unilever, a multinational company which produces a range of well-known consumer brands including Persil washing powder and the Carte D'Or range of ice creams, held a series of one- and two-day strikes across twelve of the company's UK sites in protest at the decision to close its final salary pension scheme and move current employees to a less generous career average arrangement. Unilever argued that the costs of maintaining the final salary scheme had become prohibitive, particularly as people were living longer in retirement. However, the unions claimed that the highly profitable company could easily afford to maintain it, but preferred to increase returns to its shareholders instead. One of the plants affected by the strikes—in Crumlin, South Wales—makes Pot Noodle snacks. An electrician at the site, Alan Shears, said: 'The reason [given] was that people were going to live longer and the fund was very poor [but] people have been living longer for a long time and the fund is in a healthy state . . . The real reason is they want to make the business more profitable for them and then sell it on'. The Unite union posted a video on YouTube explaining the basis for the strikes: http://www.youtube.com/watch?v=6AF6OVP-OHo

Following the strikes, in April 2012 the dispute was settled after the company made considerable improvements to the replacement career average scheme, though workers remained deeply dissatisfied. This case illustrates how strikes can occur when workers who are organized in a trade union have a collective grievance which, to them, is sufficiently serious to warrant taking action to withdraw their labour. In such circumstances strikes are used as a bargaining tool, undertaken in order to put pressure on employers to withdraw or amend decisions that have aggrieved workers. While the strikes did not lead to the retention of the final salary scheme, without them it is unlikely that Unilever would have improved the terms of the new pension arrangements. See BBC News Online (2012b, 2012c).

9.2 The nature and purpose of strikes

Understandably, strikes—the withdrawal by workers of their labour—dominate analyses of conflict in employment relations. They are the 'most obvious manifestation' of labour conflict (Hyman 1975: 186), being relatively more open, visible and important, in turn, making them more worthy of measurement and more measurable' (Gall and Hebdon 2008: 597). A strike can be defined as 'a temporary stoppage of work by a group of employees in order to express a grievance or to enforce a demand' (Griffin 1939, cited in Hyman 1977: 17). There are five dimensions of strikes that warrant specific attention:

- First, strikes are a form of 'industrial action'. The term 'industrial action' refers to those manifestations of labour conflict that involve explicitly collective behaviour by workers.

- Second, strikes are generally organized by trade unions, on the basis that when workers mobilize on a collective basis they will enjoy greater bargaining leverage over employers and governments. Strike action is difficult to uphold without the presence of a union, which can mobilize workers, organize the action, and coordinate responses to the efforts of employers and governments to prevent, or counteract the effects of, strikes (Hyman 1989).

- Third, strikes are designed to be a temporary act; employees withdraw their labour based on the understanding that work will be resumed once the dispute that has caused the strike is resolved.

- Fourth, strikes involve a stoppage of work. As a manifestation of conflict in employment relations, they can therefore be distinguished from other forms of industrial action, such as the overtime ban, which we consider later on in this chapter.

- Fifth, strikes are a form of behaviour that is undertaken by workers with a specific purpose in mind: to get a dismissed colleague reinstated for example, or to secure an increase in pay. Strikes, then, generally have a calculative, purposive character (Hyman 1977, 1989). They rarely arise without a reason, even if it is only implicit.

There are two broad types of strikes—'economic' strikes and 'political' strikes (Gall and Hebdon 2008). The former are directed mainly at employers and concern issues such as pay, benefits, and working conditions, matters which have economic consequences for the firms and workers involved. The Unilever pensions strike is an example of an economic strike.

Political strikes, though, are generally targeted at governments, and concern broader policy issues. In the UK there is strict legislation in place which prevents unions from organizing strikes over political matters. Elsewhere in Europe, though, such action is commonplace; indeed there would seem to be a trend towards using strikes to achieve political rather than economic goals, evident in the growing frequency of general strikes—those involving workers from more than one industry, who withdraw their labour on a mass scale in protest against government policies (Kelly 2011).

A distinction can also be made between official and unofficial strikes. Official strike activity is that which, once it has been approved by its appropriate decision-making machinery, has the formal, or official, backing of a trade union. Unofficial strikes, however, occur when employees withdraw their labour, perhaps by walking off the job, without receiving the formal support of their union.

Since unofficial strike action is often of rather a short duration, involving relatively few workers, it is sometimes portrayed as being largely spontaneous behaviour undertaken in order to redress an immediate grievance (Knowles 1952), hence the popularity of the term 'wildcat strike' to describe such activity (Gouldner 1955). However, unofficial strikes cannot be treated as if they are spontaneous; their occurrence reflects the ongoing efforts of employees to resist potentially damaging changes to their working conditions, or to improve their position and power, in the context of the wage–work bargain (Cronin 1979). Such activity demands organization, and hence calculation. The organized basis of unofficial action was evident in January 2009 when union activists helped to coordinate the apparently spontaneous walk-outs around the country in support of workers at the Lindsey oil refinery in their dispute over the use of foreign labour (Gall 2012b)—see Contesting employment relations 9.1.

Contesting employment relations 9.1: Unofficial strike action—Lindsey oil refinery

One of the most notable major examples of an unofficial strike occurred in early 2009 when a number of companies around the UK suffered disruption after thousands of workers walked off their jobs to demonstrate their support for striking workers at the Lindsey oil refinery in Lincolnshire, who were protesting about the use of foreign labour. Construction work on the expansion of the refinery, owned by the French oil company Total, was subcontracted to an Italian firm which had brought in its own workforce to do the job. Against a background of rising unemployment, many workers were angry that the work on the refinery was being undertaken by foreign staff, at lower rates of pay, instead of local workers. According to Stephen Briggs, one of the protesting workers, while they 'have got nothing against foreign workers, the fact is that there are a lot of people out of work and are looking for jobs' (BBC News Online 2009a).

Two implications arise from the purposeful and organized nature of strike activity. First, the notion sometimes advanced by governments and employers that strikes are abnormal, a deviation from the normal character of stable, ordered, and peaceful employment relations, cannot be upheld. In the context of an exploitative employment relationship, the withdrawal of their labour by employees is a rational form of behaviour designed to achieve a particular purpose: to alter the terms of the wage–work bargain in a way, or ways, favourable to them (Hyman 1977). It also reflects the capacity of workers to act collectively, to mobilize in pursuit of their interests through the vehicle of a trade union (Cronin 1979; Hyman 1989). This highlights the second main implication of the strike being an activity that is both purposeful and organized; that is the importance of the collective organization of workers in trade unions. Without the presence of a strong union that is able to mobilize workers, organize the action, and coordinate resistance to employer efforts to defeat it, effective strike activity is hard to uphold (Edwards 1983; Hyman 1989).

Section summary and further reading

- Given the inherent potential for conflict that characterizes the employment relationship, it is understandable that strikes, the collective withdrawal by workers of their labour, are a feature of employment relations.

- Strikes are the most obvious and visible manifestation of industrial conflict. They are purposive and calculative types of behaviour in employment relations, undertaken to pursue a demand or express a grievance.

- Strikes can occur for economic reasons, concerned with matters relating to pay, working conditions, and other workplace-related issues, or on political grounds, relating to matters of government policy (though political strikes are unlawful in the UK).

- Official strikes are those that have the formal, explicit backing of a trade union. Unofficial strikes, however, occur when employees withdraw their labour, perhaps by walking off the job, without receiving the formal support of their union.

The classic introduction to the topic is Hyman's book on Strikes (Hyman 1977, and other editions). Gall and Hebdon 2008) provide a good account of the nature and purpose of strike activity in their book chapter on conflict at work.

9.3 Strike trends

Having outlined what strikes are, and how they are to be understood as a feature of employment relations, in this section the focus is on strike trends. The starting point is an outline of some issues relating to measuring the level of strike activity, before considering the main strike trends in more detail and looking to account for them. Evidence from around the world indicates that strikes are a global phenomenon, with strike activity seemingly on the rise in many countries.

9.3.1 Measuring strikes

Strikes are often taken as a measure of the level of labour conflict because they are apparently easy to quantify. There are three main ways of ascertaining the level of strike activity in any given period, usually over the course of a year:

- The duration of strike activity is measured by calculating the number of working days not worked due to strike activity.
- The breadth of strike activity is calculated by measuring the number of workers involved.
- The frequency of strike activity is determined by totalling up the number of strikes, or stoppages, in any given year.

Unless the total number of days not worked amounts to 100 or more, strikes involving fewer than ten workers, or lasting less than one day, are excluded from official data (ONS 2012b). While official strike data can be used constructively to map trends in strike activity over time (Edwards 1995), they should nonetheless be treated with caution (Hyman 1977; Godard 2011). Managers sometimes do not record strikes, for example (Batstone, Boraston, and Frenkel 1978). Generally, government statistics understate levels of labour conflict, not least because they are only concerned with strikes, and disregard other types of industrial action by trade unions, like overtime bans (Gall and Hebdon 2008). Moreover, an infrequent number of very large strikes can disproportionately affect the statistics. This was evident during 2011 when a small number of major public sector strikes, especially the action taken on 30 November that year by twenty-seven unions in protest over proposed changes to pensions, contributed to a nearly four-fold increase in the duration of strike activity compared to the previous year.

9.3.2 The declining level of strike activity

That said, though, one of the most prominent features of employment relations has been the diminution in the level of strike activity since the 1970s. Table 9.1 shows that strike levels peaked during the 1970s, when on average each year there were well over 2,000 recorded strikes and over 12 million working days not worked as a consequence. While the 1980s were characterized by occasional large-scale strikes, in industries such as steel making and coal mining, as workers and their unions fought rationalization initiatives that threatened their jobs, livelihoods, and communities (Gilbert 1996)—the nine-month miners' strike in 1984–5

Table 9.1 The level of strike activity in Britain, 1946–99

	Strikes	Workers involved (000s)	Days not worked (000s)
1946–52	1,698	444	1,888
1953–59	2,340	790	3,950
1960–68	2,372	1,323	3,189
1969–73	2,974	1,581	12,497
1974–79	2,412	1,653	12,178
1980–85	1,276	1,213	9,806
1986–89	893	781	3,324
1990–94	334	223	824
1995–99	193	180	495

Annual averages

Sources: Edwards (1995); Office for National Statistics, http://www.statistics.gov.uk

being the most famous example—the decade saw a marked diminution of strike activity, as measured by the frequency, breadth, and duration of strikes.

During the 1990s the decline in the amount of strike activity continued, a trend which persisted into the 2000s, when it reached historically low levels. Table 9.2 provides further details of strike levels between 2000 and 2012. The year 2005 saw the lowest recorded number of working days not worked due to strike activity—157,000—while the lowest number of strikes, just ninety-two, was recorded some five years later, in 2010. Yet, despite the overall historically low levels of strike activity during the 2000s, there were notable annual fluctuations. Some years have seen a marked upsurge in strikes. In 2002, for example, over 1.3 million working days were not worked, largely as a result of two major public sector strikes involving local government workers and firefighters. While the decline in the level of strike activity is an international phenomenon (Wallace and O'Sullivan 2006; Vandaele 2011), it does seem to have been more pronounced in the UK than elsewhere.

Why has the incidence of strike activity fallen to such low levels in contemporary employment relations? Clearly, the changing composition of employment has been an important factor. Levels of employment in traditionally strike-prone industries, such as coal mining and the docks for example, have fallen considerably. Job growth has been concentrated in private sector service industries where trade unionism is weaker and strike action less commonplace. That said, though, the idea that workers in certain occupations and industries are particularly 'strike-prone' (e.g. Kerr and Siegel 1954) often fails to stand up to critical scrutiny (Edwards 1977). Strike levels may vary considerably from workplace to workplace even within the same industry.

The rise of service-based economies is sometimes associated with the diminution of labour conflict, since workers supposedly enjoy fewer opportunities to engage in collective solidarity (Wallace and O'Sullivan 2006). But too great an emphasis on the compositional explanation means that the capacity of service sector workers to mobilize and challenge the interests of their employers is under-appreciated. In particular, workers in the public

Table 9.2 The level of strike activity in Britain, 2000–12

	Strikes	Workers involved (000s)	Days not worked (000s)
2000	212	183	499
2001	194	180	525
2002	146	943	1,323
2003	133	151	499
2004	130	293	905
2005	116	93	157
2006	158	713	755
2007	142	745	1,041
2008	144	511	756
2009	98	209	455
2010	92	103	365
2011	149	1,530	1,390
2012	181	250	259

Source: Office for National Statistics, http://www.statistics.gov.uk

services have demonstrated an increased readiness to take strike action. During the 2000s, public sector disputes—among post office workers, college lecturers, local government workers, civil servants, and firefighters in particular—increasingly dominated the strike statistics. Much of their action, moreover, was often relatively short, or discontinuous, in nature, such as a series of one- or two-day strikes for example, something which increases the pressure on the employer while reducing the costs to the employee of striking, in particular loss of wages.

Another reason for the diminution of strike activity concerns changes in the economic climate. As we saw in Chapter 2, greater competitive pressures, often associated with globalization, have undermined the bargaining power of labour. They also mean that employers have a greater incentive to avoid potentially disruptive strikes (Piazza 2005). Increasingly mobile global capital can use the threat of relocation to pacify labour, for example, helping to engender a more 'disciplined' and thus quiescent workforce (Vandaele 2011).

A further reason that can be posited for the decline of strike activity is that the rise of sophisticated forms of HRM, manifest particularly in the use of high commitment management practices, has generated a more cooperative climate at work, rendering strikes and other manifestations of labour conflict unnecessary. Workers, the assumption goes, are increasingly engaged at work, more committed to their employing organizations, and are thus less likely to have reason to challenge the interests of their employers (Emmott 2005; CBI 2011a). The main difficulty with this explanation for the decline in the level of strike activity is that, as was shown in Chapter 5, there is little evidence that a high commitment approach to managing employment relations has become commonplace. Indeed, claims that the management of employment relations has been transformed along cooperative lines are belied by the large extent to which employees are actually disengaged at work (Coats 2010).

Therefore it seems doubtful that the level of strike activity has diminished because workers are more contented. What does seem to have changed, though, is that many employers are managing employment relations more assertively. They concentrate on fostering a workplace climate in which it is made apparent to employees that, given greater competitive pressures, their cooperation is essential in order to prevent job losses and the erosion of pay and working conditions—something which underpins the use of partnership agreements as discussed in Chapter 6.

Perhaps the most important reason for the decline of strike activity, and one that is related to the compositional, economic, and managerial factors already mentioned, concerns the changing balance of power between trade unions and employers (see Godard 2011). The decline in their membership and organizational capacities has rendered the unions less capable of undertaking effective industrial action. Many union leaders have placed their faith in partnership and cooperative employment relations as the route to greater influence, largely because they are operating from a position of weakness. Moreover, the highly restrictive legal framework imposes substantial constraints on the ability of unions to organize effective strike action (see Section 9.4), though its precise effects are difficult to gauge.

One key question is whether or not the diminution of strike activity evident between the 1980s and the 2000s will continue in the future. As you can see from Table 9.2, there was a marked increase in recorded strike activity during 2011, with nearly 1.4 million working days not worked. Much of this increase was the result of strikes in the public sector

⊡ Contesting employment relations 9.2: The 2011 strikes at Southampton City Council

From 2010, the potential for conflict in the public sector began to attract greater attention given the prospect of cuts to public services needed to reduce the UK government's budget deficit. Since staff costs constitute a large proportion of public expenditure, any significant attempts to reduce government spending are likely to involve some combination of wage freezes, reductions in employment levels, and/or changes to terms and conditions, including raised pension contributions. This austerity drive generated marked instances of labour conflict across the public sector. One of the most prominent examples concerns the series of strikes during 2011 at Southampton City Council that occurred in response to the then Conservative-led local authority's decision to impose a pay cut, originally of up to 5.5 per cent for staff earning more than £17,500 per year, as part of a cost-cutting initiative designed to realize some £76 million worth of savings over five years. It did this by terminating existing employment contracts and re-hiring staff on new contracts with a lower salary. It claimed that up to 400 jobs would be lost otherwise. Workers and unions reacted furiously to the pay cuts, with refuse collectors, social workers, port staff, and parking wardens among others all taking part in strike action at various times of the year, causing significant disruption as a result. The unions, who also instigated legal action against the council over its alleged failure to consult properly, claimed that the council had sufficient funds in its reserves to avoid both job losses and pay cuts. After Labour took control of the council following the local elections of May 2012, it negotiated a settlement of the dispute with the unions, which involved a phased reversal of the pay cuts imposed by its Conservative predecessor.

Sources: BBC News Online (2012d); Milmo (2012).

among schoolteachers, civil servants, lecturers, and others in response to government austerity measures that have resulted in pay cuts/freezes, the erosion of pension rights, and job losses. In local government, proposals by some councils to impose pay cuts resulted in some notable disputes, that at Southampton being a particularly prominent example (see Contesting employment relations 9.2). The biggest strike in the UK for over thirty years occurred on 30 November 2011, when twenty-seven unions held a one-day stoppage involving hundreds of thousands of public sector workers in protest at pension changes. It included the National Association of Headteachers, which organized its first ever strike.

Like previous years, most working days not worked in 2011 (92 per cent) because of strikes were in the public sector; however, some 40 per cent of actual stoppages occurred in the private sector, in companies like Unilever, particularly over issues around pay, pensions, and jobs. Since the late 2000s strikes have affected a wide range of sectors, including transport, energy, local newspapers, and manufacturing, where workers are organized in unions and have the motivation and capacity to take action to challenge their employers' actions. So care needs to be taken not to assume that strikes are solely a public sector phenomenon.

On the one hand, there is some evidence that this resurgence of strike activity ebbed during 2012, when just 259,000 days were not worked as a result of strikes. On the other hand, however, the actual number of strikes (181) reached its highest level in over a decade. Perhaps the most eye-catching strike incident during 2012 was the one-day action organized in June that year by the British Medical Association over pensions, the first strike among doctors for some forty years. Do not forget that much of the high number of days not worked because of strikes during 2011 came about as a result of the massive one-day national public strike on 30 November that year. The data indicate that 2012 was marked by a higher number of smaller strikes.

9.3.3 **Strikes—a global phenomenon**

The decline in the level of recorded strike activity between the 1970s and the 2000s was not just restricted to the UK; internationally, there was also a marked fall in the incidence of strikes (Wallace and O'Sullivan 2006; Vandaele 2011). Particularly where unions are relatively weak, globalization seems to have been a major cause of the diminution in strike levels, given its tendency to erode the power of organized labour (Piazza 2005). Yet care must be taken not to write off strikes. During the 2000s, there was evidence of increased strike activity in a number of major countries linked to demands from workers for higher wages. In Russia, for example, the number and intensity of strikes grew during this period, as workers in the automobile and energy sectors tried to use their growing bargaining power to press for higher wages, against a background of economic growth and raised expectations (Greene and Robertson 2010; Ashwin 2011). For similar reasons, the 2000s also saw rising strike levels in the major Latin American economies of Argentina and Brazil. Economic growth and governments run by parties sympathetic to trade unions helped to enhance workers' bargaining power, which their unions used to mobilize support for strikes in pursuit of higher wages (Etchemendy and Collier 2007; Sénen González and Medwid 2009; Boito and Marcelino 2011).

From a global perspective, it is apparent that strike activity and other forms of labour un-rest have not disappeared. A number of major disputes have occurred in South Africa, for example. In 2010 there was a massive three-week public sector strike which involved nearly a million and a half workers taking action in pursuit of higher pay. During 2012–13, moreover, there was widespread disruption in the country's mining sector as a result of massive strikes by miners in pursuit of improved pay and conditions, some of which were violently sup-pressed. In some countries, such as South Korea and Indonesia, strikes have been a major feature of efforts by workers' movements to challenge authoritarian employers and govern-ments, helping to instigate democratic political change (Koo 2001; La Botz 2001). One of the major challenges facing the rulers of Dubai, part of the United Arab Emirates, for example, is how to deal with the widespread labour unrest evident among its largely migrant construc-tion workforce (see International perspective 9.3).

 International perspective 9.3: Strikes and labour unrest in Dubai

During the 2000s, the emirate of Dubai in the Middle East was one of the fastest growing places in the world, with scores of new hotel complexes, luxury apartments, and shopping centres going up to service a growing tourism and leisure industry. The construction industry boomed. With 160 storeys, one building, the Burj Dubai Tower, was the tallest in the world when it was completed. The construction workforce is overwhelmingly made up of migrant labourers from countries such as India, Pakistan, and Bangladesh who travel to Dubai in the belief that finding work will make them prosperous. The reality is often excessive working hours, under oppressive conditions, in temperatures that sometimes reach 50 degrees. Low and unpaid wages often leave many of the workers, who share rooms in concrete barrack compounds, heavily in debt. They are often required to surrender their passports, so are not free to leave. Any form of industrial action by workers is illegal in Dubai, and there is no right to join a trade union. Workers who do make a fuss are treated as troublemakers and deported. During 2006 and 2007, however, some major instances of labour conflict were reported as construction workers took strike action and protested over low pay, inadequate accommodation, and poor working conditions. This demonstrates that even where the odds are heavily stacked against it, action by workers who want to improve the conditions under which they labour is always possible.

The economic recession of the late 2000s, and the austerity policies devised by many governments as a response to it, have generated increases in strike activity, particularly in emerging Latin American economies, such as Argentina, Brazil, and Chile (ILO 2011). Europe has also been affected by an upsurge in labour unrest linked to the unfavourable economic climate and austerity policies. In 2010–11, for example, mass strikes occurred in France, Greece, Italy, Spain, and Portugal as workers took to the streets to protest against government austerity measures (Vandaele 2011).

It is often thought that economic globalization, by diminishing workers' bargaining power, has been a major cause of the international decline in strike activity. Yet in so far as it has eroded people's working conditions, the process of economic globalization may in fact have both increased the extent, and extended the dimensions, of labour conflict. For one thing, neo-liberal policies associated with globalization have generated a con-siderable amount of labour unrest in their own right; the case of Bolivia is particularly notable (Kohl and Farthing 2005). Moreover, the development of export-oriented manu-facturing industries in countries such as China, and the concomitant need for cheap labour on a massive scale, has produced a highly propitious environment for labour conflict (Silver 2003). Economic reforms, in particular the development of capitalist market rela-tions, have generated widespread incidents of labour conflict, including strikes, over mat-ters such as unpaid wages and employer violations of labour regulations (see Lee 2007; Cooke 2008; Chan 2010; Friedman and Lee 2010). In some more advanced parts of the economy, rising expectations have encouraged workers to contemplate strike action in pursuit of higher wages. For example, in 2010 a wave of strikes affected car and electronics plants over demands for substantial pay rises. Striking workers in Honda won pay rises of 20–30 per cent as a result of their action.

 ### Section summary and further reading

- There are a number of ways in which the level of strike activity can be measured, though the accuracy of the data should be treated with caution. Nevertheless, the amount of strike activity in Britain would seem to have fallen to historically very low levels indeed.

- A number of factors appear to be responsible for the diminution of strike levels, including compositional change and, in particular, changes in the balance of power at the workplace resulting in weaker unions who, given the more restrictive legal framework, are less capable of initiating or organizing effective strikes.

- The economic recession, and governmental austerity measures designed to tackle it, have contributed to a resurgence of strike activity, though how long it will last is open to question.

- Strike activity would seem to be on the rise in many parts of the world; indeed the process of economic globalization has intensified labour unrest in some countries.

The government's Office for National Statistics publishes strike data on its website, and publishes an annual overview (ONS 2012b)—http://www.ons.gov.uk/ons/rel/bus-register/labour-disputes/annual-article-2011/art--labour-disputes-annual-article-2011.html

Godard (2011) provides a thoughtful analysis of the factors underlying the decline of strikes. See Silver (2003) for the implications of globalization for labour unrest. Wallace and O'Sullivan (2006) look at international data.

9.4 The legal regulation of strikes and industrial action

Unlike many other European countries, in Britain workers have never enjoyed a 'right' to go on strike, although under the influence of the European Court of Human Rights (ECHR) this may be changing (Ewing and Hendy 2010). Under the common law, based on the primacy of freedom of contract and the importance of property rights, workers who strike or undertake any form of industrial action generally act in breach of their employment contracts. Trade unions that organize industrial action potentially transgress the common law in a range of areas; most notably they commit the offence of inducing workers to breach their contracts.

During the late nineteenth and early twentieth centuries, legislation was enacted that gave unions and their officials immunities from criminal prosecution for organizing industrial ac-tion, and from civil proceedings for damages by employers, as long as the action was 'in con-templation or furtherance of a trade dispute' (Wedderburn 1986). The concept of 'immunities' gave the misleading impression that trade unions were above the law, and attracted much judicial hostility (Wedderburn 1991). In reality, all they did was ensure that the common law of contract and property rights did not make the conduct of employment relations impossible to uphold in practice (Davies and Freedland 1993).

Without these immunities, trade unions would have been in no position to bargain effectively on behalf of their members. The only alternative was a system of positive rights for workers and their unions, something that was contrary to the preference for voluntarism and autonomous self-regulation that characterized employment relations in Britain. However, during the 1980s and 1990s the Conservative governments enacted six major pieces of legislation restricting the capacity of trade unions to undertake lawful industrial action. The main focus of their interventions was to reduce the scope of the immunities that enabled unions to organize industrial action within the boundaries of the law (Dunn and Metcalf 1996; Dickens and Hall 2003). Among other things, legislation was enacted that:

- obliged unions to win majority support for industrial action from the workers concerned in a properly constituted secret postal ballot, and give employers at least seven days' notice of the action;
- prohibited any form of 'secondary' industrial action, meaning that it is only lawful when it involves a 'primary' dispute between workers and their own employer;
- enabled employers and other aggrieved parties to sue a union for damages arising out of unlawful industrial action; and
- gave employers greater scope to dismiss workers taking industrial action.

The legislation was a major element of the Conservatives' efforts to challenge the power of the unions in Britain. After 1997, Labour retained the bulk of the anti-strike legislation it inherited from its Conservative predecessors in government, and showed no inclination to repeal any of it, despite representations by union leaders (Davies and Freedland 2007).

The extent to which the restrictive legal framework weakened the capacity of trade unions to mount effective strikes was evident in a number of high-profile disputes, particularly in the newspaper publishing and transport sectors, during the 1980s and 1990s (Gennard 1984; McIlroy 1991). However, employers can sometimes be reluctant to invoke the law when facing industrial action by trade unions on the basis that legal action would only inflame the dispute, making it harder to resolve. Nevertheless, the complex legislation governing industrial action ballots gives employers plenty of scope to challenge—and thus delay—any planned action, even if their substantive case turns out to be weak (McIlroy 1999). This was evident in some high-profile industrial disputes when employers pounced upon minor discrepancies over how the ballot was conducted, or the notice required to be given to employers was arranged, to instigate court proceedings and win injunctions from sympathetic judges prohibiting the strike from going ahead. See the end-of-chapter case study for a particularly egregious example from December 2009, when British Airways cabin crew were prevented from holding a strike, despite a 92 per cent vote in favour, because of some relatively minor balloting irregularities which would not have affected the outcome anyway. In April 2010, Network Rail prevented a strike of railway signal staff from going ahead after successfully applying for a High Court injunction on the basis of a tiny number of discrepancies in the ballot. The then TUC general secretary, Brendan Barber, responded to the judgment by saying that it was 'becoming increasingly easy for employers, unhappy at the prospect of a dispute, to rely on the courts to intervene and nullify a democratic ballot for industrial action on a mere technicality'.

The impact of the restrictive legal framework on union behaviour is by no means straightforward though. Where workplace union organization is relatively strong, the obligation to hold a ballot before taking industrial action can work to a union's advantage. A large vote in favour, for example, can be used to exert pressure on employers to grant concessions. In situations where they are confident that they have the support of the workforce, canny union officials sometimes use ballots to strengthen their bargaining power in negotiations with employers (Undy et al. 1996). One of the most disruptive industrial disputes of recent years did not actually involve a strike taking place at all. Following votes in favour of strike action by tanker drivers across a number of companies in early 2012, in a dispute over demands for more common industry working standards, there was panic buying at petrol stations across the UK, albeit exacerbated by some inept government advice that motorists should stockpile petrol.

It is difficult to quantify the contribution made by the restrictive legislative framework to the declining level of strike activity in the UK. Many other European countries have also seen falling strike levels, suggesting that broader economic and industrial trends, the changing composition of the workforce, and the reduction of the number of people employed in 'strike-prone' industries in particular, have exercised more influence (Dunn and Metcalf 1996). Yet the indirect effects of the anti-strike laws, in particular the large degree to which they restrict the capacity of the unions to challenge employers' actions, have certainly contributed to the decline in the incidence of strikes and industrial action over recent decades.

Nevertheless, the 2010 coming to power of a Conservative-dominated coalition government has provided a fillip to those, particularly employers' organizations, who believe that further legal restrictions are desirable, raising the prospect of possible new laws relating to strikes and industrial action. The Confederation of British Industry (CBI 2010a, 2010b), for example, suggests that industrial action should only be legal when a given threshold—at least 40 per cent—of all union members eligible to be balloted vote in favour of it, not just a simple majority of those who actually do vote as at present; it has called for employers to be allowed to use agency workers to cover for striking workers. Moreover, the coalition reportedly sees some merit in measures that would oblige unions to maintain a minimum level of service during a dispute, as a way of moderating the potentially disruptive effects of public sector strikes arising out of austerity measures (Curtis 2011). Although the government has—so far at least—not formally announced an intention to enact new anti-strike laws, there is clearly no shortage of ideas about what to do should this position change.

Yet, even without any further changes, the law already circumscribes unions' ability to organize strikes and industrial action to an extreme degree—in ways that contravene recognized labour standards. Particularly when it comes to ballots and notice periods, already the 'law appears to impose obligations that appear impossible in practice for trade unions to comply with' (Ewing and Hendy 2010: 21). International bodies, including International Labour Organization (ILO) committees, have expressed concerns that the existing law negates workers' freedom of association, and undermines the ability of unions to organize workers and bargain effectively. The prohibition of all forms of secondary action is viewed as particularly objectionable; workers in the UK are also considered to have insufficient protection from dismissal when taking lawful industrial action. In the past, successive governments ignored international criticism of the UK's strike laws; however, recent judgments from the ECHR, which articulate the right to bargain collectively essentially as a human right, with the freedom to take industrial action an essential component of that right, may provide unions with an opportunity to challenge aspects of the current legal framework (Ewing and Hendy 2010).

 Section summary and further reading

- Workers in the UK do not enjoy the 'right' to strike; rather they enjoy certain protections when taking industrial action, as do unions when organizing it, as long as it is lawful and in furtherance of a trade dispute.

- Conservative governments of the 1980s and 1990s enacted some major changes to the law governing strikes and industrial action, making it much more restrictive, which Labour largely left unchanged after 1997. The laws are so strict that it is virtually impossible for a union to organize industrial action which is wholly lawful in every respect.

- Although some (e.g. employers' organizations and Conservative politicians) clearly believe that the law governing strikes and industrial action needs to be made more restrictive, as it is the legal framework contravenes recognized international labour standards in some important ways.

For further information about the legal framework, see McIlroy (1991, 1999), Dickens and Hall (2003), and Davies and Freedland (2007: 110–4).

9.5 Understanding labour conflict: insights from mobilization theory

While broader industrial, economic, and political factors clearly affect the level of strike activity, it is important to recognize that the causes of strikes are rooted in the dynamics of the relationship between managers and workers in particular workplace environments. Strikes, then, are both social and political phenomena (Batstone, Boraston, and Frenkel, 1978; Hyman 1989). They happen primarily because workers mobilize collectively in order to resist or influence decisions made by their employers. Thus their occurrence constitutes a political challenge to the established order of the organization.

To understand why strikes take place, then, attention must be directed at the way in which workers, organized in trade unions, perceive the need to undertake industrial action, and the effectiveness with which they are able to do so (Shorter and Tilly 1974). Broader structural factors clearly exercise an influence on strike levels in as much as they generate grievances or a more general sense of disaffection; but whether or not such discontent produces a strike in a particular organization or workplace depends on the mobilizing capacity of the workers involved, as well as their willingness and opportunity to take action (Batstone, Boraston, and Frenkel 1978). Strikes are social and political phenomena, whose manifestation is contingent on the capacity of workers, organized in trade unions, to mobilize and defend their conditions or challenge their employer, albeit within particular contexts. This helps to explain variations in strike activity between different organizations and workplaces. For example, at times the further education sector in England and Wales has been greatly disrupted by industrial action, but the level of strike activity varies considerably between colleges, reflecting variations in the mobilizing capacities of the lecturers' union at different sites (Williams 2003).

A focus on the capacity of workers to organize themselves collectively in response to problems at work, and engage in some form of industrial action to redress them, is central to the contribution that mobilization theory makes to an understanding of changes in the level of strike activity. The fall in the incidence of strikes does not reflect greater contentment at work, and thus a diminution in the potential for labour conflict; rather, in the absence of trade unions, where discontent arises, it is expressed in different forms, as exemplified by the sharp rise in the number of complaints made by aggrieved employees to employment tribunals, for example concerning matters such as unfair dismissal and discrimination (see Chapter 10).

In the largely non-union hotel industry, the unilateral exercise of managerial authority is the source of numerous grievances among employees concerning their perceived unfair treatment, many of which are submitted to tribunals (Head and Lucas 2004). Far from declining, the potential for conflict in employment relations has been increasing. Given evidence that people are willing to act collectively to pursue their interests in society (Kelly 1998), how, then, can the decline in the level of strike activity be explained?

Mobilization theory helps us to understand the social processes that enable, and constrain, the development of collective industrial action. It 'directs our attention to the social relations of the workplace and the processes by which employees perceive and respond to injustice and assert their rights' (Kelly 1998: 51). Mobilization theory holds that it is not enough for workers just to hold a grievance for industrial action such as a strike to arise. Rather, the workers concerned must hold a collective sense of injustice, recognize that their interests are different to those of their employer (agency), and attribute the source of their grievance to the actions of their employer. Moreover, a mechanism needs to exist, in the form of union activists, that channels the discontent into collective action (see Figure 9.1). Thus mobilization theory seeks to explain the circumstances under which individual grievances take on a collective dimension, inform the collective organization of workers, and result in collective industrial action (Kelly 1998, 2005b).

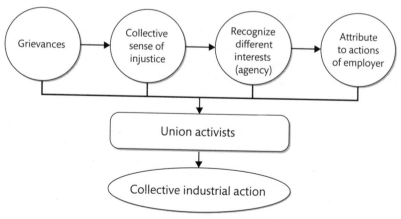

Figure 9.1 Mobilization theory

What, then, is the relevance of mobilization theory to understanding levels of labour conflict and strike activity in contemporary employment relations? First, it suggests that the absence of strikes does not imply that industrial harmony prevails in workplaces. Mobilization theory shows that effective collective action by workers is a highly contingent process, something that takes root in particular circumstances, and often in the face of determined employer opposition, even where a demonstrable conflict of interest exists.

Given a supportive political context and legislative framework, employers enjoy plenty of scope to counter-mobilize, and thus impede the capacity of workers to engage in collective action. In the case of Japanese manufacturer Nippon CTV, for example, this was done by developing a cooperative relationship with a moderate trade union. Despite the manifest discontent experienced by workers, the company's approach effectively stifled the emergence of any collective action to improve working conditions. Although workers engaged in individual acts of resistance—some refused to wear the company's blue jackets, for example—they rarely took on a collective dimension (Delbridge 1998).

Mobilization theory, then, acknowledges the important role of the counter-mobilization efforts by employers and governments in opposing strikes and labour conflict (Kelly 2011). There are a number of ways in which such counter-mobilization can manifest itself. Employers often draw on the highly restrictive legal framework in their efforts to prevent industrial action from occurring, or at least reduce its potency. Another response to strikes is to threaten, and in some cases actually impose, sanctions on striking workers. For example, in the 2009–11 British Airways cabin crew dispute the airline responded to the initial strike action by revoking staff travel concessions.

The second contribution of mobilization theory is its emphasis that collective action by workers can take a variety of forms and is thus not just restricted to strikes (Kelly 2011). This is a theme that informs the discussion of non-strike manifestations of labour conflict in Section 9.6. In non-union environments, for example, where the organization of strikes faces insuperable difficulties, there is evidence that collective action by workers, such as protests over changes to people's jobs for example, may impel managers to rethink their proposals or even back down entirely (see Scott 1994; Dundon and Rollinson 2004).

'Living wage' campaigns, aimed at improving the wages of poorly paid service sector workers such as contract cleaners, have tended not to use strikes, largely because these workers are relatively easily replaced and therefore lack sufficient bargaining power. Instead, they rely on civic campaigns, street protests, petitions, and demonstrations, which are used to mobilize public opinion and put pressure on companies who use such workers, often through subcontracting arrangements, to change their practices (see Waldinger et al. 1998; Erickson et al. 2002; Silver 2003: 109–10). See Contesting employment relations 9.4 for evidence from the UK.

The third way in which mobilization theory enhances our understanding of labour conflict is through the importance it attaches to leadership: the role activists play in using the existence of grievances to mobilize workers, and to encourage them to challenge the interests of, or even contemplate collective action against, their employer. In France, for example, activists in some railway unions have played a prominent part in fostering mobilization among contract cleaners, in pursuit of better pay and conditions (Connolly 2010).

Contesting employment relations 9.4: 'Living wage' campaigns in London

Innovative forms of collective action have been pioneered by the London Citizens movement, an alliance of faith organizations, labour unions, and community bodies, which campaigns to ensure that workers in the UK's capital are paid a 'living wage'—£8.55 in London and £7.45 in the rest of the UK (2012–13 figures)—see Chapter 7. It mobilizes on behalf of low-paid cleaning and catering staff working in major companies and public sector organizations but who are often employed by outside contractors. Activities have involved demonstrations, picketing, and even the mass occupation of a branch of the HSBC bank in one instance, which are designed to embarrass client organizations, since public attention is drawn to the low pay and poor working conditions endured by many of the people who, indirectly, work for them. Protests by living wage activists were a key feature of efforts to get HSBC bank to enter into discussions over the implementation of a living wage (Holgate 2009; Wills 2008), which it conceded in London in 2005, and extended to the rest of the UK in 2012. By 2010, over 100 organizations in London had committed to the living wage as a result of the campaign. During 2012, the living wage campaign reached the department store chain John Lewis, whose flagship Oxford Street store was the target of a one-day strike by minimum wage contract cleaners who were demanding to be paid the living wage.

The study of workers' responses to the closure of two South Wales garment factories—owned by Dewhirst and Burberry respectively—by Blyton and (Jenkins 2012a) provides two further insights about mobilization theory. First, their research demonstrates the dynamic and reflexive nature of mobilization. It is not something which is simply driven by union activists in a unilinear fashion; rather, mobilization is a process, one which is affected and strengthened by the activities of the workers themselves. Thus the 'process of engaging in collective action was itself transformative, increasing solidarity, cementing ideas of injustice and influencing its leaders as well as being under their apparent direction' (Blyton and Jenkins 2012a: 18). Their second insight is to demonstrate the importance of external linkages and interactions to successful mobilization. The mobilization of the Burberry workers was marked by the involvement of politicians, outside unions, and, in particular, grabbed the attention of the media—factors that were largely absent in the Dewhirst case.

Some aspects of mobilization theory as articulated by Kelly (1998, 2005b) have attracted critical scrutiny. Drawing on insights from a study of car factories in Argentina, Atzeni (2009), for example, questions the role attributed to workers' feelings of 'injustice', seeing this as a subjective concept which, since it varies from individual to individual, is not something capable of generating collective action. Rather, mobilization, where it occurs, is the product of the material social and economic conditions experienced by workers collectively which generates solidarity. Atzeni (2009) also raises a query about the role of activists, suggesting that when it comes to labour conflict activism can emerge out of mobilization, rather than just initiating it.

These critical points notwithstanding, by highlighting the potential constraints on collective action in workplaces, as well as pointing to the features that make it possible, mobilization theory makes an important contribution to our understanding of employment relations and the nature of labour conflict. It recognizes that the potential for conflict exists in all employment relationships. Yet the extent to which this latent conflict is expressed, and also the means of its expression, is contingent on the pattern of relationships between workers and their managers in particular workplace settings, the nature and actions of the workforce itself, including the extent to which strong social relationships exist (see Blyton and Jenkins 2012a), and the influence of external linkages and interactions.

 ## Section summary and further reading

- It is important to understand the causes of strikes with reference to the mobilizing capacity of workers and their unions. Mobilization theory can be used to understand the circumstances which generate labour conflict, with its focus on how individual grievances, which stem from a sense of injustice, become manifest in collective industrial action.

- Mobilization theory provides a number of important insights when it comes to understanding labour conflict. It shows us that collective action by workers is a highly contingent process, often constrained by the counter-mobilization efforts of employers and governments; that collective action by workers is not just confined to strike action; and that the leadership provided by activists plays a crucial part in translating grievances into instances of actual labour conflict.

For the relevance of mobilization theory as applied to employment relations, see Kelly's (1998) book *Rethinking Industrial Relations*, or his book chapter (Kelly 2005b). Atzeni (2009) provides a sympathetic critical engagement with Kelly's version of mobilization theory.

9.6 Other forms of labour conflict

While strikes are the most conspicuous form of conflict in employment relations, they are by no means the only one. In this section, then, the concept of labour conflict is broadened to encompass other manifestations. Following Scott et al.'s (1963) study of the coal mining industry, it is conventional to distinguish between 'organized' and 'unorganized' forms of conflict in the workplace. The latter is distinguished by its spontaneous, individualistic character, and sometimes goes under the label of 'organizational misbehaviour' (Ackroyd and Thompson 1999). Workers respond to the demands of the work environment through some form of resistance, by undertaking actions that allow them individually to express their frustration, through committing sabotage for example, or by distancing themselves from the causes of their problems, like going absent or quitting their jobs.

Organized forms of conflict, though, are imbued with a more formal, collective, and purposeful character, undertaken in order to challenge and change managerial decisions, not merely to enable workers to cope with them. Such conflict is 'far more likely to form part of a conscious strategy to change the situation which is identified as the source of discontent' (Hyman 1977: 53). Although a strike is the most obvious manifestation of organized conflict, other forms of collective industrial action short of a strike, including overtime bans and work-to-rules for example, are used by workers collectively, usually in trade unions, to influence organizational decision-making. See Table 9.3 for the main forms of 'organized' and 'unorganized' labour conflict.

9.6.1 Forms of organized labour conflict

Forms of organized labour conflict other than strikes are often referred to as 'action short of a strike', or as 'cut-price' (Flanders 1975) methods of industrial action. While they are types of

Table 9.3 The main forms of 'organized' and 'unorganized' labour conflict

'Organized' conflict	'Unorganized' conflict
Strikes	Fiddles
Protests, demonstrations, and occupations	Sabotage
Lock-outs	Absenteeism
'Cut-price' industrial action	Quitting
Working-to-rule	
Go-slows	
Overtime bans	

behaviour designed to disrupt an employer's ability to produce goods and services, as a strike does, they do not involve a complete withdrawal of labour. These are forms of action in which workers mostly continue to undertake their duties. There are three main types of cut-price industrial action:

- The 'go-slow' occurs in situations where workers carry on performing their jobs, but do so at a much slower pace than normal. In 2003, for example, in a dispute over safety, London Underground train drivers threatened to limit their speeds to 25 miles per hour, well below normal.

- The 'work-to-rule' generally involves a refusal by workers to undertake some aspect, or aspects, of their job in order to disrupt the normal production of goods or delivery of a service. In September 2012, for example, the main teachers' unions launched action 'short of a strike' in their dispute over pay and conditions. Among other things, this included a boycott of meetings outside standard working hours, restrictions on involvement in performance management and classroom observation activities, and a refusal to provide cover for absent staff, invigilate exams, or supervise pupils during their lunch break.

- The 'overtime ban' is another example of industrial action short of a strike: since many organizations rely on their workers undertaking overtime to maintain production levels or to ensure that services are maintained, overtime bans, where workers collectively refuse to participate in overtime working, can be extremely disruptive to the organization. In April 2012, for example, Imperial Tobacco workers in Nottingham instituted a ban on overtime to protest against the introduction of a fee for workplace car parking. Moreover, as mentioned in Chapter 8, rail unions have used bans on Sunday overtime working as a bargaining lever.

Like strikes, these forms of industrial action are designed and undertaken with a purpose, to challenge managerial decisions for example, or to put pressure on an employer to adjust the terms of the wage–work bargain in a way that benefits the workforce. Nevertheless, they are seen as less risky forms of action than strikes. Moreover, workers do not lose as much in wages as they would if they were to go on strike. Like strikes, though, go-slows, working-to-rule, and overtime bans require organization and coordination, generally through the activities of a trade union (Edwards 1995).

In rare circumstances it is employers, not the union, who initiate industrial action, by instituting a 'lock-out' of the workforce—in effect sending staff home and refusing to pay them—as a means of trying to bring about an end to a dispute. One of the most prominent recent examples of a lock-out occurred in October 2011 when the Australian airline Qantas shut down its operations for two days, grounding all domestic and international flights, until ordered to re-open by the Australian government agency responsible for regulating employment relations. The company's actions were designed to try and force an end to a long-running dispute with many of its staff, who had mounted a series of strikes in protest against restructuring proposals that threatened their jobs.

Cut-price industrial action can be an effective way for organized groups of workers to challenge managerial decision-making, express a grievance, or enforce a demand in contemporary employment relations. As we have seen, schoolteachers sometimes enforce effective work-to-rules by refusing to provide cover for absent colleagues, or by refusing to help undertake tests, among other things. While they may be relatively uncommon—not least because managers have taken a more assertive approach to dealing with cut-price industrial action, by deducting wages for 'partial performance' for example—instances like these demonstrate that organized labour conflict should not be equated simply with strike activity, even if the two seem to be complementary rather than used as alternatives (Dix, Sisson, and Forth 2009).

Simply focusing on established, conventional forms of collective industrial action would seem to indicate that labour conflict has markedly diminished in importance. However, there are some emerging signs that traditional forms of contention, namely the strike and other manifestations of collective industrial action organized by trade unions, which are generally rooted in specific workplaces, are becoming supplanted by alternative forms of conflict, such as protests, demonstrations, and other types of direct action. When the Homeform Group, the owner of Moben Kitchens, went into administration in June 2011, with the loss of over 500 jobs, workers held protests outside its Manchester head office demanding unpaid wages.

The economic recession seems to have stimulated manifold instances of direct action by workers in an effort to forestall workplace closures and preserve their jobs, encompassing protests and occupations (Gall 2010a, 2011a). In the spring of 2009, for example, workers who had been employed by the car parts firm Visteon, which had gone into administration, secured an enhanced redundancy package after mounting an occupation of two of its sites, in Belfast and Enfield. While the workers would not get their jobs back, their willingness to challenge the terms on which they had been dismissed ensured that they at least got increased financial compensation for losing their employment. See Chapter 10 for additional examples of workers challenging redundancy decisions by engaging in conflict. In France, some workers have taken a particularly innovative form of collective industrial action in protest against proposed plant closures and job cuts by employers (see International perspective 9.5).

It is not that labour conflict in general has become less relevant; rather that a particular type of labour conflict—collective action organized by unions in particular workplaces—has diminished in importance. There are signs that labour conflict may be becoming increasingly subsumed within broader political struggles, rather than be manifest in organized, temporary withdrawals of labour in the form of strikes as has largely been the case in the

International perspective 9.5: The 'bossnapping' phenomenon

Between 2008 and 2010 there was a series of incidents in France which involved workers holding their senior managers captive for a short time in order to protect their jobs or improve their redundancy settlements—actions which, despite being clearly illegal, not only attracted widespread popular support but also met with little opposition from the authorities. In 2008, for example, Mike Bacon, the head of car parts firm BRS, was held captive by workers over a weekend. Their action was prompted by the company's decision to move production from its factory in France to a plant in Slovakia. During 2009 and 2010 there were further incidents of such 'bossnapping'. Senior managers of multinational companies including Sony and Caterpillar were temporarily held captive following the announcement of plant closures or job losses (Gall 2011b). In March 2009 the French head of office equipment firm 3M, Luc Rousselet, was released following two days and nights of captivity after the company agreed to re-negotiate redundancy terms for its staff—to the disgust of many workers, who felt that more concessions could have been extracted. One French trade union leader claimed that holding bosses captive in this way was often the 'only remaining bartering tool' workers have. Bossnapping is a rational—albeit defensive—form of behaviour. Workers use direct action of this kind in an effort to prevent job losses or to improve their severance terms, not as part of a revolutionary challenge to the existing order. It can be viewed as a 'ritualized, symbolic form of protest aimed at securing publicity and public sympathy for the plight of those facing redundancy' (Parsons 2013: 305). The bossnapping phenomenon is not new to France. However, factory closures, exacerbated by the economic recession, prompted a spate of such incidents, behaviour which was widely seen to be a legitimate response from workers fighting against the adverse effects of neo-liberal economic globalization (Parsons 2013).

past (Godard 2011). Consider, for example, the rise of the 'Occupy' movement, encompassing broad-based protests and campaigns designed, directly or indirectly, to challenge employers. Mobilization is based around the need to promote social and economic justice, such as reducing inequality, including the urgency of tackling the privileged treatment accorded to corporate interests (van Gelder 2011). This reflects the 'growing tendency for workers to take action outside the workplace and against targets that are not their direct employers' (Mason 2012: 71).

9.6.2 Forms of unorganized labour conflict

Clearly, levels of strike activity and also other conventional forms of organized industrial action, compared to the past, have become less common. Yet we need to view labour conflict more broadly, encompassing forms of unorganized conflict and organizational misbehaviour. Here, fiddling, sabotage, absenteeism, and quitting are considered—four types of employee behaviour that are often held to exemplify unorganized conflict in employment relations in as much as they are spontaneous or unconsidered acts undertaken by individual workers in order to enable them to cope with the frustrations and pressures of the working environment. Before considering these, however, some initial questions arise that will help to inform the reader's understanding of the nature and dimensions of unorganized labour conflict.

First, to what extent do the types of worker behaviour considered here conflict with managerial objectives? Can they really be interpreted as labour conflict, along with more purposeful and organized activities such as strikes and overtime bans for example?

Second, how far are the behaviours associated with so-called unorganized forms of conflict spontaneous, lacking in purpose, and thus distinct from organized activity? Is it wise, therefore, to make a rigid distinction between organized and unorganized forms of conflict?

Third, unorganized types of labour conflict are often portrayed as alternatives to strikes or other manifestations of organized action (Knowles 1952), the implication being that if conflict in the employment relationship is not expressed by means of, say, a strike, it will simply take another form. Are different manifestations of conflict to be regarded as alternatives? Or do they act in concert, complementing one another?

Fiddles

Fiddling can encompass a wide range of illicit activities, ranging from employee theft to actions that alter the terms of the wage–work bargain to the benefit of the workers. Much of the early interest in fiddles focused on the latter. Roy (1952) and Lupton (1963) examined the way in which workers, through the process of 'making-out', collectively manipulated piece-rates, that is the amount they were paid per item of production, by regulating their effort. In as much as it influences the wage–work bargain in a way that runs counter to the interests of the employer, such activities are unambiguously an expression of conflict at work (Edwards 1992).

The term 'fiddling' is also used to describe more illicit behaviours at work. McIntosh and Broderick (1996) examine the practice of 'totting' among refuse collectors, something that was commonplace before the increased work pressures created by contracting out the collection service rendered it more difficult to operate. It involved 'sifting through bags and bins in search of "valuables" or "sellables" which were then either kept or sold—many refuse collectors regularly took part in car boot sales' (cited in Noon and Blyton 2007: 249).

The most well-known account of employee fiddles is contained in Mars's book *Cheats at Work* (Mars 1982). He examines the way in which the characteristics of particular jobs encourage certain types of employee fiddle to emerge. Supermarket workers, for example, being closely supervised and monitored, tend to be opportunistic in their fiddling behaviour, making the most of opportunities such as the chance to secure a free bar of chocolate as and when they arise. Other groups of workers, sales staff for instance, tend to have developed well-articulated and sophisticated fiddling techniques, often collectively, such as the manipulation of expenses claims for example.

Many fiddles, then, are underpinned by a collective ethos and cannot be seen simply as a spontaneous reaction on the part of an individual worker; they are often informed by collectively generated norms and assumptions that govern the limits of what is, and what is not, acceptable. This is evident from a Swedish hotel cleaner's experience of working life in a Finnish hotel. She describes the intense nature of the work and the pressures cleaners are under to service guest rooms in the limited time available. In order to cope, the cleaners resort to 'cheating', drawing on a repertoire of tricks designed to lighten their workloads without managers or guests noticing. For example:

> The best time-gaining trick is to refrain from changing the bed sheets when a new guest is arriving, although it is possible only if they still look fresh and are not too crumpled. The

changing of sheets and the making of the bed is the most time-consuming and heavy work task and when I can get away with not doing that is a real victory.

(Lundberg and Karlsson 2011: 146)

They also steal hotel equipment and supplies, food and drink from minibars, and occasionally items left behind by guests. It is not so much that the cleaners want these goods; rather, the action of stealing in its own right gives them a sense of satisfaction and helps to ease the pressures of work.

The thefts become a positive trait of our working day as we get something else than the boring work tasks to think about. Stealing has become a game and through it we have found some meaning in work. Not once do [we] feel that we are doing something morally wrong—rather our bitterness at our working conditions justifies more thefts. Considering all the stress and hard work we think we actually deserve some free soap.

(Lundberg and Karlsson 2011: 146)

Hence there is a difficulty with seeing fiddles as an unambiguously unorganized form of conflict; many of the most effective workplace fiddles are the product of the collective effort by workers to secure for themselves a more favourable working environment, or to increase the rewards from employment.

To what extent, though, can fiddling really be conceptualized as a form of labour conflict? Workers who participate in fiddles are engaged in activities that would appear to run counter to the interests of their employer, but 'making-out' sometimes operates in ways that support managerial objectives (Edwards 1986). Moreover, one of the most prominent features of studies of workplace fiddling is the often high level of managerial toleration of, or indulgence towards, such behaviour.

Why should managers tolerate such activities? For one thing, fiddles help to sustain employee morale in an otherwise mundane working environment, and thus help make the task of supervision less burdensome. In some industries, like hospitality for example, toleration of fiddles enables managers to keep wages low. They can also be extremely difficult to eradicate. As long as fiddling is kept within what managers consider to be appropriate limits, and does not overly damage the interests of the business, it is often tolerated on the basis that if challenged it would only reappear in another, perhaps more damaging, guise elsewhere (Edwards 1988).

Sabotage

One of the main difficulties presented by employee sabotage is defining what it is. Sabotage at work, which has been the subject of a number of academic studies (e.g. Taylor and Walton 1971; Brown 1977), is often portrayed rather narrowly as involving the deliberate vandalism or breaking of machinery. The term 'often conjures up the image of people engaged in wilful acts of destruction' (Noon and Blyton 2007: 264).

Some writers, however, prefer a broader, more inclusive definition, such that the term 'sabotage can be used to refer to any type of employee behaviour that does not comply with managerial objectives', such as the fiddles just discussed for example (see 'Fiddles'). By this reckoning, incidents of sabotage cannot just be seen as the product of individual frustration with the pressures of work, but may also, in some circumstances, have a collective dimension, being used by organized groups of workers to alter the terms of the wage–work bargain in their favour (Dubois 1979).

Rather than acting as an alternative to more conventional forms of industrial action, sabotage may complement them. During 1999, for example, incidents of sabotage were a feature of industrial disputes in Spain. They included 'the cutting of electric cables during a rail dispute, engine drivers destroying the safety mechanism in their cabs, and striking shipyard workers immobilizing the bridge giving access to the Bay of Cadiz' (Rigby and Marco Aledo 2001: 291).

Given its association with the breaking and destruction of machinery, sabotage is sometimes thought to be something that is specific to manufacturing industry and thus, given the diminution of manufacturing employment in countries like Britain and the United States, of little importance now. Nevertheless, reports of alleged sabotage still occur. In 2001, for example, the US Federal Bureau of Investigation (FBI) was called in to investigate a suspected incident of sabotage involving damaged wiring at Boeing's Renton plant in Washington state, which manufactures the 737 series aircraft. Workers at the plant faced an uncertain future since the company had announced its intention to relocate some production and other activities away from the state.

Incidents of sabotage, broadly defined, can be found in many parts of the service sector and, in so far as they cause the quality of service offered to customers to deteriorate, potentially damage the interests of the business (see Insight into practice 9.6). In his study of employment relations in McDonalds, Royle (2000) discovered employees engaged in competitions to see which of them could perspire the most over the company's food products. Even the reluctance of customer-facing staff to relate to customers in the approved manner, for example by not smiling when they are supposed to (see Fuller and Smith 1991), can be interpreted as a form of sabotage.

 Insight into practice 9.6: Employee sabotage in the contemporary service sector

The most extensive analysis of sabotage in the contemporary service sector is Harris and Ogbonna's (2002) study of four firms in the hospitality industry. They use the term 'service sabotage' to refer to behaviours by workers and managers 'that are intentionally designed negatively to affect service', and report that over 85 per cent of the customer service employees they interviewed admitted to having committed 'some form of service sabotage behaviour' in the preceding week (Harris and Ogbonna 2002: 166, 168). One waiter explained how he might deal with a rude customer: 'There are lots of things that you do that no one but you will ever know—smaller portions, dodgy wine, a bad beer—all that and you serve it with a smile! Sweet revenge!' (quoted in Harris and Ogbonna 2002: 169). The researchers encountered examples of service sabotage behaviour involving hygiene issues: 'ranging from spitting in consumables to adding dirt to food to spoiling guest rooms in a discreet fashion (an unpleasant example including the wiping of a used tissue around the rim of a drinking glass)' (Harris and Ogbonna 2002: 171). While some of these activities were the product of an attempt on the part of the individual worker concerned to deal with the pressures of the working environment, such as the demands of rude customers for example, others were far from spontaneous affairs, with employees collectively complicit in such behaviours, sometimes with the tacit approval of their managers.

Absenteeism

Dealing with absenteeism appears to be a much greater challenge for managers in contemporary employment relations than confronting strikes. The employers' organization the Confederation of British Industry (CBI) asserts that staff absence costs UK businesses some £17 billion a year, with 16 per cent of this not being the result of genuine illness or injury, but rather attributable to skiving by workers—at a cost of £2.7 billion (CBI 2011b). We have to take care with claims about the costs of sickness absence, not least because the research which underpins them is often lacking in rigour. Moreover, few of the costs to society of work-related injury and ill-health are borne by employers (Taylor et al. 2010). Nevertheless, there is a widely held assumption that much sickness absence is not the product of genuine illness or injury, but rather can be attributed to the laziness of many workers, who are therefore prone to 'absenteeism' (Ackroyd and Thompson 1999).

Rather than laziness, however, perhaps more accurately absenteeism often reflects workers' dissatisfaction with the conditions of their labour, and can thus constitute a form of withdrawal from work (Hill and Trist 1953, cited in Nichols 1997). The frustrations, pressures, and tensions that confront individuals in the working environment are relieved by taking an occasional spontaneous 'sickie'. In this way, absenteeism may be viewed as the archetypal form of unorganized labour conflict.

Yet the observation that absence rates vary according to sector, organization, and department suggests that, as a form of conflict, absenteeism cannot be understood purely in individualistic terms. For one thing, studies of absenteeism indicate the presence of absence 'norms', tacitly accepted, perhaps even institutionalized, and collectively held assumptions concerning acceptable levels of attendance. This was traditionally the case in the docks, for example (Turnbull and Sapsford 1992). Moreover, perspectives that treat absenteeism as a means by which individuals withdraw themselves from work generally ignore the powerful influence of structural factors, such as the nature of the work environment, or the incidence of injuries and ill-health at work (Nichols 1997). Where the work process is organized in such a way that workers enjoy little autonomy or control over their labour, or where the pace of work is intense and relentless, such as in some call centres for example, it can damage people's physical and mental well-being (Taylor et al. 2003).

Absenteeism may be used as a tactic by organized groups of workers to alter the terms of the wage–work bargain or to resist managerial challenges to jobs and working conditions (see Insight into practice 9.7). For example, in his study of a plant manufacturing agrochemicals and dyestuffs, Heyes (1997) demonstrates how the introduction of an annualized hours system undermined the practice of 'knocking'. In one of its manifestations, knocking would involve a worker reporting sick in order to generate lucrative overtime opportunities for a colleague. At a later date, the roles would be reversed and the joint proceeds shared.

There are, however, some problems with viewing absenteeism as a manifestation of conflict at work. For one thing, in the majority of cases absenteeism is the product of ill-health and not a reaction to unpleasant working conditions or part of a protest against management decisions. Moreover, the extent to which absenteeism can be conceptualized as a form of labour conflict often depends on the context in which it occurs. For the poorly organized women workers in the clothing factories studied by Edwards and (Scullion 1982), for example, absenteeism was an 'escape valve', giving them the opportunity to relieve the

Insight into practice 9.7:   Worker resistance and labour conflict in a call centre

The case of PhoneCo, a call centre located in Northern Ireland, indicates the degree to which workers are able to collectively resist managerial control, and the endemic state of conflict, even without the presence of a strong trade union. In a highly pressurized and demanding working environment, sales workers cheated the system by engaging in the activity of 'slammin'—that is, pretending to be involved in sales encounters: going absent while actually at work. Workers also challenged managerial control by avoiding work—'scammin': absenting themselves on smoking breaks, for example, regardless of whether or not they smoked. Efforts by managers to clamp down on unauthorized absence simply exacerbated the shared sense of grievance felt by the workers. Ostensibly unorganized forms of behaviour were in fact underpinned by a strong collective identity which enabled the workforce to challenge managerial control more effectively.

Source: Mulholland (2004)

tensions associated with an authoritarian working environment and the tedium of their jobs, while posing little challenge to managerial control. In the engineering factories in the study, though, the well-organized male workforce enjoyed an important degree of collective control over the pace of their work, and thus had less of a need to use absenteeism as a means of escaping their jobs.

Quitting

Perhaps the most unambiguously unorganized and individualistic expression of labour conflict, and the most explicit manifestation of withdrawal from work, is the practice of leaving, or quitting, one's job as a reaction against unpleasant working conditions. Thus high levels of labour turnover are often interpreted as evidence of a conflict-ridden working environment.

In one of the call centres studied by Beynon et al. (2002), managers reported that in the preceding three months 300 staff had resigned, suggesting an annual turnover rate of some 130 per cent. The causes were obvious. For one thing, working conditions were exceptionally onerous. 'Managers talked of "burn-out" and frequently expressed scepticism over whether anyone could effectively perform the job for an extended period' (Beynon et al. 2002: 152). Workers also found the unsocial working hours distinctly unappealing. A further factor was the organization's reliance on large numbers of agency-supplied temporary workers, many of whom left because it was unlikely that they would be offered a permanent contract.

For many workers, particularly those based in industries where unions are weak, and thus more organized forms of conflict are inappropriate, resigning from one's job is one of the few ways of expressing one's grievances. In the US fast-food industry, for example, young 'workers generally do not see fast-food work as a long-term career, so quitting is a more common response to dissatisfaction with wages, working conditions, or management than is a collective effort to improve the work' (Leidner 2002: 18).

But there are problems in equating quitting with conflict in an over-deterministic way. For one thing, many workers voluntarily resign their jobs not out of dissatisfaction with the conditions of their labour, but because of superior employment opportunities elsewhere (Edwards and Scullion 1982; Edwards 1995). A high turnover rate may operate to the benefit of management since it gives them greater flexibility to adjust staff numbers to meet fluctuations in demand, and thus secure control over costs, particularly in labour-intensive customer service industries, like hospitality for example. Here, turnover levels are contingent on the characteristics of the workforce. Whereas turnover among the bar workers may be very high, as businesses compete to recruit a mainly young, student labour force, it is often much lower among hotel housekeeping staff. Workers in these positions are generally mature women whose employment is structured around childcare responsibilities. They enjoy fewer opportunities to find alternative jobs, have established relatively stable working arrangements, and are thus less likely to consider quitting, even though the conditions of their jobs are no better, and often somewhat worse, than those of the bar workers (Adam-Smith, Norris, and Williams 2003).

9.6.3 'Unorganized' labour conflict—an assessment

Having considered the main types of so-called unorganized labour conflict, what conclusions can be drawn about the nature of conflict at work? Five points are particularly worthy of note. First, in order to understand the significance of conflict in contemporary employment relations it is necessary to look beyond the level of strike activity, and even other cut-price forms of industrial action, and consider the implications of fiddles, sabotage, absenteeism, and quitting. The fall in the incidence of collective industrial action cannot therefore be equated with a decline in labour conflict. Declining trade unionism means that workers increasingly lack traditional routes to express their discontent at work; alternative manifestations of conflict, of the kind considered in this section, may provide non-unionized workers with an effective means of expressing their demands (van den Broek and Dundon 2012). Moreover, the internet gives workers scope to develop innovative new ways of challenging and contesting managerial decision-making (see Employment relations reflection 9.8).

Employment relations reflection 9.8:   Virtual labour conflict

The growth of the internet has enabled workers to engage in new and innovative forms of labour conflict, both individually and collectively. On an individual level, anonymous personal web logs (or 'blogs') can be used by workers to mock, criticize, and challenge aspects of how their organization operates, and are thus to be viewed as an expression of industrial conflict (J. Richards 2008). One relatively mild example of the genre is the blog maintained by someone working for Pizza Hut: http://pizza-hut-team-member.blogspot.com. Bloggers need to be careful though, else they could end up losing their jobs. In 2005, for example, Joe Gordon, who worked for the bookseller Waterstones, was sacked after the company claimed his blogging had brought the company into disrepute.

Trade unions have tentatively begun to see the potential of the internet as a tool for challenging employers. In 2007, IBM attracted a considerable amount of negative publicity after members of its Italian workforce organized a 'virtual strike' in the online community Second Life. The protest arose after IBM Italy withdrew a pay benefit worth some $1000 per year. Instead of using conventional industrial action to try and get the decision changed, the Italian union representing the workers opted to disrupt IBM's area on Second Life. Workers from twenty-three countries joined the action, using their online representations of themselves, or 'avatars' as they are called, to protest and picket against IBM within the firm's own 'virtual world'. While the exact impact of the dispute is hard to judge, soon afterwards the head of IBM Italy left his post, and a new pay agreement was negotiated which restored the workers' pay benefit.

Sources: Barkham (2005); ITUC (2007)

Second, the analytical distinction between so-called organized and unorganized forms of conflict is rarely so clear-cut in practice (Blyton and Turnbull 2004). Seemingly spontaneous and individualistic behaviour, such as absenteeism for example, is often underpinned by collectively established norms governing appropriate levels of absence.

Third, the types of behaviour we have considered as examples of unorganized conflict often appear to operate in ways that benefit managers. They may tolerate a certain amount of fiddling, for example, or some relatively minor sabotage, if it helps them to maintain control in the workplace. That such activities occur cannot be taken as evidence of conflict since the way in which they function may not hinder, and can even act to support, management objectives. Moreover, in so far as they enable people to cope more easily with the pressures, demands, and frustrations of their jobs, these activities help to reconcile workers with the exploitative nature of the system of wage labour. Thus a 'given form of behaviour can, then, involve aspects of accommodation and adaptation to a system of work relations as well as being in conflict with or a form of resistance against it' (Edwards 1986: 76). Whether or not a particular type of behaviour can be labelled as conflict depends on the particular context in which it exists, and the meanings which workers and managers attach to it (Edwards and Scullion 1982).

Fourth, what is meant by the concept of labour conflict? Quitting one's job because the working environment is particularly unpleasant, for example, or behaving towards customers in a way that does not comply with managerial wishes because one is dissatisfied with one's working conditions both reflect the antagonism that characterizes the employment relationship. But in general these are expressions of frustration; they are not intended to challenge managerial decisions or to influence the terms of the wage–work bargain in the purposeful manner of a strike or an overtime ban.

Fifth, it is clear that rather than acting as alternatives, different manifestations of labour conflict often complement one another (Turnbull and Sapsford 1992). This can be seen in the case of sabotage incidents, for example, which are sometimes used by groups of workers to supplement other forms of industrial action during the course of a dispute.

 ## Section summary and further reading

- Strikes are not the only manifestation of collective industrial action by workers. Labour conflict can take the form of so-called 'cut-price' forms of industrial action, such as overtime bans for example, or the range of different behaviours that come under the label of 'unorganized' conflict, including fiddling and sabotage among other things.

- The conventional distinction made between 'organized' and 'unorganized' forms of conflict is hard to uphold in practice. Seemingly spontaneous and individual behaviour, such as sabotage for example, is often underpinned by collective norms and expectations. Moreover, it frequently exists in conjunction with, rather than as a substitute for, more ostensibly collective and organized activities.

- One must be cautious about ascribing the label of 'conflict' to behaviours such as fiddling, sabotage, absenteeism, and quitting. They may operate to the advantage of managers. Whether or not such types of behaviour can be classified as conflict depends on the context in which they occur, and the meanings the participants attach to them.

For discussions of labour conflict, how it can be understood, and the various examples of behaviour that constitute it, see Edwards (1988, 1992). Mars's *Cheats at Work* (Mars 1982) is an engaging analysis of various types of fiddling behaviour. Good overviews of workplace conflict can also be found in Blyton and Turnbull (2004) and Noon and Blyton (2007).

9.7 Conclusion

Labour conflict is a major feature of contemporary employment relations. Since the employment relationship is characterized by a 'basic antagonism' between an employer and an employee there is always the potential for conflict to arise (Edwards 1986). The fall in the level of strike activity cannot be equated with a decline in the level of labour conflict. The low number of strikes in contemporary employment relations is the product of a number of factors: restrictive government legislation; changes in the composition of employment, and lower levels of employment in 'strike-prone' industries; a more assertive and interventionist managerialism; and the declining level of unionization. Some of these developments, compositional change for example, are an international phenomenon; others, like the highly restrictive legislative framework, are more specific to the UK. Thus the declining level of strike activity has not come about because the potential for conflict has diminished in importance, but rather it is the expression of a number of political, economic, and industrial developments.

From a global perspective, labour conflict remains a central feature of contemporary employment relations. Strike activity has not vanished. It is increasingly evident in emerging economies, such as China. Moreover, there is evidence that economic globalization is a major source of labour unrest around the world. Therefore the need to understand strikes, why they occur, and their significance, remains of pressing importance in contemporary employment relations. Mobilization theory is an important tool for identifying the factors that contribute to, and also those that constrain, strikes. It also holds that labour conflict should not be equated with strikes. Other forms of collective action, such as protests and demonstrations for example, are perhaps more effective ways of redressing grievances for workers in sectors where there is little tradition of robust trade unionism or where proposed workplace closures mean that conventional strikes are not viable. Labour conflict can also be expressed in a range of so-called 'unorganized' behaviours, such as sabotage and quitting. Moreover, as is shown in Chapter 10, where the focus in on how labour disputes are resolved, the increase in the number of complaints submitted to employment tribunals by aggrieved workers is a further sign of the prevalence of conflict at work.

 Assignment and discussion questions

1. Discuss the view that 'the decline in strike activity means that labour conflict is not an important feature of contemporary employment relations'.

2. Why has the incidence of strike activity fallen since the 1970s?

3. What have been the main effects of the economic recession on strikes and labour conflict?

4. How does mobilization theory explain why strikes occur?

5. How far is it sensible to distinguish between 'organized' and 'unorganized' forms of labour conflict?

 Visit the Online Resource Centre that accompanies this book to develop your understanding of this chapter, and keep up to date with the latest developments in this area.
www.oxfordtextbooks.co.uk/orc/williams3e/

Chapter case study: The BA cabin crew dispute 2009–11

In December 2009 a planned twelve-day strike during the Christmas and New Year period by British Airways (BA) cabin crew, represented by the Unite trade union over planned staffing cuts, was prevented from going ahead after the High Court ruled that the ballot of cabin crew was unlawful. Although the union won support for the action in a strike ballot, with a 92 per cent vote in favour, BA went to court complaining about balloting irregularities. The High Court granted its request for an injunction against the union after around 900 cabin crew were balloted despite having taken voluntary redundancy. Unite criticized the verdict as a 'bad day for democracy', and said that it would hold a fresh ballot in the dispute over cuts in staffing levels. In February 2010 it announced the result of its re-ballot of BA cabin crew in their dispute over the imposition of changes to staffing arrangements and working practices—an overwhelming majority (81 per cent) of those balloted voted in favour of strike action. On 20 March 2010 the first three-day strike by BA cabin crew started, following the failure of last-minute efforts to reach a negotiated settlement. The Unite union claimed that the action grounded a significant number of planes. However, BA asserted that its contingency plans meant that a large proportion of passengers were still able to reach their destinations. A week later, cabin crew staff employed by BA started a second period of strike action, this time for four days. BA claimed that it was able to fly a greater proportion of passengers than during the first three-day strike. However, there were concerns, which BA denied, that the company's hard line approach to the dispute was predicated on a desire to break the power of the union.

The last of a series of five-day strikes by British Airways cabin crew came to an end in June 2010. Attempts to resolve the dispute failed, sometimes acrimoniously. Unite then planned to issue a new ballot for industrial action, focusing on some of the unresolved issues that had prevented an agreement—namely the withdrawal of concessionary travel arrangements from staff who had participated in the strikes and the alleged victimization of union activists by the company. Subsequent talks between BA and the union indicated that a potential settlement of the dispute might be in the offing. However, in November 2010 Unite called off plans to ballot cabin crew members on the terms of an agreement because of strong opposition from its members to the proposed deal, postponing the prospect of a settlement to the long-running dispute. On 21 December 2010, Unite announced that it intended to commence a ballot of members for industrial action over matters arising from earlier strikes that had yet to be resolved, including the restoration of staff travel concessions and disciplinary issues. While BA cabin crew voted four to one in favour of further strikes, in early 2011 the airline argued that the ballot's irregularities made it legally invalid, forcing the union to back down. Further talks between the company and the union then took place, as a result of which the terms of a settlement were agreed. The dispute was finally ended in June 2011 after a ballot of cabin crew staff resulted in them voting overwhelmingly in favour of an agreement negotiated between Unite and BA management which restored travel concessions to striking staff and included a two-year pay deal worth up to 7 per cent.

Sources: BBC News Online 2011*a*); Milmo (2011)

Questions

Why was the BA cabin crew dispute so prolonged and difficult to settle? What do you think led to the eventual settlement of the dispute?

10 Resolving labour conflict

 Chapter objectives

The main objectives of this chapter are to:

- examine the main features of processes designed to resolve labour conflict in employment relations;
- investigate the role of grievance and disciplinary procedures as employment relations processes;
- explore the nature of the redundancy process in employment relations; and
- critically assess the role of the system of employment tribunals.

10.1 Introduction

Having looked at labour conflict in Chapter 9, the focus of this chapter is on employment relations processes, particularly those used to resolve labour conflict and employment disputes. The starting point, in Section 10.2, is with arrangements for resolving collective disputes—those arising between trade unions and employers—encompassing the process of negotiation and the part played by external, third-party arrangements for collective dispute resolution, including the Advisory, Conciliation, and Arbitration Service (ACAS). In Section 10.3 attention switches to processes for handling disputes that arise when employees have complaints about their treatment, or are alleged to have breached organizational rules in some way—namely grievance and disciplinary procedures. The section which follows (Section 10.4) is concerned with the nature of redundancy as an employment relations process. While a supposedly fair and justifiable way of dismissing staff when the amount of work has declined, redundancy has become a convenient way for employers to implement job cuts, prompting challenges by workers and unions. The focus of the final main section (Section 10.5) is on the system of employment tribunals, quasi-judicial bodies that adjudicate over claims brought by workers that their employment rights have been breached. Although successive governments have tried to reduce the number of tribunal cases, claiming that they constitute too much of a burden on employers, the main problem with the tribunal system is its failure to make sure that employment rights are effectively enforced.

Introductory case study: Redundancy compensation for Woolworths ex-staff

In November 2008 the major high street retail chain Woolworths went into administration. After failing to find a buyer for the business, the administrator had closed all of the company's stores by January 2009, with the loss of nearly 30,000 jobs. However, the shop workers' union USDAW claimed that the administrator had failed to comply with an EU-derived law relating to 'collective redundancy' situations, that requires employers to consult in advance with representatives of recognized unions, or with elected staff representatives where there is no union presence, when proposing to make at least twenty people redundant. USDAW took legal cases on behalf of the ex-Woolworths workers. In January 2012, an employment tribunal ruled in USDAW's favour that the administrator of Woolworths had failed to meet its legal obligation to consult with the unions in advance of the redundancies going ahead. It awarded £67.8 million in compensation to be shared between around 24,000 former Woolworths workers, who would each receive up to eight weeks' worth of wages (capped at £400 per week). Because Woolworths no longer exists, the compensation in this case is paid by the government. USDAW leaders were pleased with the outcome of the case, although they criticized the fact that some 3,000 ex-Woolworths staff who had been employed in smaller stores would not receive any compensation. Under UK law, a collective redundancy situation is determined by the size of the workplace (in this case the individual store), not the organization as a whole. However, the union had this decision reversed on appeal. This case shows the important role of the law in employment relations, and how it influences processes like redundancy. It draws attention to the part played by employment tribunals in adjudicating claims by workers that employment rights have been breached. Moreover, the case also highlights some of the drawbacks of the system for pursuing redress, in particular how some former Woolworths workers were unjustly excluded from receiving compensation.

Sources: USDAW (2012, 2013)

10.2 Resolving collective disputes

Collective disputes are those that occur between employers and a trade union as the collective representative of the workforce. They generally occur over matters relating to pay and conditions and, as Chapter 9 demonstrated, have the potential to give rise to disruptive conflict, perhaps in the form of a strike. The purpose of this section is to consider the main ways in which employment relations actors try to resolve collective disputes. While negotiation is a commonly used process, where this fails to produce a settlement collective disputes procedures frequently provide for assistance from an external, third-party source. The Advisory, Conciliation, and Arbitration Service (ACAS) helps to conciliate in disputes, and also refers them to arbitration where relevant.

10.2.1 Negotiating agreements in employment relations

When thinking about negotiation, perhaps the first thing that comes to mind is an image of trade unions and employers sitting across a table from each other bargaining over pay and employment conditions. Such collective negotiation continues to be an important facet of employment relations; however it is important to bear in mind that the concept of negotiation has a much broader meaning, inasmuch as it characterizes the relationship that individuals have with their employers as well. The basis of the employment relationship as a 'negotiated order', marked by an ongoing process of 'dialogue, day-to-day consensus building, and "give and take" ' (Sisson 2010: 150), was considered in Chapter 1. What this means is that, given its indeterminate nature, employers do not enjoy complete control over the workers they have hired to undertake a job; inevitably there is some discretion enjoyed by both parties over the nature and pace of work, how it is remunerated, and the conditions under which it is performed: matters which are thus open to negotiation (Brown 2010). Negotiation can be defined as 'a collection of processes that individuals as well as groups use to define and rede-fine the terms of their interdependence with other parties—it is especially important where this interdependency is characterized by uncertainty and incompleteness as in the case of the employment relationship' (Sisson 2010: 148).

Attempts to resolve disputes in employment relations generally involve some form of nego-tiated settlement. The resolution of individual grievances at work is often achieved by means of a negotiated compromise. This demonstrates the relevance of power to the bargaining process. In a non-union environment, without union representation the aggrieved employee enjoys little power to influence the terms of the eventual settlement; where an effective union is present it is more likely that management will be obliged to make concessions. Negotiation, then, is an important feature of employment relations; by enabling disputes to be resolved, either individually or collectively, it helps to ensure that differences of interest are contained, institutionalized, and thus prevented from causing too much disruption, particularly through instances of labour conflict.

For present purposes, this analysis of the process of negotiation will focus on its role in resolving collective disputes—those arising between employers and trade unions. Walton and McKersie (1965) distinguished between two broad types of negotiation—'distributive' and 'in-tegrative' bargaining. Distributive bargaining 'deals with issues where one party's goals are in basic conflict with those of another' (Sisson 2010: 152): being concerned with resolving conflicts of interest about how resources should be divided up. The most obvious example concerns trade union pay claims; what the union is successful in winning in the form of higher pay for the workforce, the employer loses, because of their increased costs. Distributive bar-gaining, then, often has a rather confrontational dimension (Brown 2010).

'Integrative bargaining', though, embodies a more cooperative approach to negotiation. This often occurs where employers and unions negotiate over how to deal with workplace issues and problems, such as health and safety. This is viewed as a 'positive-sum' approach, because in theory both parties benefit from engaging in the negotiation exercise, in contrast to the 'zero-sum' nature of distributive bargaining, with its assumption that the outcome will produce a winner and a loser (Brown 2010: 264). Greater competitive pressures seem to have facilitated a shift from distributive to integrative bargaining, because of the onus placed on reducing costs and restructuring work and employment arrangements, and the weakened state of the trade unions (Sisson 2010); the rise to prominence of 'partnership agreements' (see Chapter 6) exemplifies this more cooperative dimension of relations between manage-ment and unions.

What does negotiation actually entail? In essence, it is a means of resolving disputes by concluding a mutually acceptable agreement. It is a social process in which the parties argue with one another, try to convince each other of the merits of their respective cases, come to appreciate the virtues of their opponent's position, and thus draw closer together so that a settlement is made possible (Torrington 1991; Martin 1992). Without compromises, or 'trade-offs', in which a party will offer to back down in one area in return for a perhaps more important concession from their opponent, negotiation will not resolve a dispute. But each side will attempt to wrest more concessions from its opponents than it is obliged to concede in return. As well as being a social process, then, the practice of negotiation exemplifies the struggle for control that characterizes relations between employers and unions.

What determines the extent to which an employer or trade union emerges victorious from a negotiation event? Clearly, the expertise and skills of the participants exercise an influence on the outcome of negotiations, particularly their knowledge of relevant issues, how effectively they can process and handle information, and their ability to persuade their opponent of the strengths of their case. Preparation is also important. Not only do effective negotiators rigorously plan the issues on which they are prepared to trade, in exchange for something more worthwhile, and those they are not, but they also consider the likely arguments and negotiating position of their opponents. Another important influence over the outcomes of negotiation exercises concerns the nature of the relationship that exists between the negotiators (Brown 2010). Where it is strong and levels of mutual trust are high, an agreement is more likely, because negotiators will feel more at ease when it comes to highlighting areas for possible compromise. However, union representatives in particular have to be careful to make sure they keep their distance from managers, and refrain from agreeing with them too readily. This is because the 'history of trade unionism is littered with negotiators who were considered to have "sold out" by developing too close a relationship with management' (Brown 2010: 267).

Two other important features of negotiation in employment relations were identified by Walton and McKersie (1965). The first of these concerns what they called 'intra-organizational bargaining'. What this means is that both employers and unions have to manage the expectations of, and secure consensus from, their own sides. As Sisson (2010: 159) observes, 'wherever groups of people are involved, there are usually quite fundamental differences of opinion or position between the members'. Managers representing the employer's side have to be concerned with what outcomes of the negotiation process are acceptable to their colleagues across the organization as a whole, and may take active steps to shape their expectations—particularly through effective communication. Trade unions often find trying to maintain an intra-organizational consensus particularly challenging, because of the importance of securing acceptance of any agreement from the workforce as a whole. In situations where negotiators find themselves overly restricted by the demands of their respective sides, fewer compromises are likely to emerge, reducing the likelihood of a negotiated agreement (Brown 2010: 266).

The second other feature of negotiation considered by Walton and McKersie (1965) concerns what they termed 'attitudinal structuring'. This is best seen as a process whereby negotiators 'seek to influence the wider climate of opinion and expectation, not least of the opposing side' (Brown 2010: 264). Negotiation is thus a matter of 'influencing and shaping preferences' (Sisson 2010: 156). The negotiating event itself is characterized by the efforts of each party to influence the attitudes of the opposing sides; adjournments are often useful in helping a party to discuss and, if necessary, adjust its position, and can also help to maintain unity among the negotiating team (Walton and McKersie 1965). However, the process of attitudinal structuring can operate at a wider level. For example, managers may use communication and employee involvement arrangements (see Chapter 5) in an attempt to shape and influence the attitudes and expectations of the workforce—before, during, and after a negotiating event (Sisson 2010). By emphasizing the difficulty of the competitive environment, for example, managers can lower any expectations of a high pay award being in the offing, making this more difficult for the union to achieve when it comes to the actual negotiation event. The presence of attitudinal structuring highlights the important extent to which the outcomes of negotiation are influenced by the prevailing balance of power between the employer and the union. If the latter is not in a position to convince its members to contemplate taking industrial action in pursuit, say, of a higher pay claim (perhaps because managers have successfully conveyed the message that under current market conditions it is unfeasible), then its power to achieve its negotiating outcomes will be lower (Brown 2010).

The concept of bargaining power refers to the ability of a party to induce its opponent to make concessions it would otherwise not entertain. Clearly, the skills and expertise of a negotiating team, and the extent to which it is able to control a negotiation event, are important sources of power (Martin 1992). But the nature of the environment also influences negotiation outcomes. For example, if an employer is struggling to increase capacity to meet a rapid influx of orders, other things being equal, it will be less capable of resisting a union pay demand, given the importance of avoiding potentially disruptive industrial action. Thus environmental variables provide employers and unions with latent bargaining power, influencing their capacity to secure negotiation outcomes.

Government intervention in industrial disputes can have a crucial influence on the bargaining power of the parties to a negotiating exercise. In the case of the UK firefighters' dispute that occurred between 2002 and 2004, over their claim for a £30,000 pay deal, the willingness of the Fire Brigades Union (FBU) to take strike action put the employers' side in a rather weak position. Extensive governmental efforts to defeat the FBU, however, strengthened the employers' bargaining position, prolonging the dispute, and eventually concluded it in a way that satisfied the union's leaders, and could be interpreted as qualified success—but it caused a lot of grassroots discontent among the FBU's activists (Seifert and Sibley 2005).

But the extent to which one side's latent bargaining power is translated into their ability to wrest concessions from their opponents depends on how effectively they can use it: in other words their mobilizing capacity (Martin 1992). Unions which are in a position to make credible threats of strikes or industrial action in pursuit of their objectives, because of their ability to mobilize their members, will enjoy greater bargaining power. In a study of a dispute over contracts of employment in the further education sector, Williams (2004) demonstrates the way in which environmental change—the removal of colleges from local authority control in particular—weakened the bargaining power of the main trade union relative to that enjoyed by the college employers. But the main cause of the union's difficulties, and a factor prolonging the dispute, was the superior mobilizing capacity of the employers' leaders, and the way they used the characteristics of the more commercial environment in which the colleges operated to resist union demands.

10.2.2 Collective disputes procedures

Procedures for resolving collective disputes between unions and employers are a long-standing feature of employment relations (see Hyman 1972). Such procedures are best viewed as formal arrangements that set out the method for resolving disputes and, as such, 'provide a framework within which workplace industrial relations are conducted' (Brown 1981: 42). The 1970s saw a rise in the incidence of disputes procedures (Kessler 1993), a reflection of the pluralist character of reform in employment relations during that period. There is evidence that collective disputes procedures remain an important feature of employment relations. They are present in around a third (35 per cent) of all workplaces, and in three-quarters (73 per cent) of workplaces with a recognized union (van Wanrooy et al. 2013: 27).

Collective disputes procedures set out the arrangements that exist to resolve disputes between employers and trade unions. For example, the procedure in NHS Direct (which was agreed with the recognized unions in 2007) emphasizes the importance of resolving disputes which involve groups of workers quickly, fairly, and 'at the lowest possible level'. It specifies that disputes should proceed through a series of stages, starting at the level of the line manager, and the means by which they should be raised. Where a dispute cannot be resolved at line manager level, it progresses to a higher stage, ultimately to a sub-committee of the NHS Direct Trust Board. The procedure also sets out the arrangements for hearing a dispute. For example, the lead union or staff representative is expected to present the case, which is followed by an opportunity for the relevant manager and their representative to put questions and then also outline their case. In general, the mere fact of having a collective disputes procedure is not associated with a lower level of industrial action; however, their presence makes conflict much easier to resolve when it does occur (Dix, Sisson, and Forth 2009).

The majority of collective disputes procedures provide for some sort of third-party intervention in circumstances where a dispute cannot be settled internally, through external conciliation, mediation, or arbitration. The nature of this intervention can vary markedly. The main purpose of conciliation, for example, is to 'facilitate independent collective bargaining' (Brown 2010: 268). It is concerned with helping the parties to a dispute to reach their own agreement by intervening to draw them closer together (Wood 1992). This can involve just helping to improve the flow of information between the parties in a rather passive fashion, or it may take on a more active character, with the conciliator playing a prominent part in shaping the terms of any eventual settlement (Brown 2010).

The process of mediation is similar to conciliation, but the third-party person plays a more active role, with the scope to make recommendations in particular (Wood 1992). There is growing interest in how mediation can be used to settle disputes between individual workers and employers (see Section 10.5). With arbitration, a dispute is submitted to a third party, an individual arbitrator or sometimes an arbitration board, who, after weighing up the arguments of the two sides and taking into account any other relevant information, decides the issue. It is often used where negotiation and conciliation have both failed to resolve a dispute, particularly in the area of pay. In general, arbitration awards are not legally binding; like collective agreements, they are binding in honour only. Disputes procedures that make reference to arbitration will specify whether it can be invoked unilaterally (that is, by just of one of the parties), or jointly (with the necessary agreement of both).

International perspective 10.1:   The development of labour arbitration in China

As mentioned in Chapter 9, employment relations in China is marked by extensive and rising levels of labour conflict as workers combine to challenge the adverse consequences of economic reforms on their jobs and livelihoods. As a result, the Chinese authorities have tried to develop new methods of resolving labour disputes, including arbitration arrangements, to keep labour unrest under control (Chan 2010). Between 1996 and 2004 there was a more than five-fold increase in the number of labour disputes dealt with by arbitration, from 47,591 to 260,471. Evidently, 'arbitration has become increasingly popular . . . as the preferred mechanism for resolving labour disputes in China' (Shen 2007: 536). The effectiveness of existing arbitration arrangements, however, is limited by their lack of independence from government control, something which reduces their legitimacy as employment relations institutions.

Governments have long recognized the advantages to be gained by facilitating machinery for resolving disputes. State intervention in this area, which dates from the late nineteenth century, was predicated on the need to ensure that potentially harmful industrial action could be resolved without it causing the country too much economic disruption (Wood 1992). The use of state-supported conciliation and arbitration facilities for resolving disputes was envisaged as a last resort, to be initiated only with the agreement of both parties once all other methods had been exhausted (Mumford 1996). Such third-party intervention was primarily conceived of as a way of 'supporting and facilitating collective bargaining and assisting voluntary resolution of disputes' (Dickens 2012a: 31). Third-party arrangements for resolving disputes are commonplace in many countries (Brown 2010). See International perspective 10.1 for details of the development of arbitration arrangements in China.

10.2.3 The role of ACAS in resolving collective disputes

The establishment of the Advisory, Conciliation, and Arbitration Service (ACAS) during the 1970s signalled the rise of a more interventionist approach to dispute resolution by the state. ACAS is a tripartite body, independent of government, and is overseen by a council comprising an equal number of representatives from employers and the trade unions (Brown 2010). On its formation, ACAS 'was given the general duty of promoting the improvement of industrial relations, and in particular of encouraging the extension of collective bargaining and the development and, where necessary, the reform of collective bargaining machinery' (Kessler 1993: 220). In particular, it was empowered to provide conciliation facilities, to make any necessary arrangements for mediation and arbitration, and to provide advice on effective personnel and employment relations practice.

Perhaps the most impressive achievement of ACAS is the way in which, as a tripartite body, it managed to endure the period of Conservative rule between 1979 and 1997. As Chapter 3 showed, not only were Conservative governments hostile to tripartism, but they were also keen to encourage the exercise of greater managerial prerogative, to undermine the power of trade unions, and to challenge the significance of collective bargaining. Thus the pluralist ethos, which during the 1960s and 1970s had encouraged greater state involvement in resolving disputes through procedures (Kessler 1993), was supplanted by a more unitary emphasis on the primacy of employer action.

Three factors have contributed to the resilience of ACAS, its tripartite character notwithstanding. First, it has effectively demonstrated its independence—from government, employers, and the unions alike (Wood 1992). Second, ACAS attracts the continued support of many employers. Third, the main priorities of ACAS have changed in important ways, from an early focus on the improvement of collective employment relations and a duty to promote collective bargaining, to a greater concern with resolving individual disputes, providing advice about workplace problems (see Section 10.5.3), and with working to stop problems from arising in the first place (Hawes 2000; Dix and Oxenbridge 2004). ACAS affirms that its role is to 'help prevent disputes and, when disputes do occur, to help resolve them with the agreement of the parties' (ACAS 2007b: 2). While the duty of ACAS to promote collective bargaining was revoked in 1992, it is still considered to be 'broadly sympathetic' to the process because of its tripartite structure (Brown 2010: 268).

During the 1980s and 1990s the amount of collective conciliation work undertaken by ACAS involving efforts to resolve collective disputes between an employer and trade union declined markedly (Goodman 2000). Nevertheless, it remains an important feature of the organization's role. In 2011–12, for example, ACAS provided collective conciliation in 972 cases, nearly half of them concerning disputes over pay. For instance, ACAS conciliation was evident in the British Airways and Unilever strikes mentioned in Chapter 9. In the overwhelming majority of such cases (91 per cent) ACAS either resolved the dispute or helped the parties to reach their own settlement (ACAS 2012). ACAS also operates a panel of independent arbitrators; the relatively small proportion of disputes that cannot be resolved as a result of conciliation are given to an arbitrator to decide on (Brown 2010).

How, then, does collective conciliation work? It is, above all, a voluntary process; ACAS cannot compel the parties to cooperate (Goodman 2000). Once underway, the integrity, and therefore the effectiveness, of conciliation work is predicated on the impartiality of the conciliator and the need to secure the trust and confidence of both parties (IRS 2001). ACAS conciliators often become involved in a dispute before the formal reference to conciliation is made. By 'running alongside' the dispute, they are able to understand its dimensions, and thus consider potential aspects of a settlement, more quickly (Dix and Oxenbridge 2004). Most conciliation work progresses in a series of so-called 'side meetings', during which the respective parties discuss, hone, and adjust their positions separately in response to the contributions of the conciliator, before they are subject to further bargaining at the negotiating table (IRS 2001). Conciliators work to try and get the respective parties to focus on, and develop a more effective understanding of, the nature of their dispute and its causes. By providing a 'fresh eye', an 'important part of the conciliator's task is getting each party, independently and alone, to describe and analyze the issues, testing and rephrasing and probing ambiguities in order to clarify the disputant parties' thinking' (Brown 2010: 268).

Conciliators work with each of the parties to help them reach their own agreement. They do this:

> by acting as an intermediary in the exchange of information and ideas, by keeping the parties communicating, clarifying issues, establishing common ground, identifying barriers to progress, eroding unrealistic expectations, pointing to the costs and disadvantages if the dispute is not settled, developing possible solutions and creating confidence that

an acceptable solution will be found. The conciliator has no powers other than those of reason and persuasion.

(Goodman 2000: 38)

ACAS conciliation is generally held in high esteem. Employers and unions appreciate the way in which ACAS conciliators are able to explain, challenge, and test their negotiating positions and thus open up potential areas of agreement (Dix and Oxenbridge 2004). Nevertheless, while collective conciliation remains a key feature of the work of ACAS, much of its activity has now become focused on resolving disputes between individual workers and their employers (see Section 10.5).

 Section summary and further reading

- Attempts to resolve disputes between employers and unions generally involve some kind of negotiated settlement. The nature of any settlement is strongly influenced by the extent of the respective parties' bargaining power. The characteristics of the environment give the parties a degree of latent power, but the outcome of negotiations is largely determined by how effectively they mobilize to make use of it.

- There is a long history of state support for third-party dispute-resolution machinery, in order to ensure that potentially damaging disputes can be settled without causing too much disruption. ACAS provides collective conciliation, and arranges access to arbitration in disputes between employers and trade unions.

For perspectives on negotiations and the skills needed for effective negotiation, see Torrington (1991). Both Sisson (2010: Chapter 5) and Brown (2010: 263–7) provide good overviews of the process of negotiation in employment relations. The evolution of third-party arrangements for dispute resolution is covered by Wood (1992) and Hawes (2000).

10.3 Resolving individual disputes: grievance and discipline in employment relations

Having considered procedures for resolving collective disputes, the purpose of this section is to examine arrangements for handling instances of workplace conflict that involve employees as individuals. Employers commonly operate formal procedures for dealing with employee grievances, and for disciplining and dismissing staff deemed to have breached organizational rules. While the focus of such arrangements is on addressing issues ostensibly relating to individual employees, it is important to bear in mind that when such conflict at work arises it may not be something which is just related to a single person, but can have a more collective dimension.

10.3.1 The purpose of grievance and disciplinary procedures

Procedures for handling employee grievances and for disciplining and dismissing staff ostensibly exist to provide a formal means for resolving individual disputes that have arisen from breaches of organizational rules or acceptable standards of conduct. Disciplinary procedures set out the arrangements for dealing with employees who are suspected of contravening organizational rules in some way, for example by being persistently late for work. Employees may also have cause to complain about the managerial interpretation of organizational rules, particularly if they feel they have been treated unfairly in some way, by being denied access to promotion opportunities for example. Therefore, grievance procedures are designed to offer a formal means of resolving a dispute that arises when an individual employee has a complaint regarding their treatment at work.

Before the 1960s, few organizations had their own written procedures for dealing with grievances and disciplinary issues (Edwards 2005). Since then, though, there has been a remarkable increase in the growth of formal arrangements for handling such matters. In 2011, 88 per cent of workplaces had a formal procedure for dealing with individual employee grievances, and 89 per cent had a procedure covering discipline and dismissal (van Wanrooy et al. 2013).

Grievance procedures generally establish a process which aggrieved employees can use to express their complaint. They usually specify the need for a statement from the individual concerned outlining their grievance; make provision for a hearing at which the employee can discuss their complaint with one or more managerial representatives; and state what happens (e.g. any right to appeal) if the outcome of the hearing does not satisfy the complainant. Grievances typically concern issues such as poor relationships with managers and colleagues, pay and grading, bullying and harassment, and discrimination.

Generally, disciplinary procedures set the appropriate standards of conduct expected from employees and delineate areas of unsatisfactory activity; provide a process that managers should use to investigate allegations of offending behaviour; outline the constitution of any disciplinary hearing, including the right of employees to voice their response to any allegations made against them; and indicate the relevant sanctions to be used in the event of a confirmed breach of discipline. For minor offences, such as a small number of illegitimate absences, the penalty might be a verbal warning by an employee's immediate supervisor, or a written warning. Where the offence is repeated, or in instances of gross misconduct, which can include matters such as sexual harassment for example, the disciplinary procedure might provide for dismissal. Workers have a right to be accompanied in a grievance or disciplinary meeting, including those concerned with hearing an appeal, by a fellow worker or a trade union representative.

Why have formal grievance and disciplinary procedures become so commonplace in organizations? For one thing, they are necessary mechanisms for managing instances of conflict that arise in the workplace, something that can be highly disruptive for employers if left unchecked. A second reason is that formal procedures for handling grievances and disciplinary cases help to define the authority of managers, and thus enhance managerial control. Grievance machinery, for example, enables employee complaints to be dealt with in a seemingly fair and consistent manner. This can help to enhance perceptions of procedural justice among employees, improving their attachment to their employers (Klass 2010). Formal disciplinary procedures also have a number of managerial benefits. Their presence demonstrates that punishing an employee, by dismissing them for example, is a fair outcome, the result of following due process, and not just an arbitrary decision. They also enable managers to establish appropriate standards of performance and conduct expected of employees (Klass 2010; ACAS 2011). Thus it is important to see grievance and disciplinary procedures less as arrangements for resolving disputes, and more as methods of maintaining managerial control in organizations. Grievance procedures, for example, rarely seem to lead to issues being handled in a way that satisfies aggrieved workers (Abbott 2007).

The third reason for the growth of formal procedures for handling grievances and disciplinary issues is that they can provide employers with a defence in cases of litigation by current and former employees (Klass 2010). The use of an appropriate formal procedure to discipline or dismiss employees, and a formal grievance procedure to enable staff to raise complaints and then have them resolved, either helps employers to avoid litigation, or enables them to defend employment tribunal claims more effectively (see Section 10.5)

10.3.2 **Discipline in action: critical perspectives**

It is important not to see procedures as impartial devices, designed to reconcile the interests of employees and employers by effectively resolving instances of workplace conflict for the good of all in the organization. This is particularly evident with regard to the matter of workplace discipline. Disciplinary procedures are explicitly managerial tools. By giving legitimacy to decisions to impose sanctions on employees, their presence is designed to buttress managerial authority (Fenley 1986). Disciplinary procedures largely reflect managerial aspirations and, by formalizing the application of workplace discipline, help persuade employees that the rules elaborated within them should be obeyed. In his study of a British-based Japanese television plant, Nippon CTV, Delbridge (1998) demonstrates the effectiveness of disciplinary rules in regulating workplace order. During induction, new recruits were instilled with the need to comply with the firm's rules, particularly those concerning absenteeism and punctuality.

Following on from this, it would be wrong to assume that the formalization of disciplinary practice has provided workers with added protection against arbitrary discipline. Managers frequently fail to follow their own procedures. Workers who have been subject to disciplinary proceedings tend to feel that managers had assumed their guilt beforehand and paid little attention to anything they might say in mitigation (Rollinson et al. 1997). Particularly in small firms, managers make up their minds to dismiss an employee before any disciplinary hearing takes place (Earnshaw, Marchington, and Goodman 2000), while a study of workplace discipline among nurses identified numerous procedural irregularities, including reports that managers were prepared to lie during disciplinary cases in order to get their desired outcome (Cooke 2006).

The 'consensus' approach holds that there has been a shift over time away from a generally punitive style of discipline towards a greater emphasis on using disciplinary procedures to correct and improve workers' behaviour (Henry 1982). However, the exercise of discipline continues to be marked by a 'punitive' rather than a 'corrective' ethos. In other words, the emphasis is on getting workers to obey managerial rules for fear of the punishment, such as dismissal, that would result from any failure to comply (Fenley 1998), rather than helping them to identify any failings and thus improve their behaviour. Studies which consider the experience of workers tend to bear this out. 'For a large proportion of those formally disciplined, the process was not seen as a persuasive one designed to get them to observe rules, but as an event which gave the manager an opportunity to take retribution, or administer a deterrent to limit future transgressions' (Rollinson et al. 1997: 298). Cooke's (2006) study of nursing demonstrates not only that disciplinary action against staff was commonplace, but also that it was undertaken largely for punitive reasons, whatever managers said about the need to improve performance or protect patient care. See Insight into practice 10.2 for examples of workers being punished for supposed misuse of social media.

 Insight into practice 10.2: Discipline and social media

The prevalence of a punitive approach to workplace discipline is evident when it comes to responses by some employers to comments made by employees on social media sites such as Facebook and Twitter. In some cases, individuals have been disciplined and/or dismissed for posting messages revealing that they have been engaged in work-related misbehaviour—for example, 'tweeting' that they are out shopping, having phoned in sick. More controversially, employees have also been subject to disciplinary action, and even dismissal, for posting online comments which their employer claims has caused it reputational damage. In one notable case, Apple Store worker Samuel Crisp made negative comments about his employer and its products on his 'private' Facebook page; however, one of his Facebook 'friends' saw the comments and alerted Crisp's manager. Crisp was sacked for gross misconduct as a result. His 2011 claim for unfair dismissal was rejected by an employment tribunal on the grounds that, while it might seem harsh, Apple does have a clear social media policy prohibiting its employees from making critical comments about the brand and its products, something that is particularly important for a company whose image is a key feature of its success. Writing anything that could be interpreted as negative about an employer or its products can result in dismissal. In 2011 David Rowat was sacked by his retail employer Argos after returning from work and posting these comments on his Facebook page: 'Had a great day back at work after my hols who am I kidding!!' and 'Back to the shambles that is work'.

Sources: Barnett (2011); Smith (2011)

The final critical point to make about discipline concerns the care that needs to be taken not to overlook the importance of informal expectations and understandings, given the nature of work and employment relationships as a wage–work bargain (Edwards 2005). Formal procedures for disciplining staff suspected of transgressing organizational rules, and the application of formal sanctions like warnings as a result, are commonplace features of workplace life. In practice, however, workplace rules, whether or not they are obeyed, and how far managers choose to enforce them, are contingent on the relationship that exists between managers and workers in specific settings. Discipline, then, 'means more than the application of sanctions by management' (Edwards and Whitston 1994: 320). Workplace rules are not laid down by managers and then obeyed by workers, in an overly clear-cut manner. Rather, they are interpreted, and then adjusted, by managers and workers as part of the continuing process of negotiation and re-negotiation that characterizes the employment relationship as a wage–work bargain.

Andrew Scott (1994) offers a good example of this in his account of employment relations in a non-union chocolate factory. On coming across evidence that workers were leaving to go home before the end of a shift, and without tidying the changing room first, managers instituted a 'first and last hour' rule. Anyone leaving the production line during the first and last hours of their shift without their manager's approval would receive a written warning. During the first few weeks of the new rule's existence, a number of workers received warnings as a result of breaching it. Having to ask permission to go to the toilet, for example, was, for the workers, a distasteful experience, and most considered the rule to be 'silly' and 'unfair' (Scott 1994: 113). Nor did the rule find favour among all the managers, who 'found it inconvenient and tiresome to spend two hours of each day making sure their staff did not slip away without permission' (Scott 1994: 113). Not all managers, then, enforced the rule, though its continued existence in the rule-book meant that it could always be re-imposed should they wish to enforce their authority more rigorously at any time.

 ## Section summary and further reading

- Formal procedures for handling employee grievances and for dealing with alleged breaches of workplace discipline help employers to manage employment relations more effectively: by providing a seemingly non-arbitrary method of resolving workplace conflict, defining the authority of managers, and providing a defence against litigation.

- Grievance and disciplinary procedures help to maintain managerial control, rather than act as impartial methods of resolving workplace disputes. The practice of discipline at work often has a marked punitive and arbitrary character. It is important to recognize the role played by informal expectations and understandings in producing workplace discipline.

Klass (2010) provides the best general overview of grievance and discipline. ACAS (2011) publishes advice and guidance about handling grievance and disciplinary issues. For a critical overview, see Edwards (2005).

10.4 Redundancy and employment relations

Losing one's job, or the threat of losing one's job, is perhaps the most unsettling of experiences for workers in employment relations. It also demonstrates in a stark fashion the difference of interest that marks the employment relationship: between an employer, whose decision it is to terminate someone's employment, and the employee, who has to bear the consequences of losing a job. This section considers the nature of redundancy as an employment relations process, one that enables employers to dismiss staff in a supposedly fair and justifiable way. However, efforts by working people to challenge redundancy decisions illustrate the contested basis of work and employment relationships.

10.4.1 The nature and causes of redundancy

'Redundancy' in employment relations refers to situations where an employer plans to dismiss employees because fewer employees are needed to undertake a specific set of work activities in a particular area, in return for financial compensation. In law, it is a potentially fair reason for dismissing staff, and employers only have to demonstrate that changing business circumstances mean that fewer employees are required, not that there has been a reduction in the amount of actual work. A redundancy situation can arise when there is no change, or even an increase, in the amount of work required, if the needs of the business mean that job losses are needed to produce efficiency savings.

Prior to the 1960s, the concept of redundancy scarcely registered in employment relations. Nevertheless, the term started to become more widely used as some employers, who wanted to reduce employment levels, offered financial payments to compensate workers for the loss of their jobs (Mukherjee 1973; Fryer 1981). Unions often strongly opposed management proposals to discharge employees and, in situations where dismissals appeared to be unavoidable, insisted on 'last-in, first-out', or 'LIFO', as the principal selection criterion. In other words, those who had the least length of service with the firm would be chosen to go first.

Policy-makers increasingly viewed the strength of union opposition to such dismissals as an obstacle to the efficient functioning of the economy, since something needed to be done to encourage workers in declining industrial sectors to move to parts of the economy that were experiencing growth. During the 1960s legislation was introduced to make it easier for employers to institute redundancies. It recognized that workers hold property rights in their jobs, stipulating that cash compensation, in the form of severance payments based on age and length of service, be awarded to those made redundant by their employer (Anderman 1986). But the main aim was to promote economic efficiency by enabling the more rational use of labour in a climate of full employment (Mukherjee 1973).

Although redundancy legislation appeared to satisfy the twin rationales of stimulating greater economic efficiency, while at the same time providing displaced workers with cash compensation for the loss of their jobs, it was nonetheless infused by 'a clear managerial agenda' (Turnbull and Wass 1997: 30). The legislation was underpinned by a desire to make it easier for employers to dismiss employees, in that it was designed to reduce both union opposition to dismissals, and the workplace disputes that they often provoked, thus strengthening managerial prerogative (Fryer 1973, 1981).

Having outlined what redundancy means, and examined some key elements of the policy background, we now need to consider the principal causes of redundancy situations in employment relations. A number of specific reasons for redundancies can be identified:

- Industrial decline: (e.g. during the 1980s and 1990s hundreds of thousands of jobs were eliminated as the importance of traditional industries like coal mining dwindled).

- Declining demand for an organization's products or services (e.g. in January 2013 the car manufacturer Honda announced its plans for 800 job losses at its Swindon plant in the UK because of falling demand).

- New technology is often introduced in a way that displaces jobs (e.g. during the 1960s and 1970s the process of containerization caused the decline of many jobs in the docks).

- Organizational restructuring (e.g. in 2011 the multinational drugs company Pfizer announced it was to close its research and development facility in Sandwich, south-east England with the loss of some 2,400 jobs).

- Business insolvency: unless a new buyer is found quickly, job losses ensue when a firm goes out of business (e.g. the closure of Woolworths stores in early 2009).

Generally, though, redundancies are instituted in order to maintain or improve organizational competitiveness, helping employers benefit from the cost savings associated with any resulting efficiency gains (Cascio 2010). In the public sector, austerity measures have resulted in widespread redundancies, particularly across local government. Following the private equity

Table 10.1 The level and rate of redundancies in the UK, 2001–12

	Redundancy level*	Redundancy rate**
2001	177,000	7.4
2002	185,000	7.6
2003	158,000	6.4
2004	141,000	5.7
2005	143,000	5.7
2006	138,000	5.5
2007	127,000	5.0
2008	163,000	6.4
2009	234,000	9.3
2010	152,000	6.2
2011	153,000	6.2
2012	149,000	6.0

* Quarterly averages

** The number of redundancies per 1,000 employees

Source: Labour Force Survey, http://www.statistics.gov.uk

takeover of the AA (see Chapter 5) the new management team made around 3,000 job losses as part of its efforts to rationalize the company and extract greater value from it (Clark 2010). This last point highlights an increasingly important aspect of how redundancies are used as a cost-cutting measure, not as a way of responding to poor performance, but rather as a means of enhancing performance by improving competitiveness. Redundancy has therefore become a popular means of instituting efficiency savings through cuts in labour costs, becoming far removed from its original stated purpose of improving the economy-wide supply of labour (Blyton and Turnbull 2004).

Redundancies have become an established part of the employment relations landscape, linked in particular to the economic recessions of the early 1980s and early 1990s when millions of workers lost their jobs as a result of business closures and rationalization programmes (Gallie et al. 1998). Although the incidence of redundancies diminished during the late 1990s and early 2000s, linked to the growth of the economy, in 2008 and 2009 there was a marked increase in the number of people being made redundant as a result of the economic recession sparked by the financial crisis. Table 10.1 shows changes in both the level and the rate of redundancies over the period 2002–12. The redundancy rate (the number of redundancies per 1,000 employees) fluctuated around the 7.5 mark in the early 2000s, before falling to 5.0 in 2007. It then rose to 9.3 in 2009 before subsiding again to 6.0 in 2012. The proportion of workplaces that had made some staff redundant during the previous year doubled from 7 per cent in 2004 to 14 per cent in 2011 (van Wanrooy et al. 2013). Further job cuts in the public sector, arising from the coalition government's deficit-reduction programme, seem likely to increase the redundancy rate as sectors including central and local government, health, and the police feel the pinch of austerity. The government's own independent Office for Budgetary Responsibility estimates that the number of public sector jobs will fall by over 900,000 between 2010–11 and 2017–18 (OBR 2012). It is important to bear in mind that the official redundancy figures do not include other measures used to reduce staff numbers, such as so-called early retirement for example, which may be a form of disguised redundancy (Worrall, Cooper, and Campbell 2000). Moreover, see Chapter 2 for details of how employers have used measures such as wage freezes and moratoriums on filling vacancies as alternatives to job losses when it comes to cutting costs.

10.4.2 The process of redundancy and its consequences

One of the most important aspects of redundancy in employment relations concerns the substantial discretion enjoyed by managers over the decision to shed labour, who should be dismissed, and how and when they should go. Redundancy has become a convenient way for managers to dismiss staff. Judicial interpretations of the relevant legislation largely support the supremacy of managerial prerogative over redundancy decisions (Turnbull 1988; Turnbull and Wass 1997). The concept of redundancy, moreover, has been treated increasingly loosely, to such an extent that it is taken to apply to an employer's decision that fewer employees are required to undertake particular work, without any obligation to demonstrate that the amount of work has in fact diminished (Lewis 1993: 72). The up-front financial costs of making severance payments are rarely onerous for employers (Turnbull 1988); in 2013, the maximum statutory payout that an individual was entitled to receive stood at £13,500, and they would have to have amassed least twenty years' service in their job and be over the age of 41 to receive this much.

The process of redundancy also enables managers to restructure their workforces in ways that benefit the employer's interest. It 'is a time when new standards can be laid down as the organization gears up to operating in a changed environment' (Lewis 1993: 39). This is particularly evident from the selection criteria used to pick people for redundancy, which can be used to communicate and reinforce managerial priorities (Cascio 2010). They are used by employers to streamline their workforces in a desirable manner through the use, for example, of supposedly more objective factors, such as performance, ability, skills, and disciplinary and attendance records, rather than LIFO. This can disadvantage certain groups of workers. In the docks industry, for example, Turnbull and Wass (1994) observed that older workers, those who are medically restricted in some way and thus unable to undertake a full range of tasks, and union activists were over-represented among those selected for redundancy. Managers may also override supposedly objective scoring systems in order to exercise discretion over who stays and who goes (Donnelly and Scholarios 1998).

One of the ways in which management can intensify their control over redundancy exercises is to encourage workers to depart voluntarily, with the promise of an enhanced cash payment if they agree to go of their own volition. This must seem odd. One would assume that voluntary redundancy, as opposed to being made compulsorily redundant, at least gives workers some discretion. In reality, however, it is not as simple as that; voluntary redundancy is marked by a combination of managerial control and employee choice which varies from situation to situation (Clarke 2007)—see Insight into practice 10.3. If the redundancy decision is genuinely voluntary, then employees with more up-to-date and marketable skills, those who may feel more optimistic about securing a position with an alternative employer, are the ones who are most likely to be lost to the organization (Cascio 2010). Ostensibly voluntary redundancy programmes are subject to extensive managerial influence over selection (Wass 1996). Managers may reserve the right to refuse applications for voluntary redundancy from people they would prefer to keep, particularly if they have 'certain skills, knowledge or capabilities deemed essential to the firm' (Turnbull and Wass 1997: 33).

 Insight into practice 10.3: Voluntary redundancy—managerial control or employee choice?

Clarke (2007) identifies two features of voluntary redundancy that distinguish it from a compulsory approach: employees supposedly exercise choice over whether or not they leave the organization; and enhanced severance payments are used as an incentive to encourage people to volunteer. Her study of the voluntary redundancy experiences of Australian workers found that the extent of genuine employee choice varied considerably. Some workers resented the way in which they were effectively forced out, with little alternative but to leave. Others, however, offered a more positive assessment of the voluntary redundancy process. This was particularly the case among workers who, realizing that alternative positions were unavailable, welcomed the opportunity to 'escape' demanding jobs with an enhanced severance payment.

On the other hand, they may actively encourage—and indeed impose—voluntary redundancy on people they do want to be rid of. Thus it is not inappropriate to refer to the concept of 'forced' voluntary redundancy in many cases (Turnbull 1988). Donnelly and Scholarios (1998) encountered a number of instances where simply enquiring about the possibility of voluntary arrangements resulted in the workers concerned being targeted for compulsory redundancy. In some cases, the alternative to voluntary redundancy is the acceptance of new terms and conditions of employment that provide for more flexible working and limit pay increases (Hudson 2002). In practice, then, there is often little to distinguish voluntary from compulsory redundancy (Burchell et al. 1999). Indeed, the term 'voluntary redundancy' may be 'something of a misnomer' (Turnbull 1988; Turnbull and Wass 1997) in so far as it communicates the misleading impression that workers can exercise much choice over whether they go or not.

Evidently, redundancy exercises offer managers an opportunity to strengthen their prerogative and, moreover, institute efficiency gains at the expense of workers' jobs. This is largely unaffected by the obligation to consult with representatives of the workforce. Where employers propose to dismiss twenty or more employees within a ninety-day period (forty-five days where it is proposed to dismiss 100 or more employees—reduced from ninety days by the coalition in 2013) they are obliged to consult with union representatives if there is a recognized trade union present, or with elected employee representatives if there is not. In theory, such consultation should be meaningful and be undertaken with a view to reaching an agreement over matters such as ways of avoiding the need for dismissals, reducing the number of people to be dismissed, and alleviating the consequences of dismissal for affected staff. Failure to undertake appropriate consultation can lead to employees being awarded compensation, as in the case of Woolworths (see the introductory case study).

There is some evidence that appropriate consultation, especially where union representatives are involved, may encourage managers to reform their proposals, for example by getting an employer to substitute voluntary redundancy for compulsory measures (Hall and Edwards 1999). However, just two-fifths (40 per cent) of consultation initiatives actually result in any kind of change to management proposals (van Wanrooy et al. 2013). The decision to make redundancies is generally taken before any consultation commences (Turnbull and Wass 2000). In only a minority of cases does consultation actually result in fewer redundancies occurring (van Wanrooy et al. 2013). Moreover, firms often avoid their obligation to consult and 'operate outside the law by using voluntary severance arrangements and offering enhanced severance payments' (Turnbull and Wass 1997: 32) to encourage staff to depart, in lieu of consultation.

Redundancy programmes are commonly initiated not because there has been a diminution in what workers are expected to do, but as a means of generating cost savings, or of instituting greater workplace flexibility (Worrall, Cooper, and Campbell 2000; Hudson 2002). Perhaps unsurprisingly, redundancy 'is probably the most evocative and fear-inducing form of organizational change for many workers' (Worrall, Cooper, and Campbell 2000: 648). Those who have been made redundant often face a period of unemployment or are forced to accept jobs that offer worse pay and conditions than those to which they are accustomed (Harris 1987; Donnelly and Scholarios 1998; Turnbull and Wass 2000). In a review of practice in three sectors—the docks, the steel industry, and coal mining—Turnbull and Wass (1997) found that workers who had been made redundant were often subsequently re-hired on a self-employed, contract, or casual basis, on drastically inferior conditions of service.

In 2005 the MG Rover car plant at Longbridge near Birmingham closed, with the loss of around 6,000 jobs. While most of those made redundant found alternative employment or took up self-employment, their pay and conditions were generally markedly inferior, with many ending up facing financial difficulties (De Ruyter, Bailey, and Mahdon 2010). Generally, the people who are most likely to be made redundant—older workers for example, or those with health problems—are those who have relatively greater difficulty in finding new ones (Turnbull 1988; Turnbull and Wass 1997).

 ## Contesting employment relations 10.4: Challenging redundancies

Redundancy can be a major source of labour conflict. Workers and unions often challenge and contest management proposals to instigate redundancies. In 2006, for example, the car parts manufacturer Dura Automotive Systems announced that its plant in Llanelli, South Wales would close by the end of that year. The company claimed that rising costs, competitive pressures, and over-capacity had combined to make the plant uneconomic. The workforce, unhappy about the low level of proposed redundancy payments, took strike action which resulted in management having to increase the compensation on offer by some £4 million. Other groups of workers, including BBC journalists, have also gone on strike in protest against redundancies. Economic recession provoked some notable instances of workers contesting proposed job losses, including protests and direct action. In France, for example, some workers and trade unionists occupied their workplaces and organized 'bossnapping' events (see Chapter 9). Factory occupations also occurred in the UK. In the summer of 2009, for example, Vestas, a company which made wind turbines at its plant on the Isle of Wight, announced the closure of the factory with the loss of over 500 jobs. Before the shutdown was completed, however, some of its workers took control of the factory and blockaded themselves inside for over a fortnight.

The ease with which employers can make people redundant in Britain, relative to other European countries, and the large extent to which managers enjoy prerogative over the redundancy process, shapes the experience of workers in important ways. The perceived cost of losing one's job is a major source of insecurity, given the resulting likelihood of worse employment conditions in a new one, or even unemployment (Turnbull and Wass 2000). A growing sense of insecurity has permeated the workforce, particularly as job losses and the threat of job losses have come to affect hitherto relatively comfortable middle-class occupations, including managerial and professional employment (McGovern et al. 2007). That said, decisions by employers to make redundancies, and also the terms on which those redundancies are then put into effect, do not go unchallenged by workers. They do not necessarily respond to redundancy threats passively, but often contest proposed job losses through various forms of labour conflict, including direct action such as protests and occupations (Gall 2011a)—see Contesting employment relations 10.4.

 ### Section summary and further reading

- Redundancy is a way in which employers can dismiss employees in circumstances where fewer employees are required to undertake work in a particular area. It is a salient feature of employment relations given the extent to which organizations use it as a means of shedding jobs for the purpose of realizing efficiency savings.

- Managers have considerable scope to exercise their prerogative during redundancy programmes. Not only do they enjoy discretion over the decision to shed labour, who should be dismissed, and how and when they should go, but they are also rarely hindered by the obligation to consult with trade union or employee representatives.

- For people who have been made redundant, the aftermath is often characterized by periods of unemployment, or employment in jobs that offer worse pay and conditions than those to which they had hitherto been accustomed. Understandably, then, workers and unions often keenly contest redundancy proposals.

Cascio (2010) provides a good up-to-date overview of the issues relating to redundancy. For a managerial perspective on redundancy, see Lewis (1993). Turnbull and Wass (1997) offer a more critical interpretation of management's control of the redundancy process, situating it within an assessment of the public policy framework.

10.5 The system of employment tribunals

Many countries operate specialist arrangements for dealing with cases arising out of disputes between workers and employers. In the UK, employment tribunals (ETs)—independent quasi-judicial bodies comprising a legally qualified chair and two lay representatives—adjudicate on claims brought by workers against their current or former employers. The purpose of this section is to examine the nature and development of the ET system, and to assess the motivations behind, and the key implications of, efforts by successive governments to reform it, largely by trying to reduce the number of claims. Whereas in the past workers generally tried to settle employment cases collectively, through trade union negotiation, the growth in the number of ET claims reflects the increased importance of individual rights at work (see Chapter 3) and the greater role of the law in resolving disputes (Renton 2012).

10.5.1 **The nature and development of the tribunal system**

Since the 1960s, employment tribunals (ETs), which were called industrial tribunals until 1998, have dealt with individual disputes between an employee and his or her employer, with the number of their jurisdictions having increased markedly over time. They are the main mechanism available to workers who wish to pursue redress for breaches of their legal employment rights. Tribunals were originally conceived as relatively informal forums within which employers and employees could resolve disputes cheaply and quickly without the formalities associated with traditional courts of law (Hepple 1992). The 'emphasis on informality and official encouragement to tribunals to eschew legalism is part of the distinguishing of tribunals from the ordinary courts and of promoting simple informal justice' (Dickens et al. 1985: 83).

A key imperative was the importance of reducing the incidence of conflict arising from employment disputes, especially those relating to the dismissal of employees (Renton 2012). Reflecting the growth in the scope of employment legislation, over the years tribunals have accumulated an increasing number of jurisdictions: claims relating to sex, race, and disability discrimination; the non-payment of wages; and complaints about the failure of employers to pay the National Minimum Wage. The most common type of complaint, though, still concerns unfair dismissal. Redress is generally in the form of compensation; it is extremely rare for workers judged to have been unfairly dismissed to get their job back, for example (Morris 2012; Renton 2012).

Partly because of the increasing number of jurisdictions over which they can adjudicate, during the 1990s and 2000s the number of claims submitted to tribunals rose substantially. In 1980 there were 41,000 tribunal claims; by 2000–1 the number had risen to over 100,000, and by 2009–10 nearly 240,000. Table 10.2 provides details of the total number of ET claims for 2008–9 to 2011–12, and highlights the most common jurisdictions within which claims fall—including unfair dismissal, unauthorized deductions from wages, and breaches of contract. ET claims can cover more than one jurisdiction; a worker claiming unfair dismissal, for example, might contend that sex discrimination was also present. Although the number of claims declined after 2009–10 to 186,300, this still represented an increase of over 80 per cent since the start of the 2000s. Anyway the fall in the number of claims was largely a function of fewer multiple claims being submitted. It is not possible for workers to engage in 'class actions', where a single case is taken through the system in a way that is representative of many other workers in the same position. Instead, if they want redress individual workers need to put in their own claims, although ETs can then deal with them together. Such multiple claims are particularly common in disputes around equal pay and sex discrimination (Morris 2012; Renton 2012). During the 2000s there was a marked increase in the number of sex discrimination and equal pay claims, largely as a result of actions initiated by women in local government and the health service looking for financial restitution after years of inequality (see Chapter 4). The high number of claims relating to the Working Time Directive (see Table 10.2) is largely the product of multiple claims from airline pilots.

10.5.2 **Reforming the tribunal system**

Employers' bodies and business lobbyists often claim that an excessive number of unwarranted ET claims impose a heavy burden. By having to contest them, employers incur

Table 10.2 Total employment tribunal claims, and by jurisdiction; selected jurisdictions, 2008-9—2011-12

	2008-9	2009-10	2010-11	2011-12
Total ET claims	151,000	236,000	218,100	186,300
Unfair dismissal	52,700	57,400	47,900	46,300
Equal pay	45,700	37,400	34,600	28,800
Unauthorized deductions from wages	33,800	75,500	71,300	51,200
Breach of contract	32,800	42,400	34,600	32,100
Working Time Directive	24,000	95,200	114,000	94,700
Sex discrimination	18,600	18,200	18,300	10,800
Redundancy—failure to inform and consult	14,000	7,500	7,400	8,000
Redundancy pay	10,800	19,900	16,000	14,700
Disability discrimination	6,600	7,500	7,200	7,700
Race discrimination	5,000	5,700	5,000	4,800
Discrimination—age	3,800	5,200	6,800	3,700
Discrimination—religion or belief	710	1,000	880	940
National Minimum Wage	600	500	520	510
Discrimination—sexual orientation	600	710	640	610

Source: Ministry of Justice (2012)

substantial costs, not just in potentially having to engage lawyers, but also in the amount of management time and resources expended (Emmott 2001). Some prefer to reach a financial settlement before a claim reaches a tribunal hearing to prevent costs from escalating, although such action may also reflect a weak case. The Confederation of British Industry (CBI 2011c) contends that the ET system is too slow, cumbersome, and legalistic; moreover, multi-jurisdictional claims, particularly those concerning equal pay and discrimination, have become too complex. There is some evidence that ETs may not sufficiently take into account the circumstances of small firms in particular when adjudicating cases; tribunal judgments do not reflect their preference for managing staff in flexible and informal ways (Earnshaw, Marchington, and Goodman 2000).

Concerns have also been raised about the supposedly large degree to which disgruntled employees use the tribunal system to claim unwarranted monetary compensation. Business leaders sometimes claim that the number of tribunal applications reflects a growing 'compensation culture' in which people are increasingly prone to 'have a punt', and thus secure financial awards to which they are not entitled (Shackleton 2002). There is particular concern about many weak cases brought by disgruntled workers, which lack any real merit, but which employers are obliged to defend at considerable cost (CBI 2011c). The intervention of 'no-win, no-fee' lawyers is particularly resented. Right-wing critics of tribunals, and especially the growth in the number of jurisdictions, contend that the regulatory burden they impose on businesses damages economic competitiveness. It has been claimed that the 'tribunal system has grown piecemeal to a size where it now imposes significant costs on the economy as a whole—in terms of uncertainty, tension and stress at work, erosion of trust, addition to business costs and, most importantly, discouragement of job creation' (Shackleton 2002: 113).

Yet the claims made by employers and business lobbyists about the supposed burden of the ET system generally rest on rather weak grounds; views and assertions often masquerade as evidence (Renton 2012). One of the most prominent charges levelled at the ET system is that it is characterized by an excessive amount of legalism—that the tribunals have departed from their original purpose of resolving disputes in a speedy, relatively informal, and non-expensive manner without the formalism of courts of law, the legal arguments that dominate them, and the participation of lawyers. Yet legalism can be interpreted in a positive way in as much as it captures the importance tribunals attach to legal standards, rules, and consistency in their decisions (Macmillan 1999). Perhaps, then, some degree of legalism is inevitable (Dickens et al. 1985), and even desirable. It is somewhat ironic that complaints about excessive legalism in tribunals come from employers since they are more likely to have legal representation than complainants (Dickens et al. 1985; Hayward et al. 2004).

Another difficulty concerns complaints from employers and pro-business lobbyists that the growth in the number of claims to tribunals is the product of a 'compensation culture' in which employees are increasingly prone to make spurious and vexatious claims against their employers in the hope of gaining unwarranted financial recompense. However, 'contrary to anecdote, the number of unmeritorious claims is few' (Morris 2012: 17), and many of the costs to employers arise from defending cases they are destined to lose (Renton 2012). Workers generally face substantial obstacles to bringing tribunal claims, let alone winning them, even when they have legitimate cause for dispute. Only around one in twenty workers with a genuine grievance actually submits an ET claim, and most of those who do so do not get as far as a tribunal hearing itself (Renton 2012).

In her study of non-union workers, Pollert (2005) found that people with employment problems generally did nothing about them. Either they had little awareness of their employment rights, or the prospect of the financial costs involved in bringing a claim acted as a deterrent. Given the lack of legal aid, without union support or the help of under-funded and over-stretched law centres and Citizens Advice Bureaux, claimants have to bear their own costs. Problems of costs, delays, and excessive legalism are generally of greater concern for workers, who are often put off from making a claim, or pursuing it to a hearing, because of what Renton (2012) calls the 'tribunal obstacle race'.

Nevertheless, successive governments have been sympathetic to business concerns about the alleged burden of the ET system. During the 2000s, Labour took steps to try to reduce the number of claims made against employers, for example by weeding out supposedly weak or 'misconceived' cases before a tribunal hearing is convened (Colling 2004, 2010; Pollert 2007). It also put more of an emphasis on reducing the number of ET claims arising in the first place, through the provision of incentives to encourage greater internal resolution of claims. Since 2009, for example, tribunals have the power to adjust the amount of compensation due to successful claimants by up to 25 per cent depending on the extent to which they have behaved 'unreasonably' in relation to the relevant ACAS code of practice. Yet a major problem with encouraging the internal resolution of complaints is that it potentially restricts employees' access to justice, by giving managers too much control over the resolution of legitimate employment disputes (Colling 2004). When it comes to government efforts to reform the ET system, much of the emphasis is placed on reducing costs and promoting efficiency savings in a way that makes it harder for workers to assert their legal rights to be treated justly and fairly at work (Dickens 2012a).

Amidst the concerns of employers that employees now have too many rights at work, something which is said to discourage them from hiring new staff and place an impediment on job growth (see Legislation and policy 10.5), since 2010 the coalition government has accelerated efforts to reform the system of ETs. With the aim of ensuring that businesses feel more confident about hiring staff, it has put an increased emphasis on resolving disputes within the workplace, and at an earlier stage, thus hoping to reduce the number of claims taken to a tribunal (Tailby et al. 2011). By means of the Enterprise and Regulatory Reform Act 2013 the coalition took steps to: encourage alternative methods of resolving disputes, for example through the greater use of mediation and ACAS conciliation (see Section 10.5.3); introduce a 'rapid resolution scheme' for resolving supposedly straightforward disputes; and promote the more extensive use of 'settlement agreements', a means of ending employment relationships which involve employers giving departing employees a severance payment in exchange for them agreeing to waive their right to make an ET claim (BIS 2012f). The Act also introduced a stricter cap on the compensation due to workers who have won unfair dismissal cases and introduced measures to enhance the efficiency of tribunal procedures. The coalition's most controversial measures, though, were the 2012 increase in the qualifying period before a worker can claim they have been unfairly dismissed, from one year in a job, to two years, and the 2013 introduction of a system of fees under which workers could have to pay up to nearly £1200 to make a claim to an employment tribunal hearing, refundable only if they are successful.

LEGISLATION AND POLICY 10.5: The Beecroft report

Despite the lack of any supporting evidence, the coalition government's approach to employment relations policy is informed by the neo-liberal belief that employment rights are a major obstacle to promoting employment growth because their existence makes employers reluctant to hire new staff (see Chapter 3). This was the main message of a 2011 report written by venture capitalist Adrian Beecroft for prime minister David Cameron which, while ostensibly not for public consumption, attracted widespread coverage after initially being leaked to a national newspaper. The Beecroft report called for 'radical changes' to the system of employment law. The proposal that attracted most attention, however, concerned the suggestion that the right of employees to claim unfair dismissal should be abolished, something that was justified on the basis that employers should be able to rid themselves of perceived under-performing employees more easily (Jameson 2012). Beecroft (2011) proposed that the right not to be unfairly dismissed should be replaced by a system of 'compensated no fault dismissal', under which employers could fire supposedly unproductive staff as long as they were provided with a pay-off and given appropriate notice. Disagreement within government—the Liberal Democrats opposed this element of Beecroft's report—meant that the proposed abolition of the right not to be unfairly dismissed was not taken up. However, Beecroft's influence can be seen when it comes to coalition measures designed to make it easier for employers to dismiss employees, through arrangements like 'settlement agreements' for example.

The effectiveness of these measures is questionable, not least because of their likely consequences. For example, sacked workers who are not eligible to claim unfair dismissal may look to make a claim on the grounds of discrimination, for which there is no qualifying period. A more profound issue concerns the greater obstacles these measures put in the way of aggrieved workers who want to pursue their legal rights at work. The introduction of the system of fees is clearly predicated on the belief that there are too many unwarranted tribunal claims that lack merit (Renton 2012), a view which, while expressed robustly by employers' bodies and business lobbyists, has little evidential support. Its most likely effect, though, will be to limit drastically the access of workers, whose employment rights have been breached, to justice (TUC 2012e). Moreover, the increase in the qualifying period for unfair dismissal will plainly 'reduce the rights of vulnerable workers' (Renton 2012: 138). Knowing that workers will now find it more difficult to make an ET claim is likely to give encouragement to unscrupulous employers keen to avoid meeting their legal obligations by exploiting their staff in ways that breach employment law (Tailby et al. 2011).

10.5.3 The role of ACAS and 'alternative' forms of dispute resolution

The role of ACAS in resolving collective disputes between employers and trade unions was examined in Section 10.2. However, stimulated by a considerable increase in statutory individual employment rights (e.g. anti-discrimination laws, minimum wage, etc.), much of the work of ACAS now involves trying to resolve disputes between an individual employee and his or her employer (Sisson and Taylor 2006). In particular, it is under a statutory duty to offer conciliation when an employee makes a complaint against his or her employer to an employment tribunal. ACAS intervention operates as a 'very cost-effective filter', reducing the number of cases dealt with by tribunal hearings (Dickens 2012a: 36). Around 60 per cent of tribunal claims are settled or withdrawn before reaching a hearing. ACAS may resolve a dispute at the conciliation stage by passing on to the complainant an employer's offer of a financial settlement, for example, or by highlighting the potential weaknesses of a case. 'Once the conciliation officer has unearthed what is motivating the claim and what is really concerning the claimant, this may facilitate settlement, especially where what is sought is less costly to the employer than any possible tribunal remedy' (Dickens 2012a: 39). Among other things, ACAS conciliators discuss the features of the case with the parties, point out how tribunals have dealt with similar cases in the past, and act as an intermediary between the sides in trying to promote a settlement. The purpose of conciliation is partly to 'explain the way tribunals operate and what they take into account in deciding claims', helping the parties to make a realistic judgement of the likely outcome (Dickens 2012a: 39). As with collective conciliation (see Section 10.2), its purpose is to help workers and employers reach their own compromise settlement.

As mentioned already, the growth in the number of tribunal applications during the 2000s was a matter of some concern for employers' bodies and business lobbyists, who claim that it has placed too much of a burden on businesses. As part of their efforts to reduce the number of tribunal hearings, governments have attempted to strengthen the role of conciliation when it comes to settling individual employment disputes. In 2009, for example, Labour introduced a voluntary 'pre-claim conciliation' arrangement. In 2011–12 ACAS dealt with

20,000 cases through this method, 78 per cent of which did not result in a tribunal claim (ACAS 2012: 8). The coalition government has placed an emphasis on 'early conciliation', and has legislated to ensure that all potential ET claims have to be initially taken to ACAS for this purpose. Since it makes a major contribution to reducing their workload, individual concili-ation activity helps to keep the costs of running the system of employment tribunals under control (Hawes 2000).

The skill, sensitivity, and competence of ACAS conciliators tend to be highly regarded (Latreille, Latreille, and Knight 2007). Nevertheless, a criticism of conciliation is that, by en-couraging the parties to reach their own settlement before a dispute gets as far as a tribunal, or by encouraging people to withdraw their complaint, it militates against effective justice. In other words, there 'is a conflict between the search for compromise, which is at the centre of conciliation and the pursuit of rights' (Dickens 2012a: 38). Workers who have experienced unlawful treatment might end up being discouraged from securing redress at a tribunal when an employer has breached their legal rights.

In addition to its encouragement for conciliation, the coalition also envisions a stronger role for mediation in resolving employment disputes, something which ACAS can also fa-cilitate. Along with conciliation and arbitration, mediation is generally viewed as a form of 'alternative' dispute resolution, in the sense that it provides for a non-legalistic settlement of disputes (Dickens 2012a). It has some features in common with conciliation—particu-larly the emphasis on helping the parties concerned to reach their own agreement. Media-tion involves a non-judgemental approach whereby an 'impartial third party, the mediator, helps two or more people in dispute to attempt to reach an agreement. Any agreement comes from those in dispute, not from the mediator' (CIPD/ACAS 2008: 8). Whereas with arbitration and conciliation the main concern is with resolving disputes arising from peo-ple's past behaviour, with mediation there is a greater emphasis on trying to influence future behaviour by tackling potential sources of conflict (Ridley-Duff and Bennett 2011). For this reason, the intervention of a mediator is seen as particularly appropriate when it comes to disputes arising from poor working relationships (Dickens 2012a). By help-ing to reduce the incidence of employee grievances and the potential for costly tribunal claims, the use of mediation is claimed to be beneficial for employers. Some organizations, such as the retail company Arcadia, owner of the TopShop and TopMan chains of stores, have developed in-house mediation schemes as a result (CIPD 2011b). However, although a majority of grievance and disciplinary procedures make provision for mediation, it is relatively little used in practice (van Wanrooy et al. 2013). Managers may be reluctant to contemplate using mediation to resolve workplace disputes because of its up-front opera-tional costs and the perceived challenge it poses to their authority (IDS 2009). Unions are also sometimes wary of mediation, seeing it as something which can be used to prevent workers from asserting their legal rights to redress when they have experienced injustice or poor treatment at work.

In addition to the growing emphasis on resolving individual employment disputes, the work of ACAS has become increasingly focused on preventing disputes from arising in the first place (Dix and Oxenbridge 2004). ACAS is frequently used as a source of employment relations advice. Employment relations reflection 10.6 provides details of its helpline service; by giving workers and employers effective advice and guidance it has helped to reduce the number of tribunal applications (Dickens 2012a). ACAS also works in an advisory capacity

> **Employment relations reflection 10.6:** The ACAS helpline service
>
> The provision of information and advice about employment matters has become one of ACAS' most important activities. Much of the information is available in publications, many of which can be accessed by going to the ACAS website (http://www.acas.org.uk). However, a growing amount of advice and information is being disseminated through its telephone helpline service. The helpline is open to, and used by, both workers and employers. There has been a growing demand for the impartial and confidential information and advice offered by the service. In 2011–12 it received 925,000 calls. The topics on which advice and information are most frequently sought are grievances, discipline, and dismissals—34 per cent of calls (ACAS 2012). The complex nature of the helpline adviser role has come in for praise. 'The skill of the help-line advisers is key in disentangling the various problems, identifying the key point, providing the relevant information and, where appropriate, pointing them towards other sources of help and advice' (Sisson and Taylor 2006: 29).

with employers and trade unions on projects designed to improve the quality of employment relations (Purcell 2000; Dix and Oxenbridge 2004). A growing aspect of ACAS' work involves supporting 'workplace effectiveness', by taking action to demonstrate that 'good' relations between employers and employees can boost business performance, for example through carefully designed attendance management policies that help to reduce employee absence levels (ACAS 2010). It has also been concerned to promote the value of its work among small businesses, overcoming the 'hard-to-shift perception that ACAS is all about dispute resolution' (ACAS 2007a: 22). Such a focus on 'workplace effectiveness' is an indication of how far ACAS has moved away from a pluralist approach of promoting collective bargaining, towards a more unitary concern with supporting harmonious employment relations climates. However, the inherent potential for conflict in the employment relationship means that the process of dispute resolution remains an important feature of the role of ACAS. Its conciliation work in individual disputes, and the advice and guidance it provides through its publications and the helpline, mean that the demand for the services of ACAS remains high.

10.5.4 Employment tribunal reform: critical perspectives

The policy of attempting to reduce the number of ET claims is based on some dubious assumptions, most notably that their rise is linked to the growth of a compensation culture in which workers are increasingly keen to take action against employers for financial gain. While the notion that workers are becoming more keen to 'take a punt' in order to pursue unmerited compensation at the expense of virtuous and over-burdened employers is superficially attractive, it is far from the truth, and conceals a more complex set of contributory factors. One, no doubt, is simply that the number of jurisdictions for which tribunals enjoy responsibility has grown markedly (Pollert 2007). Much of the increase in the number of tribunal claims has come about because of a growth in the coverage of individual legal employment rights, particularly in respect of equality and discrimination issues, where the law tends to be rather complex. Those relating to equal pay, in particular, are often submitted on a multiple basis, further increasing the number of registered claims (Dix, Sisson, and Forth 2009; Morris 2012).

A second reason for the growth in the number of tribunal claims is that it reflects persistent high levels of discontent at work. Just because strikes and other forms of organized labour conflict have declined in significance (see Chapter 9) does not mean that the potential for conflict in general in the employment relationship has diminished. It remains important but, due to the reduced salience of trade unions and collective bargaining, becomes more commonly expressed in different ways. In this sense, then, the high level of tribunal claims reflects the 'strong sense of many employees that work itself is a hostile environment characterised by unequal power relationships which require the intervention of an outside force to prevent unfair treatment', and which are an inevitable source of disputes (Renton 2012: 100). The rise in tribunal claims therefore signals a climate of growing discontent at work, with conflict on the increase, rather than the somewhat nebulous notion of a compensation culture (Tailby et al. 2011).

Linked to this, the rise in the number of tribunal claims also reflects the growth in the number of people employed in those parts of the private services sector where the management of work and employment relations is often conducted in a harsh and arbitrary manner by small employers, and unions are weak, thus generating more claims (Dickens 2000c). In the largely non-union hotel industry, for example, the unilateral exercise of managerial prerogative is the cause of numerous complaints to tribunals from employees who feel they have been treated harshly (Head and Lucas 2004). Most tribunal claims relate to the treatment of workers in workplaces with no union recognition (Dickens 2012a). Where a union is present, it is more likely that any grievances can be resolved internally through negotiation and agreement, making resort to an ET unnecessary (Knight and Latreille 2000). Evidently, the decline in the level of unionization and the increasing proportion of employment in sectors of the economy where unions are weak have been partly responsible for the upsurge in the number of tribunal claims by individual workers (Hawes 2000; Dickens 2012a). Even right-wing critics of the tribunal system concede that the rise in the number of applications to tribunals partly reflects the decline in unionization (Shackleton 2002: 45). One potentially highly effective way of reducing the number of tribunal claims made by individual workers about their treatment at work would be to extend and strengthen the presence of unions; however, employers are unlikely to find this very palatable (Renton 2012).

Another area of critique concerns the belief held by employers' bodies, business lobbyists, and the coalition government that employees have too many rights, relative to employers. This is used to justify placing restrictions on the capacity of workers to pursue redress through the ET system. Given the magnitude of workplace conflict, though, perhaps the most surprising thing is not that there are so many tribunal claims, but so few. People in low-paid, insecure, and 'vulnerable' employment, often migrant workers in industries such as cleaning, catering, and social care who rarely enjoy union representation, face particular problems in trying to bring ET claims. For one thing, the high cost of legal representation is a disincentive. Moreover, such workers may lack awareness of their employment rights, or be insufficiently confident about asserting them (TUC 2008; Pollert 2009). Vulnerable workers may also be reluctant to institute tribunal claims against employers because they are fearful of the potential consequences. According to an employment rights adviser: 'They are stopped by the fear that even though they might have the strongest case in the world, once the next employer who they go to finds out they took the previous employer to the tribunal, the chances of getting a job go out of the window' (TUC 2008: 132). The coalition government's changes to the tribunal system will reduce still further the ability of many workers to assert their statutory rights. Only around a fifth of tribunal claims get as far as a hearing anyway, with most being either withdrawn or settled beforehand, sometimes as a result of ACAS intervention (Tailby et al. 2011).

For the approximately 12–13 per cent of all claimants who actually win their case at a tribunal, restitution is often limited. Even when complainants win their case for unfair dismissal, the tribunals' power to order their re-employment is rarely used (Morris 2012); financial compensation is the most common form of restitution. Contrary to the impression one might have gained from accounts of isolated, but high-profile, sex discrimination cases which have resulted in professional women receiving large financial settlements, most awards are relatively modest (Morris 2012; Renton 2012). In 2011–12 the median compensation award for a successful unfair dismissal claim was just £4,560; for sex discrimination it was £6,476 (Ministry of Justice 2012). Moreover, the unwillingness of some employers to pay compensation awards appears to be a growing problem (Renton 2012). In England and Wales, a tribunal award can only be enforced by obtaining a County Court or High Court judgment—a complex and expensive procedure, although a 2010 change may make it easier for workers to secure the compensation to which they are entitled. One study showed that some two-fifths of workers who had been awarded compensation by an ET had received no payment (Morris 2012: 21). Citizens Advice Bureaux report dealing with between 650 and 700 cases of non-payment each year.

Therefore, it is important to be cautious when employers and business lobbyists make exaggerated claims about the alleged burden of the employment tribunal system. Rather than complain about the time and energy that has to be expended in defending a claim, employers might be better off ensuring that their staff have as few as grounds as possible for complaint in the first place, by taking a less punitive approach to discipline for example, or by handling equality and diversity issues more effectively. They might also consider strengthening employee representation arrangements, by recognizing a trade union for example, allowing grievances to be resolved internally more readily.

The main problem with the system of employment tribunals, then, is not that it is too burdensome for employers, but that it does not deliver effective justice to workers who have grievances at work, or are treated in a harsh and arbitrary manner by their employers. Workers are rarely in a position to assert their legal employment rights effectively, and their chances of success are low even if they do embark on litigation (Colling 2010). Efforts by successive governments to reduce the number of ET claims, and thus weaken employees' access to justice, reflects a neo-liberal belief that economic competitiveness is best achieved by diluting employment regulation (Pollert 2007). However, there are growing calls for more effective enforcement of individual employment rights, moving away from an approach where the onus is on aggrieved individuals to make a complaint themselves, towards a system marked by greater proactive enforcement by state agencies (TUC 2008; Citizens Advice 2011; Dickens 2012b)—see the end-of-chapter case study.

Section summary and further reading

- Employment tribunals were conceived as relatively quick, informal, inexpensive, and accessible forums for resolving disputes between an individual employee and his or her employer, and for giving workers redress for breaches of their employment rights.

- The increase in the number of tribunal claims has prompted complaints from employers' bodies and business lobbyists that the tribunal system imposes an excessive burden on employers, particularly in relation to the costs associated with defending cases. However, there is little evidence to support the view that many tribunal claims lack merit, and thus need to be discouraged.

- ACAS has a major role in trying to resolve individual disputes between workers and employers, particularly by conciliating settlements. One of the ways in which governments have tried to reduce the number of tribunal hearings is by encouraging greater use of conciliation and mediation. However, there is concern that such 'alternative' methods of dispute resolution may preclude aggrieved workers from securing justice.

- Successive governments have attempted to reform the system of employment tribunals, with the focus mainly concerned with reducing the number of claims. The coalition government's measures, which include a new system of fees for registering claims, are likely to reduce workers' access to justice and erode the extent to which they are able to ensure that their employment rights are respected. The main problem with tribunals is their failure to provide justly aggrieved employees with adequate redress.

David Renton provides a highly readable and well-informed critique of the employment tribunal system in his 2012 book *Struck Out* (Renton 2012). He also blogs on the topics of tribunals and employment rights (at: http://www.struckout.co.uk/). Both Colling (2010) and Morris (2012) cover employment tribunals in their respective book chapters. See Dickens (2012a) for the role of ACAS and 'alternative' forms of dispute resolution.

10.6 Conclusion

One of the key features of work and employment relationships is that they are marked by the presence of an inherent potential conflict of interest between a worker and an employer. The form which this conflict takes when it appears, and the factors that influence it, were the focus of Chapter 9. In this chapter the concern has been with examining the role of processes in employment relations designed to prevent conflict from becoming manifest in disputes, either collectively or individually, or with resolving it when it does. As has been evident, a key purpose of these processes is to contain, accommodate, and institutionalize conflict in a pluralist fashion. Negotiation is designed to reconcile differences of interest in employment relations, with the involvement of third parties providing help through arrangements like conciliation where necessary. Yet procedures for dealing with grievances, disciplinary cases, and redundancy largely come under the control of management, and are used primarily for managerial purposes—by making it easier to realize efficiency gains through job cuts, for example. Of course, managerial prerogative is limited by the existence of legal employment standards, such as the right not to be unfairly dismissed, for example, or the right not to be discriminated against for reasons of sex, race, disability, and so on. Workers who believe that their rights have been contravened are—in theory at least—able to pursue redress by taking a case to an employment tribunal. However, there are a number of major obstacles preventing workers from properly exercising their rights. Many lack knowledge and awareness of their statutory entitlements, or are fearful of the consequences of pursuing a claim. Moreover, the financial compensation awarded in successful cases is rather modest, giving the lie to suggestions by employers' bodies and business lobbyists that a supposed 'compensation culture' is responsible for the growth in tribunal claims during the 2000s. While the quantity of legal employment rights may have increased, much more needs to be done to ensure that they are enforced effectively.

 ## Assignment and discussion questions

1. What are the main factors that influence the outcomes of negotiation exercises in employment relations?

2. What is the purpose of grievance and disciplinary procedures? To what extent does their presence protect workers from arbitrary managerial actions?

3. In what ways do redundancy exercises help to strengthen managerial control in workplaces?

4. Critically assess the effectiveness of the system of employment tribunals as a means of enforcing the employment rights of workers.

5. What are the main functions of ACAS? How has the role of ACAS evolved since it was established in the 1970s?

 Visit the Online Resource Centre that accompanies this book to develop your understanding of this chapter, and keep up to date with the latest developments in this area. **www.oxfordtextbooks.co.uk/orc/williams3e/**

 ## Chapter case study: Enforcing employment rights

One of the most important current issues in work and employment relations concerns the difficulties many workers face when it comes ensuring that employers uphold their legal employment rights. The system of employment tribunals relies on individual workers themselves being in a position to pursue redress for breaches of their rights by making a complaint. However, they may lack knowledge and awareness of their rights, or be fearful of employer intimidation and of losing their job if they do submit a tribunal claim (Citizens Advice 2011). The problems with this 'passive, complaint-driven approach' (Dickens 2012b: 215) have generated a growing amount of interest in how employment rights can be enforced more effectively. The last Labour government took some limited measures to improve workers' awareness of their rights (Dickens 2012b). In 2009 it established a new Pay and Work Rights Helpline, which covers five areas of employment where some element of proactive enforcement of employment rights already exists: non-payment of the National Minimum Wage (NMW); employment agencies; people working in agriculture and/or for gangmasters; and the 48-hour maximum limit on the length of the working week. In its first year of existence, the Helpline fielded 73,500 calls, at least two-thirds of which were from workers. An initial evaluation of the Helpline found that it appeared to play a useful part in handling queries, especially from vulnerable workers, in respect of the five areas covered (Rutherford and Achur 2010). According to Morris (2012: 26), while it is 'only the first step in the enforcement process, the Helpline provides a welcome contribution to assisting compliance with the limited range of employment rights with which it is concerned'.

While not unwelcome, the establishment of the Helpline is far from sufficient on its own to tackle widespread flouting of employment rights by unscrupulous employers. Dickens (2012b: 215), for example, calls for a greater emphasis on proactive enforcement of employment law through the involvement of state agencies—going 'beyond simply providing *individual* redress for breaches of rights once they occur, to helping produce the kind of workplaces where breaches are less likely to occur in the first place'. Some agency-led enforcement of employment rights currently exists: the Health and Safety Executive enforces workplace health and safety standards, for example, while HMRC has a role in pursuing employers who try to avoid paying the NMW. However, the overall system of enforcement lacks coherence, and is incomplete (Dickens 2012b: 216). One of the biggest problems faced by many vulnerable workers is the failure of their employer to provide paid holidays; but this is an issue which, because it is not currently a matter for agency enforcement, lies outside the scope of the Pay and Work Rights Helpline (Citizens Advice 2011). Enforcement of rights at work would be made more effective if there was an overarching agency responsible for making sure that employers complied with employment law, perhaps through a proactive system of inspection (Dickens 2012b). The charity Citizens Advice, for example, has called for the establishment of a single Fair Employment Agency, in order to 'simplify the enforcement framework and enhance the protection of vulnerable workers', whose employers often flout the law (Citizens Advice 2011: 3). The aim would be to 'give exploited vulnerable workers a visible, simple and effective alternative to the employment tribunal system, and ensure a level playing field for law-abiding employers, by consolidating the workplace enforcement bodies that lie behind the new helpline into a single Fair Employment Agency. This new agency should be provided with the powers and resources both to secure individual workers their key statutory rights, and to tackle the illegal practices of rogue employers more generally', something that would help to reduce the number of tribunal claims (Citizens Advice 2011: 10). However, there seems little prospect of such a change being implemented while the coalition government remains in office. Although it acknowledges problems with the current system for enforcing employment rights, the coalition's broader deregulatory agenda (see Chapter 3) means that it is unlikely to contemplate establishing a more robust approach in this area (Dickens 2012b).

Question

To what extent do you agree with the view that a more proactive and comprehensive system of enforcing employment rights is desirable?

Part 5

....

Conclusion

....

Conclusion

To a large extent, employment relations as a field of study is concerned with how work and employment relationships are regulated. In the past, it was dominated by a focus on joint regulation, particularly by collective bargaining between employers and employers' associations, and trade unions. However, one of the most prominent trends since the 1980s has been the diminution of joint regulation, as evidenced by the contraction of collective bargaining coverage (see Chapter 7), particularly in the private sector. This is associated with declining levels of unionization (see Chapter 6) and the fall in the incidence of union recognition (see Chapter 5)—trends which have been driven by the greater reluctance of employers to contemplate joint regulation alongside the changing composition of employment, such that employment growth has been concentrated in sectors where joint regulation is relatively scarce. Nevertheless, the continuing importance of collective bargaining as a means of regulating work and employment relationships should not be overlooked. It is still a commonplace feature of public sector employment relations, for example. Moreover, many major private sector employers maintain joint regulatory arrangements. Where it remains, however, collective bargaining has become less influential, its coverage has narrowed, and it has taken on a more consensual dimension, as is evident from the growing number of partnership agreements (see Chapter 6).

There is now much more of a concern with the efforts of employers to regulate work and employment relationships unilaterally, through relevant managerial policies and practices. Chapter 7, for example, showed how greater managerial attempts to exercise control over pay is a prominent feature of contemporary employment relations, particularly through the use of more variable payment systems. There has been much interest in the potential of the 'sophisticated HRM' approach to transform employment relations by generating greater organizational commitment and engagement among employees (see Chapter 5). However, insights drawn from a 'political economy' perspective on HRM highlight the fragile basis of commitment-based approaches (Thompson 2011). Most importantly, it demonstrates the difficulties and obstacles managers face in trying to enhance the commitment and engagement of employees, given demands placed on organizations for short-term financial success. Managers might emphasize the importance of commitment and engagement, but often come under pressure to ensure that labour is cheaper, more flexible, and disposable in the interests of short-term profitability.

It is important to recognize how managers have *attempted* to regulate work and employment relationships unilaterally, not that they have necessarily been successful in doing so. The nature of the employment relationship as a wage–work bargain implies that their efforts are invariably influenced by the need to respond to their employees' interests, or to secure their consent and cooperation. Custom and practice expectations remain an important feature of employment relations. The exercise of managerial prerogative is always an aspiration and, given that the employment relationship *is* a relationship in which managers must, to some degree, gain workers' cooperation, can never be fully realized in practice.

A further important regulatory development concerns the growing influence of the law on work and employment relationships, especially under Labour between 1997 and 2010. Employment protection and the rights of working people have become much more dependent on the law, as opposed to the situation in the past, when joint regulation was more influential (Dickens and Hall 2010). The growth in statutory employment rights has not just been the product of national-level legislation, like the National Minimum Wage (NMW) (see Chapter 7) and the statutory union recognition procedure (see Chapter 5). Following the Labour government's agreement to sign up to the 'Social Chapter' in 1997, European Union (EU) legislation increasingly came to affect work and employment relations. The work of the trade unions is increasingly concerned with campaigning for better legal rights for workers, with ensuring that existing statutory protections are upheld, and with using them as a base from which to bargain for improvements, such as over work–life balance arrangements (see Chapter 4).

Employers' bodies and business lobbyists frequently complain that the legal framework relating to employment matters has become too onerous and burdensome; in particular, the system of employment tribunals attracts a large amount of criticism for the costs it imposes on employers (see Chapter 10). Yet the framework of law is in fact highly favourable to employers. For one thing, while there may have been a considerable increase in the quantity of new employment laws and regulations during the 2000s, they had relatively little impact. Labour was concerned to enact legislation in a 'minimalist' way, so that it imposed as few constraints on business as possible. This was consistent with the neo-liberal assumptions that characterized Labour's policy framework, in particular the importance of deregulated labour markets as a source of economic competitiveness. Moreover, arrangements for enforcing employment rights remain weak. They depend too much on the preparedness of the worker concerned to exercise his or her rights, with all the risks that entails. In this context, there is growing interest in developing mechanisms, such as the greater use of proactive inspection arrangements, to ensure that employers abide by their legal obligations when it comes to how they treat their staff; this is part of a concern with making statutory employment rights more effective (Dickens 2012*b*) (see Chapter 10).

Influenced by the entreaties of employers' bodies and business lobbyists, since taking office the coalition has instituted a wide-ranging programme of employment deregulation, the outcome of which will be to make it manifestly more difficult for workers to assert their statutory employment rights. The coalition claims that employment protection laws are a major obstacle to economic recovery, because they discourage employers from taking on new staff and growing. Yet the government's own evidence for this assertion is weak, to say the least (e.g. Jordan et al. 2013). A more important driver, it seems, is ideology. The coalition's approach to employment relations matters takes the form of a 'reasserted neo-liberalism' (Grimshaw and Rubery 2012); employment regulation, because it impedes the actions of employers, is viewed as undesirable. The harsh economic climate has also helped to undermine the legal regulation of work and employment relationships. This is manifest in the growing incidence of 'bogus' self-employment arrangements, which relieve employers of their obligation to offer a wide range of employment rights (see Chapter 2), and the increasing use of 'free labour', such as internships, which enable employers to avoid the costs of complying with the NMW (see Chapter 7). Because alternative employment opportunities are so scarce, workers often have little choice other than to accept such arrangements.

Yet employment relations cannot simply be understood as the study of how work and employment relationships are regulated, since such an approach does not adequately capture the dynamic nature of the subject matter. This book is informed by the view that studying employment relations must involve a concern with not only how workers experience their employment relationships, but also how they contest and challenge their terms. This gives us a better, and more rounded, perspective on employment relations. For one thing, it is important to recognize that workers' experiences influence the regulation of work and employment relationships. The growth of pay inequality, for example, and related concerns about the prevalence of low pay in the economy, helped to stimulate efforts to secure the minimum wage (see Chapter 7). Moreover, governments have improved statutory provisions relating to family-friendly working arrangements partly in response to pressure from workers experiencing difficulties in combining paid employment with family responsibilities (see Chapter 4).

What, then, is to be said when it comes to making an overall assessment of workers' experiences in employment relations? On a positive note, it would seem that investment by employers in voice arrangements (see Chapter 5) means that workers are better informed about workplace and organizational decisions than in the past. They also seem to be more attached to their employing organizations: three-quarters of employees agree or strongly agree that they feel some loyalty to their organization (van Wanrooy et al. 2013). More negatively, however, it seems that genuine employee involvement and participation is rather limited in practice; workers have few opportunities actually to influence workplace or organizational decision-making. On a more profound note, there is little evidence that the sophisticated HRM agenda has had a positive effect on the experience of workers (Coats 2010). Persistently poor levels of employee engagement have been attributed to the low-trust climate that pervades many organizations (Sanders 2012), in part reflecting a growing perception that senior managers are increasingly distant from, and uninterested in, the well-being of the majority of their staff (see Chapter 5). Excessive and unjustifiable pay rises for senior executives, at a time when most workers are seeing a real-terms decline in wages, has not only increased the gap between the pay of those at the top and those further down the earnings hierarchy (see Chapter 7), but has also contributed to the diminution of trust in employment relations.

The economic downturn has had a marked adverse effect on the experiences of working people. As mentioned already, most people have suffered a slump in their real wages, of a kind not seen in over half a century. While the level of unemployment has not risen by as much as expected, many workers have suffered from a prolonged period of 'under-employment', for example by not being given sufficient hours (TUC 2012b). Employment has become more insecure and precarious, particularly for certain groups of workers such as young workers and migrant workers (see Chapter 2). Moreover, workers often come under pressure to forego their statutory employment rights and protections in order to secure a job, for example by being falsely categorized as 'self-employed' (see Chapter 2). One of the main contributions of this book, then, has been to offer a perspective on work and employment relations that differs from conventional human resource management (HRM) texts. These rarely, if at all, consider the experiences of workers and as a result often present a rather anodyne and insufficiently complex understanding of what happens in workplaces.

This concern with exploring the experiences of workers demonstrates that, whatever their other characteristics, work and employment relationships are marked by a basic antagonism between a generally powerful employer, who is driven by the need to manage staff in as efficient a way as possible, and a relatively powerless individual worker, who, in addition to having an interest in the success of their organization, is also concerned with being treated fairly and having some say over workplace and organizational decisions (Budd 2004). This difference of interests means that there is always the potential for conflict to arise in employment relations (Edwards 1986). This is made evident at a number of points in the book. For example, the discussion of organizing unionism in Chapter 6 demonstrates the potential for unionization among groups of workers who often have considerable and well-justified grievances about the way they are treated at work but have traditionally not been attracted to trade unions. Even in small, non-union firms, where one might expect managerial authority to be absolute, managers must accommodate the demands of workers. They are obliged to negotiate informally with workers over such matters as the organization and pace of work (Ram 1994; Dundon and Rollinson 2004)—see Chapter 5. Workers, then, are never entirely passive actors; they always enjoy some, however limited, capacity to challenge and contest the terms of their employment relationships.

The topic of labour conflict was given a substantial amount of attention in Chapter 9. Clearly, the strike is the most visible manifestation of such conflict (Hyman 1975). Among the reasons for the decline of strike activity are: the diminishing proportion of employment in 'strike-prone' industries; the contraction of trade union organization; the articulation of a more assertive management style that aims to make strikes superfluous; and, in particular, the enactment of a whole raft of restrictive legislation. The legal framework places numerous obstacles in the way of trade unions hoping to undertake industrial action, including opportunities for employers to apply to the courts for injunctions that prevent it. However, there is some evidence that the harsh economic climate has been responsible for an increase in the level of strike activity, as unionized workers challenge proposed cuts to jobs, pay, and pensions, particularly in public sector organizations. Just because there has been a decline in the level of strike activity it does not follow that conflict is no longer an important feature of employment relations. Mobilization theory, by focusing on how employees acquire a sense of grievance and the way grievances are translated into collective action, suggests that the capacity of unions to organize workers and mobilize around their discontents is a crucial determinant of whether or not industrial action occurs (Kelly 1998). There are a variety of behaviours at work that can come under the umbrella of labour conflict, including sabotage and absenteeism for example. The harsh economic situation has prompted instances of direct action by workers protesting against plant closures and job cuts (Gall 2011a). Moreover, the growth in the number of employment tribunal claims during the 2000s is a reflection of high levels of discontent among workers—further evidence of the potential for conflict at work (see Chapter 10).

While the decline of joint regulation has given employers more opportunities to attempt to regulate the employment relationship on a unilateral basis, the inherent potential for conflict it contains means that workers will always need, and demand, independent means of expressing their interests. During periods of economic difficulty, the inherent potential conflict of interest that lies at the heart of work and employment relationships becomes more evident. While some firms have clearly tried to reduce the scope for job losses, by using short-term working or temporary lay-offs to cope with falling demand, ultimately workers are disposable. How many otherwise profitable companies have used the economic recession as an excuse to cut jobs? For all the supposed efforts by employers to engage staff, and to secure their cooperation with, and commitment to, organizational goals, the terms of people's employment relationships are, and will remain, contested. Moreover, austerity measures devised in response to the economic crisis have been responsible for a wave of social and labour unrest around the world (ILO 2011). All this suggests, then, that in future work and employment relationships will remain a source of potential conflict. Moreover, the continuing economic downturn is likely to be a source of further disputes as workers struggle to retain their jobs, seek to improve the terms on which their employment is terminated, or protest against government and employer policies that threaten their livelihoods.

The potential for conflict lies at the heart of employment relations. The legal regulation of employment relationships (e.g. anti-strike laws, minimum wages, etc.), joint regulation (union recognition agreements), and efforts at unilateral regulation by employers (e.g. voice mechanisms like company councils) can all help to contain it. They prevent the basic antagonism that marks the employment relationship from manifesting itself in the form of disputes, industrial action, or other kinds of conflictual behaviour. Ultimately, though, the imbalance of power that exists between a relatively powerful employer and a relatively powerless individual employee, and the different interests that they have, means that employment relations has to be concerned with the ways in which employment relationships are contested, as well as how they are experienced and regulated.

Key terms and concepts

Agenda for Change: a national pay and grading scheme that covers employees in the National Health Service.

Annualized hours: arrangements that specify the number of hours to be worked by employees over a year, in return for a guaranteed wage.

Arbitration: a process of resolving disputes in which an independent third party proposes a settlement based on information supplied by, and the arguments of, the respective parties.

Coercive comparisons: a process used by multinational companies to compare the performance data of plants in different countries in order to exert pressure on under-performing plants to improve.

Collective agreements: agreements that are the outcomes of collective bargaining exercises.

Collective bargaining: this term is used to refer to the process by which pay and other conditions of employment are regulated jointly by an employer, or employers' association, and one or more trade unions.

Conciliation: a process of resolving disputes in which an independent third party helps the parties to reach their own settlement.

Convergence: an approach to understanding the impact of globalization which emphasizes the growing degree of uniformity in employment relations arrangements around the world.

Custom and practice: tacit and informal expectations and understandings that govern behaviour at work.

Divergence: an approach to understanding the impact of globalization which emphasizes the persistence of national-level diversity in the employment relations arrangements of different countries.

Employers' association: a body that represents the employment and employment relations interests of a collective group of employers, often on an industry-wide basis.

Employee involvement and participation: arrangements that enable workers to exercise influence over organizational or workplace decisions, or that allow managers to communicate with their staff.

Employment tribunal: a quasi-judicial body that deals with complaints from workers that employers have failed to uphold their employment rights.

Equality bargaining: trade union initiatives that are designed to reduce disadvantage at work through interventions targeted at employers.

Equal opportunity: an approach to reducing employment disadvantage which focuses on the use of formal procedures to ensure that people are treated the same regardless of their social and personal characteristics.

European Employment Strategy: an EU-level initiative designed to tackle unemployment, social exclusion, and labour market disadvantage by promoting employability and better quality jobs.

European works councils: arrangements that exist in multinational companies for informing and consulting with employee and trade union representatives at a European level.

Globalization: refers to the growing interconnectedness of economic activities across and beyond national borders.

Hard regulation: the use of legally binding methods to secure policy objectives.

Harmonization: a process whereby any differences in non-wage terms and conditions of employment between different groups of staff in the same organization are reduced and eradicated.

Horizontal segregation: the over-representation of a specific category of workers in some occupations, and their under-representation in others.

Industrial action: a term that is generally used to refer to more 'organized' manifestations of labour conflict, such as working to rule, and the strike.

International labour standards: arrangements for regulating the terms and conditions of employment relationships above and beyond individual nation states.

Joint consultation: a form of workplace and organizational decision-making under which managers submit their proposals to employees, or their representatives, to gauge their views, but retain the right to make the final decision.

Joint regulation: a term used to refer to the process by which terms and conditions of employment are determined jointly, as a result of bargaining between employers, or employers' associations, and one or more trade unions.

Juridification: a term used to refer to the way in which aspects of economic and social policy are regulated by the law.

Labour codes of conduct: voluntary arrangements under which multinational companies agree to uphold certain specified labour standards across their supply chains.

Labour conflict: a term that is generally used to refer to the broad range of behaviours that express the antagonistic basis of the employment relationship.

Management style: the set of underlying principles that govern how employees are managed in particular organizations.

Managerial prerogative: managers' belief that they should exercise unilateral control over workplace relations.

Managing diversity: an approach to reducing employment disadvantage which is concerned with recognizing and celebrating individual differences between employees.

Mediation: a non-judgemental approach to resolving disputes, where the mediator helps the parties to reach an agreement.

Mobilization theory: a theoretical perspective used to explain why individual grievances are translated into collective action against employers.

Multinational company: a firm that invests in, and is responsible for, subsidiaries located in territories beyond its home country base.

Multi-employer bargaining: this term applies to situations where collective bargaining takes place between a collective group of employers, usually in the form of an employers' association, and one or more trade unions.

Negotiation: a process of resolving employment disputes through the presentation of arguments and compromise.

Neo-liberalism: a political and economic perspective which holds that economic prosperity is best achieved through deregulated markets, privatization, and weak trade unions.

Neo-unitary: a variant of the unitary perspective in which the emphasis is placed on the use of sophisticated human resource management practices to elicit employees' commitment.

Open Method of Coordination: a means of realizing the social and employment objectives of the European Union through voluntary, non-legally binding methods.

Overtime ban: a form of labour conflict which involves workers collectively refusing to undertake paid or unpaid overtime arrangements.

Partnership agreement: a term used to describe a formal relationship between an employer and a union that is based on the importance of cooperation and shared interests, rather than conflict.

Pay review body: independent bodies whose purpose is to make non-binding recommendations to government concerning the pay of particular groups of public sector workers.

Performance-related pay: an arrangement for determining pay that links an element of a worker's reward to some measure of their performance at work.

Pluralist: a perspective on employment relations that recognizes that employers and employees may have conflicting interests, but that these can be resolved to the mutual benefit of both by means of formal procedures, bargaining relationships with trade unions in particular.

Positive action: measures designed to correct the under-representation of certain groups of workers through interventions which help their employment prospects.

Positive discrimination: measures designed to correct the under-representation of certain groups of workers by giving them preferential treatment—unlawful in the UK.

Procedural agreement: a type of agreement that sets out the rules, or procedure, governing the relationship between the parties to it (such as the issues to be determined by collective bargaining, for example).

Protectionism: a political and economic perspective which holds that jobs in one's own country should be given priority over those in other countries.

Race to the bottom: an escalating process of weakened labour protections, caused by the tendency for multinationals to prefer investing in locations with low employment costs.

Radical: a perspective on employment relations that recognizes that employers and employees have potentially conflicting interests, which are so deep-rooted that when disputes arise they are incapable of being resolved to the mutual satisfaction of both parties.

Redundancy: a term used to refer to the dismissal of workers on the grounds that the number of workers required in a particular area has diminished.

Regime competition: the process by which multinational companies use investment and disinvestment decisions to encourage countries to dilute their labour regulations.

Secondary industrial action: sometimes referred to as 'sympathy' action, this term is used to describe action undertaken by one group of workers, who are not involved in a dispute with their own employer, to support another group of workers who are engaged in a dispute with their employer.

Self-employment: a form of employment under which an individual worker works for him- or herself, and not under the control of another employer.

Shop steward: a term that is often used in the UK to refer to unpaid union representatives in the workplace.

Social class: hierarchical divisions in society which reflect differences in people's access to material resources and that influence their life chances.

Social clause: the part of a trade agreement that deals with non-economic matters, such as employment standards.

Social dialogue: a term that is used particularly by the European Union to refer to discussions, consultations, exchanges of information, and negotiations between the social partners.

Social dumping: a term that is used to refer to situations where multinational corporations redirect investment, and therefore jobs, to locations where the costs of employment are lower.

Social partners: a term that is commonly applied by the European Union to the representative bodies of employees, trade unions, and employers.

Soft regulation: the use of non-legally binding methods to secure policy objectives (e.g. guidelines, targets).

Sophisticated human resource management: an approach to managing people at work based on engaging employees and winning their commitment to the organization, as a means of driving improvements in business performance.

Status divide: refers to the differential treatment in respect of non-wage terms and conditions of employment accorded to different groups of workers in the same organization.

Statutory union recognition procedure: a legislative basis for establishing union recognition under certain defined circumstances.

Strike: the temporary withdrawal of labour by a group of workers, undertaken in order to express a grievance or to enforce a demand.

Substantive agreement: a type of agreement that covers the substance, or the outcomes, of a collective bargaining encounter.

Teamworking: a form of employee involvement and participation under which workers are organized collectively into specific groups for the purposes of making a product or delivering a service, sometimes with a degree of autonomy and self-management.

Team briefing: a form of employee involvement and participation which involves front-line managers or supervisors sharing information with, and sometimes responding to queries from, their immediate staff.

Trade union: a collective organization of working people which works to improve their terms and conditions of employment.

Tripartism: a term used to refer to arrangements that facilitate the involvement of three parties—the government, unions, employers—in economic and social policy-making.

Union derecognition: the act of an employer who decides not to maintain union recognition.

Union recognition: the act of an employer who agrees to enter into a formal relationship, usually involving collective bargaining, with a trade union.

Unitary: a perspective on employment relations that emphasizes the harmony of interests that exist between employers and their employees.

Vertical segregation: the over-representation of a specific category of workers in low-paid and poorly skilled jobs, and their under-representation in managerial roles.

Voluntarism: a term that is used to describe the absence of state intervention in relations between employers and their employees, and between employers and trade unions.

Voluntary redundancy: a form of redundancy whereby workers supposedly put themselves forward for dismissal, in return for an enhanced severance payment.

Work intensification: a term that is used to describe the process of greater work effort.

Work-to-rule: a form of industrial action where the workers involved refuse to carry out a part, or parts, of their normal duties while continuing to attend work.

Bibliography

Abbott, B. (2004). 'Worker representation through the Citizens' Advice Bureaux', in G. Healy, E. Heery, P. Taylor, and W. Brown (eds.), *The Future of Worker Representation*. London: Routledge, 245–63.

Abbott, B. (2007). 'Workplace and employment characteristics of the Citizens Advice Bureau clients'. *Employee Relations*, 29/3: 262–79.

Ackers, P. (2011). 'Finding the future in the past? The social philosophy of Oxford industrial relations pluralism', in K. Townsend and A. Wilkinson (eds.), *The Edward Elgar Research Handbook on Work and Employment Relations*. Cheltenham: Edward Elgar, 45–66.

Ackers, P. and Payne, J. (1998). 'British trade unions and social partnership: rhetoric, reality and strategy'. *International Journal of Human Resource Management*, 9/3: 529–50.

Ackers, P. and Wilkinson, A. (2003). 'Introduction: the British industrial relations tradition—formation, breakdown and salvage', in P. Ackers and A. Wilkinson (eds.), *Understanding Work and Employment: Industrial Relations in Transition*. Oxford: Oxford University Press, 1–27.

Ackers, P. and Wilkinson, A. (2005). 'British industrial relations paradigm: a critical outline history and prognosis'. *Journal of Industrial Relations*, 47/4: 443–56.

Ackroyd, S. and Proctor, S. (1998). 'British manufacturing organization and workplace industrial relations: some attributes of the new flexible firm'. *British Journal of Industrial Relations*, 36/2: 163–83.

Ackroyd, S. and Thompson, P. (1999). *Organizational Misbehaviour*. London: Sage.

Adam-Smith, D., Norris, G., and Williams, S. (2003). 'Continuity or change? The implications of the National Minimum Wage for work and employment in the hospitality industry'. *Work, Employment and Society*, 17/1: 29–45.

Adnett, N. and Hardy, S. (2005). *The European Social Model: Modernisation or Evolution?* Cheltenham: Edward Elgar.

Advisory, Conciliation, and Arbitration Service (ACAS) (2007a). *Annual Report and Accounts 2006/07*. London: ACAS.

Advisory, Conciliation, and Arbitration Service (ACAS) (2007b). *Corporate Plan 2007-2010*. London: ACAS.

Advisory, Conciliation and Arbitration Service (ACAS) (2010). *Managing Attendance and Employee Turnover*. London: ACAS.

Advisory, Conciliation and Arbitration Service (ACAS) (2011). *Discipline and Grievances at Work: The ACAS Guide*. London: ACAS.

Advisory, Conciliation, and Arbitration Service (ACAS) (2012). *Annual Report and Accounts 2011-12*. London: ACAS.

Ahlstrand, B. (1990). *The Quest for Productivity: A Case Study of Fawley after Flanders*. Cambridge: Cambridge University Press.

Aitkenhead, M. and Liff, S. (1991). 'The effectiveness of equal opportunities policies', in J. Firth-Cozens and M. West (eds.), *Women at Work*. Buckingham: Open University Press, 26–41.

Alderman, K. and Carter, N. (1994). 'The Labour party and the trade unions: loosening the ties'. *Parliamentary Affairs*, 47/3: 321–37.

Almond, P., Edwards, T., Colling, T., Ferner, A., Gunnigle, P., Müller-Camen, M., Quintanilla, J., and Wächter, H. (2005). 'Unravelling home and host country effects: an investigation of the HR policies of an American multinational in four European countries'. *Industrial Relations*, 44/2: 276–306.

Alston, P. (2004). '"Core labour standards" and the transformation of the international labour rights regime'. *European Journal of International Law*, 15/3: 457–521.

Anderman, S. (1986). 'Unfair dismissals and redundancy', in R. Lewis (ed.), *Labour Law in Britain*. Oxford: Basil Blackwell, 415–47.

Anderson, B. (2010). 'Migration, immigration controls and the fashioning of precarious workers'. *Work, Employment and Society*, 24/2: 300–17.

Anderson, L. (2003). 'Sound bite legislation: the Employment Act 2002 and the new flexible working "rights" for parents'. *Industrial Law Journal*, 32/1: 37–42.

Anderson, P. (2009). 'Intermediate occupations and the conceptual and empirical limitations of the hourglass economy thesis'. *Work, Employment, and Society*, 23/1: 169–80.

Anderson, P. (2011). *The New Old World* (paperback edn). London: Verso.

Anner, M., Greer, I., Hauptmeier, M., Lillie, N., and Winchester, N. (2006). 'The industrial determinants of transnational solidarity: global interunion politics in three sectors'. *European Journal of Industrial Relations*, 12/7: 7–27.

Applebaum, E., Bailey, T., Berg, P., and Kalleberg, A. (2000). *Manufacturing Advantage: Why High-Performance Work Systems Pay Off*. Ithaca NY: Cornell University Press.

Arrowsmith, J. (2002). 'The struggle over working time in nineteenth and twentieth century Britain'. *Historical Studies in Industrial Relations*, 13: 83–117.

Arrowsmith, J. (2007). 'Why is there not more "annualised hours" working in Britain?'. *Industrial Relations Journal*, 38/5: 423–38.

Arrowsmith, J. (2009). 'Regulating pay: the UK's national minimum wage', in S. Corby, S. Palmer, and E. Lindop (eds.), *Rethinking Reward*. Basingstoke: Palgrave Macmillan, 120–38.

Arrowsmith, J. and Marginson, P. (2010). 'The decline of incentive pay in British manufacturing'. *Industrial Relations Journal*, 41/4: 289–311.

Arrowsmith, J. and Marginson, P. (2011). 'Variable pay and collective bargaining in British retail banking'. *British Journal of Industrial Relations*, 49/1: 54–79.

Arrowsmith, J., Nicholaisen, H., Bechter, B., and Nonell, R. (2010). 'The management of variable pay in European banking'. *The International Journal of Human Resource Management*, 21/15: 2716–40.

Arrowsmith, J. and Sisson, K. (1999). 'Pay and working time: towards organization-based systems?'. *British Journal of Industrial Relations*, 37/1: 57–75.

Arrowsmith, J. and Sisson, K. (2000). 'Managing working time', in S. Bach and K. Sisson (eds.), *Personnel Management* (3rd edn). Oxford: Blackwell, 287–313.

Ashley, L. (2010). 'Making a difference? The use (and abuse) of diversity management at the UK's elite law firms'. *Work, Employment, and Society*, 24/4: 711–27.

Ashwin, S. (2011). 'Russian unions after communism: a study in subordination', in G. Gall, A. Wilkinson, and R. Hurd (eds.), *The International Handbook of Labour Unions: Responses to Neo-Liberalism*. Cheltenham: Edward Elgar, 187–206.

Aston, J., Hill, D., and Tackey, N. (2006). *The Experience of Claimants in Race Discrimination Employment Tribunals*. DTI Employment Research Series No. 55 London: DTI.

Atkinson, A. and McKay, S. (2005). *Child Support Reform: The Views and Experiences of CSA Staff and New Clients*. Department for Work and Pensions Research Report No. 232. London: Department for Work and Pensions.

Atzeni, M. (2009). 'Searching for injustice and finding solidarity? A contribution to the mobilization theory debate'. *Industrial Relations Journal*, 40/1: 5–16.

Auerbach, S. (1990). *Legislating for Conflict*. Oxford: Clarendon.

Bach, S. (2010). 'Public sector industrial relations: the challenge of modernisation', in T. Colling and M. Terry (eds.), *Industrial Relations: Theory and Practice* (3rd edn). Chichester: John Wiley, 151–77.

Bach, S. (2011). 'Assistant roles in a modernised public service: towards a new professionalism?', in S. Corby and G. Symon (eds.), *Working for the State*. Basingstoke: Palgrave Macmillan, 129–46.

Bach, S. (2012). 'Shrinking the state or the Big Society? Public service employment relations in an era of austerity'. *Industrial Relations Journal*, 43/5: 399–415.

Bach, S., and Kessler, I., (2012). *The Modernisation of the Public Sector and Employee Relations: Targeted Change*. Basingstoke: Palgrave Macmillan.

Bach, S., Kessler, I., and Heron, P., (2006). 'Changing job boundaries and workforce reform: the case of teaching assistants'. *Industrial Relations Journal*, 37/1: 2–21.

Bach, S., Kolins Givan, R., and Forth, J., (2009). 'The public sector in transition', in W. Brown, A. Bryson, J. Forth, and K. Whitfield (eds.), *The Evolution of the Modern Workplace*. Cambridge: Cambridge University Press, 307–31.

Bacon, N. (1999). 'Union derecognition and the new human relations: a steel industry case study'. *Work, Employment and Society*, 13/1: 1–17.

Bacon, N. and Hoque, K. (2012). 'The role and impact of trade union equality representatives in Britain'. *British Journal of Industrial Relations*, 50/2, 239–62.

Bacon, N. and Samuel, P. (2009). 'Partnership agreement adoption and survival in the British private and public sectors'. *Work, Employment and Society*, 23/2: 231–48.

Bacon, N. and Wright, M. (2008). 'Private equity: friend or foe? The case for'. *People Management*, 21 August: 21–2.

Bacon, N., Wright, M., Scholes, L., and Meuleman, M. (2010). 'Assessing the impact of private equity on industrial relations in Europe'. *Human Relations*, 63/9: 1343–70.

Badigannavar, V. and Kelly, J. (2004). 'Labour-management partnership on the public sector', in J. Kelly and P. Willman (eds.), *Union Organization and Activity*. London: Routledge, 110–28.

Badigannavar, V. and Kelly, J. (2005). 'Why are some union organizing campaigns more successful than others?'. *British Journal of Industrial Relations*, 43/3: 515–35.

Badigannavar, V. and Kelly, J. (2011). 'Partnership and organizing: an empirical assessment of two contrasting approaches to union revitalization in the UK'. *Economic and Industrial Democracy*, 32/1: 5–27.

Bain, G. and Price, R. (1983). 'Union growth: dimensions, determinants and destiny', in G. Bain (ed.), *Industrial Relations in Britain*. Oxford: Basil Blackwell, 3–33.

Bairstow, S. (2004). *'Outing the Unions': Sexual Identity, Membership Diversity and the British Trade Union Movement*. Unpublished PhD thesis, University of Portsmouth.

Baldamus, W. (1961). *Efficiency and Effort*. London: Tavistock.

Baldry, C., Bain, P., and Taylor, P. (1998). ' "Bright satanic offices": intensification, control and team Taylorism', in P. Thompson and C. Warhurst (eds.), *Workplaces of the Future*. Basingstoke: Macmillan, 163–83.

Baldry, C., Bain, P., Taylor, P., Hyman, J., Scholarios, D., Marks, A., Watson, A., Gilbert, K., Gall, G., and Bunzel, D. (2007). *The Meaning of Work in the New Economy*. Basingstoke: Palgrave Macmillan.

Bara, A. and Arber, S. (2009). 'Working shifts and mental health–findings from the British Household Panel Survey (1995–2005)'. *Scandinavian Journal of Work, Environment, and Health*, 35/5: 361–7.

Barkham, P. (2005). 'Blogger sacked for sounding off'. *The Guardian*, 12 January, http://www.guardian.co.uk/technology/2005/jan/12/books.newmedia

Barley, S. and Kunda, G. (2004). *Gurus, Hired Guns, and Warm Bodies*. Princeton NJ: Princeton University Press.

Barnard, C. (2009). ' "British jobs for British workers": the Lindsey Oil Refinery dispute and the future of local labour clauses in an integrated EU market'. *Industrial Law Journal*, 38/3: 245–77.

Barnard, C. (2012). 'The financial crisis and the Euro Plus Pact: a labour lawyer's perspective'. *Industrial Law Journal*, 41/1: 98–114.

Barnard, C., Deakin, S., and Hobbs, R. (2003). 'Opting out of the 48-hour week: employer necessity or individual choice? An empirical study of the operation of article 18(1)(b) of the Working Time Directive in the UK'. *Industrial Law Journal*, 32/4: 223–52.

Barnes, C. (1992). 'Disability and employment'. *Personnel Review*, 21/6: 55–73.

Barnett, E. (2011). 'Employers warned about snooping on staff via social networks'. *The Telegraph*, 1 September, http://www.telegraph.co.uk/technology/news/8734904/Employers-warned-about-snooping-on-staff-via-social-networks.html

Barrientos, S., Mayer, F., Pickles, J., and Posthuma, A. (2011). 'Decent work in global production networks: framing the policy debate'. *International Labour Review*, 150/3–4: 299–317.

Barrientos, S. and Smith, S. (2006). *The ETI Code of Labour Practice: Do Workers Really Benefit?* University of Sussex: Institute of Development Studies.

Bassett, P. (1987). *Strike Free*. London: Papermac.

Batstone, E., Boraston, I., and Frenkel, S. (1978). *The Social Organization of Strikes*. Oxford: Basil Blackwell.

BBC Democracy Live (2012). 'Westminster Hall Debate', 26 April, http://news.bbc.co.uk/democracylive/hi/house_of_commons/newsid_9715000/9715541.stm

BBC News Online (2009a). 'Striking workers stand firm on British jobs', 4 February, http://news.bbc.co.uk/1/hi/england/humber/7869873.stm

BBC News Online (2009b). 'Restaurant tipping law to change', 1 October, http://news.bbc.co.uk/1/hi/business/7533863.stm

BBC News Online (2009c). 'Job cuts at Mini spark angry rows', 16 February, http://news.bbc.co.uk/1/hi/business/7891913.stm

BBC News Online (2009d). 'Sacked Mini workers express anger', 16 February, http://news.bbc.co.uk/1/hi/business/7892174.stm

BBC News Online (2009e). 'Cap on junior doctor hours starts', 1 August, http://news.bbc.co.uk/1/hi/health/8177878.stm

BBC News Online (2010). 'Cut working week to 21 hours, urges think tank', 13 February, http://news.bbc.co.uk/1/hi/business/8513783.stm

BBC News Online (2011a). 'Q&A: what's the BA dispute about?', 12 May, http://www.bbc.co.uk/news/business-11868081

BBC News Online (2011b). 'MP Charlotte Leslie wants to scrap doctors hours rule'. 13 May, http://www.bbc.co.uk/news/uk-england-bristol-13386320

BBC News Online (2012a). 'Five million paid less than living wages, says KPMG', 29 October, http://www.bbc.co.uk/news/business-20104177

BBC News Online (2012b). 'Unilever to face more pension action, workers warn', 31 January, http://www.bbc.co.uk/news/business-16786204

BBC News Online (2012c). 'Unilever pension dispute breakthrough', 12 April, http://www.bbc.co.uk/news/business-17687807

BBC News Online (2012d). 'Southampton council pay cuts will be reversed', 16 August, http://www.bbc.co.uk/news/uk-england-hampshire-19288806

BBC News Online (2013a). 'GMB union holds protests at Amazon sites', 13 February, http://www.bbc.co.uk/news/uk-21444710

BBC News Online (2013b). 'Back-to-work scheme breached laws, says Court of Appeal', 12 February, http://www.bbc.co.uk/news/business-21426928

BBC Panorama (2011). *All Work and Low Pay*, 3 October, http://www.bbc.co.uk/programmes/b015r35d

BBC Panorama (2013). *Blacklist Britain*, 10 June, http://www.bbc.co.uk/programmes/b02xcn7d

Beaumont, P. (1981). 'Trade union recognition: the British experience 1976–1980'. *Employee Relations*, 3/6: 2–39.

Beaumont, P. and Harris, R. (1990). 'Union recruitment and organising attempts in Britain in the 1980s'. *Industrial Relations Journal*, 21/4: 274–86.

Beauregard, T. and Henry, L. (2009). 'Making the link between work-life balance practices and organizational performance'. *Human Resource Management Review*, 19/1: 9–22.

Beecroft, A. (2011). *Report on Employment Law*. London: BIS. http://www.bis.gov.uk/assets/biscore/employment-matters/docs/r/12-825-report-on-employment-law-beecroft.pdf

Behrend, H. (1957). 'The effort bargain'. *Industrial and Labor Relations Review*, 10/4, 503–15.

Bennett, F. and Lister, R. (2010). *The 'Living Wage': The Right Answer to Low Pay?* London: Fabian Society.

Bercusson, B. (1978). *Fair Wages Resolutions*. London: Mansell.

BERR (2008). *Agency Working in the UK: A Review of the Evidence*. Employment Relations Research Series No. 93, London: Department for Business, Enterprise, and Regulatory Reform.

Bewley, H. (2006). 'Raising the standard? The regulation of employment, and public sector employment policy'. *British Journal of Industrial Relations*, 44/2: 351–72.

Bewley, H. and Fernie, S. (2003). 'What do unions do for women?', in H. Gospel and S. Wood (eds.), *Representing Workers*. London: Routledge, 92–118.

Beynon, H. (1973). *Working for Ford*. Harmondsworth: Penguin.

Beynon, H. (ed.) (1985). *Digging Deeper: Issues in the Miners' Strike*. London: Verso.

Beynon, H., Grimshaw, D., Rubery, J., and Ward, K. (2002). *Managing Employment Change*. Oxford: Oxford University Press.

Bhagwati, J. (2004). *In Defense of Globalization*. Oxford: Oxford University Press.

Bieling, H.-J. (2012). 'EU facing the crisis: social and employment policies in times of tight budgets'. *Transfer: European Review of Labour and Research*, 18/3: 255–71.

Blakemore, K. and Drake, R. (1996). *Understanding Equal Opportunity Policies*. Hemel Hempstead: Harvester-Wheatsheaf.

Blanchflower, D. and Bryson, A. (2009). 'Trade union decline and the economics of the workplace', in W. Brown, A. Bryson, J. Forth, and K. Whitfield (eds.), *The Evolution of the Modern Workplace*. Cambridge: Cambridge University Press, 48–73.

Blanden, J., Machin, S., and Van Reenen, J. (2006). 'Have unions turned the corner? New evidence on recent trends in union recognition in UK firms'. *British Journal of Industrial Relations*, 44/2: 169–90.

Blyton, P. (2011). 'Working time, work-life balance and inequality', in P. Blyton, E. Heery, and P. Turnbull (eds.), *Reassessing the Employment Relationship*. Basingstoke: Palgrave Macmillan, 299–317.

Blyton, P., Heery, E., and Turnbull, P. (2011). 'Reassessing the employment relationship: an introduction', in P. Blyton, E. Heery, and P. Turnbull (eds.), *Reassessing the Employment Relationship*. Basingstoke: Palgrave Macmillan, 1–17.

Blyton, P. and Jenkins, J. (2012a). 'Mobilizing protest: insights from two factory closures'. *British Journal of Industrial Relations*, early view: DOI:10.1111/j. 1467-8543. 2012.00906.x

Blyton, P. and Jenkins, J. (2012b). 'Life after Burberry: shifting experiences of work and non-work life following redundancy', *Work, Employment and Society*, 26/1, 26–41.

Blyton, P. and Turnbull, P. (2004). *The Dynamics of Employee Relations* (3rd edn). Basingstoke: Palgrave Macmillan.

Bogg, A. (2012). 'The death of statutory union recognition in the United Kingdom'. *Journal of Industrial Relations*, 54/3: 409–25.

Boito, A. and Marcelino, P. (2011). 'Decline in unionism? An analysis of the new wave of strikes in Brazil'. *Latin American Perspectives*, 38/5: 62–73.

Bolton, S. (2004). *Emotion Management in the Workplace*. Basingstoke: Palgrave Macmillan.

Bolton, S. and Houlihan, M. (eds.) (2007). *Searching for the Human in Human Resource Management*. Basingstoke: Palgrave Macmillan.

Bonner, C. and Gollan, P. (2005). 'A bridge over troubled water: a decade of representation at South West Water'. *Employee Relations*, 27/3: 238–58.

Booth, R. (2012). 'Addison Lee minicabs serving ministers despite pledge to illegally use bus lanes'. *The Guardian*, 17 April, http://www.guardian.co.uk/uk/2012/apr/17/addison-lee-ministers-bus-lanes

Boxall, P. and Macky, K. (2009). 'Research and theory on high-performance work systems: progressing the high-involvement stream'. *Human Resource Management Journal*, 19/1, 3–23.

Boxall, P. and Purcell, J. (2011). *Strategy and Human Resource Management* (3rd edn). Basingstoke: Palgrave Macmillan.

Boyd, C. (2001). 'HRM in the airline industry: strategies and outcomes'. *Personnel Review*, 30/4: 438–53.

Boyd, S. (2012). 'Amazon is a tax avoider because Amazon is a predatory, anti-union employer'. *Union-News.co.uk*, 13 April, http://union-news.co.uk/2012/04/amazon-is-a-tax-avoider-because-amazon-is-a-predatory-anti-union-employer/

Bradley, H. (1989). *Men's Work, Women's Work*. Cambridge: Polity.

Bradley, H. (1999). *Gender and Power in the Workplace*. Basingstoke: Macmillan.

Bradley, H., Erickson, M., Stephenson, C., and Williams, S. (2000). *Myths at Work*. Cambridge: Polity.

Bradley, H. and Healy, G. (2008). *Ethnicity and Gender at Work*. Basingstoke: Palgrave Macmillan.

Bradley, H., Healy, G., and Mukherjee, N. (2002). *Inclusion, Exclusion and Separate Organisation—Black Women Activists in Trade Unions*. ESRC Future of Work Programme, Working Paper No. 25 Swindon: ESRC.

Brannen, P. (1983). *Authority and Participation in Industry*. London: Batsford.

Brewer, M., Muriel, A., Phillips, D., and Sibieta, L. (2008). *Poverty and Inequality in the UK: 2008. IFS Commentary No. 105* London: Institute for Fiscal Studies.

Bridgford, J. and Stirling, J. (1994). *Employee Relations in Europe*. Oxford: Blackwell.

Brinkley, I. (2012). 'Technology is stretching the working day, but it doesn't have to be bad news', *The Guardian*, 27 June, http://www.guardian.co.uk/commentisfree/2012/jun/27/technology-stretching-working-day-bad-news?INTCMP=SRCH

Brinkley, I., Coats, D., and Overell, S. (2007). *7 out of 10: Labour under Labour*. London: Work Foundation.

British Universities Industrial Relations Association (BUIRA) (2009). 'What's the point of industrial relations?', in R. Darlington (ed.), *What's the Point of Industrial Relations? In Defence of Critical Social Science*. London: British Universities Industrial Relations Association, 46–59.

Brodtkorb, T. (2012). 'Statutory union recognition in the UK: a work in progress'. *Industrial Relations Journal*, 43/1: 70–84.

Bronfenbrenner, K. and Juravich, T. (1998). 'It takes more than house calls: organizing to win with a comprehensive union-building strategy', in K. Bronfenbrenner, S. Friedman, R. Hurd, R. Oswald, and R. Seeber (eds.), *Organizing to Win: New Research on Union Strategies*. Ithaca NY: ILR Press, 19–36.

Brown, D. (2001). 'Labor standards: where do they belong on the international trade agenda?'. *Journal of Economic Perspectives*, 15/3: 89–112.

Brown, D. and Crossman, A. (2000). 'Employer strategies in the face of a national minimum wage: an analysis of the hotel sector'. *Industrial Relations Journal*, 31/3: 206–19.

Brown, G. (1977). *Sabotage*. Nottingham: Spokesman.

Brown, W. (1973). *Piecework Bargaining*. London: Heinemann.

Brown, W. (ed.) (1981). *The Changing Contours of British Industrial Relations*. Oxford: Basil Blackwell.

Brown, W. (2000). 'Putting partnership into practice in Britain'. *British Journal of Industrial Relations*, 38/2: 299–316.

Brown, W. (2009). 'The process of fixing the British National Minimum Wage, 1997–2007'. *British Journal of Industrial Relations*, 47/2: 429–43.

Brown, W. (2010). 'Negotiation and collective bargaining', in T. Colling and M. Terry (eds.), *Industrial Relations: Theory and Practice* (3rd edn). Chichester: John Wiley, 255–74.

Brown, W. (2011). 'Industrial relations under New Labour, 1997–2010: a post mortem'. *Journal of Industrial Relations*, 47/2: 402–13.

Brown, W., Bryson, A., and Forth, J. (2009). 'Competition and the retreat from collective bargaining', in W. Brown, A. Bryson, J. Forth, and K. Whitfield (eds.), *The Evolution of the Modern Workplace*. Cambridge: Cambridge University Press, 22–47.

Brown, W., Deakin, S., Hudson, M., and Pratten, C. (2001). 'The limits of statutory union recognition'. *Industrial Relations Journal*, 32/3: 180–94.

Brown, W., Marginson, P., and Walsh, J. (1995). 'Management: pay determination and collective bargaining', in P. Edwards (ed.), *Industrial Relations: Theory and Practice in Britain*. Oxford: Blackwell, 123–50.

Brown, W., Marginson, P., and Walsh, J. (2003). 'The management of pay as the influence of collective bargaining declines', in P. Edwards (ed.), *Industrial Relations* (2nd edn). Oxford: Blackwell, 189–213.

Brown, W. and Marsden, D. (2011). 'Individualization and growing diversity of employment relationships', in D. Marsden (ed.), *Employment in the Lean Years: Policy and Prospects for the Next Decade*. Oxford: Oxford University Press, 73–86.

Brown, W. and Nash, D. (2008). 'What has been happening to collective bargaining under New Labour?'. *Industrial Relations Journal*, 39/2: 91–103.

Brown, W. and Nolan, P. (1988). 'Wages and labour productivity: the contribution of industrial relations research to the understanding of pay determination'. *British Journal of Industrial Relations*, 26/3: 339–61.

Brown, W. and Walsh, J. (1991). 'Pay determination in Britain in the 1980s; the anatomy of decentralization'. *Oxford Review of Economic Policy*, 7/1: 44–59.

Brown, W. and Walsh, J. (1994). 'Managing pay in Britain', in K. Sisson (ed.), *Personnel Management* (2nd edn). Oxford: Blackwell, 437–64.

Brownlie, N. (2012). *Trade Union Membership 2011.* London: Department for Business, Innovation, and Skills.

Budd, J. (2004). *Employment with a Human Face: Balancing Efficiency, Equity, and Voice.* Ithaca NY: Cornell University Press.

Budd, J. (2011). *The Thought of Work.* Ithaca NY: Cornell University Press.

Budd, J. and Bhave, D. (2008). 'Values, ideologies and frames of reference in industrial relations', in P. Blyton, N. Bacon, J. Fiorito, and E. Heery (eds.), *The SAGE Handbook of Industrial Relations.* London: Sage, 92–112.

Budd, J., Gollan, P., and Wilkinson, A. (2010). 'New approaches to employee voice and participation'. *Human Relations,* 63/3: 1–8.

Bulut, T. and Lane, C. (2011). 'The private regulation of labour standards and rights in the global clothing industry: an evaluation of its effectiveness in two developing countries'. *New Political Economy,* 16/1: 41–71.

Burchell, B. (2002). 'The prevalence and redistribution of job insecurity and work intensification', in B. Burchell, D. Ladipo, and F. Wilkinson (eds.), *Job Insecurity and Work Intensification.* London: Routledge, 61–76.

Burchell, B., Day, D., Hudson, M., Ladipo, D., Mankelow, R., Nolan, J., Reed, H., Wichert, I., and Wilkinson, F. (1999). *Job Insecurity and Work Intensification.* York: Joseph Rowntree Foundation.

Burchill, F. (2000). 'The pay review body system: a comment and a consequence'. *Historical Studies in Industrial Relations,* 10/3: 141–57.

Butcher, T. (2012). 'Still evidence-based? The role of policy evaluation in recession and beyond: the case of the National Minimum Wage'. *National Institute Economic Review,* 219/1: R26–R40.

Butler, P. (2009). 'Non-union employee representation: exploring the riddle of managerial strategy'. *Industrial Relations Journal,* 40/3: 198–214.

Butler, P., Glover, L., and Tregaskis, O. (2011). ' "When the going gets tough" . . . Recession and the resilience of workplace partnership'. *British Journal of Industrial Relations,* 49/4: 666–87.

Butler, P., Tregaskis, O., and Glover, L. (2013). 'Workplace partnership and employee involvement— contradictions and synergies: evidence from a heavy engineering case study'. *Economic and Industrial Democracy,* 34/1: 5–24.

Byford, I. (2009). 'Union renewal and young people: some positive indications from British supermarkets', in G. Gall (ed.), *Union Organising: Current Practice, Future Prospects.* London, Palgrave Macmillan, 223–38.

Byford, I. (2011). 'The effectiveness of the organising model in higher education'. *Employee Relations,* 33/3: 289–303.

Cam, S. (2012). 'Involuntary part-time workers in Britain: evidence from the Labour Force Survey'. *Industrial Relations Journal,* 43/3: 242–59.

Cantin, É. (2008). 'Making the "workshop of the world": China and the international division of labour', in M. Taylor (ed.), *Global Economy Contested: Power and Conflict Across the International Division of Labour.* Abingdon: Routledge, 51–76.

Carley, M. (1993). 'Social dialogue', in M. Gold (ed.), *The Social Dimension: Employment Policy in the European Community.* Basingstoke: Macmillan, 105–34.

Carley, M. and Hall, M. (2000). 'The implementation of the European Works Councils Directive'. *Industrial Law Journal,* 29/2: 103–24.

Carr, F. (1999). 'Local bargaining in the National Health Service: new approaches to employee relations'. *Industrial Relations Journal,* 30/3: 197–211.

Carter, B. (2000). 'Adoption of the organising model in British trade unions: some evidence from Manufacturing, Science and Finance (MSF)'. *Work, Employment and Society,* 14/1: 117–36.

Carter, B., Danford, A., Howcroft, D., Richardson, H., Smith, A., and Taylor, P. (2011). ' "All they lack is a chain": lean and the new performance management in the British civil service'. *New Technology, Work, and Employment,* 26/2: 83–97.

Carter, B. and Fairbrother, P. (1999). 'The transformation of British public-sector industrial relations: from 'model employer' to marketised relations'. *Historical Studies in Industrial Relations,* 7: 119–46.

Cascio, W. (2010). 'Downsizing and redundancy', in A. Wilkinson, N. Bacon, T. Redman, and S. Snell (eds.), *The SAGE Handbook of Human Resource Management.* London: Sage, 337–48.

Cassell, C. and Lee, B. (2009). 'Trade unions learning representatives: progressing partnership?'. *Work, Employment, and Society,* 23/2: 213–30.

Castells, M. (2001). *The Internet Galaxy.* Oxford: Oxford University Press.

Central Arbitration Committee (CAC) (2012). *Annual Report, 2011–2012.* London: CAC.

Certification Office (2012). *Annual Report by the Certification Officer 2011–12.* London: Certification Office for Trade Unions and Employers' Associations.

Chan, C. K.-C. (2010). *The Challenge of Labour in China: Strikes and the Changing Labour Regime in Global Factories.* Abingdon: Routledge.

Channel Four (2010). *Dispatches: Fashion's Dirty Secret*. 8 November, http://www.channel4.com/programmes/dispatches/episode-guide/series-75/episode-1

Charles, N. (1986). 'Women and trade unions', in Feminist Review (ed.), *Waged Work: A Reader*. London: Virago, 160–85.

Charlwood, A. (2007). 'The de-collectivisation of pay setting in Britain 1990–98: incidence, determinants and impact'. *Industrial Relations Journal*, 38/1: 33–50.

Charlwood, A. and Forth, J. (2009). 'Employee representation', in W. Brown, A. Bryson, J. Forth, and K. Whitfield (eds.), *The Evolution of the Modern Workplace*. Cambridge: Cambridge University Press, 74–96.

Charlwood, A. and Terry, M. (2007). '21st-century models of employee representation: structures, processes, and outcomes'. *Industrial Relations Journal*, 38/4: 320–37.

Chartered Institute of Personnel and Development (CIPD) (2010). *Creating an Engaged Workforce*. London: CIPD. http://www.cipd.co.uk/NR/rdonlyres/DD66E557-DB90-4F07-8198-87C3876F3371/0/Creating_engaged_workforce.pdf

Chartered Institute of Personnel and Development (CIPD) (2011*a*). *Economic Rights and Wrongs of Employment Regulation*. London: CIPD. http://www.cipd.co.uk/binaries/5547_Work_Horizons.pdf

Chartered Institute of Personnel and Development (CIPD) (2011*b*). *Conflict Management*. London: CIPD. http://www.cipd.co.uk/binaries/5461_Conflict_manage_SR_WEB.pdf

Chartered Institute of Personnel and Development (CIPD) (2012*a*). *Employee Outlook Survey, Autumn 2012*. London: CIPD. http://www.cipd.co.uk/binaries/6030%20EmpOutlook%20Autumn%202012%20WEB.pdf

Chartered Institute of Personnel and Development (CIPD) (2012*b*). *The Rise in Self-Employment*, London: CIPD. http://www.cipd.co.uk/NR/rdonlyres/3F9AF376-FD99-4A57-8C3E-71E145FC0311/0/5757WorkAudit2012WEB.pdf

Chartered Institute of Personnel and Development (CIPD) (2013). *Labour Market Outlook: Winter 2012–13*. London: CIPD. http://www.cipd.co.uk/binaries/6123%20LMO%20Winter%202012-13%20(WEB)%20with%20centenary%20logo.pdf

Chartered Institute of Personnel and Development/Advisory, Conciliation and Arbitration Service (CIPD/ACAS) (2008). *Mediation: An Employer's Guide*. London: CIPD.

China Labor Watch (2012). *Beyond Foxconn: Deplorable Working Conditions Characterize Apple's Entire Supply Chain*, http://www.chinalaborwatch.org/pdf/2012627-5.pdf

Citizens Advice (2011). *Give us a Break! The CAB Service's Case for a Fair Employment Agency*. London: Citizens Advice.

Clark, I. (2008). 'Private equity: friend or foe? The case against'. *People Management, 21 August*: 18–20.

Clark, I. (2009). 'Owners and managers: disconnecting managerial capitalism? Understanding the private-equity business model'. *Work, Employment and Society*, 23/4: 775–86.

Clark, I. (2010). 'Private equity, 'union recognition' and value extraction at the Automobile Association: the GMB as an emergency service?'. *Industrial Relations Journal*, 42/1: 36–50.

Clark, N. (2011). 'Migration and work: discrimination obligatory', in T. Wright and H. Conley (eds.), *The Gower Handbook of Discrimination at Work*. Farnham: Gower, 139–54.

Clarke, M. (2007). 'Choices and constraints: individual perceptions of the voluntary redundancy experience'. *Human Resource Management Journal*, 17/1: 76–93.

Claydon, T. (1996). 'Union de-recognition: a re-examination', in I. Beardwell (ed.), *Contemporary Industrial Relations: A Critical Analysis*. Oxford: Oxford University Press, 151–74.

Clegg, H. (1975). 'Pluralism in industrial relations'. *British Journal of Industrial Relations*, 13/3: 309–16.

Clegg, H. (1979). *The Changing System of Industrial Relations in Great Britain*. Oxford: Basil Blackwell.

Clegg, H., Fox, A., and Thompson, A. (1964). *A History of British Trade Unions since 1889. Volume I, 1889–1910*. Oxford: Clarendon.

Coates, D. (2000). 'New Labour's industrial and employment policy', in D. Coates and P. Lawler (eds.), *New Labour in Power*. Manchester: Manchester University Press, 122–35.

Coates, K. and Topham, T. (1980). *Trade Unions in Britain*. Nottingham: Spokesman.

Coats, D. (2007). *The National Minimum Wage. Retrospect and Prospect*. London: Work Foundation.

Coats, D. (2010). *Time to cut the Gordian Knot—the Case for Consensus and Reform of the UK's Employment Relations System*. London: Smith Institute.

Cockburn, C. (1989). 'Equal opportunities: the short and long agenda'. *Industrial Relations Journal*, 20/3: 213–25.

Cockburn, C. (1991). *In the Way of Women*. Basingstoke: Macmillan.

Colgan, F. (1999). 'Recognising the lesbian and gay constituency in UK trade unions: moving forward in UNISON'. *Industrial Relations Journal*, 30/5: 444–63.

Colgan. F., Creegan, C., McKearney, A., and Wright, T. (2007). 'Equality and diversity policies and practices at work: lesbian, gay, and bisexual workers'. *Equal Opportunities International*, 26/3: 590–609.

Colgan, F. and Ledwith, S. (2000). 'Diversity, identities and strategies of women trade union activists'. *Gender, Work and Organization*, 7/4: 242–57.

Colgan, F. and Ledwith, S. (2002). 'Gender and diversity: reshaping union democracy'. *Employee Relations*, 24/2: 167–89.

Colgan, F. and McKearney, A. (2012). 'Visibility and voice in organisations: lesbian, gay, bisexual, and transgendered employee networks'. *Equality, Diversity, and Inclusion: An International Journal*, 31/4: 359–78.

Colgan, F. and Wright, T. (2011). 'Lesbian, gay, and bisexual equality in a modernizing public sector 1997–2010: opportunities and threats'. *Gender, Work, and Organization*, 18/5: 548–70.

Colling, T. (2004). 'No claim, no pain? The privatization of dispute resolution in Britain'. *Economic and Industrial Democracy*, 25/4: 555–79.

Colling, T. (2010). 'Legal institutions and the regulation of workplaces', in T. Colling and M. Terry (eds.), *Industrial Relations: Theory and Practice*. Chichester: John Wiley, 323–46.

Colling, T. and Dickens, L. (1989). *Equality Bargaining—Why Not?*. London: HMSO.

Colling, T. and Dickens, L. (1998). 'Selling the case for gender equality: deregulation and equality bargaining'. *British Journal of Industrial Relations*, 36/3: 389–411.

Colling, T. and Dickens, L. (2001). 'Gender equality and trade unions: a new basis for mobilisation?', in M. Noon and E. Ogbonna (eds.), *Equality, Diversity and Disadvantage in Employment*. Basingstoke: Palgrave Macmillan, 136–55.

Colling, T. and Terry, M. (2010). 'Work, the employment relationship and the field of industrial relations', in T. Colling and M. Terry (eds.), *Industrial Relations: Theory and Practice* (3rd edn). Chichester: John Wiley, 3–25.

Commons, J. (1924). *Legal Foundations of Capitalism*. New York: Macmillan.

Compa, L. (2001). 'Free trade, fair trade and the battle for labor rights', in L. Turner, H. Katz, and R. Hurd (eds.), *Rekindling the Movement: Labor's Quest for Relevance in the Twenty-first Century*. Ithaca NY: Cornell University Press, 314–38.

Confederation of British Industry (CBI) (2010a) *Making Britain the Place to Work: An Employment Agenda for the New Government*. London: CBI.

Confederation of British Industry (CBI) (2010b) *Keeping the Wheels Turning: Modernising the Legal Framework of Industrial Relations*. CBI Briefing Paper. London: CBI.

Confederation of British Industry (CBI) (2011a). *Thinking Positive: The 21st Century Employment Relationship*. London: CBI.

Confederation of British Industry (CBI) (2011b). *Healthy Returns? Absence and Workplace Health Survey* 2011. London: CBI.

Confederation of British Industry (CBI) (2011c). *Settling the Matter: Building a More Effective and Efficient Tribunal System*. London: CBI.

Conley, H. (2011). 'The road to equality: legislating for change?', in T. Wright and H. Conley (eds.), *The Gower Handbook of Discrimination at Work*. Farnham: Gower, 23–31.

Conley, H. (2012). 'Using equality to challenge austerity: new actors, old problems'. *Work, Employment and Society*, 26/2: 34–59.

Connolly, H. (2010). 'Organizing and mobilizing precarious workers in France: the case of cleaners in the railways', in C. Thornley, S. Jeffreys, and B. Appay (eds.), *Globalization and Precarious Forms of Production and Employment: Challenges for Workers and Unions*. Cheltenham: Edward Elgar, 182–98.

Cooke, F.-L. (2005). *HRM, Work, and Employment in China*. London: Routledge.

Cooke, F.-L. (2008). 'The changing dynamics of employment relations in China: an evaluation of the rising level of labour disputes'. *Journal of Industrial Relations*, 50/1: 111–38.

Cooke, H. (2006). 'Examining the disciplinary process in nursing: a case study approach'. *Work, Employment and Society*, 20/4: 687–707.

Corby, S. (2000). 'Employee relations in the public services: a paradigm shift?'. *Public Policy and Administration*, 15/3: 60–74.

Corby, S., Palmer, S., and Lindop, E. (2009). 'Trends and tensions: an overview', in S. Corby, S. Palmer, and E. Lindop (eds.), *Rethinking Reward*. Basingstoke: Palgrave Macmillan, 3–20.

Crail, M. (2007). 'Employers make liberal use of working time regulations opt-out', *Personnel Today*, 26 November, http://www.personneltoday.com/articles/2007/11/26/43407/employers-make-liberal-use-of-working-time-regulations-opt-out.html

Creegan, C. and Robinson, C. (2008). 'Prejudice and the workplace', in A. Park, J. Curtice, K. Thomson, M. Phillips, M. Johnson, and E. Clery (eds.), *British Social Attitudes: The 24th Report*. London: Sage, 127–38.

Cremers, J. (2010). 'Rules on working conditions in Europe: subordinated to freedom of services?'. *European Journal of Industrial Relations*, 16/3: 293–306.

Cremers, J., Erik Dølvik, J., and Bosch, G. (2007). 'Posting of workers in the single market: attempts to prevent social dumping and regime competition in the EU'. *Industrial Relations Journal*, 38/6: 524–41.

Crompton, R. and Sanderson, K. (1990). *Gendered Jobs and Social Change*. London: Unwin Hyman.

Cronin, J. (1979). *Industrial Conflict in Modern Britain*. London: Croom Helm.

Crouch, C. (1995). 'The state: economic management and incomes policy', in P. Edwards (ed.), *Industrial Relations: Theory and Practice in Britain*. Oxford: Blackwell, 229–54.

Crouch, C. (1996). 'Review essay. Atavism and innovation: labour legislation and public policy since 1979 in historical perspective'. *Historical Studies in Industrial Relations*, 2: 111–24.

Crouch, C. (2005). *Capitalist Diversity and Change*. Oxford: Oxford University Press.

Croucher, R. and Cotton, E. (2009). *Global Unions, Global Business*. Hendon: Middlesex University Press.

Croucher, R. and White, G. (2007). 'Enforcing a National Minimum Wage'. *Policy Studies*, 28/2: 145–61.

Cullinane, N., Donaghey, J., Dundon, T., and Dobbins, T. (2012). 'Different rooms, different voices: double-breasting, multi-channel representation and the managerial agenda'. *International Journal of Human Resource Management*, 23/2: 368–84.

Cullinane, N. and Dundon, T. (2012). 'Unitarism and employer resistance to trade unionism'. *The International Journal of Human Resource Management*, DOI: 10.1080/09585192.2012.667428

Cully, M., Woodland, S., O'Reilly, A., and Dix, G. (1999). *Britain at Work*. London: Routledge.

Cunningham, R., Lord, A., and Delaney, L. (1999). 'Next Steps' for equality? The impact of organizational change on opportunities for women in the civil service'. *Gender, Work and Organization*, 6/2: 67–78.

Cunnison, S. and Stageman, J. (1993). *Feminizing the Unions*. Aldershot: Avebury.

Curtis, P. (2011). 'Strike laws could be toughened, warn ministers', *The Guardian*, 15 June, http://www.guardian.co.uk/politics/2011/jun/15/strike-laws-ministers?INTCMP=SRCH

Cushen, J. and Thompson, P. (2012). 'Doing the right thing? HRM and the angry knowledge worker'. *New Technology, Work, and Employment*, 27/2: 79–92.

Daly, M. (2012). 'Paradigms in EU social policy: a critical account of Europe 2020'. *Transfer: European Review of Labour and Research*, 18/3: 273–84.

Danford, A. (1998). 'Teamworking and labour regulation in the autocomponents industry'. *Work, Employment and Society*, 12/3: 409–31.

Danford, A., Richardson, M., Stewart, P., Tailby, S., and Upchurch, M. (2004). 'Partnership, mutuality and

the high-performance workplace: a case study of union strategy and worker experience in the aircraft industry', in G. Healy, E. Heery, P. Taylor, and W. Brown (eds.), *The Future of Worker Representation*. Basingstoke: Palgrave Macmillan, 167–86.

Danford, A., Richardson, M., Stewart, P., Tailby, S., and Upchurch, M. (2005). *Partnership and the High Performance Workplace*. Basingstoke: Palgrave Macmillan.

Danford, A., Richardson, M., and Upchurch, M. (2002). ' "New unionism", organising and partnership: a comparative analysis of union renewal strategies in the public sector'. *Capital and Class*, 26/1: 1–27.

Daniel, W. and Millward, N. (1983). *Workplace Industrial Relations in Britain*. London: Heinemann.

Daniels, G. (2009). ' In the field: a decade of organizing', in G. Daniels and J. McIlroy (eds.), *Trade Unions in a Neo Liberal World: British Trade Unions under New Labour*. Abingdon: Routledge, 254–82.

Daniels, G. and McIlroy, J. (eds.) (2009). *Trade Unions in a Neo Liberal World: British Trade Unions under New Labour*. Abingdon: Routledge.

Darlington, R. (2012). 'The interplay of structure and agency dynamics in strike activity'. *Employee Relations*, 45/5: 518–33.

Davies, A. and Thomas, R. (2000). 'Gender and human resource management: a critical review'. *International Journal of Human Resource Management*, 11/6: 1125–36.

Davies, Lord (2011). *Women on Boards*, https://www.gov.uk/government/uploads/system/uploads/attachment_data/file/31480/11-745-women-on-boards.pdf

Davies, P. and Freedland, M. (1993). *Labour Legislation and Public Policy*. Oxford: Clarendon.

Davies, P. and Freedland, M. (2007). *Towards a Flexible Labour Market*. Oxford: Oxford University Press.

De Menezes, L. and Kelliher, C. (2011). 'Flexible working and performance: a systematic review of the evidence for a business case'. *International Journal of Management Reviews*, 13/4: 452–74.

De Ruyter, A., Bailey. D., and Mahdon, M. (2010). 'Changing lanes or stuck in the slow lane? Employment precariousness and labour market status of MG Rover workers four years after closure', in C. Thornley, S. Jeffreys, and B. Appay (eds.), *Globalization and Precarious Forms of Production and Employment: Challenges for Workers and Unions*. Cheltenham: Edward Elgar, 214–29.

Dean, D. and Liff, S. (2010). 'Equality and diversity: the ultimate industrial relations concern', in T. Colling and M. Terry (eds.), *Industrial Relations: Theory and Practice* (3rd edn). Chichester: John Wiley, 422–46.

Deery, S., Iverson, R., and Walsh, J. (2010). 'Coping strategies in call centres: work intensity and the role of co-workers and supervisors'. *British Journal of Industrial Relations*, 48/1: 181–200.

Delbridge, R. (1998). *Life on the Line in Contemporary Manufacturing*. Oxford: Oxford University Press.

Department for Business, Innovation and Skills (BIS) (2011). *Flexible, Effective, Fair: Promoting Economic Growth Through a Strong and Efficient Labour Market*. London: BIS.

Department for Business, Innovation and Skills (BIS) (2012a) *Employment Law Review: Annual Update* 2012. London: BIS.

Department for Business, Innovation and Skills (BIS) (2012b) *Dealing with Dismissal and 'Compensated No Fault Dismissal' for Micro Businesses: Call for Evidence*. London: BIS.

Department for Business, Innovation and Skills (BIS) (2012c) *Employer's Charter*. London: BIS.

Department for Business, Innovation and Skills (BIS) (2012d). *Implementing Employee Owner Status: Government Response to Consultation*. London: BIS. https://www.gov.uk/government/uploads/system/uploads/attachment_data/file/68731/12-1338-implementing-employee-owner-status-government-response.pdf

Department for Business, Innovation and Skills (BIS) (2012e). *Executive Pay: Shareholder Voting Rights Consultation*. London: BIS. https://www.gov.uk/government/uploads/system/uploads/attachment_data/file/31372/12-639-executive-pay-shareholder-voting-rights-consultation.pdf

Department for Business, Innovation and Skills (BIS) (2012f) *Enterprise and Regulatory Reform Bill: Policy Paper*. London: BIS. http://www.bis.gov.uk/assets/biscore/corporate/docs/e/12-1235-enterprise-and-regulatory-reform-bill-policy-paper

Department for Business, Innovation and Skills (BIS) (2013). *National Minimum Wage: Final Government Evidence to the Low Pay Commission* 2012. London: BIS. https://www.gov.uk/government/publications/national-minimum-wage-final-government-evidence-to-the-low-pay-commission-2012

Department for Business, Innovation and Skills/Her Majesty's Revenue and Customs (BIS/HMRC), (2013) *National Minimum Wage Compliance and Enforcement: Report for 18 Months to 30 September 2012*. London: BIS/HMRC. https://www.gov.uk/government/uploads/system/uploads/attachment_data/file/49986/13-280-national-minimum-wage-compliance-report-for-2011-12.pdf

Department of Trade and Industry (DTI) (1998). *Fairness at Work*. London: HMSO.

Department of Trade and Industry (DTI) (2005). *Code of Practice: Access and Unfair Practices during Recognition Ballots*. London: DTI.

Department of Trade and Industry (DTI) (2006). *Success at Work*. London: DTI.

Department for Work and Pensions (DWP) (2011). *The Government Response to the Löfstedt Report*. London: DWP.

Dex, S. and Forth, J. (2009). 'Equality and diversity at work', in W. Brown, A. Bryson, J. Forth, and K. Whitfield (eds.), *The Evolution of the Modern Workplace*. Cambridge: Cambridge University Press, 230–55.

Dicken, P. (2007). *Global Shift: Mapping the Contours of the World Economy* (5th edn). London: Sage.

Dickens, L. (1992). 'Anti-discrimination legislation: exploring and explaining the impact on women's employment', in W. McCarthy (ed.), *Legal Intervention in Industrial Relations: Gains and Losses*. Oxford: Basil Blackwell, 103–46.

Dickens, L. (1994). 'The business case for women's equality: is the carrot better than the stick?'. *Employee Relations*, 16/8: 5–18.

Dickens, L. (1997). 'Gender, race and employment equality in Britain: inadequate strategies and the role of industrial relations actors'. *Industrial Relations Journal*, 28/4: 282–91.

Dickens, L. (1999). 'Beyond the business case: a three-pronged approach to equality action'. *Human Resource Management Journal*, 9/1: 9–19.

Dickens, L. (2000a). 'Still wasting resources? Equality in employment', in S. Bach and K. Sisson (eds.), *Personnel Management* (3rd edn). Oxford: Blackwell, 137–69.

Dickens, L. (2000b). 'Collective bargaining and the promotion of gender equality at work: opportunities and challenges for trade unions'. *Transfer*, 6/2: 193–208.

Dickens, L. (2000c). 'Doing more with less: Acas and individual conciliation', in B. Towers and W. Brown (eds.), *Employment Relations in Britain: 25 Years of the Advisory, Conciliation and Arbitration Service*. Oxford: Blackwell, 67–91.

Dickens, L. (2007). 'The road is long: thirty years of equality legislation in Britain'. *British Journal of Industrial Relations*, 45/3: 463–94.

Dickens, L. (2012a). 'Employment tribunals and alternative dispute resolution', in L. Dickens (ed.), *Making Employment Rights Effective: Issues of Enforcement and Compliance*. Oxford: Hart Publishing, 29–47.

Dickens, L. (2012b). 'Fairer workplaces: making employment rights effective', in L. Dickens (ed.), *Making Employment Rights Effective: Issues of Enforcement and Compliance*. Oxford: Hart Publishing, 205–28.

Dickens, L. and Hall, M. (2003). 'Labour law and industrial relations: a new settlement?', in P. Edwards (ed.), *Industrial Relations* (2nd edn). Oxford: Blackwell, 124–56.

Dickens, L. and Hall, M. (2006). 'Fairness—up to a point. Assessing the impact of New Labour's employment legislation'. *Human Resource Management Journal,* 16/4: 338–56.

Dickens, L. and Hall, M. (2009). 'Legal regulation and the changing workplace', in W. Brown, A. Bryson, J. Forth, and K. Whitfield (eds.), *The Evolution of the Modern Workplace.* Cambridge: Cambridge University Press, 332–52.

Dickens, L. and Hall, M. (2010). 'The changing legal framework of employment relations', in T. Colling and M. Terry (eds.), *Industrial Relations: Theory and Practice* (3rd edn). Chichester: John Wiley, 298–322.

Dickens, L., Jones, M., Weekes, B., and Hunt, M. (1985). *Dismissed: a Study of Unfair Dismissal and the Industrial Tribunal System.* Oxford: Basil Blackwell.

Dickens, R., Gregg, P., Machin, S., Manning, A., and Wadsworth, J. (1993). 'Wages councils: was there a case for abolition?'. *British Journal of Industrial Relations,* 31/4: 515–29.

Dickens, R. and Manning, A. (2003). 'Minimum wage, minimum impact', in R. Dickens, P. Gregg, and J. Wadsworth (eds.), *The Labour Market under New Labour.* Basingstoke: Palgrave Macmillan, 201–13.

Dix, G. and Oxenbridge, S. (2004). 'Coming to the table with Acas: from conflict to co-operation'. *Employee Relations,* 26/5: 510–30.

Dix, G., Sisson, K., and Forth, J. (2009). 'Conflict at work: the changing pattern of disputes', in W. Brown, A. Bryson, J. Forth, and K. Whitfield (eds.), *The Evolution of the Modern Workplace.* Cambridge: Cambridge University Press, 176–200.

Doherty, L. (2004). 'Work-life balance initiatives: implications for women'. *Employee Relations,* 26/4: 433–52.

Dølvik, J. E. and Visser, J. (2009). 'Free movement, equal treatment and workers' rights: can the European Union solve its trilemma of fundamental principles?'. *Industrial Relations Journal,* 40/6: 491–509.

Donaghey, J., Cullinane, N., Dundon, T., and Dobbins, T. (2012). 'Non-union employee representation, union avoidance and the managerial agenda'. *Economic and Industrial Democracy,* 33/2: 163–83.

Donaghey, J. and Teague, P. (2006). 'The free movement of workers and social Europe: maintaining the European ideal'. *Industrial Relations Journal,* 37/6: 652–66.

Donnelly, M. and Scholarios, D. (1998). 'Workers' experiences of redundancy: evidence from Scottish defence-dependent companies'. *Personnel Review,* 27/4: 325–42.

Donnelly, R. (2011). 'The organization of working time in the knowledge economy: an insight into the working time patterns of consultants in the UK and the USA', *British Journal of Industrial Relations,* 49/S1: s93–s114.

Doogan, K. (2009). *New Capitalism?* Cambridge: Polity.

Dorey, P. and Denham, A. (2011). ' "O brother, where art thou?" The Labour party leadership election of 2010'. *British Politics,* 6: 286–316.

Druker, J. and White, G. (2009). 'Introduction', in G. White and J. Druker (eds.), *Reward Management: A Critical Text* (2nd edn). Abingdon: Routledge, 1–22.

Dubois, P. (1979). *Sabotage in Industry.* Penguin: Harmondsworth.

Duhigg, C. and Barboza, D. (2012). 'In China, human costs are built into an iPad'. *The New York Times,* 25 January, http://www.nytimes.com/2012/01/26/business/ieconomy-apples-ipad-and-the-human-costs-for-workers-in-china.html

Dundon, T., González-Pérez, M.-A., and McDonough, T. (2007). 'Bitten by the Celtic Tiger: immigrant workers and industrial relations in the new 'glocalized' Ireland'. *Economic and Industrial Democracy,* 28/4: 501–22.

Dundon, T. and Rollinson, D. (2004). *Employment Relations in Non-Union Firms.* London: Routledge.

Dundon, T., Wilkinson, A., Marchington, M., and Ackers, P. (2005). 'The management of voice in non-union organisations: managers' perspectives'. *Employee Relations,* 27/3: 307–19.

Dunleavy, P. and O'Leary, B. (1987). *Theories of the State: The Politics of Liberal Democracy.* Basingstoke: Macmillan.

Dunlop, J. (1958). *Industrial Relations Systems.* New York: Holt.

Dunn, S. and Gennard, J. (1984). *The Closed Shop in British Industry.* London: Macmillan.

Dunn, S. and Metcalf, D. (1996). 'Trade union law since 1979', in I. Beardwell (ed.), *Contemporary Industrial Relations: A Critical Analysis.* Oxford: Oxford University Press, 66–98.

Earnshaw, J., Marchington, M., and Goodman, J. (2000). 'Unfair to whom? Discipline and dismissal in small establishments'. *Industrial Relations Journal,* 31/1: 62–73.

Eaton, J. (2000). *Comparative Employment Relations.* Cambridge: Polity.

Edwards, P. (1977). 'The Kerr-Siegel hypothesis of strikes and the isolated mass: a study of the falsification of sociological knowledge'. *Sociological Review,* 25/3: 551–74.

Edwards, P. (1983). 'The pattern of collective industrial action', in G. Bain (ed.), *Industrial Relations in Britain*. Oxford: Basil Blackwell, 209–34.

Edwards, P. (1986). *Conflict at Work*. Oxford: Basil Blackwell.

Edwards, P. (1988). 'Patterns of conflict and accommodation', in D. Gallie (ed.), *Employment in Britain*. Oxford: Basil Blackwell, 187–217.

Edwards, P. (1992). 'Industrial conflict'. *British Journal of Industrial Relations*, 30/3: 361–404.

Edwards, P. (1995). 'Strikes and industrial conflict', in P. Edwards (ed.), *Industrial Relations: Theory and Practice in Britain*. Oxford: Blackwell, 434–60.

Edwards, P. (2003). 'The employment relationship and the field of industrial relations', in P. Edwards, (ed.), *Industrial Relations* (2nd edn). Oxford: Blackwell, 1–36.

Edwards, P. (2005). 'Discipline and attendance: a murky aspect of people management', in S. Bach (ed.), *Managing Human Resources* (4th edn). Oxford: Blackwell, 375–97.

Edwards, P. and Ram, M. (2006). 'Surviving on the margins of the economy: working relationships in small, low-wage firms'. *Journal of Management Studies*, 43/4: 895–916.

Edwards, P., Ram, M., Sen Gupta, S., and Tsai, C.-J. (2006). 'The structuring of working relationships in small firms: towards a formal framework'. *Organization*, 13/5: 701–24.

Edwards, P. and Scullion, H. (1982). *The Social Organisation of Industrial Conflict*. Oxford: Basil Blackwell.

Edwards, P. and Whitston, C. (1994). 'Disciplinary practice: a study of railways in Britain, 1860–1988'. *Work, Employment and Society*, 8/3: 317–37.

Edwards, R. (1979). *Contested Terrain: The Transformation of the Workplace in the Twentieth Century*. London: Heinemann.

Edwards, T. (2011): 'The transfer of employment practices across borders in multinational companies', in A.-W. Harzing and A. Pinnington (eds.), *International Human Resource Management* (3rd edn). London: Sage, 267–90.

Edwards, T., Colling, T., and Ferner, A. (2007). 'Conceptual approaches to the transfer of employment practices in multinational companies: an integrated approach'. *Human Resource Management Journal*, 17/3: 201–17.

Edwards, T. and Ferner, A. (2002). 'The renewed "American challenge": a review of employment practice in US multinationals'. *Industrial Relations Journal*, 33/2: 94–111.

Egels-Zandén, N. (2007). 'Suppliers' compliance with MNCs' codes of conduct: behind the scenes at Chinese toy suppliers'. *Journal of Business Ethics*, 75: 45–62.

Elger, T. (1990). 'Technical innovation and work reorganisation in British manufacturing in the 1980s: continuity, intensification or transformation?'. *Work, Employment and Society, special issue*: 67–101.

Elger, T. and Smith, C. (2005). *Assembling Work*. Oxford: Oxford University Press.

Elliott, K. and Freeman, R. (2003). *Can Labor Standards Improve under Globalization?*. Washington DC: Institute for International Economics.

Emmott, M. (2001). 'Tribunals are judged wanting'. *The Guardian*, 12 March.

Emmott, M. (2005). *What is Employee Relations?* London: CIPD.

Equal Opportunities Commission (EOC) (2005). *Greater Expectations: Summary Final Report of the EOC's Investigation into Pregnancy Discrimination*. London: EOC.

Equal Opportunities Commission (EOC) (2006). *Moving on up? Bangladeshi, Pakistani, and Black Caribbean Women at Work*. London: EOC.

Equality and Human Rights Commission (EHRC) (2009). *Working Better: Phase 1 Report*. London: EHRC.

Equality and Human Rights Commission (EHRC) (2010). *Triennial Review 2010: How Fair is Britain?* London: EHRC.

Erickson, C., Fisk, C., Milkman, R., Mitchell, D., and Wong, K. (2002). 'Justice for Janitors in Los Angeles: lessons from three rounds of negotiation'. *British Journal of Industrial Relations*, 40/3: 543–67.

Erickson, M., Bradley, H., Stephenson, C., and Williams, S. (2009). *Business in Society*. Cambridge: Polity.

Esbenshade, J. (2004). *Monitoring Sweatshops: Workers, Consumers and the Global Apparel Industry*. Philadelphia PA: Temple University Press.

Etchemendy, S. and Collier, R. B. (2007). 'Down but not out: union resurgence and segmented neocorporatism in Argentina (2003–2007)'. *Politics and Society*, 35/3: 363–401.

Eurofound (2010). *Extending Flexicurity—the Potential of Short-Time Working Schemes*. Dublin: European Foundation for the Improvement of Living and Working Conditions.

Eurofound (2012) *Working Time in the EU*. Dublin: European Foundation for the Improvement of Living and Working Conditions.

European Commission (2010). *Europe 2020: A Strategy for Smart, Sustainable, and Inclusive Growth*. Brussels: EC.

European Commission (2012). 'Women on boards: Commission proposes 40 per cent objective'. European Commission press release, 14 November, http://europa.eu/rapid/press-release_IP-12-1205_en.htm

European Commission (2013). 'Europe 2020 in a nutshell'. 13 May, http://ec.europa.eu/europe2020/europe-2020-in-a-nutshell/

European Industrial Relations Observatory (EIRO) (2002). 'Diageo Concludes Innovative EWC Agreement'. *EIRO online*, http://www.eurofound.europa.eu/eiro/2002/11/feature/ie0211204f.htm

European Industrial Relations Observatory (EIRO) (2010). 'Commission consults social partners on Working Time Directive review'. *EIRO online*, http://www.eurofound.europa.eu/eiro/2010/04/articles/eu1004011i.htm

European Industrial Relations Observatory (EIRO) (2012). 'Social partners launch review of Working Time Directive'. *EIRO online*, http://www.eurofound.europa.eu/eiro/2011/11/articles/eu1111051i.htm

European Trade Union Confederation (ETUC) (2011). *Athens Manifesto*. Brussels: ETUC.

European Trade Union Confederation (ETUC) (n.d.). *Economic Freedoms vs Workers' Rights: The Viking, Laval, Rüffert and Luxembourg Judgments*. Brussels: ETUC.

Evans, C., Harvey, G., and Turnbull, P. (2012). 'When partnerships don't "match-up": an evaluation of labour-management partnerships in the automotive components and civil aviation industries'. *Human Resource Management Journal*, 22/1: 60–75.

Ewing, K. (2009). *Ruined Lives: Blacklisting in the UK Construction Industry*. London: UCATT.

Ewing, K. (2010). 'Labour leaves blacklisted high and dry'. *The Guardian*, 10 March, http://www.guardian.co.uk/commentisfree/2010/mar/10/labour-leaves-blacklisted-high-dry

Ewing, K. (2011). 'What today's charter of workers' rights looks like'. *The Guardian*, 31 January, http://www.guardian.co.uk/commentisfree/2011/jan/31/cable-abuse-vulnerable-workers

Ewing, K. and Hendy, J. (2010). 'The dramatic implications of *Demir* and *Baykara*'. *Industrial Law Journal*, 39/1: 2–51.

Ewing, L. (2011). 'Anti-blacklist campaigner Steve Acheson's picket pledge'. *BBC News Online*, http://www.bbc.co.uk/news/uk-england-14080162

Fair Labor Association (FLA) (2012). *Independent Investigation of Apple Supplier, Foxconn Report Highlights*, http://www.fairlabor.org/sites/default/files/documents/reports/foxconn_investigation_report.pdf

Fair Pay Network (2012). *Face the Difference: The Impact of Low Pay in National Supermarket Chains*. London: Fair Pay Network.

Fair Work Commission (2013). *Power, Pay, Progression and Justice at Work*. Unions21 Fair Work Commission, Report 1. London: Unions21.

Fairbrother, P. (1996). 'Workplace trade unionism in the state sector', in P. Ackers, C. Smith, and P. Smith (eds.), *The New Workplace and Trade Unionism*. London: Routledge, 110–48.

Fairhurst, D. (2008). 'Am I "bovvered?" Driving a performance culture through to the front line'. *Human Resource Management Journal*, 18/4: 321–6.

Farnham, D. and Pimlott, J. (1995). *Understanding Industrial Relations* (4th edn). London: Cassell.

Farrell, C. and Morris, J. (2004). 'Resigned compliance: teacher attitudes towards performance-related pay in schools'. *Educational Management Administration and Leadership*, 32/1: 81–104.

Farrell, C. and Morris, J. (2009). 'Still searching for the evidence? Evidence-based policy, performance pay, and teachers'. *Journal of Industrial Relations*, 51/1: 75–94.

Fawcett Society (2012). *The Impact of Austerity on Women*. London: Fawcett Society. http://uat.fawcettsociety.org.uk/wp-content/uploads/2013/02/The-Impact-of-Austerity-on-Women-19th-March-2012.pdf

Felstead, A., Gallie, D., Green, F., and Inanc, H. (2013). *Work Intensification in Britain: First Findings from the Skills and Employment Survey 2012*. Cardiff: ESRC Centre for Learning and Life Chances in Knowledge Economies and Societies.

Felstead, A. and Jewson, N. (1999). 'Flexible labour and non-standard employment: an agenda of issues', in A. Felstead and N. Jewson (eds.), *Global Trends in Flexible Labour*. Basingstoke: Macmillan, 1–20.

Felstead, A. and Jewson, N. (2000). *In Work, at Home*. London: Routledge.

Fenley, A. (1986). 'Industrial discipline: a suitable case for treatment'. *Employee Relations*, 8/3: 1–30.

Fenley, A. (1998). 'Models, styles and metaphors: understanding the management of discipline'. *Employee Relations*, 20/4: 349–64.

Ferner, A. (2003). 'Foreign multinationals and industrial relations innovation in Britain', in P. Edwards (ed.), *Industrial Relations* (2nd edn). Oxford: Blackwell, 81–104.

Ferner, A. (2010). 'HRM in multinational companies', in A. Wilkinson, N. Bacon, T. Redman, and S. Snell (eds.), *The SAGE Handbook of Human Resource Management*. London: Sage, 541–60.

Ferner, A. and Edwards, P. (1995). 'Power and the diffusion of organizational change within multinational corporations'. *European Journal of Industrial Relations*, 1/2: 229–57.

Ferner, A., Edwards, T., and Tempel, A. (2012). 'Power, institutions and the cross-national transfer of employment practices in multinationals'. *Human Relations*, 65/2: 163–87.

Fernie, S. (2005). 'The future of British unions: introduction and conclusions', in S. Fernie and D. Metcalf (eds.), *Trade Unions: Resurgence or Demise?* London: Routledge, 1–18.

Fine, J. (2006). *Worker Centers: Organizing Communities at the Edge of the Dream*. Ithaca NY: ILR Press.

Fitzgerald, I. and Hardy, J. (2010). ' "Thinking outside the box"? Trade union organizing strategies and Polish migrant workers in the United Kingdom'. *British Journal of Industrial Relations*, 48/1: 131–50.

Flanagan, R. (2006). *Globalization and Labor Conditions: Working Conditions and Worker Rights in a Global Economy*. New York: Oxford University Press.

Flanders, A. (1964). *The Fawley Productivity Agreements*. London: Faber and Faber.

Flanders, A. (1974). 'The tradition of voluntarism'. *British Journal of Industrial Relations*, 12/3: 352–70.

Flanders, A. (1975). *Management and Unions*. London: Faber and Faber.

Flanders, A. and Clegg, H. (eds.) (1964). *The System of Industrial Relations in Great Britain*. Oxford: Basil Blackwell.

Fleming, P., Harley, B., and Sewell, G. (2004). 'A little knowledge is a dangerous thing: getting below the surface of the growth of "knowledge work" in Australia'. *Work, Employment and Society*, 18/4: 725–47.

Forde, C. (2001). 'Temporary arrangements: the activities of employment agencies in the UK'. *Work, Employment and Society*, 15/3: 631–44.

Forde, C., MacKenzie, R., and Robinson, A. (2008). '"Help wanted". Employers' use of temporary agencies in the UK construction industry'. *Employee Relations*, 30/6: 679–98.

Foster, D. (2007). 'Legal obligation or personal lottery? Employee experiences of disability and the negotiation of adjustments in the public sector workplace'. *Work, Employment and Society*, 21/1: 67–84.

Foster, D. (2011). 'Understanding workplace adjustments for disabled employees', in T. Wright and H. Conley (eds.), *The Gower Handbook of Discrimination at Work*. Farnham: Gower, 173–84.

Foster, J. and Woolfson, C. (1986). *The Politics of the UCS Work-in*. London: Lawrence and Wishart.

Fougner, T. and Kurtoğlu, A. (2011). 'Transnational labour solidarity and social movement unionism: insights from and beyond a women workers' strike in Turkey'. *British Journal of Industrial Relations*, 49/S2: s353–75.

Fox, A. (1966). *Industrial Sociology and Industrial Relations*. Research Paper No. 3, Royal Commission on Trade Unions and Employers' Associations. London: HMSO.

Fox, A. (1974). *Beyond Contract: Work, Power and Trust Relations*. London: Faber and Faber.

Fox, A. (1985a). *History and Heritage: The Social Origins of the British Industrial Relations System*. London: Allen and Unwin.

Fox, A. (1985b) *Man Mismanagement* (2nd edn). London: Hutchinson.

Fraser, J. and Gold, M. (2001). ' "Portfolio workers": autonomy and control among freelance translators'. *Work, Employment and Society*, 15/4: 679–97.

Fredman, S. (2001). 'Equality: a new generation?'. *Industrial Law Journal*, 30/2: 145–68.

Freeman, R. and Diamond, W. (2003). 'Young workers and trade unions', in H. Gospel and S. Wood (eds.), *Representing Workers: Union Recognition and Membership in Britain*. London: Routledge, 29–50.

Frege, C. (2006). 'International trends in unionization', in M. Morley, P. Gunnigle, and D. Collins (eds.), *Global Industrial Relations*. London: Routledge, 221–38.

Frege, C. (2008). 'The history of industrial relations as a field of study', in P. Blyton, N. Bacon, J. Fiorito, and E. Heery (eds.), *The SAGE Handbook of Industrial Relations*. London: Sage, 92–112.

Frenkel, S. (2001). 'Globalization, athletic footwear commodity chains and employment relations in China'. *Organization Studies*, 22/4: 531–62.

Frenkel, S. (2006). 'Towards a theory of dominant interests, globalization, and work', in M. Korczynski, R. Hodson, and P. Edwards (eds.), *Social Theory at Work*. Oxford: Oxford University Press, 388–423.

Frenkel, S. and Kim, S. (2004). 'Corporate codes of labour practice and employment relations in sports shoe contractor factories in South Korea'. *Asia Pacific Journal of Human Resources*, 42/1: 6–31.

Frenkel, S. and Scott, D. (2002). 'Compliance, collaboration, and codes of labor practice: the Adidas connection'. *California Management Review*, 45/1: 29–49.

Friedman, A. (1977). *Industry and Labour: Class Struggle at Work and Monopoly Capitalism*. London: Macmillan.

Friedman, E. and Lee, C. K. (2010). 'Remaking the world of Chinese labour: a 30-year retrospective'. *British Journal of Industrial Relations*, 48/3: 507–33.

Fryer, R. (1973). 'Redundancy, values and public policy'. *Industrial Relations Journal*, 4/2: 2–19.

Fryer, R. (1981). 'State, redundancy and the law', in R. Fryer, A. Hunt, D. McBarnet, and B. Moorhouse (eds.), *Law, State, and Society*. London: Croom Helm, 136–59.

Fuller, L. and Smith, V. (1991). 'Consumers' reports: management by customers in a changing economy'. *Work, Employment and Society*, 5/1: 1–16.

Gall, G. (2003a). 'Employer opposition to union recognition', in G. Gall (ed.), *Union Organizing*. London: Routledge, 79–96.

Gall, G. (2003b). 'Marxism and industrial relations', in P. Ackers and A. Wilkinson (eds.), *Understanding Work and Employment: Industrial Relations in Transition*. Oxford: Oxford University Press, 316–24.

Gall, G. (2005). 'Union organizing in the "new economy" in Britain'. *Employee Relations*, 27/2: 208–25.

Gall, G. (2007). 'Trade union recognition in Britain: an emerging crisis for trade unions?'. *Economic and Industrial Democracy*, 28/1: 78–109.

Gall. G. (2010a). 'Resisting recession and redundancy: contemporary worker occupations in Britain'. *Working USA*, 13/1: 107–32.

Gall, G. (2010b). 'The first ten years of the third statutory union recognition procedure in Britain'. *Industrial Law Journal*, 39/4: 444–8.

Gall, G. (2010c). 'Statutory union recognition provisions as stimulants to employer anti-unionism in three Anglo-Saxon countries'. *Economic and Industrial Democracy*, 31/1: 7–33.

Gall, G. (2011a). 'Contemporary workplace occupations in Britain: motivations, stimuli, dynamics and outcomes'. *Employee Relations*, 33/6: 607–23.

Gall, G. (2011b). 'Worker resistance and responses to the crisis of neo-liberal capitalism'. *Employee Relations*, 33/6: 588–91.

Gall, G. (2011c). 'Why revisit the Working Time Directive?' *The Guardian*, 21 November, http://www.guardian.co.uk/commentisfree/2011/nov/21/working-time-directive-lisbon-treaty?INTCMP=SRCH

Gall, G. (2012a). 'Union recognition in Britain: the end of legally induced voluntarism?'. *Industrial Law Journal*, 41/4: 407–38.

Gall, G. (2012b). 'The engineering construction strikes in Britain, 2009'. *Capital and Class*, 36/3: 411–31.

Gall, G. and Fiorito, J. (2011). 'The backward march of labour halted? Or, what is to be done with "union organising"? The cases of Britain and the USA'. *Capital and Class*, 35/2: 233–51.

Gall, G. and Hebdon, R. (2008). 'Conflict at work', in P. Blyton, N. Bacon, J. Fiorito, and E. Heery (eds.), *The SAGE Handbook of Industrial Relations*. London: Sage, 588–605.

Gall, G. and McKay, S. (2001). 'Facing 'fairness at work': union perception of employer opposition and response to union recognition'. *Industrial Relations Journal*, 32/2: 94–113.

Gallie, D. (2005). 'Work pressure in Europe 1996–2001: trends and determinants'. *British Journal of Industrial Relations*, 43/4: 351–75.

Gallie, D., White, M., Cheng, Y., and Tomlinson, M. (1998). *Restructuring the Employment Relationship*. Oxford: Clarendon.

Gamble, J. (2011). *Multinational Retailers and Consumers in China: Transferring Organizational Practices from the United Kingdom and Japan*. Basingstoke: Palgrave Macmillan.

Garrahan, P. and Stewart, P. (1992). *The Nissan Enigma*. London: Mansell.

Gateways to the Professions Collaborative Forum (2011). *Common Best Practice Code for High-Quality Internships*, http://www.bis.gov.uk/assets/BISCore/higher-education/docs/C/11-1068-common-best-practice-code-for-quality-internships.pdf

Gatrell, C. (2005). *Hard Labour: The Sociology of Parenthood*. Maidenhead: Open University Press.

Geary, D. (1985). *Policing Industrial Disputes, 1893 to 1985*. Cambridge: Cambridge University Press.

Geary, J. and Trif, A. (2011). 'Workplace partnership and the balance of advantage: a critical case analysis'. *British Journal of Industrial Relations*, 49/S1: s44–s69.

Gennard, J. (1984). 'The implications of the Messenger Newspaper Group dispute'. *Industrial Relations Journal*, 15/3: 7–20.

Gilbert, D. (1996). 'Strikes in postwar Britain', in C. Wrigley (ed.), *A History of British Industrial Relations 1939–1979*. Cheltenham: Edward Elgar, 128–61.

Glover, J. and Kirton, G. (2006). *Women, Employment, and Organizations*. London: Routledge.

Godard, J. (2004). 'A critical assessment of the high-performance paradigm'. *British Journal of Industrial Relations*, 42/2: 349–78.

Godard, J. (2011). 'What has happened to strikes?'. *British Journal of Industrial Relations*, 49/2: 282–305.

Gold, M. (1993). 'Overview of the Social Dimension', in M. Gold (ed.), *The Social Dimension: Employment Policy in the European Community*. Basingstoke: Macmillan, 10–40.

Goldthorpe, J. (1977). 'Industrial Relations in Great Britain: a critique of reformism', in T. Clarke and L. Clements (eds.), *Trade Unions under Capitalism*. Glasgow: Fontana, 184–224.

Goldthorpe, J. and Jackson, M. (2007). 'Intergenerational class mobility in contemporary Britain: political concerns and empirical findings'. *British Journal of Sociology*, 58/4: 525–46.

Gollan, P. (2003). 'All talk but no voice: employee voice at the Eurotunnel call centre'. *Economic and Industrial Democracy*, 24/4: 509–41.

Gollan, P. (2007). *Employee Representation in Non-union Firms*. London: Sage.

Gollan, P. (2010). 'Employer strategies towards non-union collective voice', in A. Wilkinson, P. Gollan, M. Marchington, and D. Lewin (eds.), *The Oxford Handbook of Participation in Organizations*. Oxford: Oxford University Press, 212–35.

Gollan, P. and Lewin, D. (2013). 'Employee representation in non-union firms: an overview'. *Industrial Relations, 52/* S1: 173–93.

Gollan, P. and Wilkinson, A. (2007). 'Implications of the EU Information and Consultation Directive and the Regulations in the UK—prospects for the future of employee representation'. *International Journal of Human Resource Management*, 18/7: 1145–58.

Goodman, J. (2000). 'Building bridges and settling differences: collective conciliation and arbitration under Acas', in B. Towers and W. Brown (eds.), *Employment Relations in Britain: 25 Years of the Advisory, Conciliation and Arbitration Service*. Oxford: Blackwell, 31–65.

Gospel, H. (1992). *Markets, Firms and the Management of Labour in Modern Britain*. Cambridge: Cambridge University Press.

Gospel, H. and Druker, J. (1998). 'The survival of national bargaining in the electrical contracting industry: a deviant case?'. *British Journal of Industrial Relations*, 36/2: 249–67.

Gospel, H. and Willman, P. (2003). 'Dilemmas in worker representation: information, consultation and negotiation', in H. Gospel and S. Wood (eds.), *Representing Workers*. London: Routledge, 144–63.

Goss, D. (1991). *Small Business and Society*. London: Routledge.

Goss, D. and Adam-Smith, D. (2001). 'Pragmatism and compliance: employer responses to the Working Time Regulations'. *Industrial Relations Journal*, 32/3: 195–208.

Gouldner, A. (1955). *Wildcat Strike*. London: Routledge and Kegan Paul.

Gratton, L., Hope-Hailey, V., Stiles, P., and Truss, C. (1999). *Strategic Human Resource Management: Corporate Rhetoric and Employee Reality*. Oxford: Oxford University Press.

Gray, J. (2010). 'Progressive, like the 1980s'. *London Review of Books*, 21 October, 3–7.

Grayson, R. (2010). *The Liberal Democrat Journey to a Lib-Con Coalition—and Where Next?* London: Compass.

Green, F. (1997). 'Union recognition and paid holiday entitlement'. *British Journal of Industrial Relations*, 35/2: 243–55.

Green, F. (2001). 'It's been a hard day's night: the concentration and intensification of work in late twentieth century Britain'. *British Journal of Industrial Relations*, 39/1: 53–80.

Green, F. (2003). 'The demands of work', in R. Dickens, P. Gregg, and J. Wadsworth (eds.), *The Labour Market under New Labour*. Basingstoke: Palgrave Macmillan, 137–49.

Green, F. (2006). *Demanding Work*. Princeton NJ: Princeton University Press.

Green, F. (2011). 'Job quality in Britain under the Labour Government', in P. Gregg and J. Wadsworth (eds.), *The Labour Market in Winter: The State of Working Britain*. Oxford: Oxford University Press, 111–28.

Green, F., Huxley, K., and Whitfield, K. (2010). 'The employee experience of work', in A. Wilkinson, N. Bacon, T. Redman, and S. Snell (eds.), *The SAGE Handbook of Human Resource Management*. London: Sage, 377–92.

Green, F. and Whitfield, K. (2009). 'Employees' experience of work', in W. Brown, A. Bryson, J. Forth, and K. Whitfield (eds.), *The Evolution of the Modern Workplace*. Cambridge: Cambridge University Press, 201–29.

Greene, A.-M. (2003). 'Women and industrial relations', in P. Ackers and A. Wilkinson (eds.), *Understanding Work and Employment*. Oxford: Oxford University Press, 305–15.

Greene, A.-M. and Kirton, G. (2009). *Diversity Management in the UK: Organizational and Stakeholder Experiences*. Abingdon: Routledge.

Greene, A.-M. and Kirton, G. (2011). 'Diversity management meets downsizing: the case of a government department'. *Employee Relations*, 33/1: 22–39.

Greene, S. and Robertson, G. (2010). 'Politics, justice and the new Russian strike'. *Communist and Post-Communist Studies*, 43/1: 73–95.

Greenhouse, S. (2008). *The Big Squeeze: Tough Times for the American Worker*. New York: Alfred Knopf.

Greer, I. and Hauptmeier, M. (2008). 'Political entrepreneurs and co-managers: labour transnationalism at four multinational auto companies'. *British Journal of Industrial Relations*, 46/1: 76–97.

Griffin, J. (1939). *Strikes: A Study in Quantitative Economics*. New York: Colombia University Press.

Grimshaw, D., Earnshaw, J., and Hebson, G. (2003). 'Private sector provision of supply teachers: a case of legal swings and professional roundabouts'. *Journal of Education Policy*, 18/3: 267–88.

Grimshaw, D. and Rubery, J. (2010). 'Pay and working time: shifting contours of the employment relationship', in T. Colling and M. Terry (eds.), *Industrial Relations: Theory and Practice* (3rd edn). Chichester: John Wiley, 349–77.

Grimshaw, D. and Rubery, J. (2012). 'The end of the UK's liberal collectivist social model? The implications of the coalition government's policy during the austerity crisis'. *Cambridge Journal of Economics*, 36/1: 105–26.

Guégnard, C. and Mériot, S.-A. (2009). 'Housekeepers and the siren call of hotel chains', in S. Bolton and M. Houlihan (eds.), *Work Matters: Critical Reflections on Contemporary Work*. Basingstoke: Palgrave Macmillan, 97–113.

Guest, D. (2011). 'Human resource management and performance: still searching for some answers'. *Human Resource Management Journal*, 21/1: 3–13.

Guest, D., Brown, W., Peccei, R., and Huxley, K. (2008). 'Does partnership at work increase trust? An analysis based on the 2004 Workplace Employment Relations Survey'. *Industrial Relations Journal*, 39/2: 124–52.

Guest, D. and Peccei, R. (2001). 'Partnership at work: mutuality and the balance of advantage'. *British Journal of Industrial Relations*, 39/2: 207–36.

Gumbrell-McCormick, R. and Hyman, R. (2010). 'Works councils: the European model of industrial democracy?', in A. Wilkinson, P. Gollan, M. Marchington, and D. Lewin (eds.), *The Oxford Handbook of Participation in Organizations*. Oxford: Oxford University Press, 286–314.

Gunnigle, P., Turner, T., and D'Art, D. (1998). 'Counterpoising collectivism: performance-related pay and industrial relations in greenfield sites'. *British Journal of Industrial Relations*, 36/4: 565–79.

Hakim, C. (1988). 'Self-employment in Britain: recent trends and current issues'. *Work, Employment and Society*, 2/4: 421–50.

Hale, A. and Wills, J. (eds.) (2005). *Threads of Labour: Garment Industry Supply Chains from the Workers' Perspective*. Oxford: Blackwell.

Hall, M. (1994). 'Industrial relations and the social dimension of European integration: before and after Maastricht', in R. Hyman and A. Ferner (eds.), *New Frontiers in European Industrial Relations*. Oxford: Blackwell, 281–311.

Hall, M. (2005). 'Using a multi-level consultation framework: the case of B&Q', in J. Storey (ed.), *Adding Value through Information and Consultation*. Basingstoke: Palgrave Macmillan, 240–53.

Hall, M. (2006). 'A cool response to the ICE Regulations? Employer and trade union approaches to the new legal framework for information and consultation'. *Industrial Relations Journal*, 37/5: 456–72.

Hall, M. and Edwards, P. (1999). 'Reforming the statutory redundancy consultation procedure'. *Industrial Law Journal*, 28/4: 299–318.

Hall, M., Hutchinson, S., Purcell, J., Terry, M., and Parker, J. (2013). 'Promoting effective consultation? Assessing the impact of the ICE Regulations'. *British Journal of Industrial Relations*, 51/2: 355–81.

Hall, M. and Marginson, P. (2005). 'Trojan horses or paper tigers? Assessing the significance of European Works Councils', in B. Harley, J. Hyman, and P. Thompson (eds.), *Participation and Democracy at Work*. Basingstoke: Palgrave Macmillan, 204–21.

Hall, M. and Purcell, J. (2012). *Consultation at Work: Regulation and Practice*. Oxford: Oxford University Press.

Hall, M. and Terry, M. (2004). 'The emerging system of statutory worker representation', in G. Healy, E. Heery, P. Taylor, and W. Brown (eds.), *The Future of Worker Representation*. Basingstoke: Palgrave Macmillan, 207–28.

Hall, P. and Soskice, D. (2001). 'An introduction to varieties of capitalism', in P. Hall and D. Soskice (eds.), *Varieties of Capitalism: The Institutional Foundations of Comparative Advantage*. Oxford: Oxford University Press, 1–68.

Hamann, K. and Kelly, J. (2008). 'Varieties of capitalism and industrial relations', in P. Blyton, N. Bacon, J. Fiorito, and E. Heery (eds.), *The SAGE Handbook of Industrial Relations*. London: Sage, 129–48.

Hammer, N. (2005). 'International framework agreements: global industrial relations between rights and bargaining'. *Transfer*, 4/5: 511–30.

Handy, C. (1994). *The Empty Raincoat*. London: Hutchinson.

Harris, C. (1987). *Redundancy and Recession*. Oxford: Basil Blackwell.

Harris, J. (2012). 'Self-employed business opportunity? No thanks'. *The Guardian*, 22 January, http://www.guardian.co.uk/commentisfree/2012/jan/22/self-employment-proper-jobs-cameron?INTCMP=SRCH

Harris, L. and Ogbonna, E. (2002). 'Exploring service sabotage: the antecedents, types and consequences of frontline, deviant, antiservice behaviors'. *Journal of Service Research*, 4/3: 163–83.

Hassel, A. (2008). 'The evolution of a global labor governance regime'. *Governance*, 21/2: 231–51.

Hawes, W. (2000). 'Setting the pace or running alongside? Acas and the changing employment relationship', in B. Towers and W. Brown (eds.), *Employment Relations in Britain: 25 Years of the Advisory, Conciliation and Arbitration Service*. Oxford: Blackwell, 1–30.

Haynes, P. and Allen, M. (2001). 'Partnership as union strategy: a preliminary evaluation'. *Employee Relations*, 23/2: 164–93.

Hayter, S. and Weinberg, B. (2011). 'Mind the gap: collective bargaining and wage inequality', in S. Hayter (ed.), *The Role of Collective Bargaining in the Global Economy: Negotiating for Social Justice*. Cheltenham: Edward Elgar, 136–86.

Hayward, B., Fong, B., and Thornton, A. (2007). *The Third Work-Life Balance Survey: Main Findings*. Employment Relations Research Series No. 86 London: Department for Business, Enterprise, and Regulatory Reform.

Hayward, B., Peters, M., Rousseau, N., and Seeds, K. (2004). *Findings from the Survey of Employment Tribunal Applications 2003. Employment Relations Research Series No. 33* London: Department of Trade and Industry.

Head, J. and Lucas, R. (2004). 'Employee relations in the non-union hotel industry: a case of "determined opportunism"?'. *Personnel Review*, 33/6: 693–710.

Health and Safety Executive (HSE) (2008). *Working Together to Reduce Stress at Work: A Guide for Employees*. London: HSE.

Healy, G., Bradley, H., and Mukherjee, N. (2004). 'Individualism and collectivism revisited: a study of black and minority ethnic women'. *Industrial Relations Journal*, 35/5: 451–66.

Healy, G. and Kirton, G. (2000). 'Women, power and trade union government in the UK'. *British Journal of Industrial Relations*, 38/3: 343–60.

Healy, G., Kirton, G., and Noon, M. (2010). 'Inequalities, intersectionality and equality and diversity initiatives: the conundrums and challenges of researching equality, inequalities, and diversity', in G. Healy, G. Kirton, and M. Noon (eds.), *Equality, Inequalities, and Diversity: Contemporary Challenges and Strategies*. Basingstoke: Palgrave Macmillan, 1–17.

Healy, G. and Oikelome, F. (2007). 'Equality and diversity actors: a challenge to traditional industrial relations?'. *Equal Opportunities International*, 26/1: 44–65.

Heery, E. (1997). 'Performance-related pay and trade union de-recognition'. *Employee Relations*, 19/3: 208–21.

Heery, E. (1998a). 'A return to contract? Performance related pay in a public service'. *Work, Employment and Society*, 12/1: 73–95.

Heery, E. (1998b). 'Campaigning for part-time workers'. *Work, Employment and Society*, 12/2: 351–66.

Heery, E. (1998c). 'The relaunch of the Trades Union Congress'. *British Journal of Industrial Relations*, 36/3: 339–60.

Heery, E. (2006). 'Equality bargaining: where, who, why?'. *Gender, Work, and Organization*, 13/6: 522–42.

Heery, E. (2009a). 'The representation gap and the future of worker representation'. *Industrial Relations Journal*, 40/4: 324–36.

Heery, E. (2009b). 'Worker voice and reward management', in G. White and J. Druker (eds.), *Reward Management: A Critical Text* (2nd edn). Abingdon: Routledge, 100–19.

Heery, E., Bacon, N., Blyton, P., and Fiorito, J. (2008). 'Introduction: the field of industrial relations', in P. Blyton, N. Bacon, J. Fiorito, and E. Heery (eds.), *The SAGE Handbook of Industrial Relations*. London: Sage, 1–32.

Heery, E. and Frege, C. (2006). 'New actors in industrial relations'. *British Journal of Industrial Relations*, 44/4: 601–4.

Heery, E. and Simms, M. (2008). 'Constraints on union organising in the United Kingdom'. *Industrial Relations Journal*, 39/1: 24–42.

Heery, E. and Simms, M. (2010). 'Employer responses to union organising: patterns and effects'. *Human Resource Management Journal*, 20/1: 3–22.

Heery, E. and Simms, M. (2011). 'Seizing an opportunity? Union organizing campaigns in Britain, 1998-2004'. *Labor History*, 52/1: 23–47.

Heery, E., Simms, M., Simpson, D., Delbridge, R., and Salmon, J. (2000a). 'Organizing unionism comes to the UK'. *Employee Relations*, 22/1: 38–57.

Heery, E., Simms, M., Delbridge, R., Salmon, J., and Simpson, D. (2000b). 'The TUC's Organising Academy: an assessment'. *Industrial Relations Journal*, 31/5: 400–15.

Heery, E., Simms, M., Delbridge, R., Salmon, J., and Simpson, D. (2000c). 'Union organizing in Britain: a survey of policy and practice'. *International Journal of Human Resource Management*, 11/5: 986–1007.

Heery, E., Simms, M., Delbridge, R., Salmon, J., and Simpson, D. (2003). 'Trade union recruitment policy in Britain: form and effects', in G. Gall (ed.), *Union Organizing: Campaigning for Union Recognition*. London: Routledge, 56–78.

Held, D. and McGrew, A. (2007). *Globalization/Anti-Globalization*. Cambridge: Polity.

Henry, S. (1982). 'Factory law: the changing disciplinary technology of industrial social control'. *International Journal of the Sociology of Law*, 10/8: 365–83.

Hepple, B. (1992). 'The fall and rise of unfair dismissal', in W. McCarthy (ed.), *Legal Intervention in Industrial Relations: Gains and Losses*. Oxford: Blackwell, 79–102.

Hepple, B. (2005). *Labour Laws and Global Trade*. Oxford: Hart Publishing.

Herod, A., Peck, J., and Wills, J. (2003). 'Geography and industrial relations', in P. Ackers and A. Wilkinson (eds.), *Understanding Work and Employment: Industrial Relations in Transition*. Oxford: Oxford University Press, 176–92.

Heyes, J. (1997). 'Annualised hours and the "knock": the organisation of working time in a chemicals plant'. *Work, Employment and Society*, 11/1: 65–81.

Heyes, J. and Gray, A. (2001). 'The impact of the National Minimum Wage on the textiles and clothing industry'. *Policy Studies*, 22/2: 83–98.

High Pay Commission (2011). *Cheques with Balances: Why Tackling High Pay is in the Public Interest*. London: High Pay Commission.

Hill, J. and Trist, E. (1953). 'A consideration of industrial accidents as a means of withdrawal from the work situation'. *Human Relations*, 6/4: 357–80.

Hinton, J. (1973). *The First Shop Stewards' Movement*. London: Allen and Unwin.

Hirst, P., Thompson, G., and Bromley, S. (2009). *Globalization in Question* (3rd edn). Cambridge: Polity.

HM Government (2010). *The Coalition: Our Programme for Government*. London: Cabinet Office.

HM Government (2011a). *Consultation on Modern Workplaces*. http://www.bis.gov.uk/assets/biscore/employment-matters/docs/c/11-699-consultation-modern-workplaces.pdf

HM Government (2011b). *Opening Doors, Breaking Barriers: A Strategy for Social Mobility*. London: Cabinet Office.

HM Government (2012a) *Consultation on Modern Workplaces: Modern Workplaces Consultation— Government Response on Flexible Working*, http://www.bis.gov.uk/assets/biscore/employment-matters/docs/m/12-1269-modern-workplaces-response-flexible-working

HM Government (2012b) *Consultation on Modern Workplaces: Modern Workplaces Consultation— Government Response on Flexible Parental Leave*, http://www.bis.gov.uk/assets/biscore/employment-matters/docs/m/12-1267-modern-workplaces-response-flexible-parental-leave

HM Treasury (2011). *Autumn Statement 2011*. Cm 8231. London: HMSO.

HM Treasury and Department of Trade and Industry (DTI) (2003). *Balancing Work and Family Life: Enhancing Choice and Support for Parents*. London: HM Treasury/DTI.

Hochschild, A. (1983). *The Managed Heart*. London: University of California Press.

Holgate, J. (2005). 'Organizing migrant workers: a case study of working conditions and unionization in a London sandwich factory'. *Work, Employment and Society*, 19/3: 463–80.

Holgate, J. (2009). 'Contested terrain: London's living wage campaign and the tensions between community and union organising', in J. McBride and I. Greenwood (eds.), *Community Unionism: A Comparative Analysis of Concepts and Contexts*. Basingstoke: Palgrave Macmillan, 49–74.

Holloway, L. (2012). 'The Equality and Human Rights Commission is being destroyed'. *The Guardian*, 24 August, http://www.guardian.co.uk/commentisfree/2012/aug/24/coalition-destroy-equality-human-rights-commission

Holmes, C. and Mayhew, K. (2012). *The Changing Shape of the UK Job Market and its Implications for the Bottom Half of Earners*. London: Resolution Foundation.

Holmes, E. and Oakley, M. (2012). *Local Pay, Local Growth: Reforming Pay Setting in the Public Sector*. London: Policy Exchange.

Holt, H. and Grainger, H. (2005). *Results of the Second Flexible Working Employee Survey*. DTI Employment Relations Research Series No. 39 London: DTI.

Hoque, K. and Bacon, N. (2011). 'Assessing the impact of Union Learning Representatives on training: evidence from a matched sample of ULRs and managers'. *Work, Employment and Society*, 25/2: 218–33.

Hoque, K. and Noon, M. (2004). 'Equal opportunities policy and practice in Britain: evaluating the 'empty shell' hypothesis'. *Work, Employment and Society*, 18/3: 481–506.

House of Commons Employment Committee (1994). *The Future of the Unions*. Third Report Volume II, *Minutes of Evidence*. London: HMSO.

Howell, C. (2004). 'Is there a third way for industrial relations?'. *British Journal of Industrial Relations*, 42/1: 1–22.

Howell, C. (2005). *Trade Unions and the State*. Princeton NJ: Princeton University Press.

Hudson, M. (2002). 'Flexibility and the reorganisation of work', in B. Burchell, D. Ladipo, and F. Wilkinson (eds.), *Job Insecurity and Work Intensification*. London: Routledge, 39–60.

Huselid, M. (1995). 'The impact of human resource management practices on turnover, productivity, and corporate financial performance'. *Academy of Management Journal*, 38/3: 635–72.

Hussein, S. (2011). 'Estimating probabilities and numbers of direct care workers paid under the National Minimum Wage in the UK: a Bayesian approach'. *Social Care Workforce Periodical*, 16, http://www.kcl.ac.uk/sspp/kpi/scwru/pubs/periodical/issues/scwp16.pdf

Huzzard, T. and Docherty, P. (2005). 'Between global and local: eight European Works Councils in retrospect and prospect'. *Economic and Industrial Democracy*, 26/4: 541–68.

Hyman, J., Baldry, C., Scholarios, D., and Bunzel, D. (2003). 'Work-life imbalance in call centres and software development'. *British Journal of Industrial Relations*, 41/2: 215–39.

Hyman, J. and Marks, A. (2008). 'Frustrated ambitions: the reality of balancing work and life for call centre employees', in C. Warhurst, D. Eikhof, and A. Haunschild (eds.), *Work Less, Live More: Critical Analysis of the Work-Life Boundary*. Basingstoke: Palgrave Macmillan, 191–209.

Hyman, J. and Mason, B. (1995). *Managing Employee Involvement and Participation*. London: Sage.

Hyman, J. and Summers, J. (2004). 'Lacking balance? Work-life employment practices in the modern economy'. *Personnel Review*, 33/4: 418–29.

Hyman, R. (1971). *The Workers' Union*. Oxford: Clarendon Press.

Hyman, R. (1972). *Disputes Procedure in Action*. London: Heinemann.

Hyman, R. (1975). *Industrial Relations: A Marxist Introduction*. London: Macmillan.

Hyman, R. (1977). *Strikes* (2nd edn). Glasgow: Fontana/Collins.

Hyman, R. (1987). 'Strategy or structure? Capital, labour and control'. *Work, Employment and Society*, 1/1: 25–55.

Hyman, R. (1989). *The Political Economy of Industrial Relations*. Basingstoke: Macmillan.

Hyman, R. (1994). 'Changing trade union identities and strategies', in R. Hyman and A. Ferner (eds.), *New Frontiers in European Industrial Relations*. Oxford: Blackwell, 108–39.

Hyman, R. (1996). 'Is there a case for statutory works councils in Britain?', in A. McColgan (ed.), *The Future of Labour Law*. London: Cassell, 64–84.

Hyman, R. (2001a). 'The Europeanisation—or the erosion—of industrial relations?'. *Industrial Relations Journal*, 32/4: 280–94.

Hyman, R. (2001b). *Understanding European Trade Unionism: Between Market, Class and Society*. London: Sage.

Hyman, R. (2003). 'The historical evolution of British industrial relations', in P. Edwards (ed.), *Industrial Relations* (2nd edn). Oxford: Blackwell, 37–57.

Hyman, R. (2005). 'Trade unions and the politics of the European Social Model'. *Economic and Industrial Democracy*, 26/1: 9–40.

Hyman, R. (2010). 'British industrial relations: the European Dimension', in T. Colling and M. Terry (eds.), *Industrial Relations: Theory and Practice*, (3rd edn). Chichester: John Wiley, 54–79.

Hyman, R. (2011). *Trade Unions, Lisbon and Europe 2020: From Dream to Nightmare*, LSE 'Europe in Question' Discussion Paper Series, No. 45 London: LSE.

Incomes Data Services (IDS) (2009). Discipline, Grievance, and Mediation. *IDS HR Studies*, 906.

Incomes Data Services (IDS) (2011a). 'Employee consultation'. *IDS HR Studies*, 949, September.

Incomes Data Services (IDS) (2011b). *The Impact of the National Minimum Wage on Pay Setting since 1994: A Report for the Low Pay Commission*, http://www.lowpay.gov.uk/lowpay/research/pdf/IDSFinal.pdf

Incomes Data Services (IDS) (2012). *Crowding Out: Fact or Fiction?* London: Incomes Data Services.

Independent Commission on Social Mobility (2009). *Report of the Independent Commission on Social Mobility*, http://www.mnarey.co.uk/resources/Social%20Mobility%20(Narey%20Report)%20Final.pdf

Industrial Relations Services (IRS) (2001). 'We don't need no litigation'. *Employment Trends*, 719: 4–16.

Inman, P. (2013). 'Big rise in firms hiring staff on zero-hour contracts'. *The Guardian*, 2 April, http://www.guardian.co.uk/law/2013/apr/02/rise-staff-zero-hour-contracts

International Labour Organization (ILO) (2009): *Rules of the Game: A Brief Introduction to International Labour Standards* (revised edn). Geneva: ILO.

International Labour Organisation (ILO) (2011). *World of Work Report 2011: Making Markets Work for Jobs*. Geneva: International Institute for Labour Studies.

International Labour Organization (ILO) (2012). *World of Work Report 2012: Better Jobs for a Better Economy*. Geneva: ILO, International Institute for Labour Studies.

International Trade Union Confederation (ITUC) (2007). *Massive 'Virtual Strike' against IBM*. News Release, 28 September, http://www.ituc-csi.org/massive-virtual-strike-against-ibm.html?lang=en

International Trade Union Confederation (ITUC) (2008). *Annual Survey of Violations of Trade Union Rights*. Brussels: ITUC.

International Trade Union Confederation (ITUC) 2012: *Annual Survey of Violations of Trade Union Rights 2012*, http://survey.ituc-csi.org/

Ipsos Mori/Community Links (2012). *Non-Compliance with the National Minimum Wage: Research Report Prepared for the LPC*, http://www.lowpay.gov.uk/lowpay/research/pdf/Ipsos_Mori_Non-compliance_of_the_NMW_020212_FINAL.pdf

Jagodzinski, R. (2011). 'EWCs after 15 years—success or failure?'. *Transfer*, 17/2: 203–16.

James, G. (2011). 'The law relating to pregnancy and maternity leave', in T. Wright and H. Conley (eds.), *The Gower Handbook of Discrimination at Work*. Farnham: Gower, 47–56.

James, P., Tombs, S., and Whyte, D. (2013). 'An independent review of British health and safety regulation? From common sense to non-sense'. *Policy Studies*, 34/1: 36–52.

James, S. and Lloyd, C. (2008). 'Too much pressure? Retailer power and occupational health and safety in the food processing industry'. *Work, Employment and Society*, 22/4: 713–30.

Jameson, H. (2012). 'The Beecroft Report: pandering to popular perceptions of over-regulation'. *Political Quarterly*, 83/4: 838–43.

Jefferys, S. (2000). 'A "Copernican Revolution" in French industrial relations: are the times a' changing?'. *British Journal of Industrial Relations*, 38/2: 241–60.

Jefferys, S. (2003). *Liberté, Égalité and Fraternité at Work: Changing French Employment Relations*. Basingstoke: Palgrave Macmillan.

Jenkins, S. and Delbridge, R. (2007). 'Disconnected workplaces: interests and identities in the "high performance" factory', in S. Bolton and M. Houlihan (eds.), *Searching for the Human in Human Resource Management*. Basingstoke: Palgrave Macmillan, 195–218.

Jenkins, J. and Turnbull, P. (2011). 'Can workers of the world unite? Globalization and the employment relationship', in P. Blyton, E. Heery, and P. Turnbull (eds.), *Reassessing the Employment Relationship*. Basingstoke: Palgrave Macmillan, 195–224.

Jewson, N. and Mason, D. (1986). 'The theory and practice of equal opportunities policies: liberal and radical approaches'. *Sociological Review*, 34/2: 307–34.

Johnstone, S., Ackers, P., and Wilkinson, A. (2009). 'The British partnership phenomenon: a ten year review'. *Human Resource Management Journal*, 19/3: 260–79.

Johnstone, S., Wilkinson, A., and Ackers, P. (2010). 'Critical incidents of partnership: five years' experience at NatBank'. *Industrial Relations Journal*, 41/4: 382–98.

Jones, G. (2005). *Multinationals and Global Capitalism: From the Nineteenth to the Twenty-First Century*. Oxford: Oxford University Press.

Jones, T. and Ram, M. (2010). 'Review article: ethnic variations on the small firm labour process'. *International Small Business Journal*, 28/2: 163–73.

Jordan, B. (1985). *The State: Authority and Autonomy*. Oxford: Blackwell.

Jordan, E., Thomas, A., Kitching, J., and Blackburn, R. (2013). *Employment Regulation. Part A: Employer Perceptions and the Impact of Employment Regulation. Employment Relations Research Series No. 123* London: Department of Business, Innovation, and Skills.

Kahn-Freund, O. (1964). 'Legal framework', in A. Flanders and H. Clegg (eds.), *The System of Industrial Relations in Great Britain*. Oxford: Basil Blackwell, 42–127.

Kahn-Freund, O. (1977). *Labour and the Law* (2nd edn). London: Stevens.

Kalleberg, A. (2009). 'Precarious work, insecure workers: employment relations in transition'. *American Sociological Review*, 74/1: 1–22.

Kalman, D. (1999). 'Collective wisdom'. *People Management*, 25 February: 37–43.

Kamenou, N., Netto, G., and Fearfull, A. (2012). 'Ethnic minority women in the Scottish labour market: employers' perceptions'. *British Journal of Management*, DOI:10.1111/j. 1467-8551. 2012.00811.x

Kandola, B. and Fullerton, J. (1994). *Managing the Mosaic: Diversity in Action*. London: IPD.

Katz, H. and Darbishire, O. (2000). *Converging Divergences: Worldwide Changes in Employment Systems*. Ithaca NY: ILR Cornell University Press.

Kaufman, B. (2010a). 'The theoretical foundation of industrial relations and its implications'. *Industrial and Labor Relations Review*, 64/1: 74–108.

Kaufman, B. (2010b). 'SHRM theory in the post-Huselid era: why it is fundamentally misspecified'. *Industrial Relations*, 49/2: 286–313.

Kaufman, B. (2011). 'The future of employment relations: insights from theory', in K. Townsend and A. Wilkinson (eds.), *The Edward Elgar Research Handbook on Work and Employment Relations*. Cheltenham: Edward Elgar, 13–44.

Kaufman, B. (2012). 'History of the British Industrial Relations field reconsidered: getting from the Webbs to the new employment relations paradigm'. *British Journal of Industrial Relations*, early view, DOI: 10.1111/j. 1467-8543. 2012.00907.x

Kaufman, B. (2013). 'Keeping the commitment model in the air during turbulent times: employee involvement at Delta Airlines'. *Industrial Relations*, 52/ S1: 343–77.

Kaufman, B. and Taras, D. (2010). 'Employee participation through non-union forms of employee representation', in A. Wilkinson, P. Gollan, M. Marchington, and D. Lewin (eds.), *The Oxford Handbook of Participation in Organizations*. Oxford: Oxford University Press, 258–85.

Keller, B. (2003). 'The European social partners: projects and future perspectives', in D. Foster and P. Scott (eds.), *Trade Unions in Europe: Meeting the Challenge*. Brussels: Peter Lang, 115–43.

Keller, B. and Sörries, B. (1999). 'The new European social dialogue: old wine in new bottles?'. *Journal of European Social Policy*, 9/2: 111–25.

Keller, B. and Weber, S. (2011). 'Sectoral social dialogue at EU level: problems and prospects of implementation'. *European Journal of Industrial Relations*, 17/3: 227–43.

Kelliher, C. and Anderson, D. (2010). 'Doing more with less? Flexible working practices and the intensification of work'. *Human Relations*, 63/1: 83–106.

Kelly, J. (1998). *Rethinking Industrial Relations*. London: Routledge.

Kelly, J. (2005a). 'Social partnership agreements in Britain', in M. Stuart and M. Martinez Lucio (eds.), *Partnership and Modernisation in Employment Relations*. London: Routledge, 188–209.

Kelly, J. (2005b). 'Social movement theory and union revitalization in Britain', in S. Fernie and D. Metcalf (eds.), *Trade Unions: Resurgence or Demise?* London: Routledge, 62–82.

Kelly, J. (2011). 'Theories of collective action and union power', in G. Gall, A. Wilkinson, and R. Hurd (eds.), *The International Handbook of Labour Unions: Responses to Neo-Liberalism*. Cheltenham: Edward Elgar, 13–28.

Kelly, J. and Badigannavar, V. (2004). 'Union organizing', in J. Kelly and P. Willman (eds.), *Union Organization and Activity*. London: Routledge, 32–50.

Kelly, J. and Heery, E. (1994). *Working for the Union: British Trade Union Officers*. Cambridge: Cambridge University Press.

Kenny, M. (2009). 'Taking the temperature of the UK's political elite', *Parliamentary Affairs*, 62: 149–61.

Kerr, C., Dunlop, J., Harbison, F., and Myers, C. (1962). *Industrialism and Industrial Man*. London: Heinemann.

Kerr, C. and Siegel, A. (1954). 'The inter-industry propensity to strike', in A. Kornhauser, R. Dubin, and A. Ross (eds.), *Industrial Conflict*. New York: McGraw-Hill, 189–212.

Kersley, B., Alpin, C., Forth, J., Bryson, A., Bewley, H., Dix, G., and Oxenbridge, S. (2006). *Inside the Workplace: Findings from the 2004 Workplace Employment Relations Survey*. London: Routledge.

Kessler, I. (2000). 'Remuneration systems', in S. Bach and K. Sisson (eds.), *Personnel Management* (3rd edn). Oxford: Blackwell, 264–86.

Kessler, I. and Purcell, J. (1995). 'Individualism and collectivism in theory and practice: management style and the design of pay systems', in P. Edwards (ed.), *Industrial Relations: Theory and Practice in Britain*. Oxford: Blackwell, 337–67.

Kessler, S. (1993). 'Procedures and third parties'. *British Journal of Industrial Relations*, 31/2: 211–25.

Kessler, S. (1994). 'Incomes policy'. *British Journal of Industrial Relations*, 32/2: 181–99.

Kim, D.-O. and Bae, J. (2005). 'Workplace innovation, employment relations and HRM: two electronics companies in South Korea'. *The International Journal of Human Resource Management*, 17/7: 1277–302.

Kirkpatrick, I. and Hoque, K. (2006). 'A retreat from permanent employment? Accounting for the rise of professional agency work in UK public services'. *Work, Employment and Society*, 20/4: 649–66.

Kirton, G. (1999). 'Sustaining and developing women's trade union activism: a gendered project?'. *Gender, Work and Organization*, 6/4: 213–23.

Kirton, G. and Greene, A.-M. (2002). 'The dynamics of positive action in UK trade unions: the case of women and black members'. *Industrial Relations Journal*, 33/2: 157–72.

Kirton, G. and Greene, A.-M. (2009). 'The costs and opportunities of doing diversity work in mainstream organisations'. *Human Resource Management Journal*, 19/2: 159–75.

Kirton, G. and Greene, A.-M. (2010). *The Dynamics of Managing Diversity: A Critical Approach* (3rd edn). Oxford: Butterworth-Heinemann.

Kirton, G. and Healy, G. (1999). 'Transforming union women: the role of women trade union officials in union renewal'. *Industrial Relations Journal*, 30/1: 31–45.

Kirton, G. and Healy, G. (2013). 'Commitment and collective identity of long-term union participation: the case of women union leaders in the UK and USA'. *Work, Employment and Society*, 27/2: 195–212.

Klass, B. (2010). 'Discipline and grievances', in A. Wilkinson, N. Bacon, T. Redman, and S. Snell (eds.), *The SAGE Handbook of Human Resource Management*. London: Sage, 322–35.

Klein, N. (2000). *No Logo*. London: Flamingo.

Knight, K. and Latreille, P. (2000). 'Discipline, dismissals and complaints to employment tribunals'. *British Journal of Industrial Relations*, 38/4: 533–55.

Knowles, K. (1952). *Strikes—a Study in Industrial Conflict*. Oxford: Basil Blackwell.

Knox, A. (2010). ' "Lost in translation": an analysis of temporary work agency employment in hotels'. *Work, Employment and Society*, 24/3: 449–67.

Kochan, T., Eaton, A., McKersie, R., and Adler, P. (2009). *Healing Together: The Labor-Management Partnership at Kaiser Permanente*. Ithaca NY: Cornell University Press.

Kochan, T. A. and Osterman, P. (1994). *The Mutual Gains Enterprise*. Boston: Harvard University Press.

Kodz, J., Harper, H., and Dench, S. (2002). *Work–Life Balance: Beyond the Rhetoric*. Institute of Employment Studies Report No. 384 Brighton: IES.

Kohl, B. and Farthing, L. (2005). *Impasse in Bolivia*. London: Zed Books.

Koo, H. (2001). *Korean Workers: The Culture and Politics of Class Formation*. Ithaca NY: Cornell University Press.

Korczynski, M. (2002). *Human Resource Management in Service Work*. Basingstoke: Palgrave.

KPMG (2012). *Living Wage Research for KPMG*. http://www.kpmg.com/uk/en/issuesandinsights/ articlespublications/newsreleases/pages/one-in-five-uk-workers-paid-less-than-the-living-wage.aspx

Krugman, P. (2012). *End this Depression Now!* New York: W. W. Norton.

Kumar, K. (1986). *Prophecy and Progress: The Sociology of Industrial and Post-industrial Society*. Harmondsworth: Penguin.

Kuruvilla, S. and Verma, A. (2006). 'International labor standards, soft regulation, and national government roles'. *Journal of Industrial Relations*, 48/1: 41–58.

Kwarteng, K., Patel, P., Raab, D., Skidmore, C., and Truss, E. (2012). *Britannia Unchained: Global Lessons for Growth and Prosperity*. Basingstoke: Palgrave Macmillan.

La Botz, D. (2001). *Made in Indonesia: Indonesian Workers since Suharto*. Cambridge MA: South End Press.

Langlois, M. and Lucas, R. (2005). 'The adaptation of hospitality and retail firms to the NMW: a focus on the impact of age-related clauses'. *Industrial Relations Journal*, 36/1: 77–92.

Lansley, S. (2010). *Unfair to Middling: How Middle Income Britain's Shrinking Wages Fuelled the Crash and Threaten Recovery*. London: TUC.

Lansley, S. (2011). *Britain's Livelihood Crisis*. London: TUC.

Lansley, S. (2012). *All in this Together? An Audit of the Impact of the Downturn on the Workforce*. London: TUC.

Lapavitsas, C. (2011). 'Theorizing financialization'. *Work, Employment and Society*, 25/4: 611–26.

Latreille, P., Latreille, J., and Knight, K. (2007). 'Employment tribunals and Acas: evidence from a survey of representatives'. *Industrial Relations Journal*, 38/2: 136–54.

Leadbeater, C. (1999). *Living on Thin Air*. London: Viking.

Lecher, W., Rüb, S., and Weiner, K.-P. (2001). *European Works Councils: Development, Types, and Networking*. Aldershot: Ashgate.

Lee, C.-K. (2007). *Against the Law: Labor Protests in China's Rustbelt and Sunbelt*. Berkeley CA: University of California Press.

Lee, S. (2009). 'Introduction: David Cameron's political challenges', in S. Lee and M. Beech (eds.), *The Conservatives under David Cameron: Built to Last?* Basingstoke: Palgrave Macmillan, 1–17.

Lee, S. (2011). '"We are all in this together": the coalition agenda for British modernization', in S. Lee and M. Beech (eds.), *The Cameron-Clegg Government: Coalition Politics in an Age of Austerity*. Basingstoke: Palgrave Macmillan, 3–23.

Legge, K. (2001). 'Silver bullet or spent round? Assessing the meaning of the "high commitment management"/ performance relationship', in J. Storey (ed.), *Human Resource Management: A Critical Text* (2nd edn). London: Thomson Learning, 21–36.

Legge, K. (2005). *Human Resource Management: Rhetoric and Realities* (2nd edn). Basingstoke: Palgrave Macmillan.

Leidner, R. (2002). 'Fast-food work in the United States', in T. Royle and B. Towers (eds.), *Labour Relations in the Global Fast-Food Industry*. London: Routledge, 8–29.

Leighton, P. and Wynn, M. (2011). 'Classifying employment relationships—more sliding doors of a better regulatory framework?' *Industrial Law Journal*, 40/1: 5–44.

Leisink, P. (1999). 'Introduction', in P. Leisink (ed.), *Globalization and Labour Relations*. Cheltenham: Edward Elgar, 1–24.

Leopold, J. (1997). 'Trade unions, political fund ballots and the Labour party'. *British Journal of Industrial Relations*, 35/1: 23–38.

Leopold, J. (2006). 'Trade unions and the third round of political fund balloting'. *Industrial Relations Journal*, 37/3: 190–208.

Lewis, P. (1993). *The Successful Management of Redundancy*. Oxford: Blackwell.

Lewis, S. (1997). '"Family friendly" employment policies: a route to changing organizational culture or playing about at the margins?'. *Gender, Work and Organization*, 4/1: 13–23.

Liff, S. (1997). 'Two routes to managing diversity: individual differences or social group characteristics?'. *Employee Relations*, 19/1: 11–26.

Liff, S. (1999). 'Diversity and equal opportunities: room for a constructive compromise?'. *Human Resource Management Journal*, 9/1: 65–75.

Liff, S. (2003). 'The industrial relations of a diverse workforce', in P. Edwards (ed.), *Industrial Relations* (2nd edn). Oxford: Blackwell, 420–46.

Liff, S. and Wacjman, J. (1996). '"Sameness" and "difference" revisited: which way forward for equal opportunity initiatives?'. *Journal of Management Studies*, 33/1: 79–94.

Liff, S. and Ward, K. (2001). 'Distorted views through the glass ceiling: the construction of women's understandings of promotion and senior management positions'. *Gender, Work and Organization*, 8/1: 19–36.

Lillie, N. and Martinez Lucio, M. (2004). 'International trade union revitalization: the role of national union approaches', in C. Frege and J. Kelly (eds.), *Varieties of Unionism*. Oxford: Oxford University Press, 159–80.

Lindstrom, N. (2010). 'Service liberalization in the enlarged EU: a race to the bottom or the emergence of transnational political conflict?'. *Journal of Common Market Studies*, 48/5: 1307–27.

Littleton, S. (1992). *The Wapping Dispute*. Aldershot: Avebury.

Lloyd, C. (2001). 'What do employee councils do? The impact of non-union forms of representation on trade union organisation'. *Industrial Relations Journal, 32/4*: 313–27.

Locke, R., Kochan, T., Romis, M., and Qin, F. (2007). 'Beyond corporate codes of conduct: work organization and labour standards at Nike's suppliers'. *International Labour Review, 146/1–2*: 21–40.

Löfstedt, R. (2011). *Reclaiming Health and Safety for All: An Independent Review of Health and Safety Legislation*. Cm 8219. London: Department of Work and Pensions.

Logan, J. (2006). 'The union avoidance industry in the United States'. *British Journal of Industrial Relations, 44/4*: 651–75.

Loveday, B., Williams, S., and Scott, P. (2008). 'Workforce modernization in the police service: prospects for reform?' *Personnel Review, 37/4*: 361–74.

Low Pay Commission (LPC) (2004). *The National Minimum Wage: Protecting Young Workers*. Fifth report of the Low Pay Commission. London: HMSO.

Low Pay Commission (LPC) (2010). *National Minimum Wage: Low Pay Commission Report 2010*. Cm 7823. London: The Stationery Office.

Low Pay Commission (LPC) (2011). *National Minimum Wage: Low Pay Commission Report 2011*. Cm 8023. London: The Stationery Office.

Low Pay Commission (LPC) (2012). *National Minimum Wage: Low Pay Commission Report 2012*. Cm 8302. London: The Stationery Office.

Low Pay Commission (LPC) (2013). *National Minimum Wage: Low Pay Commission Report 2013*. Cm 8565. London: The Stationery Office.

Luce, S. (2004). *Fighting for a Living Wage*. New York: Cornell University Press.

Ludlum, S. and Taylor, A. (2003). 'The political representation of the labour interest'. *British Journal of Industrial Relations, 41/4*: 727–49.

Lundberg, H. and Karlsson, J. (2011). 'Under the clean surface: working as a hotel attendant'. *Work, Employment and Society, 25/1*, 141–8.

Lupton, T. (1963). *On the Shop Floor*. Oxford: Pergamon.

Macalister, T. and Pidd, H. (2009). 'Uproar in Cowley as BMW confirms 850 job cuts at Mini factory'. *The Guardian*, 16 February, http://www.theguardian.com/business/2009/feb/16/bmw-mini-job-cuts

McBride, A. (2000). 'Promoting representation of women within UNISON', in M. Terry (ed.), *Redefining Public Sector Unionism: UNISON and the Future of Trade Unions*. London: Routledge, 100–18.

McBride, A. (2001). *Gender Democracy in Trade Unions*. Aldershot: Ashgate.

McBride, J. and Greenwood, I. (eds.) (2009). *Community Unionism: A Comparative Analysis of Concepts and Contexts*. Basingstoke: Palgrave Macmillan.

McCarthy, W. (1964). *The Closed Shop in Britain*. Oxford: Basil Blackwell.

McColgan, A. (2000). 'Missing the point? The Part-time Workers (Prevention of Less Favourable Treatment) Regulations 2000 (SI 2000, No 1551)'. *Industrial Law Journal, 29/3*: 260–7.

MacDonald, R. and Coffield, F. (1991). *Risky Business? Youth and the Enterprise Culture*. Basingstoke: Falmer Press.

McDowell, L., Batvitzky, A. and Dyer, S. (2012). 'Global flows and local labour markets: precarious employment and migrant workers in the UK', in J. Scott, S. Dex, and A. Pagnol (eds.), *Gendered Lives: Gender Inequalities in Production and Reproduction*. Cheltenham: Edward Elgar, 123–51.

MacDuffie, J.-P. (1995). 'Human resource bundles and manufacturing performance: organizational logic and flexible production systems in the world auto industry'. *Industrial and Labor Relations Review, 48/2*: 195–221.

McGovern, P., Hill, S., Mills, C., and White, M. (2007). *Market, Class, and Employment*. Oxford: Oxford University Press.

McIlroy, J. (1991). *The Permanent Revolution? Conservative Law and the Trade Unions*. Nottingham: Spokesman.

McIlroy, J. (1998). 'The enduring alliance? Trade unions and the making of New Labour'. *British Journal of Industrial Relations, 36/4*: 537–64.

McIlroy, J. (1999). 'Unfinished business—the reform of strike legislation in Britain'. *Employee Relations, 21/6*: 521–39.

McIlroy, J. (2009). 'Under stress but still enduring: the contentious alliance in the age of Tony Blair and Gordon Brown', in G. Daniels and J. McIlroy (eds.), *Trade Unions in a Neo Liberal World: British Trade Unions under New Labour*. Abingdon: Routledge, 165–201.

McIlroy, J. and Daniels, G. (2009). 'An anatomy of British trade unionism since 1997: organization, structure and factionalism', in G. Daniels and J. McIlroy (eds.), *Trade Unions in a Neo Liberal World: British Trade Unions under New Labour*, Abingdon: Routledge, 127–64.

McIntosh, I. and Broderick, J. (1996). 'Neither one thing nor the other: compulsory competitive tendering and Southburg Cleansing services'. *Work, Employment and Society, 10/3*: 413–30.

McIvor, A. (1996). *Organised Capital*. Cambridge: Cambridge University Press.

McKay, S. (2001). 'Annual review article2000.Between flexibility and regulation: rights, equality and protection at work'. *British Journal of Industrial Relations*, 39/2: 285–303.

McKay, S. (2006). *Satanic Mills or Silicon Islands? The Politics of High-Tech Production in the Philippines*. Ithaca NY: Cornell University Press.

McKay, S. and Markova. E. (2010). 'The operation and management of agency workers in conditions of vulnerability'. *Industrial Relations Journal*, 41/5: 446–60.

McKinlay, A. and McNulty, D. (1992). 'At the cutting edge of new realism: the engineers' 35 hour week campaign'. *Industrial Relations Journal*, 23/3: 205–13.

McLoughlin, I. and Gourlay, S. (1994). *Enterprise without Unions*. Buckingham: Open University Press.

Machin, S. (1999). 'Wage inequality in the 1970s, 1980s and 1990s', in P. Gregg and J. Wadsworth (eds.), *The State of Working Britain*. Manchester: Manchester University Press, 185–205.

Machin, S. (2000). 'Union decline in Britain'. *British Journal of Industrial Relations*, 38/4: 631–45.

Machin, S. (2011). 'Changing wage structures: trends and explanations', in D. Marsden (ed.), *Employment in the Lean Years*. Oxford: Oxford University Press, 151–67.

MacLeod, D. and Clarke, N. (2009). *Engaging for Success: Enhancing Performance through Employee Engagement*. London: BIS.

Macmillan, J. (1999). 'Employment tribunals: philosophies and practicalities'. *Industrial Law Journal*, 28/1: 33–56.

Malik, S. (2012). 'Unemployed bussed in to steward river pageant'. *The Guardian*, 4 June, http://www.guardian.co.uk/uk/2012/jun/04/jubilee-pageant-unemployed

Malik, S. (2013). 'MPs blast government's flagship Work Programme'. *The Guardian*, 22 February, http://www.guardian.co.uk/society/2013/feb/22/mps-blast-work-programme?INTCMP=SRCH

Malik, S., Ball, J., and Davies, L. (2012). 'Jobseekers forced to clean private homes and offices for nothing'. *The Guardian*, 29 February, http://www.guardian.co.uk/politics/2012/feb/24/jobseekers-unpaid-work-placements

Manning, A. (2011). 'Minimum wages and wage inequality', in D. Marsden (ed.), *Employment in the Lean Years*. Oxford: Oxford University Press, 134–50.

Manning, A. (2012). *Minimum Wage: Maximum Impact*. London: Resolution Foundation.

Marchington, M. (1989). 'Joint consultation in practice', in K. Sisson (ed.), *Personnel Management*. Oxford: Basil Blackwell, 378–402.

Marchington, M. (1994). 'The dynamics of joint consultation', in K. Sisson (ed.), *Personnel Management* (2nd edn). Oxford: Blackwell, 662–93.

Marchington, M. (2001). 'Employee involvement at work', in J. Storey (ed.), *Human Resource Management: A Critical Text* (2nd edn). London: Thomson Learning, 232–52.

Marchington, M. (2008). 'Employee voice systems', in P. Boxall, J. Purcell, and P. Wright (eds.), *The Oxford Handbook of Human Resource Management*. Oxford: Oxford University Press, 231–50.

Marchington, M. and Harrison, E. (1991). 'Customers, competitors and choice: employee relations in food retailing'. *Industrial Relations Journal*, 22/4: 286–99.

Marchington, M. and Parker, P. (1990). *Changing Patterns of Employee Relations*. Hemel Hempstead: Harvester Wheatsheaf.

Marchington, M. and Wilkinson, A. (2005). 'Direct participation and involvement', in S. Bach (ed.), *Managing Human Resources*. Oxford: Blackwell, 398–423.

Marginson, P. (2009). 'Performance pay and collective bargaining: a complex relationship', in S. Corby, S. Palmer, and E. Lindop (eds.), *Rethinking Reward*. Basingstoke: Palgrave Macmillan, 102–19.

Marginson, P. (2012). '(Re)assessing the shifting contours of Britain's collective industrial relations'. *Industrial Relations Journal*, 43/4: 332–47.

Marginson, P., Gilman, M., Jacobi, O., and Krieger, H. (1998). *Negotiating European Works Councils: An Analysis of Agreements under Article 13*. Luxembourg: Office of Official Publications of the European Community.

Marginson, P. and Meardi, G. (2009). *Multinational Companies and Collective Bargaining*. Dublin: European Foundation for the Improvement of Living and Working Conditions. http://www.eurofound.europa.eu/docs/eiro/tn0904049s/tn0904049s.pdf

Marginson, P. and Meardi, G. (2010). 'Multinational companies: transforming national industrial relations?', in T. Colling and M. Terry (eds.), *Industrial Relations: Theory and Practice* (3rd edn). Chichester: John Wiley, 207–30.

Marginson, P. and Sisson, K. (1994). 'The structure of transnational capital in Europe: the emerging Euro-company and its implications for industrial relations', in R. Hyman and A. Ferner (eds.), *New Frontiers in European Industrial Relations*. Oxford: Blackwell, 15–51.

Marginson, P. and Sisson, K. (2004). *European Integration and Industrial Relations: Multi-Level Governance in the Making*. Basingstoke: Palgrave Macmillan.

Marks, A., Findlay, P., Hine, J., McKinlay, A., and Thompson, P. (1998). 'The politics of partnership? Innovation in employment relations in the Scottish spirits industry'. *British Journal of Industrial Relations*, 36/2: 209–26.

Marlow, S. (2002). 'Regulating labour management in small firms'. *Human Resource Management Journal*, 12/3: 25–43.

Mars, G. (1982). *Cheats at Work*. London: Allen and Unwin.

Mars, G. and Mitchell, P. (1976). *Room for Reform? A Case Study of Industrial Relations in the Hotel Industry*. Milton Keynes: Open University Press.

Marsden, D. (1999). *A Theory of Employment Systems*. Oxford: Oxford University Press.

Marsden, D. (2009). *The Paradox of Performance Related Pay Systems: Why do we Keep Adopting them in the Face of Evidence that they Fail to Motivate?* Centre for Economic Performance, Discussion Paper No. 946 London: Centre for Economic Performance.

Marsden, D. and French, S. (1998). *What a Performance: Performance Related Pay in the Public Services*. London: London School of Economics, Centre for Economic Performance.

Marsh, D. (1992). *The New Politics of British Trade Unionism*. Basingstoke: Macmillan.

Marshall, D. and Laws, D. (2004). *The Orange Book: Reclaiming Liberalism*. London: Profile Books.

Martin, A. and Ross, G. (1999). 'In the line of fire: the Europeanization of Labor representation', in A. Martin and G. Ross (eds.), *The Brave New World of European Labor*. Oxford: Berghahn, 312–67.

Martin, R. (1992). *Bargaining Power*. Oxford: Clarendon.

Martin, R., Smith, P., Fosh, P., Morris, H., and Undy, R. (1995). 'The legislative reform of union government 1979–94'. *Industrial Relations Journal*, 26/2: 146–55.

Mason, P. (2009). *Meltdown: The End of the Age of Greed*. London: Verso.

Mason, P. (2012). *Why it's Kicking Off Everywhere: The New Global Revolutions*. London: Verso.

Meardi, G. (2012). *Social Failures of EU Enlargement: A Case of Workers Voting with their Feet*. Abingdon: Routledge.

Meardi, G., Marginson, P., Fichter, M., Frybes, M., Stanojević, M., and Tóth, A. (2009). 'Varieties of multinationals: adapting employment practices in Central Eastern Europe'. *Industrial Relations*, 48/3: 489–511.

Merk, J. (2009). 'Jumping scale and bridging space in the era of corporate social responsibility: cross-border labour struggles in the global garment industry'. *Third World Quarterly*, 30/3: 599–615.

Messenger, J. (2011). 'Working time trends and developments in Europe', *Cambridge Journal of Economics*, 35/2: 295–316.

Metcalf, D. (1999). 'The British National Minimum Wage'. *British Journal of Industrial Relations*, 37/2: 171–201.

Metcalf, D. (2005). 'Trade unions: resurgence or perdition? An economic analysis?', in S. Fernie and D. Metcalf (eds.), *Trade Unions: Resurgence or Demise?* London: Routledge, 83–117.

Metcalf, D. (2008). 'Why has the British National Minimum Wage had little or no impact on employment?' *Journal of Industrial Relations*, 50/3: 489–512.

Milburn, A. (2012). *Fair Access to Professional Careers: A Progress Report by the Independent Reviewer on Social Mobility and Child Poverty*. London: Cabinet Office.

Miliband, R. (1973). *The State in Capitalist Society*. London: Quartet.

Milkman, R. (ed.) (2000). *Organizing Immigrants: The Challenge for Unions in Contemporary California*. Ithaca NY: Cornell University Press.

Millward, N., Bryson, A., and Forth, J. (2000). *All Change at Work*. London: Routledge.

Millward, N., Stevens, D., Smart, N., and Hawes, W. (1992). *Workplace Industrial Relations in Transition*. Aldershot: Dartmouth.

Milmo, D. (2011). 'British Airways settles cabin crew dispute'. *The Guardian*, 22 June, http://www.guardian.co.uk/business/2011/jun/22/british-airways-and-unite-settle-cabin-crew-dispute

Milmo, D. (2012). 'Unions and Southampton council go head to head over cuts'. *The Guardian*, 24 January, http://www.guardian.co.uk/society/2012/jan/24/southampton-council-strikes-royston-smith

Milne, S. (2004). *The Enemy Within: Thatcher's Secret War against the Miners* (2nd edn). London: Verso.

Milne, S. (2012). 'Blacklisting is the scandal that now demands action'. *The Guardian*, 4 December, http://www.guardian.co.uk/commentisfree/2012/dec/04/blacklisting-scandal-corporate-spying

Ministry of Justice (2012) *Employment Tribunal and EAT Statistics, 2011–12*. http://www.justice.gov.uk/statistics/tribunals/employment-tribunal-and-eat-statistics-gb

Minkin, L. (1991). *The Contentious Alliance: Trade Unions and the Labour Party*. Edinburgh: Edinburgh University Press.

Moore, S. (2004). 'Union mobilization and employer counter-mobilization in the statutory recognition process', in J. Kelly and P. Willman (eds.), *Union Organization and Activity*. London: Routledge, 7–31.

Moore, S. (2011). *New Trade Union Activism: Class Consciousness or Social Identity?* Basingstoke: Palgrave Macmillan.

Morris, G. (2012). 'The development of statutory employment rights in Britain and enforcement mechanisms', in L. Dickens (ed.), *Making Employment Rights Effective: Issues of Enforcement and Compliance.* Oxford: Hart Publishing, 7–28.

Mosley, L. (2011). *Labor Rights and Multinational Corporations.* New York: Cambridge University Press.

Mueller, F. and Purcell, J. (1992). 'The Europeanization of manufacturing and the decentralization of bargaining: multinational management strategies in the European automobile industry'. *International Journal of Human Resource Management*, 3/1: 15–24.

Mukherjee, S. (1973). *Through No Fault of Their Own: Systems for Handling Redundancies in Britain, France and Germany.* London: PEP.

Mulholland, K. (2004). 'Workplace resistance in an Irish call centre: slammin', scammin' smokin' an' leavin' '. *Work, Employment and Society*, 18/4: 709–24.

Mumford, K. (1996). 'Arbitration and ACAS in Britain: a historical perspective'. *British Journal of Industrial Relations*, 34/2: 287–305.

Munck, R. (2011). 'Unions, globalisation and internationalism: results and prospects', in G. Gall, A. Wilkinson, and R. Hurd (eds.), *The International Handbook of Labour Unions: Responses to Neo-Liberalism.* Cheltenham: Edward Elgar, 291–310.

Munro, A. (1999). *Women, Work and Trade Unions.* London: Mansell.

Myerscough, P. (2013). 'Short cuts'. *London Review of Books*, 3 January: 25.

Nash, D. (2006). 'Recent industrial relations developments in the United Kingdom: continuity and change under New Labour 1997–2005'. *Journal of Industrial Relations*, 48/3: 401–14.

Neathy, F. and Arrowsmith, J. (2001). *The Implementation of the Working Time Regulations.* Employment Relations Research Series No. 11 London: DTI.

Neumark, D. and Wascher, W. (2008). *Minimum Wages.* Cambridge MA: MIT Press.

New Economics Foundation (NEF) (2010) *21 Hours: Why a Shorter Working Week can help us all to Flourish in the 21st Century*, http://www.neweconomics.org/publications/21-hours

Newsome, K., Thompson, P., and Commander, J. (2009). 'The forgotten factories: supermarket suppliers and dignity at work in the contemporary economy', in S. Bolton and M. Houlihan (eds.), *Work Matters: Critical Reflections on Contemporary Work.* Basingstoke: Palgrave Macmillan, 145–61.

Nichols, T. (1986). *The British Worker Question.* London: Routledge and Kegan Paul.

Nichols, T. (1997). *The Sociology of Industrial Injury.* London: Mansell.

Nichols, T. and Sugur, N. (2004). *Global Management, Local Labour: Turkish Workers and Modern Industry.* Basingstoke: Palgrave Macmillan.

Niforou, C. (2012). 'International framework agreements and industrial relations governance: global rhetoric versus local realities'. *British Journal of Industrial Relations*, 50/2: 352–73.

Nolan, J. (2002). 'The intensification of everyday life', in B. Burchell, D. Ladipo, and F. Wilkinson (eds.), *Job Insecurity and Work Intensification.* London: Routledge, 112–36.

Nolan, P. and Slater, G. (2003). 'The labour market: history, structure and prospects', in P. Edwards (ed.), *Industrial Relations* (2nd edn). Oxford: Blackwell, 58–80.

Nolan, P. and Wood, S. (2003). 'Mapping the future of work'. *British Journal of Industrial Relations*, 41/2: 165–74.

Noon, M. (2007). 'The fatal flaws of diversity and the business case for ethnic minorities'. *Work, Employment and Society*, 21/4: 773–84.

Noon, M. and Blyton, P. (2007). *The Realities of Work* (3rd edn). Basingstoke: Palgrave Macmillan.

Noronha, E. and D'Cruz, P. (2009). 'Engaging the professional: organising call centre agents in India'. *Industrial Relations Journal*, 40/3: 215–34.

O'Brien, R. (2002). 'The varied paths to minimum global labour standards', in J. Harrod and R. O'Brien (eds.), *Global Unions? Theory and Strategies of Organized Labour in a Global Political Economy.* London: Routledge, 221–34.

O'Brien-Smith, F. and Rigby, M. (2010). 'The work–life balance strategies of USDAW: mobilising collective voice'. *Industrial Relations Journal*, 41/3, 206–17.

O'Connell Davidson, J. (1994). 'What do franchisors do? Control and commercialisation in milk distribution'. *Work, Employment and Society*, 8/1: 23–44.

O'Connor, S. (2013). 'Amazon unpacked'. *FT Magazine*, 8 February, http://www.ft.com/cms/s/2/ed6a985c-70bd-11e2-85d0-00144feab49a.html#slide1

Office for Budgetary Responsibility (OBR) (2012). *Economic and Fiscal Outlook: December 2012.* Cm 8481. London: HMSO.

Office for National Statistics (ONS) (2011) *Hours Worked in the Labour Market–2011.* Newport: Office for National Statistics. http://www.ons.gov.uk/ons/dcp171776_247259.pdf

Office for National Statistics (ONS) (2012a). 'Gender pay gap falls to 9.6 per cent in 2012'. *ONS News Release*, 22 November, http://www.ons.gov.uk/ons/dcp29904_288163.pdf

Office for National Statistics (ONS) (2012b). *Labour Disputes, Annual Article 2011*. Newport: Office for National Statistics. http://www.ons.gov.uk/ons/dcp171766_276223.pdf

Office for National Statistics (ONS) (2013). 'Self-employed up 367,000 in four years, mostly since 2011', http://www.ons.gov.uk/ons/dcp29904_299038.pdf

Ogbonna, E. and Harris, L. (2002). 'Institutionalization of tipping as a source of managerial control'. *British Journal of Industrial Relations*, 40/4: 725–52.

Organisation for Economic Cooperation and Development (OECD) (2010). *Economic Policy Reforms: Going for Growth 2010*. Paris: OECD.

Osler, D. (2002). *Labour Party PLC*. London: Mainstream Publishing.

O'Sullivan, M. and Gunnigle, P. (2009). 'Bearing all the hallmarks of oppression—union avoidance in Europe's largest low-cost airline'. *Labor Studies Journal*, 34/2: 252–70.

Oswick, C. and Noon, M. (2012). 'Discourses of diversity, equality, and inclusion: trenchant formulations or transient fashions?' *British Journal of Management*, early view: DOI: 10.1111/j. 1467-8551.2012.00830.x

Oxenbridge, S. and Brown, W. (2002). 'The two faces of partnership? An assessment of partnership and co-operative employer/trade union relationships'. *Employee Relations*, 24/3: 262–7.

Oxenbridge, S. and Brown, W. (2004). 'A poisoned chalice? Trade union representatives in partnership and co-operative employer-union relationships', in G. Healy, E. Heery, P. Taylor, and W. Brown (eds.), *The Future of Worker Representation*. Basingstoke: Palgrave Macmillan, 187–206.

Oxenbridge, S. and Brown, W. (2005). 'Developing partnership relationships: a case of leveraging power', in M. Stuart and M. Martinez Lucio (eds.), *Partnership and Modernisation in Employment Relations*. London: Routledge, 83–100.

Oxenbridge, S., Brown, W., Deakin, S., and Pratten, C. (2003). 'Initial responses to the Employment Relations Act 1999'. *British Journal of Industrial Relations*, 41/2: 315–34.

Pai, H.-H. (2008). *Chinese Whispers: The True Story Behind Britain's Hidden Army of Labour*. London: Penguin.

Pakulski, J. and Waters, M. (1996). *The Death of Class*. London: Sage.

Palley, T. (2004). 'The economic case for international labour standards'. *Cambridge Journal of Economics*, 28/1: 21–36.

Papadakis, K. (ed.) (2011). *Shaping Global Industrial Relations: The Impact of International Framework Agreements*. Basingstoke: Palgrave Macmillan.

Parker, J. (2002). 'Women's groups in British unions'. *British Journal of Industrial Relations*, 40/1: 23–48.

Parsons, N. (2013). 'Legitimizing illegal protest: the permissive ideational environment and "bossnappings" in France'. *British Journal of Industrial Relations*, 51/2: 288–309.

Pass, S. (2005). 'On the line'. *People Management*, 15 September: 38–40.

Patel, S. (2011). *Research into Employers' Attitudes and Behaviour Towards Compliance with the UK National Minimum Wage (NMW) Legislation*. Employment Relations Research Series, No. 121. London: Department for Business, Innovation and Skills.

Paterson, T. (2013). 'Amazon "used neo-Nazi guards to keep immigrant workforce under control" in Germany'. *The Independent*, 14 February, http://www.independent.co.uk/news/world/europe/amazon-used-neonazi-guards-to-keep-immigrant-workforce-under-control-in-germany-8495843.html

Pendleton, A., Whitfield, K., and Bryson, A. (2009). 'The changing use of contingent pay at the modern British workplace', in W. Brown, A. Bryson, J. Forth, and K. Whitfield (eds.), *The Evolution of the Modern Workplace*. Cambridge: Cambridge University Press, 256–84.

Pennycook, M. (2012). *What Price a Living Wage? Understanding the Impact of a Living Wage on Firm-Level Wage Bills*. London: Institute of Public Policy Research and Resolution Foundation.

Pennycook, M. and Whittaker, M. (2012). *Low Pay Britain 2012*. London: Resolution Foundation.

Perkins, S. and White, G. (2010). 'Modernising pay in the UK public services: trends and implications'. *Human Resource Management Journal*, 20/3: 244–57.

Perlin, R. (2011). *Intern Nation*. London: Verso.

Pfeffer, J. (1998). *The Human Equation*. Boston MA: Harvard Business School Press.

Piazza, J. (2005). 'Globalizing quiescence: globalization, union density and strikes in 15 industrialized countries'. *Economic and Industrial Democracy*, 26/2: 289–314.

Pierson, C. (1996). *The Modern State*. London: Routledge.

Platman, K. (2004). ' "Portfolio careers" and the search for flexibility in later life'. *Work, Employment and Society*, 18/3: 573–99.

Pochet, P. and Degryse, C. (2010). 'Social policies of the European Union'. *Global Social Policy*, 10/2: 248–57.

Polanyi, K. (1957). *The Great Transformation*. Boston: Beacon Press.

Pollert, A. (1981). *Girls, Wives, Factory Lives*. Basingstoke: Macmillan.

Pollert, A. (2005). 'The unorganised worker: the decline in collectivism and new hurdles to individual employment rights'. *Industrial Law Journal*, 34/3: 217–38.

Pollert, A. (2007). 'Individual employment rights: paper tigers—fierce in appearance but missing in tooth and claw'. *Economic and Industrial Democracy*, 28/1: 110–39.

Pollert, A. (2009). 'The reality of vulnerability amongst Britain's non-unionised workers with problems at work', in S. Bolton and M. Houlihan (eds.), *Work Matters: Critical Reflections on Contemporary Work*. Basingstoke: Palgrave Macmillan, 60–80.

Pollert, A. and Charlwood, A. (2009). 'The vulnerable worker in Britain and problems at work'. *Work, Employment and Society*, 23/2: 343–62.

Poole, M. (1986). *Towards a New Industrial Democracy: Workers' Participation in Industry*. London: Routledge and Kegan Paul.

Poole, M. and Mansfield, R. (1993). 'Patterns of continuity and change in managerial attitudes and behaviour in industrial relations, 1980–1990'. *British Journal of Industrial Relations*, 31/1: 11–35.

Poster, W. (2007). 'Who's on the line? Indian call center agents pose as Americans for US-outsourced firms'. *Industrial Relations*, 46/2: 271–304.

Poynter, G. (2000). *Restructuring in the Service Industries: Management Reform and Workplace Relations in the UK Service Sector*. London: Mansell.

Price, R. (1983). 'White-collar unions: growth, character and attitudes in the 1970s', in R. Hyman and R. Price (eds.), *The New Working Class? White Collar Workers and their Unions*. London: Macmillan, 147–83.

Price, R. (1989). 'The decline and fall of the status divide?', in K. Sisson (ed.), *Personnel Management in Britain*. Oxford: Blackwell, 271–95.

Proctor, S. (2008). 'New forms of work and the high performance paradigm', in P. Blyton, N. Bacon, J. Fiorito, and E. Heery (eds.), *The SAGE Handbook of Industrial Relations*. London: Sage, 149–69.

Prosser, T. (2011). 'The implementation of the Telework and Work-related Stress agreements: European social dialogue through "soft" law?'. *European Journal of Industrial Relations*, 17/3: 245–60.

Pun, N. (2005). 'Global production, company codes of conduct, and labor conditions in China: a case study of two factories'. *The China Journal*, 54: 101–13.

Purcell, J. (2000). 'After collective bargaining? ACAS in the age of human resource management', in B. Towers and W. Brown (eds.), *Employment Relations in Britain: 25 Years of the Advisory, Conciliation and Arbitration Service*. Oxford: Blackwell, 163–80.

Purcell, J. (2012). 'The limits and possibilities of employee engagement'. Warwick Papers in Industrial Relations, 96. Warwick: Industrial Relations Research Unit, University of Warwick.

Purcell, J. and Hall, M. (2012). *Voice and Participation in the Modern Workplace: Challenges and Prospects*. ACAS Future of Workplace Relations discussion paper series. London: ACAS.

Purcell, J. and Hutchinson, S. (2007). 'Front-line managers as agents in the HRM-performance causal chain: theory, analysis, and evidence'. *Human Resource Management Journal*, 17/1: 3–20.

Purcell, J. and Kinnie, N. (2007). 'HRM and business performance', in P. Boxall, J. Purcell, and P. Wright (eds.), *The Oxford Handbook of Human Resource Management*. Oxford: Oxford University Press, 533–51.

Purcell, J., Kinnie, N., Hutchinson, S., Rayton, B., and Swart, J. (2003). *Understanding the People and Performance Link: Unlocking the Black Box*. London: CIPD.

Purcell, J., Kinnie, N., Swart, J., Rayton, B., and Hutchinson, S. (2009). *People Management and Performance*. Abingdon: Routledge.

Purcell, J., Purcell, K., and Tailby, S. (2004). 'Temporary work agencies: here today, gone tomorrow?'. *British Journal of Industrial Relations*, 42/4: 705–25.

Rainnie, A. (1989). *Industrial Relations in Small Firms*. London: Routledge.

Ram, M. (1994). *Managing to Survive*. Oxford: Blackwell.

Ram, M. and Edwards, P. (2003). 'Praising Caesar not burying him: what we know about employment relations in small firms'. *Work, Employment and Society*, 17/4: 719–30.

Ram, M. and Edwards, P. (2010). 'Industrial relations in small firms', in T. Colling and M. Terry (eds.), *Industrial Relations: Theory and Practice* (3rd edn). Chichester: John Wiley, 231–52.

Ram, M., Edwards, P., Gilman, M., and Arrowsmith, J. (2001). 'The dynamics of informality: employment relations in small firms and the effects of regulatory change'. *Work, Employment and Society*, 15/4: 845–61.

Ram, M., Edwards, P., and Jones, T. (2007). 'Staying underground: informal work, small firms, and employment regulation in the United Kingdom'. *Work and Occupations*, 34/3: 318–44.

Ramesh, R. (2013). 'How private care firms have got away with breaking the law on pay'. *The Guardian*, 14 June, http://www.guardian.co.uk/society/2013/jun/13/care-firms-law-on-pay?INTCMP=SRCH

Redfern, D. (2007). 'An analysis of the role of European Works Councils in British workplaces'. *Employee Relations*, 29/3: 292–305.

Reed, H. and Latorre, M. (2009). *The Economic Impacts of Migration on the UK Labour Market*. Economics of Migration Working Paper 3. London: Institute for Public Policy Research.

Rees, G. and Fielder, S. (1992). 'The services economy, subcontracting and the new employment relations: contract catering and cleaning'. *Work, Employment and Society*, 6/3: 347–68.

Rees, T. (1992). *Women and the Labour Market*. London: Routledge.

Renton, D. (2012). *Struck Out: Why Employment Tribunals Fail Workers and What can be Done*. London: Pluto Press.

Resolution Foundation (2012a). *What a Drag: The Chilling Impact of Unemployment on Real Wages*. London: Resolution Foundation. http://www. resolutionfoundation.org/publications/what-drag-chilling-impact-unemployment-real-wages/

Resolution Foundation (2012b). *Who Gains from Growth? Living Standards to 2020*. London: Resolution Foundation. http://www.resolutionfoundation.org/ media/media/downloads/Who_Gains_from_Growth.pdf

Resolution Foundation (2012c). *Gaining from Growth: The Final Report of the Commission on Living Standards*. London: Resolution Foundation. http:// www.resolutionfoundation.org/media/media/ downloads/Gaining_from_growth_-_The_final_report_ of_the_Commission_on_Living_Standards.pdf

Resolution Foundation (2013). *Squeezed Britain 2013*. London: Resolution Foundation. http://www. resolutionfoundation.org/media/media/downloads/ Resolution-Foundation-Squeezed-Britain-2013_1.pdf

Richards, J. (2008). 'Because I need somewhere to vent: the expression of conflict through work blogs'. *New Technology, Work, and Employment*, 23/1–2: 95–110.

Richards, L. (2008). *Union-Free America: Workers and Anti-Union Culture*. Champaign IL: University of Illinois Press.

Richards, W. (2001). 'Evaluating equal opportunities initiatives: the case for a "transformative" agenda', in M. Noon and E. Ogbonna (eds.), *Equality, Diversity and Disadvantage in Employment*. Basingstoke: Palgrave Macmillan, 15–31.

Ridley-Duff, R. and Bennett, A. (2011). 'Towards mediation: developing a theoretical framework to understand alternative dispute resolution'. *Industrial Relations Journal*, 42/2: 106–23.

Rigby, M. and Marco Aledo, M. (2001). 'The worst record in Europe? A comparative analysis of industrial conflict in Spain'. *European Journal of Industrial Relations*, 7/3: 287–305.

Rigby, M. and O'Brien-Smith, F. (2010). 'Trade union interventions in work-life balance'. *Work, Employment and Society*, 24/2: 203–20.

Riisgaard, L. (2005). 'International framework agreements: a new model for securing workers rights?'. *Industrial Relations*, 44/4: 707–37.

Robinson, P. (1999). 'Exploring the relationship between flexible employment and labour market regulation', in A. Felstead and N. Jewson (eds.), *Global Trends in Flexible Labour*. Basingstoke: Macmillan, 84–99.

Robinson, P. (2010). 'Do voluntary labour initiatives make a difference for the conditions of workers in global supply chains?'. *Journal of Industrial Relations*, 52/5: 561–73.

Roche, W. and Teague, P. (2012). 'Business partners and working the pumps: human resource managers in the recession'. *Human Relations*, 65/10: 1333–58.

Rollinson, D., Handley, J., Hook, C., and Foot, M. (1997). 'The disciplinary experience and its effects on behaviour'. *Work, Employment and Society*, 11/2: 281–311.

Roper, I., Cunningham, I., and James, P. (2003). 'Promoting family-friendly policies: is the basis of the government's ethical standpoint viable?'. *Personnel Review*, 32/2: 211–30.

Ross, R. and Schneider, R. (1992). *From Equality to Diversity*. London: Pitman.

Roy, D. (1952). 'Quota restriction and goldbricking in a machine shop'. *American Journal of Sociology*, 5/5: 427–42.

Royal College of Physicians (RCP) (2012). *Hospitals on the Edge*, http://www.rcplondon.ac.uk/sites/default/ files/documents/hospitals-on-the-edge-report.pdf

Royal Commission (1968). *Report of the Royal Commission on Trade Unions and Employers' Associations*. London: HMSO.

Royle, T. (2000). *Working for McDonalds in Europe: The Unequal Struggle?* London: Routledge.

Royle, T. (2011). 'Regulating global capital through public and private codes: an analysis of international labour standards and corporate voluntary initiatives', in M. Barry and A. Wilkinson (eds.), *Research Handbook of Comparative Employment Relations*. Cheltenham: Edward Elgar, 421–40.

Royle, T. and Towers, B. (eds.) (2002). *Labour Relations in the Global Fast-Food Industry*. London: Routledge.

Rubery, J. and Edwards, P. (2003). 'Low pay and the National Minimum Wage', in P. Edwards (ed.), *Industrial Relations* (2nd edn). Oxford: Blackwell, 447–69.

Rubery, J. and Grimshaw, D. (2003). *The Organization of Employment: An International Perspective*. Basingstoke: Palgrave Macmillan.

Russell, A. (1992). *Harmonisation of Employment Conditions in Britain: Some Causes and Consequences.* Aberystwyth Economics Research Papers, 92–08. Aberystwyth: University College of Wales, Department of Economics and Agricultural Economics.

Rutherford, I. and Achur, J. (2010). *Survey of Pay and Work Rights Helpline Callers.* Employment Relations Research Series No. 113 London: BIS.

Rutherford, S. (1999). 'Equal opportunities policies—making a difference'. *Women in Management Review*, 14/6: 212–9.

Samuel, P. (2005). 'Partnership working and the cultivated activist'. *Industrial Relations Journal*, 36/1: 59–76.

Samuel, P. (2007). 'Partnership consultation and employer domination in two British life and pensions firms'. *Work, Employment and Society*, 21/3: 459–77.

Samuel, P. and Bacon, N. (2010). 'The contents of partnership agreements in Britain 1990–2007'. *Work, Employment and Society*, 24/3: 430–48.

Sanders, D. (2012). *Placing Trust in Employee Engagement.* Employment Relations Comment. London: ACAS.

Sargeant, M. (2010). 'The UK national minimum wage and age discrimination'. *Policy Studies*, 31/3: 351–64.

Schlosser, E. (2002). *Fast Food Nation.* London: Penguin.

Scholarios, D. and Marks, A. (2004). 'Work-life balance and the software worker'. *Human Resource Management Journal*, 14/2: 54–74.

Scott, A. (1994). *Willing Slaves? British Workers under Human Resource Management.* Cambridge: Cambridge University Press.

Scott, W., Mumford, E., McGivering, I., and Kirkby, J. (1963). *Coal and Conflict.* Liverpool: Liverpool University Press.

Seidman, G. (2007). *Beyond the Boycott: Labor Rights, Human Rights and Transnational Activism.* New York: Russell Sage Foundation.

Seidman, G. (2011). 'Workers' rights, union rights and solidarity across borders'. *International Labor and Working-Class History*, 80/1: 169–75.

Seierstad, C. (2011). 'Strategies for equality: the Norwegian experience of the use of gender quotas in the private sector', in T. Wright and H. Conley (eds.), *The Gower Handbook of Discrimination at Work.* Farnham: Gower, 279–92.

Seifert, R. and Sibley, T. (2005). *United They Stood: The Story of the 2002–2004 Firefighters' Strike.* London: Lawrence and Wishart.

Sénen González, C. and Medwid, B. (2009). 'The revitalization of trade unions and the re-emergence of industrial conflict in Argentina: the case of the oil industry '. *Journal of Industrial Relations*, 51/5: 709–22.

Seymour, R. (2013). 'China's trade union reforms aim to control its militant workforce'. *The Guardian*, 5 February, http://www.guardian.co.uk/commentisfree/2013/feb/05/china-trade-union-reform-militancy

Shackleton, J. (2002). *Employment Tribunals: Their Growth and the Case for Radical Reform.* Hobart Paper No. 145 London: Institute of Economic Affairs.

Shelley, T. (2007). *Exploited: Migrant Labour in the New Global Economy.* London: Zed Books.

Shen, J. (2007). *Labour Disputes and their Resolution in China.* Oxford: Chandos Publishing.

Sherman, R. (2011). 'Beyond interaction: customer influence on housekeeping and room service work in hotels', *Work, Employment and Society*, 25/1: 19–33.

Shorter, E. and Tilly, C. (1974). *Strikes in France.* Cambridge: Cambridge University Press.

Silver, B. (2003). *Forces of Labor: Workers' Movements and Globalization since 1870.* Cambridge: Cambridge University Press.

Simms, M. (2003). 'Union organizing in a not-for-profit organization', in G. Gall (ed.), *Union Organizing: Campaigning for Union Recognition.* London: Routledge, 97–113.

Simms, M. (2007). 'Interest formation in greenfield union organising campaigns'. *Industrial Relations Journal*, 38/5: 439–54.

Simms, M. and Charlwood, A. (2010). 'Trade unions: power and influence in a changed context', in T. Colling and M. Terry (eds.), *Industrial Relations: Theory and Practice* (3rd edn). Chichester: John Wiley, 125–48.

Simms, M. and Holgate, J. (2010a). 'TUC Organizing Academy 10 years on: what has been the impact on British unions?'. *The International Journal of Human Resource Management*, 21/3: 355–70.

Simms, M. and Holgate, J. (2010b). 'Organising for what? Where is the debate on the politics of union organising?'. *Work, Employment and Society*, 24/1: 157–68.

Simms, M., Holgate, J., and Heery, E. (2013). *Union Voices: Tactics and Tensions in UK Organizing.* Ithaca NY: Cornell University Press.

Sisson, K. (1987). *The Management of Collective Bargaining.* Oxford: Basil Blackwell.

Sisson, K. (2008). *Putting the Record Straight: Industrial Relations and the Employment Relationship.* Warwick Papers in Industrial Relations, No. 88. Warwick: University of Warwick, Industrial Relations Research Unit.

Sisson, K. (2009). *Why Employment Relations Matter.* Warwick Papers in Industrial Relations, No. 92. Warwick: University of Warwick, Industrial Relations Research Unit.

Sisson, K. (2010). *Employment Relations Matters*, http://www2.warwick.ac.uk/fac/soc/wbs/research/irru/

Sisson, K. and Brown, W. (1983). 'Industrial relations in the private sector: Donovan re-visited', in G. Bain (ed.), *Industrial Relations in Britain*. Oxford: Basil Blackwell, 137–54.

Sisson, K. and Purcell, J. (2010). 'Management: caught between competing views of the organization', in T. Colling and M. Terry (eds.), *Industrial Relations: Theory and Practice* (3rd edn). Chichester: John Wiley, 83–105.

Sisson, K. and Storey, J. (2000). *The Realities of Human Resource Management*. Buckingham: Open University Press.

Sisson, K. and Taylor, J. (2006). 'The Advisory, Conciliation, and Arbitration Service', in L. Dickens and A. Neal (eds.), *The Changing Institutional Face of British Employment Relations*. Alphen aan den Rign: Kluwer Law International, 25–36.

Smethurst, S. (2007). 'Fair traders'. *People Management*, 29 November, 28–31.

Smith, C., Child, J., and Rowlinson, M. (1990). *Reshaping Work: The Cadbury Experience*. Cambridge: Cambridge University Press.

Smith, H. (2011). 'Apple sacks worker for ranting about iPhone on Facebook'. *Metro*, 29 November, http://metro.co.uk/2011/11/29/apple-sacks-worker-samuel-crisp-over-iphone-facebook-rants-237567/

Smith, P. (2001). *Unionization and Union Leadership: The Road Haulage Industry*. London: Continuum.

Smith, P. and Morton, G. (1994). 'Union exclusion—next steps'. *Industrial Relations Journal*, 25/1: 3–14.

Smith, P. and Morton, G. (2006). 'Nine years of New Labour: neo-liberalism and workers' rights'. *British Journal of Industrial Relations*, 44/3: 401–20.

Smith, P. and Morton, G. (2009). 'Employment legislation: New Labour's neoliberal legal project to subordinate trade unions', in G. Daniels and J. McIlroy (eds.), *Trade Unions in a Neo Liberal World: British Trade Unions under New Labour*. Abingdon: Routledge, 205–29.

Som, A. (2008). 'Innovative human resource management and corporate performance in the context of economic liberalization in India'. *The International Journal of Human Resource Management*, 19/7: 1278–97.

Sommerlad, N. (2009). 'Daily Mirror and Unite Fair Tips campaign wins pay rise for thousands of waiting staff'. *Daily Mirror*, 1 October, http://blogs.mirror.co.uk/investigations/2009/10/daily-mirror-and-unite-fair-ti.html

Sommerlad, N. (2010). 'Hermes Parcelnet bosses get perks and sick pay denied to their workers'. *Daily Mirror*, 29 July, http://blogs.mirror.co.uk/investigations/2010/07/hermes-parcelnet-bosses-get-pe.html

Sommerlad, N. (2013). 'Self-employed Hermes courier loses her job after 14 years with no comeback'. *Daily Mirror*, 31 January, http://blogs.mirror.co.uk/investigations/2013/01/self-employed-hermes-courier-l.html

Standing, G. (2008). 'The ILO: an agency for globalization?'. *Development and Change*, 39/3: 355–84.

Standing, G. (2010). 'The International Labour Organization'. *New Political Economy*, 15/2: 307–18.

Standing, G. (2011). *The Precariat: The New Dangerous Class*. London: Bloomsbury.

Stanworth, C. and Stanworth, J. (1995). 'The self-employed without employees—autonomous or atypical?'. *Industrial Relations Journal*, 26/3: 221–9.

Stevis, D. and Boswell, T. (2007). 'International framework agreements: opportunities and challenges for global unionism', in K. Bronfenbrenner (ed.), *Global Unions: Challenging Transnational Capital through Cross-border Campaigns*. Ithaca NY: Cornell University Press, 174–94.

Stewart, M. (2011). 'The National Minimum Wage after a decade', in D. Marsden (ed.), *Employment in the Lean Years*. Oxford: Oxford University Press, 121–33.

Stiglitz, J. (2002). *Globalization and its Discontents*. London: Allen Lane.

Stiglitz, J. (2010). *Freefall: Free Markets and the Sinking of the Global Economy*. London: Allen Lane.

Storey, J. (1983). *Managerial Prerogative and the Question of Control*. London: Routledge and Kegan Paul.

Storey, J. (1985). 'The means of management control'. *Sociology*, 19/2: 193–211.

Streeck, W. (1997). 'Industrial citizenship under regime competition: the case of the European Works Councils'. *Journal of European Public Policy*, 4/4: 643–64.

Stuart, M. and Martinez Lucio, M. (2005). 'Partnership and modernisation in employment relations: an introduction', in M. Stuart and M. Martinez Lucio (eds.), *Partnership and Modernisation in Employment Relations*. London: Routledge, 1–22.

Suff, R. and Williams, S. (2004). 'The myth of mutuality? Employee perceptions of partnership at Borg Warner'. *Employee Relations*, 26/1: 30–43.

Sullivan, W. (2011). 'The role of trade unions in fighting racial discrimination', in T. Wright and H. Conley (eds.), *The Gower Handbook of Discrimination at Work*. Farnham: Gower, 129–38.

Sumption, M. and Somerville, W. (2010). *The UK's New Europeans: Progress and Challenges Five Years After Accession*. London: Equality and Human Rights Commission/Migration Policy Institute.

Sweiry, D. and Willitts, M. (2012). *Attitudes to Age in Britain 2010/11*. Sheffield: Department of Work and Pensions.

Syrpis, P. (2008). 'The Treaty of Lisbon: much ado . . . but about what?'. *Industrial Law Journal*, 37/3: 219–35.

Tailby, S. and Pollert, A. (2011). 'Non-unionized young workers and organizing the unorganized'. *Economic and Industrial Democracy*, 32/3: 499–522.

Tailby, S., Pollert, A., Warren, S., Danford, A., and Wilton, N. (2011). 'Under-funded and overwhelmed: the voluntary sector as worker representation in Britain's individualised industrial relations system'. *Industrial Relations Journal*, 42/3: 273–92.

Tailby, S., Richardson, M., Danford, A., Stewart, P., and Upchurch, M. (2005). 'Workplace partnership and work-life balance: a local government case study', in D. Houston (ed.), *Work-life Balance in the 21st Century*. Basingstoke: Palgrave Macmillan, 189–210.

Tattersall, A. (2009). 'Using their sword of justice: the NSW Teachers Federation and its campaigns for public education between 2001 and 2004', in J. McBride and I. Greenwood (eds.), *Community Unionism: A Comparative Analysis of Concepts and Contexts*. Basingstoke: Palgrave Macmillan, 161–86.

Taylor, L. and Walton, P. (1971). 'Industrial sabotage: motives and meanings', in S. Cohen (ed.), *Images of Deviance*. Harmondsworth: Penguin, 219–45.

Taylor, M. (2012). 'Campaigners hold protest to highlight "low pay" at Sainsbury's'. *The Guardian*, 29 May, http://www.guardian.co.uk/society/2012/may/29/sainsburys-low-pay-protest-paralympics

Taylor, P. and Bain, P. (2005). ' "India calling to the far away towns": the call centre labour process and globalization'. *Work, Employment and Society*, 19/2: 261–82.

Taylor, P., Baldry, C., Bain, P., and Ellis, V. (2003). ' "A unique working environment": health, sickness and absence in UK call centres'. *Work, Employment and Society*, 17/3: 435–58.

Taylor, P., Cunningham, I., Newsome, K., and Scholarios, D. (2010). ' "Too scared to go sick"—reformulating the research agenda on sickness absence'. *Industrial Relations Journal*, 41/4: 270–88.

Taylor, P. and Ramsay, H. (1998). 'Unions, partnership and HRM: sleeping with the enemy?'. *International Journal of Employment Studies*, 6/1: 115–43.

Taylor, S. (1998). 'Emotional labour and the new workplace', in P. Thompson and C. Warhurst (eds.), *Workplaces of the Future*. Basingstoke: Macmillan, 84–103.

Taylor-Gooby, P. and Stoker, G. (2011). 'The coalition programme: a new vision for Britain or politics as usual?'. *The Political Quarterly*, 82/1: 4–15.

Teague, P. (1989). *The European Community: The Social Dimension*. London: Kogan Page.

Teague, P. (1999). *Economic Citizenship in the European Union*. London: Routledge.

Teigen, M. (2012). 'Gender quotas for corporate boards in Norway: innovative gender equality policy', in C. Fagan, M. González Menéndez, and S. Gómez Ansón (eds.), *Women on Corporate Boards and in Top Management: European Trends and Policy*. Basingstoke: Palgrave Macmillan, 70–90.

Terry, M. (1983). 'Shop steward development and managerial strategies', in G. Bain, (ed.), *Industrial Relations in Britain*. Oxford: Basil Blackwell, 67–91.

Terry, M. (1996). 'Negotiating the government of UNISON: union democracy in theory and practice'. *British Journal of Industrial Relations*, 34/1: 87–110.

Terry, M. (1999). 'Systems of collective representation in non-union firms in the UK'. *Industrial Relations Journal*, 30/1: 16–30.

Terry, M. (2004). ' "Partnership": a serious strategy for the UK trade unions?', in A. Verma and T. Kochan (eds.), *Unions in the 21st Century: An International Perspective*. Basingstoke: Palgrave Macmillan, 205–19.

Terry, M. (2010). 'Employee representation', in T. Colling and M. Terry (eds.), *Industrial Relations: Theory and Practice* (3rd edn). Chichester: John Wiley, 275–97.

Thompson, P. (2003). 'Disconnected capitalism: or why employers can't keep their side of the bargain'. *Work, Employment and Society*, 17/2: 359–78.

Thompson, P. (2011). 'The trouble with HRM'. *Human Resource Management Journal*, 21/4: 355–67.

Thompson, P., Newsome, K., and Commander, J. (2013). ' "Good when they want to be": migrant workers in the supermarket supply chain'. *Human Resource Management Journal*, 23/2: 129–43.

Thompson, P. and Warhurst, C. (1998). 'Hands, hearts and minds: changing work and workers at the end of the century', in P. Thompson and C. Warhurst (eds.), *Workplaces of the Future*. Basingstoke: Macmillan, 1–24.

Thornley, C. (1998). 'Contesting local pay: the decentralisation of collective bargaining in the NHS'. *British Journal of Industrial Relations*, 36/3: 413–34.

Thorpe, A. (1999). 'The Labour party and the trade unions', in J. McIlroy, N. Fishman, and A. Campbell (eds.), *British Trade Unionism and Industrial Politics, Volume Two: The High Tide of Trade Unionism, 1964–79*. Aldershot: Ashgate, 133–50.

Timming, A. (2007). 'European Works Councils and the dark side of managing worker voice'. *Human Resource Management Journal*, 17/3: 248–64.

Tipping, S., Chanfreau, J., Perry, J., and Tait, C. (2012). *The Fourth Work–Life Balance Employee Survey*. Employment Relations Research Series No. 122 London: BIS.

Tolliday, S. and Zeitlin, J. (eds.) (1991). *The Power to Manage? Employers and Industrial Relations in Comparative-Historical Perspective*. London: Routledge.

Torrington, D. (1991). *Management Face to Face*. Hemel Hempstead: Prentice Hall.

Towers, B. (1997). *The Representation Gap: Change and Reform in the British and American Workplace*. Oxford: Oxford University Press.

Trades Union Congress (TUC) (1997). *General Council Report*. London: TUC.

Trades Union Congress (TUC) (2007). *Migrant Agency Workers in the UK*. London: TUC.

Trades Union Congress (TUC) (2008). *Hard Work, Hidden Lives*. Report of the Commission on Vulnerable Employment. London: TUC. http://www.vulnerableworkers.org.uk

Trades Union Congress (TUC) (2009). *Slaying the Working Time Myths*. London: TUC. http://www.tuc.org.uk/extras/workingtimemyths.pdf

Trades Union Congress (TUC) (2010). *Fair Work: Fighting Poverty through Decent Jobs*. London: TUC. http://www.tuc.org.uk/fairwork/fairworkreport.pdf

Trades Union Congress (TUC) (2011). *Unpaid Overtime gives a £29bn Boost to the UK Economy*, http://www.tuc.org.uk/workplace/tuc-20389-f0.cfm

Trades Union Congress (TUC) (2012a). *German Lessons: Developing Industrial Policy in the UK*. London: TUC. http://www.tuc.org.uk/tucfiles/204/GermanLessonsEdit.pdf

Trades Union Congress (TUC) (2012b). *Under-employment Crisis: A TUC Analysis of Under-employment Across the UK*. London: TUC. http://www.tuc.org.uk/tucfiles/367/Underemployment%20report.pdf

Trades Union Congress (TUC) (2012c). *TUC Equality Audit 2012*. London: TUC. http://www.tuc.org.uk/equality/index.cfm?mins=107&minors=24

Trades Union Congress (TUC) (2012d). *Why Postcode Pay Doesn't Add Up*, http://www.tuc.org.uk/industrial/tuc-21728-f0.cfm

Trades Union Congress (TUC) (2012e). *Priced Out: The Impact of Employment Tribunal Fees on Access to Justice*. London: TUC. http://www.tuc.org.uk/tucfiles/249/PricedOutMoJfeesconsultation.pdf

Trades Union Congress (TUC) (2013). 'Rising job levels since recession driven by surge in self-employment', *TUC Press Release*, 22 January, http://www.tuc.org.uk/economy/tuc-21841-f0.cfm

Tremblay, D.-G. and Genin, E. (2010). 'IT self-employed workers between constraint and flexibility'. *New Technology, Work, and Employment*, 25/1: 34–48.

Truss, C. (2001). 'Complexities and controversies in linking HRM with organizational outcomes'. *Journal of Management Studies*, 38/8: 1121–49.

Tsai, C.-J., Sengupta, S., and Edwards, P. (2007). 'When and why is small beautiful? The experience of work in the small firm'. *Human Relations*, 60/12: 1779–1807.

Tsogas, G. (2000). 'Labour standards and the generalized system of preferences of the European Union and the United States'. *European Journal of Industrial Relations*, 6/3: 349–70.

Tsogas, G. (2001). *Labor Regulation in a Global Economy*. New York: M. E. Sharpe.

Tsogas, G. (2009). 'International labour regulation: what have we really learnt so far?'. *Relations Industrielles/Industrial Relations*, 64/1: 75–94.

Turnbull, P. (1988). 'Leaner and possibly fitter: the management of redundancy in Britain'. *Industrial Relations Journal*, 19/3: 201–13.

Turnbull, P. (2006). 'The war on Europe's waterfront—repertoires of power in the port transport industry'. *British Journal of Industrial Relations*, 44/2: 305–26.

Turnbull, P. and Sapsford, D. (1992). 'A sea of discontent: the tides of organised and "unorganized" conflict on the docks'. *Sociology*, 26/2: 291–309.

Turnbull, P. and Wass, V. (1994). 'The greatest game no more—redundant dockers and the demise of "dock work"'. *Work, Employment and Society*, 8/4: 487–506.

Turnbull, P. and Wass, V. (1997). 'Job insecurity and labour market lemons: the (mis)management of redundancy in steel making, coal mining and port transport'. *Journal of Management Studies*, 34/1: 27–51.

Turnbull, P. and Wass, V. (2000). 'Redundancy and the paradox of job insecurity', in E. Heery and J. Salmon (eds.), *The Insecure Workforce*. London: Routledge, 57–77.

Turnbull, P. and Wass, V. (2011). 'Earnings inequality and employment', in P. Blyton, E. Heery, and P. Turnbull (eds.), *Reassessing the Employment Relationship*. Basingstoke: Palgrave Macmillan, 273–98.

Turner, H., Clack, G., and Roberts, G. (1967). *Labour Relations in the Motor Industry*. London: George Allen and Unwin.

Undy, R. (2008). *Trade Union Merger Strategies: Purpose, Process, and Performance*. Oxford: Oxford University Press.

Undy, R., Fosh, P., Morris, H., Smith, P., and Martin, R. (1996). *Managing the Unions*. Oxford: Clarendon.

Union of Shop, Distributive, and Allied Workers (USDAW) (2012). 'USDAW wins £67 million compensation for former Woolworths workers'.

USDAW News Release, 20 January, http://www. usdaw.org.uk/newsevents/news/2012/jan/ usdawwins%C2%A367millioncompens.aspx

Union of Shop, Distributive, and Allied Workers (USDAW) (2013). 'USDAW wins more than £5 million for ex-Woolies and Ethel Austin Staff in landmark legal case'. *USDAW News Release*, 31 May, http:// www.usdaw.org.uk/newsevents/news/2013/may/ usdawwinsmorethan5million.aspx

United Nations Conference on Trade and Development (UNCTAD) (2009). *World Investment Report: Transnational Corporations, Agricultural Production and Development*. New York and Geneva: United Nations.

Unlock Democracy (2012). *Donations to Political Parties Analysis, 1st Quarter, 2012*, http://action. unlockdemocracy.org.uk/page/-/publications/ Donations%20Report%20Q1%202012.pdf

Upchurch, M. (2009). 'Some conclusions from a survey of BUIRA members on the teaching of industrial relations in British universities', in R. Darlington (ed.), *What's the Point of Industrial Relations? In Defence of Critical Social Science*. London: British Universities Industrial Relations Association, 77–83.

Upchurch, M. and Donnelly, E. (1992). 'Membership patterns in USDAW 1980–1990: survival as success?'. *Industrial Relations Journal*, 23/1: 60–8.

van den Broek, D. and Dundon, T. (2012). '(Still) up to no good: reconfiguring worker resistance and misbehaviour in an increasingly unorganized world'. *Relations Industrielles/Industrial Relations*, 67/1: 97–121.

van Gelder, S. (ed.) (2011). *This Changes Everything: Occupy Wall Street and the 99% Movement*. San Francisco CA: Berrett-Koehler Publishers.

van Roozendaal, G. (2002). *Trade Unions and Global Governance: The Debate on a Social Clause*. London: Continuum.

van Wanrooy, B., Bewley, H., Bryson, A., Forth, J., Freeth, S., Stokes, L., and Wood, S. (2013). *The 2011 Workplace Employment Relations Study: First Findings*. London: Department for Business, Innovation, and Skills.

Vandaele, K. (2011). *Sustaining or Abandoning 'Social Peace'? Strike Developments and Trends in Europe since the 1990s*. European Trade Union Institute Working Paper 2011.05. Brussels: ETUI.

Vargas-Silva, C. (2012). *Briefing: Migration Flows of A8 and other EU Migrants to and from the UK*. Oxford: University of Oxford Migration Observatory.

Virdee, S. and Grint, K. (1994). 'Black self-organization in trade unions'. *Sociological Review*, 42/2: 202–26.

Virtanen, M., Ferrie, J., Singh-Manoux, A., Shipley, M., Vahtera, J., Marmot, M., and Kivmäki, M. (2010). 'Overtime work and incident coronary heart disease: the Whitehall II participative cohort study'. *European Heart Journal*, 31/14: 1737–44.

Visser, F. and Williams, L. (2006). *Work–Life Balance: Rhetoric vs Reality*. London: Work Foundation.

Wacjman, J. (2000). 'Feminism facing industrial relations in Britain'. *British Journal of Industrial Relations*, 38/2: 183–201.

Waddington, J. (2003). 'Trade union organization', in P. Edwards (ed.), *Industrial Relations* (2nd edn). Oxford: Blackwell, 214–56.

Waddington, J. (2006). 'The performance of European Works Councils in engineering: perspectives of the employee representatives'. *Industrial Relations*, 45/4: 681–708.

Waddington, J. (2011a). *European Works Councils: A Transnational Industrial Relations Institution in the Making*. Abingdon: Routledge.

Waddington, J. (2011b). 'European works councils: the challenge for labour'. *Industrial Relations Journal*, 42/6: 508–29.

Waddington, J. and Hoffman, R. (2003). 'Trade unions in Europe: reform, organisation and restructuring', in D. Foster and P. Scott (eds), *Trade Unions in Europe: Meeting the Challenge*. Brussels: Peter Lang, 33–63.

Waddington, J. and Kerr, A. (2002). 'Unions fit for young workers?'. *Industrial Relations Journal*, 33/4: 298–315.

Wailes, N., Bamber, J., and Lansbury, R. (2011). 'International and comparative employment relations: an introduction', in G. Bamber, R. Lansbury, and N. Wailes (eds), *International and Comparative Employment Relations: Globalisation and Change*. London: Sage, 1–35.

Walby, S. (1997). *Gender Transformations*. London: Routledge.

Waldinger, R., Erickson, C., Milkman, R., Mitchell, D., Valenzuela, A., Wong, K., and Zeitlin, M. (1998). 'Helots no more: a case study of the Justice for Janitors campaign in Los Angeles', in K. Bronfenbrenner, S. Friedman, R. Hurd, R. Oswald, and R. Seeber (eds), *Organizing to Win: New Research on Union Strategies*. Ithaca NY: ILR Press, 102–19.

Wall, T. and Wood, S. (2005). 'The romance of human resource management and business performance, and the case for big science'. *Human Relations*, 58/4: 429–62.

Wallace, J. and O'Sullivan, M. (2006). 'Contemporary strike trends since 1980: peering through the wrong end of a telescope', in M. Morley, P. Gunnigle, and D. Collings (eds), *Global Industrial Relations*. London: Routledge, 273–91.

Wallis, E., Stuart, M., and Greenwood, I. (2005). '"Learners of the workplace unite!": an empirical examination of the UK trade union learning representative initiative'. *Work, Employment and Society*, 19/2: 283–304.

Walsh, J. (2007). 'Equality and diversity in British workplaces: the 2004 Workplace Employment

Relations Survey'. *Industrial Relations Journal*, 38/4: 303–19.

Walsh, J. (2010). 'Working time and work-life balance', in A. Wilkinson, N. Bacon, T. Redman, and S. Snell (eds.), *The SAGE Handbook of Human Resource Management*. London: Sage, 491–506.

Walton, R. and McKersie, R. (1965). *A Behavioral Theory of Labor Negotiations*. New York: McGraw-Hill.

War on Want (2006). *Fashion Victims: The True Cost of Cheap Clothes at Primark, Asda, and Tesco*. London: War on Want. http://www.waronwant.org/attachments/Fashion%20Victims.pdf

War on Want (2008). *Fashion Victims II: How UK Clothing Retailers are Keeping Workers in Poverty*. London: War on Want. http://www.waronwant.org/attachments/Fashion%20Victims%20II.pdf

War on Want (2010). *Taking Liberties: The Story Behind the UK High Street*. London: War on Want/Labour Behind the Label. http://www.waronwant.org/attachments/Taking%20Liberties.pdf

Warhurst, C. (2008). 'The knowledge economy, skills and government labour market intervention'. *Policy Studies*, 29/1: 71–86.

Warhurst, C., Eikhof, D., and Haunschild, A. (2008). 'Out of balance or just out of bounds? Analysing the relationship between work and life', in C. Warhurst, D. Eikhof, and A. Haunschild (eds.), *Work Less, Live More: Critical Analysis of the Work–Life Boundary*. Basingstoke: Palgrave Macmillan, 1–21.

Warhurst, C. and Thompson, P. (2006). 'Mapping knowledge in work: proxies or practices?'. *Work, Employment and Society*, 20/4: 787–800.

Warnecke, T. and De Ruyter, A. (2010). 'Positive economic freedom: an enabling role for international labor standards in developing countries?'. *Journal of Economic Issues*, 44/2: 385–92.

Warren, T., Pascall, G., and Fox, E. (2010). 'Gender equality in time: low-paid mothers' paid and unpaid work in the UK'. *Feminist Economics*, 16/3: 193–219.

Wass, V. (1996). 'Who controls selection under "voluntary" redundancy? The case of the Redundant Mineworkers Payments Scheme'. *British Journal of Industrial Relations*, 34/2: 249–65.

Webb, J. (1997). 'The politics of equal opportunity'. *Gender, Work and Organization*, 4/3: 159–69.

Webb, J. and Liff, S. (1988). 'Play the white man: the social construction of fairness and competition in equal opportunity policies'. *Sociological Review*, 36/3: 532–51.

Webb, S. and Webb, B. (1920a). *Industrial Democracy*. London: Longmans, Green and Co.

Webb, S. and Webb, B. (1920b). *The History of Trade Unionism* (revised edn). London: Longmans, Green and Co.

Webster, E., Lambert, R., and Bezuidenhout, A. (2008). *Grounding Globalization: Labour in the Age of Insecurity*. Oxford: Blackwell Publishing.

Wedderburn, D. and Craig, C. (1974). 'Relative deprivation in work', in D. Wedderburn (ed.), *Poverty, Inequality and Class Structure*. Cambridge: Cambridge University Press, 141–64.

Wedderburn, Lord (1986). *The Worker and the Law* (3rd edn). Harmondsworth: Penguin.

Wedderburn, Lord (1989). 'Freedom of association and philosophies of labour law'. *Industrial Law Journal*, 18: 1–38.

Wedderburn, Lord (1991). *Employment Rights in Britain and Europe*. London: Lawrence and Wishart.

Wedderburn, Lord (1995). *Labour Law and Freedom*. London: Lawrence and Wishart.

White, G. (2000). 'The pay review body system: its development and impact'. *Historical Studies in Industrial Relations*, 9: 71–100.

White, M., Hill, S., Mills, C., and Smeaton, D. (2004). *Managing to Change?* Basingstoke: Palgrave Macmillan.

Wilkinson, A. and Dundon, T. (2010). 'Direct employee participation', in A. Wilkinson, P. Gollan, M. Marchington, and D. Lewin (eds.), *The Oxford Handbook of Participation in Organizations*. Oxford: Oxford University Press, 167–85.

Wilkinson, A. and Fay, C. (2011). 'New times for employee voice?'. *Human Resource Management*, 50/1: 65–74.

Wilkinson, M. (2012). 'Out of sight, out of mind: the exploitation of migrant workers in 21st century Britain'. *Journal of Poverty and Social Justice*, 20/1: 13–21.

Wilkinson, R. and Pickett, K. (2009). *The Spirit Level: Why More Equal Societies Almost Always do Better*. London: Allen Lane.

Williams, S. (1997). 'The nature of some recent trade union modernization policies'. *British Journal of Industrial Relations*, 35/4: 495–514.

Williams, S. (2003). 'Conflict in the colleges: industrial relations in further education since incorporation'. *Journal of Further and Higher Education*, 27/3: 307–16.

Williams, S. (2004). 'Accounting for change in public sector industrial relations: the erosion of national bargaining in further education in England and Wales'. *Industrial Relations Journal*, 35/3: 233–48.

Williams, S., Abbott, B., and Heery, E. (2011a). 'New and emerging actors in work and employment relations: the case of civil society organisations', in K. Townsend and A. Wilkinson (eds.), *The Edward Elgar Research Handbook on Work and Employment Relations*. Cheltenham: Edward Elgar, 130–49.

Williams, S., Abbott, B., and Heery, E. (2011b). 'Non-union worker representation through civil society organisations: evidence from the UK'. *Industrial Relations Journal*, 42/1: 69–85.

Williams, S., Adam-Smith, D., and Norris, G. (2004). 'Remuneration practices in the UK hospitality industry in the age of the National Minimum Wage'. *Service Industries Journal*, 24/1: 171–86.

Williams, S., Bradley, H., Devadason, R., and Erickson, M. (2013). *Globalization and Work*. Cambridge: Polity.

Williams, S. and Scott, P. (2010). 'Shooting the past? The modernisation of Conservative Party employment relations policy under David Cameron'. *Industrial Relations Journal*, 41/1: 4–16.

Williams, S. and Scott, P. (2011). 'The contingent basis of Conservative Party modernisation under David Cameron: the trajectory of employment relations policy'. *Parliamentary Affairs*, 54/3: 513–29.

Willman, P. (1989). 'The logic of "market share" trade unionism: is membership decline inevitable?'. *Industrial Relations Journal*, 20/4: 260–70.

Willman, P., Gomez, R., and Bryson, A. (2009). 'Voice at the workplace: where do we find it, why is it there and where is it going?', in W. Brown, A. Bryson, J. Forth, and K. Whitfield (eds.), *The Evolution of the Modern Workplace*. Cambridge: Cambridge University Press, 97–119.

Willmott, H. (1993). 'Strength is ignorance; slavery is freedom: managing culture in modern organizations'. *Journal of Management Studies*, 30/4: 515–52.

Wills, J. (2000). 'Great Expectations: three years in the life of a European Works Council'. *European Journal of Industrial Relations*, 6/1: 85–107.

Wills, J. (2002). 'Bargaining for the space to organize in the global economy: a review of the Accor-IUF trade union rights agreement'. *Review of International Political Economy*, 9/4: 675–700.

Wills, J. (2004). 'Trade unionism and partnership in practice: evidence from the Barclays-Unifi agreement'. *Industrial Relations Journal*, 35/4: 329–43.

Wills, J. (2008). 'Making class politics possible: organising contract cleaners in London'. *International Journal of Urban and Regional Research*, 32/2: 305–23.

Winchester, D. and Bach, S. (1995). 'The state: the public sector', in P. Edwards (ed.), *Industrial Relations: Theory and Practice in Britain*. Oxford: Blackwell, 304–34.

Winchester, D. and Bach, S. (1999). 'Britain: the transformation of public service employment relations', in S. Bach, L. Bordogna, G. DellaRocca, and D. Winchester (eds.), *Public Service Employment Relations in Europe: Transformation, Modernisation or Inertia?* London: Routledge, 22–55.

Wolf, A. (2010). *More than we Bargained for: The Social and Economic Costs of National Wage Bargaining*. London: CentreForum.

Wolf, M. (2004). *Why Globalization Works*. New Haven CT: Yale University Press.

Women and Work Commission (2006). *Shaping a Fairer Future: Final Report of the Women and Work Commission*. London: Women and Equality Unit.

Wood, J. (1992). 'Dispute resolution—conciliation, mediation and arbitration', in W. McCarthy (ed.), *Legal Intervention in Industrial Relations: Gains and Losses*. Oxford: Blackwell, 241–73.

Wood, S. and Bryson, A. (2009). 'High involvement management', in W. Brown, A. Bryson, J. Forth, and K. Whitfield (eds.), *The Evolution of the Modern Workplace*. Cambridge: Cambridge University Press, 151–75.

Wood, S. and de Menezes, L. (1998). 'High commitment management in the UK: evidence from the Workplace Industrial Relations Survey, and Employers' Manpower and Skills Practices Survey'. *Human Relations*, 51/4: 485–515.

Wood, S. and Goddard, J. (1999). 'The statutory union recognition procedure in the Employment Relations Bill: a comparative analysis'. *British Journal of Industrial Relations*, 37/2: 203–45.

Wood, S., Moore, S., and Ewing, K. (2003). 'The impact of the trade union recognition procedure under the Employment Relations Act 2000–2', in H. Gospel and S. Wood (eds.), *Representing Workers*. London: Routledge, 119–43.

Woolfson, C. (2007). 'Labour standards and migration in the New Europe: post-communist legacies and perspectives'. *European Journal of Industrial Relations*, 13/2: 199–218.

Woolfson, C., Thörnqvist, C., and Sommers, J. (2010). 'The Swedish model and the future of labour standards after Laval'. *Industrial Relations Journal*, 41/4: 333–50.

Worrall, L., Cooper, C., and Campbell, F. (2000). 'The new reality for UK managers: perpetual change and employment instability'. *Work, Employment and Society*, 14/4: 647–68.

Wright, A. (2011). ' "Modernizing" away gender pay inequality? Some evidence from the local government sector on using job evaluation'. *Employee Relations*, 33/2: 159–78.

Young, Lord (2010). *Common Sense, Common Safety*. London: HM Government.

Yu, X. (2008). 'Impacts of corporate code of conduct on labor standards: a case study of Reebok's athletic footwear supplier factory in China'. *Journal of Business Ethics*, 81/3: 513–29.

Zhang, Y.-C. and Li, S.-L. (2009). 'High performance work practices and firm performance: evidence from the pharmaceutical industry in China'. *The International Journal of Human Resource Management*, 20/11: 2331–48.

Index